T0124358

Langenscheidt
Universal Dictionary

Spanish

Spanish – English
English – Spanish

Langenscheidt

1. Auflage 2012 (1,04 - 2023)
© PONS Langenscheidt GmbH,
Stöckachstraße 11, 70190 Stuttgart 2012
All Rights Reserved.

www.langenscheidt.com

Print: Druckerei C. H. Beck, Nördlingen
Printed in Germany

ISBN 978-3-12-514033-2

Contents
Índice

Abbreviations / Abreviaturas........................ 4
La pronunciación del inglés 8
Spanish – English / Español – Inglés................ 11
English – Spanish / Inglés – Español............... 273
Los verbos irregulares ingleses 570
Numbers / Numerales............................... 573

Abbreviations
Abreviaturas

stands for the headword	~	sustituye la voz-guía
and	&	y
see	☞	véase
registered trademark	®	marca registrada
adjective	*adj*	adjetivo
adverb	*adv*	adverbio
agriculture	AGR	agricultura
anatomy	ANAT	anatomía
Argentina	*Arg*	Argentina
architecture	ARQUI	arquitectura
article	*art*	artículo
astronomy	AST	astronomía
astrology	ASTR	astrología
attributive	*atr*	atributivo
motoring	AUTO	automóvil
aviation	AVIA	aviación
biology	BIO	biología
Bolivia	*Bol*	Bolivia
botany	BOT	botánica
British English	*Br*	inglés británico
Central America	*C.Am.*	América central
Chile	*Chi*	Chile
Colombia	*Col*	Colombia
commerce, business	COM	comercio
computers, IT term	COMPUT	informática
conjunction	*conj*	conjunción
Southern Cone	*CSur*	Cono Sur
sports	DEP	deporte
contemptuous	*desp*	despectivo

education (schools, universities)	EDU	educación, enseñanza (sistema escolar y universitario)
electronics, electronic engineering	ELEC	electrónica, electrotecnia
Spain	*Esp*	España
familiar, colloquial	F	familiar
feminine	*f*	femenino
feminine noun and adjective	*f/adj*	sustantivo femenino y adjetivo
railroad	FERR	ferrocarriles
figurative	*fig*	figurativo
financial	FIN	finanzas
physics	FÍS	física
formal	*fml*	formal
photography	FOT	fotografía
feminine plural	*fpl*	femenino plural
feminine singular	*fsg*	femenino singular
gastronomy	GASTR	gastronomía
geography	GEOG	geografía
geology	GEOL	geología
grammatical	GRAM	gramática
historical	HIST	histórico
IT term	INFOR	informática
interjection	*int*	interjección
interrogative	*interr*	interrogativo
invariable	*inv*	invariable
law	JUR	jurisprudencia
Latin America	*L.Am.*	América Latina
law	LAW	jurisprudencia
masculine	*m*	masculino
masculine noun and adjective	*m/adj*	sustantivo masculino y adjetivo
nautical	MAR	navegación, marina

mathematics	MAT	matemáticas
mathematics	MATH	matemáticas
medicine	MED	medicina
meteorology	METEO	meteorología
Mexico	*Mex*	México
Mexico	*Méx*	México
masculine and feminine	*m/f*	masculino y femenino
masculine and feminine plural	*m/fpl*	masculino y femenino plural
military	MIL	militar
mineralogy	MIN	mineralogía
motoring	MOT	automóvil
masculine plural	*mpl*	masculino al plural
music	MUS	música
music	MÚS	música
noun	*n*	sustantivo
nautical	NAUT	navegación, náutica
negative	*neg*	negativo
noun plural	*npl*	sustantivo al plural
noun singular	*nsg*	sustantivo al singular
oneself	o.s.	sí mismo
popular, slang	P	popular
past participle	*part*	participio (del pasado)
Peru	*Pe*	Perú
pejorative	*pej*	peyorativo
photography	PHOT	fotografía
physics	PHYS	física
painting	PINT	pintura
plural	*pl*	plural
politics	POL	política
preposition	*prep*	preposición
pronoun	*pron*	pronombre
preposition	*prp*	preposición

psychology	PSI	psicología
psychology	PSYCH	psicología
chemistry	QUÍM	química
radio	RAD	radio
railroad	RAIL	ferrocarriles
relative	*rel*	relativo
religion	REL	religión
River Plate	*Rpl*	Río de la Plata
South America	S.Am.	América del Sur
singular	*sg*	singular
someone	s.o.	alguien
sports	SP	deporte
Spain	*Span*	España
something	*sth*	algo, alguna cosa
subjunctive	*subj*	subjuntivo
bullfighting	TAUR	tauromaquia
also	*tb*	también
theater, theatre	TEA	teatro
technology	TÉC	técnica, tecnología
technology	TECH	técnica, tecnología
telecommunications	TELEC	telecomunicaciones
theater, theatre	THEA	teatro
typography, typesetting	TIP	tipografía
transportation	TRANSP	transportes
television	TV	televisión
vulgar	V	vulgar
auxiliary verb	*v/aux*	verbo auxiliar
verb	*vb*	verbo
Venezuela	*Ven*	Venezuela
intransitive verb	*v/i*	verbo intransitivo
impersonal verb	*v/impers*	verbo impersonal
transitive verb	*v/t*	verbo transitivo
West Indies	W.I.	Antillas
zoology	ZO	zoología

La pronunciación del inglés

A. Vocales y diptongos

[ɑː]   sonido largo parecido al de *a* en *raro*: *far* [fɑːr].

[ʌ]   *a* abierta, breve y oscura, que se pronuncia en la parte anterior de la boca sin redondear los labios: *butter* [ˈbʌtər], *come* [kʌm], *blood* [blʌd].

[æ]   sonido breve, bastante abierto, algo parecido al de *a* en *parra*: *fat* [fæt], *ran* [ræn].

[ɒː]   vocal larga, bastante cerrada, entre *a* y *o*; más cercana a la *a* que a la *o*: *fall* [fɒːl], *fault* [fɒːlt].

[e]   sonido breve, medio abierto, parecido al de *e* en *perro*: *bed* [bed], *less* [les], *hairy* [ˈheɪ].

[aɪ]   sonido parecido al de *ai* en *estáis*, *baile*: *I* [aɪ], *lie* [laɪ], *dry* [draɪ].

[aʊ]   sonido parecido al de *au* en *causa*, *sauce*: *house* [haʊs], *now* [naʊ].

[eɪ]   *e* medio abierta, pero más cerrada que la *e* de *hablé*; suena como si le siguiese una [ɪ] débil, sobre todo en sílaba acentuada: *date* [deɪt], *play* [pleɪ].

[ə]   'vocal neutra', siempre átona; parecida al sonido de la *a* final de *cada*: *about* [əˈbaʊt], *connect* [kəˈnekt].

[iː]   sonido largo, parecido al de *i* en *misa*, *vino*: *scene* [siːn], *sea* [siː], *feet* [fiːt], *ceiling* [ˈsiːlɪŋ].

[ɪ]   sonido breve, abierto, parecido al de *i* en *silba*, *tirria*, pero más abierto: *big* [bɪg], *city* [ˈsɪtɪ].

[oʊ]   *o* larga, más bien cerrada, sin redondear los labios ni levantar la lengua: *note* [noʊt], *boat* [boʊt], *below* [bɪˈloʊ].

[ɔː]	vocal larga, bastante cerrada; es algo parecida a la *o* de *por*: *abnormal* [æb'nɔːrml], *before* [bɪ'fɔːr].
[ɔɪ]	diptongo cuyo primer elemento es una *o* abierta, seguido de una *i* abierta pero débil; parecido al sonido de *oy* en *doy*: *voice* [vɔɪs], *boy* [bɔɪ].
[ɜː]	forma larga de la 'vocal neutra' (ə), algo parecida al sonido de *eu* en la palabra francesa *leur*: *word* [wɜːrd], *girl* [gɜːrl].
[uː]	sonido largo, parecido al de *u* en *cuna*, *duda*: *fool* [fuːl], *shoe* [ʃuː], *you* [juː], *rule* [ruːl].
[ʊ]	*u* pura pero muy rápida, más cerrada que la *u* de *burra*: *put* [pʊt], *look* [lʊk].

B. Consonantes

[b]	como la *b* de *cambiar*: *bay* [beɪ], *brave* [breɪv].
[d]	como la *d* de *andar*: *did* [dɪd], *ladder* ['lædər].
[f]	como la *f* de *filo*: *face* [feɪs], *baffle* ['bæfl].
[g]	como la *g* de *golpe*: *go* [gou], *haggle* ['hægl].
[h]	se pronuncia con aspiración fuerte, sin la aspereza gutural de la *j* en *Gijón*: *who* [huː], *ahead* [ə'hed].
[j]	como la *y* de *cuyo*: *you* [juː], *million* ['mɪljən].
[k]	como la *c* de *casa*: *cat* [kæt], *kill* [kɪl].
[l]	como la *l* de *loco*: *love* [lʌv], *goal* [goul].
[m]	como la *m* de *madre*: *mouth* [mauθ], *come* [kʌm].
[n]	como la *n* de *nada*: *not* [nɑːt], *banner* ['bænər].
[p]	como la *p* de *padre*: *pot* [pɑːt], *top* [tɑːp].
[r]	Cuando se pronuncia, es un sonido muy débil, más bien semivocal, que no tiene nada de la vibración fuerte que caracteriza la *r* española; se articula elevando la punta de la lengua hacia el

paladar duro: *rose* [roʊz], *pride* [praɪd], *there* [ðer].

[s]	como la *s* de *casa*: *sit* [sɪt], *scent* [sent].
[t]	como la *t* de *pata*: *take* [teɪk], *patter* ['pætər].
[v]	inexistente en español; a diferencia de *b*, *v* en español, se pronuncia juntando el labio inferior con los dientes superiores: *vein* [veɪn], *velvet* ['velvɪt].
[w]	como la *u* de *huevo*: *water* ['wɒːtər], *will* [wɪl].
[z]	como la *s* de *mismo*: *zeal* [ziːl], *hers* [hɜːrz].
[ʒ]	inexistente en español; como la *j* en la palabra francesa *jour*: *measure* ['meʒər], *leisure* ['liːʒər]. Aparece a menudo en el grupo [dʒ], que se pronuncia como el grupo *dj* de la palabra francesa *adjacent*: *edge* [edʒ], *gem* [dʒem].
[ʃ]	inexistente en español; como *ch* en la palabra francesa *chose*: *shake* [ʃeɪk], *washing* ['wɒːʃɪn]. Aparece a menudo en el grupo [tʃ], que se pronuncia como la *ch* en *mucho*: *match* [mætʃ], *natural* ['nætʃrəl].
[θ]	como la *z* de *zapato* en castellano: *thin* [θɪn], *path* [pæθ].
[ð]	forma sonorizada del anterior, algo como la *d* de *todo*: *there* [ðer], *breathe* [briːð].
[ŋ]	como la *n* de *banco*: *singer* ['sɪŋər], *tinker* ['tɪŋkər].

A

a ◇ *dirección* to; **al este de** to the east of; **ir ~ la cama / al cine** go to bed / to the movies ◇ *situación* at; **al sol** in the sun; **está ~ cinco kilómetros** it is five kilometers away ◇ *tiempo:* **~ las tres** at three o'clock; **estamos ~ quince de febrero** it's February fifteenth; **~ los treinta años** at the age of thirty **~ la española** the Spanish way; **~ mano** by hand; **~ pie** on foot; **~ 50 kilómetros por hora** at fifty kilometers an hour ◇ *precio:* **¿~ cómo o cuánto está?** how much is it? ◇ *objeto indirecto:* **dáselo ~ tu hermano** give it to your brother ◇ *objeto directo:* **vi ~ mi padre** I saw my father ◇ *para introducir pregunta:* **¿~ que no lo sabes?** I bet you don't know; **~ ver...** OK ...

abad *m* abbot

abajo 1 *adv* ◇ *situación* below, underneath; *en edificio* downstairs; **ponlo ahí ~** put it down there; **el cajón de ~ siguiente** the drawer below; *último* the bottom drawer ◇ *dirección* down; *en edificio* downstairs; **empuja hacia ~** push down ◇ *con cantidades:* **de diez para**

~ ten or under **2** *int:* **¡~ los traidores!** down with the traitors!

abalanzarse rush *o* surge forward; **~ sobre algo / alguien** pounce on sth / s.o.

abandonar leave; *objeto, a alguien* abandon; *a esposa, hijos* desert; *idea, actividad* give up; **abandonarse** let o.s. go; **~ a** abandon o.s. to; **abandono** *m* abandonment; DEP *de carrera* retirement; **en un estado de ~** in a state of neglect

abanicar fan; **abanicarse** fan o.s.; **abanico** *m* fan; *fig* range

abaratar reduce the price of; *precio* reduce

abarcar cover; *L.Am. (acaparar)* hoard; **~ con la vista** take in

abarrotado packed; **abarrotes** *mpl L.Am.* groceries; **(tienda de) ~** grocery store, *Br* grocer's

abastecer supply (**de** with); **abastecimiento** *m* supply

abatible collapsible, folding *atr;* **abatimiento** *m* gloom; **abatir** *edificio* knock down; *árbol* cut down; AVIA shoot *o* bring down; *fig* kill; *(deprimir)* depress

abdicación *f* abdication; **abdicar** abdicate

abecé *m fig* ABCs *pl, Br* ABC

abedul *m* birch

abeja *f* ZO bee; **abejorro** *m* bumblebee

abertura *f* opening

abeto *m* fir (tree)

abierto 1 *part* ☞ **abrir 2** *adj* open

abismo *m* abyss; *fig* gulf

ablandar *tb fig* soften

abnegación *f* self-denial; **abnegado** selfless

abogado,-a *m/f* a lawyer; *en tribunal superior* attorney, *Br* barrister; **no le faltaron ~s** *fig* there were plenty of people who defended him; **abogar: ~ por alguien** defend; *algo* advocate

abolición *f* abolition; **abolir** abolish

abominable abominable; **abominar** detest, loathe

abonable COM payable; **abonado,-a** *f* subscriber; *a teléfono, gas, electricidad* customer; *a ópera, teatro* season-ticket holder; **abonar** COM pay; AGR fertilize; *Méx* pay on account; **el terreno** *fig* sow the seeds; **abonarse** *a espectáculo* buy a season ticket (**a** for); *a revista* take out a subscription (**a** to); **abono** *m* COM payment; AGR fertilizer; *para espectáculo, transporte* season ticket

abordar MAR board; *tema, asunto* broach, raise; *proble-ma* tackle, deal with; *a una persona* approach

aborigen 1 *adj* native, indigenous **2** *m/f* native

aborrecer loathe, detest; **aborrecimiento** *m* loathing

abortar 1 *v/i* MED miscarry; *de forma provocada* have an abortion **2** *v/t plan* foil; **aborto** *m* miscarriage; *provocado* abortion; *fig* F freak F

abrasar 1 *v/t burn, 2 v/i del sol* burn; *de bebida, comida* be boiling hot; **abrasarse: ~ de sed** F be parched F; **~ de calor** F be sweltering F

abrazar hug; **abrazarse** embrace; **abrazo** *m* hug; **un ~** *en carta* best wishes; **más íntimo** love

abrelatas *m inv* can opener, *Br tb* tin opener

abreviar shorten; *palabra* abbreviate; *texto* abridge; **abreviatura** *f* abbreviation

abridor *m* bottle opener

abrigar wrap up; *esperanzas* hold out; *duda* entertain; **abrigarse** wrap up warm; **abrigo** *m* coat; *(protección)* shelter; **ropa de ~** warm clothes; **al ~ de** in the shelter of

abril *m* April

abrir 1 *v/t* open; *túnel* dig; *grifo* turn on **2** *v/i de persona* open up; *de ventana, puerta* open; **en un ~ y cerrar de ojos** in the twinkling of an eye

abrochar, abrocharse do up; *cinturón de seguridad* fasten

abrumar overwhelm (**con** *o* **de** with)

abrupto *terreno* rough; *pendiente* steep; *tono, respuesta* abrupt; *cambio* sudden

absolución *f* absolution

absolutamente absolutely; **no entendió ~ nada** he didn't understand a thing; **absoluto** absolute; **en ~** not at all

absolver JUR acquit; REL absolve

absorber absorb; (*consumir*) take; COM take over; **absorción** *f* absorption; COM takeover

abstemio 1 *adj* teetotal **2** *m*, **-a** *f* teetotaler; *Br* teetotaller

abstención *f* abstention; **abstenerse** refrain (**de** from); POL abstain; **abstinencia** *f* abstinence; **síndrome de ~** MED withdrawal symptoms *pl*

abstracción *f* abstraction; **hacer ~ de** exclude; **abstracto** abstract; **abstraer** abstract; **abstraerse** shut o.s. off (**de** from); **abstraído 1** *adj* preoccupied; **~ en algo** engrossed in sth **2** *part* ☞ **abstraer**

absurdo 1 *adj* absurd **2** *m*: **es un ~ que** it's absurd that

abuchear boo

abuela *f* grandmother; **abuelo** *m* grandfather; **~s** grandparents

abultar be bulky; **no abulta casi nada** it takes up almost

no room at all

abundancia *f* abundance; **comida en ~** plenty of food; **abundante** plentiful, abundant; **abundar** be plentiful *o* abundant

aburrido (*que aburre*) boring; (*que se aburre*) bored (**de** with); **aburrimiento** *m* boredom; **aburrir** bore; **aburrirse** get bored (**de** with)

abusar: *de* abuse; *persona* take advantage of; **~ sexualmente de** sexually abuse; **abuso** *m* abuse; **~s deshonestos** indecent assault

a.C. (*= antes de Cristo*) BC (*= before Christ*)

acá here; **de ~ para allá** from here to there; **de entonces para ~** since then

acabado *m* finish; **acabar** finish; **acabé haciéndolo yo** I finished up *o* ended up doing it myself; **~ con** put an end to; *caramelos* finish off; *persona* destroy; **~ de hacer algo** have just done sth; **va a ~ mal** F *persona* he'll come to no good; **esto va a ~ mal** F this is going to end badly; **acabarse** *de actividad* finish, end; *de pan, dinero* run out; **se nos ha acabado el azúcar** we've run out of sugar; **¡se acabó!** that's that!

academia *f* academy; **~ de idiomas** language school

acallar *tb fig* silence

acalorado *fig* heated; **estar ~** be agitated; **acalorar** *fig* in-

flame; acalorarse (*enfadarse*) get worked up; (*sofocarse*) get embarrassed

acampada *f* camp; **ir de ~** go camping; **acampar** camp

acantilado *m* cliff

acaparar hoard, stockpile; *tiempo* take up; *interés* capture; (*monopolizar*) monopolize

acariciar caress; *perro* stroke; *idea* toy with

acarrear carry; *fig* give rise to, cause; **acarreo** *m* transportation

acaso perhaps; **por si ~** just in case

acatamiento *m* compliance (**de** with); **acatar** comply with, obey

acatarrarse catch a cold

acaudalado wealthy, well-off

acceder (*ceder*) agree (**a** to), accede (**a** to) *fml*; **~ a** *lugar* gain access to; *cargo* accede to *fml*

accesible accessible; **acceso** *m tb* INFOR access; *de fiebre* attack; *de tos* fit; **de difícil ~** inaccessible; **accesorio 1** *adj* incidental **2** *m* accessory

accidentado 1 *adj terreno* rough; *viaje* eventful **2** *m*, **-a** *f* casualty; **accidental** (*no esencial*) incidental; (*casual*) chance *atr*; **accidente** *m* accident; (*casualidad*) chance; GEOG feature; **~ de tráfico** o **de circulación** road traffic accident; **~ laboral** industrial accident

acción *f* action; **acciones** COM stock, shares; **poner en ~** put into action; **accionar** activate; **accionista** *m/f* stockholder, shareholder

acebo *m* holly

aceite *m* oil; **~ de girasol** / **oliva** sunflower / olive oil; **aceitera** TÉC oilcan; GASTR cruet; **aceituna** *f* olive

aceleración *f* acceleration; **acelerador** *m* accelerator; **acelerar** *v/t motor* rev up; *fig* speed up; **aceleró el coche** she accelerated **2** *v/i* accelerate

acento *m* accent; (*énfasis*) stress, emphasis; **acentuar** stress; *fig* accentuate, emphasize

aceptable acceptable; **aceptación** *f* acceptance; (*éxito*) success; **aceptar** accept

acequia *f* irrigation ditch

acera *f* sidewalk, *Br* pavement; **ser de la otra ~** F be gay

acerbo sharp

acerca: ~ de about

acercar bring closer; **~ a alguien a un lugar** give s.o. a ride o *Br* lift somewhere; **acercarse** approach; (*ir*) go; *de grupos, países* come closer together; *de fecha* draw near; **¡acércate!** come closer

acero *m* steel; **~ inoxidable** stainless steel

acertado *comentario* apt;

elección good, wise; **estar muy ~** be dead right; **acertante** *m/f de apuesta* winner; **acertar 1** *v/t respuesta* get right; *al hacer una conjetura* guess **2** *v/i* be right; **acertijo** *m* riddle, puzzle

achacar attribute (**a** to)

achaque *m* ailment

achicar make smaller; MAR bail out; **achicarse** get smaller; *fig* feel intimidated

acidez *f* acidity; **~ de estómago** heartburn; **ácido 1** *adj tb fig* sour, acid **2** *m* acid

acierto *m* idea good idea; *respuesta* correct answer; *habilidad* skill

aclamación *f* acclaim; **aclamar** acclaim

aclarar 1 *v/t problema* clarify, clear up; *ropa, vajilla* rinse **2** *v/i de día* break; *del tiempo* clear up; **aclararse**: **~ la voz** clear one's throat; **no me aclaro** I don't understand; *por cansancio etc* I can't think straight

aclimatarse acclimatize, become acclimatized

acné *m* acne

acobardar daunt; **acobardarse** get frightened

acogedor welcoming; *lugar* cozy, *Br* cosy; **acoger** receive; *en casa* take in; **acogerse**: **~ a algo** have recourse to sth; **acogida** *f* reception

acolchar quilt, pad

acometer 1 *v/t* attack; *tarea* tackle **2** *v/i* attack; **~ contra algo** attack sth

acomodado well-off; **acomodador** *m* usher; **acomodar** adapt; *a alguien* accommodate

acompañamiento *m* accompaniment; **acompañante** *m/f* companion; MÚS accompanist; **acompañar** (*ir con*) go with, accompany *fml*; (*permanecer con*) keep company; MÚS, GASTR accompany

acondicionador *m* conditioner; **acondicionar** *un lugar* equip, fit out; *pelo* condition

acongojar grieve, distress

aconsejable advisable; **aconsejar** advise

acontecer take place, occur; **acontecimiento** *m* event

acoplar *piezas* fit together

acorazado armored, *Br* armoured; **acorazar** armorplate, *Br* armour-plate; **acorazarse** *fig* protect o.s.

acordar agree; **acordarse** remember; **¿te acuerdas de él?** do you remember him?; **acorde 1** *adj*: **~ con** in keeping with **2** *m* MÚS chord

acordeón *m* accordion

acordonar cordon off

acortar 1 *v/t* shorten **2** *v/i* take a short cut

acosar hound, pursue; *con preguntas* bombard; **acoso** *m fig* hounding, harassment;

~ sexual sexual harassment

acostar put to bed; **acostarse** go to bed; (*tumbarse*) lie down; **~ con alguien** go to bed with s.o.

acostumbrado (*habitual*) usual; **estar ~ a algo** be used to sth; **acostumbrar 1** *v/t* get used (**a** to) **2** *v/i*: **acostumbraba a venir** he used to come; **acostumbrarse** get used (**a** to)

acotar *terreno* fence off; *texto* annotate

acrecentar increase

acreditado well-known, reputable; **acreditar** *diplomático etc* accredit (**como** as); (*avalar*) prove; **acreditarse** get a good reputation

acreedor *m*, **~a** *f* creditor; **acreencia** *f LAm.* credit

acróbata *m/f* acrobat

acta(s) *f(pl)* minutes *pl*

actitud *f* (*disposición*) attitude; (*posición*) position

activar activate; (*estimular*) stimulate; **actividad** *f* activity; **activo 1** *adj* active; **en ~** on active service **2** *m* COM assets *pl*

acto *m* (*acción*), TEA act; *ceremonia* ceremony; **~ seguido** immediately afterward; **en el ~** instantly

actor *m* actor; **actriz** *f* actress

actuación *f* TEA performance; (*intervención*) intervention; **actual** present, current; **un tema muy ~** a very topical issue; **actualidad** *f* current situation; **en la ~** at present, presently; (*hoy en día*) nowadays; **~es** current affairs; **actualizar** bring up to date, update; **actualmente** currently

actuar (*obrar*, *ejercer*), TEA act; MED work, act

acuarela *f* watercolor, *Br* watercolour

acuario *m* aquarium

Acuario *m/f inv* ASTR Aquarius

acuático aquatic; **deporte ~** water sport

acuchillar stab

acudir come; **~ a alguien** turn to s.o.; **~ a las urnas** go to the polls

acueducto *m* aqueduct

acuerdo *m* agreement; **estar de ~ con** agree with; **llegar a un ~**, **ponerse de ~** come to *o* reach an agreement; **de ~ con algo** in accordance with sth; **¡de ~!** alright!, OK!

acumulador *m* ELEC accumulator, storage battery; **acumular**, **acumularse** accumulate

acuñar *monedas* mint; *expresión* coin

acuoso watery

acupuntura *f* acupuncture

acusación *f* accusation; **acusado** *m*, **-a** *f* defendant; **acusar** accuse (**de** of); JUR charge (**de** with); (*manifestar*) show; **~ recibo de** acknowledge receipt of; **acuse**

m: **~ de recibo** acknowledg(e)ment

acústico acoustic

adaptación *f* adaptation; **~ cinematográfica** movie version; **adaptador** *m* adaptor; **adaptar, adaptarse** adapt (**a** to)

adecuado suitable, appropriate

adelantado advanced; **por ~** in advance; **ir ~ de un reloj** be fast; **adelantamiento** *m* AUTO passing maneuver, *Br* overtaking manoeuvre; **adelantar 1** *v/t mover* move forward; *reloj* put forward; AUTO pass, *Br* overtake; *dinero* advance; *(conseguir)* achieve, gain **2** *v/i de un reloj* be fast; *(avanzar)* make progress; AUTO pass, *Br* overtake; **adelantarse** *mover* move forward; *(ir delante)* go on ahead; *de estación, cosecha* be early; *de un reloj* gain; **se me adelantó** she got there first; **adelante en espacio** forward; **seguir ~** carry on, keep going; *¡~!* come in; **más ~** *en tiempo* later on; **de ahora en ~** from now on; **salir ~** *fig: de persona* succeed; *de proyecto* go ahead; **adelanto** *m tb* COM advance

adelfa *f* BOT oleander

adelgazar 1 *v/t* lose **2** *v/i* lose weight

además 1 *adv* as well, besides **2** *prp*: **~ de** as well as

adentro 1 *adv* inside; **mar ~** out to sea; **~ de** *L.Am.* inside **2** *mpl*: **para sus ~s** to oneself

aderezar *con especias* season; *ensalada* dress; *fig* liven up; **aderezo** *m* GASTR seasoning; *para ensalada* dressing

adeudado in debt; **adeudar** owe; **~ en cuenta** debit an account; **adeudarse** get into debt

adherir stick; **adherirse** *a superficie* stick (**a** to), adhere (**a** to) *fml*; **~ a una organización** become a member of *o* join an organization; **~ a una idea** support an idea; **adhesión** *f* adhesion; **adhesivo** *m/adj* adhesive

adicción *f* addiction; **~ a las drogas** drug addiction

adición *f* MAT addition; *Rpl en restaurante* check, *Br* bill; **adicional** additional; **adicionar** MAT add, add up

adicto 1 *adj* addicted (**a** to); **ser ~ al régimen** be a supporter of the regime **2** *m*, **-a** *f* addict

adiestrar train

adinerado wealthy

adiós 1 *int* goodbye, bye; *al cruzarse* hello **2** *m* goodbye; **decir ~** say goodbye (**a** to)

aditivo *m* additive

adivinar guess; *de adivino* foretell; **adivino** *m* fortune teller

adjetivo *m* adjective

adjudicar award

adjunto 1 *adj* deputy *atr*; **profesor ~** assistant teacher; *en universidad* associate professor, *Br* lecturer **2** *m*, **-a** *f* assistant **3** *adv*: **~ le remitimos** please find enclosed

administración *f* administration; *de empresa etc* management; **~ pública** civil service; **administrador** *m*, **~a** *f* administrator; *de empresa etc* manager; **administrar** *medicamento* administer, give; *empresa* run, manage; *bienes* manage; **administrativo 1** *adj* administrative **2** *m*, **-a** *f* administrative assistant

admirable admirable; **admiración** *f* admiration; **signo de ~** exclamation mark; **admirador** *m*, **~a** *f* admirer; **admirar** admire; *(asombrar)* amaze; **admirarse** be amazed (**de** at *o* by)

admisible admissible; **admisión** *f* admission; **admitir** *(aceptar)* accept; *(reconocer)* admit

ADN (= **ácido desoxirribonucleico**) DNA (= deoxyribonucleic acid)

adobar GASTR marinate

adobe *m* adobe

adolescencia *f* adolescence; **adolescente** *m/f* adolescent

adonde where

adónde where

adopción *f* adoption; **adoptar** adopt; **adoptivo** *padres* adoptive; *hijo* adopted

adoquín *m* paving stone

adorable lovable, adorable; **adorar** love, adore; REL worship

adormecedor soporific; **adormecerse** doze off

adornar decorate; **adorno** *m* ornament; *de Navidad* decoration

adquirir acquire; *(comprar)* buy; **adquisición** *f* acquisition; **hacer una buena ~** make a good purchase; **adquisitivo**: **poder ~** purchasing power

adrede on purpose, deliberately

adrenalina *f* adrenaline

aduana *f* customs; **aduanero 1** *adj* customs *atr* **2** *m*, **-a** *f* customs officer

aducir *argumentos* give, put forward; *(alegar)* claim

adueñarse: **~ de** take possession of

adulación *f* flattery; **adulador** flattering *atr*; **adular** flatter

adúltera *f* adulteress; **adulterar** adulterate; **adulterio** *m* adultery; **adúltero 1** *adj* adulterous **2** *m* adulterer

adulto 1 *adj* adult; **edad -a** adulthood **2** *m*, **-a** *f* adult

adverbio *m* adverb

adversario *m*, **-a** *f* adversary, opponent; **adverso** adverse; **adversidad** *f* adversity, hard times *pl*

advertencia *f* warning; **advertir** warn (**de** about); *(notar)* notice

adviento *m* REL Advent

adyacente adjacent

aéreo air *atr*, *vista*, *fotografía* aerial; **compañía -a** airline

aerodeslizador *m* hovercraft; **aerodinámico** aerodynamic; **aeródromo** *m* airfield, aerodrome; **aerograma** *m* air mail letter; **aeromozo** *m*, **-a** *f L.Am.* flight attendant; **aeronáutica** *f* aeronautics; **aeronave** *f* airplane, *Br* aeroplane; **aeropuerto** *m* airport; **aerosol** *m* aerosol; **aerotaxi** *m* air taxi

afable pleasant, affable

afamado famous

afán *m* (*esfuerzo*) effort; (*deseo*) eagerness; **sin ~ de lucro** *organización* not-for-profit; **afanarse** make an effort

afear: **~ algo / a alguien** make sth / s.o. look ugly

afección *f* MED complaint, condition; **afectado** (*afligido*) upset (*por* by); (*amanerado*) affected; **afectar** affect; (*conmover*) upset, affect; (*fingir*) feign; **afectivo** emotional; **afecto** *m* affection; **tener ~ a alguien** be fond of s.o.; **afectuoso** affectionate

afeitado *m* shave; **afeitadora** *f* electric razor; **afeitar** shave; *barba* shave off; **afeitarse** shave, have a shave

afeminado effeminate

aferrado stubborn

afición *f* love (*por* of); (*pasa-*

tiempo) pastime, hobby; **la ~** DEP the fans; **aficionado 1** *adj*: **ser ~ a** be interested in **2** *m*, **-a** *f* enthusiast; *no profesional* amateur; **aficionarse** become interested (**a** in)

afilado sharp; **afilador** *m* sharpener; **afilar** sharpen; *L.Am.* F (*halagar*) butter up F; *S.Am.* (*seducir*) seduce

afiliación *f* affiliation (**a** to), becoming a member (**a** to); **afiliado** *m* member; **afiliarse**: **~ a** become a member of, join

afinar MÚS tune; *punta* sharpen; *fig* fine-tune

afinidad *f* affinity

afirmación *f* statement; *declaración positiva* affirmation; **afirmar** state, declare; **afirmativo** affirmative

aflicción *f* grief, sorrow

afligir afflict; (*apenar*) upset; *L.Am.* F (*golpear*) beat up; **afligirse** get upset

aflojar 1 *v/t nudo* loosen; F *dinero* hand over **2** *v/i de tormenta* abate; *de viento, fiebre* drop

afluencia *f fig* influx, flow; **horas de ~** peak times; **afluente** *m* tributary; **afluir** flock, flow

afónico: **está ~** he has lost his voice

afortunadamente fortunately, luckily; **afortunado** lucky, fortunate

afrenta *f* insult, affront;

afrentar insult, affront

África Africa; **africano 1** *adj*
African **2** *m*, **-a** *f* African;
afroamericano 1 *adj* African-American **2** *m*, **-a** *f* African-American; **afroantilla-
no, afrocaribeño 1** *adj* Af-
ro-Caribbean **2** *m*, **-a** *f* Af-
ro-Caribbean

afrontar face (up to)

afuera outside; **afueras** *fpl*
outskirts

agacharse bend down; (*acu-
clillarse*) crouch down;
L.Am. (*rendirse*) give in

agalla *f* ZO gill; **tener ~s** F
have guts F

agarradera *f L.Am.* handle

agarrado *fig* F mean, stingy
F; **agarrar 1** *v/t* (*asir*) grab;
L.Am. (*tomar*) take; *L.Am.*
(*atrapar, pescar*), *resfriado*
catch; *L.Am. velocidad* pick
up; **~ una calle** *L.Am.* go
along a street **2** *v/i* (*asirse*)
hold on; *de planta* take root;
L.Am. por un lugar go; **agar-
ró y se fue** he upped and
went; **agarrarse** (*asirse*) hold
on; *L.Am. a golpes* get into a
fight

agasajar fête

agencia *f* agency; **~ inmo-
biliaria** real estate office, *Br*
estate agency; **~ de viajes**
travel agency

agenda *f diario* diary; *programa* schedule; *de mitin* agenda

agente *m/f* agent; **~ de cambio y bolsa** stockbroker; **~**

de policía police officer

ágil agile

agitación *f* POL unrest; **agitar**
shake; *brazos, pañuelo* wave;
fig stir up

aglomeración *f de gente*
crowd; **aglomerar** pile up

agobiado *fig* stressed out; **~
de trabajo** snowed under
with work; **agobiante** oppressive

agolparse crowd together

agonía *f* agony; **agonizante**
dying; **agonizar** *de persona*
be dying; *de régimen* be
crumbling

agosto *m* August

agotado exhausted (*vendido*)
sold out; **agotador** exhausting; **agotamiento** *m* exhaus-
tion; **agotar** exhaust; **agotarse** (*cansarse*) exhaust
o.s.; (*terminarse*) run out;
(*venderse*) sell out

agraciado *persona* attractive

agradable pleasant, nice;
agradar: *me agrada la idea*
fml I like the idea; *nos ~ía
mucho que...* *fml* we would
be delighted if ...

agradecer: **~ algo a alguien**
thank s.o. for sth; *te lo agradezco* I appreciate it; *te lo
agradecido* grateful, appreciative; **agradecimiento** *m* appreciation; **agrado** *m*: *ser
del ~ de alguien* be to
s.o.'s liking

agrandar make bigger

agrario land *atr*, agrarian; *política agricultural*

agravante 1 *adj* JUR aggravating *atr* **2** *f* aggravating factor; **agravar** make worse, aggravate; **agravarse** get worse, deteriorate

agraviar offend, affront; **agravio** *m* offense, *Br* offence

agregado *m*, **-a** *f* en *universidad* senior lecturer; *en colegio* senior teacher; POL attaché; ~ **cultural** cultural attaché

agregar add

agresión *f* aggression; **agresividad** *f* aggression; **agresivo** aggressive; **agresor** *m*, ~**a** *f* aggressor

agriarse *de vino* go sour; *de carácter* become bitter

agrícola agricultural, farming *atr*; **agricultor** *m*, ~**a** *f* farmer; **agricultura** *f* agriculture

agridulce bittersweet

agrietarse crack; *de manos, labios* chap

agrio *fruta* sour; *disputa, carácter* bitter

agrios *mpl* BOT citrus fruit

agrónomo: ingeniero ~ agriculture specialist, agronomist

agrupar group, put into groups

agua *f* water; ~ **corriente** running water; ~ **dulce** fresh water; ~ **mineral** mineral water; ~ **oxigenada** (hydrogen) peroxide; ~ **potable** drinking water; **es** ~ **pasada** it's

water under the bridge; **se me hace la boca** ~ it makes my mouth water; ~**s residuales** effluent, sewage

aguacate *m* BOT avocado

aguacero *m* downpour

aguafiestas *m/f inv* party pooper F

aguafuerte *m* etching

aguamarina *f* aquamarine

aguantar 1 *v/t un peso* bear, support; *respiración* hold; *(soportar)* put up with; **no lo puedo** ~ I can't stand o bear it **2** *v/i* hang on; **aguantarse** *contenerse* keep quiet; **me tuve que aguantar** *conformarme* I had to put up with it; **aguante** *m* patience; *física* stamina

aguar *fiesta* spoil

aguardar 1 *v/t* wait for **2** *v/i* wait

aguardiente *m fruit-based alcoholic spirit*

aguarrás *m* turpentine

agudeza *f de sonido* high pitch; MED intensity; *(perspicacia)* sharpness; ~ **visual** sharp-sightedness; **agudo** acute; *(afilado)* sharp; *sonido* high-pitched; *(perspicaz)* sharp

aguijón *m* ZO sting; *fig* spur

águila *f* eagle; **¿**~ **o sol?** *Méx* heads or tails?

aguja *f* needle; *de reloj* hand

agujerear make holes in; **agujero** *m* hole

agujetas *fpl* stiffness; **tener** ~ be stiff

aguzar sharpen; **~ el oído** prick up one's ears

ahí there; **está por ~** it's (somewhere) over there; *dando direcciones* it's that way

ahijada *f* goddaughter; **ahijado** *m* godson

ahínco *m* effort; **trabajar con ~** work hard

ahogado *en agua* drowned; **ahogar** *(asfixiar)* suffocate; *en agua* drown; AUTO flood; *protestas* stifle; **ahogarse** choke; *(asfixiarse)* suffocate; *en agua* drown; AUTO flood; **ahogo** *m* breathlessness

ahondar: **~ en algo** go into sth in depth

ahora now; *(pronto)* in a moment; **~ mismo** right now; **por ~** for the time being; **~ bien** however; **desde ~, de ~ en adelante** from now on; **¡hasta ~!** see you soon

ahorcar hang; **ahorcarse** hang o.s.

ahorrador 1 *adj* thrifty **2** *m, ~a f* saver, investor; **ahorrar 1** *v/t* save; **~ algo a alguien** save s.o. sth **2** *v/i* save (up); **ahorro** *m* saving; **~s** savings; **caja de ~s** savings bank

ahumado smoked; *cristal ~* tinted glass; **ahumar** smoke

airado angry

airbag *m* AUTO airbag; **airbus** *m* AVIA airbus

aire *m* air; **~ acondicionado** air-conditioning; **al ~ libre** in the open air; **a mi ~** in my own way; **hace mucho ~** it is very windy; **airear** *tb fig* air

airoso: salir ~ de algo do well in sth

aislado isolated; **aislante 1** *adj* insulating **2** *m* insulator; **aislar** isolate; ELEC insulate; **aislador** *m* insulator; **aislamiento** *m* TÉC, ELEC insulation; *fig* isolation

ajado *flores* withered; *(desgastado)* worn

ajedrez *m* chess

ajeno *propiedad, problemas etc* someone else's; **me era totalmente ~** it was completely alien to me; **estar ~ a** be unaware of; **por razones ~as a nuestra voluntad** for reasons beyond our control

ajetrearse F get het up; **ajetreo** *m* bustle

ajo *m* BOT garlic; **estar en el ~** F be in the know F

ajuar *m de novia* trousseau

ajustable adjustable; **ajustado** tight; **ajustar 1** *v/t máquina etc* adjust; *tornillo* tighten; *precio* set; **~ cuentas** fig settle a score **2** *v/i* fit; **ajuste** *m:* **~ de cuentas** settling of scores

ajusticiar execute

al *prp* **a** *y art* **el. ~ entrar** on coming in, when we / they *etc* came in

ala *f* wing; MIL flank; **~ delta** hang glider

alabanza *f* acclaim; **alabar**

praise, acclaim

alabastro *m* alabaster

alacena *f* larder

alacrán *m* ZO scorpion

alado winged

alambique *m* still

alambrado *m* wire netting

alambre *m* wire; **~ de espino o de púas** barbed wire

alarde *m* show, display

alargador *m* TÉC extension cord, *Br* extension lead; **alargar** lengthen; *prenda* let down; *en tiempo* prolong; *mano, brazo* stretch out; **alargarse** *de sombra, día* get longer

alarido *m* shriek

alarma *f* alarm; **dar la voz de ~** raise the alarm; **alarmar** alarm; **alarmarse** become alarmed

alba *f* dawn

albahaca *f* BOT basil

albañil *m* bricklayer

albarán *m* delivery note

albaricoque *m* BOT apricot; **albaricoquero** *m* apricot tree

albergue *m* refuge, shelter; **~ juvenil** youth hostel

albóndiga *f* meatball

albornoz *m* bathrobe

alborotador *m.* **~a** *f* rioter; **alborotar 1** *v/t* stir up; *(desordenar)* disturb **2** *v/i* make a racket; **alboroto** *m* commotion

albufera *f* lagoon

álbum *m* album

alcachofa *f* BOT artichoke; *de*

ducha shower head

alcalde *m*, **-esa** *f* mayor; **alcaldía** *f* mayor's office, city hall

alcance *m* reach; *de arma etc* range; *de medida* scope; *de tragedia* extent, scale; **al ~ de la mano** within reach; **dar ~ a alguien** catch up with s.o.

alcanfor *m* camphor

alcantarillado *m* sewer system; *de sumideros* drainage system

alcanzar 1 *v/t* reach; *a alguien* catch up with; *cantidad* amount to **2** *v/i en altura* reach; *en cantidad* be enough; **~ a oír** manage to hear

alcaparra *f* BOT caper

alcázar *m* fortress

alcoba *f* *S.Am.* bedroom

alcohol *m* alcohol; **~ de quemar** denatured alcohol, *Br* methylated spirits *sg*; **alcoholemia** *f* blood alcohol level; **prueba de ~** drunkometer test, *Br* Breathalyzer® test; **alcohólico 1** *adj* alcoholic **2** *m*, **-a** *f* alcoholic; **alcoholismo** *m* alcoholism

aldaba *f* doorknocker

aldea *f* (small) village

aleación *f* alloy

alegar 1 *v/t motivo* cite; **~ que** claim that **2** *v/i L.Am. (discutir)* argue; *(quejarse)* moan; **alegato** *m* JUR *fig* speech; *Andes* argument

alegoría *f* allegory

alegrar make happy; (*animar*) cheer up; (*alegrarse* cheer up; F *bebiendo* get tipsy; ~ **por alguien** be pleased for s.o. (*de* about); **alegre** happy; F *bebido* tipsy; **alegría** *f* happiness

alejamiento *m* removal, separation; *fig* distancing

alejar (*animar*) encourage; *esperanzas* cherish

alemán 1 *m*/*adj* German **2** *m*, **-ana** *f persona* German; **3** *m idioma* German; **Alemania** Germany

alentar (*animar*) encourage; *esperanzas* cherish

alergia *f* allergy; **alérgico** allergic (*a* to)

alerta 1 *adv:* **estar** ~ be on the alert **2** *f* alert; **dar la** ~ raise the alarm; **poner en** ~ alert

aleta *f* ZO fin; *de buzo* flipper; *de la nariz* wing

aletear flap its wings

alevosía *f* treachery

alfabético alphabetical; **alfabeto** *m* alphabet

alfalfa *f* BOT alfalfa

alfarería *f* pottery; **alfarero** *m*, **-a** *f* potter

alféizar *m* sill, windowsill

alférez *m* second lieutenant

alfil *m* bishop

alfiler *m* pin; ~ **de gancho** *Arg* safety pin

alfombra *f* carpet; *más pequeña* rug; **alfombrado** *m L.Am.* carpeting, carpets *pl*; **alfombrilla** *f* mouse mat

alga *f* BOT alga; *marina* seaweed

álgebra *f* algebra

álgido *fig* decisive

algo 1 *pron* something; *en frases interrogativas o condicionales* anything; ~ **es** ~ it's something, it's better than nothing **2** *adv* rather, somewhat

algodón *m* cotton

alguacil *m*, ~**esa** *f* bailiff

alguien somebody, someone; *en frases interrogativas o condicionales* anybody, anyone

algún *en frases interrogativas o condicionales* some; *en frases interrogativas o condicionales* any; ~ **día** some day

alguno 1 *adj* some; *en frases interrogativas o condicionales* any; **no la influyó de modo** ~ it didn't influence her in any way; **¿has estado alguna vez en ...?** have you ever been to ...? **2** *pron: persona* someone, somebody; ~**s opinan que...** some people think that ...; ~ **se podrá usar** *objeto* we'll be able to use some of them

alhaja *f* piece of jewelry *o Br* jewellery; *fig* gem; ~**s** jewelry

aliado *m*, **-a** *f* ally; **alianza** *f* POL alliance; (*anillo*) wedding ring; **aliarse** form an alliance

alias *m inv* alias

alicatado *m* tiling, tiles *pl*

alicates *mpl* pliers

aliciente *m* (*estímulo*) incentive; (*atractivo*) attraction

aliento *m* breath; *fig* encouragement

aligerar *carga* lighten; **~ el paso** quicken one's pace

alijo *m* MAR consignment

alimentación *f* (*dieta*) diet; *acción* feeding; ELEC power supply; **alimentar 1** *v/t* feed; ELEC power **2** *v/i* be nourishing; **alimento** *m* (*comida*) food; **tiene poco ~** it has little nutritional value; **alimentario, alimenticio** food *atr*, **industria ~a** food industry; **producto ~** foodstuff

alinear align

aliñar dress

alisar smooth

alistar MIL draft; **alistarse** enlist; *L.Am.* (*prepararse*) get ready

aliviar alleviate, relieve; **alivio** *m* relief

aljibe *m* cistern, tank

allá *de lugar* (over) there; **~ por los años veinte** back in the twenties; **más ~** further on; **más ~ de** beyond; **el más ~** the hereafter; **~ ella** F that's up to her

allanar (*alisar*) smooth; (*aplanar*) level (out); *obstáculos* overcome

allegado *m*, **-a** *f* relation, relative

allí there; **por ~** over there; *dando direcciones* that way; **¡~ está!** there it is!

alma *f* soul

almacén *m* warehouse; (*tienda*) store, shop; **grandes almacenes** department store; **almacenar** *tb* INFOR store

almanaque *m* almanac

almeja *f* ZO clam

almendra *f* almond; **almendro** *m* almond tree

almíbar *m* syrup

almidón *m* starch; **almidonar** starch

almirante *m* admiral

almohada *f* pillow; **consultarlo con la ~** sleep on it; **almohadilla** *f* small cushion; TÉC pad

almorranas *fpl* piles

almorzar *al mediodía* have lunch; *a media mañana* have a mid-morning snack; **almuerzo** *m* *al mediodía* lunch; *a media mañana* mid-morning snack; **~ de trabajo** working lunch

alojamiento *m* accommodations *pl*, *Br* accommodation; **alojar** accommodate; **alojarse** stay

alondra *f* ZO lark

alpargata *f* Esp espadrille

alpinismo *m* mountaineering; **alpinista** *m/f* mountaineer, climber

alquilar *de usuario* rent; *de dueño* rent out; **alquiler** *m* *acción*: *de coche etc* rental; *de casa* renting; *dinero* rental, *Br* rent; **~ de coches** car rental, *Br tb* car hire

alquitrán *m* tar

alrededor 1 *adv* around **2** *prp*: **~ de** around; **alrededores** *mpl* surrounding area

alta *f* MED discharge; **darse de ~ en** *organismo* register

altanería f arrogance, disdain; **altanero** arrogant

altar m altar

altavoz m loudspeaker

alteración f alteration; **alterado** persona upset; ~ **genéticamente** genetically altered o modified; **alterar** alter; a alguien upset; **el orden público** cause a breach of the peace; **alterarse** get upset (por because of)

altercado m argument

alternar 1 v/t alternate **2** v/i mix; **alternativa** f alternative; **alternativo** alternative; **alterno** alternate; **corriente -a** ELEC alternating current

alterne f M hospitality in hostess bars; **bar de ~** hostess bar; **chica de ~** hostess

altiplanicie f, **altiplano** m high plateau; **El Altiplano** the Bolivian plateau, the Bolivian Altiplano

altisonante high-flown

altitud f altitude

altivo haughty

alto[1] **1** adj persona tall; precio, número, montaña high; **-as presiones** high pressure; ~ **horno** blast furnace; **clase -a** high class; **en -a mar** on the high seas; **en voz ~a** out loud **2** adv speak loudly; **hablar** ~ speak loudly; **pasar por** ~ overlook; **poner más** ~ TV, RAD turn up **3** m (altura) height; Chi pile

alto[2] m halt; (pausa) pause; **hacer un** ~ stop; ~ **el fuego**

ceasefire

altoparlante m L.Am. loudspeaker

altramuz m lupin

altura f MAT height; MÚS pitch; AVIA altitude, height; GEOG latitude; **a estas ~s** by this time; **estar a la ~ de algo** be up to sth

alubia f BOT kidney bean

alucinar 1 v/i hallucinate **2** v/t F amaze; **alucine** m ~ F amazing; **alucinógeno** m hallucinogen

alud m avalanche

aludir: ~ **a** allude to

alumbrado 1 adj lit **2** m lighting; **alumbramiento** m birth; **alumbrar 1** v/t (dar luz a) light (up) **2** v/i give off light

aluminio m aluminum, Br aluminium; **papel de** ~ aluminum foil

alumno m, **-a** f student

alunizar land on the moon

alusión f allusion (a to)

alza f rise; **en** ~ **en bolsa** rising; **alzamiento** m MIL, POL uprising; **alzar** barrera, brazo lift, raise; precios raise

ama f (dueña) owner; ~ **de casa** housewife; ~ **de llaves** housekeeper

amabilidad f kindness; **amable** kind (con to)

amaestrar train

amago m threat; **hizo** ~ **de levantarse** she made as if to get up; ~ **de infarto** minor heart attack

amainar de lluvia ease up

amamantar bebé breastfeed; cría feed

amanecer 1 v/i get light; de persona wake up **2** m dawn

amansar break in, tame; **amansarse** become tame, become quieter

amante 1 adj lover; **es ~ de ...** he's fond of ... **2** m/f lover

amar love

amaraje m AVIA landing on water; **amarar** AVIA land on water

amargar ocasión spoil; **~ a alguien** make s.o. bitter; **amargo** tb fig bitter; **amargura** f tb fig bitterness

amarillento yellowish; **amarillo** m/adj yellow

amarra f MAR mooring rope; **tener buenas ~s** fig have contacts; **amarrar** L.Am. (atar) tie; **amarre** m MAR mooring, berth

amasar pan knead; fortuna amass

amazona f horsewoman

Amazonas: **el ~** the Amazon

ambages mpl: **decirlo sin ~** say it straight out

ámbar m amber; **el semáforo está en ~** the lights are yellow, Br the lights are at amber

ambición f ambition; **ambicionar** aspire to; **ambicioso** ambitious

ambientador m air freshener; **ambiental** environmental; **ambiente 1** adj: **me-**dio ~ environment; **temperatura ~** room temperature **2** m (entorno) environment; (situación) atmosphere

ambiguo m buffet

ambigüedad f ambiguity; **ambiguo** ambiguous

ámbito m area; (límite) scope

ambos, ambas 1 adj both **2** pron both (of us / you / them)

ambulancia f ambulance; **ambulante 1** adj traveling, Br travelling **2** m/f L.Am. (vendedor) street seller; **ambulatorio 1** adj MED out-patient atr **2** m out-patient clinic

amén 1 m amen **2** prp: **~ de** as well as

amenaza f threat; **~ de bomba** bomb scare; **amenazador** threatening; **amenazante** threatening; **amenazar 1** v/t threaten (con, de with) **2** v/i: **~** con threaten to

ameno enjoyable

América America; **América Central** Central America; **América Latina** Latin America; **América del Norte** North America; **América del Sur** South America; **americana** f American (woman); prenda jacket; **americano** m/adj American

ametralladora f machine gun

amianto m asbestos

amiba f ameba, Br amoeba

amígdala f tonsil; **amigdali-**

tis *f* tonsillitis

amigo 1 *adj* friendly; **ser ~ de algo** be fond of sth **2** *m*, **-a** *f* friend; **hacerse ~s** make friends

aminorar reduce; **~ la marcha** slow down

amistad *f* friendship; **~es** friends; **amistoso** friendly; **partido ~** DEP friendly (game)

amnistía *f* amnesty

amo *m* (*dueño*) owner; HIST master

amodorramiento *m* drowsiness

amoldar adapt (*a* to); **amoldarse** adapt (*a* to)

amonestación *f* warning; DEP caution; **amonestar** reprimand; DEP caution

amoníaco, amoniaco *m* ammonia

amontonar pile up; **amontonarse** pile up; *de gente* crowd together

amor *m* love; **~ mío** my love, darling; **~ propio** self-respect; **hacer el ~** make love; **amoroso** amorous

amortiguador *m* AUTO shock absorber; **amortiguar** *impacto* cushion; *sonido* muffle

amortización *f* repayment, redemption; **amortizar** pay off

amparar protect; (*ayudar*) help; **amparo** *m* protection; (*cobijo*) shelter; **al ~ de** under the protection of

amperio *m* ampere, amp

ampliación *f de casa, carretera* extension; FOT enlargement; **ampliar** *plantilla* increase; *negocio* expand; *plazo, edificio* extend; FOT enlarge; **amplificación** *f* amplification; **amplificador** *m* amplifier; **amplificar** amplify; **amplio** *casa* spacious; *gama, margen* wide; *falda* full; **amplitud** *f* breadth

ampolla *f* MED blister; (*botellita*) vial, *Br* phial

amputar amputate

amueblar furnish

amuleto *m* charm

analfabeto 1 *adj* illiterate **2** *m*, **-a** *f* illiterate

analgésico 1 *adj* painkilling, analgesic **2** *m* painkiller, analgesic

análisis *m inv* analysis; **~ de mercado** market research; **~ de sangre** blood test; **analista** *m/f* analyst; **analizar** analyze

analogía *f* analogy; **analógico** analog, *Br* analogue; **análogo** analogous

ananá(s) *m S.Am.* pineapple

anaquel *m* shelf

anarquía *f* anarchy

anatomía *f* anatomy

anca *f* haunch; **~s de rana** frogs' legs

ancho 1 *adj* wide, broad; **a sus -as** at ease, relaxed **2** *m* width; **~ de vía** FERR gauge; **dos metros de ~** two meters wide

anchoa *f* anchovy

anchura f width

anciana f old woman; **ancianidad** f old age; **anciano 1** adj old **2** m old man

ancla f anchor; **anclar** anchor

andamio m scaffolding

andar v/i (caminar) walk; (funcionar) work; **andando** on foot; **~ bien / mal** fig go well / badly; **~ con cuidado** be careful; **~ en algo** (buscar) rummage in sth; **~ haciendo algo** be doing sth; **¡anda!** come on! **2** v/t walk

andén m platform; L.Am. sidewalk, Br pavement

Andes mpl Andes; **andinismo** m L.Am. mountaineering, climbing; **andinista** m/f L.Am. mountaineer, climber; **andino** Andean

andrajoso ragged

anécdota f anecdote

anejo m attached **2** m annex, Br annexe

anemia f anemia, Br anaemia; **anémico** anemic, Br anaemic

anestesia f anesthesia Br anaesthesia

anexión f POL annexation; **anexionar** POL annex; **anexo 1** adj attached **2** m edificio annex, Br annexe

anfiteatro m amphitheater, Br amphitheatre; de teatro dress circle

anfitrión m host; **anfitriona** f hostess

ánfora f L.Am. POL ballot box; HIST amphora

ángel m angel; **~ custodio** guardian angel

angina f: **~s** sore throat, strep throat; **~ de pecho** angina

angosto narrow

angostura f angostura

anguila f eel; **angula** f elver

angular 1 adj angular; **piedra ~** cornerstone **2** m TÉC angle iron; **gran ~** FOT wide-angle lens sg; **ángulo** m MAT, fig angle; **anguloso** angular

angustia f anguish; **angustiar** distress; **angustiarse** agonize (**por** over); **angustioso** agonizing

anhelar long for; **anhelo** m longing, desire (**de** for)

anidar nest

anilla f ring; **cuaderno de ~s** ring binder

anillo m ring

ánima f REL soul; TÉC bore

animación f liveliness; en películas animation; **hay mucha ~** it's very lively; **animado** lively; **animador** m host; **~ turístico** events organizer; **animadora** f hostess; DEP cheerleader

animal 1 adj animal atr, fig stupid **2** m tb fig animal; **~ doméstico** mascota pet; de granja domestic animal

animar cheer up; (alentar) encourage; **animarse** cheer up

ánimo m spirit; (coraje) encouragement; **estado de ~** state of mind; **con ~ de** with the intention of; **¡~!** cheer up!

animosidad f animosity
animoso spirited
aniquilar annihilate
anís m BOT aniseed; *bebida* anisette
aniversario m anniversary
ano m ANAT anus
anoche last night; **antes de ~** the night before last; **anochecer 1** v/i get dark **2** m dusk
anomalía f anomaly; **anómalo** anomalous
anónimo 1 adj anonymous **2** m poison pen letter
anorak m anorak
anormal abnormal
anotar note down
ansia f yearning; (*inquietud*) anxiousness; **ansiar** yearn for, long for; **ansiedad** f anxiety; **ansioso** anxious; **está ~ por verlos** he's longing to see them
ante¹ m suede; ZO moose; *Méx* (*postre*) egg and coconut dessert
ante² prp posición before; *dificultad* faced with; **~ todo** above all
anteanoche the night before last
anteayer the day before yesterday
antebrazo m forearm
antecedente m precedent; **~s penales** previous convictions; **poner a alguien en ~s** put s.o. in the picture; **anteceder** precede, come before; **antecesor** m, **~a** f predecessor
antelación f: **con ~** in advance
antemano: **de ~** beforehand
antena f de radio, televisión antenna, Br aerial; ZO antenna; **~ parabólica** satellite dish
anteojos mpl binoculars
antepasado m, **-a** f ancestor
antepecho m de ventana sill; (*barandilla*) parapet
anteponer: **~ algo a algo** put sth before sth
anterior previous, former; **anterioridad** f: **con ~** before, previously; **con ~ a** before
antes 1 adv before; **cuanto ~, lo ~ posible** as soon as possible; **poco ~** shortly before; **~ que nada** first of all **2** prp: **~ de** before
antesala f lobby
antibala(s) bulletproof
antibiótico m antibiotic
anticiclón m anticyclone
anticipación f anticipation; **con ~** in advance; **anticipado** pago advance atr, *elecciones* early; **por ~** in advance; **anticipar** *sueldo* advance; *fecha, viaje* move up, Br bring forward; *información* give a preview of
anticonceptivo m contraceptive
anticongelante m antifreeze
anticuado antiquated; **anticuario** m antique dealer
antideslizante non-slip
antídoto m MED antidote; fig

cure
antifaz *m* mask
antigüedad *f* age; *en el trabajo* length of service; **~es** antiques; **antiguo** old; *del pasado remoto* ancient
antipatía *f* antipathy, dislike; **antipático** disagreeable, unpleasant
antirrobo *m* AUTO antitheft device
antiséptico *m/adj* antiseptic
antiterrorista *brigada* antiterrorist *atr*; **la lucha ~** the fight against terrorism
antojarse: se le antojó salir he felt like going out; **se me antoja que...** it seems to me that ...; **antojo** *m* whim; *de embarazada* craving; **a mí ~** as I please
antología *f* anthology; **de ~** *fig* F incredible F
antorcha *f* torch
antro *m* F dive F, dump F
antropófago *m*, **-a** *f* cannibal
anual annual; **anualidad** *f* annual payment
anuario *m* yearbook
anublarse cloud over
anudar knot
anular[1] cancel; *matrimonio* annul; *gol* disallow
anular[2] *adj* ring-shaped; **dedo ~** ring finger
anunciar announce; COM advertise; **anuncio** *m* announcement; *(presagio)* sign; COM advertisement; **~ luminoso** illuminated sign; **~s por palabras, pequeños**

~s classified advertisements
anverso *m* obverse
añadidura *f*: **por ~** in addition; **añadir** add
añejo mature
año *m* year; **~ bisiesto** leap year; **~ fiscal** fiscal year, Br financial year; **~ luz** light year; **~ nuevo** New Year; **¿cuándo cumples ~s?** when's your birthday?; **¿cuántos ~s tienes?** how old are you?; **a los diez ~s** at the age of ten; **los ~s veinte** the twenties
añoranza *f* yearning (**de** for); **añorar** miss
apacible mild-mannered
apaciguar pacify, calm down
apadrinar be godparent to; *político* support, back; *artista etc* sponsor; **~ a la novia** give the bride away
apagado *fuego* out; *luz* off; *persona* dull; *color* subdued; **apagar** *televisor, luz* turn off; *fuego* put out; **apagarse de luz** go off; *de fuego* go out; **apagón** *m* blackout
apalear beat
apañado F resourceful; **apañarse** manage; **apañárselas** manage, get by
aparador *m* sideboard; *Méx (escaparate)* shop window
aparato *m* piece of equipment; *doméstico* appliance; BIO, ANAT system; *de partido político* machine; **al ~** TELEC speaking; **aparatoso** spectacular

aparcamiento *m* parking lot, *Br* car park; **~ subterráneo** underground parking garage, *Br* underground car park; **aparcar 1** *v/t* park; *proyecto* shelve **2** *v/i* park

aparecer appear

aparejador *m*, **~a** *f* architectural technician; **aparejo** *m*: **~s de pesca** fishing gear; **aparejar** prepare; *caballo* saddle; MAR rig; **traer aparejado** entail, bring with it

aparentar pretend; **no aparenta la edad que tiene** she doesn't look her age; **aparente** (*evidente*) apparent; *L.Am.* (*fingido*) feigned; **aparición** *f* appearance; (*fantasma*) apparition; **apariencia** *f* appearance; **en ~** outwardly

apartado *m* section; **~ de correos** PO box; **apartamento** *m* apartment, *Br* flat; **apartamiento** *m* separation; *L.Am.* (*apartamento*) apartment, *Br* flat; **apartar** separate; *para después* set aside; *de un sitio* move away (**de** from); **~ a alguien de hacer algo** dissuade s.o. from doing sth; **apartarse** move aside (**de** from); **~ del tema** stray from the subject; **aparte** to one side; (*por separado*) separately; **~ de** aside from, *Br* apart from; **punto y ~** new paragraph

apasionado 1 *adj* passionate

2 *m/f* enthusiast; **apasionar** fascinate; **apasionarse** develop a passion (**por** for)

apatía *f* apathy; **apático** apathetic

apearse get off, alight *fml*

apedrear throw stones at; *matar* stone

apego *m* attachment

apelación *f* JUR appeal; **apelar** *tb* JUR appeal (**a** to)

apellido *m* surname; **~ de soltera** maiden name

apenar sadden

apenas 1 *adv* hardly, scarcely **2** *conj* as soon as

apéndice *m* appendix; **apendicitis** *f* appendicitis

aperitivo *m comida* appetizer; *bebida* aperitif

apero *m utensilio* implement; *L.Am.* (*arneses*) harness

apertura *f* opening; FOT aperture; POL opening up

apestar 1 *v/t* stink out F **2** *v/i* reek (**a** of)

apetecer: **¿qué te apetece?** what do you feel like?; **apetecible** appetizing

apetito *m* appetite; **apetitoso** appetizing

ápice *m*: **ni un ~** *fig* not an ounce; **no ceder ni un ~** *fig* not give an inch

apicultura *f* beekeeping

apilar pile up

apio *m* BOT celery

apisonadora *f* steamroller; **apisonar** roll

aplacar *hambre* satisfy; *sed* quench; *a alguien* calm down

aplanar level, flatten; ~ **las calles** *C.Am., Pe* hang around the streets; **aplanarse** *fig* (*descorazonarse*) lose heart

aplastar *tb fig* crush

aplaudir *v/i* applaud, clap **2** *v/t tb fig* applaud; **aplauso** *m* round of applause

aplazar *visita* put off, postpone; *Arg* fail

aplicable applicable; **aplicación** *f* application; **aplicar** apply

aplique *m* wall light

apoderado *m* COM agent; **apoderar**(**se**) take possession *o* control (**de** of)

apodo *m* nickname

apoplejía *f* apoplexy; **ataque de** ~ stroke

aportar contribute; ~ **pruebas** JUR provide evidence

apostar 1 *v/t* bet (**por** on) **2** *v/i* bet; ~ **por algo** opt for sth

apóstol *m* apostle

apoyar lean (**en** against), rest (**en** against); (*respaldar, confirmar*) support; **apoyo** *m fig* support

app *f* IT app

apreciable (*visible*) appreciable, noticeable; (*considerable*) considerable, substantial; **apreciación** *f* appreciation; **apreciado** valued; **apreciar** appreciate; (*sentir afecto por*) be fond of; **aprecio** *m* respect

apremio *m* pressure

aprender, aprenderse learn; **aprendiz** *m*, ~**a** *f* apprentice, trainee; **aprendizaje** *m* apprenticeship

aprestar, aprestarse get ready

apresurar hurry; **apresurarse** hurry up; ~ **a hacer algo** hurry *o* rush to do sth

apretado tight; **apretar 1** *v/t botón* press; (*pellizcar, pinzar*) squeeze; *tuerca* tighten; ~ **el paso** quicken one's pace; ~ **los puños** clench one's fists **2** *v/i de ropa, zapato* be too tight

aprieto *m* predicament

aprisa quickly

aprisionar *fig* trap

aprobación *f* approval; *de ley* passing; **aprobado** *m* EDU pass; **aprobar** approve; *comportamiento, idea* approve of; *examen* pass

apropiación *f* appropriation

apropiado appropriate, suitable; **apropiarse**: ~ **de algo** take sth

aprovechable usable; **aprovechado 1** *adj desp* opportunistic **2** *m*, ~**a** *f desp* opportunist; **aprovechamiento** *m* exploitation, use; ~ **de residuos** of waste material; **aprovechar 1** *v/t* take advantage of; *tiempo, espacio* make good use of **2** *v/i* take the opportunity (**para** to); **¡que aproveche!** enjoy your meal!

aprovisionamiento *m* provi-

sioning, supply; **aprovisio-
nar** provision, supply; **apro-
visionarse** stock up (*de* on)
aproximación *f* approxima-
tion; (*acercamiento*) approach; *en lotería* consolation prize; **aproximada-
mente** approximately; **aproximado** approximate; **apro-
ximar** bring closer; **aproximarse** approach; **aproxima-
tivo** approximate, rough
aptitud *f* aptitude (*para* for),
flair (*para* for); *apto* suitable (*para* for); *para servicio
militar* fit; EDU pass
apuesta *f* bet
apuntado pointed
apuntador *m*, **~a** *f* TEA
prompter
apuntalar *edificio* shore up;
fig prop up
apuntar 1 *v/t* (*escribir*) note
down; TEA prompt; *en curso
etc* put down (*en*, *a* on; *para*
for); **~ con el dedo** point at o
to **2** *v/i con arma* aim; **apun-
te** *m* note
apuñalar stab
apurado *L.Am.* (*con prisa*) in
a hurry; (*pobre*) short (*of*
cash); **apurar 1** *v/t vaso* finish
off; *a alguien* pressure **2** *v/i
Chi: no me apura* I'm not in
a hurry for it; **apurarse**
worry; *L.Am.* (*darse prisa*)
hurry (up); **apuro** *m* predicament; *vergüenza* embar-
rassment; *L.Am.* rush; *me
da* **~** I'm embarrassed
aquejado: *estar* **~** *de* be suf-

fering from
**aquel, aquella, aquellos,
aquellas** that; *pl* those
**aquél, aquélla, aquéllos,
aquéllas** that (one); *pl* those
(ones)
aquello that
aquí here; *en el tiempo* now;
desde **~** from here; *por* **~**
here
árabe 1 *m/f & adj* Arab **2** *m
idioma* Arabic
Arabia Saudí Saudi Arabia
arado *m* plow, *Br* plough
arancel *m* tariff; **arancelario**
tariff *atr*
arándano *m* blueberry
araña *f* ZO spider; *lámpara*
chandelier
arañar scratch; **arañazo** *m*
scratch
arar plow, *Br* plough
arbitraje *m* arbitration; **arbitrar** *en fútbol, boxeo* referee;
en tenis, béisbol umpire; *en
conflicto* arbitrate; **arbitrario** arbitrary; **árbitro** *m en
fútbol, boxeo* referee; *en tenis, béisbol* umpire; *en conflicto* arbitrator
árbol *m* tree; **~ genealógico**
family tree
arbusto *m* shrub, bush
arca *f* chest; **~ de Noé** Noah's
Ark
arcada *f* MED: *me provocó* **~s**
it made me retch
arcaico archaic
arcángel *m* archangel
arce *m* BOT maple
arcén *m* shoulder, *Br* hard

shoulder

archifamoso very famous

archipiélago *m* archipelago

archivador *m* file cabinet, *Br* filing cabinet; **archivar** *documentos* file; *asunto* shelve; **archivo** *m* archive; INFOR file

arcilla *f* clay

arco *m* ARQUI arch; MÚS bow; *L.Am.* DEP goal; ~ **iris** rainbow

arder burn; *estar muy caliente* be very hot; *ardiente persona, amor* passionate; *defensor* ardent; *bebida* scalding

ardilla *f* squirrel

ardor *m entusiasmo* fervor, *Br* fervour; ~ **de estómago** heartburn

arduo arduous

área *f* area; DEP ~ **de castigo** *o* **de penalty** penalty area; ~ **de servicio** service area

arena *f* sand; ~**s movedizas** quicksand; **arenoso** sandy

arenque *m* herring

arete *m L.Am. joya* earring

Argel Algiers; **Argelia** Algeria; **argelino 1** *adj* Algeria **2** *m*, **-a** *f* Algerian

Argentina Argentina; **argentino 1** *adj* Argentinian **2** *m*, **-a** *f* Argentinian

argolla *f L.Am.* ring

argucia *f* clever argument; **argüir** argue; **argumentación** *f* argumentation; **argumentar** argue; **argumento** *m razón* argument; *de libro etc* plot

aria *f* aria

aridez *f* aridity, dryness; **árido** arid, dry; *fig* dry

Aries *m/f inv* ASTR Aries

arisco unfriendly

arista *f* MAT edge; BOT beard

aristocracia *f* aristocracy; **aristocrático** aristocratic

arma *f* weapon; ~ **blanca** knife; ~ **de fuego** firearm; **alzarse en** ~**s** rise up in arms; **armada** *f* navy; **armadura** *f* armor, *Br* armour; **armamento** *m* armaments *pl*; **armar** MIL arm; TÉC assemble; ~ **un escándalo** F make a scene

armario *m* closet, *Br* wardrobe; ~ **de cocina** cabinet, *Br* cupboard

armazón *f* skeleton, framework

armería *f* gunstore

armiño *m* ZO stoat; *piel* ermine

armisticio *m* armistice

armonía *f* harmony; **armónica** *f* harmonica, mouth organ; **armónico** *m/adj* harmonic

arnés *m* harness; *para niños* leading strings *pl*, *Br* leading reins *pl*

aro *m* hoop; *L.Am.* (*pendiente*) earring

aroma *m* aroma; *de flor* scent; **aromático** aromatic

arpa *f* harp; **arpista** *m/f* harpist

arpón *m* harpoon

arquear *espalda* arch; *cejas*

raise

arqueo *m* MAR capacity; COM: **~ (de caja)** cashing up

arqueología *f* archeology, *Br* archaeology

arquitecto *m*, **-a** *f* architect; **arquitectura** *f* architecture

arrabal *m* poor outlying area

arraigado entrenched

arrancar 1 *v/t planta, página* pull out; *vehículo* start (up); *(quitar)* snatch **2** *v/i de vehículo, máquina* start (up); INFOR boot (up); *(huir)* run away; **arranque** *m* AUTO starter; *(energía)* drive; *(ataque)* fit

arrasar 1 *v/t por el suelo*, INFOR drag *(por* along); *(llevarse)* carry away **2** *v/i por el suelo* trail on the ground; **arrastrarse** crawl; *fig (humillarse)* grovel *(delante de* to); **arrastre** *m*: **estar para el ~** *fig* F be fit to drop F

arrebatador breathtaking; **arrebatar** snatch *(a* from); **arrebatarse** get excited; **arrebato** *m* fit

arrecife *m* reef

arredrarse be intimidated *(ante* by)

arreglado neat; **si empieza a llover estamos ~s** if it starts to rain, that'll be just dandy; **arreglar** *(reparar)* fix, repair; *(ordenar)* tidy (up); *(solucionar)* sort out; MUS arrange; **~ cuentas** settle up; *fig* settle scores; **arreglarse** get ready; *de problema* get sorted out; *(apañarse)* manage; **arreglárselas** manage; **arreglo** *m (reparación)* repair; *(solución)* solution; *(acuerdo)*, MUS arrangement; **~ de cuentas** settling of scores; **con ~ a** in accordance with

arremeter: ~ contra charge *(at)*; *fig (criticar)* attack

arrendamiento *m* renting; **arrendar** *L.Am. (dar en alquiler)* rent (out); *(tomar en alquiler)* rent; **se arrienda** for rent; **arrendatario** *m*, **-a** *f* tenant

arrepentirse be sorry; *(cambiar de opinión)* change one's mind; **~ de algo** regret sth

arrestar arrest; **arresto** *m* arrest

arriba 1 *adv* up; *en edificio* upstairs; **el cajón de ~** siguiente the next drawer up, the drawer above; *último* the top drawer; **~ del todo** right at the top; **sigan hacia ~** keep going up; **me miró de ~ abajo** she looked me up and down; **de diez para ~** ten or above **2** *int* long live

arribada *f*, **arribaje** *m* MAR arrival; **arribar** MAR arrive, put in

arribista *m/f* social climber

arriesgar risk

arrimar move closer

arrinconar *(acorralar)* corner; *libros etc* put away; *persona* cold-shoulder

arroba *f* INFOR "at" symbol

arrodillarse kneel (down)

arrogancia f arrogance; **arrogante** arrogant

arrojar throw; *resultado* produce; (*vomitar*) throw up; **arrojarse** throw o.s.; **arrojo** m bravery

arrollador overwhelming; **arrollar** AUTO run over; *fig* crush

arropar wrap up; *fig* protect

arroyo m stream; *sacar a alguien del ~ fig* lift s.o. out of the gutter

arroz m rice; **~ con leche** rice pudding

arruga f wrinkle; **arrugar** wrinkle

arruinar ruin

arsenal m arsenal

arsénico m arsenic

arte m (pl f) art; **~ dramático** dramatic art; **bellas ~s** fine art; **malas ~s** guile

artefacto m (*dispositivo*) device

arteria f artery

arterio(e)sclerosis f arteriosclerosis

artesa f trough

artesana f craftswoman; **artesanía** f (handi)crafts pl; **artesano** m craftsman

articulación f ANAT, TÉC joint; *de sonidos* articulation; **articulado** articulated; **articular** articulate

artículo m article; COM product, item

artífice m author

artificial artificial

artificio m trick; (*artefacto*) device; **artificioso** sly; (*falto de naturalidad*) affected

artillería f artillery

artista m/f artist; **artístico** artistic

artritis f arthritis

artrosis f rheumatoid arthritis

arveja f Rpl, Chi, Pe pea

arzobispo m archbishop

as m tb fig ace

asa f handle

asado m/adj roast

asalariado m, -a f wage earner; *de empresa* employee

asaltar attack; *banco* rob; **asalto** m attack (**a** on); *robo* robbery, raid; *en boxeo* round

asamblea f *reunión* meeting; *ente* assembly

asar roast; **~ a la parrilla** broil, Br grill

ascendente 1 adj rising, upward **2** m ASTR ascendant; **ascender 1** v/t a empleado promote **2** v/i de temperatura etc rise; de montañero climb; DEP, en trabajo be promoted (**a** to); **ascendiente** m ancestor; **ascensión** f ascent; **ascenso** m de temperatura, precios rise (**de** in); de montaña ascent; DEP, en trabajo promotion; **ascensor** m elevator, Br lift; **ascensorista** m/f elevator operator

asceta m/f ascetic; **ascético** ascetic

asco m disgust; **me da ~** I find

it disgusting; **¡qué ~!** how disgusting!

ascua f ember; **estar en** o **sobre ~s** be on tenterhooks

asediar tb fig besiege

asegurado 1 adj insured **2** m, -a f insured; **aseguradora** f insurance company; **asegurar** (afianzar) secure; (prometer) assure; (garantizar) guarantee; COM insure; **asegurarse** make sure

asemejarse: ~ a look like

asentimiento m approval, agreement; **asentir** agree (**a** to); **con la cabeza** nod

aseo m cleanliness; (baño) restroom, toilet

asequible precio affordable; obra accessible

asesinar murder; POL assassinate; **asesinato** m murder; POL assassination; **asesino** m, -a f murderer; POL assassin

asesor m, -a f consultant, advisor, Br adviser; **~ de imagen** public relations consultant

asesoramiento m advice; **asesorar** advise; **asesoría** f consultancy

asfalto m asphalt

asfixia f asphyxiation; **asfixiar, asfixiarse** asphyxiate, suffocate

así 1 adv (de este modo) like this; (de ese modo) like that; **~ no más** S.Am. just like that; **~ pues** so; **~ que** so; **~ de grande** this big; **~ ~** so

so **2** conj: **~ como** al igual que while, whereas

Asia Asia; **asiático 1** adj Asian **2** m, -a f Asian

asiduidad f frequency; **con ~** con frecuencia regularly; **asiduo** regular

asiento m seat; **tomar ~** take a seat

asignar allocate; persona, papel assign; **asignatura** f subject

asilado m, -a f POL asylum seeker; **asilo** m home, institution; POL asylum; **~ de ancianos** old people's home

asimilar assimilate

asimismo (también) also; (igualmente) likewise

asistencia f (ayuda) assistance; a lugar attendance (**a** at); **~ en carretera** AUTO roadside assistance; **~ médica** medical care; **asistenta** f cleaner; **asistente** m/f (ayudante) assistant; **~ social** social worker; **los ~s** those present; **asistir 1** v/t help, assist **2** v/i be present

asma f asthma; **asmático** asthmatic

asno m ZO donkey; persona idiot

asociación f association; **asociar** associate

asomarse lean out (**por** of)

asombrar amaze, astonish; **asombro** m amazement, astonishment; **asombroso** amazing, astonishing

asomo m: **ni por ~** no way

aspecto *m de persona, cosa* look, appearance; *(faceta)* aspect; **tener buen ~** look good

aspereza *f* roughness; **áspero** *superficie* rough; *sonido* harsh; *persona* abrupt

aspiraciones *fpl* aspirations

aspirador *m*, **~a** *f* vacuum cleaner; **aspirante** *m/f a cargo* candidate (**a** for); *a título* contender (**a** for); **aspirar 1** *v/t* suck up; *al respirar* inhale, breathe in **2** *v/i*: **~ a** aspire to

aspirina *f* aspirin

asquear *m* disgust; **asqueroso 1** *adj (sucio)* filthy; *(repugnante)* revolting, disgusting **2** *m*, **-a** *f* creep

asta *f* flagpole; *(pitón)* horn

asterisco *m* asterisk

astilla *f* splinter; **~s** *para fuego* kindling; **hacer ~s algo** *fig* smash sth to pieces

astillero *m* shipyard

astracán *m* astrakhan

astro *m* AST, *fig* star; **astrología** *f* astrology; **astrólogo** *m*, **-a** *f* astrologer; **astronauta** *m/f* astronaut; **astronave** *f* spaceship; **astronomía** *f* astronomy

astucia *f* shrewdness, astuteness; **astuto** shrewd, astute

asumir assume; *(aceptar)* accept, come to terms with

asunto *m* matter; F *(relación)* affair; **~s exteriores** foreign affairs; **no es ~ tuyo** it's none of your business

asustar frighten, scare

atacar attack

atajar 1 *v/t* check the spread of, contain; *L.Am. pelota* catch **2** *v/i* take a short cut; **atajo** *m L.Am.* short cut

atalaya 1 *f* watchtower **2** *m/f* sentinel

ataque *m (agresión)* attack; *(acceso)* fit; **~ cardíaco** o **al corazón** heart attack; **le dio un ~ de risa** she burst out laughing

atar tie (up); *fig* tie down

atardecer 1 *v/i* get dark **2** *m* dusk

atareado busy

atasco *m* traffic jam

ataúd *m* coffin, casket

ate *m Méx* quince jelly

atención 1 *f* attention; *(cortesía)* courtesy; **¡~!** your attention, please!; **llamar la ~ a alguien** *reñir* tell s.o. off; *por ser llamativo* attract s.o.'s attention; **prestar ~** pay attention (**a** to)

atender 1 *v/t a enfermo* look after; *en tienda* attend to **2** *v/i* pay attention (**a** to)

atenerse: **~ a normas** abide by; *consecuencias* accept; **saber a qué ~** know where one stands

atentado *m* attack **(contra, a** on); **~ terrorista** terrorist attack; **~ con coche bomba** car bomb attack

atento attentive; **estar ~ a** pay attention to

atenuante JUR extenuating; **atenuar** lessen, reduce

ateo 1 adj atheistic **2** m, -a f atheist

aterrizaje m AVIA landing; ~ **forzoso** o **de emergencia** emergency landing; **aterrizar** land

aterrorizar terrify; (amenazar) terrorize

atestado overcrowded

atestiguar JUR testify; fig bear witness to

ático m piso top floor; apartamento top floor apartment o Br flat; (desván) attic

atizar fuego poke; pasiones stir up; **le atizó un golpe** she hit him

atleta m/f athlete; **atletismo** m athletics

atmósfera f atmosphere

atolondrado scatterbrained

atómico atomic; **átomo** m atom; **ni un ~ de** fig not an iota of

atónito astonished, amazed

atontado dazed, stunned

atormentar torment

atornillar screw on

atosigar pester

atracadero m MAR mooring; **atracar 1** v/t banco hold up; a alguien mug; Chi F make out with **F 2** v/i MAR dock

atracción f attraction

atraco m robbery; de persona mugging

atractivo 1 adj attractive **2** m appeal, attraction; **atraer** attract

atrapar catch, trap

atrás posición at the back, behind; movimiento back; **años** ~ years ago o back; **hacia** ~ back, backward; **quedarse** ~ get left behind; **atrasado** en estudios, pago behind (**en** in o with); reloj slow; pueblo backward; **ir** ~ de un reloj be slow; **atrasar 1** v/t reloj put back; fecha postpone, put back **2** v/i de reloj lose time; **atraso** m backwardness; COM ~**s** arrears

atravesar cross; (perforar), crisis go through

atrevido daring; **atreverse** dare

atribuir attribute (**a** to); **atributo** m attribute

atril m lectern

atrocidad f atrocity

atropellado in a rush; **atropellar** knock down; **atropello** m running over; escándalo outrage

atroz appalling, atrocious

ATS (= **ayudante técnico sanitario**) registered nurse

atún m tuna (fish)

aturdido in a daze

audacia f audacity; **audaz** bold, audacious

audible audible

audición f TEA audition; JUR hearing

audiencia f audience; JUR court; **índice de** ~ TV ratings pl

audífono m hearing aid; **audiovisual** audiovisual

audioguía *f* audioguide, audio guide

auditivo auditory; *problema* hearing *atr*

auditor *m*, **~a** *f* auditor; **auditorio** *m* (*público*) audience; *sala* auditorium

aula *f* classroom; *en universidad* lecture hall, *Br* lecture theatre

aumentar 1 *v/t* increase **2** *v/i* increase, go up; **aumento** *m* increase (**de** in); *de sueldo* raise, *Br* rise; **ir en ~** be increasing

aun even; **~ así** even so

aún still; *en oraciones negativas* yet; *en comparaciones* even; **~ no** not yet

aunque although, even though; + *subj* even if

aureola *f* halo

auricular *m de teléfono* receiver; **~es** headphones, earphones

auscultar: **~ a alguien** listen to s.o.'s chest

ausencia *f de persona* absence; *no existencia* lack (**de** of); **ausentarse** leave, go away; **ausente** absent

austeridad *f* austerity; **austero** austere

austral southern

Australia Australia; **australiano 1** *adj* Australian **2** *m*, **-a** *f* Australian

Austria Austria; **austriano 1** *adj* Austrian **2** *m*, **-a** *f* Austrian

auténtico authentic

autismo *m* autism

auto *m* JUR order; *L.Am.* AUTO car

autoadhesivo self-adhesive

autobanco *m* ATM, cash machine

autobiografía *f* autobiography

autobús *m* bus

autocar *m* bus

autocaravana *f* camper van

autocine *m* drive-in movie theater

autodefensa *f* self-defense, *Br* self-defence

autodisparador *m* FOT automatic shutter release

autoescuela *f* driving school

autógrafo *m* autograph

automático automatic

automóvil *m* car, automobile; **automovilismo** *m* driving; **automovilista** *m/f* motorist

autonomía *f* autonomy; *en España* autonous region

autopista *f* freeway, *Br* motorway

autopsia *f* autopsy

autor *m*, **~a** *f* author; *de crimen* perpetrator

autoridad *f* authority; **autorización** *f* authority; **autorizar** authorize; **autorizado** (*permitido*) authorized; (*respetado*) authoritative

autorradio *m* car radio

autoservicio *m* supermarket; *restaurante* self-service restaurant

autostop *m* hitchhiking; **hacer ~** hitchhike; **autostopis-**

ta *m/f* hitchhiker

autovía *f* divided highway, *Br* dual carriageway

auxiliar 1 *adj* auxiliary; *profesor* assistant **2** *m/f* assistant; ~ *de vuelo* stewardess, flight attendant **3** help; **auxilio** *m* help; **primeros ~s** first aid

aval *m* guarantee

avalancha *f* avalanche

avance *m* advance

avanzar advance, move forward; MIL advance (**hacia** on)

avaricia *f* avarice; **avaro 1** *adj* miserly **2** *m*, *-a f* miser

ave *f* bird; *S.Am.* (*pollo*) chicken; ~ *de presa o de rapiña* bird of prey

avellana *f* hazelnut

avena *f* oats *pl*

avenencia *f* agreement

avenida *f* avenue

aventura *f* adventure; *riesgo* venture; *amorosa* affair; *opinión* venture; **aventurar** risk; **aventurero** adventurous

avergonzar (*aborchornar*) embarrass; **le avergüenza algo reprensible** she's ashamed of it; **avergonzarse** be ashamed (**de** of)

avería *f* TÉC fault; AUTO breakdown; **averiado** broken down

averiguar find out

aversión *f* aversion

avestruz *m* ostrich

aviación *f* aviation; MIL air force; **aviador** *m*, *-a f* pilot,

aviator

avicultura *f* poultry farming

avidez *f* eagerness; **ávido** eager (**de** for), avid (**de** for)

avión *m* plane; **por ~** *mandar una carta* (by) airmail; **avioneta** *f* light aircraft

avisador *m* warning light; *sonoro* alarm; *L.Am.* (*anunciante*) advertiser; **avisar** *notificar* let know, tell; *de peligro* warn; (*llamar*) send for; **aviso** *m* notice; (*advertencia*) warning; *L.Am.* (*anuncio*) advertisement; **hasta nuevo ~** until further notice; **sin previo ~** without any warning

avispa *f* wasp

avispado bright, sharp

axila *f* armpit

ay ow!, ouch!; *de susto* oh!

ayer yesterday; ~ *por la mañana* yesterday morning

ayuda *f* help, assistance; **ayudante** *m/f* assistant; **ayudar** help

ayunar fast; **ayunas: estoy en ~** I haven't eaten anything

ayuntamiento *m* city council, town council; *edificio* city hall

azafata *f* flight attendant; ~ *de congresos* hostess

azafrán *m* saffron

azahar *m* orange / lemon blossom

azotea *f* flat roof

azúcar *m* (*also f*) sugar; ~ *glas* confectioner's sugar, *Br* icing sugar

azufre *m* sulfur, *Br* sulphur

azul 1 *adj* blue; ~ *celeste* sky-blue; ~ *marino* navy(-blue) **2** *m* blue

azulejo *m* tile

B

B.A. (= *Buenos Aires*) Buenos Aires

babero *m* bib

babor *m* MAR port

baca *f* AUTO roof rack

bacalao *m* cod

bache *m* pothole; *fig* rough patch

bachiller *m/f* high school graduate; **bachillerato** *m Esp* high school leaver's certificate

bacteria *f* bacteria

bagatela *f* trinket

bahía *f* bay

bailador 1 *adj*: **ser muy** ~ love dancing **2** *m*, ~*a f* dancer; **bailaor** *m*, ~*a f* flamenco dancer; **bailar** dance; **bailarín** *m*, **-ina** *f* dancer; **baile** *m* dance; *fiesta* formal ball; ~ *de salón* ballroom dancing

baja *f* fall, drop; **estar de** ~ **(por enfermedad)** be off sick; ~*s* MIL casualties; **bajada** *f* fall, drop; **bajar 1** *v/t* lower; *precio* lower; *escalera* go down; ~ *algo de arriba* get sth down **2** *v/i* go down; *de intereses* fall, drop

bajeza *f* (*calidad*) baseness; (*acto*) despicable thing to do

bajo 1 *adj* low; *persona* short;

bass; *piso* first floor, *Br* ground floor **3** *adv cantar*, *hablar* quietly, softly; *volar* low **4** *prp* under; *tres grados* ~ *cero* three degrees below zero

bala *f* bullet; **ni a** ~ *L.Am.* F no way

balance *m* COM balance; **balancear** *caderas* swing; **balancearse** swing, sway; MAR rock; **balancín** *m* TÉC rocker; (*mecedora*) rocking chair; **balanza** *f* scales *pl*; ~ *comercial* balance of trade; ~ *de pagos* balance of payments

balbucear, balbucir stammer; *de niño* babble

balcón *m* balcony

balde: **de** ~ for nothing; **en** ~ in vain

baldío *adj* uncultivated; *fig* useless **2** *m* uncultivated land

baldosa *f* floor tile

Baleares *fpl* Balearics; **baleárico** Balearic

baliza *f* MAR buoy

ballena *f* ZO whale

ballet *m* ballet

balneario *m* spa

balón *m* ball; **baloncesto** *m*

basketball; **balonmano** *m* handball; **balonvolea** *m* volleyball

balsa *f* raft

bálsamo *m* balsam

baluarte *m* stronghold; *persona* pillar, stalwart

bambú *m* bamboo

banal banal

banana *f L.Am., Rpl, Pe, Bol* banana

banca *f actividad* banking; *conjunto de bancos* banks *pl; en juego* bench; ~ *electrónica* on-line banking

banco *m* COM bank; *para sentarse* bench; ~ *de arena* sand bank; ~ *de datos* data bank

banda *f* MÚS, *(grupo)* band; *de delincuentes* gang; *(cinta)* sash; *en fútbol* touchline; ~ *sonora* soundtrack

bandeja *f* tray

bandera *f* flag; **banderilla** *f* TAUR banderilla *(dart stuck into bull's neck during bullfight)*; **banderola** *f* flag

bandido *m*, **-a** *f* bandit

bandolero *m*, **-a** *f* bandit

banquero *m*, **-a** *f* banker

banquete *m* banquet; ~ *de bodas* wedding reception

banquillo *m* JUR dock; DEP bench

bañador *m* swimsuit; **bañar** bathe; **bañarse** have a bath; *en el mar* go for a swim; **bañera** *f* (bath)tub, bath; **bañera de hidromasaje** whirlpool, Jacuzzi®; **baño** *m* en la *bañera* bath; *en el mar* swim; *esp L.Am.* bathroom; *(ducha)* shower; **baño de sangre** blood bath; **baño de sol** sunbathing session; **baños de sol** sunbathing

baqueta *f* MÚS drumstick

bar *m* bar

baraja *f* deck of cards

barajar 1 *v/t naipes* shuffle; *fig* consider **2** *v/i* quarrel

baranda *f* en *billar* cushion

barandilla *f* handrail, banister

baratear sell off

baratija *f* trinket

barato cheap

barba *f* beard

barbacoa *f* barbecue

barbaridad *f* barbarity; *costar una* ~ cost a fortune; *¡qué* ~*!* what a thing to say / do!; **bárbaro 1** *adj F* tremendous, awesome F; *¡qué* ~*!* amazing! F **2** *m*, **-a** *f* F punk F

barbero *m* barber

barbilla *f* chin

barbudo bearded

barca *f* boat; **barcaza** *f* barge; **barco** *m* boat; *más grande* ship; ~ *de vela* sailing ship

barítono *m* baritone

barman *m* bartender, *Br* barman

barniz *m* varnish; **barnizar** varnish

barómetro *m* barometer

barquero *m* boatman

barquillo *m* wafer; *Méx,*

C.Am. ice-cream cone

barra *f* de metal, *en bar* bar; *de cortinas* rod; **~ de labios** lipstick; **~ de pan** baguette; **~ espaciadora** space-bar; **~ de herramientas** INFOR tool bar; **~ invertida** backslash

barraca *f* (*chabola*) shack; *de tiro* stand; *de feria* stall; *L.Am*. (*deposito*) shed; **~s** *L.Am*. shanty town

barranco *m* ravine

barredera 1 *f* street sweeper **2** *adj*: **red** *m* trawl net

barrena *f* gimlet; AVIA: **entrar en ~** go into a spin

barrera *f* barrier; **~ del sonido** sound barrier

barricada *f* barricade

barriga *f* belly; **rascarse la ~** fig F sit on one's butt F

barril *m* barrel

barrio *m* neighborhood, *Br* neighbourhood, area; **~ de chabolas** *Esp* shanty town

barro *m* mud

barroco *m/adj* baroque

barruntar suspect

barullo *m* uproar, racket

basar base (**en** on)

báscula *f* scales

base *f* QUÍM, MAT, MIL base; **~ de datos** INFOR database; **~s** *de concurso* etc conditions; **a ~ de** by dint of; **básico** base

basílica *f* basilica

básquetbol *m L.Am*. basketball

bastante 1 *adj* enough; *número o cantidad considerable*

plenty of; **2** *adv* quite, fairly; **bebe ~** she drinks quite a lot; **bastar** be enough; **basta con uno** one is enough; **¡basta!** that's enough!

bastos *mpl* suit in Spanish deck of cards

basura *f tb* fig trash, *Br* rubbish; **cubo de la ~** trash can, *Br* rubbish bin; **basurero** *m* garbage collector, *Br* dustman

bata *f* robe, *Br* dressing gown; MED (white) coat; TÉC lab coat

batalla *f* battle; **batallón** *m* battalion

batata *f* BOT sweet potato

batería *f* MIL, ELEC, AUTO battery; MÚS drums, drum kit; **~ de cocina** set of pans; **aparcar en ~** AUTO parallel park

batida *f* de caza beating; *de policía* search

batido 1 *adj camino* well-trodden **2** *m* GASTR milkshake; **batidora** *f* mixer

batiente *m* jamb

batir beat; *nata* whip; *récord* break

batuta *f* MÚS baton; **llevar la ~** fig F be the boss F

baúl *m* chest, trunk; *L.Am*. AUTO trunk, *Br* boot

bautismo *m* baptism, christening; **bautizar** baptize, christen; *barco* name; *vino* F water down; **bautizo** *m* baptism, christening

baya *f* berry

bayeta f cloth

baza f en naipes trick; fig trump card

bazar m hardware and fancy goods store; mercado bazaar

bazo m ANAT spleen

beatificar REL beatify; **beatitud** f beatitude; **beato 1** adj desp overpious **2** m, -a f desp over-pious person

bebé m baby

bebedor m, ~a f drinker; **beber** drink; **bebida** f drink

beca f scholarship, grant

béchamel f béchamel (sauce)

beige beige

béisbol m baseball

belén m nativity scene

belga m/f & adj Belgian; **Bélgica** Belgium

Belice Belize; **beliceño 1** adj Belizean **2** m, -a f Belizean

bélico war atr; **belicoso** warlike, bellicose; fig persona belligerent

belleza f beauty; **bello** beautiful

bemol m MÚS flat

bencina f benzine; Pe, Bol (gasolina) gas, Br petrol

bendecir bless

beneficencia f charity; **beneficiar** benefit; **beneficiarse** benefit (de, con from); **beneficio** m benefit; COM profit; Rpl slaughterhouse; CAm. coffee-processing plant; **en ~ de** in aid of; **beneficioso** beneficial; **benéfico** charity atr

benévolo benevolent; kind; (indulgente) lenient

benigno MED benign

berberecho m ZO cockle

berenjena f egg plant, Br aubergine

bermudas mpl, fpl Bermuda shorts

berro m BOT watercress

berza f BOT cabbage

besar kiss; **beso** m kiss

bestia 1 f beast **2** m/f fig F brute F; mujer bitch F; **bestial** F tremendous F; **bestialidad** f act of cruelty

besugo m ZO bream; fig F idiot

betún m shoe polish

biberón m baby's bottle

Biblia f Bible; **bíblico** biblical

biblioteca f library; mueble bookcase; **bibliotecario** m, -a f librarian

bicarbonato m: ~ (de sodio) bicarbonate of soda

bicho m bug; (animal) creature; fig F persona nasty piece of work; ~s vermin; **¿qué ~ te ha picado?** what's eating you?

bici f F, **bicicleta** f bicycle; **ir o montar en ~** go cycling; **~ de montaña** mountain bike; **~ eléctrica** e-bike, electric bicycle

bidé m bidet

bidón m drum

biela f TÉC connecting rod

bien 1 m good; **~es** goods, property; **~es de consumo** consumer goods; **~es in-**

muebles real estate **2** *adv*
well; *(muy)* very; *más ~*
rather; *o ~... o...* either ...
or ...; *¡está..!* it's OK!, it's
alright!; *¡~ hecho!* well
done!

bienal 1 *adj* biennial **2** *f* biennial event

bienaventurado REL blessed;
bienestar *m* wellness; *cen-*
tro m de ~ wellness center,
Br wellness centre; *hotel m*
de ~ wellness hotel; **bienes-**
tar *m* well-being; **bienhe-**
chor 1 *adj* beneficent **2** *m*
benefactor; **bienvenida** *f*
welcome; *dar la ~ a alguien*
welcome s.o.; **bienvenido**
welcome

bife *m Rpl* steak

biftec *m* steak

bifurcarse fork

bigamia *f* bigamy

bigote *m* mustache, *Br* moustache; *~s de gato etc* whiskers

bigudí *m* hair curler

bikini *m* bikini

bilateral bilateral

bilingüe bilingual

bilis *f* bile; *fig* F bad mood

billar *m* billiards; *~ america-*
no pool

billete *m* ticket; *~ abierto*
open ticket; *~ de autobús*
bus ticket; *~ de banco* bill,
Br banknote; *~ de ida, ~*
sencillo one-way ticket, *Br*
single (ticket); *~ de ida y*
vuelta round-trip ticket, *Br*
return (ticket); **billetero** *m*
billfold, *Br* wallet

billón *m* trillion

bimensual twice-monthly

bimotor 1 *adj* twin-engined **2**
m twin-engined plane

biodegradable biodegradable

biografía *f* biography; **bio-**
gráfico biographical

biología *f* biology; **biológico**
biological; AGR organic

biombo *m* folding screen

biopsia *f* MED biopsy

biquini *m* bikini

birria *f* F piece of junk F; *va*
hecha una ~ F she looks a
real mess

bis *m* encore; *9 ~* 9A

bisabuela *f* great-grand-
mother; **bisabuelo** *m*
great-grandfather

bisagra *f* hinge

bisiesto: *año ~* leap year

bisnieta *f* great-granddaugh-
ter; **bisnieto** *m* great-grand-
son

bisoñé *m* hairpiece, toupee

bisté, bistec *m* steak

bisturí *m* MED scalpel

bisutería *f* costume jewelry *o*
Br jewellery

bizco cross-eyed

bizcocho *m* sponge (cake)

blanca *f* persona white; MÚS
half-note, *Br* minim; *estar*
sin ~ fig F be broke F; **blan-**
co 1 *adj* white; *(diana)*, fig target; *arma -a* knife **2** *m* persona white; *(diana)*, fig target; *dar en el ~* hit the nail
on the head; **Blancanieves**
f Snow White; **blancura** *f*

whiteness

blando soft; **blandura** f softness

blanquear whiten; *pared* whitewash; *dinero* launder

blasfemar curse, swear; REL blaspheme; **blasfemia** f REL blasphemy

blindado armored, Br armoured; *puerta* reinforced; ELEC shielded; **blindaje** m *de vehículo* armor o Br armour plating

bloc m pad

bloque m block; POL bloc; ~ **de apartamentos** apartment building, Br block of flats; **en** ~ en masse; **bloquear** block; DEP obstruct; *(atascar)* jam; MIL blockade; COM freeze; **bloqueo** m blockade

blusa f blouse

boa f boa constrictor

boato m ostentation

bobada f piece of nonsense

bobina f bobbin; FOT reel, spool; ELEC coil

bobo 1 *adj* silly, foolish 2 *m*, -**a** f fool

boca f mouth; ~ **a** ~ mouth to mouth; ~ **de metro** subway entrance; ~ **abajo** face down; ~ **arriba** face up; **se me hace la** ~ **agua** my mouth is watering; **bocacalle** f side street; **bocadillo** m sandwich; **bocado** m mouthful, bite; **bocajarro**: **a** ~ at point-blank range; fig *decir* point-blank; **bocazas** m/f

inv F loudmouth F

boceto m sketch

bochorno m sultry weather; *fig* embarrassment; **bochornoso** *tiempo* sultry; *fig* embarrassing

bocina f MAR, AUTO horn

bocio m MED goiter, Br goitre

boda f wedding

bodega f wine cellar; MAR, AVIA hold; L.Am. bar; C.Am., Pe, Bol grocery store

bodegón m PINT still life

bofetada f slap

boga f: **estar en** ~ fig be in fashion

boicot m boycott; **boicotear** boycott

boina f beret

boj m BOT box

bola f ball; TÉC ball bearing; *de helado* scoop; F *(mentira)* fib F; ~ **de nieve** snowball

bolera f bowling alley

bolero 1 m MÚS bolero **2** m/f Méx bootblack

boleta f L.Am. ticket; *(pase)* passt; *(voto)* ballot paper; **boletería** f L.Am. ticket office; *en cine, teatro* box office; **boletero** m, -**a** f L.Am. ticket clerk; *en cine, teatro* box office employee

boletín m bulletin, report; ~ **de evaluación** report card; ~ **meteorológico** weather report; **boleto** m L.Am. ticket; ~ **de autobús** L.Am. bus ticket; ~ **de ida y vuelta** L.Am., ~ **redondo** Méx round-trip ticket, Br return

bólido *m fig* racing car

bolígrafo *m* ball-point pen

Bolivia Bolivia; **boliviano 1** *adj* Bolivian **2** *m*, **-a** *f* Bolivian

bollería *f* bakery

bollo *m* bun; (*abolladura*) bump

bolo *m* pin; *C.Am.*, *Méx* christening present; **bolos** *mpl* bowling

bolsa *f* bag; COM stock exchange; *L.Am.* (*bolsillo*) pocket; **~ de agua caliente** hot-water bottle

bolsillo *m* pocket; **meterse a alguien en el ~** F win s.o. over; **bolso** *m* purse, *Br* handbag

bomba *f* bomb; TÉC pump; *S.Am.* gas station; **~ de relojería** time bomb; **caer como una ~** *fig* F come as a bombshell; **pasarlo ~** F have a great time; **bombardear** bomb; **bombardero** *m* bomber; **bombear** *líquido* pump; *balón* lob

bombero *m*, **-a** *f* firefighter

bombilla *f* light bulb; *Rpl* metal straw for the mate gourd

bombón *m* chocolate; *fig* F babe F; **bombona** *f* cylinder; **bombonería** *f* candy store, *Br* sweet shop

bonachón good-natured

bondad *f* goodness, kindness; **tenga la ~ de** please be so kind as to; **bondadoso** caring

boniato *m* sweet potato

bonificación *f* (*gratificación*) bonus; (*descuento*) discount; **bonificar** (*gratificar*) give a bonus to; (*descontar*) give a discount of

bonito 1 *adj* pretty **2** *m* ZO tuna

bono *m* voucher; COM bond

boquerón *m* anchovy

boquiabierto *fig* F speechless

boquilla *f* MÚS mouthpiece; **~ de manguera** nozzle

borbotar bubble

borda *f* MAR gunwale; **echar por la ~** throw overboard

bordado 1 *adj* embroidered **2** *m* embroidery; **bordar** embroider; **~ algo** *fig* do sth brilliantly

borde *m* edge; **al ~ de** *fig* on the verge *o* brink of

bordillo *m* curb, *Br* kerb

bordo *m*: **a ~** on board

borla *f* tassel

borrachera *f* drunkenness; **agarrar una ~** get drunk; **borracho 1** *adj* drunk **2** *m*, **-a** *f* drunk

borrador *m* eraser; *de texto* draft; (*boceto*) sketch; **borrar** erase; INFOR *tb* delete; *pizarra* clean; *recuerdo* blot out

borrasca *f* area of low pressure

borrego *m* lamb

borrón *m* blot; *mancha extendida* smudge; **hacer ~ y cuenta nueva** *fig* wipe the slate clean; **borroso**

blurred, fuzzy

bosque *m* wood; *grande* forest

bosquejar *dibujo* sketch; *fig plan* outline; **bosquejo** *m* sketch; *fig* outline

bostezar yawn; **bostezo** *m* yawn

bota *f* boot; **~ de montar** riding boot

botadura *f* MAR launch

botánica *f* botany; **botánico 1** *adj* botanical **2** *m*, **-a** *f* botanist

botar 1 *v/t* MAR launch; *pelota* bounce; *L.Am.* (*echar*) throw; *L.Am.* (*desechar*) throw out; *L.Am.* (*despedir*) fire **2** *v/i* *de pelota* bounce

bote *m* (*barco*) boat; *L.Am.* (*lata*) can; (*tarro*) jar; **~ de la basura** *Méx* trash can, *Br* rubbish bin; **~ salvavidas** lifeboat; **de ~ en ~** packed out

botella *f* bottle

botellero *m* wine rack

botica *f* pharmacy, *Br tb* chemist's (shop); **boticario** *m*, **-a** *f* pharmacist, *Br tb* chemist

botijo *m* container with a spout for drinking from

botín *m* loot; *calzado* ankle boot

botiquín *m* medicine chest; *estuche* first-aid kit

botón *m* button; BOT bud; **botones** *m* inv bellhop, bellboy

bóveda *f* vault

bovino bovine

boxeador *m*, **~a** *f* boxer; **boxear** box; **boxeo** *m* boxing

boya *f* buoy; *de caña* float; **boyante** *fig* buoyant

bozal *m* *para perro* muzzle

bracero *m*, **-a** *f* agricultural laborer *o Br* labourer; **de ~** arm in arm

bragas *fpl* panties

braguета *f* fly

bramar roar; *del viento* howl; **bramido** *m* roar

brandy *m* brandy

branquia *f* ZO gill

brasa *f* ember; **a la ~** GASTR char-broiled, *Br* char-grilled; **brasero** *m* brazier; *eléctrico* electric heater

Brasil Brazil; **brasileño 1** *adj* Brazilian **2** *m*, **-a** *f* Brazilian

bravo *animal* fierce; *mar* rough; *persona* brave; *L.Am.* (*furioso*) angry; **¡~!** well done!; *en concierto etc* bravo!; **bravura** *f* *de animal* ferocity; *de persona* bravery

braza *f* breaststroke; **brazalete** *m* bracelet; (*banda*) armband; **brazo** *m* arm; **con los ~s abiertos** with open arms

brea *f* tar, pitch

brecha *f* breach; *fig* F gap; MED gash F

bregar struggle; *trabajar* work hard

breve brief; **en ~** shortly; **brevedad** *f* briefness, brevity

brezo *m* BOT heather

bribón *m*, **-ona** *f* rascal

bricolaje *m* do-it-yourself,

buitre

DIY

brida f de caballo bridle; TÉC clamp; **a toda ~** at top speed

brillante 1 adj bright; fig brilliant **2** m diamond; **brillar** f shine; **brillo** m shine; de estrella, luz brightness; **dar** o **sacar ~ a algo** polish sth; **brillantez** f brilliance

brincar jump up and down; **brinco** m F leap, bound; **dar ~s** jump

brindar 1 v/t offer **2** v/i drink a toast (**por** to); **brindis** m inv toast

brío m fig F verve, spirit; **brioso** F spirited, lively

brisa f MAR breeze

británico 1 adj British **2** m, -a f Briton, Brit F

broca f TÉC drill bit

brocado m brocade

brocha f brush

broche m broach, Br brooch; (cierre) fastener; L.Am. (pinza) clothes pin

broma f joke; **en ~** as a joke; **gastar ~s** play jokes; **bromear** joke; **bromista** m/f joker

bronce m bronze; **bronceado 1** adj tanned **2** m suntan; **bronceador** m suntan lotion; **broncearse** get a tan

bronco voz harsh, gruff

bronquial bronchial; **bronquios** mpl bronchial tubes; **bronquitis** f bronchitis

brotar BOT sprout, bud; fig appear, arise; **brote** m BOT shoot; MED, fig outbreak;

~s de bambú bamboo shoots; **~s de soja** beansprouts

bruja f witch; **brujo** m wizard; **brujería** f witchcraft

brújula f compass

bruma f mist; **brumoso** misty

brusco sharp, abrupt

brutal brutal; P fiesta incredible F; **brutalidad** f brutality; **bruto 1** adj brutish; (inculto) ignorant; (torpe) clumsy; COM gross **2** m, -a f brute, animal

bucal oral

buceador m, **-a** f diver; **bucear** dive; fig delve (**en** into)

buche m de ave crop; de persona F belly F

bucle m (rizo) curl; INFOR loop

budín m pudding

budismo m Buddhism

buenaventura f fortune

bueno good; (bondadoso) kind; (sabroso) nice; **por las -as** willingly; **de -as a primeras** without warning; **ponerse ~** get well; **¡~!** well!; **¿~?** Méx hello; **-a voluntad** goodwill; **¡-as!** hello!; **~s días** good morning; **-as noches** good evening; **-as tardes** good evening

buey m ox

búfalo m buffalo

bufanda f scarf; fig F perk

bufete m lawyer's office

buhardilla f attic

búho m owl

buitre m vulture

bujía *f* AUTO spark plug

bulbo *m* bulb

Bulgaria Bulgaria; **búlgaro 1** *adj* Bulgarian **2** *m*, **-a** *f* Bulgarian **3** *m idioma* Bulgarian

bullicio *m* din; (*actividad*) bustle; **bullir** boil; *de lugar* swarm (*de* with)

bulo *m* F rumor, *Br* rumour

bulto *m* package; MED lump; *en superficie* bulge; (*silueta*) vague shape; (*pieza de equipaje*) piece of baggage

buñuelo *m Esp* fritter

buque *m* ship; **~ de guerra** warship

burbuja *f* bubble

burdel *m* brothel

burdo rough

burgués 1 *adj* middle-class, bourgeois **2** *m*, **-esa** *f* member of the bourgeoisie; **burguesía** *f* middle class, bourgeoisie

burla *f* joke; (*engaño*) trick;

hacer **~ de alguien** F make fun of s.o.; **burlar** F get around; **burlarse** make fun (*de* of); **burlesco** *tono* joking; *gesto* rude

burlón 1 *adj* mocking **2** *m*, **-ona** *f* mocker

burocracia *f* bureaucracy; **burócrata** *m/f* bureaucrat; **burocrático** bureaucratic

burro *m* donkey

bus *m* bus

busca 1 *f* search; **en ~ de** in search of **2** *m* F pager; **buscar** search for, look for; **búsqueda** *f* search

busto *m* bust

butaca *f* armchair; TEA seat

butano *m* butane

butifarra *f* type of sausage

buzo *m* diver

buzón *m* mailbox, *Br* postbox; INFOR mailbox; **~ de voz** TELEC voice mail; **buzoneo** *m* direct mailing

C

C (= *Centígrado*) C (= Centigrade); (= *compañía*) Co. (= Company); **c** (= *calle*) St. (= Street)

cabal: *no estar en sus ~es* not be in one's right mind

cabalgadura *f* mount; **cabalgar** ride; **cabalgata** *f* procession

caballa *f* ZO mackerel

caballería *f* MIL cavalry; (*caballo*) horse

caballería *f* MIL cavalry; (*caballo*) horse

caballero 1 *adj* gentlemanly **2** *m* gentleman; HIST knight; *trato* sir; (*servicio de*) **~s** men's room, gents; *en tienda de ropa* menswear; **caballeroso** gentlemanly

caballete *m* PINT easel; TÉC trestle

caballo *m* horse; *en ajedrez* knight; **~ balancín** rocking horse; *a ~ entre* halfway between; *montar* o *andar Rpl a ~* ride (a horse); *ir a ~* go on horseback

cabaña *f* cabin

cabaret *m* cabaret

cabecear 1 *v/i* nod **2** *v/t el balón* head; **cabecera** *f* head; *de periódico* masthead; *de texto* top

cabecilla *m/f* ringleader

cabellera *f* hair; *de cometa* tail

cabello *m* hair; **cabelludo** hairy

caber fit; *caben tres litros* it holds three liters; *cabemos todos* there's room for all of us; *no cabe duda* fig there's no doubt

cabestrillo *m* MED sling

cabestro *m* halter

cabeza 1 *f* head; *de ajo* bulb of garlic; *~ (de ganado)* head of (cattle); *~ nuclear* nuclear warhead; *el equipo a la ~* o *en ~* the team at the top **2** *m/f*: *~ de familia* head of the family; *~ de turco* scapegoat; *~ rapada* skinhead

cabezota pig-headed

cabida *f* capacity; *dar ~ a* hold

cabina *f* cabin; *~ telefónica* phone booth

cabizbajo dejected

cable *m* ELEC cable; MAR line, rope; *echar un ~ a alguien* give s.o. a hand; **cablear** wire up

cabo *m* end; GEOG cape; MAR rope; MIL corporal; *al ~ de*

after; *de ~ a rabo* F from start to finish; *llevar a ~* carry out

cabra *f* goat; *estar como una ~* F be nuts F; **cabrearse** P get mad F; **cabritilla** *f* kid (skin)

cabrón *m* V bastard P, son of a bitch V

cacahuate *m* Méx peanut

cacahuete *m* peanut

cacao *m* cocoa; *de labios* lip salve

cacarear 1 *v/i de gallo* crow; *de gallina* cluck **2** *v/t* F crow about F

cacería *f* hunt

cacerola *f* pan

cacharro *m* pot; *Méx, C.Am.* F *(trasto)* piece of junk; *Méx, C.Am.* F coche junkheap; **lavar los ~s** *Méx, C.Am.* wash the dishes

cachear frisk; **cacheo** *m* frisk

cachete *m* cheek

cacho *m* F bit; *Rpl (cuerno)* horn; *Ven, Col* F *(marijuana)* joint F; *jugar al ~ Bol, Pe* play dice

cachondeo *m*: *estar de ~* F be joking; *tomar a ~* F take as a joke; **cachondo** F *(caliente)* horny F; *(gracioso)* funny

cachorro *m* pup

cacique *m* chief; POL local political boss; *fig* F tyrant

caco *m* F thief

cactus *m inv* cactus

cada each; *con énfasis en la totalidad* every; *~ uno, ~ cual* each one; **~ vez** every time, each time; **~ vez más** more and more; **~ tres días** every three days; **uno de ~ tres** one out of every three

cadáver *m* (dead) body, corpse

cadena *f* chain; *de perro* leash; TV channel; **~ perpetua** life sentence

cadencia *f* MÚS rhythm

cadera *f* hip

cadete *m* MIL cadet; *Rpl, Chi* office junior, errand boy

caducar expire; **caducidad** *f*: **fecha de ~** expiration date, *Br* expiry date; *de alimentos, medicinas* use-by date; **caduco** BOT deciduous; *persona* senile; *belleza* faded

caer fall; **me cae bien / mal** *fig* I like / don't like him; **dejar ~ algo** drop sth; **estar al ~** be about to arrive; **~ enfermo** fall ill

café *m* coffee; *(bar)* café; **~ instantáneo** instant coffee; **~ solo** black coffee; **cafeína** *f* caffeine; **cafetera** *f* coffee maker; *para servir* coffee pot; **cafetería** *f* coffee shop

cagar V have a shit P; **cagarse** shit o.s. P

caída *f* fall

caído 1 *adj* fallen; *hombros* sagging; **~ de ánimo** downhearted **2** *mpl*: **los ~s** MIL the fallen

caimán *m* ZO alligator; *Méx, C.Am.* útil monkey wrench

caja *f* box; *de reloj, ordenador*

case; COM cash desk; *en supermercado* checkout; **~ de ahorros** savings bank; **~ de cambios** gearbox; **~ de caudales**, **~ fuerte** safe; **~ de cerillas** matchbox; **~ de música** music box; **~ postal** post office savings bank; **~ registradora** cash register; **cajero** *m*, **-a** *f* cashier; *de banco* teller; **~ automático** ATM

cajón *m* drawer; *L.Am.* casket, coffin

cal *f* lime

cala *f* cove

calabacín *m* zucchini, *Br* courgette; **calabaza** *f* pumpkin

calabozo *m* cell

calado soaked

calamar *m* squid

calambre *m* ELEC shock; MED cramp

calamidad *f* calamity

calar 1 *v/t (mojar)* soak; *persona, conjura* see through **2** *v/i de zapato* leak; *de ideas* take root; **~ hondo en** make a big impression on; **calarse de motor** stall; **~ hasta los huesos** get soaked to the skin

calavera *f* skull

calcar trace

calceta *f*: **hacer ~** knit; **calcetín** *m* sock

calcio *m* calcium

calco *m* tracing; *fig* copy

calcomanía *f* decal, *Br* transfer

calculable calculable; **calculadora** *f* calculator; **calcular**

tb fig calculate; **cálculo** *m* calculation; MED stone; ~ **biliar** gallstone; ~ **renal** kidney stone

caldear warm up; *ánimos* inflame

caldera *f* boiler; *Rpl, Chi* kettle; **calderilla** *f* small change

calderón *m* MÚS *tb* signo pause

caldo *m* GASTR stock; ~ **de cultivo** fig breeding ground

calefacción *f* heating; ~ **central** central heating; **calefactor** *m* heater

calendario *m* calendar; *(programa)* schedule

calentador *m* heater; ~ **de agua** water heater; **calentamiento** *m*: ~ **global** global warming; **calentar** heat (up); ~ **a alguien** fig provoke s.o.; **calentura** *f* fever

calidad *f* quality; **en** ~ **de médico** as a doctor

cálido *tb* fig warm

caliente hot; F *(cachondo)* horny F; **en** ~ in the heat of the moment

calificación *f* description; EDU grade, *Br* mark; **calificado** qualified; *trabajador* skilled; **calificar** describe *(de)* as; EDU grade, *Br* mark; **calificativo 1** *adj* qualifying **2** *m* description

callado quiet; **callar 1** *v/i* go quiet; *(guardar silencio)* be quiet; **¡calla!** be quiet!, shut up! **2** *v/t* silence

calle *f* street; DEP lane; **calle-**

jón *m* alley; ~ **sin salida** blind alley; fig dead end; **callejear** stroll (around the streets); **callejero 1** *adj* street *atr* **2** *m* street directory

callista *m/f* podiatrist, *Br* chiropodist

callo *m* callus; ~**s** GASTR tripe

calma *f* calm; **calmante 1** *adj* soothing **2** *m* MED sedative; **calmar** calm (down)

calor *m* heat; fig warmth; **hace mucho** ~ it's very hot; **tengo** ~ I'm hot; **caloría** *f* calorie

calumnia *f* oral slander; *por escrito* libel; **calumniar** *oralmente* slander; *por escrito* libel; **calumnioso** oral slanderous; *por escrito* libelous

caluroso hot; fig warm

calva *f* bald patch

calvicie *f* baldness; **calvo 1** *adj* bald **2** *m* bald man

calzada *f* road (surface); **calzado** *m* footwear; **calzador** *m* shoe horn

calzón *m* DEP shorts *pl*; *L.Am. de hombre* shorts *pl*, *Br* (under)pants *pl*; *L.Am. de mujer* panties *pl*

calzoncillos *mpl* shorts, *Br* (under)pants

cama *f* bed; ~ **de matrimonio** double bed; **irse a la** ~ go to bed

camaleón *m* chameleon

cámara *f* FOT, TV camera; *(sala)* chamber; ~ **de comercio e industria** chamber of commerce and industry; **a ~ lenta** in slow motion; **~ de vídeo** video camera

camarada m/f comrade; **de trabajo** colleague, co-worker

camarera f waitress; **camarero** m waiter

camarón m L.Am. shrimp, Br prawn

camarote m MAR cabin

cambiable changeable; **cambiante** changing; **tiempo** changeable; **cambiar 1** v/t change (**por** for); **compra** exchange (**por** for) **2** v/i change; **~ de lugar** change places; **~ de marcha** AUTO shift gear, Br change gear; **cambiarse** change; **~ de ropa** change (one's clothes); **cambio** m change; COM exchange rate; **~ de marchas** AUTO gear shift, Br tb gear change; **~ de sentido** U-turn; **a ~ de** in exchange for; **en ~** on the other hand; **~ climático** climate change

camello 1 m ZO camel **2** m/f F (vendedor de drogas) dealer

camerino m TEA dressing room

caminar walk; fig move; **caminando** on foot; **camino** m (senda) path; (ruta) way; **a medio ~** halfway; **de ~ a** on the way to; **por el ~** on the way; **abrirse ~** fig make one's way; **ir por buen / mal ~** fig be on the right / wrong track; **ponerse en ~** set out

camión m truck, Br tb lorry;

Méx bus; **camionero** m, -a f truck driver, Br tb lorry driver; Méx bus driver; **camioneta** f van

camisa f shirt; **camiseta** f T-shirt; **camisón** m nightdress

camorra f F fight; **armar ~** F cause trouble

campamento m camp

campana f bell; **~ extractora** extractor hood; **campanada** f chime; **campanario** m bell tower

campaña f campaign

campechano down-to-earth

campeón m, -ona f champion; **campeonato** m championship; **de ~** F terrific F

campesino 1 adj rural, country atr **2** m, -a f farmer; muy pobre peasant; **campestre** rural, country atr

camping m campground, Br tb campsite

campista m/f camper

campo m field; DEP field, Br tb pitch; (estadio) stadium, Br tb ground; **el ~** (área rural) the country; **~ de batalla** battlefield; **~ de golf** golf course; **~ visual** MED field of vision; **a ~ traviesa**, **a través** cross-country

camposanto m cemetery

camuflaje m camouflage; **camuflar** camouflage

cana f gray o Br grey hair

Canadá m Canada; **canadiense** m/f & adj Canadian

canal m channel; TRANSP canal; **canalizar** channel

canalla *m* swine F, rat F

canalón *m* gutter

Canarias *fpl* Canaries; *Islas ~* Canary Islands

canario 1 *adj* Canary *atr* **2** *m* ZO canary

canasta *f* basket; *juego* canasta; **canasto** *m* basket

cancelar cancel; *deuda, cuenta* settle, pay

cáncer *m* cancer; **Cáncer** *m/f inv* ASTR Cancer

cancha *f* DEP court; *L.Am. de fútbol* field, *Br tb* pitch; *~ de tenis* tennis court; *¡~! Rpl* F gangway! F

canciller *m* Chancellor; *S.Am. de asuntos exteriores* Secretary of State, *Br* Foreign Minister

canción *f* song; *siempre la misma ~* F the same old story F

candado *m* padlock

candela *f* *L.Am.* fire; *¿me das~?* have you got a light?

candelero *m*: *estar en el ~* be in the limelight

candidato *m*, *-a* *f* candidate; **candidatura** *f* candidacy

cándido naive

canela *f* cinnamon

cangrejo *m* crab

canguro 1 *m* ZO kangaroo **2** *m/f* F baby-sitter

canica *f* marble

canilla *f* *L.Am.* faucet, *Br* tap

canje *m* exchange; **canjear** exchange (*por* for)

canoa *f* canoe

canonizar canonize

cansado tired; **cansar** tire; *(aburrir)* bore; **cansarse** get tired; *(aburrirse)* get bored; *~ de algo* get tired of sth

cantábrico: *(mar) Cantábrico* Bay of Biscay

cantante *m/f* singer; **cantar 1** *v/t & v/i* sing **2** *m*: *ése es otro ~ fig* F that's a different story

cántaro *m* pitcher; *llover a ~s* F pour down

cantautor *m*, *~a* *f* singer-songwriter

cantera *f* quarry

cantidad *f* quantity, amount; *había ~ de* there was (*pl* were) a lot of

cantina *f* canteen

canto¹ *m* singing; *de pájaro* song

canto² *m* edge; *(roca)* stone; *~ rodado* boulder

cantor 1 *adj* singing; *niño ~* choirboy; *pájaro ~* songbird **2** *m*, *~a* *f* singer

caña *f* BOT reed; *(tallo)* stalk; *cerveza* small glass of beer; *L.Am.* straw; *muebles de ~* cane furniture; *~ de azúcar* sugar cane; *~ de pescar* fishing rod

cáñamo *m* hemp; *L.Am.* marijuana plant

cañería *f* pipe

caño *m* pipe; *de fuente* spout

cañón *m* cannon; *antiaéreo, antitanque etc* gun; *de fusil* barrel; GEOG canyon **2** *adj* F fantastic F

caoba *f* mahogany

caos *m* chaos; **caótico** chaotic

capa *f* layer; *prenda* cloak; ~ **de ozono** ozone layer; ~ **de pintura** coat of paint

capacidad *f* capacity; *(aptitud)* competence

capataz *m* foreman; **capataza** *f* forewoman

capaz able *(de* to); **ser** ~ **de** be capable of

capilar capillary *atr*; **loción** hair *atr*

capilla *f* chapel; ~ **ardiente** chapel of rest

capital **1** *adj importancia* prime; **pena** ~ capital punishment **2** *f de país* capital **3** *m* COM capital; **capitalismo** *m* capitalism; **capitalista** **1** *adj* capitalist **2** *m/f* capitalist

capitán *m* captain; **capitanear** captain

capitulación *f* capitulation, surrender; *(pacto)* agreement; **capitular** surrender, capitulate

capítulo *m* chapter

capó *m* AUTO hood, *Br* bonnet

capota *f* AUTO top, *Br* hood

capricho *m* whim; **caprichoso** capricious

Capricornio *m/f inv* ASTR Capricorn

cápsula *f* capsule; ~ **espacial** space capsule

captar understand; RAD pick up; *negocio* take; **captura** *f* capture; *en pesca* catch; **tasa** **de** ~**s** fishing quota; **capturar** capture

cara *f* face; *(expresión)* look; *fig* nerve; ~ **a algo** facing sth; ~ **a** face to face; **de** ~ **a** facing; *fig* with regard to; **dar la** ~ face the consequences; **echar algo en** ~ **a alguien** remind s.o. of sth; **tener buena / mala** ~ *de comida* look good / bad; *de persona* look well / sick; **de** ~ **o cruz** heads or tails

caracol *m* snail; **¡~es!** wow! *F*; *enfado* damn! *F*

carácter *m* character; **característica** *f* characteristic; **característico** characteristic *(de* of*)*; **caracterizar** characterize; TEA play

caradura *f* *F* guy / woman with a nerve, *Br* cheeky devil *F*

carajillo *m* coffee with a shot of liquor

caramba wow!; *enfado* damn! *F*

caramelo *m* dulce candy, *Br* sweet; *(azúcar derretida)* caramel

carátula *f* *de disco* jacket; *L.Am. de reloj* face

caravana *f* *(remolque)* trailer, *Br* caravan; *de tráfico* traffic jam; *Méx (reverencia)* bow

carbohidrato *m* carbohydrate

carbón *m* coal; **carbonizar** char; **carbono** *m* carbon

carburador *m* AUTO carburetor, *Br* carburettor; **carbu-**

rante *m* fuel

carcajada *f* laugh, guffaw; **reír a ~s** roar with laughter

cárcel *f* prison; **carcelero** *m*, **-a** *f* warder, jailer

carcoma *f* woodworm

cardenal *m* REL cardinal; (*hematoma*) bruise

cardíaco, cardiaco cardiac; **cardiólogo** *m*, **-a** *f* cardiologist

cardo *m* BOT thistle

carecer: ~ de algo lack sth; **carencia** *f* lack (**de** of)

careo *m* confrontation

carestía *f* high cost

careta *f* mask

carga *f* load; *de buque* cargo; MIL, ELEC charge; (*responsabilidad*) burden; **~ fiscal o impositiva** tax burden; **ser una ~ para alguien** be a burden to s.o.; **cargado** loaded (**de** with); *aire* stuffy; *ambiente* tense; *café* strong; **cargamento** *m* load; **cargar 1** *v/t arma, camión* load; *batería, acusado* charge; COM charge (**en** to); L.Am. (*traer*) carry; **esto me carga** L.Am. P I can't stand this **2** *v/i* (*apoyarse*) rest (**sobre** on); (*fastidiar*) be annoying; **~ con algo** carry sth; **cargarse con peso, responsabilidad** weigh o.s. down; F (*matar*) bump off; F (*romper*) wreck F

cargo *m* position; JUR charge; **alto ~** *persona* high-ranking official; **está a ~ de Gómez** Gómez is in charge of it; **ha-**

cerse ~ de algo take charge of sth

Caribe *m* Caribbean; **caribeño** Caribbean

caricatura *f* caricature

caricia *f* caress

caridad *f* charity

caries *f* MED caries

cariño *m* affection, fondness; **hacer ~ a alguien** L.Am. (*acariciar*) caress s.o.; (*abrazar*) hug s.o.; **¡~!** darling!; **con ~** with love; **cariñoso** affectionate

carioca of / from Rio de Janeiro

caritativo charitable

carlinga *f* cockpit

carnaval *m* carnival

carne *f* meat; *de persona* flesh; **~ de gallina** *fig* goose bumps *pl*; **~ picada** ground meat, Br mince

carnero *m* ram

carnet *m* card; **~ de conducir** driver's license, Br driving licence; **~ de identidad** identity card

carnicería *f* butcher's; *fig* carnage; **carnicero** *m*, **-a** *f* butcher

caro expensive, dear; **costar ~** *fig* cost dear

carpa *f de circo* big top; ZO carp; L.Am. *para acampar* tent; L.Am. *de mercado* stall

carpeta *f* file

carpintería *f* carpentry; *de obra* joinery; **carpintero** *m* carpenter; *de obra* joiner

carrera *f* race; EDU degree

course; *profesional* career; *a las ~s* at top speed; *~s de coches* motor racing

carreta *f* cart; **carrete** *m* FOT (roll of) film; *~ de hilo* reel of thread

carretera *f* highway, (main) road; *~ de circunvalación* beltway, *Br* ring road; **carretilla** *f* wheelbarrow

carril *m* lane; *~-bici* cycle lane; *~-bus* bus lane

carrito *m* cart, *Br* trolley; *~ de bebé* buggy; **carro** *m* cart; *L.Am.* car; *L.Am.* (*taxi*) taxi, cab; *~ de combate* tank; *~-patrulla L.Am.* patrol car

carrocería *f* AUTO bodywork

carta *f* letter; GASTR menu; (*naipe*) (playing) card; (*mapa*) chart; *~ certificada o registrada* registered letter; *~ urgente* special-delivery letter; *a la ~* a la carte; *dar ~ blanca a alguien* give s.o. carte blanche; **poner las ~s boca arriba** *fig* put one's cards on the table; **carta-bomba** *f* letter bomb; **cartabón** *m* set square

cartel *m* poster; **estar en ~ de** *película* be on

cartelera *f* billboard; *de periódico* listings *pl*

cartera *f* wallet; (*maletín*) briefcase; COM, POL portfolio; *de colegio* knapsack, *Br* satchel; *L.Am.* purse, *Br* handbag; *mujer* mailwoman, *Br* postwoman; **cartero** *m* mailman, *Br* postman

cartón *m* cardboard; *de tabaco* carton; *~ piedra* pap(i)er-mâché

cartucho *m de arma* cartridge

cartuja *f* monastery

casa *f* house; (*hogar*) home; *en ~* at home; *a casa* home; *voy a casa de Marta* I'm going to Marta's (house); *~ cuna* children's home; *~ de huéspedes* rooming house, *Br* boarding house; *~ matriz* head office; *~ de socorro* first aid post

casado married; **casamiento** *m* marriage; *casar* fig match (up); *~ con* go with; *casarse* get married; *~ con alguien* marry s.o.

cascada *f* waterfall

cascanueces *m inv* nutcrackers

cascar crack; *algo quebradizo* break; *fig* F whack F; *~la* peg out F

cáscara *f de huevo* shell; *de naranja, limón* peel

casco *m* helmet; *de barco* hull; (*botella vacía*) empty (bottle); *edificio* empty building; *de caballo* hoof; *de vasija* fragment; *~s* (*auriculares*) headphones; *~ urbano* urban area; *~s azules* MIL blue berets, UN peacekeeping troops

casera *f* landlady; **casero 1** *adj* home-made; *comida ~a* home cooking **2** *m* landlord

caseta *f* hut; *de feria* stall

casete *m* (*also f*) cassette

casi almost, nearly; *en frases negativas* hardly

casilla *f en formulario* box; *en tablero* square; *de correspondencia* pigeon hole; *S.Am.* post office box

casino *m* casino

caso *m* case; *en ~ de que*, *~ de* in the event that, in case of; *hacer ~* take notice; *en todo ~* in any case, in any event; *en el peor de los ~s* if the worst comes to the worst; *en último ~* as a last resort

caspa *f* dandruff

cassette *m* (*also f*) cassette

casta *f* caste

castaña *f* chestnut; **castaño 1** *adj color* chestnut, brown **2** *m color* chestnut (tree); *color* chestnut, brown; **castañuela** *f* castanet; *estar como unas ~s* F be over the moon F

castellano 1 *adj* Castilian **2** *m*, *-a f* Castilian **3** *m* (Castilian) Spanish

castidad *f* chastity

castigar punish; **castigo** *m* punishment

castillo *m* castle; *~ de fuegos artificiales* firework display

castizo pure

casto chaste

castor *m* beaver

castrar castrate; *fig* emasculate

casual chance *atr*; **casualidad** *f* chance, coincidence; *por o de ~* by chance

catalán 1 *adj* Catalan **2** *m*, *-ana f* Catalan **3** *m idioma* Catalan

catalizador *m* catalyst; AUTO catalytic converter

catálogo *m* catalog, *Br* catalogue

catar taste

catarata *f* GEOG waterfall; MED cataract

catarro *m* cold; *inflamación* catarrh

catástrofe *f* catastrophe; *~ climática* climate catastrophe

catear F flunk F

cátedra *f* EDU chair

catedral *f* cathedral

catedrático *m*, *-a f* EDU head of department

categoría *f* category; *social, de local, restaurante* class; (*estatus*) standing; *actor de primera ~* first-rate actor; **categórico** categorical

catolicismo *m* (Roman) Catholicism; **católico 1** *adj* (Roman) Catholic **2** *m*, *-a f* (Roman) Catholic

catorce fourteen

catre *m* bed

caucho *m* rubber; *L.Am.* (*neumático*) tire, *Br* tyre

caución *f* guarantee, security

caudal *m de río* volume of flow; *fig* wealth

caudillo *m* leader

causa *f* cause; (*motivo*) reason; JUR lawsuit; *a ~ de* because of; **causar** cause

cáustico *tb fig* caustic

cautela f caution; **cauteloso** cautious

cautivar fig captivate; **cautiverio** m, **cautividad** f captivity; **cautivo 1** adj captive **2** m, **-a** f captive

cauto cautious

cava m cava, sparkling wine

cavar dig

caverna f cavern

caviar m caviar

cavidad f cavity

caza 1 f hunt; actividad hunting; **~ mayor / menor** big / small game; **andar a la ~ de algo / alguien** be after sth / s.o. **2** m AVIA fighter; **cazador** m hunter; **cazadora** f prenda jacket; **cazar 1** v/t animal hunt; información track down; (pillar, captar) catch; **~ un buen trabajo** get o.s. a good job **2** v/i hunt; **ir a ~** go hunting

cazo m saucepan

cazuela f pan; de barro, vidrio casserole

c/c (= **cuenta corriente**) C/A (= checking account)

CD m (= **disco compacto**) CD; reproductor CD-player; **CD-ROM** m CD-ROM

cebada f barley

cebar fatten; anzuelo bait; L.Am. mate prepare; **cebo** m bait

cebolla f onion; **cebolleta** f, **cebollino** m planta scallion, Br spring onion

cebra f zebra; **paso de ~** crosswalk, Br zebra crossing

cecear en acento regional pronounce Spanish "s" as "th"; como defecto lisp

ceder 1 v/t give up; (traspasar) transfer, cede; **~ el paso** AUTO yield, Br give way **2** v/i give way, yield; de viento, lluvia ease off

cedro m cedar

cédula f L.Am. identity document

cegar blind; tubería block; **ceguera** f tb fig blindness

ceja f eyebrow

cejar give up

celador m, **-a** f orderly; de cárcel guard; de museo attendant

celda f cell

celebración f celebration; **celebrar** misa celebrate; reunión, fiesta have, hold; **célebre** famous; **celebridad** f fame; persona celebrity

celeste light blue, sky blue; **celestial** celestial; fig heavenly

celibato m celibacy; **célibe** m/f & adj celibate

celo m zeal; (cinta adhesiva) Scotch® tape, Br Sellotape®; **en ~** ZO in heat; **~s** jealousy; **tener ~s de** be jealous of; **celoso** jealous

célula f cell; **celular** cellular; **celulitis** f cellulite; **celulosa** f cellulose

cementerio m cemetery

cemento m cement

cena f dinner

cenar 1 v/t: **~ algo** have sth for

dinner **2** *v/i* have dinner

cenicero *m* ashtray

Cenicienta *f* Cinderella

ceniza *f* ash; **~s** ashes

censo *m* census; **~ electoral** voting register, electoral roll; **~ar** *v/t* censor; **censura** *f* censorship; **censurar** censor; *tratamiento* condemn

cent (= **céntimo**) cent

centavo *m* cent

centella *f* spark; (*rayo*) flash of lightning

centenario 1 *adj* hundred-year-old *atr* **2** *m* centennial, *Br* centenary

centésimo 1 *adj* hundredth **2** *m*, **-a** *f* hundredth

centígrado centigrade; **centímetro** *m* centimeter, *Br* centimetre

céntimo *m* cent; **estar sin un ~** not have a red cent *F*

centinela *m/f* sentry; *de banda criminal* lookout

centolla *f*, **centollo** *m* ZO spider crab

central 1 *adj* central **2** *f* head office; **~ atómica** *o* **nuclear** nuclear power station; **~ eléctrica** power station; **~ telefónica** telephone exchange; **~ térmica** thermal power station; **centralita** *f* TELEC switchboard; **centralizar** centralize; **centrar** *tb* DEP center, *Br* centre; *esfuerzos* focus (**en** on); **centrarse** concentrate (**en** on); **céntrico** central; **centrifugadora**

f centrifuge; *para ropa* spin-dryer; **centrifugar** spin; **centro** *m* center, *Br* centre; **~ comercial** (shopping) mall, *Br tb* shopping centre; **~ urbano** *en señal* town center; **Centroamérica** Central America; **centroamericano** Central American

ceñido tight; **ceñirse: ~ a algo** *fig* stick to sth

cepa *f* de vid stock

cepillar brush; **cepillo** *m* brush; **~ de dientes** toothbrush

cera *f* wax

cerámica *f* ceramics

cerca¹ *f* fence

cerca² *adv* near, close; **de ~** close up; **~ de** near, close to; (*casi*) nearly

cercado *m* fence

cercanía *f*: **tren de ~s** suburban train; **cercano** nearby; **~ a** close to, near to; **cercar** surround; *con valla* fence in

cerciorarse make sure (**de** of)

cerco *m* ring; *de puerta* frame; *L.Am.* fence; **poner ~ a** lay siege to

cerda *f* animal sow; *fig F persona* pig *F*; *de brocha* bristle; **cerdo** *m* hog, *Br* pig; *fig F persona* pig *F*

cereal *m* cereal; **~es** (breakfast) cereal

cerebelo *m* ANAT cerebellum; **cerebral** cerebral; **cerebro**

m ANAT brain; *fig*: *persona* brains *sg*

ceremonia *f* ceremony; **ceremonial** *m/adj* ceremonial; **ceremonioso** ceremonious

cereza *f* cherry; **cerezo** *m* cherry (tree)

cerilla *f* match

cero *m* zero, *Br tb* nought; *en fútbol etc* zero, *Br* nil; *en tenis* love; **bajo / sobre ~** below / above zero; **empezar desde ~** *fig* start from scratch

cerrado closed; *persona* narrow-minded; (*túmido*) introverted; *cielo* overcast; **curva -a** tight curve; **cerradura** *f* lock; **cerrajero**, **-a** *f* locksmith; **cerrar 1** *v/t* close; *tubería* block; *grifo* turn off; **~ con llave** lock **2** *v/i* close

cerro *m* hill

cerrojo *m* bolt; **echar el ~** bolt the door

certamen *m* competition

certero accurate

certeza *f* certainty

certidumbre *f* certainty

certificado 1 *adj carta* registered **2** *m* certificate; **certificar** certify; *carta* register

cervecería *f* bar

cerveza *f* beer; **~ de barril** *o* **de presión** draft, *Br* draught (beer); **fábrica de ~** brewery

cesación *f* cessation; **cesar** stop; **no ~ de hacer algo** keep on doing sth; **sin ~** non-stop

cesárea *f* MED Cesarean, *Br*

Caesarean

cese *m* cessation

cesión *f* transfer

césped *m* lawn

cesta *f* basket; **~ de la compra** shopping basket; **cesto** *m* large basket

chabacano vulgar, tacky F

chabola *f* shack; **barrio de ~s** shanty town

chacal *m* jackal

chacha *f* F maid

cháchara *f* chatter

chafar squash; *cosa erguida* flatten; F *planes etc* ruin

chaflán *m* corner

chal *m* shawl

chalado F crazy F (*por* about)

chalet *m* chalet; **~ adosado** house sharing one or more walls with other houses; **~ pareado** duplex, *Br* semi-detached house

chalupa *f* MAR small boat; *Méx* stuffed tortilla

chamaca *f* C.Am., *Méx* girl; **chamaco** *m* C.Am., *Méx* boy

chamba *f* *Méx* F job

champán *m*, **champaña** *m* champagne

champiñón *m* mushroom

champú *m* shampoo

chamuscar scorch; *pelo* singe

chance 1 *m* L.Am. chance; **dame ~** let me have a try **2** *conj* *Méx* perhaps

chancho *m* L.Am. hog, *Br* pig; *carne* pork

chanchullo *m* F trick, scam F

chancleta *f* thong; *S.Am.*

baby girl

chándal *m* sweats *pl*, *Br* tracksuit

chantaje *m* blackmail; **chantajear** blackmail

chanza *f* wisecrack

chapa *f* (*tapón*) cap; (*plancha*) sheet (of metal); (*insignia*) badge; *AUTO* bodywork; **chapado** plated; **~ a la antigua** old-fashioned

chaparro *Méx* small

chaparrón *m* downpour; *fig F* **de insultos** barrage

chapistería *f* *AUTO* body shop

chapotear splash

chapucear botch

chapucero 1 *adj* shoddy **2** *m*, **-a** *f* shoddy worker

chapurrear: **~ el francés** speak poor French

chapuza *f* shoddy piece of work; (*trabajo menor*) odd job

chapuzar duck; **chapuzarse** dive in; **chapuzón** *m* dip; **darse un ~** go for a dip

chaqué *m* morning coat; **chaqueta** *f* jacket; **~ de punto** cardigan; **chaquetón** *m* three-quarter length coat

charanga *f* brass band

charca *f* pond; **charco** *m* puddle

charcutería *f* delicatessen

charla *f* chat; *organizada* talk; **charlar** chat

charnela *f* hinge

charol *m* patent leather

cháter charter *atr*

chasco *m* joke; **llevarse un ~** be disappointed

chasis *m inv* *AUTO* chassis

chasquear: *látigo* crack

chatarra *f* scrap; **chatarrero** *m*, **-a** *f* scrap merchant

chato *nariz* snub; *L.Am.* *nivel* low

chaval *m* F kid F, boy; **chavala** *f* F kid F, girl

chaveta *f* TÉC (*cotter*) pin; **estar ~** F be nuts F; **perder la ~** F go off one's rocker F

checo 1 *adj* Czech **2** *m*, **-a** *f* Czech **3** *m idioma* Czech

cheque *m* check, *Br* cheque; **~ sin fondos** bad check (*Br* cheque); **~ de viaje** traveler's check, *Br* traveller's cheque; **chequear** check; **chequeo** *m* MED check-up; **chequera** *f* checkbook, *Br* chequebook

chic *m/adj* chic

chica *f* girl

chicharrones *mpl* cracklings, *Br* pork scratchings

chichón *m* bump

chicle *m* chewing gum

chico 1 *adj* small, little **2** *m* boy

chiflado F crazy F (**por** about)

Chile Chile; **chileno 1** *adj* Chilean **2** *m*, **-a** *f* Chilean

chillar shriek; *de cerdo* squeal; **chillón 1** *adj voz* shrill; *color* loud **2** *m*, **-ona** *f* loudmouth

chimenea *f* chimney; *de salón* fireplace

chimpancé *m* chimpanzee

China China; **china** f Chinese woman; Rpl serving girl; Rpl (niñera) nursemaid

chinche m ZO bedbug; L.Am. (chincheta) thumbtack, Br drawing pin

chincheta f thumbtack, Br drawing pin

chinela f slipper

chinesco Chinese; **chino 1** adj Chinese **2** m Chinese man; idioma Chinese; **trabajo de ~s** F hard work

chip m INFOR chip

chipirón m baby squid

chiquilla f girl, kid F; **chiquillo** m boy, kid F; **chiquillada** f childish trick

chirimoya f custard apple

chirona f: **en ~** F in the can F, inside F

chirriar squeak; **chirrido** m squeak

chisme m F bit of gossip; objeto doodad F, Br doodah F; **chismorrear** F gossip; **chismoso 1** adj gossipy **2** m, -a f F gossip

chispa f spark; (cantidad pequeña) spot; fig F wit; **chispear** spark; fig sparkle; de lluvia spit

chisporrotear de leña crackle; de aceite spit

chiste m joke

chistera f top hat

chistoso funny

chivarse F rat F (**a** to); **chivato** m, -a f F stool pigeon F

chivo m ZO kid; C.Am., Méx wages pl

chocante startling; que ofende shocking; (extraño) odd; L.Am. (antipático) unpleasant; **chocar** crash (**con, contra** into); **~le a alguien** surprise s.o.; (ofender) shock s.o.; **~ con un problema** come up against a problem

chocho F senile; **estar ~ con** dote on

chocolate m chocolate; F (hachís) hash F

chófer L.Am., **chofer** m driver

chollo m F bargain

choque m collision, crash; DEP, MIL clash; MED shock

chorizo m chorizo (spicy cured sausage); F thief; Rpl (filete) rump steak

chorrear gush out, stream; (gotear) drip; **chorro** m líquido jet, stream; fig stream; C.Am. faucet, Br tap

choza f hut

christmas m Christmas card

chubasco m shower

chuchería f knick-knack; (golosina) candy, Br sweet

chufa f BOT tiger nut

chuleta f GASTR chop

chulo F fantastic F; Méx (guapo) attractive; (presuntuoso) cocky F

chumbera f C.Am. prickly pear

chupada f suck; de cigarrillo puff; **chupado** F (delgado) skinny; F (fácil) dead easy F; L.Am. F drunk; **chupar** suck; (absorber) soak up;

chupete *m de bebé* pacifier, *Br* dummy; *(sorbete)* Popsicle®, *Br* ice lolly

chupi *adj* great F, fantastic F

churrasco *m Rpl* steak

churro *m* fritter; *(chapuza)* botched job

chusco 1 *adj* funny **2** *m* piece of bread

chusma *f desp* rabble *desp*

chutar DEP shoot;; **chutarse** F *con drogas* shoot up F

Cía. (= **Compañía**) Co. (= Company)

ciática *f* MED sciatica

ciber... cyber...

cicatriz *f* scar; **cicatrizar** scar

ciclismo *m* cycling; **ciclista** *m/f* cyclist; **ciclo** *m* cycle; *de cine* season; **ciclomotor** *m* moped

ciclón *m* cyclone

cicuta *f* BOT hemlock

ciega *f* blind woman; **ciego 1** *adj* blind; **a -as** blindly **2** *m* blind man

cielo *m* sky; REL heaven; *ser un ~* F be an angel F; *~ raso* ceiling

cien a *o* one hundred

ciencia *f* science; *~ ficción* science fiction; *a ~ cierta* for certain, for sure; **científico 1** *adj* scientific **2** *m*, *-a f* scientist

cieno *m* silt

ciento a *o* one hundred; *el cinco por ~* five percent

cierre *m* fastener; *de negocio* closure; *~ centralizado* AUTO central locking; *~ relám-*

pago *L.Am.* zipper, *Br* zip

cierto certain; *es ~* it's true; *~ día* one day; *por ~* incidentally; *estar en lo ~* be right

ciervo *m* deer; *~ volante* stag beetle

cifra *f* figure; **cifrar** write in code; *~ su esperanza en* pin one's hopes on; **cifrarse:** *~ en* amount to

cigala *f* ZO crayfish

cigarra *f* ZO cicada

cigarrillo *m* cigarette; **cigarro** *m* cigar; *L.Am.* cigarette

cigüeña *f* ZO stork

cigüeñal *m* AUTO crankshaft

cilindrada *f* AUTO cubic capacity; **cilíndrico** cylindrical; **cilindro** *m* cylinder

cima *f* summit; *fig* peak

cimentar lay the foundations of; *fig* base (*en* on); **cimientos** *mpl* foundations

cinc *m* zinc

cincel *m* chisel; **cincelar** metal engrave; *piedra* chisel

cinco five; **cincuenta** fifty

cine *m* movies *pl*, cinema; **cineasta** *m/f* film-maker

cínico 1 *adj* cynical **2** *m*, *-a f* cynic; **cinismo** *m* cynicism

cinta *f* ribbon; *de música, vídeo* tape; *~ adhesiva* adhesive tape; *~ aislante* friction tape, *Br* insulating tape; *~ métrica* tape measure; *~ de vídeo* video tape

cintura *f* waist; **cinturón** *m* belt; *~ de seguridad* AUTO seatbelt

ciprés *m* BOT cypress

circo *m* circus

circuito *m* circuit; *corto ~* ELEC short circuit; circulación *f* movement; FIN, MED circulation; AUTO traffic; circular 1 *adj* circular 2 *v/i* circulate; AUTO drive, travel; *de persona* move (along); círculo *m* circle; *~ vicioso* vicious circle

circunferencia *f* circumference

circunscribir limit (*a* to)

circunspecto circumspect, cautious

circunstancia *f* circumstance

circunvalación *f*: (*carretera de*) *~* beltway, *Br* ring-road

ciruela *f* plum; *~ pasa* prune

cirugía *f* surgery; *~ estética* cosmetic surgery; cirujano *m*, *-a f* surgeon

cisne *m* ZO swan

cisterna *f* de WC cistern

cita *f* appointment; *de texto* quote, quotation; *citar a reunión* arrange to meet; *a juicio* summon; (*mencionar*) mention; *de texto* quote; citarse arrange to meet; citación *f* JUR summons *sg*, subpoena

cítrico *m* citrus fruit

ciudad *f* town; *más grande* city; *Ciudad de México* Mexico City; *~ universitaria* university campus; ciudadanía *f* citizenship; *~ europea*, *~ de la Unión Europea* EU citizenship; ciudadano *m*, *-a f* citizen; ciudadela *f* citadel

cívico civic; civil civil; *casarse por lo ~* have a civil wedding; civilización *f* civilization; civilizado civilized; civilizar civilize; civilizarse become civilized

clamar: *~ por algo* clamor *o Br* clamour for sth; clamor *m* roar; *fig* clamor, *Br* clamour

clandestino POL clandestine, underground

claqué *m* tap-dancing

clara *f* de huevo white; *bebida* shandy-gaff, *Br* shandy

claraboya *f* skylight

claridad *f* light; *fig* clarity; clarificar clarify

clarín *m* bugle

clarinete *m* clarinet

claro *tb fig* clear; *color* light; (*luminoso*) bright; *salsa* thin; *¡~!* of course!; *hablar ~* speak plainly

clase *f* class; (*variedad*) kind, sort; *~ particular* private class; *dar ~ (s)* teach

clásico classical

clasificación *f* DEP league table; clasificar classify; clasificarse DEP qualify; *~ tercero* come in third

claudicar give in

claustro *m* ARQUI cloister

cláusula *f* clause

clausura *f* de acto closing ceremony; *de bar, local* closure; REL cloister; clausurar *acto oficial* close; *por orden oficial* close down

clavar stick (*en* into); clavos

drive (**en**) into); **uñas** sink (**en** into); ~ **a alguien por algo** F overcharge s.o. for sth

clave 1 f key; **en** ~ in code **2** adj (*importante*) key

clavel m BOT carnation

clavícula f ANAT collarbone

clavija f ELEC pin

clavo m def nail; GASTR clove; CSur F *persona* dead loss F; **dar en el** ~ hit the nail on the head

claxon m AUTO horn

clemencia f clemency, mercy; **clemente** clement, merciful

clérigo m priest, clergyman

clic m INFOR click; **hacer** ~ **en** click on

clienta, cliente m/f de tienda customer; de empresa client; **clientela** f clientele, customers pl

clima m climate; **climatizador** m air conditioner

clínica f clinic

clip m para papeles paperclip; para el pelo bobby pin, Br hairgrip

cloaca f tb fig sewer

clon m clone; **clonación** f; **clonar** clone

cloro m chlorine

cloroformo m chloroform

club m club; ~ **náutico** yacht club

clueca f broody hen

coagularse coagulate; de sangre clot

coalición f coalition

coartada f JUR alibi

cobarde 1 adj cowardly **2** m/f coward; **cobardía** f cowardice

cobaya m/f guinea pig

cobertizo m shed; **cobertura** f cover; TV etc coverage

cobra f cobra

cobrador m, ~**a** f a domicilio collector; **cobrar 1** v/t charge; subsidio, pensión receive; deuda collect; cheque cash; salud, fuerzas recover; importancia acquire **2** v/i be paid, get paid

cobre m copper

cobro m charging; de subsidio receipt; de deuda collection; de cheque cashing

cocaína f cocaine; **cocainómano** m, ~**a** f cocaine addict

cocer cook; en agua boil; al horno bake

coche m car; Méx (taxi) cab, taxi; ~ **de caballos** horse-drawn carriage; ~ **cama** sleeping car; ~ **comedor** L.Am. dining car; ~ **de línea** (long-distance) bus; ~**s compartidos** car sharing; **cochecito** m: ~ **de niño** stroller, Br pushchair; **cochebomba** m car bomb; **cochecito** m: ~ **de niño** stroller, Br pushchair; **coche-literas** m sleeping car; **coche-restaurante** m restaurant car

cochina f sow; F *persona* pig F; **cochino 1** adj filthy, dirty; (*asqueroso*) disgusting **2** m hog, Br pig; F *persona* pig F; **cochinillo** m suck-

(l)ing pig

cocido 1 adj boiled **2** m stew
cocina f habitación kitchen; aparato cooker, stove; actividad cooking; **cocinar** cook; **cocinero** m, -a f cook
coco m BOT coconut; monstruo bogeyman F
cocodrilo m crocodile
cocotero m coconut palm
cóctel m cocktail
codicia f greed; **codiciar** covet; **codicioso** greedy
código m, ~ **de barras** barcode; ~ **postal** zip code, Br postcode
codo m elbow; ~ **con** ~ fig F side by side; **hablar por los** ~**s** F talk nineteen to the dozen F
codorniz f quail
cofre m de tesoro chest; para alhajas jewelry o Br jewellery box
coger 1 v/t (asir) take (hold of); del suelo pick up; ladrón, enfermedad catch; TRANSP catch, take; (entender) get; L.Am. V screw V **2** v/i en un espacio fit; L.Am. V screw V; ~ **por la primera y la derecha** take the first right
cogida f TAUR goring
coherencia f coherence; **coherente** coherent; **ser** ~ **con** be consistent with
cohete m rocket
coincidencia f coincidence; **coincidir** coincide
coito m intercourse
cojear de persona limp, hob-

ble; de mesa wobble
cojín m cushion; **cojinete** m TÉC bearing
cojo lame; mesa wobbly
col f cabbage; ~ **de Bruselas** Brussels sprout
cola[1] f (pegamento) glue
cola[2] f (de animal) tail; de gente line, Br queue; L.Am. F de persona butt F; **hacer** ~ stand in line, Br queue
colaboración f collaboration; **colaborador** m, ~a f collaborator; en periódico contributor; **colaborar** collaborate
colación f: **traer** o **sacar** a ~ bring up
colador m colander; para té etc strainer
colapsar paralyze; tráfico bring to a standstill; **colapso** m collapse; **provocar un** ~ **en la ciudad** bring the city to a standstill
colarse en un lugar get in; en una fiesta gatecrash; en una cola cut in line, Br push in
colcha f L.Am. bedspread; **colchón** m mattress; fig buffer
colección f collection; **coleccionar** collect; **coleccionista** m/f collector; **colecta** f collection; **colectivo 1** adj collective **2** m L.Am. bus; Méx, C.Am. taxi
colega m/f colleague; F pal
colegiado m, -a f DEP referee
colegio m school; ~ **profesio-**

nal professional institute

cólera 1 *f* anger; *montar en ~* get into a rage 2 *m* MED cholera

colgador *m* *L.Am.* hanger; **colgar** 1 *v/t* hang; TELEC put down 2 *v/i* hang (*de* from); TELEC hang up; **colgarse** hang o.s.; INFOR IT lock up; *~ de algo* hang from sth; *~ de alguien* hang onto s.o.

colibrí *m* hummingbird

cólico *m* colic

coliflor *f* cauliflower

colilla *f* cigarette end

colina *f* hill

colindante adjoining

colisión *f* collision; *fig* clash; **colisionar** collide (*con* with)

collar *m* necklace; *para animal* collar

colmena *f* beehive

colmillo *m* eye tooth; *de perro* fang; *de elefante* tusk

colmo *m*: *¡es el ~!* this is the last straw!; *para ~* to cap it all

colocación *f* positioning, placing; (*trabajo*) position; **colocar** put, place; *~ a alguien en un trabajo* get s.o. a job

Colombia Colombia; **colombiano** 1 adj Colombian 2 *m*, *-a f* Colombian

Colón Columbus

colonia *f* colony; *perfume* cologne; *~ de verano* summer camp; **colonizar** colonize

color *m* color, *Br* colour; *~ café* coffee-colored; *L.Am.* brown; *televisión en ~* color TV; *víveres* red; **colorear** color, *Br* colour

colosal colossal

columna *f* column; *~ vertebral* ANAT spinal column

columpio *m* swing

coma 1 *f* GRAM comma 2 *m* MED coma

comadre *f L.Am.* godmother; **comadrona** *f* midwife

comandancia *f* distrito command; (*cuartel*) command headquarters *sg o pl*; *Méx* police station; **comandante** *m* MIL commander; *rango* major; AVIA captain

comarca *f* area

combate *m* combat; MIL engagement; DEP fight; *fuera de ~* out of action; **combatir** fight

combinación *f* combination; *prenda* slip; *hacer ~* TRANSP change; **combinado** *m* cocktail; **combinar** combine

combustible *m* fuel; **combustión** *f* combustion

comedia *f* comedy; **comediante** *m* actor

comedor *m* dining room

comentar comment on

comenzar begin

comer 1 *v/t* eat; *a mediodía* have for lunch 2 *v/i* eat; *a mediodía* have lunch; *dar de ~ a alguien* feed s.o.

comercial 1 *adj* commercial; *de negocios* business *atr*; *el*

déficit ~ the trade deficit **2** m/f representative; **comercializar** market, sell; *desp* commercialize; **comerciante** m/f trader; ~ **al por menor** retailer; **comerciar** trade, do business; **comercio** m trade; *local* store, shop

comestible 1 *adj* eatable, edible **2** m foodstuff; ~**s** food

cometa 1 m comet **2** f kite

cometer commit; *error* make; **cometido** m task

cómic m comic; **cómico 1** *adj* comical **2**, -a f comedian

comida f (*comestibles*) food; *ocasión* meal

comienzo m beginning

comillas *fpl* quotation marks

comisaría f precinct, *Br* police station; **comisario** m commissioner; *de policía* captain, *Br* superintendent; **comisión** f committee; *de gobierno*, (*recompensa*) commission

comité m committee

como 1 *adv* as; **así** ~ as well as; **había** ~ **cincuenta** there were about fifty **2** *conj* if; ~ **si** as if; ~ **no llegó, me fui solo** as o since she didn't arrive, I went by myself

cómo how; ¡~ **me gusta!** I really like it; **¿~ dice?** what did you say?; ¡~ **no!** *Méx* of course!

comodidad f comfort

comodín m *en naipes* joker

cómodo comfortable

compacto compact

compadecer feel sorry for

compañero m, -a f companion; *en una relación, un juego* partner; ~ **de trabajo** co-worker, colleague; ~ **de clase** classmate; **compañía** f company; **hacer** ~ **a alguien** keep s.o. company

comparable comparable; **comparación** f comparison; **comparar** compare

comparecer appear

comparsa 1 f TEA: **la** ~ the extras *pl* **2** m/f TEA extra; *fig* rank outsider

compartimento m FERR car, *Br* compartment

compartir share (**con** with)

compás m MAT compass; MÚS rhythm; **al** ~ to the beat

compasión f compassion; **compasivo** compassionate

compatible INFOR compatible

compatriota m/f compatriot

compendio m summary

compensación f compensation; **compensar 1** *v/t* compensate (**por** for) **2** *v/i fig* be worthwhile

competencia f (*habilidad*) competence; *entre rivales* competition; (*incumbencia*) area of responsibility; ~ **desleal** unfair competition; **competente** competent

competición f DEP competition; **competidor 1** *adj* rival **2** m, -a f competitor; **competir** compete (**con** with); **competitivo** competitive

complaciente obliging, helpful

complejo 1 adj complex **2** m PSI complex; **~ de inferioridad** inferiority complex

complementario complementary; **complemento** m complement; **~s de moda** fashion accessories

completar complete; **completo** complete; *autobús, teatro* full; **por ~** completely

complicación f complication; **complicar** complicate

cómplice m/f accomplice; **complicidad** f complicity

componente m component; **componer** make up, comprise; *sinfonía, poema etc* compose; *algo roto* fix; **componerse be made up (de** of); *L.Am.* MED get better

comportamiento m behavior, *Br* behaviour; **comportar** involve, entail; **comportarse** behave

composición f composition; **compositor** m, **~a** f composer

compota f compote

compra f purchase; **ir de ~s** go shopping; **~s online** online shopping; **comprador** m, **~a** f buyer, purchaser; **comprar** buy, purchase; **compraventa** f buying and selling

comprender understand; *(abarcar)* include; **comprensible** understandable; **comprensión** f understanding

de texto, auditiva comprehension; **comprensivo** understanding

compresa f sanitary napkin; *Br* sanitary towel; **compresión** f tb INFOR compression; **compresor** m compressor; **comprimido** m MED pill; **comprimir** compress

comprobación f check; **comprobante** m proof; *(recibo)* receipt; **comprobar** check; *(darse cuenta de)* realize

comprometer compromise; *(obligar)* commit; **comprometerse** promise (**a** to); *a una causa* commit o.s.; *de novios* get engaged; **compromiso** m commitment; *(obligación)* obligation; *(acuerdo)* agreement; *(apuro)* awkward situation

computadora f *L.Am.* computer; **~ de escritorio** desktop (computer); **~ personal** personal computer; **~ portátil** laptop; **computar** count; *(calcular)* calculate

común common; **por lo ~** generally; **comunal** communal; **elecciones ~es** *L.Am.* municipal elections

comunicación f communication; TRANSP link; **comunicar 1** v/t TRANSP connect, link; **~ algo a alguien** inform s.o. of sth **2** v/i communicate; TELEC be busy

comunidad f community; **~ autónoma** autonomous region

comunión f REL communion

comunismo m Communism; **comunista** m/f & adj Communist

con with; **pan ~ mantequilla** bread and butter; **~ todo eso** in spite of all that; **~ tal de que** provided that, as long as; **~ hacer eso** by doing that

cóncavo concave

concebir conceive

conceder concede; *entrevista, permiso* give; *premio* award

concejal m, **~a** f councilor, Br councillor; **concejo** m council

concentración f concentration; *de personas* gathering; **concentrar** concentrate

concepción f BIO, fig conception; **la Inmaculada Concepción** REL the Immaculate Conception; **concepto** m concept; **en ~ de algo** COM (in payment) for sth; **bajo ningún ~** on no account

concerniente: **~ a** concerning, regarding; **en lo ~ a** with regard to; **concernir** concern; **en lo que concierne a...** as far as ... is concerned

concertar cita arrange; *precio* agree; *esfuerzos* coordinate

concertino m/f MÚS concertmaster, Br leader (of the orchestra)

concesión f concession; COM dealership; **concesionario** m dealer

concha f ZO shell

conciencia f conscience; **a ~** conscientiously; **con plena ~ de** fully conscious of; **concienzudo** conscientious

concierto m MÚS concert; *fig* agreement

conciliación f JUR reconciliation; **conciliar** reconcile; **~ el sueño** get to sleep

concilio m council

conciso concise

concluir conclude; **conclusión** f conclusion; **en ~** in short; **concluyente** conclusive

concordar 1 v/t reconcile **2** v/i agree (**con** with)

concretar specify; (*hacer concreto*) realize; **concretarse** materialize; *de esperanzas* be fulfilled; **concreto 1** adj specific; (*no abstracto*) concrete; **en ~** specifically **2** m L.Am. concrete

concurrencia f audience; *de circunstancias* combination; **concurrido** crowded; **concursante** m/f competitor; **concursar** compete; **concurso** m competition; COM tender

concurrir: **~ a** attend

conde m count

condecoración f decoration; **condecorar** decorate

condena f JUR sentence; (*desaprobación*) condemnation; **condenar** JUR sentence (**a** to); (*desaprobar*) condemn

confitar

condensador *m* condenser; **condensar** condense; *libro* abridge

condesa *f* countess

condescendiente *actitud* accommodating; *desp* condescending

condición *f* condition; *a ~ de que* on condition that; *estar en condiciones de* be in a position to; **condicional** *m/adj* conditional; **condicionar**: *~ algo en* make sth conditional on

condimentar flavor, *Br* flavour; **condimento** *m* seasoning

condiscípulo *m*, *-a f* en universidad fellow student; *en colegio* fellow student, *Br* fellow pupil

condón *m* condom

conducción *f* AUTO driving; *de calor*, *electricidad* conduction; *(tuberías)* piping; *(cables)* cables *pl*

conducir 1 *v/t vehículo* drive; *(dirigir)* lead (*a* to); ELEC, TÉC conduct **2** *v/i* drive; *de camino* (*a* to); *conducta f* conduct; **conducto** *m* pipe; *fig* channel; *por ~ de* through; **conductor** *m*, *-a f* driver; *~ de orquesta* L.Am. conductor

conectar connect

conejillo *m*: *~ de Indias* tb fig guinea pig; **conejo** *m* rabbit

conexión *f* connection

confección *f* making; *de vestidos* dressmaking; *de trajes* tailoring; **confeccionar** make

confederación *f* confederation

conferencia *f* lecture; *(reunión)* conference; TELEC long-distance call; **ferenciante** *m/f* lecturer; **conferir** award

confesar 1 *v/t* REL confess; *delito* confess to, admit **2** *v/i* JUR confess; **confesarse** confess; *(declararse)* admit to being; **confesión** *f* confession; **confesionario** *m* confessional; **confeso** self-confessed; **confesor** *m* REL confessor

confiado trusting; **confianza** *f* confidence; *~ en sí mismo* self-confidence; *de ~ persona* trustworthy; *amigo de ~* close friend; **confiar 1** *v/t* secreto confide (*a* to); *~ algo a alguien* entrust s.o. with sth, entrust sth to s.o. **2** *v/i* trust (*en* in); *(estar seguro)* be confident (*en* of); **confidencia** *f* confidence; **confidencial** confidential; **confidente 1** *m* *(soplón)* informer; *(amigo)* confidant **2** *f* *(soplón)* informer; *(amiga)* confidante

configuración *f* configuration; **configurar** shape; INFOR set up, configure

confirmación *f* confirmation; **confirmar** confirm

confiscación *f* confiscation; **confiscar** confiscate

confitar crystallize

confitería *f* candy store, *Br* confectioner's

confitura *f* preserve

conflictivo *época, zona* troubled; *persona* troublesome; **conflicto** *m* conflict

confluencia *f de ríos* confluence; *de calles* junction; **confluir** meet, converge

conformar 1 *v/t (constituir)* make up; *(dar forma a)* shape **2** *v/i* agree (**con** with); **conformarse** make do (**con** with); **conforme 1** *adj* satisfied (**con** with) **2** *prp:* **~ a** in accordance with; **conformidad** *f (acuerdo)* agreement; *(consentimiento)* consent; **de o en ~ con** in accordance with

confort *m* comfort; **confortable** comfortable; **confortar:** **~ a** comfort

confrontación *f* confrontation; **confrontar** compare; *a personas* bring face to face; *peligro, desafío* face up to; **confrontarse:** **~ con** face up to

confundir confuse; *(equivocar)* mistake (**con** for); **confundirse** make a mistake; **~ de calle** get the wrong street; **confusión** *f* confusion; **confuso** confused

congelación *f* freezing; **~ de precios** price freeze; **congelado** frozen; **congelador** *m* freezer; **congelar** freeze

congeniar get on well (**con** with)

congénito congenital

congestión *f* MED congestion; **~ del tráfico** traffic congestion

congoja *f* anguish

congraciarse ingratiate o.s. (**con** with)

congratulaciones *fpl* congratulations; **congratular** congratulate; **congratularse:** **~ de o por algo** congratulate o.s. on sth

congregar bring together; **congresista** *m/f* conference *o* convention delegate, conventioneer; **congreso** *m* conference, convention; **Congreso en EE.UU.** Congress; **~ de los diputados** lower house of Spanish parliament

congruencia *f* consistency; MAT congruence

cónico conical

conífera *f* BOT conifer

conjetura *f* conjecture

conjugación *f* GRAM conjugation; *fig* combination; **conjugar** GRAM conjugate; *fig* combine

conjunción *f* GRAM conjunction; **conjuntivitis** *f* MED conjunctivitis; **conjunto 1** *adj* joint **2** *m de personas, objetos* collection; *de prendas* outfit; MAT set; **en ~** as a whole

conjuración *f* plot, conspiracy

conllevar entail

conmemoración *f* commemoration; **conmemorar** commemorate

conmigo with me

conmoción f shock; (agitación) upheaval; **conmocionar** shock; **conmocionarse** be moved; **conmovedor** moving; **conmover** move

conmutador m ELEC switch; L.Am. TELEC switchboard

cono m cone

conocer know; por primera vez meet; (reconocer) recognize; dar a ~ make known; **conocerse** know one another; por primera vez meet (one another); a sí mismo know o.s.; **se conoce que** it seems that; **conocido 1** adj well-known **2** m, -a f acquaintance; **conocimiento** m knowledge; MED consciousness; **perder el ~** lose consciousness

conque so

conquista f conquest; **conquistador** m conqueror; **conquistar** conquer; persona win over

consabido usual

consagrar REL consecrate; (hacer famoso) make famous; vida devote

consciente MED conscious; ~ **de** aware of, conscious of

consecuencia f consequence; a ~ de as a result o consequence of; en ~ consequently; **consecuente** consistent; **consecutivo** consecutive; tres años ~s

three years in a row; **conseguir** get; objetivo achieve

consejero m, -a f adviser; COM director; ~ **delegado** CEO, chief executive officer; **consejo** m piece of advice; ~ **de administración** board of directors; ~ **de ministros** grupo cabinet; reunión cabinet meeting

consentimiento m consent; **consentir 1** v/t allow; a niño indulge **2** v/i: ~ **en algo** agree to sth

conserje m/f superintendent, Br caretaker

conserva f: **en** ~ canned, Br tb tinned; ~**s** canned food; **conservador** conservative; **conservante** m preservative; **conservar** conserve; alimento preserve; **conservatorio** m conservatory

considerable considerable; **consideración** f consideration; **considerar** consider

consigna f order; de equipaje baggage room, Br left luggage

consigo with him / her; (con usted, con ustedes) with you; (con uno) with you, with one fml

consiguiente consequent; **por** ~ and so, therefore

consistencia f consistency; **consistente** consistent; (sólido) solid; **consistir** consist (en of)

consolar console

consolidar consolidate

consomé *m* consommé

consonancia *f*: **en ~ con** in keeping with; **consonante** *f* consonant

consorcio *m* consortium

conspiración *f* conspiracy; **conspirar** conspire; **conspirador** *m*, **~a** *f* conspirator

constancia *f* constancy; **dejar ~ de** leave a record of; **constante** constant; **constar ser recorded; ~ de** consist of

constatación *f* verification; **constatar** verify

consternado dismayed

constipado 1 *adj*: **estar ~** have a cold **2** *m* cold; **constiparse** get a cold

constitución *f* constitution; **constitucional** constitutional; **constituir** constitute, make up; *empresa, organismo* set up

construcción *f* construction; *(edificio)* building; **constructor** *m*, **~a** *f* builder; **construir** build, construct

consuelo *m* consolation

cónsul *m/f* consul; **consulado** *m* consulate

consulta *f* consultation; MED *local* office, *Br* surgery; **consultar** consult; **consultorio** *m* MED office, *Br* surgery

consumar complete, finish; *crimen* carry out; *matrimonio* consummate; **consumición** *f* consumption; **ya pago yo la ~ en bar** I'll pay; **consumidor** *m*, **~a** *f* COM consumer; **confianza** *f* **del consumidor** consumer confidence; **consumir** consume; **consumo** *m* consumption; **de bajo ~** economical

contabilidad *f* accountancy; **llevar la ~** do the accounts; **contable** *m/f* accountant

contactar: **~ con alguien** contact s.o.; **contacto** *m* contact; AUTO ignition; **ponerse en ~** get in touch (**con** with)

contado: **al ~** in cash; **contador 1** *m* meter **2** *m*, **-a** *f* *L.Am.* accountant; **contaduría** *f* *L.Am.* accountancy

contagiar infect; **~ la gripe a alguien** give s.o. the flu; **contagiarse** get infected; **contagio** *m* contagion; **contagioso** contagious

contaminación *f* contamination; *de río, medio ambiente* pollution; **contaminante 1** *adj* polluting **2** *m* pollutant; **contaminar** contaminate; *río, medio ambiente* pollute

contar 1 *v/t* count; *(narrar)* tell **2** *v/i* count; **~ con** count on

contemplación *f*: **sin contemplaciones** without ceremony; **contemplar** look at

contemporáneo 1 *adj* contemporary **2** *m*, **-a** *f* contemporary

contenedor *m* TRANSP container; **~ de basura** dumpster, *Br* skip; **~ de vidrio** bottle bank; **contener** contain; *respiración* hold; *muchedumbre* hold back; **contenerse** control o.s.; **contenido** *m* content

contentar please; **contentarse** be satisfied (**con** with); **contento** (*satisfecho*) pleased; (*feliz*) happy

contestación *f* answer; **contestador** *m*: **~ automático** answer machine; **contestar 1** *v/t* answer, reply to **2** *v/i* reply (**a** to), answer (**a** sth); *de forma insolente* answer back

contexto *m* context

contienda *f* conflict; DEP contest

contigo with you

contiguo adjoining, adjacent

continencia *f* continence

continental continental; **continente** *m* continent

continuación *f* continuation; **a ~** (*ahora*) now; (*después*) then; **continuar** continue; **continuo** (*sin parar*) continuous; (*frecuente*) continual

contorno *m* outline

contorsión *f* contortion

contra against; **en ~ de** against

contraataque *m* counterattack

contrabajo *m* double bass

contrabandista *m/f* smuggler; **contrabando** *m* contraband, smuggled goods *pl*; *acción* smuggling; **hacer ~** smuggle; **pasar algo de ~** smuggle sth in

contracción *f* contraction

contracepción *f* contraception; **contraceptivo** *m/adj* contraceptive

contradecir contradict; **contradicción** *f* contradiction; **contradictorio** contradictory

contraer contract; **~ matrimonio** marry

contralto MÚS **1** *m* countertenor **2** *f* contralto

contraluz *f*: **a ~** against the light

contramedida *f* countermeasure

contraorden *f* countermand

contrapartida *f* COM contraentry; **como ~** fig in contrast

contraproducente counterproductive

contrario 1 *adj* contrary; *sentido* opposite; *equipo* opposing; **al ~, por el ~** on the contrary; **de lo ~** otherwise; **ser ~ a algo** be opposed to sth **2** *m*, **-a** *f* adversary, opponent

contrasentido *m* contradiction

contraseña *f* password

contrastar contrast; **contraste** *m* contrast

contratación *f de trabajadores* hiring, recruitment; **~ bursátil** trading; **contratar** contract; *trabajadores* hire

contratiempo *m* setback

contratista *m/f* contractor; **~ de obras** main contractor

contrato *m* contract

contravención *f* contravention; **contravenir** contravene

contraventana f shutter

contribución f contribution; (*impuesto*) tax; **contribuir** contribute (**a** to); **contribuyente** m/f taxpayer

control m control; (*inspección*) check; **~ remoto** remote control; **controlador** m, **-a** f: **~ aéreo** air traffic controller; **controlar** control; (*vigilar*) check; **controlarse** control o.s.

controversia f controversy; **controvertido** controversial

contumaz obstinate

contusión f bruise

convalecencia f convalescence; **convalecer** convalesce; **~ de** recover from

convencer convince; **convencimiento** m conviction

convención f convention; **convencional** conventional

conveniencia f de hacer algo advisability; **hacer algo por ~** do sth in one's own interest; **conveniente** convenient; (*útil*) useful; (*aconsejable*) advisable; **convenio** m agreement; **convenir 1** v/t agree **2** v/i be advisable; **no te conviene** it's not in your interest

convento m de monjes monastery; de monjas convent

conversación f conversation; **conversar** make conversation

conversión f conversion;

convertible 1 adj COM convertible **2** m L.Am. convertible; **convertir** convert; **convertirse:** **~ en algo** turn into sth

convexo convex

convicción f conviction; **convicto** JUR convicted

convidado m, **-a** f guest; **convidar** invite (**a** to)

convincente convincing

convivencia f living together

convocar summon; huelga call; oposiciones organize; **convocatoria** f announcement; de huelga call

convoy m convoy

convulsión f convulsion; fig upheaval; **convulsivo** convulsive

conyugal conjugal; **cónyuge** m/f spouse

coñac m (pl **~s**) brandy, cognac

cooperación f cooperation; **cooperar** cooperate; **cooperativa** f cooperative; **cooperar** cooperate

coordinación f coordination; **coordinar** coordinate

copa f de vino etc glass; DEP cup; **tomar una ~** have a drink; **~s** (en naipes) suit in Spanish deck of cards

copia f copy; **copiadora** f (photo)copier; **copiar** copy

copiloto m/f copilot

copioso copious

copla f verse; (*canción*) popular song

copo m flake; **~ de nieve**

snowflake; **~s de maíz** cornflakes

coque *m* coke

coquetear flirt

coraje *m* courage; **me da ~** *fig* F it makes me mad F

coral[1] *m* ZO coral

coral[2] *f* MÚS choir

Corán *m* Koran

corazón *m* heart; *de fruta* core; **corazonada** *f* hunch

corbata *f* tie

corchea *f* MÚS eighth note, *Br* quaver

corchete *m* hook and eye; *Chi (grapa)* staple; **~s** TIP square brackets

corcho *m* cork

corcova *f* hump(back), hunchback; **corcovado** humpbacked, hunchbacked

cordel *m* string

cordero *m* lamb

cordial cordial; **cordialidad** *f* cordiality

cordillera *f* mountain range

cordón *m* cord; *de zapato* shoelace; **~ umbilical** umbilical cord

cordura *f* sanity; *(prudencia)* good sense

Corea Korea; **coreano 1** *adj* Korean **2** *m*, **-a** *f* Korean **3** *m* idioma Korean

coreografía *f* choreography; **coreógrafo, -a** *f* choreographer

cornada *f* TAUR goring

córnea *f* cornea

corneja *f* ZO crow

córner *m* en fútbol corner (kick)

corneta *f* MIL bugle

cornudo 1 *adj* horned **2** *m* cuckold

coro *m* MÚS choir; *de espectáculo, pieza musical* chorus; **a ~** together, in chorus

corona *f* crown; **~ de flores** garland; **coronación** *f* coronation; **coronar** crown

coronel *m* MIL colonel

coronilla *f* ANAT crown; **estoy hasta la ~** F I've had it up to here F

corpiño *m* bodice; *Arg (sujetador)* bra

corporación *f* corporation; **corporal** *placer, estética* physical; *fluido* body *atr*; **corpulento** solidly built

Corpus (Christi) *m* Corpus Christi

corral *m* farmyard

correa *f* lead; *de reloj* strap

corrección *f* correction; **en el trato** correctness; **correcto** correct; *(educado)* polite; **corrector 1** *adj* correcting *atr* **2** *m*, **~a** *f*: **~ (de pruebas)** proofreader

corredor 1 *m*, **~a** *f* DEP runner; COM agent; **~ de bolsa** stockbroker **2** *m* ARQUI corridor

corregir correct

correo *m* mail, *Br tb* post; **~s** post office; **~ aéreo** airmail; **~ electrónico** e-mail; **~ de voz** voicemail; **por ~** by mail; **echar al ~** mail, *Br tb* post

correr 1 *v/i* run; *(apresurarse)*

rush; *de tiempo* pass; **~ con los gastos** pay the expenses; *a todo* **~** at top speed **2** *v/t* run; *cortinas* draw; *mueble* slide

correspondencia *f* correspondence; FERR connection; **corresponder: ~ a alguien** *de bienes* be for s.o., be due to s.o.; *de responsabilidad* be up to s.o.; *de asunto* concern s.o.; *a un favor* repay s.o.; **actuar como corresponde** do the right thing; **correspondiente** corresponding; **corresponsal** *m/f* correspondent

corretaje *m* brokerage

corrida *f*: **~ de toros** bullfight

corriente 1 *adj* (*actual*) current; (*común*) ordinary; **estar al ~** be up to date **2** *f* ELEC, *de agua* current; **~ de aire** draft, *Br* draught

corroborar corroborate

corroer corrode; *fig* eat up

corromper corrupt

corrosión *f* corrosion; **corrosivo** corrosive; *fig* caustic

corrupción *f* decay; *fig* corruption; **corrupto** corrupt

corsario *m* corsair, privateer

corsé *m* corset

cortacésped *m* lawnmower

cortado 1 *adj* cut, *calle* closed; *leche* curdled; *persona* shy; **quedarse** be embarrassed **2** *m* coffee with a dash of milk; **cortar 1** *v/t* cut; *electricidad* cut off; *calle* close **2** *v/i* cut; **cortarse** cut o.s.; *fig* F

get embarrassed; **~ el pelo** have one's hair cut; **cortáuñas** *m inv* nail clippers *pl*

corte¹ *m* cut; **~ de luz** power outage, *Br* power cut; **~ de pelo** haircut; **~ de tráfico** road closure; **me da ~** I'm embarrassed

corte² *f* court; *L.Am.* JUR (law) court; **las Cortes** Spanish parliament

cortejo *m* entourage

cortés courteous; **cortesía** *f* courtesy

corteza *f de árbol* bark; *de pan* crust; *de queso* rind

cortijo *m* farmhouse

cortina *f* curtain

corto short; **~ de vista** nearsighted; **quedarse ~** fall short; **cortocircuito** *m* ELEC short circuit; **cortometraje** *m* short (movie)

corva *f* back of the knee

corzo *m* ZO roe deer

cosa *f* thing; **como si tal ~** as if nothing had happened; **decir a alguien cuatro ~s** give s.o. a piece of one's mind; **eso es otra ~** that's something else; **¿qué pasa? – poca** what's new? – nothing much; **son ~s de la vida** that's life

cosecha *f* harvest; **cosechar** harvest; *fig* gain, win

coser sew; **ser ~ y cantar** F be dead easy F

cosmética *f* cosmetics; **cosmético** *m/adj* cosmetic

cosquillas *fpl*: **hacer ~ a al-**

guien tickle s.o.; **tener ~** be ticklish; **cosquilloso** ticklish; *fig* touchy

Costa Rica Costa Rica; **costarricense** *m/f & adj* Costa Rican

costa¹ *f:* **a ~ de** at the expense of; **a toda ~** at all costs

costa² GEOG coast

costado *m* side; **por los cuatro ~s** *fig* throughout

costar 1 *v/t* cost; *trabajo, esfuerzo etc* take **2** *v/i* in dinero cost; **me costó** it was hard work; **cueste lo que cueste** at all costs; **~ caro** *fig* cost dear

coste *m →* **costo**

costear pay for

costilla *f* ANAT rib; GASTR sparerib

costo *m* cost; **~ de la vida** cost of living; **costoso** costing

costra *f* MED scab

costumbre *f* custom; *de una persona* habit; **de ~** usual

costura *f* sewing; **costurera** *f* seamstress; **costurero** *m* sewing box

cotejar compare; **cotejo** *m* comparison

cotidiano daily

cotización *f (precio)* price; *(cuota)* contribution; *(valor)* value; **cotizar** *de trabajador* pay social security, *Br* pay National Insurance; *de acciones, bonos* be listed

coto *m:* **~ de caza** hunting reserve; **poner ~ a algo** *fig* put a stop to sth

coyuntura *f* situation; ANAT joint

C.P. (= **código postal**) zip code, *Br* post code

cráneo *m* ANAT skull, cranium

cráter *m* crater

creación *f* creation; **creador** *m*, **~a** *f* creator; **crear** create; *empresa* set up; **creativo** creative

crecer grow; **crecida** *f* rise in river level; *(inundación)* flooding; **creciente** growing; *luna* waxing; **crecimiento** *m* growth

crédito *m* COM credit; **a ~** on credit; **no dar ~ a sus oídos / ojos** F not believe one's ears / eyes

crédulo credulous

creencia *f* belief; **creer 1** *v/i* believe (**en** in) **2** *v/t* think; *(dar por cierto)* believe; **¡ya lo creo!** F you bet! F; **creerse: ~ que...** believe that ...; **se cree muy lista** she thinks she's very clever; **creíble** credible

crema *f* GASTR cream

cremación *f* cremation

cremallera *f* zipper, *Br* zip; TÉC rack

crepitar crackle

crepúsculo *m tb fig* twilight

crespo curly

cresta *f* crest

creyente 1 *adj:* **ser ~** REL believe in God **2** *m* REL believer

cría *f acción* breeding; *de zo-*

rro, león cub; *de perro* puppy; *de gato* kitten; *de oveja* lamb; **sus ~s** her young; **criada** f maid; **criadero** m *de animales* breeding establishment; *de cabras* breeding ground; *de plantas* nursery; **criado** m servant; **criador** m, **~a** f breeder; **criar** *niños* raise, bring up; *animales* breed; **criarse** grow up; **criatura** f creature; F *(niño)* baby, child

criba f sieve; **cribar** sift, sieve; *fig* select

crimen m crime; **criminal** m/f & *adj* criminal; **criminalidad** f crime

crío m, **~a** f F kid F

criollo 1 *adj* Creole **2** m, **-a** f Creole

crisantemo m BOT chrysanthemum

crisis f *inv* crisis

crispado irritated

cristal m crystal; *(vidrio)* glass; *(lente)* lens; *de ventana* pane; **~ líquido** liquid crystal; **cristalería** f *fábrica* glassworks sg; *objetos* glassware

cristiandad f Christendom; **cristianismo** m Christianity; **cristiano 1** *adj* Christian **2** m, **-a** f Christian; **Cristo** Christ

criterio m criterion; *(juicio)* judg(e)ment

crítica f criticism; **muchas ~s** a lot of criticism; **criticar** criticize; **crítico 1** *adj* critical **2** m, **-a** f critic

Croacia Croatia; **croata 1** *adj* Croatian **2** m/f Croat(ian); **3** m *idioma* Croat(ian)

cromo m QUÍM chrome; *(estampa)* picture card

crónica f chronicle; *en periódico* report

crónico MED chronic

cronista m/f reporter

cronológico chronological

cronometrar DEP time; **cronómetro** m stopwatch

croqueta f croquette

croquis m *inv* sketch

cruce m cross; *de carreteras* crossroads; **en las líneas** TELEC crossed line

crucero m cruise

crucial crucial

crucificar crucify; **crucifijo** m crucifix; **crucigrama** m crossword

crudeza f harshness; *de enfrentamiento* severity; *de lenguaje, imágenes* crudeness; **crudo 1** *adj alimento* raw; *fig* harsh; *lenguaje, imágenes* crude **2** m crude (oil)

cruel cruel; **crueldad** f cruelty

crujiente GASTR crunchy; **crujir** creak; *al arder* crackle; *de grava* crunch

cruz f cross; **Cruz Roja** Red Cross; **cruzar** cross; **cruzarse** pass one another; **~ de brazos** cross one's arms; **~ con alguien** pass s.o.

cuaderno m notebook; EDU exercise book

cuadra f stable; *L.Am. (man-*

zana) block; **cuadrado** *m/adj* square; **al ~** squared

cuadrilla *f* squad, team

cuadro *m* painting; *(grabado)* picture; *(tabla)* table; DEP team; **~ de mandos** *o* **de instrumentos** AUTO dashboard; **de** *o* **a ~s** checked

cuádruple, cuádruplo *m* quadruple

cuajada *f* GASTR curd; **cuajar** *de nieve* settle; *fig: de idea, proyecto etc* come together, jell F; **cuajarse de leche** curdle; *de nieve* settle

cual 1 *pron rel:* **el ~, la ~** *etc cosa* which; *persona* who; **por lo ~** (and) so **2** *adv* like

cualidad *f* quality

cualquier any; **~ cosa** anything; **de ~ modo** *o* **forma** anyway; **cualquiera** *persona* anyone, anybody; *cosa* any (one); **un ~** a nobody; **¡~ lo comprende!** nobody can understand it!

cuando 1 *conj* when; *condicional* if **2** *adv* when; **de ~ en ~** from time to time; **~ menos** at least

cuándo when

cuantía *f* amount, quantity; *fig* importance; **cuantioso** substantial

cuanto 1 *adj:* **~ dinero quieras** as much money as you want; **unos ~s chavales** a few boys **2** *pron all*, everything; **unas -as** a few; **todo ~** everything **3** *adv:* **~ antes, mejor** the sooner the better;

en ~ as soon as; **en ~ a** as for

cuánto 1 *interr* how much; *pl* how many; **¿a ~ están?** how much are they?; **¿a ~ estamos?** what's the date today? **2** *exclamaciones:* **¡~ gente había!** there were so many people!; **¡~ me alegro!** I'm so pleased!

cuarenta forty

cuarentena *f* quarantine; **una ~** a quarantine period

Cuaresma *f* Lent

cuartel *m* barracks *pl*; **~ general** headquarters *pl*

cuarteto *m* MÚS quartet; **~ de cuerda** string quartet

cuarto 1 *adj* fourth **2** *m (habitación)* room; *(parte)* quarter; **~ de baño** bathroom; **~ de estar** living room; **~ de hora** quarter of an hour; **de tres a ~** F third-rate; **las diez y ~** quarter after ten; *Br* quarter past ten; **las tres menos ~** a quarter to *o* of three

cuarzo *m* quartz

cuatro four

Cuba Cuba; **cubano 1** *adj* Cuban **2** *m, -a f* Cuban

cuba *f*: **estar como una ~** F be plastered F

cúbico cubic

cubierta *f* MAR deck; AUTO tire, *Br* tyre; **cubierto 1** *part* ☞ **cubrir 2** *m*; *en la mesa* place setting; **~s** flatware, *Br* cutlery

cubilete *m* cup *(for dice)*

cubitera *f bandeja* ice tray; *(cubo)* ice bucket

cubito m: **~ de hielo** ice cube

cubo m cube; recipiente bucket; **~ de la basura** garbage can, Br rubbish bin

cubrir cover (**de** with); **cubrirse** cover o.s.

cucaracha f cockroach

cuchara f spoon; **meter su** L.Am. F stick one's oar in F; **cucharada** f spoonful; **cucharilla** f teaspoon; **cucharón** m ladle

cuchichear whisper

cuchilla f razor blade; **cuchillo** m knife

cuclillas: en ~ squatting

cuco 1 m cuckoo; **reloj de ~** cuckoo clock **2** adj (astuto) sharp

cucurucho m de papel etc cone; sombrero pointed hat

cuello m ANAT neck; de camisa etc collar

cuenca f GEOG basin; **cuenco** m bowl

cuenta f (cálculo) sum; de restaurante check, Br bill; COM account; **~ atrás** countdown; **~ bancaria** bank account; **~ corriente** checking account, Br current account; **más de la ~** too much; **darse ~ de algo** realize sth; **pedir ~s a alguien** ask s.o. for an explanation; **perder la ~** lose count; **tener** o **tomar en ~** take into account

cuentagotas m inv dropper

cuentakilómetros m inv odometer, Br mileometer

cuento m (short) story; (pre-

texto) excuse; **~ chino** F tall story F; **venir a ~** be relevant

cuerda f rope; de guitarra, violín string; **~s vocales** ANAT vocal chords

cuerdo sane; (sensato) sensible

cuerno m horn; de caracol feeler; **irse al ~** F fall through, be wrecked; **poner los ~s a alguien** F be unfaithful to s.o.

cuero m leather; Rpl (fuete) whip; **en ~s** F naked

cuerpo m body; de policía force; **~ diplomático** diplomatic corps

cuervo m ZO raven, crow

cuesta f slope; **~ abajo** downhill; **~ arriba** uphill; **a ~s** on one's back

cuestión f question; **en ~ de...** in a matter of ...; **cuestionar** question; **cuestionario** m questionnaire

cueva f cave

cuidado m care; **¡~!** look out!; **andar con ~** tread carefully; **me tiene sin ~** I couldn't care less; **tener ~** be careful; **cuidadora** f Méx nursemaid; **cuidadoso** careful; **cuidar 1** v/t look after, take care of **2** v/i: **~ de** look after, take care of; **cuidarse** look after o.s., take care of o.s.; **~ de hacer algo** take care to do sth

culata f butt

culebra f ZO snake

culebrón m TV soap

culminante: punto ~ peak,

climax

culo m V ass V, Br arse V; F butt F, Br tb bum F

culpa f fault; **ser por ~ de alguien** be s.o.'s fault; **tener la ~** be to blame (**de** for); **culpable 1** adj guilty **2** m/f culprit; **culpar; ~ a alguien de algo** blame s.o. for sth

cultivador m grower; **cultivar** AGR grow; **tierra** farm; fig cultivate; **cultivo** m AGR crop; BIO culture; **cultura** f culture; **cultural** cultural; **culturismo** m bodybuilding

cumbre f tb POL summit

cumpleaños m inv birthday

cumplido m compliment; **no andarse con ~s** not stand on ceremony; **cumplidor** reliable

cumplimentar trámite carry out; **cumplimiento** m de promesa fulfillment; Br fulfilment; de ley compliance (**de** with); **cumplir 1** v/t orden carry out; promesa fulfill, Br fulfil; condena serve; **~ diez años** reach the age of ten **2** v/i: **~ con algo** carry sth out; **~ con su deber** do one's duty

cuna f tb fig cradle

cuneta f ditch

cuña f wedge

cuñada f sister-in-law; **cuñado** m brother-in-law

cuota f share; de club, asociación fee

cupo m quota

cupón m coupon

cúpula f dome; esp POL leadership

cura 1 m priest **2** f cure; (tratamiento) treatment; Méx, C.Am. F hangover; **curable** curable; **curación** f (recuperación) recovery; (tratamiento) treatment; **curar 1** v/t tb GASTR cure; (tratar) treat; herida dress; pieles tan **2** v/i MED recover (**de** from); **curarse** MED recover; Méx, C.Am. F get drunk

curiosidad f curiosity; **curioso 1** adj curious **2** m, -a f onlooker

curita f L.Am. Band-Aid®, Br Elastoplast®

cursar carrera take; orden, fax send; instancia deal with

cursi F persona affected; **cursilería** f affectation

cursillista m/f course participant; **cursillo** m short course

cursiva f italics pl

curso m course; **en el ~ de** in the course of

cursor m INFOR cursor

curtido 1 adj weather-beaten **2** m tanning; **~s** tanned hides; **curtir** tan; fig harden

curva f curve; **curvo** curved

custodia f JUR custody; **custodiar** guard

cutáneo skin atr; **cutis** m skin

cuyo, -a whose

D

daltónico color-blind, *Br* colour-blind; **daltonismo** *m* color-blindness; *Br* colour-blindness

dama *f* lady; **~ de honor** bridesmaid; *(juego de)* **~s** checkers *sg*, *Br* draughts *sg*

damasco *m* damask; *L.Am. fruta* apricot

damnificado 1 *adj* affected **2** *m*, **-a** *f* victim

danés 1 *adj* Danish **2** *m*, **-esa** *f* Dane **3** *m idioma* Danish

danza *f* dance; **danzar** *danzar* dance

dañar harm; *cosa* damage; **dañarse** harm o.s.; *de un objeto* get damaged; **dañino** harmful; *fig* malicious; **daño** *m* harm; *a un objeto* damage; **hacer~** hurt; **~s** damage; **~s y perjuicios** damages

dar 1 *v/t* give; *beneficio* yield **2** *v/i*: **dame** give it to me, give me it; **~ a** de ventana look onto; **~ con algo** come across sth; **~ de sí** de material stretch, give; **¡qué más da!** what does it matter!; **da igual** it doesn't matter

dardo *m* dart

darse *de una situación* arise

dársena *f* dock

datar **~ de** date from

dátil *m* BOT date

dato *m* piece of information; **~s** information, data *sg*; **~s personales** personal details

D.C. (= *después de Cristo*) AD (= Anno Domini)

de ◇ *origen* from; **~... a** from ... to ◇ *posesión* of; **el coche ~ mi amigo** my friend's car ◇ *material* (made) of; **un anillo ~ oro** a gold ring ◇ *contenido* of; **un vaso ~ agua** a glass of water ◇ *cualidad:* **una mujer ~ 20 años** a 20 year old woman ◇ *causa* with; **temblaba ~ miedo** she was shaking with fear ◇ *hora:* **~ noche** at night; **~ día** by day ◇ *en calidad de* as; **trabajar~ albañil** work as a bricklayer ◇ *agente* by; **~ Goya** by Goya ◇ *condición* if; **~ haberlo sabido** if I'd known

deambular wander around

debacle *f* debacle

debajo 1 *adv* underneath **2** *prp:* **(por) ~ de** under, below

debate *m* debate, discussion

debatir 1 *v/t* debate, discuss **2** *v/i* struggle

deber 1 *m* duty; **~es** homework **2** *v/t* owe **3** *v/i en presente* must, have to; *en pretérito* should have; *en futuro* (will) have to; *en condicional* should; **debe de tener quince años** he must be about 15; **debido 1** *part* → **deber 2** *adj:* **como es ~** properly; **~ a** owing to

débil weak; **debilitar** weaken; **debilidad** f

débito m COM debit

debut m début; **debutar** make one's début

década f decade

decadencia f decadence; *de un imperio* decline; **decadente** decadent; **decaer** tb fig decline; *de salud* deteriorate; **decaído 1** part ☞ **decaer 2** adj fig depressed, down F; **decaimiento** m decline; *de salud* deterioration

decapitar behead, decapitate

decatlón m DEP decathlon

decena f: *una ~ de* about ten

decencia f decency

decenio m decade

decente decent

decepción f disappointment; **decepcionar** disappoint

decidido 1 part ☞ **decidir 2** adj decisive; **estar ~** be determined (*a* to); **decidir** decide; **decidirse** make up one's mind, decide

décima f tenth; **tener ~s** MED have a slight fever

decimal decimal atr; **décimo 1** adj tenth **2** m *de lotería* share of a lottery ticket

decir 1 v/t say; *(contar)* tell; *querer ~* mean; *~ que sí* say yes; *es ~* in other words; *¡no me digas!* you're kidding!; *¡quién lo diría!* who would believe it!; *se dice que...* they say that ..., it's said that ...; *¡diga!, ¡dígame!* Esp TELEC hello

decisión f decision; fig decisiveness; **decisivo** decisive

declamar declaim

declaración f declaration; *~ de la renta o de impuestos* tax return; **prestar ~** JUR testify, give evidence; **declarar 1** v/t state; *bienes* declare; *~ culpable* find guilty **2** v/i JUR give evidence; **declararse** declare o.s.; *de incendio* break out; *~ a alguien* declare one's love for s.o.

declinar decline

declive m fig decline

decodificador m ☞ **descodificador**

decoración f decoration; *decorado* m TEA set; **decorar** decorate

decrecer decrease, diminish

decrépito decrepit; **decrepitud** f decrepitude

decretar order, decree; **decreto** m decree

dedal m thimble

dedicación f dedication; **dedicar** dedicate; *esfuerzo* devote; **dedicatoria** f dedication

dedo m finger; *~ del pie* toe; *~ gordo* thumb; *~ índice* forefinger

deducción f deduction; **deducir** deduce; COM deduct

defecto m defect; *moral* fault; INFOR default; **defectuoso** defective, faulty

defender defend

defensa 1 f JUR, DEP defense,

defensivo 90

Br defence; *L.Am.* AUTO fender, *Br* wing **2** *m/f* DEP defender; **defensivo** defensive; **defensor** *m*, **~a** *f* defender, champion; JUR defense counsel, *Br* defending counsel; **~ del pueblo** *en España* ombudsman

deficiencia *f* deficiency; **con ~ auditiva** with a hearing problem; **deficiente 1** *adj* deficient; (*insatisfactorio*) inadequate **2** *m/f* handicapped person; **déficit** *m* deficit

definición *f* definition; **definir** define; **definitivo** definitive; *respuesta* definite; **en ~** all in all

deforestación *f* deforestation; **deforestar** deforest

deformar distort; MED deform; **deforme** deformed

defraudación *f* fraud; **defraudar** disappoint; (*estafar*) defraud; **~ a Hacienda** evade taxes

defunción *f* death, demise *fml*

degenerar degenerate (**en** into)

degradación *f* degradation; MIL demotion

degustación *f* tasting; **degustar** taste

dehesa *f* meadow

dejadez *f* slovenliness; (*negligencia*) neglect

dejado 1 *part* ☞ **dejar 2** *adj* slovenly

dejar 1 *v/t* leave; (*permitir*) let, allow; (*prestar*) lend; *benefi-*

cios yield; **déjame en la esquina** drop me at the corner **2** *v/i:* **~ de hacer algo** (*parar*) stop doing sth; **no deja de fastidiarme** he keeps (on) annoying me; **dejarse** let o.s. go

delantal *m* apron

delante in front; (*más avanzado*) ahead; (*enfrente*) opposite; **por ~** ahead; **~ de** in front of; **el asiento de ~** the front seat; **delantera** *f* DEP forward line; **llevar la ~** lead; **delantero** *m*, **-a** *f* DEP forward

delatar: ~ a alguien inform on s.o.; *fig* give s.o. away; **delator** *m*, **~a** *f* informer

delegación *f* delegation; (*oficina*) local office; **~ de Hacienda** tax office; **delegado** *m*, **-a** *f* delegate; COM representative

deleitar delight; **deleite** *m* delight

deletrear spell

delfín *m* ZO dolphin

delgadez *f* de cuerpo slimness; (*esbeltez*) thinness; **delgado** slim; *lámina, placa* thin

deliberación *f* deliberation; **deliberar** deliberate (**sobre** on)

delicadeza *f* gentleness; *de acabado, tallado* delicacy; (*tacto*) tact; **delicado** delicate

delicia *f* delight; **delicioso** delightful; *comida* delicious

delimitar delimit

delincuencia f crime; **delincuente** m/f criminal

delineante m/f draftsman, Br draughtsman; **mujer draughtswoman**, Br draughtswoman; **delinear** draft; fig draw up

delirante adj delirious; fig: **idea** crazy; **delirar** be delirious; **¡tú deliras!** fig you must be crazy!; **delirio** m MED delirium; **tener ~ por el fútbol** be mad about soccer; **~s de grandeza** delusions of grandeur

delito m offense, Br offence

demanda f demand (**de** of); JUR lawsuit, claim; **demandado** m, **-a** f JUR defendant; **demandante** m/f JUR plaintiff; **demandar** JUR sue

demarcación f demarcation; **demarcar** demarcate

demás 1 adj remaining 2 adv: **lo ~** the rest; **los ~** the rest, the others; **por lo ~** apart from that; **demasiado** 1 adj too much; **antes de pl** too many 2 adv antes de adj, adv too; con verbo too much

demencia f MED dementia; fig madness; **demente** 1 adj demented, crazy 2 m/f mad person

democracia f democracy; **demócrata** 1 adj democratic 2 m/f democrat; **democrático** democratic

demoler demolish; **demolición** f demolition

demonio m demon; **¡~s!** F

hell! F, damn! F

demora f delay; **demorar 1** v/i stay on; L.Am. (tardar) be late; **no demores** don't be long 2 v/t delay

demostración f proof; de método demonstration; de fuerza, sentimiento show; **demostrar** prove; (enseñar) demonstrate; (mostrar) show; **demostrativo** demonstrative

denegar refuse

denigrar degrade; (criticar) denigrate

denominación f name; **~ de origen** guarantee of quality of a wine; **denominador** m: **~ común** tb fig common denominator; **denominar** designate

denotar show, indicate

densidad f density; **denso** bosque dense; fig weighty

dentadura f: **~ postiza** false teeth pl, dentures pl; **dentífrico** m toothpaste; **dentista** m/f dentist; **dentición** f teething; (dientes) teeth pl

dentro 1 adv inside; **por ~** inside 2 **~ de** en espacio in, inside; en tiempo in, within

denuncia f report; **poner una ~** make a formal complaint; **denunciante** m/f person who reports a crime; **denunciar** report; fig condemn, denounce

departamento m department; L.Am. (apartamento) apartment, Br flat

dependencia *f* dependence (*de* on); COM department; **~ de alguien** *en una jerarquía* report to s.o.; **eso depende** that all depends; **dependiente 1** *adj* dependent **2** *m*, **-a** *f* sales clerk, *Br* shop assistant

depilar *con cera* wax; *con pinzas* pluck; **depilatorio** *m* depilatory

deplorable deplorable; **deplorar** deplore

deporte *m* sport; **deportista** *m/f* sportsman; *mujer* sportswoman; **deportivo** sports *atr*; *actitud* sporting

deposición *f* deposition; **depositar** *tb fig* put, place; *dinero* deposit (*en* in); **depósito** *m* COM deposit; *(almacén)* store; *de agua*, AUTO tank; **~ de cadáveres** morgue, *Br* mortuary

depravado depraved; **depravar** deprave

depreciación *f* depreciation; **depreciar** lower the value of; **depreciarse** depreciate, lose value

depresión *f* depression; **deprimido** depressed; **deprimir** depress

depuración *f* purification; POL purge; **depuradora** *f* purifier; **depurar** purify; *agua* treat; POL purge

derecha *f tb* POL right; **a la ~** *posición* on the right; *dirección* to the right

derecho 1 *adj lado* right; *(recto)* straight; *C.Am.* (*recto*) straight, honest **2** *adv* straight **3** *m* *(privilegio)* right; JUR law; **del ~** on the right side; **~ de asilo** right to asylum; **~s de** *royalties*; **~s humanos** human rights; **no hay ~** it's not fair, it's not right; **tener ~ a** have a right to **4** *mpl*: **~s** fees

derivación *f* derivation; **derivar** derive (*de* from); *de barco* drift

dermatólogo *m*, **-a** *f* dermatologist

derramar spill; *luz*, *sangre* shed; *(esparcir)* scatter; **derramarse** spill; *de gente* scatter; **derrame** *m* MED: **~ cerebral** stroke

derrapar AUTO skid

derretir melt; **derretirse** melt; *fig* be besotted (*por* with)

derribar *edificio*, *persona* knock down, demolish; *avión* shoot down; **derribo** *m* *de edificio* demolition; *de persona* knocking down; *de avión* shooting down; POL overthrow

derrocar POL overthrow

derrochador *m*, **-a** *f* spendthrift; **derrochar** waste; *salud*, *felicidad* burst with; **derroche** *m* waste

derrota *f* defeat; **derrotar** MIL defeat; DEP beat, defeat

derrumbamiento *m* *acciden-*

tal collapse; *intencionado* demolition; **derrumbarse** collapse, fall down; *de una persona* go to pieces

desabrido (*soso*) tasteless; *persona* surly; *tiempo* unpleasant

desabrochar undo, unfasten

desacatar *orden* disobey; *ley, regla* break; **desacato** m JUR contempt

desacertar be wrong; **desacierto** m mistake

desaconsejar advise against

desacoplar uncouple

desacostumbrar: ~ *a alguien de algo* get s.o. out of the habit of sth; **desacostumbrarse:** ~ *a algo* get out of the habit of sth

desacreditar discredit

desacuerdo m disagreement; **estar en** ~ **con** disagree with

desafiar challenge; *peligro* defy

desafinado out of tune; **desafinar** be out of tune

desafío m challenge; *al peligro* defiance

desafortunadamente unfortunately; **desafortunado** unfortunate

desagradable unpleasant, disagreeable; **desagradecido** ungrateful; *tarea* thankless; **desagrado** m displeasure

desagüe m drain; *acción* drainage; (*cañería*) drainpipe

desahogado spacious; **desahogarse** fig F let off steam

desahuciar: ~ *a alguien* declare s.o. terminally ill; (*inquilino*) evict s.o.; **desahucio** m JUR eviction; **demanda de** ~ eviction order

desairar snub; **desaire** m snub

desalentar discourage; **desaliento** m discouragement

desalinización f desalination

desaliñado slovenly

desalmado 1 *adj* heartless **2** m, -a f heartless person

desalojar *ante peligro* evacuate; (*desahuciar*) evict; (*vaciar*) vacate

desamparado defenseless, Br defenceless; **desamparo** m neglect

desangrarse bleed to death

desanimado discouraged, disheartened; **desanimar** discourage, dishearten; **desanimarse** become discouraged o disheartened

desapacible nasty, unpleasant

desaparecer 1 v/i disappear, vanish **2** v/i L.Am. disappear F; **desaparición** f disappearance

desapercibido unnoticed

desaprensivo unscrupulous

desaprobación f disapproval; **desaprobar** disapprove of

desaprovechado wasted; **desaprovechar** *oportunidad* waste

desarmar MIL disarm; TÉC take to pieces, dismantle; **desarme** *m* MIL disarmament

desarraigar *tb fig* uproot; **desarraigo** *m fig* rootlessness

desarreglar make untidy; *horario* disrupt; **desarreglo** *m* disorder; *de horarios* disruption

desarrollar develop; *tema* explain; *trabajo* carry out; **desarrollarse** develop, evolve; (*ocurrir*) take place; **desarrollo** *m* development; *país en vías de ~* developing country

desaseado F scruffy

desasosegar make uneasy; **desasosegarse** become uneasy; **desasosiego** *m* disquiet, unease

desastre *m tb fig* disaster; **desastroso** disastrous

desatar untie; *fig* unleash

desatención *f* lack of attention, inattention; **desatender** neglect; (*ignorar*) ignore; **desatento** (*desconsiderado*) discourteous; (*distraído*) inattentive

desatinado foolish; **desatinar** (*actuando*) act foolishly; (*hablando*) talk nonsense; **desatino** *m* mistake

desatornillar unscrew

desavenencia *f* disagreement

desaventajado unfavorable, *Br* unfavourable

desayunar 1 *v/i* have breakfast **2** *v/t:* **~** *algo* have sth for breakfast; **desayuno** *m* breakfast

desbancar *fig* displace, take the place of

desbarajuste *m* mess

desbloquear *carretera* clear; *mecanismo* free up, unjam; *cuenta bancaria* unfreeze

desbordar 1 *de un río* overflow, burst; *de un multitud* break through; *de un acontecimiento* overwhelm; *fig* exceed **2** *v/i* overflow; **desbordarse** *de un río* burst its banks; *fig* get out of control

descabellado: *idea -a* F hare-brained idea

descafeinado decaffeinated; *fig* watered-down

descalabro *m* calamity

descalificación *f* disqualification; **descalificar** disqualify

descalzo barefoot

descansar rest, have a rest; *¡que descanses!* sleep well; **descanso** *m* rest; DEP half time; TEA interval; *sin ~* without a break

descapotable *m* AUTO convertible

descarado rude, impertinent

descarga *f* ELEC, MIL discharge; *de mercancías* unloading; INFOR download; **descargar** *arma*, ELEC discharge; *fig: ira etc* take out (*en, sobre* on); *mercancías* unload; INFOR download; *de responsabilidad, culpa* clear (**de** of); **descargo** *m* defense, *Br* defence

descaro *m* nerve

descarrilamiento *m* FERR derailment; **descarrilar** derail

descartar rule out

descendencia *f* descendants *pl*; **descendente** downward; *escala* descending; **descender** 1 *v/i* go down, descend; *para indicar acercamiento* come down, descend; *fig* go down, decrease; **~ de** descend from 2 *v/t escalera* go down; *para indicar acercamiento* come down; **descendiente** 1 *adj* descended 2 *m/f* descendant; **descenso** *m de precio etc* drop; *de montaña,* AVIA descent; DEP relegation

descentralizar decentralize

descifrar decipher; *fig* work out

descodificador *m* decoder; **descodificar** decode

descolgar take down; *teléfono* pick up

descolorar bleach; **descolorarse** fade; **descolorido** faded; *fig* colorless, *Br* colourless

descomedido immoderate; (*descortés*) rude

descomponer (*dividir*) break down; (*pudrir*) cause to decompose; *L.Am.* (*romper*) break; **descomponerse**

(*pudrirse*) decompose, rot; TÉC break down; *Rpl* (*emocionarse*) break down (in tears); **se le descompuso la cara** he turned pale; **descomposición** *f* breaking down; *putrefacción* decomposition; (*diarrea*) diarrhea, *Br* diarrhoea; **descompuesto 1** *part* → **arr**; **descomponer 2** *adj alimento* rotten; *cadáver* decomposed; *persona* upset; *L.Am.* tipsy; *L.Am. máquina* broken down

descomunal enormous

desconcertado disconcerted; **desconcertar** *a persona* disconcert; **desconcertarse** be disconcerted, be taken aback

desconectar 1 *v/t* ELEC disconnect 2 *v/i fig* switch off

desconfiado mistrustful, suspicious; **desconfianza** *f* mistrust, suspicion; **desconfiar** be mistrustful, be suspicious (**de** of)

descongelar *comida* thaw, defrost; *refrigerador* defrost; *precios* unfreeze

descongestionar MED clear; *tráfico* relieve

desconocer not know; **desconocido 1** *adj* unknown 2 *m, -a f* stranger; **desconocimiento** *m* ignorance

desconsiderado inconsiderate

desconsolado inconsolable; **desconsuelo** *m* grief; **des-**

consolar distress

descontar COM deduct, take off; *fig* exclude

descontento 1 *adj* dissatisfied **2** *m* dissatisfaction

desconvocar call off

descortés impolite, rude; **descortesía** *f* discourtesy, impoliteness

descoser *costura* unpick; **descoserse** *de dobladillo etc* come unstitched; *de prenda* come apart at the seams

descrédito *m* discredit; **caer en ~** be discredited

describir describe; **descripción** *f* description

descubierto 1 *part* ☞ **descubrir 2** *adj* uncovered; *persona* bareheaded; *cielos* clear; *piscina* open-air; **al ~** in the open; **quedar al ~** be exposed **3** *m* COM overdraft; **poner al ~** uncover, reveal; *estatua* unveil

descubrimiento *m* discovery; (*revelación*) revelation; **descubrir** discover; *poner de manifiesto* uncover, reveal; *estatua* unveil

descuento *m* discount; DEP stoppage time

descuidado careless; **descuidar 1** *v/t* neglect **2** *v/i*: **¡descuida!** don't worry!; **descuidarse** get careless; *en cuanto al aseo* let o.s. go; (*despistarse*) let one's concentration drop; **descuido** *m* carelessness; (*error*) mistake; (*omisión*) oversight; **en un ~** *L.Am.* in a moment of carelessness

desde 1 *prp en el tiempo* since; *en el espacio, en escala* from; **~ 1993** since 1993; **~ hace tres días** for three days; **~... hasta...** from ... to ... **2** *adv*: **~ luego** of course; **~ ya** *Rpl* right away

desdén *m* disdain, contempt; **desdeñar** scorn; **desdeñoso** disdainful, contemptuous

desdicha *f* (*desgracia*) misfortune; (*infelicidad*) unhappiness; **desdichado 1** *adj* unhappy; (*sin suerte*) unlucky **2** *m*, -**a** *f* poor soul

deseable desirable; **desear** wish for; *suerte etc* wish; **¿qué desea?** what would you like?

desecar dry

desechable disposable; **desechar** (*tirar*) throw away; (*rechazar*) reject; **desechos** *mpl* waste

desembalar unpack

desembarcar disembark; **desembarco** *m*, **desembarque** *m de personas* disembarkation; *de mercancías* landing

desembocadura *f* mouth; **desembocar** flow (*en* into); *de calle* come out (*en* into); *de situación* end up (*en* in)

desembolsar pay out; **desembolso** *m* expenditure

desembragar 2 *v/i* release the clutch, declutch; **desembrague** *m* declutching

desempaquetar unwrap

desempate m POL: *una votación de* ~ a vote to decide the winner; (*partido de*) ~ DEP decider, deciding game

desempeñar *tarea* carry out; *cargo* hold; *papel* play; **desempeño** m *de tarea, papel* performance

desempleo m unemployment

desempolvar v/t dust; fig dust off; *conocimientos teóricos* brush up

desencadenar fig trigger; **desencadenarse** fig be triggered

desencantar fig disillusion, disenchant; **desencanto** m fig disillusionment

desenchufar ELEC unplug

desenfadado self-assured; *programa* light, undemanding; **desenfado** m ease

desenfrenado frenzied, hectic; **desenfreno** m frenzy

desenganchar *caballo* unhitch; *carro* uncouple; **desengancharse** get loose; fig F kick the habit F

desengañar disillusion; **desengañarse** become disillusioned (**de** with); (*dejar de engañarse*) stop kidding o.s.; **desengaño** m disappointment

desenlace m outcome

desenmascarar fig unmask, expose

desenredar untangle; *situación confusa* straighten out,

sort out

desenvoltura f ease; **desenvuelto 1** part ☞ **desenvolver 2** adj self-confident

desenvolver unwrap; **desenvolverse** fig cope

deseo m wish; **deseoso:** ~ **de hacer algo** eager to do sth

desequilibrado 1 adj unbalanced **2** m, -a f: **ser un** ~ **mental** be mentally unbalanced; **desequilibrar** unbalance; ~ **a alguien** throw s.o. off balance

deserción f desertion; **desertar** MIL desert; **desertor** m, ~**ora** f deserter

desescombro m clearing (up), removal

desesperación f despair; **desesperado** in despair; **desesperar 1** v/t infuriate, exasperate **2** v/i despair (**de** of); **desesperarse** get exasperated

desestabilizar POL destabilize

desestimar *queja* reject

desfachatez f impertinence

desfalco m embezzlement

desfallecer faint; **desfallecimiento** m (*debilidad*) weakness; (*desmayo*) fainting fit

desfase m gap; ~ **horario** jet lag

desfavorable unfavorable, Br unfavourable

desfigurar disfigure

desfilar parade; **desfile** m parade; ~ **de modelos** o **de modas** fashion show

desgana f loss of appetite; **con ~** fig half-heartedly

desgarrador heartrending; **desgarrar** tear up; *corazón* break; **desgarro** m MED tear

desgastado worn out; **desgastar** wear out; *defensas* wear down; **desgaste** m wear (and tear)

desglose m breakdown, itemization

desgracia f misfortune; *suceso* accident; **por ~** unfortunately; **desgraciado 1** adj unfortunate; *(miserable)* wretched **2** m *(sinvergüenza)* swine F

desgravar 1 v/t deduct **2** v/i be tax-deductible

desgreñar dishevel

desguazar scrap

deshabitado uninhabited

deshacer undo; *maleta* unpack; *planes* wreck; *(suspender)* cancel; **deshacerse de** nudo de corbata, lazo etc come undone; *de hielo* melt; **~ de** get rid of; **deshecho 1** part ☞ **deshacer 2** adj F anímicamente devastated F; *de cansancio* beat F

deshelar, deshelarse thaw

desheredar disinherit

deshielo m thaw

deshonesto dishonest; **deshonra** f dishonor; *Br* dishonour; **deshonrar** dishonor, *Br* dishonour

deshora: a ~ (s) at the wrong time

desierto 1 adj empty, deserted; *isla -a* desert island **2** m desert

designación f appointment, naming; *de lugar* selection; *de candidato* designation; **designar** appoint, name; *lugar* select

desigual unequal; *terreno* uneven; **desigualdad** f inequality

desilusión f disappointment; **desilusionar** disappoint; *(quitar la ilusión)* disillusion

desinfección f disinfection; **desinfectante** m disinfectant; **desinfectar** disinfect

desintegración f tb FÍS disintegration; **desintegrarse** disintegrate; *de grupo de gente* break up

desinterés m lack of interest; *(generosidad)* unselfishness; **desinteresado** unselfish

desintoxicación f detoxification

desistir give up, stop

desleal disloyal

desleír dissolve; **desleírse** dissolve

deslenguado 1 adj foulmouthed **2** m, **-a** f foulmouthed person

desligar separate **(de** from); *fig: persona* cut off **(de** from)

desliz m fig F slip-up F; **deslizar 1** v/t slide, run **(por** along); *idea, frase* slip in **2** v/i slide; **deslizarse** slide

deslucido tarnished; *colores* dull, drab; **deslucir** tarnish; *fig* spoil; **deslucirse** de colo-

res fade; _de persona_ be discredited

deslumbrar _fig_ dazzle

desmán _m_ outrage

desmantelar dismantle

desmaquillar remove make-up from; **desmaquillarse** take one's make-up off

desmarcarse DEP lose one's marker; **~ de** distance o.s. from

desmayado _persona_ unconscious; _voz_ weak; _color_ pale; **desmayarse** faint; **desmayo** _m_ fainting fit; _sin ~_ without flagging

desmedido excessive

desmejorar 1 _v/t_ spoil **2** _v/i_ MED get worse, go downhill; **desmejorarse** MED get worse, go downhill; _(perder esplendor)_ lose one's looks

desmentido _m_ denial; **desmentir** deny; _a alguien_ contradict

desmenuzar crumble up; _fig_ break down

desmesurado excessive

desmontable easily dismantled; **desmontar** _v/t_ dismantle, take apart; _tienda de campaña_ take down **2** _v/i_ dismount

desmoronarse _tb fig_ collapse

desnivel _m_ unevenness; _entre personas_ disparity

desnudar undress; _fig_ fleece; **desnudarse** undress; **desnudez** _f_ nudity; _fig_ nakedness; **desnudismo** _m_ nudism; **desnudo 1** _adj_ naked;

(sin decoración) bare **2** _m_ PINT nude

desobedecer disobey; **desobediencia** _f_ disobedience; **desobediente** disobedient

desocupación _f L.Am._ unemployment; **desocupado 1** _adj_ _apartamento_ empty; _L.Am. sin trabajo_ unemployed **2** _mpl:_ _los ~s_ the unemployed; **desocupar** vacate

desodorante _m_ deodorant

desolación _f_ desolation; **desolado** desolate; _fig_ devastated; **desolador** devastating; **desolar** _tb fig_ devastate

desorden _m_ disorder; **desordenado** untidy, messy; _fig_ disorganized; **desordenar** make untidy

desorganización _f_ lack of organization; **desorganizado** disorganized

desorientarse get disoriented, lose one's bearings; _fig_ get confused

despachar 1 _v/t a persona, cliente_ attend to; _problema_ sort out; _(vender)_ sell; _(enviar)_ send, dispatch **2** _v/i_ meet _(con_ with); **despacho** _m_ office; _diplomático_ dispatch; **~ de billetes** ticket office

despacio slowly; _L.Am._ _(en voz baja)_ in a low voice

desparramar scatter; _líquido_ spill; _dinero_ squander; **desparramarse** spill; _fig_ scatter

despectivo contemptuous;

GRAM pejorative
despedazar tear apart
despedida f farewell; **~ de soltero** stag party; **~ de soltera** hen party; **despedir** see off; *empleado* dismiss; *perfume* give off; *de jinete* throw; **despedirse** say goodbye (**de** to)
despegar 1 v/t remove, peel off **2** v/i AVIA, fig take off; **despegue** m AVIA, fig take-off
despejado *cielo, cabeza* clear; **despejar** clear; *persona* wake up; **despejarse** *de cielo* clear up; *fig* wake o.s. up
despensa f larder
desperdicio m waste; **~s** waste; **no tener ~** be worthwhile
desperfecto m (*defecto*) flaw; (*daño*) damage
despertador m alarm (clock); **despertar 1** v/t wake; *apetito* whet; *sospecha* arouse; *recuerdo* reawaken **2** v/i wake up; **despertarse** wake (up)
despido m dismissal
despierto awake; *fig* bright
despilfarrar squander
despistado scatterbrained
desplazamiento m trip; (*movimiento*) movement; **desplazar** move; (*suplantar*) take over from; **desplazarse** travel
desplegar unfold, open out; MIL deploy
desplomarse collapse

despoblar depopulate; **despoblarse** become depopulated o deserted
despojar strip (**de** of)
despreciar look down on; *propuesta* reject; **desprecio** m contempt; (*indiferencia*) disregard; *acto* slight
desprender detach, separate; *olor* give off; **desprenderse** come off; **~ de** fig part with; *de estudio* emerge; **desprendimiento** m detachment
despreocupado (*descuidado*) careless; (*sin preocupaciones*) carefree
desprevenido unprepared; **pillar** o L.Am. **agarrar ~** catch unawares
después (*más tarde*) afterward, later; *seguido en orden* next; *en el espacio* after; **yo voy ~** I'm next; **~ de** after; **~ de que se vaya** after he's gone
desquite m compensation; **tomarse el ~** F get one's own back
destacado outstanding; **destacar** stand out
destajo m: **a ~** piecework
destapar open, take the lid off; **destaparse** uncover
desterrar exile; **destierro** m exile
destilación f distillation; **destilar** distill; fig exude
destinar *fondos* allocate (**para** for); *a persona* post (**a** to); **destinatario** m, -a f addressee; **destino** m fate; *de viaje*

etc destination; **en el ejército**
etc posting

destituir dismiss
destornillador *m* screwdriver; **destornillar** unscrew
destreza *f* skill
destrozar destroy; *emocionalmente* shatter, devastate
destrucción *f* destruction; **destructor 1** *adj* destructive; **máquina ~a de documentos** document shredder **2** *m barco* destroyer; **destruir** destroy; (*estropear*) ruin, wreck
desunión *f* lack of unity
desusado obsolete
desvalijar rob; *apartamento* burglarize, burgle
desván *m* attic
desvelar keep awake; *secreto* reveal; **desvelo** *m* sleeplessness; **~s** efforts
desventaja *f* disadvantage; **desventajoso** disadvantageous
desventura *f* misfortune; **desventurado 1** *adj* unfortunate **2** *m*, **-a** *f* unfortunate
desvergonzado shameless
desviación *f* diversion; **desviar** *golpe* deflect; *tráfico, río* divert; **~ la conversación** change the subject; **~ la mirada** look away; **~ a alguien del buen camino** lead s.o. astray; **desvío** *m* diversion
detallado detailed; **detalle** *m* detail; *fig* thoughtful gesture; **al ~** retail; **detallista**

m/f COM retailer

detectar detect; **detective** *m/f* detective; **~ privado** private detective
detención *f* detention; **orden de ~** arrest warrant; **detener** stop; *de policía* arrest, detain; **detenerse** stop
detergente *m* detergent
deteriorar damage
determinación *f* (*intrepidez*) determination; (*decisión*) decision; **determinado** certain; **determinar** determine; **determinarse** decide (**a** to)
detestar detest
detrás behind; **por ~** at the back; *fig* behind your / his *etc* back; **~ de** behind; **uno ~ de otro** one after the other; **estar ~ de algo** *fig* be behind sth
detrimento *m*: **en ~ de** to the detriment of
deuda *f* debt; **estar en ~ con alguien** *fig* be in s.o.'s debt; **agencia** *f* **de calificación de ~** FIN rating agency; **deudor** *m*, **~a** *f* debtor
devaluación *f* devaluation; **devaluar** devalue
devastar devastate
devoción *f* *tb fig* devotion
devolución *f* return; *de dinero* refund; **devolver** give back, return; *fig: visita, saludo* return; **F** (*vomitar*) throw up **F**; **devolverse** *L.Am.* go back
devorar devour
devoto 1 *adj* devout **2** *m*, **-a** *f*

devotee

DF (= *Distrito Federal*) Mexico City

día *m* day; **~ de fiesta** holiday; **~ festivo** holiday; **~ hábil** *o* **laborable** work day; **poner al ~** update, bring up to date; **a los pocos ~s** a few days later; **algún ~, un ~** some day, one day; **de ~** by day; **ya es de ~** it's light already; **el ~ menos pensado** when you least expect it; **hace mal ~ tiempo** it's a nasty day; **hoy en ~** nowadays; **todos los ~s** every day; **un ~ sí y otro no** every other day; **¡buenos ~s!** good morning

diabetes *f* diabetes; **diabético 1** *adj* diabetic **2** *m, -a f* diabetic

diablo *m* devil; **mandar a alguien al ~** tell s.o. to go to hell

diafragma *m* diaphragm

diagnóstico 1 *adj* diagnostic **2** *m* diagnosis

diagonal 1 *adj* diagonal **2** *f* diagonal (line)

diagrama *m* diagram

dialecto *m* dialect

diálogo *m* dialog, *Br* dialogue

diamante *m* diamond

diámetro *m* diameter

diapositiva *f* FOT slide, transparency

diario 1 *adj* daily **2** *m* diary; (*periódico*) newspaper; **a ~** daily

diarrea *f* MED diarrhea, *Br* diarrhoea

dibujante *m/f* draftsman, *Br* draughtsman; **mujer** draftswoman, *Br* draughtswoman; **de viñetas** cartoonist; **dibujar** draw; *fig* describe; **dibujo** *m* drawing; *estampado* pattern; **~s animados** cartoons; **película de ~ animados** animation

diccionario *m* dictionary

dicha *f* (*felicidad*) happiness; (*suerte*) good luck

dicho 1 *part* → **decir 2** *adj* said; **~ y hecho** no sooner said than done; **mejor ~** *o* rather **3** *m* saying

dichoso happy; F (*maldito*) damn F

diciembre *m* December

dictado *m* dictation; **dictador** *m*, **~a f** dictator

dictamen *m* (*informe*) report; (*opinión*) opinion; **emitir un ~** make out a report; **dictaminar** state

dictar dictate; *ley* announce; **~ sentencia** JUR pass sentence

diecinueve nineteen; **dieciocho** eighteen; **dieciséis** sixteen; **diecisiete** seventeen

diente *m* tooth; **~ de ajo** clove of garlic; **~ de león** BOT dandelion; **poner los ~s largos a alguien** make s.o. jealous

diesel *m* diesel

diestro 1 *adj* **a ~ y siniestro** *fig* F left and right **2** *m* TAUR bullfighter

dieta *f* diet; **estar a ~** be on a

diet; **~s** traveling o Br travelling expenses

diez ten

difamación f defamation; **de palabra** slander; **por escrito** libel; **difamar** slander, defame; **por escrito** libel

diferencia f difference; **a ~ de** unlike; **con ~ fig** by a long way; **diferencial** m differential; **diferenciar** differentiate; **diferente** different

diferido TV: **en ~** prerecorded; **diferir 1** v/t postpone **2** v/i differ (**de** from)

difícil difficult; **dificultad** f difficulty; **poner ~es** make it difficult

dificultar hinder

difteria f MED diphtheria

difundir spread; (*programa*) broadcast; **difundirse** spread

difunto 1 *adj* late 2 *m*, **-a** f deceased

digerir digest; **digestible** digestible; **digestión** f digestion; **digestivo** digestive

digital digital

dignarse deign; **dignidad** f dignity; **dignatario** m, **-a** f dignitary; **digno** worthy; *trabajo* decent

dilapidar waste

dilatación f dilation; **dilatar 1** v/t dilate; (*prolongar*) prolong; (*aplazar*) postpone **2** v/i Méx (*tardar*) be late; **no me dilato** I won't be long

dilema m dilemma

diligencia f diligence; *vehículo* stagecoach; **~s** JUR procedures, formalities; **diligente** diligent

diluir dilute

diluvio m downpour; *fig* deluge

dimensión f dimension; *fig* size, scale; **dimensiones** measurements

diminuto tiny, diminutive

dimisión f resignation; **dimitir** resign

Dinamarca Denmark

dinamita f dynamite

dínamo, dinamo f o L.Am. m dynamo

dinero m money; **~ en efectivo, ~ en metálico** cash

dinosaurio m dinosaur

Dios m God; **¡~ mío!** my God!; **¡por ~!** for God's sake!

diosa f goddess

diploma m diploma; **diplomacia** f diplomacy; **diplomático 1** *adj* diplomatic **2** m, **-a** f diplomat

diputación f deputation; **diputado** m, **-a** f representative, Br Member of Parliament

dique m dike, Br dyke

dirección f tb TEA, *de película* direction; COM management; POL leadership; *de coche* steering; **en carta** address; **en aquella ~** that way; **~ asistida** AUTO power steering; **~ de correo electrónico** e-mail address; **di-**

rectivo 1 *adj* governing; COM managing **2** *m*, **-a** *f* COM manager; **directo** direct; **en** ~ TV, RAD live; **director 1** *adj* leading **2** *m*, **-a** *f* manager; EDU principal, *Br* head (teacher); TEA, *de película* director; ~ **de orquesta** conductor; **directorio** *m tb* INFOR directory; **directriz** *f* guideline

dirigir TEA, *película* direct; COM manage, run; MÚS conduct; ~ **una carta a** address a letter to; ~ **una pregunta a** direct a question to; **dirigirse** make, head (**a**, **hacia** for)

discapacidad *f* disability; **discapacitado 1** *adj* disabled **2** *m*, **-a** *f* disabled person

disciplina *f* discipline; **discípulo** *m*, **-a** *f* REL, *fig* disciple

disco *m* disk, *Br* disc; MÚS record; (*discoteca*) disco; DEP discus; ~ **compacto** compact disc; ~ **duro**, *L.Am.* ~ **rígido** INFOR hard disk

discordia *f* discord; (*colección de discos*) record collection

discoteca *f* disco

discreción *f* discretion; **a** ~ **disparar** at will; **a** ~ **de** at the discretion of

discrepancia *f* discrepancy; (*desacuerdo*) disagreement; **discrepar** disagree

discreto discreet

discriminar discriminate against; (*diferenciar*) diferentiate

disculpa *f* apology; **disculpar** excuse

discurso *m* speech; *de tiempo* passage, passing

discusión *f* discussion; (*disputa*) argument; **discutir 1** *v/t* discuss **2** *v/i* argue (**sobre** about)

disentería *f* MED dysentery

diseñador *m*, **-a** *f* designer; **diseñar** design; **diseño** *m* design; ~ **gráfico** graphic design

disfraz *m para ocultar* disguise; *para fiestas* costume, fancy dress; **disfrazarse** *para ocultarse* disguise o.s. (**de** as); *para divertirse* dress up (**de** as)

disfrutar 1 *v/t* enjoy **2** *v/i* have fun, enjoy o.s.; ~ **de buena salud** be in *o* enjoy good health

disgustado upset (**con** with); **disgustar** upset; **disgustarse** get upset; **disgusto** *m*: **me causó un gran** ~ I was very upset; **llevarse un** ~ get upset; **a** ~ unwillingly

disidente *m/f* dissident

disimular 1 *v/t* disguise **2** *v/i* pretend

disipar *duda* dispel

diskette *m* diskette, floppy (disk)

dislexia *f* dyslexia; **disléxico 1** *adj* dyslexic **2** *m*, **-a** *f* dyslexic

dislocación *f* MED dislocation; *fig* distortion

disminución f decrease; **disminuido 1** adj handicapped **2** m, -a f handicapped person; **disminuir 1** v/t gastos, costos reduce, cut; velocidad reduce **2** v/i decrease, diminish

disolución f dissolution; **disolver** dissolve; manifestación break up

disparador m FOT shutter release; **disparar 1** v/t tiro, arma fire; foto take; precios send up **2** v/i shoot, fire; **dispararse** de arma, alarma go off; de precios shoot up, rocket F

disparate m F piece of nonsense; **es un ~ hacer eso** it's crazy to do that

disparo m shot

dispensar dispense; recibimiento give; (eximir) excuse (**de** from)

dispersar disperse

disponer 1 v/t (arreglar) arrange; (preparar) prepare; (ordenar) stipulate **2** v/i: **~ de algo** have sth at one's disposal; **disponible** available; **disposición** f disposition; de objetos arrangement; **~ de ánimo** state of mind; **estar a ~ de alguien** be at s.o.'s disposal

dispositivo m device

dispuesto 1 part ☞ **disponer 2** adj ready (**a** to)

disputar 1 v/t dispute; partido play **2** v/i argue (**sobre** about)

disquete m INFOR diskette, floppy (disk)

distancia f tb fig distance; **distante** tb fig distant

distensión f MED strain; fig: de ambiente easing; POL détente

distinción f distinction; **a ~ de** unlike; **distinguido** distinguished; **distinguir** distinguish (**de** from); (divisar) make out; con un premio honor, Br honour; **distintivo** m emblem; MIL insignia; **distinto** different; **~s** (varios) several

distorsión f distortion

distracción f distraction; (descuido) absent-mindedness; (diversión) entertainment; (pasatiempo) pastime; **distraer** distract; **la radio la distrae** she enjoys listening to the radio; **distraído 1** part ☞ **distraer 2** adj absent-minded; temporalmente distracted

distribución f distribution; **distribuidor** m distributor; **distribuir** distribute; beneficio share out

distrito m district

disturbio m disturbance

disuadir dissuade; POL deter; **~ a alguien de hacer algo** dissuade s.o. from doing sth

diurno day atr

divagar digress

diversidad f diversity

diversión f fun; (pasatiempo) pastime; **aquí no hay mu-**

chas diversiones there's not much to go around here; **diverso** diverse; *~s* several, various

divertido funny; (*entretenido*) entertaining; **divertir** entertain; **divertirse** have fun, enjoy o.s.

dividir divide

divino *tb fig* divine

divisa *f* currency; *~s* foreign currency

división *f* division

divorciado 1 *adj* divorced **2** *m, -a f* divorcee; **divorciarse** get divorced; **divorcio** *m* divorce

divulgar spread

doblar 1 *v/t* fold; *cantidad* double; *película* dub; MAR round; *pierna, brazo* bend; *en una carrera* pass, *Br* overtake; *~ la esquina* go around *o* turn the corner **2** *v/i* turn; **doble 1** *adj* double; *nacionalidad* dual; *~ clic* double click; *hacer ~ clic en* double click on **2** *m:* **el ~** twice as much (*de* as); **el ~ de gente** twice as many people; *~s tenis* doubles **3** *m/f en película* double

doce twelve; **docena** *f* dozen

dócil docile

doctor *m, -a f* doctor

documentación *f* documentation; *de una persona* papers; **documental** *m* documentary; **documentar** document; **documentarse** do research; **documento** *m* docu-

ment; *~ nacional de identidad* national identity card

dogma *m* dogma

dogo *m* ZO mastiff

dólar *m* dollar

dolencia *f* ailment; **doler** *tb fig* hurt; *me duele el brazo* my arm hurts; **dolido** *fig* hurt; **dolor** *m tb fig* pain; *~ de cabeza* headache; *~ de estómago* stomach-ache; *~ de muelas* toothache; **doloroso** *tb fig* painful

domador *m, ~a f* tamer; **domar** *tb tb fig* tame; *caballo* break in

doméstico 1 *adj* domestic, household *atr* **2** *m, -a f* servant

domiciliado resident; **domiciliar** pay by direct billing, *Br* pay by direct debit; **domicilio** *m* address; *repartir a ~* do home deliveries

dominación *f* domination; *desp* domineering; **dominar** dominate; *idioma* have a good command of

domingo *m* Sunday; *~ de Ramos* Palm Sunday

dominicano 1 *adj* Dominican **2** *m, -a f* Dominican

dominio *m* control; *fig* command; **ser del ~ público** be in the public domain

don[1] *m* gift; *~ de gentes* way with people

don[2] *m* Mr; *~ Enrique Sanchez* English uses the surname while Spanish uses the *first name*

donación f donation; **~ de órganos** organ donation; **donar** donate; **donativo** m donation

donde 1 adv where **2** prp esp L.Am.: **fui ~ el médico** I went to the doctor

dónde interr where?; **¿de ~ eres?** where are you from?; **¿hacia ~ vas?** where are you going?

dongle m IT dongle

doña f Mrs; **~ Estela** Mrs Sanchez English uses the surname while Spanish uses the first name

dopaje, doping m doping; **dopar** dope; **doparse** take drugs

dorada f ZO gilthead

dorado gold; *montura* gilt

dormido asleep; **quedarse ~** fall asleep; **dormilón** m, **-ona** f F sleepyhead F; **dormir 1** v/i sleep; (*estar dormido*) be asleep **2** v/t put to sleep; **~ a alguien** MED give s.o. a general anesthetic o Br anaesthetic; **dormirse** go to sleep; (*quedarse dormido*) fall asleep; (*no despertarse*) oversleep; **dormitorio** m bedroom

dorsal 1 adj dorsal **2** m DEP number; **dorso** m back

dos two; **de ~ en ~** in twos; **los ~** both; **cada ~ por tres** all the time

dosis f inv dose

dotar equip (**de** with); *fondos* provide (**de** with); *cualidades* endow (**de** with); **dote** f a novia dowry; **tener ~s para algo** have a gift for sth

draga f máquina dredge; *barco* dredger; **dragar** dredge

drama m drama; **dramatizar** dramatize; **dramaturgo** m, **-a** f playwright, dramatist

drástico drastic

drenaje m drainage; **drenar** drain

droga f drug; **~ de diseño** designer drug; **drogadicto 1** adj addicted to drugs **2** m, **-a** f drug addict; **drogarse** take drugs; **drogodependencia** f drug dependency; **droguería** f store selling cleaning and household products

ducha f shower; **ducharse** have a shower, shower

duda f doubt; **dudar 1** v/t doubt **2** v/i hesitate (**en** to); **dudoso** doubtful; (*indeciso*) hesitant

duelo m grief; (*combate*) duel

duende m imp

dueño m, **-a** f owner

dulce 1 adj sweet; *fig* gentle **2** m candy, Br sweet; **dulzura** f tb fig sweetness

duna f dune

dúplex m duplex (apartment)

duplicado m/adj duplicate; **duplicar** duplicate

duque m duke; **duquesa** f duchess

duración f duration; **duradero** lasting; *ropa, calzado* hard-wearing; **durante** *indicando duración* during; *indicando período* for; **~ seis meses** for six months; **durar** last

durazno *m L.Am.* BOT peach
dureza *f de material* hardness; *de carne* toughness; *de clima*,

fig harshness; **duro 1** *adj* hard; *carne* tough; *clima*, *fig* harsh; **~ de oído** F hard of hearing **2** *adv* hard **3** *m* five peseta coin
DVD *m* (= *disco de vídeo digital*) DVD

E

e *conj* (*instead of y before words starting with i, hi*) and
ebanista *m* cabinetmaker;
ébano *m* ebony; **ebanistería** *f* cabinetmaking
ebrio drunk
ebullición *f*: **punto de ~** boiling point
echar 1 *v/t* (*lanzar*) throw; (*poner*) put; *de un lugar* throw out; *humo* give off; *carta* mail, *Br tb* post; **~ a alguien del trabajo** fire s.o.; **~ abajo** pull down, destroy; **~ la culpa a alguien** put the blame on s.o.; **me echó 40 años** he thought I was 40 **2** *v/i*: **~ a** start to, begin to; **~ a correr** start *o* begin to run, start running; **echarse** (*tirarse*) throw o.s.; (*tumbarse*) lie down; (*ponerse*) put on; **~ a llorar** start *o* begin to cry, start crying
eclesiástico ecclesiastical, church *atr*
eclipse *m* eclipse
eco *m* echo; **tener ~** *fig* make an impact

ecografía *f* (ultrasound) scan
ecología *f* ecology; **ecológico** ecological; *alimentos* organic; (*que no daña el medio ambiente*) environmentally friendly; **ecologista** *m/f* ecologist
economía *f* economy; **ciencia** economics *sg*; **~ de mercado** market economy; **~ sumergida** black economy; **económico** economic; (*barato*) economical; **economista** *m/f* economist; **economizar** economize on, save
Ecuador Ecuador
ecuador *m* equator
ecuatorial equatorial
ecuatoriano 1 *adj* Ecuadorean **2** *m*, **-a** *f* Ecuadorean
eczema *m* eczema
edad *f* age; **la Edad Media** the Middle Ages *pl*; **la tercera ~** the over 60s; **a la ~ de** at the age of; **¿qué ~ tienes?** how old are you?, what age are you?
edición *f* edition
edicto *m* edict

edificación f construction, building; building *construct, build;* **edificio** m building
editar edit; *(publicar)* publish; **editor** m, **~a** f editor; **editorial 1** m editorial, leading article **2** f publishing company, publisher
edredón m eiderdown
educación f *(crianza)* upbringing; *(modales)* manners pl; **~ física** physical education, PE; **educado** polite; **mal ~** rude; **educativo** educational; **educar** educate; *(criar)* bring up; *voz* train
EE.UU. (= Estados Unidos) US(A) (= United States of America)
efectivo 1 adj effective; **hacer ~** COM cash **2** m: **en ~** (in) cash; **efecto** m effect; **~ invernadero** greenhouse effect; **~s secundarios** side effects; **en ~** indeed; **surtir ~** take effect, work; **efectuar** carry out
eficacia f efficiency; **eficaz** *(efectivo)* effective; *(eficiente)* efficient; **eficiencia** f efficiency; **~ energética** energy efficiency; **eficiente** efficient
efusivo effusive
egipcio 1 adj Egyptian **2** m, **~** f Egyptian; **Egipto** Egypt
egoísmo m selfishness, egoism; **egoísta 1** adj selfish, egoistic **2** m/f egoist
eje m axis; *de auto* axle; *fig* linchpin

ejecución f *(realización)* implementation, carrying out; *de condenado* execution; MÚS performance; **ejecutar** *(realizar)* carry out, implement; *condenado* execute; INFOR run, execute; MÚS play, perform; **ejecutiva** f executive; **ejecutivo 1** adj executive; **el poder ~** POL the executive **2** m executive; **el Ejecutivo** the government
ejemplar 1 adj alumno etc model atr, exemplary **2** m de libro copy; de revista issue; animal, planta specimen; **ejemplo** m example; **dar buen ~** set a good example; **por ~** for example
ejercer vlt cargo practise, Br practise; influencia exert **2** vli de profesional practice, Br practise; **ejercicio** m exercise; COM fiscal year, Br financial year; **hacer ~** exercise; **ejercitar** músculo, derecho exercise; **ejercitarse en** practice, Br practise
ejército m army
el 1 art the **2** pron: **~ de...** that of ...; **~ de Juan** Juan's; **~ que está...** the one who is ...
él sujeto he; cosa it; complemento him; cosa it; **de ~** his; **es ~** it's him
elaborar produce, make; metal etc work; plan devise, draw up

elasticidad f elasticity; **elástico 1** adj elastic **2** m elastic; (goma) elastic band

elección f choice; electo elect; **elector** m voter; electoral election atr, electoral

electricidad f electricity; **electricista** m/f electrician; **eléctrico** luz, motor electric; aparato electrical; **electrizar** tb fig electrify

electrodoméstico m electrical appliance

electrónica f electronics; **electrónico** electronic; **libro** ~ e-book, electronic book; **comercio** ~ e-business; **electrotecnia** f electrical engineering

elefante m elephant; ~ **marino** elephant seal, sea elephant

elegancia f elegance; **elegante** elegant

elegir choose; por votación elect

elemental (esencial) fundamental, essential; (básico) elementary, basic; **elemento** m element

elepé m LP, album

elevación f elevation; **elevado** high; fig elevated; **elevador** m hoist; L.Am. elevator, Br lift; **elevar** raise; **elevarse** rise; de monumento stand

eliminar eliminate; desperdicios dispose of; **eliminatoria** f DEP qualifying round, heat

élite f elite

ella sujeto she; cosa it; complemento her; cosa it; **de ~** her; **es de ~** it's hers; **es ~** it's her

ellas sujeto they; complemento them; **de ~** their; **es de ~** it's theirs; **son ~** it's them

ello it

ellos sujeto they; complemento them; **de ~** their; **es de ~** it's theirs; **son ~** it's them

elocuencia f eloquence; **elocuente** eloquent

elogiar praise; **elogio** m praise; **elogioso** full of praise, highly complimentary

El Salvador El Salvador

eludir evade, avoid

emanar 1 v/i fml emanate (**de** from) fml; fig stem (**de** from) **2** v/t exude, emit

emancipación f emancipation; **emanciparse** become emancipated

embadurnar smear (**de** with)

embajada f embassy; **embajador** m, ~**a** f ambassador

embalaje m packing; paquete packaging; **embalar** pack

embalse m reservoir

embarazada 1 adj pregnant **2** f pregnant woman; **embarazo** m pregnancy; **interrupción del** ~ termination, abortion; **embarazoso** awkward, embarrassing

embarcación f vessel, craft; **embarcadero** m wharf; **embarcar 1** v/t pasajeros board, embark; mercancías load **2** v/i board, embark; **embarcarse en barco** board, embark; *en avión* board; **~ en** *fig* embark on; **embarco** *m* embarkation

embargar JUR seize; *fig* overwhelm; **embargo** *m* embargo; JUR seizure; *sin* **~** however

embarque *m* boarding; *de mercancías* loading

embaucar trick, deceive

embelesar captivate

embellecer make more beautiful; **embellecerse** grow more beautiful

embestir charge (*contra* at)

emblema *m* emblem; **emblemático** emblematic

embolia *f* MED embolism

embolsar, embolsarse pocket

emborrachar make drunk, get drunk; **emborracharse** get drunk

emboscada *f* ambush

embotellamiento *m* traffic jam; **embotellar** bottle

embragar AUTO **1** *v/t* engage **2** *v/i* engage the clutch; **embrague** *m* AUTO clutch

embriagar *fig* intoxicate; **embriaguez** *f* intoxication

embrión *m* embryo; **embrionario** embryonic

embrollar muddle, mix up; **embrollarse** get complicated; *de hilos* get tangled up; **embrollo** *m* tangle; *fig* mess, muddle

embromar Rpl F (*molestar*) annoy

embrujar *tb fig* bewitch

embudo *m* funnel

embuste *m* lie; **embustero 1** *adj* deceitful **2** *m,* -*a f* liar

emergencia *f* emergency

emerger emerge

emigración *f* emigration; **emigrante** *m* emigrant; **emigrar** emigrate; ZO migrate

eminente eminent

emisión *f* emission; COM issue; RAD, TV broadcast; **emisora** *f* radio station; **emitir** *calor, sonido* give out, emit; *moneda* issue; *opinión* express, give; *veredicto* deliver; RAD, TV broadcast; *voto* cast

emoción *f* emotion; *¡qué* **~!** how exciting!; **emocionado** excited; **emocionante** (*excitante*) exciting; (*conmovedor*) moving; **emocionar** excite; (*conmover*) move; **emocionarse** get excited; (*conmoverse*) be moved

emotivo emotional; (*conmovedor*) moving

empalagoso sickly; *fig* sickly sweet

empalmar 1 *v/t* connect, join **2** *v/i* connect, join up (*con* with); *de idea, conversación* follow on (*con* from); **empalme** *m* TÉC connection; *de carreteras* intersection, *Br* junction

empanada *f* pie; **empanar** coat in breadcrumbs

empapado soaked; **empapar** soak; (*absorber*) soak up

empapelar wallpaper

empaquetar pack

emparedado *m* sandwich

empastar *muela* fill; *libro* bind; **empaste** *m* filling

empatar (*igualar*) tie the game, *Br* equalize; **empate** *m* tie, draw; **gol del ~** *en fútbol* equalizer

empedernido inveterate, confirmed

empedrado *m* paving; **empedrar** pave

empeine *m* instep

empeñar pawn; **empeñarse** (*endeudarse*) get into debt; (*esforzarse*) make an effort (*en* to); **~ en hacer** *obstinarse* insist on doing, be determined to do

empeño *m* (*obstinación*) determination; (*esfuerzo*) effort; *Méx* lugar pawn shop

empeoramiento *m* deterioration, worsening; **empeorar 1** *v/t* make worse **2** *v/i* deteriorate, get worse

emperador *m* emperor; *pez* swordfish; **emperatriz** *f* empress

empezar start, begin; **~ a hacer algo** start to do sth, start doing sth; **~ por hacer algo** start *o* begin by doing sth; **empiezo** *m* *S.Am.* start, beginning

empinado steep

emplasto *m* MED poultice; *fig* soggy mess

emplazamiento *m* site, location; JUR subpena, *Br* subpœna

empleado 1 *adj*: **le está bien ~** it serves him right **2** *m*, **-a** *f* employee; **~ de hogar** maid; **emplear** (*usar*) use; *persona* employ; **empleo** *m* employment; (*puesto*) job; (*uso*) use; **modo de ~** instructions *pl* for use

empobrecerse become impoverished, become poor; **empobrecimiento** *m* impoverishment

empollar F cram F, *Br* swot F; **empollón** *m* F grind F, *Br* swot F

empotrado built-in, fitted

emprendedor enterprising; **emprender** embark on, undertake; **~la con alguien** F take it out on s.o.

empresa *f* company; *fig* venture, undertaking; **empresaria** *f* businesswoman; **empresarial** business *atr*; **ciencias ~es** business studies; **empresario** *m* businessman

empujar push; *fig* urge on; **empujón** *m* push, shove; **empuje** *m* push; *fig* drive

empuñar grasp

en (*dentro de*) in; (*sobre*) on; **~ inglés** in English; **~ la calle** on the street, *Br tb* in the street; **~ casa** at home; **~ coche / tren** by car / train

enagua(s) *f(pl)* petticoat

enajenar JUR transfer; (*trastornar*) drive insane

enamorado in love (**de** with); **enamorarse** fall in love (**de** with)

enano 1 *adj* tiny; *perro, árbol*

miniature, dwarf *atr* **2** *m* dwarf

encabezamiento *m* heading; **encabezar** head; *movimiento* lead

encadenar chain (up); *fig* link together

encajar 1 *v/t piezas* fit; *golpe* take **2** *v/i* fit (**en** in; **con** with); **encaje** *m* lace

encalar whitewash

encallar MAR run aground

encantado (*contento*) delighted; *castillo* enchanted; **¡~!** nice to meet you; **encantador** charming; **encantar**: **me / le encanta** I love / he loves it; **encanto** *m* (*atractivo*) charm; **como por ~** as if by magic; **eres un ~** you're an angel

encarcelar put in prison, imprison

encarecer put up the price of; **encarecerse** become more expensive; *de precios* increase, rise; **encarecidamente: le ruego ~ que...** I beg you to … ; **encarecimiento** *m de precios* increase, rise; (*alabanza*) praise; (*empeño*) insistence

encargado *m*, **-a** *f* person in charge; *de un negocio* manager; **encargar** (*pedir*) order; **le encargué que me trajera...** I asked him to bring me …; **encargarse** (*tener responsabilidad*) be in charge; **yo me encargo de**

la comida I'll take care of the food; **encargo** *m* job, errand; COM order; **¿te puedo hacer un ~?** can I ask you to do something for me?; **hecho por ~** made to order

encarnado red; **encarnar** *cualidad etc* embody; TEA play

encéfalo *m* brain

encendedor *m* lighter; **encender 1** *v/t fuego* light; *luz, televisión* switch on, turn on; *fig* inflame, arouse; **encendido 1** *adj luz, televisión* (switched) on; *fuego* lit; *cara* red **2** *m* AUTO ignition

encerar polish, wax

encerrar lock up, shut up; (*contener*) contain

enchufar ELEC plug in; **enchufe** *m* ELEC *macho* plug; *hembra* outlet, *Br* socket; **tener ~** fig F have connections

encía *f* gum

enciclopedia *f* encyclopedia

encierro *m protesta* sit-in; *de toros* bull running

encima on top; **~ de** on top of, on; **por ~ de** over, above; **por ~ de todo** above all; **hacer algo muy por ~** do sth very quickly; **no lo llevo ~** I haven't got it on me; **ponerse algo ~** put sth on; **encimera** *f sábana* top sheet; *Esp mostrador* worktop

encina *f* holm oak

encinta pregnant

encogerse *de material* shrink; *fig*: *de persona* be intimi-

dated, cower; **~ de hombros**
shrug (one's shoulders)

encolerizarse get angry

encomendar entrust (**a** to);
encomendarse commend
o.s. (**a** to)

encomienda *f L.Am.* HIST
grant of land and labor
by colonial authorities after
the Conquest

encontrar find; **encontrarse**
(*reunirse*) meet; (*estar*) be; **~
con alguien** meet s.o., run
into s.o.; **me encuentro bien**
I'm fine

encorvado *persona, espalda*
stooped

encorvar hunch; *estantería*
buckle

encuadernación *f* binding;
encuadernar bind

encubridor *m*, **~a** *f* accessory
after the fact; **encubrir** *delincuente* harbor, *Br* harbour;
delito cover up

encuentro *m* meeting, encounter; DEP game; **salir** o
ir al ~ de alguien meet
s.o.; **~s online** online dating

encuesta *f* survey; (*sondeo*)
(opinion) poll

encurtidos *mpl* pickles

endeble weak, feeble

enderezar straighten out; **enderezarse** straighten up; *fig*
straighten o.s. out, sort o.s
out

endeudarse get into debt

endibia *f* BOT endive

endosar COM endorse; **me lo
endosó a mí** F she landed

me with it F

endulzar sweeten; (*suavizar*)
soften

endurecer harden; *fig* toughen up; **endurecerse** harden,
become harder; *fig* become
harder, toughen up

enebro *m* BOT juniper

eneldo *m* BOT dill

enema *m* MED enema

enemigo 1 *adj* enemy *atr* **2** *m*
enemy; **ser ~ de** *fig* be opposed to, be against; **enemistad** *f* enmity; **enemistarse** fall out

energético *crisis* energy *atr*,
alimento energy-giving;
energía *f* energy; **~ solar** solar power, solar energy;
enérgico energetic; *fig*
forceful, strong

enero *m* January

enfadado annoyed (**con**
with); (*encolerizado*) angry
(**con** with); **enfadar** (*molestar*) annoy; (*encolerizar*)
make angry, anger; **enfadarse** (*molestarse*) get annoyed
(**con** with); (*encolerizarse*)
get angry (**con** with); **enfado**
m (*molestia*) annoyance; (*cólera*) anger

énfasis *m* emphasis; **poner ~
en** emphasize, stress; **enfático** emphatic

enfermar 1 *v/t* drive crazy **2**
v/i get sick, *Br tb* get ill; **enfermedad** *f* illness, disease;
enfermería *f sala* infirmary,
sickbay; *carrera* nursing; **enfermero** *m*, **-a** *f* nurse; **enfer-**

mizo unhealthy; **enfermo 1** *adj* sick, ill **2** *m, -a f* sick person

enfilar *camino* take; *perlas* string

enfocar *cámara* focus; *imagen* get in focus; *fig*: *asunto* look at; **enfoque** *m fig* approach

enfrentamiento *m* clash, confrontation; **enfrentar** confront, face up to; **enfrentarse** DEP meet; **~ con alguien** confront s.o.; **~ a algo** face (up to) sth

enfrente opposite; **~ de** opposite

enfriar *vino* chill; *algo caliente* cool (down); *fig* cool; **enfriarse** (*perder calor*) get cold, go cold; (*perder demasiado calor*) get cold, go cold; (*perder demasiado calor*) MED catch a cold

enfurecerse get furious

enganchar hook; F *novia, trabajo* land F; **engancharse** get caught (**en** on); MIL sign up, enlist; **~ a la droga** F get hooked on drugs F

engañar **1** *v/t* deceive, cheat; (*ser infiel a*) cheat on; **engaño** *m* (*mentira*) deception, deceit; (*ardid*) trick; **engañoso** *persona* deceitful; *apariencias* deceptive

engatusar F sweet-talk F

engendrar father; *fig* breed, engender *fml*

englobar include, embrace

engordar **1** *v/t* put on, gain **2** *v/i de persona* put on weight;

de comida be fattening; **engorde** *m* fattening (up)

engorroso tricky

engranaje *m* TÉC gears *pl*; *fig* machinery; **engranar** mesh, engage

engrandecer enlarge; (*ensalzar*) praise; **engrandecerse** grow in stature

engrasar grease, lubricate; **engrase** *m* greasing, lubrication

engreído conceited

engrosar **1** *v/t* swell, increase **2** *v/i* put on weight

engullir bolt (down)

enhorabuena *f* congratulations *pl*; **dar la ~** congratulate (*por* on)

enigma *m* enigma; **enigmático** enigmatic

enjabonar soap

enjambre *m tb fig* swarm

enjaular cage; *fig* jail, lock up

enjuagar rinse; **enjuague** *m acto* rinsing; *líquido* mouthwash

enjugar *deuda etc* wipe out; *líquido* mop up; *lágrimas* wipe away

enjuto lean, thin

enlace *m* link, connection; **~ matrimonial** marriage

enlazar **1** *v/t* link (up), connect; *L.Am.* *con cuerda* rope, lasso **2** *v/i de carretera* link up; AVIA, FERR connect

enloquecer **1** *v/t* drive crazy *o* mad **2** *v/i* go crazy *o* mad

enlutar plunge into mourning; **enlutarse** go into

mourning
enmarañar *pelo* tangle; *asunto* complicate, muddle
enmascarar hide, disguise
enmendar *asunto* rectify, put right; JUR, POL amend; **~le la plana a alguien** find fault with what s.o. has done; **enmienda** *f* POL amendment
enmohecerse go moldy *o Br* mouldy; *de metal* rust
enmudecer 1 *v/t* silence **2** *v/i* fall silent
enojar (*molestar*) annoy; *L.Am.* (*encolerizar*) make angry; **enojarse** *L.Am.* (*molestarse*) get annoyed; (*encolerizarse*) get angry; **enojo** *m L.Am.* anger; **enojoso** (*delicado*) awkward; (*aburrido*) tedious, tiresome
enorgullecerse be proud (**de** of)
enorme enormous, huge
enredar 1 *v/t* tangle, get tangled; *fig* complicate **2** *v/i* make trouble; **enredo** *m* tangle; (*confusión*) mess, confusion; (*intriga*) intrigue; *amoroso* affair
enrejar *ventana* put bars on
enriquecer make rich; *fig* enrich; **enriquecerse** get rich; *fig* be enriched
enrojecer 1 *v/t* turn red **2** *v/i* blush, go red; **enrojecerse** go red
enrollar roll up; *cable* coil; *hilo* wind; **me enrolla** F I like it, I think it's great
ensaimada *f* GASTR *pastry in the form of a spiral*

ensalada *f* GASTR salad
ensalzar extol, praise
ensamblar assemble
ensanchar widen; *prenda* let out; **ensanche** *m de carretera* widening; *de ciudad* new suburb
ensañarse show no mercy (**con** to)
ensayar test, try (out); TEA rehearse; **ensayo** *m* TEA rehearsal; *escrito* essay; **~ general** dress rehearsal
enseguida immediately, right away
ensenada *f* inlet, cove
enseñanza *f* teaching; **~ primaria** elementary education, *Br* primary education; **~ secundaria** *o* **media** secondary education; **~ superior** higher education; **enseñar** (*dar clases*) teach; (*mostrar*) show
ensillar saddle
ensimismado deep in thought
ensordecedor deafening; **ensordecer 1** *v/t* deafen **2** *v/i* go deaf
ensuciar (get) dirty; *fig* tarnish; **ensuciarse** get dirty; *fig* get one's hands dirty
ensueño *m*: **de ~** *fig* fairy-tale *atr*, dream *atr*
entablar strike up, start
entallado tailored, fitted
entarimado *m* (*suelo*) floorboards *pl*; (*plataforma*) stage, platform; **entarimar**

floor

ente *m* (*ser*) being, entity; F (*persona rara*) oddball F; (*organización*) body

entender understand; *~ de algo* know about sth; **entenderse** understand; *a ver si nos entendemos* let's get this straight; *yo me entiendo* I know what I'm doing; *~ con alguien* get along with s.o.; **entendido 1** understood; *tengo ~ que* I understand that **2** *m*, -a *f* expert, authority; **entendimiento** *m* understanding; (*inteligencia*) mind

enterado knowledgeable, well-informed; *estar ~ de* know about; *darse por ~* get the message; **enterarse** find out, hear (*de* about); *¡para que te enteres!* F so there! F; *¡se va a enterar!* F he's in for it! F

enteramente entirely

entereza *f* fortitude

entero 1 *adj* whole, entire; (*no roto*) intact; *por ~* completely, entirely **2** *m* (*punto*) point

enterrador *m*, -a *f* gravedigger; **enterramiento** *m* burial; **enterrar** bury; *~ a todos* outlive everybody

entibiar, entibiarse *tb fig* cool down

entidad *f* entity, body

entierro *m* burial; (*funeral*) funeral

entoldado *m de tienda* awn-ing; *para fiesta* tent, *Br* marquee

entonación *f* intonation; **entonar 1** *v/t* intone, sing; *fig* F perk up **2** *v/i* sing in tune

entonces then; *por ~, en aquel ~* in those days, at that time

entorno *m* environment

entorpecer hold up, hinder; *paso* obstruct; *entendimiento* dull

entrada *f acción* entry; *lugar* entrance; *localidad* ticket; *pago* deposit; *de comida* starter; *de ~* from the outset; **entradas** *fpl* receding hairline; **entrante 1** *adj mes etc* next, coming **2** *m* GASTR starter

entrañas *fpl* entrails

entrar 1 *v/i para indicar acercamiento* come in, enter; *para indicar alejamiento* go in, enter; *caber* fit; INFOR log on *o* in; *me entró frío / sueño* I got cold / sleepy, I began to feel cold / sleepy; *este tipo no me entra* I don't like the look of the guy **2** *v/t para indicar acercamiento* bring in; *para indicar alejamiento* take in

entre *dos cosas, personas* between; *más de dos* among(st); *expresando cooperación* between; *la relación ~ ellos* the relationship between them

entreabierto half-open

entreacto *m* TEA interval

entrecortado *habla* halting; *respiración* difficult, labored, *Br* laboured

entredicho *m*: **poner en ~** call into question, question

entrega *f* handing over; *de mercancías* delivery; *(dedicación)* dedication; **~ a domicilio** (home) delivery; **~ de premios** prize-giving; **hacer ~ de algo a alguien** present s.o. with sth; **entregar** give, hand over; *trabajo, deberes* hand in; *mercancías* deliver; *premio* present; **entregarse** give o.s. up; **~ a** *fig* dedicate o.s. to

entrelazar interweave

entremeses *mpl* GASTR appetizers, hors d'oeuvres

entremeter insert

entrenador *m*, **~a** *f* coach; **entrenamiento** *m* coaching; **entrenar, entrenarse** train

entretanto meanwhile, in the meantime

entretener 1 *v/t (divertir)* entertain, amuse; *(retrasar)* detain; *(distraer)* distract **2** *v/i* be entertaining; **entretenerse** *(divertirse)* amuse o.s.; *(distraerse)* keep o.s. busy; *(retrasarse)* linger; **entretenido** *(divertido)* entertaining, enjoyable; **estar ~ ocupado** be busy; **entretenimiento** *m* entertainment, amusement

entretiempo *m*: **de ~ ropa** mid-season; *CSur DEP* half time

entrever make out, see

entrevista *f* interview; **entrevistar** interview; **entrevistarse**: **~ con alguien** meet (with) s.o.

entristecer sadden

entrometerse meddle **(en** in); **entrometido 1** *part ☞* **entrometerse 2** *adj* meddling *atr*, interfering **3** *m* meddler, busybody

entumecerse go numb, get stiff

enturbiar *tb fig* cloud

entusiasmado excited; **entusiasmar** excite, make enthusiastic; **entusiasmarse** get excited, get enthusiastic **(con** about); **entusiasmo** *m* enthusiasm; **entusiasta 1** *adj* enthusiastic **2** *m/f* enthusiast

enumerar list, enumerate

enunciar state

envasar *en botella* bottle; *en lata* can; *en paquete* pack; **envase** *m* container; *botella* (empty) bottle; **~ de cartón** carton

envejecer age

envenenar *tb fig* poison

envergadura *f* AVIA wingspan; MAR breadth; *fig* magnitude, importance; **de gran o mucha ~** *fig* of great importance

enviado *m*, **-a** *f* POL envoy; *de un periódico* reporter, correspondent; **enviar** send

envidia *f* envy, jealousy; **me da ~** I'm envious *o* jealous;

tener ~ a alguien de algo envy s.o. sth; **envidiar** envy; **~ a alguien por algo** envy s.o. sth; **envidioso** envious, jealous; **envidiable** enviable

envío m shipment

envoltorio m wrapper; **envoltura** f cover, covering; *de regalo* wrapping; *de caramelo* wrapper

envolver wrap (up); *(rodear)* surround; *(involucrar)* involve; **~ a alguien en algo** involve s.o. in sth

enyesar *pared* plaster; MED put in plaster

enzima f o m BIO enzyme

eólico wind *atr*; **parque ~** wind farm

epidemia f epidemic

epilepsia f MED epilepsy; **epiléptico 1** *adj* epileptic **2** m, **-a** f epileptic

epílogo m epilog, Br epilogue

episcopal episcopal

episodio m episode

época f time, period; *parte del año* time of year; GEOL epoch; **hacer ~** be epoch-making

equilibrado well-balanced; **equilibrar** balance; **equilibrio** m balance; FÍS equilibrium; **equilibrista** m/f acrobat; *con cuerda* tightrope walker

equinoccio m equinox

equipaje m baggage, luggage; **~ de mano** hand baggage

equipamiento m: **~ de serie** AUTO standard features pl;

equipar equip (**con** with)

equiparar put on a level (**a** o **con** with); **~ algo con algo** *fig* compare sth to sth

equipo m DEP team; *accesorios* equipment; **~ de música** o **de sonido** sound system

equitación f riding

equitativo fair, equitable

equivalente m/adj equivalent; **equivaler** be equivalent (**a** to)

equivocación f mistake; **por ~** by mistake; **equivocado** wrong; **equivocar: ~ a alguien** make s.o. make a mistake; **equivocarse** make a mistake; **te has equivocado** you are wrong o mistaken; **~ de número** TELEC get the wrong number; **equívoco 1** *adj* ambiguous, equivocal **2** m misunderstanding; *(error)* mistake

era f era

erección f erection; **erecto** erect

erguir raise, lift; *(poner derecho)* straighten; **erguirse** *de persona* stand up, rise; *de edificio* rise

erial m uncultivated land

erigir erect

erizado bristling (**de** with); **erizarse** *de pelo* stand on end; **erizo** m ZO hedgehog; **~ de mar** ZO sea urchin

ermita f chapel; **ermitaño 1** ZO hermit crab **2** m, **-a** f hermit

erosión f erosion

erótico erotic; **erotismo** m eroticism

erradicar eradicate, wipe out

errante wandering; **errar 1** v/t miss; ~ **el tiro** miss 2 v/i miss; ~ **es humano** to err is human; **errata** f mistake, error; **de imprenta** misprint, typo

erróneo wrong, erroneous fml; **error** m mistake, error; ~ **de cálculo** error of judg(e)ment

eructar belch F, burp F

erudito 1 adj learned, erudite **2** m scholar

erupción f GEOL eruption; MED rash

esa ☞ **ese**

ésa ☞ **ése**

esbeltez f slimness; **esbelto** slim

esbozar sketch; proyecto etc outline; **esbozo** m sketch; de proyecto etc outline

escabeche m type of marinade

escabroso rough; problema tricky; relato indecent

escabullirse escape, slip away

escafandra f diving suit; AST space suit

escala f tb MÚS scale; AVIA stopover; ~ **de cuerda** rope ladder; ~ **de valores** scale of values; **a** ~ to scale, lifesized

escalada f DEP climb, ascent; ~ **de los precios** increase in prices; **escalador** m, ~a f climber; **escalar** climb

escaldar GASTR blanch; manos scald

escalera f stairs pl, staircase; ~ **de caracol** spiral staircase; ~ **de incendios** fire escape; ~ **de mano** ladder; ~ **mecánica** escalator; **escalerilla** f de avión steps pl; en barco gangway

escalofriante horrifying; **escalofrío** m shiver

escalón m step; de escalera de mano rung

escalope m escalope

escama f ZO scale; de jabón, piel flake; **escamar** scale; fig make suspicious

escamotear (ocultar) hide, conceal; (negar) withhold

escandalizar shock, scandalize; **escandalizarse** be shocked; **escándalo** m scandal; (jaleo) racket, ruckus; **armar un** ~ make a scene; **escandaloso** scandalous; (ruidoso) noisy, rowdy

escandinavo 1 adj Scandinavian **2** m, -a f Scandinavian

escanear scan; **escáner** m scan

escaño m POL seat

escapada f escape; **escapar** escape (**de** from); **dejar** ~ oportunidad pass up; suspiro let out, give; **escaparse** (huir) escape (**de** from); de casa run away (**de** from); ~ **de situación** get out of

escaparate m store window

escape m de gas leak; AUTO exhaust; **salir a** ~ rush out

escarabajo *m* ZO beetle

escarbar 1 *v/i tb fig* dig around (**en** in) **2** *v/t* dig around in

escarcha *f* frost

escardar hoe

escarlata *m/adj inv* scarlet

escarmentar 1 *v/t* teach a lesson to **2** *v/i* learn one's lesson

escarnecer deride; **escarnio** *m* derision

escarpado sheer, steep

escasear be scarce; **escasez** *f* shortage, scarcity; **escaso** *recursos* limited; **andar ~ de algo** *falto* be short of sth; **-as posibilidades de** not much chance of; **falta un mes** ~ it's barely a month away

escatimar be mean with; **no ~ esfuerzos** spare no effort

escayola *m/f* (plaster) cast; **escayolar** put in a (plaster) cast

escena *f* scene; *escenario* stage; **entrar en ~** come on stage; **hacer una ~** *fig* make a scene; **escenario** *m* stage; *fig* scene; **escenificar** stage; **escenografía** *f* *arte* set design; (*decorados*) scenery

escepticismo *m* skepticism, *Br* scepticism; **escéptico 1** *adj* skeptical, *Br* sceptical **2** *m*, **-a** *f* skeptic, *Br* sceptic

esclarecer throw o shed light on; *misterio* clear up

esclavitud *f* slavery; **esclavo** *m* slave

esclusa *f* lock

escoba *f* broom; **escobilla** *f* small brush; AUTO wiper blade

escocer sting, smart

escocés 1 *adj* Scottish **2** *m* Scot, Scotsman; **escocesa** *f* Scot, Scotswoman; **Escocia** Scotland

escoger choose, select

escolar 1 *adj* school *atr* **2** *m/f* student; **escolarización** *f* education, schooling; **escolarizar** educate

escollo *m* MAR reef; (*obstáculo*) hurdle, obstacle

escolta 1 *f* escort **2** *m/f* *motorista* outrider; (*guardaespaldas*) bodyguard; **escoltar** escort

escombros *mpl* rubble

esconder hide, conceal; **esconderse** hide; **escondidas** *fpl* *S.Am.* hide-and-seek; **a ~** in secret; **escondite** *m* hiding place; *juego* hide-and-seek; **escondrijo** *m* hiding place

escopeta *f* shotgun; **~ de aire comprimido** air gun, air rifle

escoria *f* slag; *desp* dregs *pl*

Escorpio *m/f inv* ASTR Scorpio; **escorpión** *m* ZO scorpion

escotado low-cut; **escote** *m* neckline; *de mujer* cleavage

escotilla *f* MAR hatch

escozor *m* burning sensation, stinging; *fig* bitterness

escribir write; (*deletrear*)

spell; **~ a máquina** type; **escrito 1** part ☞ **escribir 2** adj written; **por ~** in writing **3** m document; **~s** writings; escritor m, **~a** f writer; escritorio m desk; **artículos de ~** stationery; escritura f writing; JUR deed; *Sagradas Escrituras* Holy Scripture

escrúpulo m scruple; **sin ~s** unscrupulous; escrupuloso (*cuidadoso*) meticulous; (*honrado*) scrupulous; (*aprensivo*) fastidious

escrutar scrutinize; *votos* count

escuadra f MAT set square; *de carpintero* square; MIL squad; MAR squadron; DEP *de portería* top corner

escuchar **1** v/t listen to; *L.Am.* (oír) hear **2** v/i listen

escudo m *arma* shield; *insignia* badge; *moneda* escudo; **~ de armas** coat of arms

escuela f school; **~ de comercio** business school; **~ de idiomas** language school; **~ primaria** elementary school; *Br* primary school

escueto succinct, concise

escultor m, **~a** f sculptor; escultura f sculpture

escupir **1** v/i spit **2** v/t spit out

escurridizo slippery; *fig* evasive; escurrir **1** v/t *ropa* wring out; *platos, verduras* drain **2** v/i *de platos* drain; *de ropa* drip-dry; escurrirse *de líquido* drain away; (*deslizarse*) slip; (*escaparse*) slip away

ese, esa, esos, esas that; *pl* those

ése, ésa, ésos, ésas *pron singular* that (one); *pl* those (ones)

esencia f essence; esencial essential

esfera f sphere; esférico **1** adj spherical **2** m DEP F ball

esforzar strain; esforzarse make an effort, try hard; esfuerzo m effort; **sin ~** effortlessly

esfumarse F *tb fig* disappear

esgrima f fencing; esgrimir *arma* wield; *fig*: *argumento* put forward

esguince m sprain

eslabón m link; **el ~ perdido** the missing link

eslogan m slogan

eslovaco **1** adj Slovak(ian) **2** m, **-a** f Slovak **3** m *idioma* Slovak; Eslovaquia Slovakia

Eslovenia Slovenia; esloveno **1** adj Slovene, Slovenian **2** m, **-a** f Slovene, Slovenian **3** m *idioma* Slovene

esmaltar enamel; **~ las uñas** put nail polish on; esmalte m enamel; **~ de uñas** nail polish, nail varnish

esmerado meticulous

esmeralda f emerald

esmerarse take great care (**en** over)

esmeril m grind

esmero m care

esnob **1** adj snobbish **2** m

snob; **esnobismo** *m* snob-bishness

eso that; *en ~* just then; *mismo, ~* es that's it, that's the way; *a ~ de las dos* at around two; *por ~* that's why; *¿y ~?* why's that?

esófago *m* ANAT esophagus, *Br* oesophagus

espabilado (*listo*) bright, smart; (*vivo*) sharp

espacial *cohete, viaje* space *atr*, FÍS, MAT spatial; **espacio** *m* space; TV *program; ~ de tiempo* space of time; *~* **vital** living space; **espacioso** spacious, roomy

espada *f* sword; **~s** (*en naipes*) suit in Spanish deck of cards

espaguetis *mpl* spaghetti *sg*

espalda *f* back; *a ~s de alguien* behind s.o.'s back; *de ~ a* with one's back to; *por la ~* from behind; *nadar a ~* swim backstroke

espantajo *m* scarecrow; *fig* sight; **espantapájaros** *m inv* scarecrow; **espantar 1** *v/t* (*asustar*) frighten, scare; (*ahuyentar*) frighten away; F (*horrorizar*) horrify; **espanto** *m* (*susto*) fright; *L.Am.* (*fantasma*) ghost; *nos llenó de ~ desagrado* we were horrified; *¡qué ~!* how awful!; *de ~* terrible; **espantoso** horrific; *para enfatizar* terrible, dreadful; *hace un calor ~* it's incredibly hot

España Spain; **español 1** *adj* Spanish **2** *m, -a f* Spaniard; *los ~es* the Spanish **3** *m idioma* Spanish; **españolismo** *m* (*afición*) love of Spain; *cualidad* Spanishness

esparadrapo *m* Band-Aid®, *Br* (sticking) plaster

esparcir *papeles* scatter; *rumor* spread; **esparcirse** *de papeles* be scattered; *de rumor* spread

espárrago *m* asparagus

esparto *m* BOT esparto grass

espasmo *m* spasm

especia *f* spice

especial special; (*difícil*) fussy; *en ~* especially; **especialidad** *f* specialty, *Br* speciality; **especialista** *m/f* specialist; *en cine* stuntman; *mujer* stuntwoman; **especializarse** specialize (*en* in); **especialmente** specially

especie *f* BIO species *sg*; (*tipo*) kind, sort

especificar specify; **específico** specific

espectacular spectacular; **espectáculo** *m* TEA show; (*escena*) sight; *dar el ~ fig* make a spectacle of o.s.; **espectador** *m, ~a f en cine etc* member of the audience; DEP spectator; (*observador*) on-looker

espectro *m* FÍS spectrum; (*fantasma*) ghost

especular speculate

espejismo *m* mirage; **espejo** *m* mirror; *~ retrovisor* rear-view mirror

espeluznante horrific, horrifying

espera f wait; *sala de ~* waiting room; *en ~ de* pending; *estar a la ~ de* be waiting for

esperanza f hope; *~ de vida* life expectancy

esperar 1 *v/t (aguardar)* wait for; *con esperanza* hope; *(suponer, confiar en)* expect **2** *v/i (aguardar)* wait

esperma f sperm

espeso thick; *vegetación, niebla* thick, dense; **espesor** m thickness

espía m/f spy; **espiar 1** *v/t* spy on **2** *v/i* spy

espiga f BOT ear, spike

espina f *de planta* thorn; *de pez* bone; *~ dorsal* spine, backbone

espinacas fpl spinach

espinilla f *de la pierna* shin; *en la piel* pimple, spot

espino m BOT hawthorn; **espinoso** tb fig thorny

espionaje m spying, espionage

espiral f/adj spiral *(atr)*

espirar exhale

espíritu m spirit; **espiritual** spiritual

espléndido splendid, magnificent; *(generoso)* generous; **esplendor** m splendor, Br splendour

espliego m lavender

esponja f sponge; **esponjoso** spongy; *toalla* soft, fluffy

espontáneo spontaneous

esposa f wife; **esposas** fpl *(manillas)* handcuffs pl; **esposo** m husband

esprint m sprint

espuma f foam; *de jabón* lather; *de cerveza* froth; *~ de afeitar* shaving foam; *~ moldeadora* styling mousse; **espumoso** frothy, foamy; *caldo* sparkling

esquela f *aviso* death notice, obituary

esqueleto m skeleton; *Méx, C.Am., Pe, Bol fig* blank form

esquema m *(croquis)* sketch, diagram; *(sinopsis)* outline, summary

esquí m ski; *deporte* skiing; *~ de fondo* cross-country skiing; *~ náutico* o *acuático* waterskiing; **esquiador** m, *~a* f skier; **esquiar** ski

esquina f corner

esquirol m/f strikebreaker, scab F

esquivar avoid, dodge F

esquizofrenia f schizophrenia; **esquizofrénico** schizophrenic

esta ☞ *este²*

estabilidad f stability; **estable** stable

establecer establish; *negocio* set up; **establecimiento** m establishment

establo m stable

estaca f stake

estación f station; *del año* season; *~ espacial* o *orbital* space station; *~ de invierno* *o* **invernal** winter resort; ~ **de servicio** service station; ~ **de trabajo** INFOR work station; **estacionamiento** *m* AUTO *acción* parking; *L.Am.* parking lot, *Br* car park; **estacionar** AUTO park

estadio *m* DEP stadium

estadística *f cifra* statistic; *ciencia* statistics *sg*

estado *m* state; MED condition; ~ **civil** marital status; **en buen** ~ in good condition; **el Estado** the State; ~ **del bienestar** welfare state; **los Estados Unidos (de América)** the United States (of America)

estadounidense 1 *adj* American, *US attr* **2** *m/f* American

estafa *f* swindle, cheat; **estafador** *m,* ~**a** *f* con artist F, fraudster; **estafar** cheat (*a* out of)

estallar explode; *de guerra* break out; *de escándalo* break; **estalló en llanto** she burst into tears; **estallido** *m* explosion; *de guerra* outbreak

estampa *f de libro* illustration; *(aspecto)* appearance; REL prayer card; **estampado** *tejido* patterned; **estampar** *sello* put; *tejido* print; *pasaporte* stamp

estampilla *f L.Am.* stamp

estancar *río* dam up; *fig* bring to a standstill; **estancarse** stagnate; *fig* come to a

standstill

estancia *f* stay; *Rpl (hacienda)* farm, ranch

estanco 1 *adj* watertight **2** *m* shop selling cigarettes etc

estándar *m* standard; **estandarizar** standardize

estandarte *m* standard, banner

estanque *m* pond

estante *m* shelf; **estantería** *f* shelves *pl*; *para libros* bookcase

estaño *m* tin

estar be; **¿está Javier?** is Javier in?; **estamos a 3 de enero** it's January 3rd; **ahora estoy con Vd.** I'll be with you in just a moment; ~ **a bien / mal con alguien** be on good / bad terms with s.o.; ~ **de ocupación** work as, be; ~ **en algo** be working on sth; ~ **para hacer algo** be about to do sth; **no** ~ **para algo** not be in a mood for sth; **está por hacer** it hasn't been done yet; **¡ya estoy!** I'm ready!; **¡ya está!** that's it!; **estarse** stay; ~ **quieto** keep still

estatal state *atr*

estatua *f* statue; **estatura** *f* height; **estatuto** *m* statute; ~**s** articles of association

este[1] *m* east

este[2], **esta, estos, estas** this; *pl* **these**

éste, ésta, éstos, éstas this (one); *pl* these (ones)

estela *f* MAR wake; AVIA, *fig*

trail

estepa f steppe

estera f mat

estéreo stereo

estéril MED sterile; *trabajo, esfuerzo etc* futile; **esterilizar** *tb persona* sterilize

esterlina: libra ~ pound sterling

esteticista m/f beautician; **estético** esthetic, *Br* aesthetic

estiércol m dung; *(abono)* manure

estigma m *tb fig* stigma

estilo m style; **algo por el ~** something like that; **son todos por el ~** they're all the same

estilográfica f fountain pen

estima f esteem, respect; **estimación** f *(cálculo)* estimate; *(estima)* esteem, respect; **estimar** respect, hold in high regard; **estimo conveniente que** I consider it advisable to

estimulante 1 *adj* stimulating **2** m stimulant; **estimular** stimulate; *(animar)* encourage; **estímulo** m stimulus; *(incentivo)* incentive

estío m *literario* summertime

estipulación f stipulation

estirar 1 *v/t (alisar)* smooth out; **estirón** m *(tirón)* tug; **dar un ~** F *de niño* shoot up

estirpe f stock

estival summer *atr*

esto this; **~ es** that is to say; **por ~** this is why; **a todo ~**

(mientras tanto) meanwhile; *(a propósito)* incidentally

estofado stewed

estómago m stomach

Estonia Estonia; **estonio 1** *adj* Estonian **2** m, **-a** f Estonian **3** m *idioma* Estonian

estorbar 1 *v/t (dificultar)* hinder **2** *v/i* get in the way; **estorbo** m hindrance

estornino m ZO starling

estornudar sneeze

estragón m BOT tarragon

estragos mpl devastation; **causar ~ entre** wreak havoc among

estrambótico F eccentric; *ropa* outlandish

estrangular strangle

estratagema f stratagem; **estrategia** f strategy; **estratégico** strategic

estrato m *fig* stratum

estrechar 1 *v/t ropa* take in; *mano* shake; **~ entre los brazos** hug, embrace; **estrecho 1** *adj* narrow; *(apretado)* tight; *amistad* close; **~ de miras** narrow-minded **2** m strait, straits pl

estrella f *tb de cine etc* star; **~ fugaz** falling star; **~ de mar** ZO starfish; **~ polar** Pole star; **estrellarse** crash *(contra* into)

estremecer shock, shake; **estremecerse** shake, tremble; *de frío* shiver; *de horror* shudder; **estremecimiento** m shaking, trembling; *de frío* shiver; *de horror* shudder

estreñimiento m constipation

estrépito m noise, racket; **estrepitoso** noisy

estrés m stress; **estresado** stressed out; **estresar** stress; **estresante** stressful

estría f en piel stretch mark

estribo m stirrup; *perder los ~s fig* fly off the handle F

estribor m MAR starboard

estricto strict

estridente shrill, strident

estrofa f stanza, verse

estropeado (*averiado*) broken; **estropear** *aparato* break; *plan* ruin, spoil

estructura f structure

estruendo m racket, din

estrujar F crumple up; *trapo* wring out; *persona* squeeze

estuche m case, box

estuco m stucco work

estudiante m/f student; **estudiar** study; **estudio** m *disciplina* study; *apartamento* studio; *Br* studio flat; *de cine, música* studio; **estudioso** studious

estufa f heater

estupefaciente m narcotic (drug); **estupefacto** stupefied, speechless

estupendo fantastic, wonderful

estupidez f *cualidad* stupidity; *acción* stupid thing; **estúpido 1** *adj* stupid **2** m, **-a f** idiot

etapa f stage

eternidad f eternity; **eterno** eternal; *la película se me hizo -a* the movie seemed to go on for ever

etiqueta f label; (*protocolo*) etiquette

eucalipto m BOT eucalyptus

Europa f Europe; **europeo 1** *adj* European **2** m, **-a f** European

euskera m/adj Basque

evacuación f evacuation; **evacuar** evacuate

evadir avoid; *impuestos* evade; **evadirse** *tb fig* escape

evaluación f evaluation, assessment; (*prueba*) test; **evaluar** assess, evaluate

evangélico evangelical; **evangelio** m gospel

evaporación f evaporation; **evaporarse** evaporate; *fig* F vanish into thin air

evasión f *tb fig* escape; *~ de capitales* flight of capital; *~ fiscal* tax evasion; **evasiva** f evasive reply; **evasivo** evasive

evento m event; **eventual** possible; *trabajo* casual, temporary; *en el caso ~ de* in the event of; **eventualidad** f eventuality

evidencia f evidence, proof; *poner en ~* demonstrate; *poner a alguien en ~* show s.o. up; **evidente** evident, clear

evitable avoidable; **evitar** avoid; (*impedir*) prevent; *molestias* save; *no puedo ~lo* I can't help it

evocar evoke

evolución f BIO evolution; (*desarrollo*) development; **evolucionar** BIO evolve; (*desarrollar*) develop

exactitud f accuracy; **exacto** accurate, exact; *¡~!* exactly!, precisely!

exageración f exaggeration; **exagerar** exaggerate

exaltado excited, worked up; **exaltarse** get excited, get worked up (*por* about)

examen m test, exam; MED examination; (*análisis*) study; **~ de conducir** driving test; **examinar** examine; **examinarse** take an exam

excavación f excavation; **excavadora** f digger; **excavar** excavate; *túnel* dig

excedente 1 adj surplus; *empleado* on extended leave of absence **2** m surplus; **exceder** exceed; **excederse** go too far, get carried away

excelencia f excellence; **Su Excelencia la...** Her Excellency the ...; **por ~** par excellence; **excelente** excellent

excéntrico 1 adj eccentric **2** m, **-a** f eccentric

excepción f exception; **a ~ de** except for; **excepcional** exceptional; **excepto** except; **exceptuar** except; **exceptuando** with the exception of, except for

excesivo excessive; **exceso** m excess; **~ de equipaje** excess baggage; **~ de velocidad** speeding; **en ~** in excess, too much

excitación f excitement, agitation; **excitante 1** adj exciting; *una bebida* **~** a stimulant **2** m stimulant; **excitar** excite; *sentimientos, sexualmente* arouse; **excitarse** get excited; *sexualmente* become aroused

exclamación f exclamation; **exclamar** exclaim

excluir leave out (**de** of), exclude (**de** from); *posibilidad* rule out; **exclusión** f exclusion; **con ~ de** with the exception of; **exclusiva** f *privilegio* exclusive rights *pl* (**de** to); *reportaje* exclusive; **exclusivo** exclusive

excomulgar REL excommunicate

excremento m excrement

excursión f trip, excursion

excusa f excuse; **~s** apologies; **excusar** excuse

exento exempt (**de** from); **~ de impuestos** tax-exempt, tax-free

exhausto exhausted

exhibición f display, demonstration; *de película* screening, showing; **exhibir** show, display; *película* screen, show; *cuadro* exhibit

exhortar exhort (**a** to)

exigencia f demand; **exigente** demanding; **exigir** demand; (*requerir*) call for, demand exiliar exile; **exiliarse** go into exile; **exilio** m exile; **en el ~** in exile

existencia f existence; (vida) life; **~s** COM supplies, stocks; **existir** exist; **existen muchos problemas** there are a lot of problems

éxito m success; **~ de taquilla** box office hit; **tener ~** be successful, be a success; **exitoso** successful

exótico exotic

expansión f expansion; (recreo) recreation; **expansivo** expansive

expatriarse leave one's country

expectación f sense of anticipation; **expectante** expectant; **expectativa** f (esperanza) expectation; **estar a la ~ de algo** be waiting for sth; **~s** (perspectivas) prospects

expedición f expedition; **expediente** m file, dossier; (investigación) investigation, inquiry; **~ académico** student record; **~ disciplinario** disciplinary proceedings pl

expedir documento issue; mercancías send, dispatch

experiencia f experience

experimentar 1 v/t try out, experiment with 2 v/i experiment (con on); **experimento** m experiment

experto 1 adj expert; **~ en hacer algo** expert at doing sth 2 m expert (en on)

expiar expiate, atone for

expirar expire

explicable explainable, explicable; **explicación** f explanation; **explicar** explain; **explicarse** (comprender) understand; (hacerse comprender) express o.s.; **explicativo** explanatory

exploración f exploration; **explorador** m, **~a** f explorer; MIL scout; **explorar** explore

explosión f explosion; **~ demográfica** population explosion; **hacer ~** go off, explode; **explosionar** explode; **explosivo** m/adj explosive

explotación f de mina, tierra exploitation, working; de negocio running, operation; de trabajador exploitation; **~ del trabajador** exploit; **explotar 1** v/t tierra, mina work, exploit; situación take advantage of, exploit; trabajador exploit 2 v/i go off, explode; fig explode

exponer teoría set out, put forward; (revelar) expose; pintura exhibit, show; (arriesgar) risk; **exponerse: ~ a algo** (arriesgarse) lay o.s. open to sth

exportación f export; **exportar** export; **exportador** m, **~a** f exporter

exposición f exhibition; **expositor** m, **~a** f exhibitor

expresar express; **expresión** f expression; **expresivo** expressive

expreso 1 adj express atr; **tren**

~ express (train) **2** *m* tren express (train); *café* espresso

exprimidor *m* lemon squeezer; *eléctrico* juicer; **exprimir** squeeze; (*explotar*) exploit

expropiar expropriate

expulsar expel, throw out F; DEP expel from the game, *Br* send off; **expulsión** *f* expulsion; DEP sending off

exquisito *comida* delicious; (*bello*) exquisite; (*refinado*) refined

éxtasis *m tb droga* ecstasy

extender *brazos* stretch out; (*untar*) spread; *tela, papel* spread out; (*ampliar*) extend; **extenderse** *de campos* stretch; *de influencia* extend; (*difundirse*) spread; (*durar*) last; *explayarse* go into detail; **extensible** extending; **extensión** *f tb* TELEC extension; *superficie* expanse, area; *informe* lengthy, long

exterior 1 *adj aspecto* external, outward; *capa* outer; *apartamento* overlooking the street; POL foreign; **la parte** ~ the outside **2** *m* (*fachada*) exterior, outside; *aspecto* exterior, outward appearance; *viajar al* ~ (*al extranjero*) travel abroad

exterminar exterminate, wipe out

externo 1 *adj aspecto* external, outward; *influencia* external, outside; *capa* outer; *deuda* foreign **2** *m, -a f* EDU

student who attends a boarding school but returns home each evening, *Br* day boy / girl

extinción *f*: **en peligro de** ~ in danger of extinction; **extinguidor** *m L.Am.*: ~ (**de incendios**) (fire) extinguisher; **extinguir** BIO, ZO wipe out; *fuego* extinguish, put out; **extinguirse** BIO, ZO become extinct, die out; *de fuego* go out; *de plazo* expire; **extintor** *m* fire extinguisher

extirpar MED remove; *vicio* eradicate, stamp out

extorsión *f* extortion

extra 1 *adj excelente* top quality; *adicional* extra; **horas** ~ overtime; **paga** ~ extra month's pay **2** *m/f de cine* extra **3** *m gasto* additional expense

extracción *f* extraction; **extracto** *m* extract; (*resumen*) summary; GASTR, QUÍM extract; ~ **de cuenta** bank statement; **extractor** *m* extractor; ~ **de humos** extractor fan

extradición *f* extradition; **extraditar** extradite

extraer extract, pull out; *conclusión* draw

extranjero 1 *adj* foreign **2** *m,* **-a** *f* foreigner; **en el** ~ abroad

extrañar *L.Am.* miss; **extrañarse** be surprised (**de** at); **extrañeza** *f* strangeness; (*sorpresa*) surprise; **extraño 1** *adj* strange, odd **2** *m, -a f*

stranger
extraordinario extraordinary
extraterrestre extraterrestrial, alien
extraviar lose, mislay; **extraviarse** get lost, lose one's way
extremar maximize
extremaunción f REL extreme unction
extremidad f end; **~es** extremities; **extremista 1** adj extreme **2** m/f POL extremist; **extremo 1** adj extreme **2** m extreme; *parte primera o última* ma end; *punto* point; **llegar al ~ de** reach the point of 3 m/f; **~ derecho / izquierdo** DEP right / left wing; **en ~** in the extreme
exuberante exuberant; *vegetación* lush
eyacular ejaculate

F

fabada f GASTR *Asturian stew with pork sausage, bacon and beans*
fábrica f plant, factory; **fabricación** f manufacturing; **fabricante** m manufacturer, maker; **fabricar** manufacture
fabuloso fabulous
faceta f fig facet
facha 1 f look; *(cara)* face **2** m/f desp fascist; **fachada** f tb fig façade
facial facial
fácil easy; **es ~ que** it's likely that; **facilidad** f ease; **tener ~ para algo** have a gift for sth; **~es de pago** credit facilities, credit terms; **facilitar** facilitate, make easier; *(hacer factible)* make possible; *medios, dinero etc* provide
factible feasible
factor m factor
factoría f esp L.Am. plant,

factory
factura f COM invoice; *de luz, gas etc* bill; **facturación** f COM invoicing; *volumen de negocio* turnover; AVIA check-in; **facturar** COM invoice, bill; *volumen de negocio* turn over; AVIA check in
facultad f faculty; *(autoridad)* authority
faena f task, job; **hacer una ~ a alguien** play a dirty trick on s.o.
fagot m MÚS bassoon
faisán m ZO pheasant
faja f *prenda interior* girdle
falda f skirt; *de montaña* side; **falda-pantalón** f divided skirt, culottes pl
falla f fault; *de fabricación* flaw; **fallar 1** v/i fail; *(no acertar)* miss; *de sistema etc* go wrong; JUR find *(en favor de* for; *en contra de* against); **~ a alguien** let

s.o. down **2** v/t JUR pronounce judg(e)ment in; *pregunta* get wrong; **~ el tiro** miss

fallecer pass away; **fallecimiento** m demise

fallo m mistake; TÉC fault; JUR judg(e)ment; **~ cardíaco** heart failure

falsedad f falseness; (*mentira*) lie; **falsificación** f de moneda counterfeiting; *de documentos, firma* forgery; **falsificar** *moneda* counterfeit; *documento, firma* forge, falsify; **falso** false; *joyas* fake; *documento, firma* forged; **jurar en ~** commit perjury

falta f (*escasez*) lack, want; (*error*) mistake; (*ausencia*) absence; *en tenis* fault; *en fútbol* foul; (*tiro libre*) free kick; **hacerle ~ a alguien** foul s.o.; **~ de** lack of, shortage of; **sin ~** without fail; **buena ~ le hace** it's about time; **echar en ~ a alguien** miss s.o.; **hacer ~** be necessary

faltar be missing; **falta una hora** there's an hour to go; **sólo falta hacer la salsa** there's only the sauce to do; **~ a** be absent from; **~ a alguien** be disrespectful to s.o.; **~ a su palabra** not keep one's word; **falto: ~ de** lacking in, devoid of; **~ de recursos** short of resources

fama f fame; (*reputación*) reputation; **tener mala ~** have a bad reputation

familia f family; **sentirse como en ~** feel at home; **familiar 1** adj family attr; (*conocido*), *lenguaje* familiar **2** m/f relation, relative

famoso 1 adj famous **2** m, -a f celebrity

fanático 1 adj fanatical **2** m, -a f fanatic; **fanatismo** m fanaticism

fanfarria f adj boastful **2** m, -ona f boaster; **fanfarronear** boast, brag

fango m fig mud

fantasía f fantasy; (*imaginación*) imagination; **joyas de ~** costume jewelry o Br jewellery; **fantasma** m ghost; **fantástico** fantastic

fardo m bundle

faringe f ANAT pharynx; **faringitis** f MED pharyngitis

farmacéutico 1 adj pharmaceutical **2** m, -a f pharmacist, Br tb chemist; **farmacia** f pharmacy, Br tb chemist's; *estudios* pharmacy; **~ de guardia** 24-hour pharmacist, Br emergency chemist; **fármaco** m medicine

faro m MAR lighthouse; AUTO headlight, headlamp; **~ antiniebla** fog light; **farol** m lantern; (*farola*) streetlight, streetlamp; *en juegos de cartas* bluff

farsa f tb fig farce; **farsante** m/f fraud, fake

fascinación f fascination; **fascinar** fascinate

fascismo m fascism; **fascista**

m/f & adj fascist

fase *f* phase

fastidiar annoy; F (*estropear*) spoil; **fastidio** *m* annoyance; **¡qué ~!** what a nuisance!; **fastidioso** annoying

fatal 1 *adj* fatal; (*muy malo*) dreadful, awful **2** *adv* very badly; **fatalidad** *f* misfortune

fatiga *f* tiredness, fatigue; **fatigado** tired; **fatigar** tire; **fatigoso** tiring

favor *m* favor, *Br* favour; **a ~ de** in favor of; **por ~** please; **hacer un ~** do a favor; **favorable** favorable, *Br* favourable; **favorecer** favor, *Br* favour; *de ropa, color* suit; **favoritismo** *m* favoritism, *Br* favouritism; **favorito 1** *adj* favorite, *Br* favourite **2** *m*, **-a** *f* favorite

fax *m* fax; **enviar u. a alguien** send s.o. a fax, fax s.o.

faz *f* face

fe *f* faith (**en** in)

fealdad *f* ugliness

febrero *m* February

febril feverish

fecha *f* date; **~ límite de consumo** best before date; **~ de nacimiento** date of birth; **fechar** date

fecundar fertilize; **fecundidad** *f* fertility; **fecundo** fertile

federación *f* federation; **federal** federal

felicidad *f* happiness; **¡~es!** congratulations!; **felicitación** *f* letter of congratula-

tions; **¡felicitaciones!** congratulations!; **felicitar** congratulate (**por** on); **feliz** happy; **¡~ Navidad!** Merry Christmas!

felpa *f* toweling, *Br* towelling

femenino *adj* feminine; *moda, equipo* women's **2** GRAM feminine; **femin(e)idad** *f* femininity; **feminismo** *m* feminism; **feminista** *m/f & adj* feminist

fenomenal 1 *adj* F fantastic F, phenomenal F **2** *adv*: **lo pasé ~** F I had a fantastic time F; **fenómeno 1** *m* phenomenon; *persona* genius **2** *adj* F fantastic F, great F

feo 1 *adj* ugly; *fig* nasty **2** *m*: **hacer un ~ a alguien** F snub s.o.

féretro *m* casket, coffin

feria *f* COM fair; *L.Am.* (*mercado*) market; *Méx* (*calderilla*) small change; **~ de muestras** trade fair; **feriado 1** *adj L.Am.*: **día ~** public holiday **2** *m L.Am.* public holiday; **ferial 1** *adj*: **recinto ~** fairground **2** *m* fair

fermentación *f* fermentation; **fermentar** ferment

ferocidad *f* ferocity; **feroz** fierce; (*cruel*) cruel

férreo *fig* big iron *atr*; *del ferrocarril* rail *atr*; **ferretería** *f* hardware store; **ferrocarril** *m* railroad, *Br* railway; **ferroviario** rail *atr*

ferry *m* ferry

fértil fertile; **fertilidad** *f* fertil-

ity; **fertilizante** *m* fertilizer;
fertilizar fertilize
ferviente *fig* fervent
festival *m* festival; ~ **cinema-**
tográfico film festival; **festi-**
vo festive
fétido fetid
feto *m* fetus
fiable trustworthy; *datos,*
máquina etc reliable; **fiado:**
al ~ F on credit; **fiador** *m*
TÉC safety catch **2** *m,* ~**a** *f*
JUR guarantor
fiambre *m* cold cut, *Br* cold
meat; P *(cadáver)* stiff P
fianza *f* deposit; JUR bail; **ba-**
jo ~ on bail
fiar give credit; **fiarse:** ~ **de al-**
guien trust s.o.; **no me fío** I
don't trust him / them *etc*
fibra *f* fiber, *Br* fibre; ~ **óptica**
optical fiber; ~ **de vidrio** fiberglass
ficha *f* file card, index card; *en*
juegos de mesa counter; *en*
un casino chip; *en damas*
checker, *Br* draught; *en aje-*
drez man, piece; TELEC token; **fichar 1** *v/t* DEP sign;
JUR open a file on **2** *v/i*
DEP sign *(por* for); **fichero**
m file cabinet, *Br* filing cabinet; INFOR file
fidelidad *f* fidelity
fideo *m* noodle
fiebre *f* fever; *(temperatura)*
temperature; ~ **del heno**
hay fever
fiel 1 *adj* faithful; *(leal)* loyal **2**
mpl: los ~**es** REL the faithful
pl

fieltro *m* felt
fiera *f* wild animal
fierro *m* L.Am. iron
fiesta *f* festival; *(reunión so-*
cial) party; *(día festivo)* public holiday; **estar de** ~ be in a
party mood
figura *f* figure; *(estatuilla)* figur-
ine; *(forma)* shape; *naipes*
face card, *Br* picture card; **fi-**
gurado figurative; **figurante**
m, -**a** *f en película* extra; TEA
walk-on; **figurar** appear **(en**
in); **figurarse** imagine
fijación *f* fixing; *(obsesión)*
fixation; **fijador** *m* FOT, PINT
fixative, fixer; *para el pelo*
hairspray; **fijar** fix; *cartel*
stick; *fecha, objetivo* set; *resi-*
dencia establish; *atención* focus; **fijarse** *(establecerse)* settle; *(prestar atención)* pay attention **(en** to); ~ **en algo**
(darse cuenta) notice sth; **fijo**
adj fixed; *trabajo* permanent;
fecha definite; TELEC **núme-**
ro *m* ~ landline (number); *m*
TELEC landline; **te llamo**
luego al ~ I'll call you later
on the landline
fila *f* line, *Br* queue; *de asien-*
tos row; **en** ~ **india** in single
file; ~**s** MIL ranks
filete *m* GASTR fillet
Filipinas *fpl* Philippines; **fili-**
pino 1 *adj* Philippine, Filipi-
no **2** *m,* -**a** *f* Filipino **3** *m idio-*
ma Filipino, Filipino
film(e) *m* movie, film; **filma-**
ción *f* filming, shooting; **fil-**
mar film, shoot

filólogo m, -a f philologist

filosofía f philosophy; **filosófico** philosophical; **filósofo** m, -a f philosopher

filtrar filter; *información* leak; **filtrarse** filter (**por** through); *de agua, información* leak; **filtro** m filter

fin m end; *(objetivo)* aim, purpose; **~ de semana** weekend; **a ~es de mayo** at the end of May; **al ~ y al cabo** at the end of the day; **en ~** anyway

final 1 adj & m final; **finalidad 1** f purpose, aim; **finalista 1** adj: **las dos selecciones ~s** the two teams that reached the final **2** m/f finalist; **finalización** f completion; **finalizado** complete; **finalizar** end, finish; **finalmente** eventually

financiación f funding; **financiar** fund, finance; **financista** m/f L.Am. financier; **finanzas** fpl finances

finca f *(bien inmueble)* property; L.Am. *(granja)* farm

finés 1 adj Finnish **2** m, **-esa** f Finn **3** m *idioma* Finnish

fineza f *cualidad* fineness; *dicho* compliment

fingir pretend, feign fml

finlandés 1 adj Finnish **2** m, **-esa** f Finn **3** m *idioma* Finnish; **Finlandia** f Finland

fino adj fine; *libro, tela* thin; *(esbelto)* slim; *modales, gusto* refined; *sentido de humor* subtle; **finura** f de cali-

dad fineness; *de tela* thinness; *(esbeltez)* slimness; *de modales, gusto* refinement; *de sentido de humor* subtlety

firma f signature; *acto* signing; COM firm; **firmar** sign

firme firm; *(estable)* steady; **en ~** COM firm; **firmeza** f firmness

fiscal 1 adj tax atr, fiscal **2** m/f district attorney, Br public prosecutor

física f physics; **físico 1** adj physical **2** m, -a f physicist **3** m de una persona physique

fisioterapia f physical therapy, Br physiotherapy

fisura f crack; MED fracture

flác(c)ido flabby

flaco thin; **punto ~** weak point

flamante *(nuevo)* brand-new

flamenco 1 adj MÚS flamenco **2** m MÚS flamenco; ZO flamingo

flaqueza f fig weakness

flash m FOT flash

flato m MED stitch

flauta f flute; *Méx* GASTR fried taco; **~ dulce** recorder; **~ travesera** (transverse) flute; **flautista** m/f flautist

flecha f arrow

flequillo m del pelo bangs pl, Br fringe

fletar charter; *(embarcar)* load

flexible flexible

flirtear flirt (**con** with)

flojo loose; *café, argumento* weak; COM *actividad* slack; *redacción* poor; L.Am. *(pere-*

zoso) lazy

flor f flower; **florecer** BOT flower. bloom; *de negocio, civilización* flourish; **florero** m vase; **florista** m/f florist; **floristería** f florist

flota f fleet; **flotador** m float; **flotar** float

fluctuación f fluctuation; **fluctuar** fluctuate

fluido 1 adj fluid; *tráfico* free-flowing; *lenguaje* fluent **2** m fluid; **fluir** flow; **flujo** m flow

fluorescente 1 adj fluorescent **2** m strip light

fluvial river atr

foca f ZO seal

foco m focus; TEA, TV spotlight; *de infección* center, Br centre; *de incendio* seat; *L.Am. (bombilla)* lightbulb; *de auto* headlight; *de calle* streetlight

fogón m *de cocina* stove; TÉC burner; *L.Am. fuego* bonfire

follaje m foliage

follar V fuck V, screw V

folleto m pamphlet

follón m argument; *(lío)* mess

fomentar foster; COM promote; *rebelión* foment, incite; **fomento** m COM promotion

fonda f cheap restaurant; *(pensión)* boarding house

fondo m bottom; *(apariencia)* end; *de pasillo* end; *(profundidad)* depth; PINT, FOT background; *de un museo* collection; COM fund; **~ de**

inversión investment fund; **~ de pensiones** pension fund; **Fondo Monetario Internacional** International Monetary Fund; **~s** money, funds; **tiene buen ~** he's got a good heart; **en el ~** deep down

fontanería f plumbing; **fontanero** m plumber

footing m DEP jogging; **hacer ~** go jogging, jog

forastero 1 adj foreign **2** m, -a f outsider, stranger

forestal forest atr

forjar metal forge

forma f form; *(apariencia)* shape; *(manera)* way; **de todas ~s** in any case, anyway; **estar en ~** be fit; **formación** f formation; *(entrenamiento)* training; **~ profesional** vocational training; **formal** formal; *niño* well-behaved; *(responsable)* responsible; **formalidad** f formality; **formar** form; *(educar)* educate

formatear format; **formato** m format

formidable huge; *(estupendo)* tremendous

fórmula f formula; **formular** *teoría* formulate; *queja* make, lodge; **formulario** m form

forraje m fodder

fortalecer tb fig strengthen; **fortaleza** f strength of character; MIL fortress; **fortificación** f fortification; **fortificar** MIL fortify

fortuito chance *atr*, accidental

fortuna *f* fortune; *(suerte)* luck; **por ~** fortunately, luckily

forzado forced; **forzar** force; *(violar)* rape; **forzoso** *aterrizaje* forced

fosa *f* pit; *(tumba)* grave; **~s nasales** nostrils

fósforo *m* QUÍM phosphorus; *L.Am.* *(cerilla)* match

foso *m* ditch; TEA, MÚS pit; *de castillo* moat

foto *f* photo; **fotocopia** *f* photocopy; **fotocopiadora** *f* photocopier; **fotocopiar** photocopy; **fotogénico** photogenic; **fotografía** *f* photography; **fotografiar** photograph; **fotógrafo** *m*, **-a** *f* photographer

fracasado 1 *adj* unsuccessful **2** *m*, **-a** *f* loser; **fracasar** fail; **fracaso** *m* failure

fracción *f* fraction; POL faction

fractura *f* MED fracture; **fracturar** MED fracture

frágil fragile

fragmento *m* fragment; *de novela*, *poema* excerpt, extract

fragua *f* forge

fraile *m* friar, monk

frambuesa *f* raspberry

francés 1 *adj* French **2** *m* Frenchman; *idioma* French; **francesa** *f* Frenchwoman; **Francia** France

franco *(sincero)* frank; *(evidente)* distinct, marked;

COM free

franela *f* flannel

franja *f* fringe; *de tierra* strip

franquear *carta* pay the postage on; *camino*, *obstáculo* clear; **franqueo** *m* postage; **franqueza** *f* frankness

frasco *m* bottle

frase *f* phrase; *(oración)* sentence; **~ hecha** set phrase

fraternal brotherly

fraude *m* fraud; **fraudulento** fraudulent

frecuencia *f* frequency; **con ~** frequently; **frecuentar** frequent; **frecuente** frequent; *(común)* common

fregadero *m* sink; **fregar** *platos* wash; *el suelo* mop; *L.Am.* F bug F; **fregona** *f* mop; *L.Am.* F pain in the neck F

freidora *f* deep fryer; **freír** fry; F *(matar)* waste P

frenar 1 *v/i* AUTO brake **2** *v/t* *fig* slow down; *impulsos* check; **freno** *m* brake; **poner ~ a algo** *fig* curb sth, check sth; **~ de mano** parking brake, *Br* handbrake

frente 1 *f* forehead **2** *m* MIL, METEO front; **de ~** colisión head-on; **de ~ al grupo** *L.Am.* facing the group; **hacer ~ a** face up to **3** *prp*: **~ a** opposite

fresa *f* strawberry

fresco 1 *adj* cool; *pescado etc* fresh; *persona* F fresh F, *Br* cheeky F **2** *m*, **-a** *f*: **¡eres un ~!** F you've got nerve!

F **3** *m* fresh air; *C.Am. bebida* fruit drink; **frescura** *f* freshness; (*frío*) coolness; *fig* nerve

fresno *m* BOT ash tree

fresón *m* strawberry

frialdad *f tb fig* coldness

fricción *f* TEC, *fig* friction

frigorífico 1 *adj* refrigerated **2** *m* icebox, *Br* fridge

frijol *m*, **frijol** *m L.Am.* bean

frío 1 *adj tb fig* cold **2** *m* cold; **tener ~** be cold

fritar *L.Am.* fry; **frito 1** *part ~* **freir 2** *adj* fried **3** *mpl*: **~s** fried food

frívolo frivolous

frontal frontal; *ataque etc* head-on; (*delantero*) front *atr*

frontera *f* border; **fronterizo** border *atr*

frotar rub

fructuoso *fig* fruitful

fruncir *material* gather; **~ el ceño** frown

frustración *f* frustration; **frustrar** frustrate; *plan* thwart; **frustrarse** fail

fruta *f* fruit; **frutal 1** *adj* fruit *atr* **2** *m* fruit tree; **frutería** *f* fruit store, *Br* greengrocer's; **frutilla** *f S.Am.* strawberry; **fruto** *m tb fig* fruit; *nuez, almendra etc* nut; **~s secos** nuts

fuego *m* fire; **¿tienes ~?** do you have a light?; **~s artificiales** fireworks; **pegar** *o* **prender ~ a** set fire to

fuel(-oil) *m* fuel oil

fuelle *m* bellows *pl*

fuente *f* fountain; *recipiente* dish; *fig* source

fuera 1 *vb* ➙ *ir, ser* **2** *adv* outside; (*en otro lugar*) away; (*en otro país*) abroad; **por ~** on the outside; **¡~!** get out! **3** *prp*: **~ de** outside; **¡sal ~ de aquí!** get out of here!; **~ del país** abroad

fuerte 1 *adj* strong; *dolor* intense; *lluvia* heavy; *aumento* sharp; *ruido* loud; *fig* P incredible **2** *adv* hard **3** *m* MIL fort; **fuerza** *f* strength; (*violencia*) force; ELEC power; **~ aérea** air force; **~ de voluntad** willpower; **~s armadas** armed forces; **~s de seguridad** security forces; **a ~ de** by (dint of)

fuga *f* escape; *de gas, agua* leak; **darse a la ~** flee; **fugarse** run away; *de la cárcel* escape; **fugaz** *fig* fleeting; **fugitivo 1** *adj* runaway *atr* **2** *m*, **-a** *f* fugitive

fulana *f* so-and-so; F (*prostituta*) hooker P; **fulano** *m* so-and-so

fulminante sudden

fumador *m*, **-a** *f* smoker; **fumar** smoke

función *f* purpose, function; *en el trabajo* duty; TEA performance; **en ~ de** according to; **funcional** functional; **funcionamiento** *m* working; **funcionar** work; **no funciona** out of order; **funcionario** *m*, **-a** *f* government employee, civil servant

funda f cover; de gafas case; de almohada pillowcase

fundación f foundation; **fundador** m, **-a** f founder

fundamental fundamental; **fundamentalismo** m fundamentalism; **fundamentalista** m/f fundamentalist; **fundamentalmente** fundamentally; **fundamento** m foundation; **~s** (nociones) fundamentals; **fundar** fig base (**en** on); **fundarse** be based (**en** on)

fundición f smelting; (fábrica) foundry; **fundir** hielo melt; metal smelt; COM merge; **fundirse** melt; de bombilla fuse; de plomos blow; COM merge; L.Am. de empresa go under

fúnebre funeral atr; fig: ambiente gloomy; **funeral** m funeral; **funeraria** f funeral parlor, Br undertaker's

funesto disastrous

funicular m funicular; (teleférico) cable car

furcia f P whore P

furgón m van; FERR boxcar, Br goods van; **~ de equipajes** baggage car, Br luggage van; **furgoneta** f van

furia f fury; **furioso** furious; **furor** m: **hacer ~** fig be all the rage F

furtivo furtive

fusible m ELEC fuse

fusil m rifle; **fusilamiento** m execution (by firing squad); **fusilar** shoot; fig F (plagiar) lift F

fusión f FÍS fusion; COM merger; **fusionar** COM merge; **fusionarse** merge

fútbol m soccer, Br football; **~ americano** football, Br American football; **~ sala** five-a-side soccer; **futbolín** m Foosball®, table football; **futbolista** m/f soccer player, Br footballer, Br football player

futuro m/adj future (atr)

G

gabardina f prenda raincoat; material gabardine

gabinete m (despacho) office; en una casa study; POL cabinet; L.Am. de médico office, Br surgery

gafas fpl glasses; **~ de sol** sunglasses

gaita f MÚS bagpipes pl

gala f gala; **traje de ~** formal

galante gallant

galardón m award; **galardonar: fue galardonado con...** he was awarded …

galería f gallery; **~ de arte** art gallery

galgo m greyhound

gallego 1 adj Galician; Rpl F Spanish **2** m, **-a** f Galician;

Rpl F Spaniard **3** *m idioma*
Galician

galleta *f* cookie, *Br* biscuit

gallina 1 *f* hen **2** *m* F chicken;
gallinero *m* henhouse

gallo *m* rooster, *Br* cock

galopar gallop; **galope** *m* gallop

gama *f* range

gamba *f* shrimp, *Br* prawn

gamberro *m*, **-a** *f* trouble-maker

gamo *m* fallow deer

gamuza *f* chamois

gana *f*: **de mala ~** unwillingly,
grudgingly; **no me da la ~**
I don't want to; **... me da ~
de ...** makes me want to; **tener ~s de (hacer) algo** feel
like (doing) sth

ganadería *f* stockbreeding;
ganadero *m*, **-a** *f* stockbreeder; **ganado** *m* cattle *pl*

ganador *m* winner; **ganancia**
f profit; **ganar 1** *v/t* win; *mediante el trabajo* earn **2** *v/i*
mediante el trabajo earn;
(vencer) win; *(mejorar)* improve; **ganarse** earn; *a alguien* win over; *~ **la vida*** earn
a living

ganchillo *m* crochet; **gancho**
m hook; *L.Am.*, *Arg fig* F
sex-appeal; **hacer ~** *L.Am.*
(ayudar) lend a hand; **tener
~** F *de un grupo, una campaña* be popular; *de una persona* have that certain something

gandul *m* lazybones *sg*

ganga *f* bargain

ganso *m* goose; *macho* gan-
der

garaje *m* garage

garantía *f* guarantee; **garantizar** guarantee

garapiñado candied

garbanzo *m* BOT chickpea

garbo *m* *al moverse* grace

garganta *f* ANAT throat;
GEOG gorge; **gargantilla** *f*
choker

gárgaras *fpl*: **hacer ~** gargle

garra *f* claw; *de ave* talon; **caer
en las ~s de alguien** *fig* fall
into s.o.'s clutches; **tener ~** F
be compelling

garrafa *f* carafe

garrapata *f* ZO tick

garza *f* ZO heron

gas *m* gas; **~es** MED gas, wind;
con ~ carbonated, *Br* fizzy;
sin ~ still

gasa *f* gauze

gaseosa *f* lemonade; **gasoducto** *m* gas pipeline; **gas-
oil, gasóleo** *m* oil; *para mo-
tores* diesel; **gasolina** *f* gas,
Br petrol; **gasolinera** *f* gas
station, *Br* petrol station

gastar *dinero* spend; *energía,
electricidad etc* use; *(llevar)*
wear; *(desperdiciar)* waste;
(desgastar) wear out; **¿qué
número gastas?** what size
do you take?; **gastarse** *dinero* spend; *de gasolina, agua*
run out of; *de pila* run down;
de ropa, zapatos wear out;
gasto *m* expense

gastronomía *f* gastronomy;
gastrónomo *m*, **-a** *f* gastro-

gestoría

nome

gata f (female) cat; *Méx* servant, maid; *a ~s* F on all fours; **gatear** crawl

gatillo m trigger

gato m cat; AUTO jack; *cuatro ~s* a handful of people

gavilán m sparrowhawk

gaviota f (sea)gull

gay m/adj gay

gazpacho m gazpacho (*cold soup made with tomatoes, peppers, garlic etc*)

gel m gel

gelatina f gelatin(e); GASTR Jell-O®, *Br* jelly

gemelo 1 adj twin atr **2** mpl: *~s* twins; *de camisa* cuff links; *prismáticos* binoculars

Géminis m/f inv ASTR Gemini

gemir moan, groan

generación f generation

generador m ELEC generator; *~ de costes* COM, FIN cost driver

general 1 adj general; *en ~* in general; *por lo ~* generally **2** m general; **generalidad** f (*mayoría*) majority; (*vaguedad*) general nature; **generalizar 1** v/t make more widespread **2** v/i generalize; **generalmente** generally

generar generate

género m (*tipo*) type; *de literatura* genre; GRAM gender; COM goods pl, merchandise

generosidad f generosity; **generoso** generous

genética f genetics; **genéticamente** genetically; *~ modificado* genetically modified; **genético** genetic; **genetista** m/f geneticist

genial brilliant, F (*estupendo*) fantastic F, great F; **genio** m genius; (*carácter*) temper; *tener mal ~* be bad-tempered

genitales mpl genitals

gente f people pl; *L.Am.* (*persona*) person

gentil kind, courteous; REL Gentile; **gentileza** f kindness; *por ~ de* by courtesy of

gentío m crowd

geografía f geography; **geográfico** geographical

geología f geology; **geológico** geological; **geólogo** m, **-a** f geologist

geometría f geometry; **geométrico** geometrical

geranio m geranium

gerencia f management; *oficina* manager's office; **gerente** m/f manager

geriatría f geriatrics

germano 1 adj Germanic **2** m, **-a** f German

germen m germ; **germinar** tb fig germinate

gesticular gesticulate

gestión f management; *gestiones* (*trámites*) formalities, procedure; **gestionar** *trámites* take care of; *negocio* manage

gesto m gesture; (*expresión*) expression

gestoría f Esp agency offering clients help with official documents

giba f hump, hunch

gigante m/adj giant (atr); **gigantesco** gigantic

gilipollas m/f inv P jerk P

gilipollez f ESP V bullshit V

gimnasia f gymnastics; **hacer** ~ do exercises; **gimnasio** m gymnasium, gym

ginebra f gin

ginecólogo m, -a f gynecologist, Br gynaecologist

gira f tour; **girar** 1 v/i turn; alrededor de algo revolve; fig (tratar) revolve (**en torno a** around) 2 v/t COM transfer; **girasol** m BOT sunflower; **giratorio** revolving; **giro** m turn; GRAM idiom; ~ **postal** COM money order

gitano 1 adj gypsy atr 2 m, -a f gypsy

glacial icy; **glaciar** m glacier

glándula f ANAT gland

glaucoma m MED glaucoma

glicerina f glycerin(e)

global global; visión, resultado overall; cantidad total; **globalización** f globalization; **globo** m aerostático, de niño balloon; terrestre globe; ~ **terráqueo** globe

gloria f glory; (delicia) delight; **estar en la** ~ F be in seventh heaven; **glorificar** glorify; **glorioso** glorious

glosa f gloss; **glosar** gloss; **glosario** m glossary

glotón 1 adj greedy 2 m, -ona f glutton

glucosa f glucose

gluten m gluten; **sin** ~ gluten-free

glúteo m gluteus

gobernador m governor; **gobernar** rule, govern; **gobierno** m government

goce m pleasure, enjoyment

gol m DEP goal

golf m DEP golf

golfillo m (street) urchin

golfista m/f golfer

golfo 1 m GEOG gulf 2 m, -a f good-for-nothing; niño little devil; **Golfo de California** Gulf of California; **Golfo de México** Gulf of Mexico

golondrina f ZO swallow

golosina f candy, Br sweet; **goloso** sweet-toothed

golpe m knock, blow; ~ **de Estado** coup d'état; **de** ~ suddenly; **no da** ~ F she doesn't do a thing; **golpear** hit

goma f (caucho) rubber; (pegamento) glue; (banda elástica) rubber band; F (preservativo) condom, rubber P; C.Am. F (resaca) hangover; ~ (**de borrar**) eraser; ~ **espuma** foam rubber

gonorrea f gonorrhea, Br gonorrhoea

gordo 1 adj fat 2 m, -a f fat person 3 m premio jackpot; **gordura** f fat

gorila m gorilla

gorra f cap; **de** ~ F for free F

gorrino m fig pig

gorrión m sparrow

gorro m cap; **estar hasta el** ~

de algo F be fed up to the back teeth with sth F

gorrón *m*, **-ona** *f* F scrounger

gota *f* drop; **ni ~** F not a drop; *de pan* not a scrap; **gotear** *filtrarse* leak; **gotera** *f* leak; *(mancha)* stain

gótico *m/adj* Gothic

gozar enjoy o.s.; **~ de** *(disfrutar de)* enjoy; *(poseer)* have, enjoy; **gozo** *m* *(alegría)* joy; *(placer)* pleasure; **gozoso** happy

grabación *f* recording; **grabado** *m* engraving; **grabadora** *f* tape recorder; **grabar** *vídeo etc* record; PINT, *fig* engrave

gracia *f*: **tener ~** *(ser divertido)* be funny; *(tener encanto)* be graceful; **me hace ~** I think it's funny; **dar las ~s a alguien** thank s.o.; **~s** thank you; **gracioso** funny

gradas *fpl* DEP stands, grandstand; **graderío** *m* stands

grado *m* degree; **de buen ~** with good grace, readily

graduación *f* TÉC *etc* adjustment; *de alcohol* alcohol content; EDU graduation; MIL rank; **gradual** gradual; **gradualmente** gradually; **graduar** TÉC *etc* adjust; **~ las gafas o la vista** have one's eyes tested; **graduarse** graduate, get one's degree

gráfico 1 *adj* graphic **2** *m* MAT graph; INFOR graphic; **grafista** *m/f* graphic designer

gragea *f* tablet, pill

gramática *f* grammar; **gramático** grammatical

gramo *m* gram

Gran Bretaña Great Britain

gran short form of **grande** *before a noun*

granada *f* BOT pomegranate; **~ de mano** MIL hand grenade

grande 1 *adj* big; **a lo ~** in style **2** *m/f* L.Am. *(adulto)* grown-up, adult; *(mayor)* eldest; **pasarlo en ~** F have a great time; **grandeza** *f* greatness; **grandioso** magnificent

grandilocuente grandiloquent

granel *m*: **vender a ~** COM sell in bulk

granizado *m* type of soft drink made with crushed ice; **granizar** hail; **granizo** *m* hail

granja *f* farm

grano *m* grain; *de café* bean; *en la piel* pimple, spot

granuja *m* rascal

grapa *f* staple; **grapadora** *f* stapler

grasa *f* BIO, GASTR fat; *lubricante, suciedad* grease; **sin ~s** fat-free; **grasiento** greasy; **graso** greasy; *carne* fatty; **de bajo contenido ~** low-fat

gratificación *f* gratification; **gratificar** reward; **gratificante** gratifying

gratinar cook au gratin

gratis free; **gratitud** f gratitude; **gratuito** free

grato pleasant

grava f gravel

gravamen m tax; **gravar** tax

grave serious; *tono* grave, solemn; *nota* low; *voz* deep; *estar ~* be seriously ill; **gravedad** f seriousness, gravity; Fís gravity

gravilla f grave

gravitación f gravitation

Grecia Greece

gremio m (*oficio manual*) trade; (*profesión*) profession

gres m (*arcilla*) earthenware; *para artesano* potter's clay

gresca f (*pelea*) fight; (*escándalo*) uproar

griego 1 adj Greek **2** m, **-a** f Greek **3** m idioma Greek

grieta f crack

grifo m adj Méx F high **2** m faucet, Br tap; Pe (*gasolinera*) gas station, Br petrol station

grillo m ZO cricket

gripe f flu, influenza

gris gray, Br grey

gritar shout, yell; **griterío** m shouting; **grito** m cry, shout; *a ~ pelado* at the top of one's voice; *pedir algo a ~s* F be crying out for sth

grosella f redcurrant

grosería f rudeness; **grosero 1** adj rude **2** m, **-a** f rude person

grúa f crane; AUTO wrecker, Br breakdown truck

grueso thick; *persona* stout

grulla f ZO crane

gruñir (*quejarse*) grumble; *de perro* growl; *de cerdo* grunt

grupo m group

gruta f cave; *artificial* grotto

guacho 1 adj S.Am. (*sin casa*) homeless; (*huérfano*) orphaned **2** m, **-a** f S.Am. sin casa homeless person; (*huérfano*) orphan

guadaña f scythe

guagua f W.I., Ven, Canaries bus; Pe, Bol, Chi (*niño*) baby

guante m glove; **guantera** f AUTO glove compartment

guapo hombre handsome, good-looking; mujer beautiful; S.Am. (*valiente*) bold, gutsy F

guarda m/f keeper; **guardabarros** m inv AUTO fender, Br mudguard; **guardabosques** m/f inv forest ranger; **guardacoches** m/f inv parking lot attendant, Br car park attendant; **guardacostas** m inv coastguard vessel; **guardaespaldas** m inv bodyguard; **guarda jurado** security guard; **guardameta** m/f DEP goalkeeper

guardar keep; *poner en un lugar* put (away); *recuerdo* have; *apariencias* keep up; INFOR save; *~ silencio* keep silent; **guardarse** keep; *~ de* refrain from

guardarropa m checkroom, Br cloakroom; (*ropa, armario*) wardrobe

guardería f nursery

guyanés

guardia 1 *f* guard; *de ~* on duty **2** *m/f* MIL guard; (*policía*) police officer; *~ civil* *Esp* civil guard; *~ de seguridad* security guard; *~ de tráfico* traffic warden

guardián 1 *adj*: *perro ~* guard dog **2** *m*, **-ana** *f* guard; *fig* guardian

guarida *f* ZO den; *de personas* hideout

guarnecer adorn (*de* with); GASTR garnish (*con* with); **guarnición** *f* GASTR accompaniment; MIL garrison

guarro **1** *adj* F (*sucio*) filthy F **2** *m tb fig* F pig

guasa *f* *L.Am.* joke; *de ~* as a joke

Guatemala Guatemala; **guatemalteco 1** *adj* Guatemalan **2** *m*, **-a** *f* Guatemalan

guateque *m* party

guay *Esp* F cool F, neat F

gubernamental governmental, government *atr*

guerra *f* war; *~ civil* civil war; *~ mundial* world war; *dar ~ a alguien* F give s.o. trouble; **guerrero 1** *adj* warlike **2** *m* warrior; **guerrilla** *f* guerillas *pl*; **guerrillero** *m* guerilla

guía **1** *m/f* guide; *~ turístico* tour guide **2** *f* *libro* guide (book); *~ telefónica* o *de teléfonos* phone book; **guiar** guide

guijarro *m* pebble

guinda *f* GASTR *L.Am.* purple **2** *f* *fresca* morello cherry; *en dulce* glacé cherry

guindilla *f* GASTR chil(l)i

guiñar: *le guiñó un ojo* she winked at him

guión *m* *de película* script; GRAM *corto* hyphen; *largo* dash

guirnalda *f* garland

guisante *m* pea; **guisar** GASTR stew, casserole; **guiso** *m* GASTR stew, casserole

guitarra *f* guitar; **guitarrista** *m/f* guitarist, guitar player

gusano *m* worm

gustar: *me gusta viajar* I like to travel, I like traveling; *¿te gusta...?* do you like ...?; *no me gusta* I don't like it; **gusto** *m* taste; (*placer*) pleasure; *a ~* at ease; *con mucho ~* with pleasure; *de buen ~* in good taste, tasteful; *de mal ~* in bad taste; *mucho o tanto ~* how do you do; **gustoso**: *hacer algo ~* do sth gladly

Guyana Francesa French Guyana; **Guyana** Guyana; **guyanés 1** *adj* Guyanese **2** *m*, **-esa** *f* Guyanese

H

haba f broad bean

Habana: La ~ Havana; **habanero 1** adj of / from Havana, Havana atr **2** m, -**a** f citizen of Havana; **habano 1** adj of / from Havana, Havana atr **2** m, -**a** f citizen of Havana; **Habana 3** m Havana (cigar)

haber 1 v/aux have; **hemos llegado** we've arrived; **he de levantarme pronto** I have to o I've got to get up early; **has de ver** Méx you ought to see it **2** v/impers: **hay** there is sg, there are pl; **hubo un incendio** there was a fire; **¿qué hay?**, Méx **¿qué hubo?** how's it going?; **hay que hacerlo** it has to be done; **no hay de qué** not at all **3** m asset; **pago** fee; **de cuenta bancaria** credit

habichuela f kidney bean

hábil skilled; (capaz) capable; (astuto) clever, smart; **habilidad** f skill; (capacidad) ability; (astucia) cleverness; **habilitar** lugar fit out; persona authorize

habitable habitable; **habitación** f room; (dormitorio) bedroom; **~ doble / individual** double / single room; **habitante** m/f inhabitant; **habitar** live (**en** in)

hábito m tb REL habit; (práctica) knack; **habitual 1** adj usual, regular **2** m/f regular; **habituar: ~ a alguien a algo** get s.o. used to sth; **habituarse: ~ a algo** get used to sth

habla f speech; **¡al ~!** TELEC speaking; **quedarse sin ~** fig be speechless; **hablada** f L.Am. piece of gossip; **~s** gossip; **hablador** talkative; Méx boastful; **habladurías** fpl gossip; **hablante** m/f speaker; **hablar** speak; (conversar) talk; **con alguien** talk to s.o., talk with s.o.; **~ de libro** etc be about; **¡ni ~!** no way!; **hablarse** speak to one another

hacendado land-owning **2** m, -**a** f land-owner

hacer 1 v/t (realizar) do; (elaborar, crear) make; **~ una pregunta** ask a question; **¡qué le vamos a ~!** that's life; **le hicieron ir** they made him go **2** v/i: **haces bien / mal en ir** you are doing the right / wrong thing by going; **me hace mal** it's making me ill; **esto hará de mesa de objeto** this will do as a table; **~ como que o como si** act as if; **no le hace** L.Am. it doesn't matter; **se me hace qué** L.Am. it seems to me that **3** v/impers: **hace calor / frío** it's hot /

cold; **hace tres días** three days ago; **desde hace un año** for a year; **hacerse** traje make; casa build o.s.; (convertirse, volverse) cook; (convertirse, volverse) get, become; **~ viejo** get old; **se hace tarde** it's getting late; **~ el sordo** pretend to be deaf; **~ a algo** get used to sth; **~ con algo** get hold of sth

hacha f ax, Br axe

hachís m hashish

hacia toward; **~ adelante** forward; **~ abajo** down; **~ arriba** up; **~ atrás** back(ward); **~ las cuatro** about four (o'clock)

hacienda f L.Am. (granja) ranch, estate

Hacienda f ministerio Treasury Department, Br Treasury; oficina Internal Revenue Service, Br Inland Revenue

hacinar stack

hada f fairy

halagar flatter; **halago** m flattery

halcón m falcon

hall m hall

hallar find; (descubrir) discover; muerte, destino meet; **hallarse** (sentirse) feel; **hallazgo** m find; (descubrimiento) discovery

halógeno halogen

halterofilia f DEP weight-lifting

hamaca f hammock; (tumbona) deck chair; L.Am. (mecedora) rocking chair

hambre f hunger; **tener ~** be hungry **morirse de ~** fig be starving; **hambriento** tb fig hungry (**de** for)

hamburguesa f hamburger

hampa f underworld

harapiento ragged; **harapo** m rag

harina f flour

hartar 1 v/t: **~ a alguien con algo** tire s.o. with sth; **~ a alguien de algo** give s.o. too much of sth; **harto 1** adj fed up F; (lleno) full (up) **2** adv very much; **delante del adjetivo** extremely; **me gusta ~** L.Am. I like it a lot

hasta 1 prp until, till; **llegó ~ Bilbao** he went as far as Bilbao; **~ ahora** so far; **~ aquí** up to here; **¿~ cuándo?** how long?; **~ que** until; **~ luego!, ¡~ la vista!** see you (later) **2** adv even

hastío m boredom

hato m L.Am. bundle

hay ☞ **haber**

haz m bundle; de luz beam

hazaña f achievement

hebilla f buckle

hebra f de hilo thread

hechizar fig bewitch; **hechizo** m spell, charm

hecho 1 part de **hacer**; **~ a mano** hand-made; **¡bien ~!** well done!; **muy ~** carne well-done **2** adj estado; **un hombre ~ y derecho** a fully grown man **3** m fact; **de ~** in fact; **hechura** f de ropa making

hectárea f hectare (*approx. 2.5 acres*)

hedor m stink, stench

helada f frost; **heladería** f ice cream parlor o Br parlour; **helado 1** adj frozen; fig icy; **quedarse ~** be stunned **2** m ice cream; **helarse** tb fig freeze

hélice f propeller

helicóptero m helicopter

helipuerto m heliport

hematoma m bruise

hembra f female

hemisferio m hemisphere

hemorragia f MED morrhage, Br haemorrhage, bleeding; **hemorroides** fpl MED hemorrhoids, Br haemorrhoids, piles

hender, henderse crack; **hendidura** f crack

heno m hay

hepático liver atr, hepatic; **hepatitis** f MED hepatitis

heredar inherit (**de** from); **heredera** f heiress; **heredero** m heir; **hereditario** hereditary

hereje m heretic; **herejía** f heresy

herencia f inheritance

herida f wound; (*lesión*) injury; **mujer** wounded woman; **mujer lesionada** injured woman; **herir** wound; (*lesionar*) injure

hermana f sister; **hermanastra** f stepsister; **hermanastro** m stepbrother; **hermandad** f de hombres brother-

hood, fraternity; **de mujeres** sisterhood; **hermano** m brother

hermoso beautiful; **hermosura** f beauty

hernia f MED hernia

héroe m hero; **heroico** heroic; **heroína** f mujer heroine; **droga** heroin

herradura f horseshoe

herramienta f tool

herrumbre f rust

hervidero m fig hotbed; **hervir 1** v/i boil; fig seethe (**de** with) **2** v/t boil

hidrato m: **~ de carbono** carbohydrate

hidráulico hydraulic

hidroavión m seaplane; **hidrocarburo** m hydrocarbon; **hidroeléctrico** hydroelectric; **hidrógeno** m hydrogen

hiedra f BOT ivy

hielo m ice

hiena f ZO hyena

hierba f grass; **mala ~** weed; **hierbabuena** f BOT mint

hierro m iron

hígado m liver

higiene f hygiene; **higiénico** hygienic

higo m BOT fig; **higuera** f BOT fig tree

hija f daughter; **hijastra** f stepdaughter; **hijastro** m stepson; **hijo** m son; **~s** children pl; **~ de puta** P son of a bitch V, bastard P; **~ único** only child

hilar 1 v/t spin **2** v/t: **~ delgado** o **fino** fig split hairs; **hilo** m

thread; ~ **dental** dental floss;
sin ~s TELEC cordless; **perder el ~** *fig* lose the thread
himno *m* hymn; ~ **nacional**
national anthem
hincapié *m:* **hacer ~** put special emphasis (**en** on)
hincha *m* F fan, supporter;
hinchado swollen; **hinchar**
inflate, blow up; *Rpl* P annoy; **hincharse** MED swell;
fig stuff o.s (**de** with); (*mostrarse orgulloso*) swell with
pride; **hinchazón** *f* swelling
hinojo *m* BOT fennel
hipermercado *m* supermarket, *Br tb* supermarket; **hipertensión** *f* MED high
blood pressure, hypertension; **hipertexto** *m* hypertext
hípica *f* equestrian sports *pl*
hipo *m* hiccups *pl*; **quitar el ~**
F take one's breath away
hipócrita 1 *adj* hypocritical **2**
m/f hypocrite
hipódromo *m* racetrack
hipopótamo *m* hippopotamus
hipoteca *f* COM mortgage; **hipotecar** COM mortgage; *fig*
compromise
hipótesis *f* hypothesis; **hipotético** hypothetical
hirviente boiling
hispánico Hispanic; **Hispanidad** *f:* **la ~** the Spanish-speaking world; **hispano 1**
adj (*español*) Spanish; (*hispanohablante*) Spanish-speaking; **en** *EE.UU.* Hispanic **2**
m, **-a** *f* (*español*) Spaniard;

(*hispanohablante*) Spanish
speaker; **en** *EE.UU.* Hispanic
histérico hysterical
historia *f* history; (*cuento*)
story; **una ~ de drogas** F
some drugs business; **déjate
de ~s** F stop making excuses; **histórico** historical;
(*importante*) historic
hito *m tb fig* milestone
hockey *m* field hockey, *Br*
hockey; ~ **sobre hielo** hockey, *Br* ice hockey
hogar *m fig* home
hoguera *f* bonfire
hoja *f* BOT leaf; *de papel* sheet;
de libro page; *de cuchillo*
blade; ~ **de afeitar** razor
blade; ~ **de cálculo** INFOR
spreadsheet; **hojalata** *f* tin;
hojear leaf through
hola hello, hi F
Holanda Holland; **holandés
1** *adj* Dutch **2** *m* Dutchman;
los holandeses the Dutch **3**
m idioma Dutch; **holandesa**
f Dutchwoman
holgado loose, comfortable;
estar ~ de tiempo have time
to spare
holgazán *m* idler
hollín *m* soot
hombre *m* man; ~ **de negocios** businessman; ~ **rana**
frogman; **¡claro, ~!** you
bet!, sure thing!; **¡~, qué alegría!** that's great!
hombrera *f* shoulder pad; MIL
epaulette; **hombro** *m* shoulder; ~ **con ~** shoulder to

shoulder
homenaje *m* homage; **homenajear** pay homage to
homeópata *m/f* homeopath
homicidio *m* homicide
homogéneo homogenous
homosexual *m/f & adj* homosexual
honda *f de cuero* sling(shot); *Rpl (tirachinas)* slingshot, *Br* catapult
hondo deep; **hondura** *f* depth
Honduras Honduras; **hondureño 1** *adj* Honduran **2** *m, -a f* Honduran
honesto honorable, *Br* honourable, decent
hongo *m* fungus
honor *m* honor, *Br* honour; **en ~ a** in honor of; **hacer ~ a** live up to; **palabra de ~** word of honor; **honorable** honorable, *Br* honourable; **honorario** honorary; **honorarios** *mpl* fees; **honra** *f* honor, *Br* honour; **honradez** *f* honesty; **honrado** honest; **honrar** honor, *Br* honour; **honrarse**: ~ **de hacer algo** be honored *o Br* honoured to do sth; **honroso** honorable, *Br* honourable
hora *f* hour; **~s extraordinarias** overtime; **~ local** local time; **~ punta** rush hour; **a la ~ de...**, *fig* when it comes to ...; **¡ya era ~!** about time too!; **tengo ~ con el dentista** I have an appointment with the dentist; **¿qué es?** what time is it?; **horario**

m schedule, *Br* timetable; **~ comercial** business hours *pl*; **~ flexible** flextime, *Br* flexitime; **~ de trabajo** (working) hours *pl*
horca *f* gallows *pl*
horchata *f drink made from tiger nuts*
horizontal horizontal; **horizonte** *m* horizon
horma *f* form, mold, *Br* mould; *de zapatos* last
hormiga *f* ant
hormigón *m* concrete; **~ armado** reinforced concrete
hormiguero *m* ant hill
hormona *f* hormone
hornillo *m de fogón* burner; *de gas* gas ring; *transportable* camping stove
horno *m* oven; **alto ~** blast furnace
horóscopo *m* horoscope
horquilla *f para pelo* hairpin
horrendo horrendous
horrible horrible, dreadful; **horror** *m* horror (**a** of); **tener ~ a** be terrified of; **me gusta ~es** F I like it a lot; **¡qué ...!** how awful!; **horroroso** terrible; *(feo)* hideous
hortaliza *f* vegetable
horticultura *f* horticulture
hospedaje *m* accommodation *pl*, *Br* accommodation; **dar ~ a alguien** put s.o. up; **hospedar** put up; **hospedarse** stay (**en** at); **hospital** *m* hospital; **hospitalario** hospitable; MED hospital *atr*; **hospitalidad** *f* hospitali-

ty

hostal m hostel; **hostelería** f hotel industry; *como curso* hotel management

hostia f REL host

hostil hostile; **hostilidad** f hostility

hotel m hotel; **~ spa** spa hotel

hoy today; *de* **~ en adelante** from now on; **~ por ~** at the present time; **~ en día** nowadays

hoyo m hole; *(depresión)* hollow; **hoyuelo** m dimple

hucha f money box

hueco 1 adj hollow; *(vacío)* empty; *fig: persona* shallow **2** m gap; *(agujero)* hole; *de ascensor* shaft

huelga f strike; **~ de celo** work-to-rule; **~ de hambre** hunger strike; **declararse en ~, ir a la ~** go on strike; **huelguista** m/f striker

huella f mark; *de animal* track; **~s dactilares** finger prints

huérfano 1 adj orphan atr **2** m, **-a** f orphan

huerta f truck farm, Br market garden; **huerto** m kitchen garden

hueso m bone; *de fruta* pit, stone; *persona* tough guy; *Méx* F cushy number F; *Méx* F *(influencia)* influence, pull F; **~ duro de roer** fig F hard nut to crack F

huésped m/f guest

huevera f para servir eggcup; *para almacenar* egg box;

huevo m egg; P *(testículo)* ball P; **~ duro** hard-boiled egg; **~ escalfado** poached egg; **~ frito** fried egg; **~ pasado por agua** soft-boiled egg; **~s revueltos** scrambled eggs; **un ~ de** P a load of F

huida f flight, escape; **huir** flee, escape (*de* from); **~ de algo** avoid sth

hule m oilcloth; *L.Am. (caucho)* rubber

hulla f coal

humanidad f humanity; **humano** human

humareda f cloud of smoke; **humear** con humo smoke; *con vapor* steam

humedad f humidity; *de una casa* damp(ness); **humedecer** dampen; **húmedo** humid; **toalla** damp

humildad f humility; **humilde** humble; *(sin orgullo)* modest; **clase social** lowly; **humillación** f humiliation; **humillante** humiliating; **humillar** humiliate

humo m smoke; *(vapor)* steam

humor m humor, Br humour; **estar de buen / mal ~** be in a good / bad mood; **sentido del ~** sense of humor; **humorista** m/f humorist; *(cómico)* comedian

hundimiento m sinking; **hundir** sink; *fig: empresa* ruin; *persona* devastate; **hundirse** sink; *fig: de empresa* collapse; *de persona* go to pieces

húngaro 1 *adj* Hungarian **2** *m*, **-a** *f* Hungarian **3** *m idioma* Hungarian; **Hungría** *f* Hungary

huracán *m* hurricane
hurtadillas *fpl*: **a ~** furtively
hurtar steal; **hurto** *m* theft
husmear F nose around F

I

ibérico Iberian; **ibero, íbero** *m*, **-a** *f* Iberian; **iberoamericano** Latin American
ibicenco Ibizan
iceberg *m* iceberg
ida *f* outward journey; (*billete de*) **~ y vuelta** round trip (ticket), *Br* return (ticket)
idea *f* idea; **no tener ni ~** not have a clue; **ideal** *m*/*adj* ideal; **idealismo** *m* idealism; **idealista 1** *adj* idealistic **2** *m*/*f* idealist; **idear** think up
idéntico identical; **identidad** *f* identity; **identificón** *f* identification; **INFOR** user name; **~ genética** genetic fingerprint; **identificar** identify; **identificarse** identify o.s.
ideología *f* ideology
idilio *m* idyll; (*relación amorosa*) romance
idioma *m* language
idiota 1 *adj* idiotic **2** *m*/*f* idiot; **idiotez** *f* stupid thing to say / do
ídolo *m tb fig* idol
idóneo suitable
iglesia *f* church
ignorancia *f* ignorance; **ignorante** ignorant; **ignorar** not

know, not be aware of
igual 1 *adj* (*idéntico*) same (*a, que* as); (*proporcionado*) equal (*a* to); (*constante*) constant; **al ~ que** like, the same as; **me da ~** I don't mind **2** *m*/*f* equal; **no tener ~** have no equal; **igualar 1** *v*/*t precio, marca* equal, match; (*nivelar*) level off; **~ algo** MAT make sth equal (*con, a* to) **2** *v*/*i* DEP tie the game, *Br* equalize; **igualdad** *f* equality; **~ de oportunidades** equal opportunities; **igualmente** equally
ilegal illegal; **ilegalidad** *f* illegality
ilegible illegible
ilegítimo unlawful; *hijo* illegitimate
ileso unhurt
ilícito illicit
ilimitado unlimited
iluminación *f* illumination; **iluminar** *edificio, calle etc* light, illuminate; *fig* light up
ilusión *f* illusion; (*deseo, esperanza*) hope; **iluso 1** *adj* gullible **2** *m*, **-a** *f* dreamer; **ilusorio** illusory
ilustración *f* illustration;

ilustrado illustrated; (*culto*) learned; **ilustrar** illustrate; (*aclarar*) explain; **ilustre** illustrious

imagen *f tb fig* image; **ser la viva ~ de** be the spitting image of; **imaginable** imaginable; **imaginación** *f* imagination; **imaginar, imaginarse** imagine; **imaginativo** imaginative

imán *m* magnet

imbécil 1 *adj* stupid **2** *m/f* idiot, imbecile

imitación *f* imitation; **imitar** imitate

impaciencia *f* impatience; **impacientarse** lose (one's) patience; **impaciente** impatient

impacto *m tb fig* impact; **~ de bala** bullet wound

impar *número* odd

imparable unstoppable

imparcial impartial

impartir impart; *clase, bendición* give

impávido fearless

impecable impeccable

impedir prevent; (*estorbar*) impede

impenetrable impenetrable

impensado unexpected

imperar rule; *fig* prevail

imperceptible imperceptible

imperdible *m* safety pin

imperdonable unpardonable, unforgivable

imperfecto *m/adj* imperfect

imperial imperial; **imperio** *m* empire; **imperioso** *necesi-*

dad pressing; *persona* imperious

impermeable 1 *adj* waterproof **2** *m* raincoat

impertérrito unperturbed, unmoved

impertinente 1 *adj* impertinent **2** *m/f*: **¡eres un ~!** you've got nerve!

ímpetu *m* impetus; **impetuoso** impetuous

implacable implacable

implantar *programa* implement; *democracia* establish; *pena de muerte* bring in; MED implant; **implantarse** be introduced

implicar mean, imply; (*involucrar*) involve; *en un delito* implicate (**en** in)

implorar beg for

imponente impressive; F terrific; **imponer 1** *v/t* impose; *miedo, respeto* inspire **2** *v/i* be imposing o impressive; **imponerse** (*hacerse respetar*) assert o.s.; DEP win; (*prevalecer*) prevail; (*ser necesario*) be imperative; **~ una tarea** set o.s. a task

impopular unpopular

importación *f* import

importancia *f* importance; **darse ~** give o.s. airs; **tener ~** be important; **importante** important; **importar** matter; **no importa** it doesn't matter; **eso a ti no te importa** that's none of your business; **¿qué importa?** what does it matter?; **¿le importa...?** do you mind …?; **importe** *m* amount; (*coste*) cost

importuno inopportune

imposibilidad *f* impossibility; **imposible** impossible

imposición *f* imposition; (*exigencia*) demand; COM deposit

impotencia *f* impotence, helplessness; MED impotence; **impotente** helpless, impotent; MED impotent

impracticable impracticable

impregnar saturate (*de* with); TÉC impregnate (*de* with)

imprenta *f taller* print shop; *arte, técnica* printing; *máquina* printing press

imprescindible essential; *persona* indispensable

impresión *f* impression; *acto* printing; (*tirada*) print run; **la sangre le da ~** he can't stand the sight of blood; **impresionante** impressive; **impresionismo** *m* impressionism; **impresionar: ~le a alguien** impress s.o.; (*conmover*) move s.o.; (*alterar*) shock s.o.; **impreso** *m* form; **~s** printed matter; **impresora** *f* INFOR printer; **~ de chorro de tinta** inkjet (printer); **~ de inyección de tinta** inkjet (printer); **~ láser** laser (printer)

imprevisto 1 *adj* unforeseen, unexpected **2** *m* unexpected event

imprimir *tb* INFOR print; *fig* transmit

improbable unlikely, improbable

improductivo unproductive

improvisar improvise

imprudente reckless, rash

impuesto *m* tax; **~ sobre el valor añadido** sales tax, *Br* value-added tax; **~ sobre la renta** income tax

impugnar challenge

impulsar TÉC propel; COM boost

impulsivo impulsive; **impulso** *m* impulse; (*empuje*) impetus; COM boost; *fig* urge, impulse; **tomar ~** take a run up

impunidad *f* impunity

imputar attribute

inacabable endless; **inacabado** unfinished

inaccesible inaccessible

inaceptable unacceptable

inadmisible inadmissible

inadvertido: pasar ~ go unnoticed

inagotable inexhaustible

inaguantable unbearable

inalámbrico 1 *adj* TELEC cordless **2** *m* TELEC cordless (telephone)

inarrugable crease-resistant

inaudito unprecedented

inauguración *f* official opening, inauguration; **inaugurar** (*officially*) open, inaugurate

incansable tireless

incapacidad *f* disability; (*falta de capacidad*) inability; (*ineptitud*) incompetence; in-

capaz incapable (*de* of)

incautarse: ~ *de* seize

incauto unwary

incendiar set fire to; **incendio** *m* fire

incentivo *m* incentive

incertidumbre *f* uncertainty

incidente *m* incident

incienso *m* incense

incierto *m* uncertain

incineración *f de cadáver* cremation

incisivo cutting; *fig* incisive; **diente** ~ incisor

incitar incite

inclinación *f* inclination; *de un terreno* slope; *muestra de respeto* bow; *fig* tendency; **inclinar** tilt; ~ **la cabeza** nod (one's head); **me inclina a creer que...** it makes me think that ...; **inclinarse** bend (down); *de un terreno* slope; *desde la vertical* lean; *en señal de respeto* bow; ~ **a** *fig* tend to, be inclined to

incluir include; **inclusive** inclusive; **incluso** even

incoherente incoherent

incoloro colorless, *Br* colourless

incomodar inconvenience; (*enfadar*) annoy; **incomodarse** feel uncomfortable; (*enfadarse*) get annoyed (*por* about); **incómodo** uncomfortable; (*fastidioso*) inconvenient

incomparable incomparable

incompatible incompatible

incompetente incompetent

incompleto incomplete

incomprensible incomprehensible

incomunicado isolated, cut off; JUR in solitary confinement

inconfundible unmistakable

inconsciente MED unconscious; (*ignorante*) unaware; (*irreflexivo*) thoughtless

inconstante fickle

incontestable indisputable

inconveniente 1 *adj* (*inoportuno*) inconvenient; (*impropio*) inappropriate **2** *m* (*desventaja*) drawback; (*estorbo*) problem; *no tengo* ~ I don't mind

incorporar incorporate; **incorporarse** sit up; ~ **a** MIL join

incorrecto incorrect, wrong; *comportamiento* impolite; **incorregible** incorrigible

incrédulo incredulous; **increíble** incredible

incremento *m* growth

incubadora *f* incubator; **incubar** incubate

inculpar JUR accuse

inculto ignorant, uneducated

incurable incurable

indecente indecent; *película* obscene

indeciso undecided; *por naturaleza* indecisive

indefinido (*impreciso*) vague; (*ilimitado*) indefinite

indemnización *f* compensation; **indemnizar** compensate (*por* for)

independencia f independence; **independiente** independent; **independientemente** independently
indescriptible indescribable
indeterminado indeterminate; (*indefinido*) indefinite
India: (la) ~ India; **indio 1** *adj* Indian **2** *m, -a* f Indian
indicación f indication; (*señal*) sign; **indicaciones** *para llegar* directions; (*instrucciones*) instructions; **indicador** *m* indicator; **indicar** show, indicate; (*señalar*) point out; (*sugerir*) suggest; **índice** *m* index; **dedo** ~ index finger; **indicio** *m* indication, sign; (*vestigio*) trace
indiferencia f indifference; **indiferente** indifferent; (*irrelevante*) immaterial
indígena 1 *adj* indigenous, native **2** *m/f* native
indigente destitute
indigestión f indigestion; **indigesto** indigestible
indignar: ~ a alguien make s.o. indignant; **indignarse** become indignant
indirecta f insinuation; (*sugerencia*) hint; **indirecto** indirect
indiscreción f indiscretion; (*declaración*) indiscreet remark; **indiscreto** indiscreet
indiscutible indisputable
indisoluble insoluble; *matrimonio* indissoluble
indispensable indispensable
indispuesto indisposed, un-

well
indistinto vague; *sonido* faint
individual individual; *cama, habitación* single; **individuo** *m* individual
indivisible indivisible
índole f nature
indolencia f laziness, indolence; **indolente** lazy, indolent
indomable *animal* untameable; *persona* indomitable
indudable undoubted
indulgencia f indulgence
indultar pardon; **indulto** *m* pardon
indumentaria f clothing
industria f industry; **industrial 1** *adj* industrial **2** *m/f* industrialist
inédito unpublished; *fig* unprecedented
ineficacia f inefficiency; *de un procedimiento* ineffectiveness; **ineficaz** inefficient; *procedimiento* ineffective
ineficiencia f inefficiency; **ineficiente** inefficient
inepto 1 *adj* inept, incompetent **2** *m, -a* f incompetent fool
inequívoco unequivocal
inesperado unexpected
inestable unstable; *tiempo* unsettled
inestimable invaluable
inevitable inevitable
inexperto inexperienced
inexplicable inexplicable
infalible infallible

infame loathsome; (*terrible*) dreadful

infamia *f* (*deshonra*) disgrace; *acción* dreadful thing to do; *dicho* slander, slur

infancia *f* infancy; **infanta** *f* infanta, princess

infantería *f* MIL infantry

infantil children's *atr*; *naturaleza* childlike; *desp* infantile, childish

infarto *m* MED heart attack

infatigable tireless, indefatigable

infección *f* MED infection; **infeccioso** infectious; **infectar** infect

infeliz 1 *adj* unhappy, miserable **2** *m/f* poor devil

inferior 1 *adj* inferior (**a** to); *en el espacio* lower (**a** than) **2** *m/f* inferior; **inferioridad** *f* inferiority

infertilidad *f* infertility

infestar infest; (*invadir*) overrun

infiel 1 *adj* unfaithful **2** *m/f* unbeliever

infierno *m* hell

ínfimo *cantidad* very small; *calidad* very poor

infinidad *f*: **~ de** countless; **infinito 1** *adj* infinite **2** *m* infinity

inflación *f* inflation

inflamable flammable; **inflamación** *f* MED inflammation; **inflamarse** MED become inflamed

inflar inflate; **inflarse** swell (up); *fig* F get conceited

inflexible *fig* inflexible

influencia *f* influence; **tener ~s** have contacts; **influir**: **~ en alguien / algo** influence s.o. / sth, have an influence on s.o. / sth; **influjo** *m* influence; **influyente** influential

infografía *f* computer graphics *pl*

información *f* information; (*noticias*) news *sg*; **informal** informal; *persona* unreliable; **informar** inform (**de**, **sobre** about); **informática** *f* information technology, IT; **informático 1** *adj* computer *atr* **2** *m*, **-a** *f* IT specialist

informe 1 *adj* shapeless **2** *m* report; **~s** (*referencias*) references

infracción *f* offense, *Br* offence

infraestructura *f* infrastructure

infrarrojo infrared

infrecuente infrequent

infructuoso fruitless

ingeniero *m*, **-a** *f* engineer; **ingenio** *m* ingenuity; (*aparato*) device; **~ azucarero** *L.Am.* sugar refinery; **ingenioso** ingenious

Inglaterra England

ingle *f* groin

inglés 1 *adj* English **2** *m* Englishman; *idioma* English; **inglesa** *f* Englishwoman

ingratitud *f* ingratitude; **ingrato** ungrateful; *tarea* thankless

ingravidez *f* weightlessness
ingrediente *m* ingredient
ingresar 1 *v/i:* ~ **en** *en universidad* go to; *en asociación* join; *en hospital* be admitted to **2** *v/t cheque* pay in; *ingreso* *m* entry; *en una asociación* joining; *en hospital* admission; COM deposit; ~**s** income
inhabitado uninhabited
inhalar inhale
inhibición *f* inhibition; JUR disqualification
inhumano inhuman
inicial *f*/*adj* initial; **iniciar** initiate; *curso* start, begin; **iniciativa** *f* initiative; **inicio** *m* start, beginning
inigualable incomparable; *precio* unbeatable
injerencia *f* interference
injuria *f* insult; **injuriar** insult
injusticia *f* injustice; **injusto** unjust
inmediaciones *fpl* immediate area (**de** of), vicinity (**de** of); **inmediatamente** immediately; **inmediato** immediate; **de** ~ immediately
inmejorable unbeatable
inmenso immense
inmigración *f* immigration; **inmigrante** *m*/*f* immigrant; **inmigrar** immigrate
inminente imminent
inmoral immoral
inmortal immortal
inmóvil *persona* motionless; *vehículo* stationary
inmueble *m* building

inmune immune; **inmunidad** *f* MED, POL immunity; **inmunizar** immunize; **inmunológico: sistema** ~ MED immune system
innato innate, inborn
innecesario unnecessary
innovación *f* innovation
innumerable innumerable, countless
inocencia *f* innocence; **inocente** innocent
inodoro *m* toilet
inofensivo inoffensive, harmless
inolvidable unforgettable
inoportuno inopportune; (*molesto*) inconvenient
inoxidable: acero ~ stainless steel
inquietar worry; **inquietarse** worry; **inquietud** *f* worry, anxiety; *intelectual* interest; **inquieto** worried
inquilino *m* tenant
inquisitivo inquisitive
insalubre unhealthy
insano unhealthy
insatisfacción *f* dissatisfaction; **insatisfactorio** unsatisfactory; **insatisfecho** dissatisfied
inscribir 1 *v/t* (*grabar*) inscribe; *en lista* register, enter; *en curso* enroll, Br enrol, register; **inscripción** *f* inscription; *en lista* registration, entry; *en curso* enrollment, Br enrolment, registration
insecticida *m* insecticide; **insecto** *m* insect

inseguridad f de una persona insecurity; de estructura unsteadiness; (peligro) dangerousness; **inseguro** insecure; estructura unsteady; (peligroso) dangerous, unsafe

insensato foolish

insensible insensitive (**a** to)

insertar insert

inservible useless

insignificante insignificant

insinuar insinuate

insípido insipid

insistir insist; **~ en hacer algo** insist on doing sth; **~ en algo** stress sth

insolación f MED sunstroke

insolencia f insolence; **insolente** insolent

insólito unusual

insoluble insoluble

insolvencia f insolvency

insomnio m insomnia

insonorizar soundproof; **insonoro** soundless

insoportable unbearable, intolerable

inspección f inspection; **inspeccionar** inspect; **inspector** m, **~a** f inspector

inspiración f inspiration; MED inhalation; **inspirar** inspire; MED inhale

instalación f acto installation; **instalaciones deportivas** sports facilities; **instalar** install, Br instal; (colocar) put; un negocio set up; **instalarse** en un sitio install o Br instal o.s.

instancia f JUR petition; (peti-

ción por escrito) application; **a ~s de** at the request of

instantánea f FOT snapshot; **instantáneo** immediate, instantaneous; **instante** m moment, instant; **al ~** right away, immediately

instinto m instinct

institución f institution; **instituir** institute; **instituto** m institute; Esp high school, Br secondary school; **~ de belleza** beauty salon; **institutriz** f governess

instrucción f education; (formación) training; MIL drill; INFOR instruction; JUR hearing; **instrucciones de uso** instructions, directions (for use); **instruido** educated; **instruir** educate; (formar) train; JUR pleito hear; **instructivo** educational

instrumento m instrument; (herramienta), fig tool; **~ musical** musical instrument

insuficiencia f lack; MED failure; **insuficiente 1** adj insufficient, inadequate **2** m EDU nota fail

insultar insult; **insulto** m insult

insuperable insurmountable

intachable faultless

intacto intact; (sin tocar) untouched

integrar integrate; equipo make up; **íntegro** whole, entire; **un hombre ~** fig a man of integrity

intelectual m/f & adj intellectual

inteligencia *f* intelligence; **inteligente** intelligent

intemperie *f*: **a la ~** in the open air

intempestivo untimely

intemporal timeless

intención *f* intention; **doble** *o* **segunda ~** ulterior motive; **intencional** intentional

intensidad *f* intensity; *(fuerza)* strength; **intensificar** intensify; **intensificarse** intensify; **intensivo** intensive; **intenso** intense; *(fuerte)* strong

intentar try, attempt; **intento** *m* attempt, try; *Méx (intención)* aim; **intentona** *f*: **~ (golpista)** POL putsch, coup

interacción *f* interaction; **interactivo** interactive

intercalar insert

intercambio *m* exchange, swap

interceder intercede *(por* for)

interceptar *tb* DEP intercept

interés *m tb* COM interest; *desp* self-interest; **sin ~** interest-free; **interesado 1** *adj* interested **2** *m*, **-a** *f* interested party; **interesante** interesting; **interesar** interest; **interesarse**: **~ por** take an interest in

interface *m*, **interfaz** *f* INFOR interface

interferencia *f* interference; **interferir 1** *v/t* interfere with **2** *v/i* interfere *(en* in)

interino substitute *atr; (provisional)* provisional, acting *atr*

interior 1 *adj* interior; *bolsillo* inside *atr;* COM, POL domestic **2** *m* interior; DEP inside-forward; **en su ~** *fig* inwardly

interlocutor *m*, **~a** *f* speaker; **mi ~** the person I was talking to

intermediario *m* COM intermediary, middle-man; **intermedio 1** *adj nivel* intermediate; *tamaño, calidad* medium **2** *m* intermission

intermitente 1 *adj* intermittent **2** *m* AUTO turn signal, *Br* indicator

internacional *m/f* & *adj* international

internado *m* boarding school

internauta *m/f* INFOR Internet user, Net surfer

internet *m* Internet; **en ~** on the Internet

interno 1 *adj* internal; POL domestic, internal **2** *m*, **-a** *f* EDU boarder; *(preso)* inmate; MED intern, *Br* houseman

interpretar interpret; TEA play; **intérprete** *m/f* interpreter

interrogación *f* interrogation; **signo de ~** question mark; **interrogar** question; **interrogatorio** *m* questioning, interrogation

interrumpir 1 *v/t* interrupt; *servicio* suspend; *vacaciones* cut short **2** *v/i* interrupt; **interrupción** *f* interruption; *de servicio* suspension; *de va-*

caciones cutting short; **sin ~**
non-stop; **interruptor** *m*
ELEC switch
intervalo *m tb* MÚS interval; *(espacio)* gap
intervención *f* intervention; *en debate* participation; *en película* appearance; MED operation; **intervenir 1** *v/i* intervene; *en debate* take part, participate; *en película* appear **2** *v/t* TELEC tap; *contrabando* seize; MED operate on
intestinal intestinal; **intestino** *m* intestine
intimidad *f* intimacy; *(lo privado)* privacy; **en la ~** in private
intimidar intimidate
íntimo intimate; *(privado)* private; *amigos* close
intolerable intolerable; **intolerante** intolerant
intoxicación *f* poisoning; **intoxicar** poison
intranquilo uneasy; *(nervioso)* restless
intransferible non-transferable
intransigente intransigent
intransitable impassable
intratable: es ~ he is impossible (to deal with)
intravenoso MED intravenous
intrépido intrepid
intriga *f* intrigue; *de novela* plot; **intrigar 1** *v/t (interesar)* intrigue **2** *v/i* plot, scheme
introducción *f* introduction;

acción de meter insertion; INFOR input; **introducir** introduce; *(meter)* insert; INFOR input
intuición *f* intuition; **intuir** sense
inundación *f* flood; **inundar** flood
inusitado unusual
inútil 1 *adj* useless; MIL unfit **2** *m/f:* **es un ~** he's useless
invadir invade; *de un sentimiento* overcome
invalidar invalidate; **invalidez** *f* disability; **inválido 1** *adj persona* disabled; *documento* invalid **2** *m*, **-a** *f* disabled person
invariable invariable
invasión *f* MIL invasion
invencible invincible; *miedo* insurmountable
invención *f* invention; **inventar** invent; **inventario** *m* inventory; **invento** *m* invention; **inventor** *m* inventor
invernadero *m* greenhouse; **invernal** winter *atr*
inverosímil unlikely
inversión *f* reversal; COM investment; **inverso** opposite; *orden* reverse; **a la -a** the other way around; **inversor** *m*, **~a** *f* investor; **invertir** reverse; COM invest **(en** in)
investigación *f* investigation; EDU, TÉC research; **~ y desarrollo** research and development; **investigador** *m*, **~a** *f* researcher; **investigar** investigate; EDU, TÉC research

invidente

invidente *m/f* blind person
invierno *m* winter
invisible invisible
invitación *f* invitation; **invitado** *m*, **-a** *f* guest; **invitar** invite (**a** to); (*convidar*) treat (**a** to)
involuntario involuntary
inyección *f* injection; **inyectar** inject
IP *f* IT IP; **dirección** *f* ~ IP address
ir 1 *v/i* go (**a** to); ~ **en avión** fly; **¡ya voy!** I'm coming!; ~ **a por algo** go and fetch sth; ~ **bien / mal** go well / badly; **iba de amarillo** she was wearing yellow; **van dos a dos** DEP the score is two all; **¿de qué va la película?** what's the movie about?; **¡qué va!** you must be joking!; F; **¡vamos!** come on!; **¡vaya!** well! **2** *v/aux*: **va a llover** it's going to rain; **ya voy comprendiendo** I'm beginning to understand; ~ **para viejo** be getting old; **irse** go (away), leave; **¡vete!** go away!; **¡vámonos!** let's go
ira *f* anger
Irak Iraq, Irak
Irán Iran; **iraní** *m/f* & *adj* Iranian
iraquí *m/f* & *adj* Iraqi, Iraki
iris *m inv* ANAT iris; **arco** ~ rainbow
Irlanda Ireland; **irlandés 1**

adj Irish **2** *m* Irishman; **irlandesa** *f* Irishwoman
ironía *f* irony; **irónico** ironic
irradiación *f* irradiation
irregular irregular; **superficie** uneven; **irregularidad** *f* irregularity; **de superficie** unevenness
irrelevante irrelevant
irreprochable irreproachable
irresistible irresistible
irresponsable irresponsible
irrevocable irrevocable
irrigar MED, AGR irrigate
irritación *f* irritation; **irritar** *tb* MED irritate; **irritarse** get irritated
irrompible unbreakable
irrumpir burst in
isla *f* island
Israel Israel; **israelí** *m/f* & *adj* Israeli
Italia Italy; **italiano 1** *adj* Italian **2** *m*, **-a** *f* Italian; **3** *m idioma* Italian
itinerancia *f* IT roaming
itinerario *m* itinerary
IVA *m* (= **impuesto sobre el valor añadido** *o* L.Am. **agregado**) sales tax, Br VAT (= value added tax)
izar hoist
izquierda *f tb* POL left; **izquierdista** POL **1** *adj* leftwing **2** *m/f* left-winger; **izquierdo** left

J

jabalí *m* ZO wild boar

jabalina *f* javelin

jabón *m* soap; **~ de afeitar** shaving soap; **jabonera** *f* soap dish

jacinto *m* hyacinth

jactarse boast (**de** about)

jadear pant

jaguar *m* ZO jaguar

jalea *f* jelly

jaleo *m* (*ruido*) racket, uproar; (*lío*) mess

Jamaica Jamaica; **jamaicano 1** *adj* Jamaican **2** *m*, **-a** *f* Jamaican

jamás never; **¿viste ~ algo así?** did you ever see anything like it?; **nunca ~** never ever; **por siempre ~** for ever and ever

jamón *m* ham; **~ de York** cooked ham; **~ serrano** cured ham

Japón *m* Japan; **japonés 1** *adj* Japanese **2** *m*, **-esa** *f* Japanese **3** *m* idioma Japanese

jaque *m* check; **~ mate** checkmate; **dar ~ a** checkmate

jaqueca *f* MED migraine

jarabe *m* syrup; *Méx* type of folk dance

jardín *m* garden; **~ de infancia** kindergarten; **jardinera** *f* jardiniere; **jardinería** *f* gardening; **jardinero** *m*, **-a** *f* gardener

jarra *f* pitcher, *Br* jug; **en ~s** with hands on hips; **jarro** *m* pitcher, *Br* jug

jaula *f* cage

jazmín *m* BOT jasmine

jefatura *f* headquarters *pl*; (*dirección*) leadership; **~ de policía** police headquarters; **jefe** *m*, **-a** *f* **de departamento**, **organización** head; (*superior*) boss; POL leader; **de tribu** chief; **~ de cocina** (head) chef; **~ de estado** head of state

jengibre *m* BOT ginger

jeque *m* sheik

jerez *m* sherry

jerga *f* jargon; (*argot*) slang

jersey *m* sweater

jibia *f* ZO cuttlefish

jilguero *m* ZO goldfinch

jinete *m* rider; *en carrera* jockey

jirafa *f* ZO giraffe

jocoso humorous, joking

joder V (*follar*) screw V, fuck V; (*estropear*) screw up V, fuck up V; *L.Am.* F (*fastidiar*) annoy

jornada *f* (working) day; *distancia* day's journey; **~ laboral** work day; **~ partida** split shift; **jornal** *m* day's wage; **jornalero** *m*, **-a** *f* day laborer, *Br* day laborer

joroba *f* hump; *fig* pain F; **jorobado** hump-backed; *fig* F in a bad way F; **jorobar** F (*molestar*) bug F; *planes* ruin

joven 1 *adj* young **2** *m/f* young man; *mujer* young woman; *los jóvenes* young people

joya *f* jewel; *persona* gem; **~s** jewelry, *Br* jewellery; **joyería** *f* jewelry store, *Br* jeweller's; **joyero** *m*, **-a** *f* jeweler, *Br* jeweller **2** *m* jewelry *o Br* jewellery box

juanete *m* MED bunion

jubilación *f* retirement; **~ anticipada** early retirement; **jubilado 1** *adj* retired **2** *m*, **-a** *f* retiree, *Br* pensioner; **jubilarse** retire; **júbilo** *m* jubilation

judía *f* BOT bean; **~ verde** green bean, runner bean

judicial judicial

judío 1 *adj* Jewish **2** *m*, **-a** *f* Jew

juego *m* game; *acción* play; *por dinero* gambling; (*conjunto de objetos*) set; **~ de azar** game of chance; **~ de café** coffee set; **~ de manos** conjuring trick; **~ de mesa** board game; **~ de sociedad** game; *Juegos Olímpicos* Olympic Games; *estar en ~* fig be at stake; *fuera de ~* DEP offside; *hacer ~ con* go with, match

juerga *f* partying F

jueves *m inv* Thursday

juez *m/f* judge; **~ de línea** in *fútbol* assistant referee; *en fútbol americano* line judge

jugada *f* play, *Br* move; *en ajedrez* move; *hacerle una ma-* la **~ a alguien** play a dirty trick on s.o.; **jugador** *m*, **-a** *f* player; **jugar 1** *v/t* play **2** *v/i* play; *con dinero* gamble; **~ al baloncesto** play basketball; *jugarse* risk; **jugarreta** *f* F dirty trick F

jugo *m* juice; **jugoso** *tb fig* juicy

juguete *m* toy; **juguetería** *f* toy store, *Br* toy shop

juicio *m* judg(e)ment; JUR trial; (*sensatez*) sense; (*cordura*) sanity; *a mi ~* in my opinion; *estar en su ~* be in one's right mind; *perder el ~* lose one's mind

julio *m* July

junco *m* BOT reed

jungla *f* jungle

junio *m* June

junta *f* POL (regional) government; *militar* junta; COM board; (*sesión*) meeting; TÉC joint; **~ directiva** board of directors; **juntar** put together; *gente* gather together; *bienes* collect; **juntarse** (*reunirse*) meet, assemble; *de pareja* empezar a salir start going out; *empezar a vivir juntos* move in together; *de caminos, ríos* meet, join; **~ con alguien** socialmente mix with s.o.; **junto 1** *adj* together **2** *prp*: **~ a** next to, near; **~ con** together with

juntura *f* TÉC joint

jurado *m* JUR jury; **juramento** *m* oath; *bajo ~* under oath; **jurar** swear; **jurídico** legal;

jurisdicción *f* jurisdiction; **jurista** *m/f* jurist

justicia *f* justice; **la ~** (*la ley*) the law; **justificante** *m de pago* receipt; *de ausencia, propiedad* certificate; **justificar** *tb* TIP justify; **justo** just, fair; (*exacto*) right, exact; **lo ~** just enough; **¡~!** right!, exactly!

juvenil youthful; **juventud** *f* youth

K

kárate *m* karate; **karateca** *m/f* karate expert

kilo *m* kilo; *fig* F million; **kilobyte** *m* kilobyte; **kilogramo** *m* kilogram, *Br* kilogramme; **kilómetro** *m* kilometer, *Br* kilometre; **kilovatio** *m* kilowatt

kiosco *m* kiosk

kiwi *m* BOT kiwi (fruit)

L

la 1 *art* the; **~ que está embarazada** the one who is the pregnant; **~ más grande** the biggest (one); **dame ~ roja** give me the red one **2** *pron complemento directo sg* her; *a usted* you; *algo* it

laberinto *m* labyrinth, maze

labia *f*: **tener mucha ~** have the gift of the gab; **labio** *m* lip

labor *f* work; (*tarea*) task, job; **hacer ~es** do needlework; **no estar por la ~** F not be enthusiastic about the idea; **laborable:** *día* ~ workday; **laboral** labor *atr*, *Br* labour *atr*; **laboratorio** *m* laboratory, lab F; **labrador** *m* farm worker; **labrar** *tierra* work; *piedra* carve

laca *f* lacquer; **~ de uñas** nail varnish o polish

lactante *madre* nursing; *bebé* being breastfed

lactosa *f* lactose; **sin ~** lactose-free; **intolerancia** *f* **a la ~** MED lactose intolerance

ladera *f* slope

lado *m* side; (*lugar*) place; **al ~** nearby; **al ~ de** beside, next to; **de ~** sideways; **ir por otro ~** go another way; **por un ~...** **por otro ~** on the one hand ... on the other hand

ladrar bark

ladrillo *m* brick

ladrón *m* thief

lagartija *f* ZO small lizard; **lagarto** *m* ZO lizard

lago *m* lake

lágrima *f* tear

laguna *f* lagoon; *fig* gap

laico lay *atr*

lamentable deplorable; **lamentablemente** regrettably; **lamentar** regret, be sorry about; *muerte* mourn; **lamentarse** complain (*de* about); **lamento** *m* whimper; *por dolor* groan

lamer lick

lámina *f* sheet

lámpara *f* lamp; ~ *de pie* floor lamp

lana *f* wool; *Méx P* dough F

lance *m* incident, episode; *de* ~ secondhand

lancha *f* launch; ~ *fueraborda* outboard

langosta *f insecto* locust; *crustáceo* spiny lobster; **langostino** *m* king prawn

lánguido languid

lanzamiento *m* MIL, COM launch; ~ *de disco* / *de martillo* discus / hammer (throw); ~ *de peso* shot put; **lanzar** throw; *cohete*, *producto* launch; *bomba* drop; **lanzarse** throw o.s. (*en* into); (*precipitarse*) pounce (*sobre* on)

lápiz *m* pencil; ~ *de ojos* eyeliner; ~ *labial* o *de labios* lipstick

largarse F clear off F; **largo 1** *adj* long; *persona* tall; *a la* ~*a* in the long run; *a lo* ~ *del día* throughout the day; *a lo* ~ *de la calle* along the street; *¡*~*!* scram! F; *pasar de* ~ go (straight) past **2** *m* length; **largometraje** *m* feature film

laringe *f* larynx

las 1 *art fpl* **la 2** *pron complemento directo pl* **las** ~ *ustedes* you; *llévate* ~ *que quieras* take the ones o those you want; ~ *de...* those of ...; ~ *de Juan* Juan's

lascivo lewd

láser *m* laser; *rayo* ~ laser beam

lástima *f* pity, shame; **lastimarse** hurt o.s.

lastre *m* ballast; *fig* burden

lata *f* can, *Br tb* tin; *fig* F drag F; *dar la* ~ F be a drag F

lateral 1 *adj tb atr* **2** *m* DEP: ~ *derecho* / *izquierdo* right / left back

latido *m* beat

latifundio *m* large estate

látigo *m* whip

latín *m* Latin; **latino** Latin; **Latinoamérica** Latin America; **latinoamericano 1** *adj* Latin American **2** *m*, *-a f* Latin American

latir beat

latitud *f* latitude

latón *m* brass

laurel *m* BOT laurel; *dormirse en los* ~*es* *fig* rest on one's laurels

lavable washable; **lavabo** *m* washbowl; **lavado** *m* washing; ~ *de cerebro* *fig* brainwashing; **lavadora** *f* washing machine; **lavandería** *f* laundry; **lavaplatos** *m inv* dishwasher; *L.Am.* (*fregadero*) sink; **lavar 1** *v/t* wash; ~ *los platos* wash the dishes; ~ *la ropa* do the laundry;

en seco dry-clean **2** *v/i* (*lavar los platos*) do the dishes; **de detergente** clean; **lavarse wash up,** *Br* have a wash; **~ los dientes** brush one's teeth; (*a ella*) (to) her; (*a usted*) wash one's hands; **lavativa** *f* MED enema; **lavavajillas** *m inv* liquido dishwashing liquid, *Br* washing-up liquid; **electrodoméstico** dishwasher

laxante *m/adj* MED laxative

lazo *m* knot; **de adorno** bow; **para atrapar animales** lasso

le *complemento indirecto* (to) him; (*a ella*) (to) her; (*a usted*) (to) you; (*a algo*) (to) it; *complemento directo* him; (*a usted*) you

leal loyal; **lealtad** *f* loyalty

lección *f* lesson

leche *f* milk; **lechería** *f* dairy; **lechero 1** *adj* dairy *atr* **2** *m* milkman

lecho *m* **tb de río** bed

lechón *m* suckling pig

lechuga *f* lettuce

lechuza *f* ZO barn-owl; *Cuba, Méx* P hooker F

lector *m*, **~a** *f* reader; **lector de libros electrónicos** IT e-book reader; **lectura** *f* reading

leer read

legación *f* legation

legal legal; *fig* F *persona* great F; **legalidad** *f* legality; **legalizar** legalize

legar leave

legendario legendary

legislación *f* legislation; legislar legislate; **legislativo** legislative

legitimar justify; *documento* authenticate; **legítimo** legitimate; (*verdadero*) authentic

lego lay *atr*; *fig* ignorant

legua *f*: **se ve a la ~** *fig* F you can see it a mile off F; *hecho* it's blindingly obvious F

legumbre *f* BOT pulse

lejanía *f* distance; **en la ~** in the distance; **lejano** distant

lejía *f* bleach

lejos 1 *adv* far (away); **Navidad queda ~** Christmas is a long way off; **a lo ~** in the distance; **ir demasiado ~** *fig* go too far; **llegar ~** *fig* go far **2** *prp*: **~ de** far from

lema *m* slogan

lencería *f* lingerie

lengua *f* tongue; **~ materna** mother tongue; **irse de la ~** let the cat out of the bag; **lenguado** *m* ZO sole; **lenguaje** *m* language

lente *f* lens; **~s de contacto** contact lenses; **lentes** *mpl* L.Am. glasses

lenteja *f* BOT lentil

lentejuela *f* sequin

lentillas *fpl* contact lenses

lentitud *f* slowness; **lento** slow; **a fuego ~** on a low heat

leña *f* (fire)wood; **echar ~ al fuego** *fig* add fuel to the fire; **leñador** *m* woodcutter

Leo *m/f inv* ASTR Leo

león *m* lion; *L.Am.* puma; **~ marino** sealion

leopardo *m* leopard

leotardo

leotardo *m de gimnasta* leotard; **~s** tights, *Br* heavy tights

lerdo (*torpe*) slow(-witted)

les *pl complemento indirecto* (to) them; (*a ustedes*) (to) you; *complemento directo* them; (*a ustedes*) you

lesbiana *f* lesbian

lesión *f* injury; **lesionar** injure

letal lethal

letón 1 *adj* Latvian **2** *m*, **-ona** *f* Latvian **3** *m idioma* Latvian; **Letonia** *f* Latvia

letra *f* letter; *de canción* lyrics *pl*; **~ de imprenta** block capital; **~ mayúscula** capital letter; **al pie de la ~** word for word; **letrado 1** *adj* learned **2** *m*, **-a** *f* lawyer

letrero *m* sign

levadura *f* yeast

levantamiento *m* raising; (*rebelión*) rising; *de embargo* lifting; **levantar** raise; *bulto* lift (up); *del suelo* pick up; *edificio, estatua* put up; *embargo* lift; **~ sospechas** arouse suspicion; **¡levanta los ánimos!** cheer up!; **levantarse** get up; (*ponerse de pie*) stand up; *de un edificio, una montaña* rise; *en rebelión* rise up; **levante** *m* east

leve slight; *sonrisa* faint

léxico *m* lexicon

ley *f* law; **con todas las de la ~** fairly and squarely

leyenda *f* legend

liar tie (up); *en papel* wrap (up); *cigarrillo* roll; *persona* confuse

libanés 1 *adj* Lebanese **2** *m*, **-esa** *f* Lebanese; **Líbano** *m* Lebanon

liberación *f* release; *de un país* liberation; **liberal** liberal; **liberar** (set) free, release; *país* liberate; *energía* release; **libertad** *f* freedom, liberty; **~ bajo fianza** JUR bail; **~ condicional** JUR probation

libertinaje *m* licentiousness

Libia Libya; **libio 1** *adj* Libyan **2** *m*, **-a** *f* Libyan

libra *f* pound; **~ esterlina** pound (sterling)

Libra *m/f inv* ASTR Libra

librar 1 *v/t* free (*de* from); *cheque* draw; *batalla* fight **2** *v/i*: **libro los lunes** I have Mondays off; **libre** free; **librecambio** *m* free trade

librería *f* bookstore; **librero** *m* bookseller; *L.Am. mueble* bookcase; **libreta** *f* notebook; **~ de ahorros** bankbook, passbook; **libro** *m* book; **~ de bolsillo** paperback (book); **~ de cocina** cookbook; **~ de familia** *booklet recording family births, marriages and deaths*

licencia *f* permit, license, *Br* licence; (*permiso*) permission; MIL leave; **~ de manejar** *o* **conducir** *L.Am.* driver's license, *Br* driving licence; **tomarse demasiadas ~s** take liberties; licenciado *m*, -a *f* graduate; licenciar MIL discharge; licenciarse graduate; MIL be discharged; licenciatura *f* EDU degree

licitar *L.Am. en subasta* bid for

licor *m* liquor, *Br* spirits *pl*

licuadora *f* blender

líder 1 *m/f* leader 2 *adj* leading

lidia *f* bullfighting

liebre *f* hare

lienzo *m* canvas

liga *f* POL, DEP league; *de medias* garter; ligamento *m* ANAT ligament; ligar 1 *v/t* bind; (*atar*) tie 2 *v/i*: **~** F pick up F

ligero 1 *adj* light; (*rápido*) rapid; *movimiento* agile; (*leve*) slight; **~ de ropa** scantily clad; **a la -a** (*sin pensar*) lightly 2 *adv* quickly

ligue *m* F: **estar de ~** be on the pick-up F

liguero *m* garter belt, *Br* suspender belt

lija *f*: *papel de* **~** sandpaper

lila *f* BOT lilac

lima *f* file; BOT lime; **~ de uñas** nail file; limar file; *fig* polish

limitar 1 *v/t* limit 2 *v/i*: **~ con** border on; limitarse limit o.s. (*a* to); límite 1 *m* limit; (*línea de separación*) boundary; **~ de velocidad** speed limit 2 *adj*: *situación* **~**

life-threatening situation

limón *m* lemon; limonada *f* lemonade; limonero *m* lemon tree

limosna *f*: **una ~, por favor** can you spare some change?

limpiabotas *m/f inv* bootblack; limpiaparabrisas *m inv* windshield wiper, *Br* windscreen wiper; limpiar clean; *con un trapo* wipe; *fig* clean up; **~ a alguien** F clean s.o. out F; limpieza *f estado* cleanliness; *acto* cleaning; **~ general** spring cleaning; **~ en seco** dry-cleaning; limpio clean; (*ordenado*) neat, tidy; *político* honest; **quedarse ~** *S.Am.* F be broke F; **sacar algo en ~** *fig* make sense of sth

linaje *m* lineage

lince *m* ZO lynx

lindante adjacent (**con** to), bordering (**con** on); lindar: **~ con algo** adjoin sth; *fig* border on sth

lindo 1 *adj* lovely; **de lo ~** a lot, a great deal 2 *adv L.Am. jugar, bailar* beautifully

línea *f* line; **en ~** on line; **aérea** airline; **mantener la ~** watch one's figure; **de primera** *fig* first-rate; **tecnología de primera ~** cutting edge technology; **entre ~s** *fig* between the lines

lingüístico linguistic

lino *m* linen; BOT flax

linterna *f* flashlight, *Br* torch
lío *m* bundle; F (*desorden*) mess; F (*jaleo*) fuss; ~ **amoroso** F affair; **hacerse un** ~ get into a muddle
liposucción *f* liposuction
liquidación *f* COM de deuda settlement; de negocio liquidation; ~ **total** clearance sale; **liquidar** *cuenta, deuda* settle; COM *negocio* wind up, liquidate; *existencias* sell off; F (*matar*) liquidate F, bump off F; **líquido 1** *adj* liquid; COM net **2** *m* liquid
lira *f* lira
lírica *f* lyric poetry
lisiado 1 *adj* crippled **2** *m* cripple
liso smooth; *terreno* flat; *pelo* straight; (*sin adornos*) plain; **-a y llanamente** plainly and simply
lisonja *f* flattery; **lisonjear** flatter
lista *f* list; ~ **de boda** wedding list; ~ **de correos** general delivery, *Br* poste restante; ~ **de espera** waiting list; **listado** *m* INFOR printout; **listín** *m*: ~ (**telefónico**) phone book
listo (*inteligente*) clever; (*preparado*) ready
listón *m* de madera strip; DEP bar
litera *f* bunk; de tren couchette
literario literary; **literatura** *f* literature
litoral 1 *adj* coastal **2** *m* coast
litro *m* liter, *Br* litre

Lituania Lithuania; **lituano 1** *adj* Lithuanian **2** *m*, -a *f* Lithuanian **3** *m* idioma Lithuanian
liviano light; (*de poca importancia*) trivial
llaga *f* ulcer
llama *f* flame; ZO llama
llamada *f* call; *en una puerta* knock; *en timbre* ring; ~ **a cobro revertido** collect call; ~ **de auxilio** distress call; **llamamiento** *m* call; **hacer un** ~ **a algo** call for sth: **llamar** call; TELEC call, *Br tb* ring; ~ **a la puerta** knock at the door; *con timbre* ring the bell; **el fútbol no me llama nada** football doesn't appeal to me in the slightest; **llamarse** be called: **¿cómo te llamas?** what's your name?
llamativo eyecatching; *color* loud
llanito *m*, -a *f* F Gibraltarian
llano 1 *adj* terreno level; *trato* natural; *persona* unassuming **2** *m* flat ground
llanta *f* wheel rim; *C.Am., Méx* (*neumático*) tire, *Br* tyre
llanto *m* sobbing
llanura *f* plain
llave *f* key; *para tuerca* wrench, *Br tb* spanner; ~ **de contacto** AUTO ignition key; ~ **inglesa** TÉC monkey wrench; ~ **en mano** available for immediate occupancy; **bajo** ~ under lock and key; **cerrar con** ~ lock; **llave-**

ro *m* key ring

llegada *f* arrival; **llegar** arrive; *(alcanzar)* reach; *la comida no llegó para todos* there wasn't enough food for everyone; *me llega hasta las rodillas* it comes down to my knees; *~ a saber* find out; *~ a ser* get to be; *~ viejo* live to a ripe old age

llenar 1 *v/t* fill; *impreso* fill out o in 2 *v/i* be filling; **lleno** full (*de* of); *pared* covered (*de* with); *~ fully*

llevar 1 *v/t* take; *ropa, gafas* wear; *ritmo* keep up; *~ las de perder* be likely to lose; *me lleva dos años* he's two years older than me; *llevo ocho días aquí* I've been here a week 2 *v/i* lead (*a* to); *llevarse* take; *susto, sorpresa* get; *~ bien / mal* get on well / badly; *se lleva el color rojo* red is fashionable

llorar cry, weep

llover rain; *llueve* it is raining

llovizna *f* drizzle; **lloviznar** drizzle

lluvia *f* rain; *Rpl* (*ducha*) shower; **lluvioso** rainy

lo 1 *art* the; *no sabes ~ difícil que es* you don't know how difficult it is 2 *pron: a él* him; *a usted* you; *algo lo* 8; *~ sé* I know 3 *pron rel: ~ que* what; *~ cual* which

lobo *m* wolf; *~ marino* seal; *~ de mar* *fig* sea dog

local 1 *adj* local **2** *m* premises *pl*; **localidad** *f* town; *TEA*

seat; **localizar** locate; *incendio* contain

loción *f* lotion

loco *adj* mad, crazy; *a lo ~* F *(sin pensar)* hastily **2** *m* madman

locomoción *f* locomotion; *medio de ~* means of transport; **locomotora** *f* locomotive

locuaz talkative, loquacious *fml*

locura *f* madness

locutor *m*, *~a* *f* RAD, TV presenter

lodo *m* mud

lógica *f* logic; **lógico** logical

logrado excellent; **lograr** achieve; *(obtener)* obtain; *~ hacer algo* manage to do sth; **logro** *m* achievement

lombarda *f* BOT red cabbage

lomo *m* back; GASTR loin

lona *f* canvas

loncha *f* slice

Londres London

longaniza *f* type of dried sausage

longitud *f* longitude; *(largo)* length

lonja *f de pescado* fish market; *(loncha)* slice

loro *m* parrot

los 1 *art mpl* the **2** *pron complemento directo pl* them; *a ustedes* you; *llévate ~ que quieras* take the ones o those you want; *~ de...* those of ...; *~ de Juan* Juan's

losa *f* flagstone

lote *m en reparto* share, part;

L.Am. (*solar*) lot; **lotería** *f* lottery; **lotero** *m*, **-a** *f* lottery ticket seller

loza *f* china

lubina *f* ZO sea bass

lubri(fi)cante 1 *adj* lubricating **2** *m* lubricant; **lubri(fi)car** lubricate

lucha *f* fight, struggle; DEP wrestling; **~ libre** DEP all-in wrestling; **luchar** fight (*por* for)

lúcido lucid, clear

luciérnaga *f* ZO glowworm

lucir 1 *v/i* shine; L.Am. (*verse bien*) look good **2** *v/t* ropa, joya wear; **lucirse** *tb irónico* excel o.s.

lucrativo lucrative; **lucro** *m* profit; **sin ánimo de ~** not-for-profit

luego 1 *adv* (*después*) later; *en orden*, *espacio* then; L.Am. (*en seguida*) right now; L.Am. *Méx* straight away **2** *conj* therefore; **~ que** L.Am. since

lugar *m* place; **~ común** cliché; **en ~ de** instead of; **en primer ~** in the first place, first(ly); **fuera de ~** out of place; **yo en tu ~** if I were you, (if I were) in your place; **dar ~ a** give rise to; **tener ~** take place

lujo *m* luxury; **lujoso** luxurious

lumbago *m* MED lumbago; **lumbar** lumbar

lumbre *f* fire; **luminoso** luminous; *lámpara*, *habitación*

bright

luna *f* moon; *de tienda* window; *de vehículo* windshield, *Br* windscreen; **~ de miel** honeymoon; **~ llena / nueva** full / new moon; **media ~** L.Am. GASTR croissant; **lunar 1** *adj* lunar **2** *m en la piel* mole; **de ~es** spotted, polka-dot

lunes *m inv* Monday

luneta *f*: **~ térmica** AUTO heated windshield, *Br* heated windscreen

lupa *f* magnifying glass; **mirar algo con ~** fig go through sth with a fine-tooth comb

luso 1 *adj* Portuguese **2** *m*, **-a** *f* Portuguese

lustrar polish; **lustre** *m* shine; *fig* luster, *Br* lustre

luto *m* mourning; **estar de ~ por alguien** be in mourning for s.o.

Luxemburgo *m* Luxembo(u)rg; **luxemburgués 1** *adj* of / from Luxemb(o)urg, Luxemb(o)urg *atr* **2** *m*, **-guesa** *f* Luxemb(o)urger

luz *f* light; **~ trasera** AUTO rear light; **luces de carretera** *o* **largas** AUTO full *o* main beam headlights; **luces de cruce** *o* **cortas** AUTO dipped headlights; **~ verde** *tb fig* green light; **arrojar** *o* **sobre algo** *fig* shed light on s.th.; **dar a ~** give birth to; **salir a la ~** fig come to light; **a todas luces** evidently

M

macabro 1 *adj* macabre **2** *m*, **-a** *f* ghoul

macarrones *mpl* macaroni *sg*

macedonia *f*: **~ de frutas** fruit salad

maceta *f* flowerpot

machacar crush; *fig* thrash

machete *m* machete

machismo *m* male chauvinism; **machista 1** *adj* sexist **2** *m* sexist, male chauvinist

macho 1 *adj* male; (*varonil*) tough; *desp* macho **2** *m* male; *apelativo* F man F, *L.Am.* (*plátano*) banana

macizo 1 *adj* solid **2** *m* GEOG massif; *Macizo de Brasil* Brazilian Highlands; **~ de flores** flower bed

madeja *f* hank

madera *f* wood; **tener ~ de** have the makings of; **madero** *m* P cop P

madrastra *f* step-mother

madre 1 *f* mother; **~ soltera** single mother **2** *adj* Méx, C.Am. F great F

madrileño 1 *adj* of / from Madrid; Madrid *atr* **2** *m*, **-a** *f* native of Madrid

madrina *f* godmother

madrugada *f* early morning; (*amanecer*) dawn; **de ~** in the small hours; **madrugador** *m*, **-a** *f* early riser; **madrugar** *L.Am.* (*quedar despierto*) stay up till the small

hours; (*levantarse temprano*) get up early

madurar 1 *v/t fig*: *idea* think through **2** *v/i de persona* mature; *de fruta* ripen; **madurez** *f* mental maturity; *edad* middle age; *de fruta* ripeness; **maduro** *mentalmente* mature; *de edad* middle-aged; *fruta* ripe

maestría *f* mastery; *Méx* EDU master's (degree); **maestro 1** *adj* master *atr* **2** *m*, **-a** *f* EDU teacher; MÚS maestro

magia *f tb fig* magic; **mágico** magic

magistrado *m* judge; **magistral** masterly

magnético magnetic

magnetofón *m* tape recorder; **magnetoscopio** *m* VCR, video (cassette recorder)

magnífico magnificent

magnitud *f* magnitude

mago *m tb fig* magician; *los Reyes Magos* the Three Wise Men

magro *carne* lean

magulladura *f* bruise

mahometano 1 *adj* Muslim **2** *m*, **-a** *f* Muslim

maíz *m* corn

majadero F **1** *adj* idiotic, stupid **2** *m* F idiot

majestad *f* majesty; **majestuoso** majestic

majo F nice; (*bonito*) pretty

mal 1 *adj* ☞ **malo 2** *adv* badly; **~ que bien** one way or the other; **¡menos ~!** thank goodness!; **ponerse a ~ con alguien** fall out with s.o.; **tomarse algo a ~** take sth badly **3** *m* MED illness; **el ~ menor** the lesser of two evils

malaria *f* MED malaria

malcriado spoilt

maldad *f* evil

maldecir curse; **maldición** *f* curse; **maldito** F damn F; **¡a ~ sea!** (god)damn it!

maleante *m/f & adj* criminal

malecón *m* breakwater

maleducado rude, bad-mannered

malentendido *m* misunderstanding

malestar *m* MED discomfort; *social* unrest

maleta *f* bag, suitcase; *L.Am.* AUTO trunk, *Br* boot; **hacer la ~** pack one's bags; **maletero** *m* trunk, *Br* boot; **maletín** *m* briefcase

maleza *f* undergrowth

malformación *f* malformation

malgastar waste

malhechor *m*, **~a** *f* criminal

malhumorado bad-tempered

malicia *f* (*mala intención*) malice; (*astucia*) cunning; **no tener ~** F be very naive; **malicioso** (*malintencionado*) malicious; (*astuto*) cunning, sly

maligno harmful; MED malignant

malintencionado malicious

malla *f* mesh; *Rpl* (*bañador*) swimsuit

Mallorca *f* Majorca; **mallorquín 1** *adj* Majorcan **2** *m*, **-quina** *f* Majorcan

malo 1 *adj* bad; *calidad* poor; (*enfermo*) sick, ill; **por las buenas** *o* **por las -as** like it or not; **por las -as** by force; **ponerse ~** fall ill **2** *m* bad guy, baddy F

malogrado *muerto* dead before one's time; **malograrse** fail; *de plan* come to nothing; *fallecer* die before one's time; *S.Am.* (*descomponerse*) break down; (*funcionar mal*) go wrong

maloliente stinking

malparado: salir ~ de algo come out badly from sth

malta *f* malt

maltratar mistreat

maltrecho weakened; *cosa* damaged

malvado evil

malversación *f:* **~ de fondos** embezzlement

Malvinas: las ~ the Falklands, the Falkland Islands

mama *f* breast

mamá *f* mom, *Br* mum

mamar suck; **dar de ~** (breast)feed

mamífero *m* mammal

mampara *f* screen

manada *f* herd; *de lobos* pack

manantial *m* spring

manar flow

mancha *f* (*dirty*) mark; *de grasa, sangre etc* stain; **manchar**

get dirty; *de grasa, sangre etc* stain

Mancha: Canal de la ~ English Channel; **la ~** La Mancha

manco *de mano* one-handed; *de brazo* one-armed

mandamás *m inv* F big shot F

mandar *v/t* order; *(enviar)* send; **~ hacer algo** have sth done **2** *v/i* be in charge; **¿mande?** *Méx* can I help you?; *Méx* TELEC hallo?; *(¿cómo?)* what did you say?

mandarina *f* mandarin (orange)

mandato *m* order; POL mandate

mandíbula *f* ANAT jaw

mandil *m* leather apron

mando *m* command; **~ a distancia** TV remote control; **tablero de ~s** AUTO dashboard; **mandón** F bossy F

manecilla *f* hand

manejar *v/t* handle; *máquina* operate; *L.Am.* AUTO drive **2** *v/i L.Am.* AUTO drive; **manejo** *m* handling; *de una máquina* operation

manera *f* way; **~s** manners; **lo hace a su ~** he does it his way; **de ~ que** so (that); **de ninguna ~** certainly not; **no hay ~ de** it is impossible to; **de todas ~s** anyway

manga *f* sleeve; **~ de riego** hosepipe; **en ~s de camisa** in one's shirtsleeves; **traer algo en la ~** F have sth up one's sleeve

mangar P pinch F

mango *m* BOT mango; *CSur* F *(dinero)* dough F; **estoy sin un ~** *CSur* F I'm broke F, I don't have a bean F

manguera *f* hose(pipe)

manguito *m* TÉC sleeve; **~s para nadar** armbands

maní *m S.Am.* peanut

manía *f (costumbre)* habit; *(antipatía)* dislike; *(obsesión)* obsession; **tiene sus ~s** she has her little ways

manicomio *m* lunatic asylum

manicura *f* manicure

manifestación *f de gente* demonstration; *(muestra)* show; *(declaración)* statement; **manifestante** *m/f* demonstrator; **manifestar** *(demostrar)* show; *(declarar)* declare, state; **manifestarse** demonstrate; **manifiesto 1** *adj* clear, manifest **2** *m* manifesto

manillar *m* handlebars *pl*

maniobra *f* maneuver, *Br* manoeuvre; **maniobrar** maneuver, *Br* manoeuvre

manipulación *f* manipulation; *(manejo)* handling; **manipular** manipulate; *(manejar)* handle

maniquí 1 *m* dummy **2** *m/f* model

manivela *f* handle

manjar *m* delicacy

mano 1 *f* hand; **~ de obra** manpower; **~ de pintura** coat of paint; **a ~ izquierda** on the lefthand side; **de se-**

gunda — second-hand; **echar una ~ a alguien** give s.o. a hand; **estar a ~s** L.Am. F be even; **traerse algo entre ~s** be plotting sth; **~s libres** hands-free 2 *m* Méx F buddy; manojo *m* handful; **~ de llaves** bunch of keys; **~ de nervios** *fig* bundle of nerves

manopla *f* mitten

manosear handle; *persona* F grope F

mansión *f* mansion

manso docile; *persona* mild

manta *f* blanket

manteca *f* fat; *Rpl* butter; **~ de cacao** cocoa butter; **~ de cerdo** lard; mantecado *m* type of cupcake, *traditionally eaten at Christmas*

mantel *m* tablecloth; **~ individual** table mat; mantelería *f* table linen

mantener (*sujetar*) hold; *techo etc* hold up; (*preservar*) keep; *conversación, relación* have; *económicamente* support; (*afirmar*) maintain; mantenerse (*sujetarse*) be held; *económicamente* support o.s.; *en forma* keep; mantenimiento *m* maintenance; *económico* support; **gimnasia de ~** gymnasium

mantequilla *f* butter

mantilla *f* de bebé shawl

manto *m* GEOL layer, stratum; (*capa*) cloak; **un ~ de nieve** a blanket of snow

mantón *m* shawl

manual *m*/adj manual; manualidades *fpl* handicrafts

manuscrito 1 *adj* handwritten 2 *m* manuscript

manutención *f* maintenance

manzana *f* apple; *de casas* block; manzanilla *f* camomile tea; manzano *m* apple tree

maña *f* skill

mañana 1 *f* morning; **por la ~** in the morning; **por la ~** tomorrow morning; **de la ~ a la noche** from morning until night; **de la noche a la ~** *fig* overnight 2 *adv* tomorrow; **~ pasado** the day after tomorrow

mapa *m* map; **~ de carreteras** road map

maqueta *f* model

maquillaje *m* make-up; maquillar make up; maquillarse put on one's make-up

máquina *f* machine; FERR locomotive; CAm., W.I. AUTO car; **~ de afeitar** (electric) shaver; **~ de coser** sewing machine; **~ de fotos** camera; **~ recreativa** arcade game; **~ de respiración asistida** life support machine; **a toda ~** at top speed; maquinaciones *fpl* scheming; maquinador 1 *adj* scheming 2 *m*, **~a** *f* schemer; maquinal *fig* mechanical; maquinar plot; maquinaria *f* machinery; maquinilla *f*: **~ de afeitar** razor; **~ eléctrica** electric razor; maquinista *m*/f FERR engineer, *Br* train driver

mar *m* (*also f*) sea; **llover a ~es** *fig* **F** pour, bucket down F; **alta ~** high seas *pl*; **Mar Bermejo** Gulf of California; **mar Caribe** Caribbean Sea

maraña *f* de hilos tangle; (*lío*) jumble

maravilla *f* marvel, wonder; BOT marigold; **a las mil ~s** marvelously, *Br* marvellously; **maravillarse** be amazed (**de** at); **maravilloso** marvelous, *Br* marvellous

marca *f* mark; COM brand; **~ registrada** registered trademark; **de ~** brand-name *atr*; **marcador** *m* DEP (*resultado*) score; (*tablero*) scoreboard; **marcapasos** *m inv* MED pacemaker; **marcar** mark; *número de teléfono* dial; *gol* score; *res* brand; *de termómetro, contador etc* read, register

marcha *f* (*salida*) departure; (*velocidad*) speed; (*avance*) progress; MIL march; AUTO gear; **~ atrás** AUTO reverse (gear); **a ~s forzadas** *fig* flat out; **a toda ~** at top speed; **ponerse en ~** get going; **marchante** *m L.Am.* regular customer; **marchar** (*progresar*) go; (*funcionar*) work; (*caminar*) walk; MIL march; **marcharse** leave, go

marchitar wilt; **marchito** *flor* withered; *juventud* faded

marco *m* de cuadro, puerta frame; *fig* framework

marea *f* tide; **~ alta** high tide; **~ baja** low tide; **~ negra** oil slick; **marearse** feel nauseous, *Br* feel sick; **marejada** *f* heavy sea; **mareo** *m* seasickness

marfil *m* ivory

margarina *f* margarine

margarita *f* BOT daisy

margen *m tb fig* margin; **al ~ de eso** apart from that; **marginal** marginal

maricón *m* P fag P, *Br* poof P; **mariconera** *f* man's handbag

marido *m* husband

marina *f* navy; **~ mercante** merchant navy

marinero *1 adj* sea *atr* **2** *m* sailor; **marino** **1** *adj* brisa sea *atr*; *planta, animal* marine; **azul ~** navy blue **2** *m* sailor

marioneta *f tb fig* puppet

mariposa *f* butterfly

mariquita *f* ladybug, *Br* ladybird

marisco *m* seafood

marítimo *adj* maritime

marmita *f* pot, pan

mármol *m* marble

marqués *m* marquis; **marquesa** *f* marchioness

marquesina *f* marquee, *Br* canopy

marrano **1** *adj* filthy **2** *m* hog, *Br* pig; F *persona* pig F

marrón *m adj* brown

marroquí *m/f & adj* Moroccan; **Marruecos** Morocco

marta *f* ZO marten

martes m inv Tuesday

martillar hammer; **martillo** m hammer; ~ **neumático** pneumatic drill

mártir m/f martyr; **martirio** m tb fig martyrdom; **martirizar** tb fig martyr

marzo m March

más 1 adj more 2 adv more; *superlativo* most; MAT plus; ~ **grande** bigger; ~ **importante** more important; **el** ~ **grande** the biggest; **el** ~ **importante** the most important; **trabajar** ~ work harder; ~ **bien** rather; **¿qué** ~**?** what else?; **no** ~ *L.Am.* ☞ **nomás**; **por** ~ **que** however much; **sin** ~ without more ado

mas conj but

masa f mass; GASTR dough

masacre f massacre

masaje m massage; **masajista** m/f masseur; **mujer** masseuse

mascar v/t chew **2** v/i *L.Am.* chew tobacco

máscara f mask; **mascarilla** f mask; *cosmética* face pack

mascota f mascot; *animal doméstico* pet

masculino masculine

masivo massive

masón m mason

masoquismo m masochism; **masoquista 1** adj masochistic **2** m/f masochist

máster m master's (degree)

masticar chew

mástil m mast; **de tienda** pole

mata f bush

matadero m slaughterhouse; **matanza** f slaughter; **matar** kill; *ganado* slaughter; **matarse** kill o.s.; *morir* be killed

matasellos m inv postmark

mate 1 adj matt **2** m en ajedrez mate; *L.Am.* (infusión) maté

matemáticas fpl mathematics, math, Br maths; **matemático 1** adj mathematical **2** m, -a f mathematician

materia f matter; (*material*) material; (*tema*) subject; ~ **prima** raw material; **en** ~ **de** as regards; **material** m/adj material

maternal maternal; **maternidad** f maternity; **casa de** ~ maternity hospital; **materno:** **por parte** -a on one's mother's side, maternal

matinal morning atr

matiz m *de ironía* touch; *de color* shade; **matizar** *comentarios* qualify

matón m bully; (*criminal*) thug

matorral m thicket

matrícula f AUTO license plate, Br numberplate; EDU registration; **matricular** register

matrimonial marriage atr, marital; **matrimonio** m marriage; *boda* wedding

matriz f matrix; ANAT womb

matutino morning atr

maxilar 1 adj maxillary **2** m jaw(bone)

máxima f maxim; **máximo** maximum

mayo *m* May

mayonesa *f* mayonnaise

mayor ◇ *comparativo*: *en tamaño* larger, bigger; *en edad* older; *en importancia* greater; *ser* ~ *de edad* be an adult; JUR be of legal age; *al por* ~ COM wholesale ◇ *superlativo*: *el* ~ *en edad* the oldest, the eldest; *en tamaño* the largest, the biggest; *en importancia* the greatest; *los* ~*es* adults; *la* ~ *parte* the majority; **mayoría** *f* majority; *alcanzar la* ~ *de edad* come of age; *la* ~ *de* the majority, most (of); **mayorista** *m/f* wholesaler

mayúscula *f* capital (letter), upper case letter

maza *f* mace

mazapán *m* marzipan

mazorca *f* cob

me *complemento directo* me; *complemento indirecto* (to) me; *reflexivo* myself

mear F pee F

mecánica *f* mechanics; **mecánico 1** *adj* mechanical **2** *m*, -**a** *f* mechanic; **mecanismo** *m* mechanism; **mecanizar** mechanize

mecanografía *f* typing; **mecanógrafo** *m*, -**a** *f* typist

mecedora *f* rocking chair

mecenas *m inv* patron, sponsor

mecer, **mercerse** rock

mecha *f* wick; *de explosivo* fuse; *del pelo* highlight; *Méx* F fear; **mechero** *m* cig-

arette lighter; **mechón** *m de pelo* lock

medalla *f* medal; **medallista** *m/f* medalist, *Br* medallist

media *f* stocking; ~**s** pantyhose *pl*, *Br* tights *pl*

mediación *f* mediation; **mediado**: *a* ~**s** *de junio* in mid-June; **mediador** *m*, -**a** *f* mediator; **mediana** *f* AUTO median strip, *Br* central reservation; **mediano** medium, average; **medianoche** *f* midnight; **mediante** by means of; **mediar** mediate

mediático media *atr*

medicamento *m* medicine, drug; **medicina** *f* medicine; **medicinal** medicinal; **médico 1** *adj* medical **2** *m/f* doctor; ~ *de cabecera o de familia* family doctor; ~ *de urgencia* emergency doctor

medida *f* measure; (*grado*) extent; *hecho a* ~ made to measure; *a* ~ *que* as

medieval medieval

medio 1 *adj* half; *tamaño* medium; (*de promedio*) average; *las tres y* -*a* half past three, three-thirty **2** *m* environment; (*centro*) middle; (*manera*) means; ~ *ambiente* environment; *por* ~ *de* by means of; *en* ~ *de* in the middle of; ~**s** *dinero* means; ~**s** *de comunicación o de información* (mass) media **3** *adv* half; *hacer algo a* -*as* half do sth; *ir a* -*as* go halves; **día por ~** *L.Am.* every other day

medioambiental environmental

mediocre mediocre

mediodía *m* midday

medir 1 *v/t* measure **2** *v/i:* **mide 2 metros de ancho / alto** it's 2 meters wide / high

meditación *f* meditation; **meditar 1** *v/t* ponder **2** *v/i* meditate

médula *f* marrow; **~ espinal** spinal cord

medusa *f* ZO jellyfish

mejicano 1 *adj* Mexican **2** *m*, **-a** *f* Mexican; **Méjico** *país* Mexico; **Méx DF** Mexico City

mejilla *f* cheek

mejillón *m* ZO mussel

mejor better; **el ~** the best; **lo ~** the best thing; **lo ~ posible** as well as possible; **a lo ~** perhaps; **mejora** *f* improvement

mejorana *f* BOT marjoram

mejorar improve; **¡que te mejores!** get well soon!; **mejoría** *f* improvement

melena *f* long hair; *de león* mane

mellizo 1 *adj* twin *atr* **2** *m*, **-a** *f* twin

melocotón *m* peach

melón *m* melon

meloso F sickly sweet

membrana *f* membrane

membrete *m* heading, letterhead; **papel con ~** letterhead, headed paper

membrillo *m* quince; **dulce de ~** quince jelly

memorable memorable

memoria *f tb* INFOR memory; *(informe)* report; **de ~** by heart; **~s** *(biografía)* memoirs; **memorizar** memorize

mención *f:* **hacer ~ de** mention; **mencionar** mention

mendigar beg for; **mendigo** *m* beggar

menear shake; *las caderas* sway; **~ la cola** wag its tail

menester *m (trabajo)* job; **~es** *F* tools, gear; **ser ~ (necesario)** be necessary

menguante decreasing; *luna* waning; **menguar** decrease; *de la luna* wane

meningitis *f* MED meningitis

menopausia *f* menopause

menor smaller; *en tamaño* smaller; *en edad* younger; **ser ~ de edad** be a minor; **al por ~** COM retail; **el ~** *en tamaño* the smallest; *en edad* the youngest

Menorca *f* Minorca; **menorquín 1** *adj* Minorcan **2** *m*, **-quina** *f* Minorcan

menos 1 *adj en cantidad* less; *en número* fewer **2** *adv comparativo en cantidad* less; *superlativo en cantidad* least: MAT minus; **es ~ guapa que Ana** she is not as pretty as Ana; **a ~ que** unless; **al ~**, **por lo ~** at least; **echar de ~** miss; **ni mucho ~** far from it; **son las dos ~ diez** it's ten of two, it's ten to two

menospreciar underestimate; (desdeñar) look down on; **menosprecio** m contempt

mensaje m message; ~ **de texto** text (message); **mensajero** m courrier

menstruación f menstruation

mensual monthly; **mensualidad** f monthly payment

menta f BOT mint

mental mental; **mentalidad** f mentality; **mente** f mind

mentar mention

mentir lie; **mentira** f lie; **mentiroso 1** adj: **ser muy** ~ tell a lot of lies **2** m, -a f liar

menú m tb INFOR menu; ~ **de ayuda** help menu

menudeo m L.Am. retail trade; **menudo 1** adj small; **¡-a suerte!** fig F lucky devil!; **a** ~ often **2** m L.Am. small change; **~s** GASTR giblets

meñique m/adj: (**dedo**) ~ little finger

meollo m fig heart

mercadería f L.Am. merchandise; **mercado** m market; **Mercado Común** Common Market; ~ **negro** black market; **mercancía** f merchandise; **mercantil** commercial

mercenario m/adj mercenary

mercería f notions pl, Br haberdashery

mercurio m mercury

merecer deserve; **no** ~ **la pena** it's not worth it

merendar have an afternoon snack

merengue m GASTR meringue

meridiano m/f meridian; **meridional 1** adj southern **2** m southerner

merienda f afternoon snack

mérito m merit

merluza f ZO hake

merma f reduction, decrease; **mermar 1** v/t reduce **2** v/i diminish

mermelada f jam

mero 1 adj mere; **el** ~ **jefe** Méx F the big boss **2** m ZO grouper

mes m month

mesa f table; **poner / quitar la** ~ set / clear the table; **meseta** f plateau; **mesilla**, **mesita** f: (**de noche**) night stand, Br bedside table

mesón m traditional rustic-style restaurant

mestizo m person of mixed race

mesura f: **con** ~ in moderation; **mesurado** moderate

meta f en fútbol goal; en carrera finish line; fig (objetivo) goal, objective

metabolismo m metabolism

metal m metal; **metálico 1** adj metallic **2** m: **en** ~ (in) cash

meteorología f meteorology; **meteorológico** weather atr, meteorological

meter put; (involucrar) involve; **meterse**: ~ **en algo** get into sth; (involucrarse) get involved in sth; **~ con alguien** pick on s.o.; **¿dónde se ha metido?** where has he got to?

meticuloso meticulous

metódico methodical; **método** m method

metro m *medida* meter, Br metre; *para medir* rule; *transporte* subway, Br underground

metrópolis f inv metropolis; **metropolitano** metropolitan

mexicano 1 adj Mexican **2** m, -a Mexican; **México** *país* Mexico; **Méx DF** Mexico City

mezcla f *sustancia* mixture; *de tabaco, café etc* blend; *acto* mixing; *de tabaco, café etc* blending; **mezclar** mix; *tabaco, café etc* blend; **~ a alguien en algo** get s.o. mixed up in sth; **mezclarse** mix; **~ en algo** get mixed up in sth

mezquino mean

mezquita f mosque

mí me; *reflexivo* myself

mi, mis my

microbio m microbe; **microbús** m minibus; **microchip** m (micro)chip; **microfilm(e)** m microfilm; **micrófono** m microphone; **~ oculto** bug; **microondas** m inv microwave; **microprocesador** m microprocessor; **microscopio** m microscope

miedo m fear (**a** of); **dar ~** be frightening; **me da ~ la os-** **curidad** I'm frightened of the dark; **tener ~ de que** be afraid that; **de ~** F awesome F; **miedoso** timid; **¡no seas tan ~!** don't be scared!

miel f honey

miembro m member; ANAT limb

mientras 1 conj while; **~ que** whereas **2** adv: **~ tanto** in the meantime

miércoles m inv Wednesday

mierda f P shit P, crap P; **una ~ de película** a crap movie P

miga f *de pan* crumb; **hacer buenas / malas ~s** fig F get on well / badly

migración f migration

milagro m miracle; **milagroso** miraculous

milicia f militia

milímetro m millimeter, Br millimetre

militar 1 adj military **2** m soldier; **los ~es** the military **3** v/i POL: **~ en** be a member of

milla f mile

millar m thousand

millón m million; **mil millones** billion; **millonario** m millionaire

mimar spoil, pamper

mímica f mime

mina f MIN mine; *Rpl* F broad F, *Br* bird F; **minar** mine; fig undermine

mineral m/adj mineral; **minería** f mining; **minero 1** adj mining **2** m miner

minifalda f miniskirt

minimizar minimize; **mínimo** *m/adj* minimum

ministerio *m* POL department; **~ de Asuntos Exteriores**, L.Am. **~ de Relaciones Exteriores** State Department, *Br* Foreign Office; **~ de Hacienda** Treasury Department, *Br* Treasury; **~ del Interior** Department of the Interior, *Br* Home Office; **ministro** *m*, **-a** *f* minister; **~ del Interior** Secretary of the Interior, *Br* Home Secretary; **primer ~** Prime Minister

minoría *f* minority

minorista COM **1** *adj* retail *atr* **2** *m/f* retailer

minuciosidad *f* attention to detail; **minucioso** meticulous, thorough

minúscula *f* small letter, lower case letter; **minúsculo** tiny, minute

minusválido 1 *adj* disabled **2** *m*, **-a** *f* disabled person; **los ~s** the disabled

minuta *f* GASTR menu; (*cuenta de los honorarios*) bill

minuto *m* minute

mío, mía mine; **el ~ / la ~** mine

miope short-sighted; **miopía** *f* short-sightedness

mirada *f* look; **echar una ~** take a look (**a** at); **mirador** *m* viewpoint; **mirar 1** *v/t* look at; (*observar*) watch; L.Am. (*ver*) see **2** *v/i* look; **~ por la ventana** look out of the window

mirlo *m* ZO blackbird

misa *f* REL mass

misal *m* missal

miserable wretched; **miseria** *f* poverty; *fig* misery; **misericordia** *f* mercy; **mísero** wretched; **sueldo** miserable

misil *m* missile

misión *f* mission; **misionero** *m*, **-a** *f* missionary

mismo 1 *adj* same; **yo ~** I myself; **me da lo ~** it's all the same to me **2** *adv*: **aquí ~** right here; **ahora ~** right now

misterio *m* mystery; **misterioso** mysterious

mística *f* mysticism; **místico** mystic(al)

mitad *f* half; **a ~ del camino** halfway; **a ~ de la película** halfway through the movie; **a ~ de precio** half-price

mitigar mitigate; **ansiedad, dolor** *etc* ease

mitin *m* POL meeting

mito *m* myth; **mitología** *f* mythology

mixto mixed; **comisión** joint

mobiliario *m* furniture

mocedad *f* youth

mochila *f* backpack; IT dongle; **mochilero** *m*, **-a** *f* backpacker

moción *f* POL motion

moco *m*: **tener ~s** have a runny nose; **mocoso** *m*, **-a** *f* F snotty-nosed kid F

moda *f* fashion; **de ~** in fashion; **estar pasado de ~** be out of fashion

modales *mpl* manners

modalidad *f* form; DEP discipline; **~ de pago** method of payment

modelar model; **modelo 1** *m* model **2** *m/f persona* model

moderación *f* moderation; **moderador** *m*, **~a** *f* TV presenter; **moderar** moderate; *impulsos* control; *velocidad, gastos* reduce; *debate* chair

modernización *f* modernization; **modernizar** modernize; **moderno** modern

modestia *f* modesty; **modesto** modest

módico *precio* reasonable

modificar modify

modismo *m* idiom

modista *m/f* dressmaker; *diseñador* fashion designer

modo *m* way; **a ~ de** as; **de ~ que** so that; **de ningún ~** not at all; **en cierto ~** in a way; **de todos ~s** anyway

mofa *f* mockery; **mofarse: ~ de** make fun of

moho *m* mold, *Br* mould; **mohoso** moldy, *Br* mouldy

mojado (*húmedo*) damp, moist; (*muy mojado*) wet; **mojar** (*humedecer*) dampen, moisten; (*empapar*) wet; *galleta* dunk, dip

mojón *m tb* fig milestone

molar P **1** *v/t*: **me mola ese tío** I like the guy a lot **2** *v/i* be cool F

molde *m* form; *Br* mould; *para bizcocho* (cake) tin; **romper ~s** fig break the mold;

moldeado *m* molding; *Br* moulding; **moldear** mold; *Br* mould; **moldura** *f* ARQUI molding; *Br* moulding

molécula *f* molecule

moler grind; *fruta* mash; **carne molida** ground meat, *Br* mince

molestar bother, annoy; (*doler*) trouble; **no ~** do not disturb; **molestarse** get upset; (*ofenderse*) take offense *o Br* offence; (*enojarse*) get annoyed; **~ en hacer algo** take the trouble to do sth; **molestia** *f* nuisance; **~s** MED discomfort; **molesto** annoying; (*incómodo*) inconvenient

molinillo *m*: **~ de café** coffee grinder *o* mill; **molino** *m* mill; **~ de viento** windmill

molleja *f de ave* gizzard; **~s** GASTR sweetbreads

molusco *m* ZO mollusk, *Br* mollusc

momentáneo momentary; **momento** *m* moment; **al ~** at once; **por el ~, de ~** for the moment

momia *f* mummy

monarca *m* monarch; **monarquía** *f* monarchy

monasterio *m* monastery

mondadientes *m inv* toothpick

mondar peel; *árbol* prune

moneda *f* coin; (*divisa*) currency; **monedero** *m* change purse, *Br* purse; **monetario** monetary

monitor¹ *m* TV, INFOR monitor

monitor[2] *m*, **~a** *f* (*profesor*) instructor

monja *f* nun; **monje** *m* monk

mono 1 *m* ZO monkey; *prenda* coveralls *pl*, *Br* boilersuit **2** *adj* pretty, cute; **monopatín** *m* skateboard; **monopolio** *m* monopoly; **monótono** monotonous

monovolumen *m* AUTO minivan, *Br* people carrier, MPV

monstruo *m* monster; (*fenómeno*) phenomenon; **monstruosidad** *f* monstrosity; **monstruoso** monstrous

montacargas *m inv* hoist

montador *m*, **~a** *f* TÉC fitter; *de película* editor; **montaje** *m* TÉC assembly; *de película* editing; TEA staging; *fig* F con F

montaña *f* mountain; **~ rusa** rollercoaster; **montañoso** mountainous

montar 1 *v/t* TÉC assemble; *tienda* put up; *negocio* set up; *película* edit; *caballo* mount; **~ la guardia** mount guard **2** *v/i*: **~ en bicicleta** ride a bicycle; **~ a caballo** ride a horse

monte *m* mountain; (*bosque*) woodland

montón *m* pile, heap; **montones de** F piles of F

montura *f de gafas* frame

monumental monumental; **monumento** *m* monument

monzón *m* monsoon

moño *m* bun

moqueta *f* (wall-to-wall) carpet

mora *f de zarza* blackberry; *de morera* mulberry

morado purple

moral 1 *adj* moral **2** *f* (*moralidad*) morals *pl*; (*ánimo*) morale; **moralidad** *f* morality

morboso perverted

morcilla *f* blood sausage, *Br* black pudding

mordaz biting; **morder** bite; **mordisco** *m* bite

moreno *pelo, piel* dark; (*bronceado*) tanned

morfina *f* morphine

morir die (**de** of); **morirse** die; **~ por** *fig* be dying for

morisco Moorish

moro 1 *adj* North African **2** *m*, **-a** *f* North African

moroso COM **1** *adj* slow to pay **2** *m*, **-a** *f* slow payer

mortal 1 *adj* mortal; *accidente, herida* fatal; *dosis* lethal **2** *m/f* mortal; **mortalidad** *f* mortality

mortero *m tb* MIL mortar

mortífero lethal

mosaico *m* mosaic

mosca *f* fly; **por si las ~s** F just to be on the safe side

Moscú Moscow

mosquearse F get hot under the collar F; (*sentir recelo*) smell a rat F

mosquitero *m* mosquito net; **mosquito** *m* mosquito

mostaza *f* mustard

mosto *m* grape juice

mostrador *m* counter; *en bar* bar; **~ de facturación** check-in desk; **mostrar** show

mote *m* nickname; MÚS, *S.Am.* boiled corn *o Br* maize

motín *m* mutiny; *en una cárcel* riot

motivar motivate; **motivo** *m* motive, reason; MÚS, PINT motif; **con ~ de** because of

moto *f* motorcycle, motorbike; **~ acuática o de agua** jet ski; **motocicleta** *f* motorcycle; **motociclista** *m/f* motorcyclist

motor *m* engine; *eléctrico* motor; **motora** *f* motorboat; **motorismo** *m* motorcycling; **motorista** *m/f* motorcyclist

motriz motor

mover move; (*agitar*) shake; (*impulsar, incitar*) drive; **movible** movable; *fig precio, opinión* fickle

móvil 1 *adj* mobile **2** *m* TELEC cell(phone), *Br* mobile (phone); **movilidad** *f* mobility; **movilizar** mobilize; **movimiento** *m* movement; COM, *fig* activity

moza *f* girl; *camarera* waitress; **mozo 1** *adj*: **en mis años ~s** in my youth **2** *m* boy; *camarero* waiter

muchacha *f* girl; **muchacho** *m* boy

muchedumbre *f* crowd

mucho 1 *adj cantidad* a lot of, lots of; *esp neg* much; **no tengo ~ dinero** I don't have much money; **~s** a lot of, lots

of, many; *esp neg* many; **no tengo ~s amigos** I don't have many friends; **tengo ~ frío** I am very cold; **es ~ coche para mí** it's too big a ca[...] for me **2** *adv* a lot; *esp neg* much; **no me gustó ~** I did[...]n't like it very much; **¿du ra / tarda ~?** does it last / take long?; **como ~** at the most; **ni ~ menos** far from it; **por ~ que** however much **3** *pron* a lot, much; **~s** a lot o[...] people, many people

mucosa *f* ANAT mucous membrane; **mucosidad** *f* mucus

muda *f de ropa* change o[...] clothes; **mudanza** *f de casa* move; **mudar** change; ZO[...] shed; **mudarse**: **~ de casa** move house; **~ de ropa** change (one's clothes)

mudo mute; *letra* silent

mueble *m* piece of furniture; **~s** furniture

mueca *f de dolor* grimace; **ha cer ~s** make faces

muela *f* tooth; ANAT molar; **~ del juicio** wisdom tooth

muelle *m* TÉC spring; MAR wharf

muerte *f* death; **muerto 1** *par* ***o morir* 2** *adj* dead **3** *m*, -a[...] dead person; **los ~s** the dead

muesca *f* notch, groove

muestra *f* sample; (*señal*) sign; (*exposición*) show

mugre *f* filth; **mugrient[...]** filthy

mujer *f* woman; (*esposa*) wife

mujeriego m womanizer

mula f ZO mule; *Méx (basura)* trash, *Br* rubbish

mulato m mulatto

muleta f crutch; TAUR cape

mulo m ZO mule

multa f fine; **multar** fine

multicine m multiplex; **multicolor** multicolored; *Br* multicoloured; **multicultural** multicultural; **multinacional** f multinational

múltiple multiple; **multiplicación** f multiplication; **multiplicar**, **multiplicarse** multiply; **múltiplo** m MAT multiple; **multisalas** m inv multiplex; **multitarea** f multitasking

multitud f crowd; **~ de** thousands of; **multitudinario** mass atr

multiuso multipurpose

mundial 1 adj world atr **2** m: **el ~ de fútbol** the World Cup; **mundo** m world; **todo el ~** everybody, everyone

munición f ammunition

municipal municipal; **municipio** m municipality

muñeca f doll; ANAT wrist; **muñeco** m doll; *fig* puppet; **~ de nieve** snowman

mural 1 adj wall atr **2** m mural; **muralla** f de ciudad wall

murciélago m ZO bat

murmurar murmur; *criticar* gossip

muro m wall

muscular muscular; **músculo** m muscle; **musculoso** muscular; **musculatura** f muscles pl

museo m museum; *de pintura* art gallery

musgo m BOT moss

música f music; **~ de fondo** background music; **musical** m/adj musical; **músico** m, **-a** f musician

muslo m thigh

mutación f BIO mutation; TEA scene change

mutilado m, **-a** f disabled person; **mutilar** mutilate

mutuo mutual

muy very; *(demasiado)* too; **~ valorado** highly valued

N

nabo m **1** adj Arg F dumb F **2** m turnip

nácar m mother-of-pearl

nacer be born; *de un huevo* hatch; *de una planta* sprout; *de un río, del sol* rise; *(surgir)* arise **(de** from); **nacido** born; **mal ~** wicked; **nacimiento** m birth; *de Navidad* crèche, nativity scene

nación f nation; **nacional** national; **nacionalidad** f nationality; **nacionalizar** COM nationalize; *persona* naturalize

nada 1 pron nothing; **no hay ~**

there isn't anything, there's nothing; ~ **más** nothing else; ~ **menos que** no less than; **¡de ~!** you're welcome, not at all; **no es** ~ it's nothing **2** *adv* not at all; **no ha llovido** ~ it hasn't rained at all **3** *f* nothingness

nadador *m*, **-a** *f* swimmer; **nadar** swim

nadie nobody, no-one; **no había** ~ there was nobody there, there wasn't anyone there

nado: atravesar a ~ swim across

naipe *m* (playing) card

nalga *f* buttock

naranja 1 *f* orange; **media** ~ F (*pareja*) other half **2** *adj* orange; **naranjo** *m* orange tree

narciso *m* BOT daffodil

narcótico *m*/*adj* narcotic; **narcotráfico** *m* drug trafficking

nariz *f* nose; **¡narices!** F nonsense!

narración *f* narration; **narrar:** ~ **algo** tell the story of sth

nasal nasal

nata *f* cream; ~ **montada** whipped cream

natación *f* swimming

natal native; **natalidad** *f* birthrate

natillas *fpl* custard

nativo *m*, **-a** *f* native

natural *adj* natural; **ser** ~ **de** come from| **2** *m*: **fruta al** ~ fruit in its own juice; **naturaleza** *f* nature; **naturalidad** *f*

naturalness; **naturalizar** naturalize; **naturalizarse** become naturalized; **naturalmente** naturally; **naturista 1** *adj* nudist, naturist; **medicina** natural **2** *m*/*f* nudist, naturist

naufragar be shipwrecked; *fig* fail; **naufragio** *m* shipwreck; **náufrago 1** *adj* shipwrecked **2** *m*, **-a** *f* shipwrecked person

náuseas *fpl* nausea

náutico nautical

navaja *f* knife

naval naval; **nave** *f* ship; **de iglesia** nave; ~ **espacial** spaceship, spacecraft; **navegable** navigable; **navegación** *f* navigation; ~ **a vela** sailing; **navegar 1** *v*/*i* sail; *por el aire, espacio* fly; ~ **por la red** *o* **por Internet** INFOR surf the Net **2** *v*/*t* sail

navegador *m* INFOR browser; **navegante** *m*/*f* navigator

Navidad *f* Christmas

naviero *m* shipowner; **navío** *m* ship

neblina *f* mist; **nebuloso** *m* hazy, nebulous

necesario necessary; **neceser** *m* toilet kit; *Br* toilet bag; **necesidad** *f* need; (*cosa esencial*) necessity; **de primera** ~ essential; **en caso de** ~ if necessary; **hacer sus** ~ F relieve o.s.; **necesitado** needy; **necesitar** need

necio brainless

necrología f, **necrológica** f obituary

neerlandés 1 adj Dutch **2** m Dutchman; idioma Dutch; **neerlandesa** f Dutchwoman

negación f negation; de acusación denial; **negar** acusación deny; (no conceder) refuse; **negarse** refuse (**a** to); **negativa** f refusal; de acusación denial; **negativo** m/adj negative

negligencia f JUR negligence; **negligente** negligent

negociación f negotiation; **negociaciones** talks; **negociante** m/f businessman; mujer businesswoman; desp money-grubber; **negociar** negotiate; (trato) deal

negra f pej black woman; MÚS quarter note, Br crotchet; L.Am. (querida) honey, dear; **negrita** f bold; **negro 1** adj black; **estar ~** F be furious **2** m pej black man; L.Am. (querido) honey, dear

nena f F little girl, kid F; **nene** m F little boy, kid F

neocelandés ☞ **neozelandés**

neoyorquino 1 adj New York atr **2** m, **-a** New Yorker

neozelandés 1 adj New Zealand atr **2** m, **-esa** f New Zealander

nervio m ANAT nerve; **nerviosismo** m nervousness; **nervioso** nervous; **ponerse ~**

get nervous; (agitado) get agitated; **poner a alguien ~** get on s.o.'s nerves

neto COM net

neumático 1 adj pneumatic **2** m AUTO tire, Br tyre

neumonía f MED pneumonia

neuralgia f neuralgia

neurólogo m, **-a** f neurologist

neurosis f inv neurosis; **neurótico** neurotic

neutral neutral; **neutralidad** f neutrality; **neutro** neutral

nevada f snowfall; **nevar** snow; **nevera** f refrigerator, fridge; **~ portátil** cooler

ni neither; **~.... ~** neither ~ nor; **~ siquiera** not even

Nicaragua f Nicaragua; **nicaragüense** m/f & adj Nicaraguan

nicho m niche

nido m nest

niebla f fog

nieta f granddaughter; **nieto** m grandson; **~s** grandchildren

nieve f snow; Méx water ice, sorbet

ninfa f nymph

ningún ☞ **ninguno**

ninguno no; **no hay -a razón** there's no reason why, there isn't any reason why

niña f girl; forma de cortesía young lady; **niñera** f nanny; **niñez** f childhood; **niño 1** adj young; desp childish **2** m boy; forma de cortesía young man; **~s** children pl; **~ de pecho** infant

nipón 1 adj Japanese **2** m, -ona f Japanese

níquel m nickel

níspero m BOT loquat

nitidez f clarity; FOT sharpness; **nítido** clear; imagen sharp

nitrógeno m nitrogen

nivel m level; (altura) height; ~ **del mar** sea level; ~ **de vida** standard of living; **nivelar** level

no no; para negar verbo not; **no entiendo** I don't understand, I do not understand; ~ **te vayas** don't go; ~ **bien** as soon as; ~ **del todo** not entirely; **ya** ~ not any more; ~ **más** L.Am. ~ **nomás**; **así** ~ **más** L.Am. just like that; **te gusta**, **¿**~**?** you like it, don't you?; **¿te ha llamado**, **¿**~**?** he called you, didn't he?

noble m/f & adj noble; **nobleza** f nobility

noche f night; **de**~, **por la** ~ at night; **¡buenas** ~**s!** saludo good evening; despedida good night; **Nochebuena** f Christmas Eve; **Nochevieja** f New Year's Eve

noción f notion; **nociones** mpl basic knowledge

nocivo harmful

nocturno night atr; ZO nocturnal; **clase** -**a** evening class

nogal m BOT walnut

nomás L.Am. just; **llévaselo** ~ just take it away; ~ **lo vio** as soon as she saw him

nombrado famous, renowned; **nombramiento** m appointment; **nombrar** mention; para un cargo appoint; **nombre** m name; GRAM noun; ~ **de familia** family name, surname; ~ **de pila** first name; ~ **de soltera** maiden name

nómina f pay slip; **nominal** nominal; **nominar** nominate

nor(d)este m northeast

noria f de agua waterwheel; en feria ferris wheel

norirlandés 1 adj of / from Northern Ireland, Northern Ireland atr **2** m, ~**esa** f man / woman from Northern Ireland

norma f standard; (regla) rule, regulation; **normal** normal; **normalizar** standardize

noroeste m northwest

norte m north

Norteamérica North America; **norteamericano 1** adj North American **2** m, -a f North American

Noruega Norway; **noruego 1** adj Norwegian **2** m, -a f Norwegian **3** m idioma Norwegian

nos complemento directo us; complemento indirecto (to) us; reflexivo ourselves

nosotros, **nosotras** we; complemento us; **ven con** ~ come with us; **somos** ~ it's us

nostalgia f nostalgia; por la patria homesickness

nota f tb MÚS note; EDU grade, mark; ~ **a pie de página** footnote; **tomar ~ de algo** make a note of sth; **notable** remarkable, notable; **notar** notice; (sentir) feel; **hacer ~ algo a alguien** point sth out to s.o.; **se nota que** you can tell that; **hacerse ~** draw attention to o.s.

notario m, **-a** f notary

noticia f piece of news; en noticiario news story; **~s** news sg; **~s de última hora** TV breaking news

notificación f notification; **notificar** notify

notorio famous, well-known

novato m, **-a** f beginner

novedad f novelty; cosa new thing; (noticia) piece of news; acontecimiento new development; **llegar sin ~** arrive safely; **novela** f novel; **~ negra** crime novel; **~ rosa** romantic novel; **novelista** m/f novelist

noveno ninth; **noventa** ninety

novia f girlfriend; el día de la boda bride

noviembre m November

novillada f bullfight featuring novice bulls; **novillo** m young bull; **vaca** heifer

novio m boyfriend; el día de la boda bridegroom; **los ~s** the bride and groom; (recién casados) the newly-weds

nube f cloud; **estar en las ~s** fig be miles away; **nublado 1**

adj cloudy **2** m storm cloud; **nublarse** cloud over; **nuboso** cloudy; **nubosidad** f clouds pl

nuca f nape of the neck

nuclear nuclear; **núcleo** m nucleus; de problema heart

nudillo m knuckle

nudismo m nudism; **nudista** m/f nudist; **playa ~** nudist beach

nudo m knot

nuera f daughter-in-law

nuestro 1 adj our **2** pron ours

Nueva York New York

Nueva Zelanda New Zealand

nueve nine

nuevo new; (otro) another; **de ~** again

nuez f BOT walnut; ANAT Adam's apple

nulo null and void; F persona hopeless; (inexistente) nonexistent

numeración f numbering; (números) numbers pl; **numerar** number; **numérico** numerical; **teclado ~** numeric keypad, number pad; **número** m number; de publicación issue; de zapato size; **~ secreto** PIN (number); **en ~s rojos** fig in the red; **montar un ~** F make a scene; **numeroso** numerous

nunca never; **jamás** o **más** never again; **más que ~** more than ever

nupcial wedding atr

nutria f ZO otter
nutrición f nutrition; **nutrir** nourish; *fig: esperanzas* cherish; **nutritivo** nutritious, nourishing
ñame m BOT yam

ñandú m ZO rhea
ñoñería f feebleness F; **ñoño 1** adj feeble F, wimpish F **2** m, -a f drip F, wimp F
ñu m ZO gnu

O

o or; **~... ~** either ... or
oasis m inv oasis
obcecado (*terco*) obstinate; (*obsesionado*) obsessed
obedecer obey; *de una máquina* respond; **~ a** fig be due to; **obediencia** f obedience; **obediente** obedient
obertura f MÚS overture
obesidad f obesity; **obeso** obese
obispo m bishop
objeción f objection; **objetar 1** v/t object; **tener algo que ~** have any objection **2** v/i become a conscientious objector
objetivo 1 adj objective **2** m objective; MIL target; FOT lens
objeto m object; **con ~ de** with the aim of
objetor m, **~a** f objector
oblea f wafer
oblicuo oblique, slanted
obligación f obligation, duty; COM bond; **obligar: ~ a alguien** oblige o force s.o. (**a** to); *de una ley* apply to s.o.; **obligarse: ~ a hacer algo** force o.s. to do sth; **obligato-**

rio obligatory
oboe m MÚS oboe
obra f work; **~s de construcción** building work; **en la vía pública** road works; **~ de arte** work of art; **~ maestra** masterpiece; **~ de teatro** play; **obrar 1** act; **obrero 1** adj working **2** m, **-a** f worker
obsceno obscene
obsequiar: ~ a alguien con algo present s.o. with sth; **obsequio** m gift
observación f observation; JUR observance; **observar** observe; **observatorio** m observatory
obsesión f obsession; **obsesionar** obsess; **obsesionarse** become obsessed (**con** with); **obsesivo** obsessive
obstaculizar hinder; **obstáculo** m obstacle
obstante: **no ~** nevertheless
obstetricia f obstetrics
obstinación f obstinacy; **obstinado** obstinate; **obstinarse** insist (**en** on)
obstrucción f obstruction, blockage; **obstruir** obstruct, block

obtener get, obtain *fml*
obturador *m* shutter
obvio obvious
oca *f* goose
ocasión *f* occasion; (*oportunidad*) chance, opportunity; **con ~ de** on the occasion of; **de ~** COM cut-price, bargain *atr*; **de segunda mano** second-hand; **ocasionar** cause
ocaso *m* del sol setting; *de un imperio* decline
occidental 1 *adj* western **2** *m/f* Westerner; **occidente** *m* west
océano *m* ocean
ochenta eighty; **ocho** eight
ocio *m* leisure time; *desp* idleness; **ocioso** idle
octava *f* MÚS octave; **octavilla** *f* leaflet; **octavo 1** *adj* eighth **2** *m* eighth; DEP **~s de final** last 16
octubre *m* October
ocular eye *atr*; **oculista** *m/f* ophthalmologist
ocultar hide, conceal; **oculto** hidden; (*sobrenatural*) occult
ocupación *f tb* MIL occupation; (*actividad*) occupation; **ocupado** busy; *asiento* taken; **ocupante** *m/f* occupant; **ocupar** occupy; (*habitar*) live in, occupy; *obreros* employ; *periodo de tiempo* spend, occupy; MIL occupy; **ocuparse**: **~ de** deal with; (*cuidar de*) look after
ocurrencia *f* occurrence;

(*chiste*) quip, witty remark; **ocurrente** witty; **ocurrir** happen, occur; **se me ocurrió** it occurred to me, it struck me
odiar hate; **odio** *m* hatred, hate; **odioso** odious, hateful
odontología *f* dentistry; **odontólogo** *m* odontologist
oeste *m* west
ofender offend; **ofenderse** take offense *o Br* offence (*por* at); **ofensa** *f* insult; **ofensiva** *f* offensive
oferta *f* offer; **~ pública de adquisición** takeover bid
oficial 1 *adj* official **2** *m/f* MIL officer; **oficina** *f* office; **~ de correos** post office; **~ de empleo** employment office; **~ de turismo** tourist office; **oficio** *m trabajo* trade; **oficioso** unofficial; **oficialista** *L.Am.* pro-government; **oficinista** *m/f* office worker
ofimática *f* INFOR office automation
ofrecer offer; **ofrecimiento** *m* offer
oftalmólogo *m*, **-a** *f* ophthalmologist
oída *f*: **conocer algo de ~s** have heard of sth; **oído** *m* hearing; **hacer ~s sordos** turn a deaf ear; **ser todo ~s** *fig* be all ears; **oír** *tb* JUR hear; (*escuchar*) listen to; **¡oye!** listen!
ojal *m* buttonhole
ojalá **¡~!** let's hope so; **¡~ venga!** I hope he comes

ojeada f glance; **ojeras** fpl bags under the eyes; **ojete 1** m eyelet **2** m/f Méx V bastard P, son of a bitch V; **ojo** m ANAT eye; **¡~!** F watch out!; **~ de la cerradura** keyhole; **a ~** roughly; **andar con ~** F keep one's eyes open F; **no pegar ~** F not sleep a wink F

ola f wave; **~ de calor** heat wave; **~ de frío** cold spell; **oleada** f fig wave, flood; **oleaje** m swell

olé olé

oleada f fig wave, flood; **oleaje** m swell

óleo m oil; **oleoducto** m (oil) pipeline; **oleoso** oily

oler smell (**a** of); **olfatear** sniff; **olfato** m sense of smell; fig nose

olimpíada, olimpiada f Olympics pl

oliva f BOT olive; **olivo** m olive tree

olla f pot; **~ exprés** o **a presión** pressure cooker

olor m smell; **agradable** tb scent; **~ corporal** BO; **oloroso** scented

olvidar forget; **olvidarse: ~ de algo** forget sth; **olvido** m oblivion

ombligo m ANAT navel

omisión f omission; **omitir** omit, leave out

omnipotente omnipotent; **omnisciente** omniscient

omóplato, omoplato m ANAT shoulder blade

once eleven

onda f wave; **estar en la ~** F be with it F; **ondear** de banderas wave; **ondulación** f undulation; **ondular 1** v/i undulate **2** v/t pelo wave

oneroso onerous

onoro sonorous

onza f ounce

OPA f (= **oferta pública de adquisición**) takeover bid

opaco opaque

ópera f MÚS opera; **~ prima** first work

operación f operation; **operador** m, **~a** f TELEC, INFOR operator; **~ turístico** tour operator; **operar 1** v/t MED operate on; cambio bring about **2** v/i operate; COM do business (**con** with); **operarse** MED have an operation (**de** on); de un cambio occur; **operario** m, **-a** f operator, operative

opereta f MÚS operetta

opinar 1 v/t think (**de** about) **2** v/i express an opinion; **opinión** f opinion

opio m opium

oponente m/f opponent; **oponer** resistencia put up (**a** to); razón, argumento put forward (**a** against); **oponerse** be opposed (**a** to); (manifestar oposición) object (**a** to)

oporto m port

oportunidad f opportunity; **oportunista 1** adj opportunistic **2** m/f opportunist; **opor**

tuno timely; *momento* oportune; *respuesta, medida* suitable

oposición f POL opposition; **oposiciones** official entrance exams

opresión f oppression; *oprimir* oppress; *botón* press; *de zapatos* be too tight for

optar *(elegir)* opt *(por* for); *~ a* be in the running for

óptica f optician, Br optician's; FÍS optics; *fig* point of view; **óptico 1** adj optical **2** m, -a f optician

optimismo m optimism; **optimista 1** adj optimistic **2** m/f optimist

óptimo ideal

opuesto **1** part ↗ **oponer 2** adj opposite

opulencia f opulence; opulento opulent

oración f REL prayer; GRAM sentence

oráculo m oracle

orador m, ~a f orator; oral oral; **prueba de inglés ~** English oral (exam)

orden **1** m order; **~ del día** agenda; **poner en ~** tidy up **2** f *(mandamiento)* order; *¡a la ~!* yes, sir; *por ~ de* by order of; **ordenado** tidy; **ordenador** m INFOR computer; **~ de escritorio** desktop (computer); **~ personal** personal computer; **~ portátil** laptop; **asistido por ~** computer aided; **ordenanza 1** f bylaw **2** m office junior, gofer

F; MIL orderly; **ordenar** *habitación* tidy up; *alfabéticamente* arrange; *(mandar)* order

ordeñar milk

ordinario ordinary; *desp* vulgar; *de ~* ordinarily

oreja f ear; **orejeras** fpl earmuffs

orfanato m orphanage

orfebre m/f goldsmith / silversmith

orgánico organic

organillo m barrel organ

organismo m organism; POL agency, organization

organista m/f organist

organización f organization; *Organización de las Naciones Unidas* United Nations; **organizador 1** adj organizing **2** m, ~a f organizer; **organizar** organize

órgano m MÚS, ANAT, *fig* organ

orgasmo m orgasm

orgía f orgy

orgullo m pride; **orgulloso** proud *(de* of)

orientación f orientation; *(ayuda)* guidance; *sentido de la ~* sense of direction

oriental **1** adj oriental, eastern **2** m/f Oriental

orientar *(aconsejar)* advise; *~ algo hacia algo* turn sth toward sth; **orientarse** get one's bearings; *de una planta* turn *(hacia* toward)

oriente m east; *Oriente* Orient; *Oriente Medio* Middle

East; **Extremo** o **Lejano Oriente** Far East

orificio m hole; *en cuerpo* orifice

origen m origin; **dar ~ a** give rise to; **original** m/adj original; **originalidad** f originality; **originar** give rise to; **originario** *(nativo)* native *(de of)*

orilla f shore; *de un río* bank

orín m rust

orina f urine; **orinal** m urinal; **orinar** urinate

ornamentar adorn; **ornamento** m ornament; **~s** REL vestments

oro m gold; **~s** *(en naipes)* suit in Spanish deck of cards

orquesta f orchestra

orquídea f BOT orchid

ortiga f BOT nettle

ortodoncia f MED orthodontics

ortodoxo orthodox

ortografía f spelling

ortopédico 1 adj orthopedic, Br orthopaedic **2** m, -a f orthopedist, Br orthopaedist

oruga f ZO caterpillar; TÉC (caterpillar) track

orujo m liquor made from the remains of grapes

orzuelo m MED stye

os *complemento directo* you; *complemento indirecto* (to) you; *reflexivo* yourselves

osado daring; **osar** dare

oscilar oscillate; *de precios* fluctuate

oscurecer 1 v/t darken; *logro,*

triunfo overshadow **2** v/i get dark; **oscuridad** f darkness

oscuro dark; *fig* obscure; **a -as** in the dark

óseo bone atr

oso m bear; **~ hormiguero** anteater; **~ panda** panda; **~ polar** polar bear

ostensible obvious

ostentar flaunt; *cargo* hold

ostra f oyster; **¡~s!** F hell! F

OTAN f (= **Organización de Tratado del Atlántico Norte**) NATO (= North Atlantic Treaty Organization)

otoñal fall atr, Br autumnal

otoño m fall, Br autumn

otorgar award; *favor* grant

otorrino F, **otorrinolaringólogo** m MED ear, nose and throat specialist

otro 1 adj *(diferente)* another *con el, la* other; **~s** other. **~s dos libros** another two books **2** pron *(adicional)* another (one); *(persona distinta)* someone o somebody else; *(cosa distinta)* another one, a different one; **~s** others **3** *siguiente:* **¡hasta -a!** see you soon **4** pron *recíproco:* **amar el uno al ~** love one another

ovación f ovation

oval, ovalado oval

ovario m ANAT ovary

oveja f sheep

ovillo m ball

ovino m sheep; **~s** sheep pl

óvulo m egg

oxidarse rust, go rusty; **óxido**

m QUÍM oxide; (*herrumbre*) rust; **oxígeno** *m* oxygen

oyente *m/f* listener

ozono *m* ozone; *capa de ~* ozone layer

P

pabellón *m* pavilion; *edificio* block; MÚS bell; MAR flag

pacer graze

paciencia *f* patience; **paciente** *m/f* & *adj* patient

pacífico 1 *adj* peaceful; *persona* peaceable **2** *m*: *el Pacífico* the Pacific; **pacifista** *m/f* & *adj* pacifist

pacotilla *f*: *de ~* third-rate, lousy F

pactar 1 *v/t* reach (an) agreement; *~ un acuerdo* reach (an) agreement **2** *v/i* reach (an) agreement; **pacto** *m* agreement, pact

padecer suffer; *~ de* have trouble with

padrastro *m* step-father; **padre** *m* father; REL Father; *~s* parents; *¡qué ~!* Méx F brilliant!; **padrenuestro** *m* Lord's Prayer; **padrino** *m* *en bautizo* godfather; (*en boda*) man who gives away the bride

paga *f* pay; *de niño* allowance, Br pocket money

pagano pagan

pagar pay; *compra, gastos, crimen* pay for; *favor* repay; *¡me las pagarás!* you'll pay for this!; **pagaré** *m* IOU

página *f* page; *~ web* web page; *~s amarillas* yellow pages

pago *m* payment; Rpl (*quinta*) piece of land

país *m* country; *los Países Bajos* the Netherlands; **paisaje** *m* landscape; **paisajista** *m/f* & *adj* landscape artist; *jardinero* landscape gardener

paisano *m*: *de ~* MIL in civilian clothes; *policía* in plain clothes

paja *f* straw; **pajar** *m* hayloft

pajarita *f* corbata bow tie; **pájaro** *m* bird; *fig* nasty piece of work F; *~ carpintero* woodpecker

pala *f* spade; *raqueta* paddle; *para servir* slice; *para recoger* dustpan

palabra *f* tb *fig* word; *bajo ~* on parole; *tomar la ~* speak; **palabrota** *f* swearword

palacio *m* palace; *~ de deportes* sports center *o* Br centre; *~ de justicia* law courts

paladar *m* palate

palanca *f* lever; *~ de cambios* AUTO gearshift, Br gear lever

palangana *f* washbowl, Br washing-up bowl

palco *m* TEA box

paleta *f* PINT palette; TÉC trowel; **paletilla** *f* GASTR

shoulder

paliar alleviate; *dolor* relieve

palidecer *de persona* turn pale; **palidez** *f* paleness; **pálido** pale

palillo *m para dientes* toothpick; *para comer* chopstick

paliza 1 *f* beating; *(derrota)* thrashing F; *(pesadez)* drag F **2** *m/f* F drag F

palma *f* palm; **dar ~s** clap (one's hands); **palmada** *f* pat; *(manotazo)* slap

palmera *f* BOT palm tree; *(dulce)* heart-shaped pastry

palmo *m* hand's breadth; **~ a ~** inch by inch

palo *m de madera etc* stick; MAR mast; *de fregar* post, upright; **~ de golf** golf club; **~ mayor** MAR mainmast; **a medio ~** L.Am. F half-drunk; **a ~ seco** *whisky* straight up, *Br* neat; **ser un ~** L.Am. F be fantastic

paloma *f* pigeon; *blanca* dove

palomita *f* Méx checkmark, *Br* tick; **~s de maíz** popcorn

palpable *fig* palpable; **palpar** feel

palpitación *f* palpitation; **palpitar** *del corazón* pound; *Rpl fig* have a hunch F

paludismo *m* MED malaria

pampa *f* pampa, prairie; **a la ~** *Rpl* in the open

pan *m* bread; **un ~** a loaf; **~ integral** wholewheat *o Br* wholemeal bread; **~ de molde** sliced bread; **~ de barra** French bread; **~ rallado**

breadcrumbs *pl*; **~ tostado** toast

pana *f* corduroy

panacea *f* panacea

panadería *f* bakery; **panadero** *m*, **-a** *f* baker

panal *m* honeycomb

Panamá Panama; **el Canal de ~** the Panama Canal; **Ciudad de ~** Panama city; **panameño 1** *adj* Panamanian **2** *m*, **-a** *f* Panamanian

pancarta *f* placard

páncreas *m inv* ANAT pancreas

pandereta *f*, **pandero** *m* tambourine

pandilla *f* group; *de delincuentes* gang

panecillo *m* (bread) roll

pánico *m* panic

pantaleta *f* C.Am., Méx panties *pl*

pantalla *f* TV, INFOR screen; *de lámpara* shade

pantalón *m*, **pantalones** *mp* pants *pl*, *Br* trousers *pl*

pantano *m* reservoir

pantanoso swampy

pantera *f* ZO panther

pantorrilla *f* ANAT calf

panty *m* pantyhose *pl*, *Br* tights *pl*

panza *f de persona* belly

pañal *m* diaper, *Br* nappy

paño *m* cloth; **~ de cocina** dishtowel; **pañuelo** *m* handkerchief

papa 1 *m* Pope **2** *f L.Am.* potato

papá *m* F pop F, dad F; **~s**

L.Am. parents; **Papá Noel**
Santa Claus
papada f double chin
papagayo m ZO parrot
papaya f BOT papaya
papel m paper; *trozo* piece of
paper; *TEA*, *fig* role; **~ de
aluminio** aluminum foil; *Br*
aluminium foil; **~ de envolver** wrapping paper; **~ de regalo** giftwrap; **~ higiénico**
toilet paper; **papelera** f
waste basket; *Br* wastepaper
basket; **papelería** f stationery store, stationer's shop
paperas fpl MED mumps
papilla f *para bebés* baby food;
para enfermos purée
paquete m package, parcel;
de cigarrillos packet
Paquistán Pakistan; **paquistaní** m/f & adj Pakistani
par f par; **a la ~ que** as well
as 2 m *abierto de ~ en ~*
wide open
para for; *dirección* toward; *¿~*
head for; **diez ~ las ocho**
L.Am. ten of eight, ten to
eight; **lo hace ~ ayudarte**
he does it (in order) to help
you; **~ que** you; **¿~ qué te
marchas?** what are you
leaving for?; **lo heredó todo
~ morir a los 30** he inherited
it all, only to die at 30
parabólica f satellite dish
parabrisas m inv AUTO windshield, *Br* windscreen; **paracaídas** m inv parachute; **pa-
racaidista** m/f parachutist;
MIL paratrooper; *para*; **para-**

choques m inv AUTO bumper
parada f stop; **~ de autobús**
bus stop; **~ de taxis** taxi
stand, *Br* taxi rank
paradero m whereabouts sg;
L.Am. (*de pie*) standing
(up); **salir bien / mal /**
come off well / badly 2 m,
-a f unemployed person
parado 1 adj unemployed;
paradójico paradoxical
parador m *Esp* parador
(*state-run luxury hotel*)
paraguas m inv umbrella
Paraguay Paraguay; **paraguayo 1** adj Paraguayan **2**
m, -a f Paraguayan
paraíso m paradise; **~ fiscal**
tax haven
paraje m place, spot
paralela f MAT parallel; DEP
~s parallel bars; **paralelo**
m/adj parallel
parálisis f tb fig paralysis; **pa-
ralítico 1** adj paralytic **2** m,
-a f person who is paralyzed;
paralizar MED paralyze; *actividad* bring to a halt; **parali-
zarse** *por miedo* be paralyzed (*por* by); *fig actividad*
be brought to a halt
paranoia f paranoia; **paranoico 1** adj paranoid **2** m,
-a f person suffering from
paranoia
parapente m hang glider; *actividad* hang gliding
parapeto m parapet
parapléjico 1 adj MED para-

plegic *m*, **-a** *f* paraplegic

parar 1 *v/t* stop; *L.Am.* (*poner de pie*) stand up **2** *v/i* stop; *en alojamiento* stay; **~ de llover** stop raining; **pararse** stop; *L.Am.* (*ponerse de pie*) stand up

pararrayos *m inv* lightning rod, *Br* lightning conductor

parásito *m* parasite

parasol *m* parasol; *en la playa* (beach) umbrella

parcela *f* lot, *Br* plot

parche *m* patch

parcial (*partidario*) bias(s)ed

parco moderate, frugal; **es ~ en palabras** he's a man of few words

pardo 1 *adj* color dun; *L.Am. desp* half-breed *desp*, *Br tb* half-caste *desp* **2** *m* color dun; *L.Am. desp* half-breed *desp*

parecer 1 *m* opinion, view; **al ~** apparently **2** *v/i* seem, look; **¿qué te parece?** what do you think?; **parecerse** resemble each other; **~ a alguien** resemble s.o.; **parecido 1** *adj* similar **2** *m* similarity

pared *f* wall

pareja *f* pair; *en una relación* couple; *de una persona* partner; *de un objeto* other one

parentela *f* relatives *pl*, family; **parentesco** *m* relationship

paréntesis *m inv* parenthesis; *fig* break; **entre ~** *fig* by the way

paridad *f* COM parity

pariente *m/f* relative

parir 1 *v/i* give birth **2** *v/t* give birth to

parking *m* parking lot, *Br* car park

parlamento *m* parliament

paro *m* unemployment; **estar en ~** be unemployed; **~ cardíaco** cardiac arrest

parodia *f* parody; **parodiar** parody

parpadear blink; **párpado** *m* eyelid

parque *m* park; *para bebé* playpen; **~ de atracciones** amusement park; **~ de bomberos** fire station; **~ natural** nature reserve; **~ temático** theme park

parqué *m* parquet

parquímetro *m* parking meter

párrafo *m* paragraph

parrilla *f* broiler, *Br* grill; **a la ~** broiled, *Br* grilled; **parrillada** *f L.Am.* barbecue

párroco *m* parish priest; **parroquia** *f* REL parish; COM clientele, customers *pl*; **parroquiano** *m*, **-a** *f* parishioner

parte 1 *m* report; **dar ~ a alguien** inform s.o. **2** *f trozo* part; JUR party; **alguna ~** somewhere; **ninguna ~** nowhere; **otra ~** somewhere else; **de ~ de** on behalf of; **en ~** partly; **en o por todas ~s** everywhere; **por otra ~** moreover; **estar de ~ de** al-

guien be on s.o.'s side; **to-mar ~ en** take part

parterre *m* flowerbed

participación *f* participation; **participante** *m/f* participant; **participar 1** *v/t una noticia* announce **2** *v/i* take part (*en* in), participate (*en* in)

particular 1 *adj clase, propiedad* private; *asunto personal, (específico)* particular; *(especial)* peculiar; **en ~** in particular **2** *m (persona)* individual; **~es** particulars; **particularidad** *f* peculiarity

partida *f en juego* game; *(remesa)* consignment; *documento* certificate; **~ de nacimiento** birth certificate; **partidario 1** *adj:* **ser ~ de** be in favour of **2** *m, -a f* supporter; **partido** *m* POL party; DEP game; **sacar ~ de** take advantage of; **tomar ~** take sides

partir 1 *v/t (dividir, repartir)* split; *(romper)* break open, split open; *(cortar)* cut **2** *v/i (irse)* leave; **a ~ de hoy** (starting) from today; **a ~ de ahora** from now on; **~ de** fig start from

parto *m* birth; *fig* creation

party line *f* chatline

parvulario *m* kindergarten

pasa *f* raisin

pasada *f con trapo* wipe; *de pintura* coat; **de ~** in passing; **¡qué ~!** F that's incredible! F; **pasado 1** *adj tiempo* last; **el lunes ~** last Monday **2** *m*

past

pasador *m para el pelo* barrette, *Br* (hair) slide; *(pestillo)* bolt; GASTR strainer

pasaje *m (billete)* ticket; MÚS, *de texto* passage; **pasajero 1** *adj temporary;* *relación* brief **2** *m, -a f* passenger

pasamano(s) *m* handrail

pasaporte *m* passport

pasar 1 *v/t* pass; *tiempo* spend; *un lugar* go past; *frontera* cross; *problemas, dificultades* experience; AUTO *(adelantar)* pass, *Br* overtake; *una película* show; **para ~ el tiempo** to pass the time; **lo bien** have a good time **2** *v/i (suceder)* happen; *en juegos* pass; **paso de coger el teléfono** F I can't be bothered to pick up the phone; **pasé a visitarla** I dropped in to see her; **~ de moda** go out of fashion; **~ por** go by; **pasa por aquí** come this way; **dejar ~ oportunidad** miss; **hacerse ~ por** pass o.s. off as; **pasaré por tu casa** I'll drop by your house; **¡pasa!** come in; **¿qué pasa?** what's happening?, what's going on?; **¿qué les pasa?** what's the matter?; **pasarse** *tb fig* go too far; *del tiempo* pass, go by; *(usar el tiempo)* spend; *de molestia, dolor* go away; **~ al enemigo** go over to the enemy; **se le pasó llamar** he forgot to call

pasarela *f de modelos* run-

way, *Br* catwalk
Pascua *f* Easter; **¡felices ~s!**
Merry Christmas!
pase *m tb* DEP. TAUR pass; *en el cine* showing; **~ de modelos** fashion show
pasearse walk; **paseo** *m* walk; **~ marítimo** seafront; **dar un ~** go for a walk
pasillo *m* corridor; *en avión, cine* aisle
pasión *f* passion
pasivo passive
pasmar amaze; **pasmarse** be amazed; **~ de frío** freeze
paso *m* step; *(manera de andar)* walk; *(ritmo)* pace, rate; *de agua* flow; *de tráfico* movement; *(cruce)* crossing; *de tiempo* passing; *(huella)* footprint; **~ a nivel** grade crossing, *Br* level crossing; **~ de peatones** crosswalk, *Br* pedestrian crossing; **~ on the way; estar de ~** be passing through
pasota F *actitud* couldn't-care-less
pasta *f sustancia* paste; GASTR pasta; P *(dinero)* dough P; **~ de dientes** toothpaste
pastel *m* GASTR cake; *pintura, color* pastel; **pastelería** *f* cake shop
pastilla *f* tablet; *de jabón* bar; **a toda ~** F at top speed F
pasto *m (hierba)* grass; **a todo ~** F for all one is worth F; **pastor** *m* shepherd; REL pastor; **~ alemán** German shepherd

pata *f* leg; **a cuatro ~s** on all fours; **meter la ~** F put one's foot in it F; **patada** *f* kick; **dar una ~** kick; **patalear** stamp one's feet
Patagonia Patagonia; **patagónico** Patagonian
patata *f* potato; **~s fritas** *de sartén* French fries, *Br* chips; *de bolsa* chips, *Br* crisps
paté *m* paté
patear *L.Am. de animal* kick
patente 1 *adj* clear, obvious **2** *f* patent; *L.Am.* AUTO license plate, *Br* numberplate
paternal paternal, fatherly; **paternidad** *f* paternity, fatherhood; **paterno** paternal
patético pitiful
patíbulo *m* scaffold
patilla *f de gafas* arm; **~s** *barba* sideburns
patín *m* skate; **~ (de ruedas) en línea** rollerblade®, in-line skate; **patinador** *m*, **~a** *f* skater; **patinaje** *m* skating; **~ artístico** figure skating; **~ sobre hielo** ice-skating; **~ sobre ruedas** roller-skating; **patinar** skate; **patinete** *m* scooter
patio *m* courtyard, patio; **~ de butacas** TEA orchestra, *Br* stalls *pl*
pato *m* ZO duck
patológico pathological
patraña *f* tall story
patria *f* homeland; **patrimonio** *m* heritage; **patriota** *m/f* patriot; **patriótico** patriotic

patrocinador m, **~a** f sponsor; **patrocinar** sponsor

patrón m (*jefe*) boss; REL patron saint; *para costura* pattern; (*modelo*) standard; MAR skipper; **patrona** f (*jefa*) boss; REL patron saint

patrulla f patrol; **patrullar** patrol

paulatino gradual

pausa f pause; *en una actividad* break; MÚS rest; **~ publicitaria** commercial break; **pausado** slow, deliberate

pava f animal (hen) turkey; F (*colilla*) cigarette butt

pavimento m pavement, Br road surface

pavo 1 adj L.Am. F stupid **2** m ZO turkey; **~ real** peacock

payaso m clown

paz f peace; **dejar en ~** leave alone

peaje m toll

peatón m pedestrian

peca f freckle

pecado m sin; **pecador** m, **~a** f sinner; **pecar** sin; **~ de ingenuo / generoso** be very naive / generous

pecho m (*caja torácica*) chest; (*mama*) breast; **tomar algo a ~** take sth to heart; **pechuga** f GASTR breast; L.Am. fig F (*caradura*) nerve F

pecoso freckled

peculiar peculiar, odd; (*característico*) typical

pedagógico educational

pedal m pedal

pedante 1 adj pedantic; (*pre-*

suntuoso) pretentious **2** m/f pedant; (*presuntuoso*) pretentious individual; **pedantería** f pedantry; (*presunción*) pretentiousness

pedazo m piece, bit; **hacer ~s** F smash to bits F

pediatra m/f pediatrician, Br paediatrician

pedicura f pedicure

pedido m order; **pedir 1** v/t ask for; (*necesitar*) need; *en restaurante* order; **me pidió que no fuera** he asked me not to go **2** v/i mendigar beg; *en restaurante* order

pedo 1 adj drunk **2** m F fart F

pegadizo catchy; **pegajoso** sticky; *fig: persona* clingy; **pegamento** m glue; **pegar 1** v/t (*golpear*) hit; (*adherir*) stick, glue; *bofetada, susto, resfriado* give **2** v/i (*golpear*) hit; (*adherir*) stick; *del sol* beat down; (*armonizar*) go (together); **pegarse** *resfriado* catch; *acento* pick up; *susto* give o.s.; **~ un golpe / un tiro** hit / shoot o.s.; **pegatina** f sticker

peinado m hairstyle; **peinar 1** v/t tb fig comb; **~ a alguien** comb s.o.'s hair; **peine** m comb; **peineta** f ornamental comb

p. ej. (= **por ejemplo**) eg (= for example)

pelaje m ZO coat; fig (*aspecto*) look; **pelar** manzana, patata etc peel

peldaño *m* step

pelea *f* fight; **pelear, pelearse** fight

peletería *f* furrier

película *f* movie, film; FOT film; ~ **del Oeste** Western; **de** ~ F awesome F

peligro *m* danger; **correr** ~ be in danger; **poner en** ~ endanger, put at risk; **peligroso** dangerous

pelirrojo red-haired, redheaded

pellejo *m de animal* skin, hide

pellizcar pinch

pelo *m de persona, de perro* hair; *de animal* fur; **a** ~ F (*sin preparación*) unprepared; **montar a** ~ ride bareback; **tomar el** ~ **a alguien** pull s.o.'s leg F

pelota 1 *f* ball; ~**s** F nuts F, balls F; **en** ~**s** P stark naked **2** *m/f* F creep F

peluca *f* wig

peluche *m* soft toy; **oso de** ~ teddy bear

peludo *persona* hairy; *animal* furry

peluquería *f* hairdressing salon, *Br* hairdresser's; **peluquero** *m*, **-a** *f* hairdresser; **peluquín** *m* hairpiece

pelusa *f* fluff

pelvis *f inv* ANAT pelvis

pena *f* (*tristeza*) sadness, sorrow; (*congoja*) grief; (*lástima*) pity; JUR sentence; ~ **capital** death penalty, capital punishment; ~ **de muerte** death penalty; **no vale** *o*

no merece la ~ it's not worth it; **¡qué** ~! what a shame *o* pity!; **a duras** ~**s** with great difficulty; **me da** ~ *L.Am.* I'm ashamed; **penal** penal; **derecho** ~ criminal law; **penalizar** penalize

pender hang (**sobre** over); **pendiente 1** *adj* unfinished; *cuenta* unpaid **2** *m* earring **3** *f* slope

péndulo *m* pendulum

pene *m* ANAT penis

penetración *f* penetration; **penetrante** *mirada* penetrating; *sonido* piercing; *frío* bitter; *herida* deep; *análisis* incisive; **penetrar** penetrate; (*entrar*) enter; *de un líquido* seep in

penicilina *f* penicillin

península *f* peninsula

penitencia *f* penitence

penoso distressing; *trabajo* laborious

pensamiento *m* thought; BOT pansy; **pensar 1** *v/t* think about; (*opinar*) think; **¡ni** ~**lo!** don't even think about it **2** *v/i* think (**en** about); **pensativo** thoughtful

pensión *f* rooming house, *Br* guesthouse; *dinero* pension; ~ **alimenticia** child support, *Br* maintenance; ~ **completa** American plan, *Br* full board; **pensionista** *m/f* pensioner

Pentecostés *m* Pentecost

penúltimo penultimate

penuria f shortage (**de** of); (*pobreza*) poverty

peña f crag, cliff; (*roca*) rock; F **de amigos** group; **peñón** m: **el Peñón de Gibraltar** the Rock of Gibraltar

peón m en ajedrez pawn; *trabajador* laborer, *Br* labourer

peor worse; **de mal en ~** from bad to worse

pepinillo m gherkin; **pepino** m cucumber

pepita f pip

pequeñez f smallness; **pequeño 1** *adj* small, little; **de ~** when I was small o little 2 m, -a f little one

pera f pear; **peral** m pear tree

perca f *pez* perch

percance m mishap

percatarse notice; **~ de algo** notice sth

percebe m ZO barnacle

percepción f perception; COM *acto* receipt; **perceptible** perceptible

percha f coat hanger; *gancho* coat hook

percibir perceive; COM *sueldo* receive

percusión f MÚS percussion

perdedor m, **-a** f loser; **perder 1** v/t *tren, avión etc* miss; *el tiempo* waste **2** v/i lose; **echar a ~** ruin; **echarse a ~** de alimento go bad; **perderse** get lost; **pérdida** f loss

perdigón m pellet

perdiz f ZO partridge

perdón m pardon; REL for-

giveness; **pedir ~** say sorry, apologize; **¡~!** sorry; **¿~?** pardon me?; **perdonar** forgive; JUR pardon; **~ algo a alguien** forgive s.o. sth; **¡perdone!** sorry; **perdone, ¿tiene hora?** excuse me, do you have the time?

perdurable enduring; **perdurar** endure

perecedero perishable; **perecer** perish

peregrinación f pilgrimage; **peregrinar** go on a pilgrimage; **peregrino** m, **-a** f pilgrim

perejil m BOT parsley

perezoso 1 *adj* lazy **2** m ZO sloth

perfección f perfection; **a la ~** perfectly, to perfection; **perfeccionar** perfect; **perfecto** perfect

pérfido treacherous

perfil m profile; **de ~** in profile, from the side

perfilar *dibujo* outline; *proyecto* put the finishing touches to; **perfilarse** emerge

perforar pierce; *calle* dig up

perfumar perfume; **perfume** m perfume; **perfumería** f perfume shop

pergamino m parchment

pericia f expertise

periferia f periphery; *de ciudad* outskirts pl

perímetro m perimeter

periódico 1 *adj* periodic **2** m newspaper; **periodismo** m journalism; **periodista** *m/f* journalist; **período, periodo** *m* period

peripecia *f* adventure

periquito *m* ZO budgerigar

perito 1 *adj* expert **2** *m*, -a *f* expert; COM *en seguros* loss adjuster

perjudicar harm, damage; **perjudicial** harmful, damaging; **perjuicio** *m* harm, damage; **sin ~ de** without affecting

perjurio *m* perjury

perla *f* pearl

permanecer remain, stay; **permanencia** *f* stay; **permanente 1** *adj* permanent **2** *f* perm

permeable permeable

permisible permissible; **permiso** *m* permission; *documento* permit; **~ de conducir** driver's license, *Br* driving licence; **~ de residencia** residence permit; **con ~** excuse me; **estar de ~** be on leave; **permitir** permit, allow

permuta *f* exchange

pernicioso harmful

pernoctar spend the night

pero 1 *conj* but **2** *m* flaw, defect; **no hay ~s que valgan** no excuses

perogrullada *f* platitude

perpendicular perpendicular

perpetrar *crimen* perpetrate, commit

perpetuar perpetuate; **perpetuo** *fig* perpetual

perplejo puzzled, perplexed

perra *f* dog; **perro** *m* dog; **~ callejero** stray; **~ guardián** guard dog; **~ lazarillo** seeing eye dog®, *Br* guide dog; **~ pastor** sheepdog; **hace un tiempo de ~s** F the weather is lousy F

persecución *f* pursuit; *(acoso)* persecution; **perseguidor** *m*, **~a** *f* persecutor; **perseguir** pursue; *delincuente* look for; *(molestar)* pester; *(acosar)* persecute

perseverancia *f* perseverance; **perseverante** persistent; **perseverar** persevere *(en* with)

persiana *f* blind

persignarse cross o.s.

persistencia *f* persistence; **persistente** persistent; **persistir** persist

persona *f* person; **quince ~s** fifteen people; **personaje** *m* TEA character; *famoso* celebrity; **personal 1** *adj* personal **2** *m* personnel, staff; **personalidad** *f* personality; **personarse** arrive, turn up; **personificar** personify, embody

perspectiva *f* perspective; *fig* point of view; **~s** outlook, prospects

perspicacia *f* shrewdness, perspicacity; **perspicaz** shrewd, perspicacious

persuadir persuade; **persuasión** *f* persuasion; **persuasivo** persuasive

pertenecer belong (*a* to); **perteneciente: ~ *a*** belonging to

pértiga *f* pole; **salto con ~** DEP pole vault

pertinaz persistent; (*terco*) obstinate

pertinente relevant, pertinent

pertrechar equip, supply (*de* with); **pertrecharse** equip o.s.; **pertrechos** *mpl* MIL equipment

perturbación *f* disturbance; **perturbado** *m*, -a *f*: (*mental*) mentally disturbed person; **perturbador** disturbing; **perturbar** disturb; *reunión* disrupt

Perú Peru; **peruano 1** *adj* Peruvian **2** *m*, -a *f* Peruvian

perversidad *f* wickedness, evil; **perversión** *f* perversion; **perverso** perverted; **pervertir** pervert

pesa *f para balanza* weight; DEP shot; *C.Am* butcher's shop

pesadez *f fig* drag *F*

pesadilla *f* nightmare

pesado **1** *adj objeto* heavy; *libro*, *clase etc* tedious, boring; *trabajo* tough **2** *m*, -a *f* bore; **¡qué ~ es!** *F* he's a real pain *F*

pesadumbre *f* grief, sorrow

pésame *m* condolences *pl*

pesar 1 *v/t* weigh **2** *v/i* be heavy; (*influir*) carry weight; *fig* weigh heavily (*sobre* on) **3** *m* sorrow; *a ~ de* in spite of, despite

pesca *f actividad* fishing; (*peces*) fish *pl*; **pescadería** *f* fish shop; **pescadero** *m*, -a *f* fish dealer, *Br* fishmonger; **pescado** *m* GASTR fish; **pescador** *m* fisherman; **pescar 1** *v/t un pez*, *resfriado etc* catch; (*intentar tomar*) fish for; *trabajo*, *marido etc* land *F* **2** *v/i* fish

pescuezo *m* neck

pese: ~ *a* despite

pesebre *m* (*comedero*) manger; (*belén*) crèche

pesimismo *m* pessimism; **pesimista 1** *adj* pessimistic **2** *m/f* pessimist

pésimo awful, terrible

peso *m* weight; *moneda* peso; *de ~ fig* weighty

pesquisa *f* investigation

pestaña *f* eyelash; **pestañear** flutter one's eyelashes; *sin ~ fig* without batting an eyelid

peste *f* MED plague; *F olor* stink *F*; **echar ~s** *F* curse and swear

pestillo *m* (*picaporte*) door handle; (*cerradura*) bolt

petardo **1** *m* firecracker **2** *m*, -a *f F* nerd *F*

petición *f* request

petrificar petrify (*tb fig*); **petrificarse** become petrified

petróleo *m* oil, petroleum; **petrolero 1** *adj* oil *atr* **2** *m* MAR oil tanker

petulancia *f* smugness; **petulante** smug

pez *m* ZO fish; ~ **espada** swordfish; ~ **gordo** F big shot F

pezón *m* nipple

piadoso pious

pianista *m/f* pianist; **piano** *m* piano; ~ **de cola** grand piano

pica *f* TAUR goad; *palo de la baraja* spade

picadero *m escuela* riding school; **picadura** *f de reptil, mosquito* bite; *de avispa* sting; *tabaco* cut tobacco

picadillo *m* GASTR *de lomo*: marinated ground meat

picado 1 *adj diente* decayed; *mar* rough, choppy; *carne* ground, *Br* minced; *verdura* minced, *Br* minced; *fig* offended **2** *m L.Am.* dive; *caer en ~ de precios* nosedive

picador *m* TAUR picador; MIN face worker

picante 1 *adj* hot, spicy; *chiste* risqué **2** *m* hot spice

picar 1 *v/t de mosquito, serpiente* bite; *de avispa* sting; *de ave* peck; *carne* grind, *Br* mince; *verdura* mince, *Br* finely chop; TAUR jab with a lance; *(molestar)* annoy **2** *v/i fig* take the bait; *L.Am. de la comida* be hot; *(producir picor)* itch; *del sol* burn

picardía *f (astucia)* craftiness, slyness; *(travesura)* mischievousness; *Méx (taco, palabrota)* swearing, swearwords *pl*

pícaro *persona* crafty, sly; *comentario* mischievous

picarse *(agujerearse)* rust; *(cariarse)* decay; F *(molestarse)* get mad F

pichón *m L.Am. pollo* chick; F *(novato)* rookie F

pico *m* ZO beak; *(boca)* mouth; *de montaña* peak; *herramienta* pickax, *Br* pickaxe; *a las tres y ~* some time after three o'clock

picor *m* itch

picotear peck

pie *m* foot; *de estatua, lámpara* base; *a ~* on foot; *de ~* standing; *no tiene ni ~s ni cabeza* I can't make head nor tail of it

piedad *f* pity; *(clemencia)* mercy

piedra *f tb* MED stone

piel *f de persona, fruta* skin; *de animal* hide, skin; *(cuero)* leather; *abrigo de ~es* fur coat

pienso *m* animal feed

pierna *f* leg; *dormir a ~ suelta* sleep like a log

pieza *f de un conjunto,* MÚS piece; *de aparato* part; TEA play; *(habitación)* room; ~ *de recambio* spare (part)

pijama *m* pajamas *pl, Br* pyjamas *pl*

pila *f* ELEC battery; *(montón)* pile; *(fregadero)* sink

pilar *m tb fig* pillar

píldora *f* pill

pileta *f Rpl* sink; *(alberca)* swimming pool

pillar (*tomar*) seize; (*atrapar*) catch; (*atropellar*) hit; *chiste* get

pillo 1 *adj* mischievous **2** *m*, **-a** *f* rascal

pilotar AVIA fly, pilot; AUTO drive; MAR steer; **piloto** *m* AVIA, MAR pilot; AUTO driver; ELEC pilot light; **~ automático** autopilot

pimentón *m* paprika; **pimienta** *f* pepper; **pimiento** *m* pepper; **me importa un ~** F I couldn't care less F

pincel *m* paintbrush

pinchadiscos *m/f* F disc jockey, DJ

pinchar 1 *v/t* prick; AUTO puncture; TELEC tap; F (*molestar*) bug F; **~le a alguien** MED give s.o. a shot **2** *v/i* prick; AUTO get a flat (tire), Br get a puncture; **pinchazo** *m herida* prick; *dolor* sharp pain; AUTO flat (tire), Br puncture; F (*fracaso*) flop F

pincho *m* GASTR bar snack

pingüino *m* ZO penguin

pino *m* BOT pine; **hacer el ~** do a handstand

pinta *f* pint; *aspecto* looks *pl*; **tener buena ~** *fig* look inviting

pintada *f* graffiti; **~s** graffiti *pl o sg*

pintar paint; **no ~ nada** *fig* F not count; **pintarse** put on one's make-up

pintor *m*, **-a** *f* painter; **~ (de brocha gorda)** (house) painter; **pintoresco** picturesque; **pintura** *f* *sustancia* paint; *obra* painting

pinza *f* clothes pin, Br clothes peg; ZO claw; **~s** tweezers; L.Am. (*alicates*) pliers

piña *f del pino* pine cone; *fruta* pineapple; **piñón** *m* BOT pine nut; TÉC pinion

pío pious

piojo *m* ZO louse; **~s** lice *pl*

pionero 1 *adj* pioneering **2** *m*, **-a** *f tb fig* pioneer

pipa *f* pipe; **~s semillas** sunflower seeds; **pasarlo ~** F have a great time

pipí *m* F pee F; **hacer ~** F pee F

pique *m* resentment; (*rivalidad*) rivalry; **irse a ~** *fig* go under

piqueta *f herramienta* pickax, Br pickaxe; *en cámping* tent peg

piquete *m* POL picket

piragüismo *m* canoeing

pirámide *f* pyramid

pirata *m/f* pirate; **~ informático** hacker; **piratería** *f* piracy

pirenaico Pyrenean; **Pirineos** *mpl* Pyrenees

piropo *m* compliment

pirotécnico fireworks *atr*

pisada *f* footstep; **huella** footprint; **pisar** step on; *uvas* tread; *fig* (*maltratar*) walk all over; *idea* steal; **~ a alguien** step on s.o.'s foot

piscina *f* swimming pool

Piscis *m/f inv* ASTR Pisces

piso *m* apartment, Br flat; (*planta*) floor

pisotear trample

pista f track, trail; (*indicio*) clue; *de atletismo* track; ~ **de aterrizaje** AVIA runway; ~ **de baile** dance floor; ~ **de tenis** / **squash** tennis / squash court

pistacho m BOT pistachio

pistola f pistol; **pistolero** m gunman

pistón m piston

pita f BOT agave, pita

pitar 1 v/i whistle; *con bocina* hoot; (*abuchear*) whistle at; *salir pitando* F dash off F **2** v/t (*penalti, falta etc*) call, Br blow for; *silbato* blow

pitillera f cigarette case; **pitillo** m cigarette; *hecho a mano* roll-up

pito m whistle; (*bocina*) horn

piyama m L.Am. pajamas pl, Br pyjamas pl

pizarra f blackboard; *piedra* slate

placa f (*lámina*) sheet; (*plancha*) plate; (*letrero*) plaque; Méx AUTO license plate, Br number plate; ~ **madre** INFOR motherboard; ~ (**dental**) plaque; ~ **de matrícula** AUTO license plate, Br number plate

placer 1 v/i please **2** m pleasure

plaga f AGR pest; MED plague; *fig* scourge; (*abundancia*) glut; **plagado** infested; (*lleno*) full; ~ **de gente** swarming with people

plan m plan

plancha f *para planchar* iron; *en cocina* broiler, Br grill; *de metal* sheet; F (*metedura de pata*) goof F; *a la* ~ GASTR broiled, Br grilled; **planchado 1** adj F **shattered** F **2** m ironing; **planchar** iron; Méx F (*dar plantón*) stand up F; L.Am. (*lisonjear*) flatter

planeador m glider; **planear 1** v/t plan **2** v/i AVIA glide

planeta m planet

planicie f plain

planificar plan

plano 1 adj flat **2** m ARQUI plan; *de ciudad* map; *en cine* shot; MAT plane; *fig* level

planta f BOT plant; (*piso*) floor; ~ **del pie** sole of the foot; **plantación** f plantation; **plantar 1** v/t *árbol etc* plant; *tienda de campaña* put up; ~ **a alguien** F stand s.o. up F

plantear *problema* pose, create; *cuestión* raise

plantilla f *para zapato* insole; (*personal*) staff; DEP squad; *para cortar*, *patrón* template

plantón m: *dar un ~ a alguien* F stand s.o. up F

plástico m plastic

plata f silver; L.Am. F (*dinero*) cash, dough F

plataforma f tb POL platform; ~ **petrolífera** oil rig

plátano m banana

platea f TEA orchestra, Br stalls pl

plateado Méx wealthy

platicar 1 *v/t L.Am.* tell **2** *v/i Méx* chat, talk

platillo *m:* **~ volante** flying saucer; **~s** MÚS cymbals

platina *f de microscopio* slide; *de estéreo* tape deck

platino *m* platinum

plató *m de película* set; TV studio

plato *m* plate; GASTR dish; **~ combinado** mixed platter; **~ hondo** soup dish; **~ preparado** ready meal; **~ principal** main course; **~ sopero** soup dish

playa *f* beach; **~ de estacionamiento** *L.Am.* parking lot, *Br* car park; **playeras** *fpl* canvas shoes

plaza *f* square; *(vacante)* job opening; *en vehículo* seat; *de trabajo* position; **~ de toros** bull ring

plazo *m period; (pago)* installment, *Br* instalment; **a corto / largo** in the short / long term; **a ~s** in installments

plegable collapsible, folding; **plegar** fold (up); **plegarse** *fig* submit (**a** to)

pleito *m* JUR lawsuit; *fig* dispute; **poner un ~ a alguien** sue s.o.

pleno 1 *adj* full; **en ~ día** in broad daylight **2** *m* plenary session

pliego 1 *vb* ☞ **plegar 2** *m* *(hoja de papel)* sheet (of paper); *(carta)* sealed letter *o* document; **pliegue** *m* fold, crease

plomero *m Méx* plumber; **plomo** *m* lead; ELEC fuse; *fig* F drag F; **sin ~** AUTO unleaded

pluma *f* feather; *para escribir* fountain pen

plural *m/adj* plural

población *f gente* population; *(ciudad)* city, town; *(pueblo)* village; *Chi* shanty town; **poblado 1** *adj* populated; *barba* bushy; **~ de** full of **2** *m (pueblo)* settlement; **poblador** *m,* **~a** *f Chi* shanty town dweller; **poblar** populate

pobre poor **2** *m/f* poor person; **los ~** the poor; **pobreza** *f* poverty

pocilga *f* pigpen, *Br* pigsty

poco 1 *adj sg* little, not much; *pl* few, not many; **un ~ de** a little; **unos ~s** a few **2** *adv* little; **trabaja ~** he doesn't work much; **estuvo ~ por aquí** he wasn't around much; **~ a ~** little by little; **dentro de ~** soon, shortly; **hace ~** a short time ago, not long ago; **por ~** nearly **3** *m:* **un ~** a little, a bit

poda AGR prune

poder 1 *v/aux capacidad* can, be able to; *permiso* can, be allowed to; *posibilidad* may, might; **no pude hablar con ella** I wasn't able to talk to her; **¿puedo ir contigo?** can *o* may I come with you?; **¡podías habérselo dicho!** you could have *o* you might have told him **2** *v/i:*

~ con (*sobreponerse a*) manage, cope with; **me puede** he can beat me; **no puedo más** I can't take any more, I've had enough; **puede ser** perhaps, maybe; **puede que** perhaps, maybe; **¿se puede?** may I come in? **3** *m tb* POL lover; **en ~ de alguien** in s.o.'s hands; **poderoso** powerful

podio *m* podium

podólogo *m*, **-a** *f* MED podiatrist, *Br* chiropodist

podrido *tb fig* rotten

poema *m* poem; **poesía** *f género* poetry; (*poema*) poem; **poeta** *m/f* poet; **poético** poetic; **poetisa** *f* poet

polaco 1 *adj* Polish **2** *m*, **-a** *f* Pole **3** *m idioma* Polish

polea *f* TÉC pulley

policía 1 *f* police **2** *m/f* police officer, policeman; **mujer** police officer, policewoman; **policíaco, policiaco** detective *atr*

polideportivo *m* sports center, *Br* sports centre

polifacético versatile, multifaceted

poligamia *f* polygamy

polilla *f* ZO moth

polio *f* MED polio

política *f* politics; **político 1** *adj* political **2** *m*, **-a** *f* politician

póliza *f* policy; **~ de seguros** insurance policy

polizón *m/f* stowaway

pollo *m* ZO, GASTR chicken

polo *m* GEOG, ELEC pole; *prenda* polo shirt; DEP polo; **Polo Norte** North Pole; **Polo Sur** South Pole

Polonia Poland

polución *f* pollution; **polucionar** pollute

polvo *m* dust; *en química, medicina etc* powder; **~s de talco** talcum powder; **echar un ~** V have a screw V; **pólvora** *f* gunpowder; **polvoriento** dusty

pomada *f* cream

pomelo *m* BOT grapefruit

pompa *f* pomp; **~ de jabón** bubble; **~s fúnebres** *ceremonia* funeral ceremony; *establecimiento* funeral home

ponedero *m* nest(ing) box

ponencia *f* presentation; EDU paper

ponente *m/f* speaker

poner put; (*añadir*) put in; RAD, TV turn on, switch on; *la mesa* set; *ropa* put on; (*escribir*) put down; *en libro etc* say; *negocio* set up; *huevos* lay; **~ a alguien furioso** make s.o. angry; **~le una multa a alguien** fine s.o.; **pongamos que** let's suppose o assume that; **ponerse** *ropa* put on; **ponte en el banco** go and sit on the bench; **se puso ahí** she stood over there; **dile que se ponga** TELEC tell her to come to the phone; **~ pálido** turn pale; **~ furioso** get angry; **~ enfermo** become o fall ill; **~ a** start to

popa *f* MAR stern

popular popular; *(del pueblo)* folk *atr*; *barrio* lower-class; **popularizar** popularize

por *motivo* for, because of; **lo hizo ~ amor** she did it out of love ◇ *medio* by; **~ avión** by air ◇ *tiempo*: **~ un segundo** L.Am. for a second; **~ la mañana** in the morning ◇ *movimiento*: **~ la calle** down the street; **~ un tunel** through a tunnel; **~ aquí** this way ◇ *posición aproximada* around, about; **está ~ aquí** it's around here (somewhere) ◇ *cambio*: **~ cincuenta pesos** for fifty pesos ◇ *otros usos*: **~ hora** an *o* per hour; **dos ~ dos** two times two; **¿~ qué?** why?

porcelana *f* porcelain, china

porcentaje *m* percentage

porche *f* porch

porción *f* portion

pormenor *m* detail

pornografía *f* pornography

poro *m* pore; **poroso** porous

porque because; **~ sí** just because

porqué *m* reason

porquería *f* filth; F *cosa de poca calidad* piece of trash F

porra *f* baton; *(palo)* club

porro *m* F joint F

porrón *m* *container from which wine is poured straight into the mouth*

portaaviones *m inv* aircraft carrier

portada *f* TIP front page; *de revista* cover; ARQUI front

portador *m*, **~a** *f* COM bearer; MED carrier

portal *m* foyer; *(entrada)* doorway

portaminas *m inv* automatic pencil, *Br* propelling pencil

portarse behave

portátil portable

portavoz *m/f* spokesman; *mujer* spokeswoman

porte *m* *(aspecto)* appearance; *(gasto de correo)* postage

porteño *Arg* **1** *adj* of Buenos Aires **2** *m*, **~a** *f* native of Buenos Aires

portería *f* reception; *casa* superintendent's apartment, *Br* caretaker's flat; DEP goal

portero *m* doorman; *de edificio* superintendent, *Br* caretaker; DEP goalkeeper; **~ automático** intercom, *Br* entryphone

pórtico *m* portico

portorriqueño 1 *adj* Puerto Rican **2** *m*, **~a** *f* Puerto Rican

Portugal Portugal; **portugués 1** *m/adj* Portuguese **2** *m*, **-esa** *f* persona Portuguese **3** *m* idioma Portuguese

porvenir *m* future

pos(t)venta after-sales *atr*

posada *f* C.Am., Méx Christmas party; *(fonda)* inn

posar mano lay, place (**sobre** on); **~ la mirada en** Méx cast; **posarse** de ave, insecto, AVIA land

pose *f* pose

poseer possess; (*ser dueño de*) own, possess; **posesión** *f* possession; **tomar ~** (*de un cargo*) POL take up office

posguerra *f* postwar period

posibilidad *f* possibility; **posibilitar** make possible; **posible** possible; **en lo ~** as far as possible; **hacer todo lo ~** do everything possible; **es ~ que...** perhaps ...

posición *f tb* MIL, *fig* position; *social* standing, status

positivo positive

postal 1 *adj* mail *atr*, postal **2** *f* postcard; **poste** *m* post

postergar postpone

posterior later, later; (*trasero*) rear *atr*, back *atr*; **posterioridad** *f*: **con ~** later, subsequently; **con ~ a** later than, subsequent to

postizo 1 *adj* false **2** *m* hairpiece

postre *m* dessert; **a la ~** in the end

postura *f tb fig* position

potable drinkable; *fig* F passable; **agua ~** drinking water

potaje *m* GASTR stew

potasio *m* potassium

pote *m* (*olla*) pot; GASTR stew

potencia *f* power; **en ~** potential; **potente** powerful

potro *m* ZO colt

práctica *f* practice; **practicable** *tarea* feasible, practicable; *camino* passable; **practicar** practice, *Br* practise; *deporte* play; **~ la equitación** ride; **práctico** practical

pradera *f* prairie, grassland; **prado** *m* meadow

pragmático pragmatic; **pragmatismo** *m* pragmatism

precario precarious

precaución *f* precaution

precedente 1 *adj* previous **2** *m* precedent; **preceder** precede

precintar *paquete* seal; *lugar* seal off; **precinto** *m* seal

precio *m* price; **precioso** (*de valor*) precious; (*hermoso*) beautiful

precipicio *m* precipice

precipitación *f* (*prisa*) hurry, haste; **precipitaciones** rain; **precipitado** hasty, sudden; **precipitar** (*lanzar*) throw, hurl; (*acelerar*) hasten; **precipitarse** rush; *fig* be hasty

precisar (*aclarar*) specify; (*necesitar*) need; **precisión** *f* precision; **preciso** precise, accurate; **ser ~** be necessary

precoz early; *niño* precocious

precursor *m*, **~a** *f* precursor, forerunner

predecesor *m*, **~a** *f* predecessor

predecir predict

predicar preach

predicción *f* prediction

predilecto favorite, *Br* favourite

predispuesto predisposed (**a** to)

predominar predominate; **predominio** *m* predominance

prefacio *m* preface, foreword

preferencia f preference;
preferente preferential;
preferido 1 part ☞ **preferir**
2 adj favorite; Br favourite;
preferir prefer

prefijo m prefix; TELEC area
code; Br dialling code

pregunta f question; **preguntar** ask; ~ **por algo** ask about
sth; ~ **por alguien** paradero
ask for s.o.; salud etc ask
about s.o.

prejuicio m prejudice

prematuro 1 adj premature **2**
m, **-a** f premature baby

premiar award a prize to; **premio** m prize

prenda f item of clothing, garment; garantía security; en
juegos forfeit

prendedor m broach, Br
brooch

prender 1 v/t a fugitivo capture; sujetar pin up; L.Am.
fuego light; L.Am. luz turn
on; ~ **fuego** a set fire to **2**
v/i de planta take; (empezar
a arder) catch; de moda catch
on

prensa f press; ~ **amarilla** gutter press; **prensar** press

preocupación f worry, concern; **preocupado** worried,
concerned (**por** about); **preocupante** worrying; **preocupar** worry, concern; **preocuparse** worry (**por** about);
~ **de** (encargarse) look after,
take care of

preparación f preparation;
(educación) education; para

trabajo training; **preparado**
ready, prepared; **preparar**
prepare, get ready; **preparativos** mpl preparations

preponderar predominate

preposición f GRAM preposition

presa f (dique) dam; (embalse)
reservoir; (víctima) prey;
L.Am. para comer bite to eat

prescribir JUR prescribe;
prescripción f JUR de contrato expiry, expiration

presencia f presence; **buena**
~ smart appearance; **pre-
senciar** witness; (estar presente a) attend, be present at

presentación f presentation;
COM launch; entre personas
introduction; **presentador**
m, ~a f TV presenter; **presentar** present; a alguien introduce; producto launch;
solicitud submit; **presentarse en sitio** show up; (darse
a conocer) introduce o.s.; a
examen take; de problema,
dificultad arise; a elecciones
run

presente 1 adj present; **tener
algo** ~ bear sth in mind; **¡~!**
here! **2** m tiempo present **3**
m/f/pl: **los** ~**s** those present

presentir foresee; **presiento
que...** I have a feeling
that …

preservar protect; **preservativo** m condom

presidencia f presidency; de
compañía presidency, Br
chairmanship; de comité

chairmanship; **presidente**
m, -**a** *f* president; *de gobierno*
premier, prime minister; *de*
compañía president, *Br*
chairman, *Br mujer* chair-
woman; *de comité* chair

presidio *m* prison

presidir be president of; *reu-*
nión chair

presión *f* pressure; ~ *sanguí*
nea blood pressure; *presio-*
nar botón press; *fig* put pressure on, pressure

preso 1 *part* ☞ **prender** 2 *m*,
-**a** *f* prisoner

prestación *f* provision; ~ *so-*
cial sustitutoria MIL community service in lieu of military service; *préstamo m*
loan; ~ *bancario* bank loan;
prestar *dinero* lend; *ayuda*
give; *L.Am.* borrow; ~ *aten-*
ción pay attention

prestidigitador *m*, ~**a** *f* con-
jurer

prestigio *m* prestige; **presti-**
gioso prestigious

presumido conceited; (*co-*
queto) vain; **presumir** 1 *v/t*
presume 2 *v/i* show off; ~
de algo boast about sth;
presume de listo he thinks
he's very clever; **presunto**
alleged, suspected; **presun-**
tuoso conceited

presuponer assume; **presu-**
puesto 1 *part* ☞ **presupo-**
ner 2 *m* POL budget

pretencioso pretentious

pretender: pretendía con-
vencerlos he was trying to

persuade them; **pretendien-**
te *m de mujer* suitor; **preten-**
sión *f L.Am.* (*arrogancia*)
vanity; *sin pretensiones*
unpretentious

pretexto *m* pretext

prevención *f* prevention;
prevenir prevent; (*avisar*)
warn (*contra* against); **pre-**
ventivo preventive, preven-
tative

prever foresee

previo previous; *sin* ~ *aviso*
without (prior) warning

previsión *f* (*predicción*) forecast; (*preparación*) foresight

prima *f de seguro* premium;
(*pago extra*) bonus

primavera *f* spring; BOT prim-
rose

primer first; **primero** 1 *adj*
first; ~**s auxilios** first aid 2
m, -**a** *f* first (one) 3 *adv* first

primitivo primitive; (*original*)
original

primo *m*, -**a** *f* cousin

primordial fundamental

princesa *f* princess

principal main, principal; *lo* ~
the main *o* most important
thing

príncipe *m* prince

principiante 1 *adj* inexperienced 2 *m/f* beginner; **prin-**
cipio *m* principle; *en tiempo*
beginning; *a* ~**s de abril** at
the beginning of April

prioridad *f* priority; **priorita-**
rio priority *atr*

prisa *f* hurry, rush; *darse* ~
hurry (up); *tener* ~ be in a

hurry o rush

prisión f prison, jail; **prisionero 1** adj captive **2** m, -a f prisoner

prismáticos mpl binoculars

privado 1 part **> privar 2** adj private; **privar:** **~ a alguien de algo** deprive s.o. of sth; **privarse** deprive o.s.; **privatizar** privatize

privilegiado privileged; (excelente) exceptional; **privilegiar** privilege; (dar importancia a) favor, Br favour; **privilegio** m privilege

proa f MAR bow

probabilidad f probability; **probable** probable, likely

probar 1 v/t teoría test, try out; (comer un poco de) taste, try; (comer por primera vez) try **2** v/i try; **~ a hacer** try doing; **probeta** f test tube

problema m problem; **problemático** problematic

procedencia f origin; **procedente: ~ de** from; **proceder 1** v/i come (**de** from); (actuar) proceed; (ser conveniente) be fitting; **~ a** proceed to; **~ contra alguien** initiate proceedings against s.o. **2** m conduct; **procedimiento** m procedure, method; JUR proceedings pl

procesamiento m: **~ de textos** word processing; **procesar** INFOR process; JUR prosecute; **procesión** f procession; **proceso** m process; JUR trial; **~ de datos / tex-**

tos data / word processing

proclamación f proclamation; **proclamar** proclaim

procurador m, -a f JUR attorney, lawyer; **procurar** try

prodigio m wonder, miracle; persona prodigy

producción f production; **producir** produce; (causar) cause; **productividad** f productivity; **productivo** productive; empresa profitable; **producto** m product; **productor** m, -a f producer

profanar defile, desecrate

profesión f profession; **profesional** m/f & adj professional; **profesor** m, -a f teacher; de universidad professor, Br lecturer

profeta m prophet

profundidad f depth; **profundo** deep; pensamiento, persona profound

programa m program, Br programme; INFOR program; EDU syllabus; **~ de estudios** syllabus, curriculum; **programador** m, -a f programmer; **programar** aparato program, Br programme; INFOR program; (planear) schedule

progresar progress, make progress; **progresivo** progressive; **progreso** m progress

prohibición f ban (**de** on); **prohibido** forbidden; **~ fumar** no smoking; **prohibir** forbid, ban

prolijo long-winded; (*minucioso*) detailed

prólogo *m* preface

prolongar extend, prolong

promedio *m* average

promesa *f* promise; **prometedor** bright, promising; **prometer** promise; **prometida** *f* fiancée; **prometido 1** *part* ☞ **prometer 2** *adj* engaged **3** *m* fiancé

prominente prominent

promoción *f* promotion; EDU year; **promocionar** promote; **promotor** *m*, **~a** *f* promoter; **~ inmobiliario** developer; **promover** promote; (*causar*) provoke, cause

promulgar *ley* promulgate

pronombre *m* GRAM pronoun

pronóstico *m* prognosis; **~ del tiempo** weather forecast

pronto 1 *adj* prompt **2** *adv* (*dentro de poco*) soon; (*temprano*) early; **de ~** suddenly; **tan ~ como** as soon as

pronunciación *f* pronunciation; **pronunciar** pronounce; (*decir*) say; **~ un discurso** give a speech

propagación *f* spread; propaganda *f* advertising; POL propaganda; **propagar** spread

propenso prone (**a** to)

propicio favorable, *Br* favourable

propiedad *f* property; **propietario** *m*, **-a** *f* owner, proprietor

propina *f* tip

propio own; (*característico*) characteristic (**de** of), typical (**de** of); (*adecuado*) suitable (**para** for); **la ~a directora** the director herself

proponer propose, suggest; **proponerse:** **~ hacer algo** decide to do sth

proporción *f* proportion; **proporcional** proportional; **proporcionar** provide, supply; *satisfacción* give

proposición *f* proposal, suggestion

propósito *m* (*intención*) intention; (*objetivo*) purpose; **a ~** on purpose; (*por cierto*) by the way

propuesta *f* proposal

propulsión *f* TÉC propulsion

prórroga *f* DEP overtime, *Br* tb extra time; **prorrogar** *plazo* extend

prosa *f* prose

proseguir carry on, continue

prospecto *m* directions for use *pl*; *de propaganda* leaflet

prosperar prosper, thrive; **prosperidad** *f* prosperity; **próspero** prosperous, thriving

prostitución *f* prostitution; **prostituta** *f* prostitute

protagonista *m*/*f* personaje main character; *actor, actriz* star; *de una hazaña* hero; *mujer* heroine

protección *f* protection; **proteger** protect (**de** from)

proteína *f* protein

protesta f protest; **protestante** m/f Protestant; **protestar 1** v/t protest **2** v/i (*quejarse*) complain (**por, de** about); (*expresar oposición*) protest (**contra, por** about, against)

protocolo m protocol

provecho m benefit; **¡buen ~!** enjoy (your meal); **sacar ~ de** benefit from; **provechoso** S.Am. beneficial

proveedor m, **~a** f supplier; **~ de (acceso a) Internet** Internet Service Provider, ISP; **proveer** supply; **~ a alguien de algo** supply s.o. with sth

proverbio m proverb

providencia f providence

provincia f province; **provincial** provincial

provisión f provision; **provisional** provisional; **provisorio** S.Am. provisional

provocar cause; *al enfado* provoke; *sexualmente* lead on; **¿te provoca un café?** S.Am. how about a coffee?; **provocativo** provocative

proxeneta m pimp

proximidad f proximity; **próximo** (*siguiente*) next; (*cercano*) near, close

proyección f MAT, PSI projection; *de película* showing; **proyectar** project; (*planear*) plan; *película* show; *sombra* cast; **proyectil** m missile; **proyecto** m plan; *trabajo* project; **~ de ley** bill; **tenir en ~ hacer algo** plan to do

sth; **proyector** m projector

prudencia f caution, prudence; **prudente** careful, cautious

prueba f tb TIP proof; JUR piece of evidence; DEP event; EDU test; **a ~ de bala** bulletproof; **poner algo a ~** put sth to the test

psicología f psychology; **psicológico** psychological; **psicólogo** m, **-a** f psychologist; **psicópata** m/f psychopath; **psiquiatra** m/f psychiatrist; **psiquiatría** f psychiatry; **psiquiátrico** psychiatric; **psíquico** psychic

púa f ZO spine, quill; MÚS plectrum, pick

publicación f publication; **publicar** publish; **publicarse** come out, be published; **publicidad** f (*divulgación*) publicity; COM advertising; (*anuncios*) advertisements pl; **publicitario 1** adj advertising atr **2** m, **-a** f advertising executive; **público 1** adj public; *escuela* public, Br state **2** m public; TEA audience; DEP spectators pl, crowd

puchero m GASTR (cooking) pot; **hacer ~s** fig pout

pudín m pudding

pudor m modesty

pudrirse rot; **~ de envidia** be green with envy

pueblo m village; *más grande* town

puente m bridge; **hacer ~**

have a day off between a weekend and a public holiday

puerco 1 *adj* dirty; *fig* filthy F **2** *m* ZO pig; **~ espín** porcupine

pueril childish, puerile

puerro *m* BOT leek

puerta *f* door; *en valla* gate; DEP goal; **~ de embarque** gate

puerto *m* MAR port; GEOG pass

Puerto Rico Puerto Rico

pues well; *fml* (*porque*) as, since; **~ bien** well; **¡~ sí!** of course!

puesta *f*: **~ a punto** tune-up; **~ de sol** sunset

puesto 1 *part →* **poner 2** *m* *lugar* place; *en mercado* stall, stand; MIL post; **~ (de trabajo)** job **3** *conj*: **~ que** since, given that

pulcro immaculate

pulga *f* ZO flea

pulgada *f* inch; **pulgar** *m* thumb

pulgón *m* ZO aphid, *Br* greenfly

pulido 1 *adj* polished **2** *m* *acción* polishing; *efecto* polish; **pulir** polish

pulmón *m* lung; **pulmonar** pulmonary, lung *atr*; **pulmonía** *f* MED pneumonia

pulpa *f* pulp

púlpito *m* pulpit

pulpo *m* ZO octopus

pulsación *f* beat; *de tecla* key stroke; **pulsar** *botón, tecla*

press

pulso *m* pulse; *fig* steady hand; **tomar el ~ a alguien** take s.o.'s pulse

pulverizador *m* spray; **pulverizar** spray; (*convertir en polvo*) pulverize, crush

puma *m* ZO puma, mountain lion

punible punishable

punta *f* tip; (*extremo*) end; *de lápiz*, GEOG point; *L.Am.* (*grupo*) group; **sacar ~ a** sharpen; **puntada** *f* stitch; **puntapié** *m* kick; **puntilla** *f*: **de ~s** on tippy-toe, *Br* on tiptoe

punto *m* point; *señal* dot; *signo de puntuación* period, *Br* full stop; *en costura, sutura* stitch; **dos ~s** colon; **~ muerto** AUTO neutral; **~ de vista** point of view; **~ y coma** semicolon; **a ~ (listo)** ready; (*a tiempo*) in time; **de ~** knitted **en ~** on the dot; **estar a ~ de** be about to; **hacer ~** knit

puntuación *f* punctuation; DEP score; EDU grade, *Br* mark; **puntual** punctual; **puntualidad** *f* punctuality; **puntualizar** (*señalar*) point out; (*aclarar*) clarify

puñal *m* dagger

puñetazo *m* punch

puño *m* fist; *de camisa* cuff; *de bastón, paraguas* handle

pupila *f* pupil

pupitre *m* desk

puré *m* purée; *sopa* cream; **~ de patatas** *o L.Am.* **papas**

mashed potatoes
pureza *f* purity
purgante *m/adj* laxative, purgative; **purgar** MED, POL purge; **purgarse** take a laxative; **purgatorio** *m* REL purgatory

purificar purify; **puro 1** *adj*
pure; *Méx (único)* sole, only;
la -a verdad the honest truth
2 *m* cigar
púrpura *f* purple
pus *m* pus
pústula *f* MED pustule
puta *f* P whore P; **putada** *f* P
dirty trick

Q

que 1 *pron rel sujeto: persona*
who, that; *cosa* which, that;
complemento: persona that,
whom *fml; cosa* that, which;
el coche ~ ves the car you
can see, the car that *o* which
you can see **2** *conj* that; *lo*
mismo ~ tú the same as
you; *más grande ~* bigger
than; *¡~ entre!* tell him to
come in; *¡~ descanses!*
sleep well; *¡~ sí!* I said yes;
¡~ no! I said no; *es ~...* the
thing is ...; *yo ~ tú* if I were
you

qué 1 *adj & pron interr* what;
¿~ día es? what day is it?
2 *adj & pron int: ¡~ moto!*
what a motorbike!; *¡~ de flo-*
res! what a lot of flowers! **3**
adv: ¡~ alto es! he's so tall!;
¡~ bien! great!

quebradizo brittle; **quebra-**
do 1 *adj* broken **2** *m* MAT
fraction; **quebrar 1** *v/t* break
2 *v/i* COM go bankrupt *o* bust
F

quedar (*permanecer*) stay; **en**
un estado be; (*sobrar*) be left;

te queda bien / mal de estilo
it suits you / doesn't suit
you; *de talla* it fits you /
doesn't fit you; *~ cerca* be
nearby; *~ con alguien* F arrange to meet (with) s.o.; *~*
en algo agree to sth; **que-**
darse stay; *~ ciego* go blind;
~ con algo keep sth; **me**
quedé sin comer I ended
up not eating
quehaceres *mpl* tasks
queja *f* complaint; **quejarse**
complain (*a* of; *de* about)
quema *f* burning; **quemadu-**
ra *f* burn; **quemar 1** *v/t* burn;
con agua scald; F *recursos*
use up; F *dinero* blow F **2**
v/i be very hot
querella *f* JUR lawsuit
querer (*desear*) want; (*amar*)
love; *~ decir* mean; *sin ~* unintentionally; **quisiera...** I
would like ...; **querido 1** *part*
☞ **querer 2** *adj* dear **3** *m*, **-a** *f*
darling
queso *m* cheese
quicio *m*: **sacar de ~ a al-**
guien F drive s.o. crazy F

quiebra f COM bankruptcy

quien *rel sujeto* who, that; *objeto* who, whom *fml*, that

quién who; **¿de ~ es este libro?** whose is this book?, who does this book belong to?

quieto still; **quietud** f peacefulness

quilate m carat

quilla f keel

química f chemistry; **químico 1** *adj* chemical **2** *m*, *-a* f chemist

quince fifteen; **quincena** f two weeks, *Br* fortnight

quiniela f lottery where the winners are decided by soccer results, *Br* football pools

quinientos five hundred

quinina f quinine

quinta f MIL draft, *Br* call-up; **es de mi ~** he's my age

quinto 1 *adj* fifth **2** *m* MIL conscript

quiosco m kiosk; **~ de prensa** newsstand, *Br* newsagent's

quirófano m operating room, *Br* operating theatre

quirúrgico surgical

quitaesmalte m nail varnish remover; **quitamanchas** *m inv* stain remover; **quitanieves** m snowplow, *Br* snowplough

quitar 1 *v/t ropa* take off, remove; *obstáculos* remove; **~ algo a alguien** take sth (away) from s.o.; **~ la mesa** clear the table **2** *v/i*: **¡quita!** get out of the way!; **quitarse** *ropa, gafas* take off; *(apartarse)* get out of the way; **~ algo / a alguien de encima** get rid of sth / s.o.

quitasol m sunshade

quizá(s) perhaps, maybe

R

rabanito m BOT wild radish; **rábano** m BOT radish

rabia f MED rabies *sg*; **dar ~ a alguien** make s.o. mad; **tener ~ a alguien** have it in for s.o.; **rabiar**: **~ de dolor** be in agony; **~ por** be dying for

rabioso MED rabid; *fig* furious

rabo m tail

racha f spell

racial racial

racimo m bunch

ración f share; *(porción)* serving, portion; **racional** rational; **racionalizar** rationalize; **racionar** ration

racismo m racism; **racista** m/f & adj racist

radar m radar

radiación f radiation; **radiactividad** f radioactivity; **radiactivo** radioactive; **radiador** m radiator; **radiante** radiant; **radiar** radiate

radical *m/f & adj* radical

radio 1 *m* MAT radius; QUÍM radium; *L.Am.* radio; **~ de acción** range **2** *f* radio; **~ despertador** clock radio; **radioaficionado** *m* radio ham; **radiocasete** *m* cassette player; **radiografía** *f* X-ray; **radiología** *f* radiology; **radiopatrulla** *f* radio patrol car; **radiotaxi** *m* radio taxi; **radioterapia** *f* radiotherapy; **radioyente** *m/f* listener

ráfaga *f* gust; *de balas* burst

rafia *f* raffia

raído threadbare

rail, raíl *m* rail

raíz *f* root; **~ cuadrada** MAT square root; **a ~ de** as a result of

raja *f* (*rodaja*) slice; (*corte*) cut; (*grieta*) crack; **rajar 1** *v/t fruta* cut, slice; *cerámica* crack; *neumático* slash **2** *v/i* F gossip; **rajarse** *fig* F back out

rallador *m* grater; **rallar** GASTR grate

rama *f* branch; POL wing; **andarse por las ~s** beat about the bush

ramera *f* whore, prostitute

ramificarse branch out

ramo *m* COM sector; **~ de flores** bunch of flowers

rampa *f* ramp; **~ de lanzamiento** launch pad

rana *f* ZO frog

rancho *m* Méx small farm; *L.Am.* (*barrio de chabolas*) shanty town

rancio rancid; *fig* ancient

ranura *f* slot

rapaz 1 *adj* predatory **2** *m*, **-a** *f* K id F

rape *m pescado* anglerfish; **al ~ pelo** cropped

rapidez *f* speed, rapidity; **rápido 1** *adj* quick, fast **2** *m* rapids *pl*

rapiña *f* pillage

raptar kidnap; **rapto** *m* kidnap

raqueta *f* racket

rareza *f* scarcity, rarity; **raro** rare

ras *m*: **a ~ de tierra** at ground level

rascacielos *m inv* skyscraper; **rascar** scratch; *superficie* scrape, scratch

rasgar tear (up); **rasgo** *m* feature; **a grandes ~s** broadly speaking

rasguñar scratch; **rasguño** *m* MED scratch

raso 1 *adj* flat, level; **soldado ~** private **2** *m material* satin; **al ~** in the open air

raspado *m* Méx water ice; **raspar 1** *v/t* scrape; *con lija* sand **2** *v/i* be rough

rastrear 1 *v/t persona* track; *bosque, zona* comb **2** *v/i* trail; **rastrillo** *m* rake; **rastro** *m* flea market; (*huella*) trace; **rastrojo** *m* stubble

rata *f* ZO rat

ratero *m*, **-a** *f* petty thief

raticida *m* rat poison

ratificar POL ratify

rato *m* time; **~s libres** spare

time; **al poco ~** after a short time o while; **todo el ~** all the time

ratón m ZO, INFOR mouse; **ratonera** f mouse trap

raya f GRAM dash; ZO ray; *de pelo ~*, Br parting; **a** o **de ~s** striped; **pasarse de la ~** overstep the mark, too far; **rayado** disco, superficie scratched

rayar 1 v/t scratch; (*tachar*) cross out **2** v/i border (**en** on)

rayo m FÍS ray; METEO (bolt of) lightning; **~ láser** laser beam; **~ X** X-ray

raza f race; *de animal* breed

razón f reason; **a ~ de precio** at; **dar la ~ a alguien** admit that s.o. is right; **entrar en ~** see sense; **perder la ~** lose one's mind; **tener ~** be right; **razonable** precio reasonable

razonar precio reasonable

reacción f reaction (**a** to); **avión ~** jet (aircraft); **reaccionar** react (**a** to); **reaccionario 1** adj reactionary **2** m, -a f reactionary

reactor m reactor; (*motor*) jet engine

real (*regio*) royal; (*verdadero*) real; **realidad** f reality; **en ~** in fact, in reality; **realista 1** adj realistic **2** m/f realist; **realizador** m, **~a** f de película director; RAD, TV producer; **realizar** tarea carry out; RAD, TV produce; COM realize

realzar highlight

reanimar revive

reanudar resume

rebaja f reduction; **~s de verano** summer sale; **rebajar** reduce

rebanada f slice

rebaño m flock

rebasar Méx AUTO pass, Br overtake

rebatir razones rebut, refute

rebeca f cardigan

rebelarse rebel; **rebelde 1** adj rebel atr **2** m/f rebel; **rebelión** f rebellion

rebosar overflow

rebotar **1** v/t bounce; (*disgustar*) annoy **2** v/i bounce; **rebote** m bounce; **de ~** on the rebound

rebozar GASTR coat

rebuscado over-elaborate

recado m errand; Rpl (*arnés*) harness; **dejar un ~** leave a message

recaer fig: de responsabilidad fall (**en** on); MED have a relapse; JUR reoffend; **recaída** f MED relapse

recalentar comida warm o heat up

recargar batería recharge; recipiente refill; **~ un 5%** charge 5% extra; **recargo** m surcharge

recauchutado m retread

recaudación f acción collection; cantidad takings pl; **recaudador** m, **~a** f collector; **recaudar** impuestos, dinero collect

recelar suspect; **~ de alguien**

not trust s.o.; **recelo** *m* mistrust; **receloso** suspicious

recepción *f* reception; **recepcionista** *m/f* receptionist; **receptor** *m* receiver

receta *f* GASTR recipe; ~ **médica** prescription; **recetar** MED prescribe

rechazar reject; MIL repel; **rechazo** *m* rejection

rechinar creak, squeak

recibir receive; **recibo** *m* (sales) receipt

reciclable recyclable; **reciclado, reciclaje** *m* recycling; **reciclar** recycle

recién newly; *L.Am. (hace poco)* just; ~ **casados** newlyweds; ~ **nacido** newborn; ~ **pintado** wet paint; ~ **llegamos** we've only just arrived; **reciente** recent

recinto *m* premises *pl*; *área* grounds *pl*

recipiente *m* container

recíproco reciprocal

recital *m* recital; **recitar** recite

reclamación *f* complaint; POL claim, demand; **reclamar 1** *v/t* claim, demand **2** *v/i* complain

reclamo *m* lure

reclinar rest; **reclinarse** lean, recline (**contra** against)

recluta *m/f* recruit; **reclutar** recruit

recobrar recover

recodo *m* bend

recogedor *m* dustpan; **recoger** pick up, collect; *habitación* tidy up; AGR harvest;

(mostrar) show; **recogida** *f* collection; ~ **de basuras** garbage collection; *Br* refuse collection; ~ **de equipajes** baggage reclaim

recolección *f* harvest; **recolectar** harvest

recomendable recommendable; **recomendación** *f* recommendation; **recomendar** recommend

recompensa *f* reward; **recompensar** reward

reconciliación *f* reconciliation; **reconciliar** reconcile; **reconciliarse** make up (**con** with), be reconciled (**con** with)

reconocer recognize; *errores* admit, acknowledge; *area* reconnoitre, *Br* reconnoitre; MED examine; **reconocido** grateful; **reconocimiento** *m* recognition; *de error* acknowledg(e)ment; MED examination, check-up; MIL reconnaissance

reconquista *f* reconquest

reconstruir *fig* reconstruct

récord 1 *adj* record(-breaking) **2** *m* record

recordar remember, recall; ~ **algo a alguien** remind s.o. of sth

recorrer *distancia* cover; *a pie* walk; *territorio, país* travel around; *camino* go along, travel along; **recorrido** *m* route; DEP round

recortar cut out; *fig* cut; **recorte** *m fig* cutback; ~ **de pe-**

ríódico cutting, clipping; **~ salarial** salary cut

recrear recreate; **recrearse** amuse o.s.; **recreativo** recreational; **juegos ~s** amusements; **recreo** m recreation; EDU recess, Br break

recriminar reproach

recrudecer worsen; **recrudecerse** intensify

rectángulo m rectangle

rectificar correct, rectify; **camino** straighten

recto straight; **(honesto)** honest

recuerdo m memory; **da ~s a Luís** give my regards to Luís

recuperación f tb fig recovery; **recuperar tiempo** make up; **algo perdido** recover; **recuperarse** recover **(de** from)

recurrir 1 v/t JUR appeal against **2** v/i: **~ a** resort to, turn to; **recurso** m JUR appeal; **material** resource; **~s humanos** human resources

red f net; INFOR, fig network; **caer en las ~es de** fig fall into the clutches of

redacción f writing; **de editorial** editorial department; EDU essay; **redactar** write, compose; **redactor** m, **~a** f editor

redada f raid

redecilla f hairnet

redención f redemption; **redimir** redeem

rédito m return, yield

redoblar redouble; **redoblarse** double; **redoble** m MÚS (drum)roll

redonda f: **a la ~** around; **redondear para más** round up; **para menos** round down; **(rematar)** round off; **redondo** round; **negocio** excellent; **caer ~** flop down

reducción f reduction; MED setting; **reducir** reduce **(a** to); MIL overcome

reeducar reeducate

reelección f reelection; **reelegir** re-elect

reembolsar refund; **reembolso** m refund; **contra ~** collect on delivery, Br cash on delivery, COD

reemplazar replace; **reemplazo** m replacement; DEP substitute; MIL recruit

reexpedir forward

referencia f reference; **~s** COM references; **referente a** referring to; **referir** tell, relate; **referirse** refer **(a** to)

refinación f refining; **refinado 1** adj tb fig refined **2** m refining; **refinamiento** m refining; **refinar** refine; **refinería** f refinery

reflejar tb fig reflect; **reflejo** m reflex; **imagen** reflection; **reflexión** f fig reflection, thought; **reflexionar** reflect on, ponder; **reflexivo** GRAM reflexive

reflujo m ebb

reforestación f reforestation; **reforestar** reforest

reforma f reform; **~s (obras)**

refurbishment; (*reparaciones*) repairs; *reformar* reform; *edificio* refurbish; (*reparar*) repair

reforzar reinforce; *vigilancia* increase, step up

refractario TÉC heat-resistant, fireproof; *fig ser ~ a algo* be against sth

refrán *m* saying

refregar scrub

refrescar 1 *v/t tb fig* refresh; *conocimientos* brush up **2** *v/i* cool down; **refresco** *m* soda, *Br* soft drink

refrigeración *f de alimentos* refrigeration; *aire acondicionado* air-conditioning; *de motor* cooling; **refrigerador** *m* refrigerator; **refrigerar** refrigerate; **refrigerio** *m* snack

refuerzo *m* reinforcement; **~s** MIL reinforcements

refugiado *m*, **-a** *f* refugee; **refugiarse** take refuge; **refugio** *m* refuge

refundir rework

refutar refute

regadera *f* watering can; *Méx* (*ducha*) shower; **regadío** *m*: *tierra de ~* irrigated land

regalar: **~ algo a alguien** give sth to s.o., give s.o. sth

regaliz *m* BOT licorice, *Br* liquorice

regalo *m* gift, present

regañar 1 *v/t* tell off **2** *v/i* quarrel

regar water; AGR irrigate

regata *f* regatta

regatear DEP get past, dodge;

no ~ esfuerzos spare no effort; **regateo** *m* haggling

regazo *m* lap

regenerar regenerate

régimen *m* POL regime; MED diet; *estar a ~* be on a diet

regio regal, majestic; *S.Am.* F (*estupendo*) great F

región *f* region; **regional** regional

regir 1 *v/t* rule, govern **2** *v/i* apply, be in force

registrar register; *casa* search; **registro** *m* register; *de casa* search; **~ civil** register of births, marriages and deaths

regla *f* (*norma*) rule; *para medir* ruler; MED period; *por ~ general* as a rule

reglamentar regulate; **reglamentario** regulation *atr*; **reglamento** *m* regulation

regocijo *m* delight

regresar 1 *v/i* return **2** *v/t Méx* return, give back; **regreso** *m* return

regulable adjustable; **regulación** *f* regulation; *de temperatura* control; **regular 1** *adj* regular; (*común*) ordinary; (*no muy bien*) so-so **2** *v/t* TÉC regulate; *temperatura* control; **regularidad** *f* regularity

rehabilitación *f* rehabilitation; ARQUI restoration; **rehabilitar** ARQUI restore

rehén *m* hostage

rehuir shy away from

rehusar refuse, decline

reimpresión *f* reprinting

reina f queen; **reinado** m reign; **reinar** tb fig reign

reincidente 1 adj repeat **2** m/f repeat offender; **reincidir** reoffend

reino m tb fig kingdom; **el Reino Unido** the United Kingdom

reintegrar, reintegrarse return (**a** to); **reintegro** m (en lotería) prize in the form of a refund of the stake money

reír, reírse laugh (**de** at)

reiterar repeat, reiterate

reivindicar claim; ~ **un atentado** claim responsibility for an attack

reja f AGR plowshare, Br ploughshare; (barrote) bar, railing; **meter entre ~s** fig F put behind bars; **rejilla** f FERR luggage rack

rejoneador m bullfighter on horseback

rejuvenecer rejuvenate

relación f relationship; **relaciones públicas** public relations, PR sg; **relacionar** relate (**con** to), connect (**con** with); **relacionarse** be connected (**con** to), be related (**con** to); (mezclarse) mix

relajación f relaxation; **relajar, relajarse** relax

relámpago m flash of lightning; **viaje** ~ flying visit

relampaguear: **relampagueó y tronó mucho** there was a lot of thunder and lightning

relativo relative; ~ **a** regarding, about

relato m short story

relax m relaxation

relegar relegate

relevar MIL relieve; ~ **a alguien de algo** relieve s.o. of sth; **relevo** m MIL change (sustituto) relief, replacement; **carrera de ~s** relay (race); **tomar el ~ de alguien** take over from s.o., relieve s.o.

relieve m relief; **poner de ~** highlight

religión f religion; **religiosa** nun; **religiosidad** f religiousness; **religioso 1** adj religious **2** m monk

relinchar neigh

rellano m landing

rellenar fill; GASTR pollo stuff; formulario fill out, fill in; **relleno 1** m GASTR stuffed; pastel filled **2** m stuffing; en pastel filling

reloj m clock; de pulsera watch, wristwatch; ~ **de sol** sundial; **relojería** f watchmaker's; **relojero** m, -a watchmaker

relucir sparkle, glitter

remachar mesa, silla rivet; orden repeat

remanente m remainder, surplus

remar row

rematar 1 v/t finish off; L.Am COM auction **2** v/i en fútbol shoot; **remate** m L.Am COM auction, sale; en fútbol shot; **ser tonto de ~** be a complete idiot

remediar remedy; **no puedo ~lo** I can't do anything about it; **remedio** m remedy; **sin ~** hopeless; **no hay más ~ que...** there's no alternative but to ...

remendar con parche patch; (zurcir) darn

remero m rower, oarsman

remesa f (envío) shipment, consignment; L.Am. dinero remittance

remiendo m (parche) patch; (zurcido) darn

remilgado fussy, finicky; re-milgo m; **tener / hacer ~s** be fussy

remisión f remission; en texto reference; **remitente** m/f sender; **remitir 1** v/t send, ship; en texto refer (**a** to) **2** v/i MED go into remission; de crisis ease (off)

remo m pala oar; deporte rowing

remodelar redesign, remodel

remojar soak; L.Am. F aconte-cimiento celebrate

remolacha f beet, Br beet-root; **~ azucarera** sugar beet

remolcador m tug; **remolcar** AUTO, MAR tow

remolino m de aire eddy; de agua whirlpool

remolque m AUTO trailer

remordimiento m remorse

remoto remote

remover (agitar) stir; L.Am. (destituir) dismiss; C.Am.,

Méx (quitar) remove

remplazar ☞ **reemplazar**

remuneración f remunera-tion; **remunerar** pay

Renacimiento m Renais-sance

renacuajo m ZO tadpole; F persona shrimp F

renal ANAT renal, kidney atr

rencor m resentment; **guar-dar ~ a alguien** bear s.o. a grudge; **rencoroso** resentful

rendición f surrender

rendido exhausted

rendija f crack; (hueco) gap

rendimiento m performance; FIN yield; (producción) out-put; **rendir 1** v/t honores pay; beneficio produce, yield **2** v/i perform; **rendirse** sur-render

renegado 1 adj renegade atr **2** m renegade; **renegar: ~ de alguien** disown s.o.; **~ de al-go** renounce sth

renglón m line; **a ~ seguido** immediately after

reno m ZO reindeer

renombrado famous, re-nowned; **renombre** m: **de ~** famous, renowned

renovación f renewal; **reno-var** renew

renta f income; de casa rent; **rentable** profitable; **rentar** (arrendar) rent out; (alquiler) rent

renuncia f resignation; **re-nunciar: ~ a** tabaco, alcohol etc give up; puesto resign; de-manda drop

reñir 1 v/t tell off **2** v/i quarrel, fight F

reo m, -a f accused

reorganizar reorganize

reparación f repair; fig reparation; **reparar 1** v/t repair **2** v/i: **~ en algo** notice sth; **reparo** m: **poner ~s a** find problems with; **repartir** (dividir) share out, divide up; productos deliver; **reparto** m (división) share-out, distribution; TEA cast; **~ a domicilio** home delivery

repasar trabajo go over again; EDU review, Br revise

repaso m de lección review, Br revision; de últimas novedades review; TÉC de motor service; **dar un ~ a alguien** tell s.o. off

repatriación f repatriation; **repatriarse** go home

repelente 1 adj fig repellent, repulsive; F niño horrible **2** m repellent; **repeler** repel

repente m: **de ~** suddenly; **repentino** sudden

repercusión f fig repercussion; **repercutir** have repercussions (**en** on)

repertorio m TEA, MÚS repertoire

repetición f repetition; **repetir** repeat

repicar 1 v/t campanas ring; castañuelas click **2** v/i ring out; **repique** m de campanas ringing; de castañuelas clicking

repisa f shelf

repleto full (**de** of)

réplica f replica

replicar reply

repoblación f repopulation, restocking

repollo m BOT cabbage

reponer existencias replace; TEA obra revive; **~ fuerzas** get one's strength back; **reponerse** recover (**de** from)

reportaje m story, report; **reportero** m, -a f reporter; **~ gráfico** press photographer

reposacabezas m inv AUTO headrest; **reposado** calm; **reposar** rest; de vino settle

reposición f TEA revival; TV repeat

reposo m rest

repostar refuel

repostería f pastries pl

reprender scold, tell off

represa f dam; (embalse) reservoir

represalia f reprisal

representación f representation; TEA performance; **en ~ de** on behalf of; **representante** m/f representative; **representar** represent; obra put on, perform; papel play: **~ menos años** look younger

represión f repression

reprimenda f reprimand

reprimir tb PSI repress

reprobable reprehensible; **reprobación** f condemnation; **reprobar** condemn; L.Am. EDU fail

reprochar reproach; **repro-**

che *m* reproach

reproducción *f* BIO reproduction; **reproducir** reproduce; **reproducirse** BIO reproduce, breed; **reproductor 1** *adj* breeding **2** *m* breeding animal

reptar creep

reptil *m* ZO reptile

república *f* republic; **República Dominicana** Dominican Republic; **republicano 1** *adj* republican **2** *m*, **-a** *f* republican

repudiar *fml* repudiate; *herencia* renounce

repuesto *m part* ☞ **reponer 2** *m* spare part; **de ~** spare

repugnancia *f* disgust, repugnance; **repugnante** disgusting, repugnant; **repugnar** disgust, repel

repulsión *f* repulsion; **repulsivo** repulsive

reputación *f* reputation; **reputado** reputable

requemar burn

requerimiento *m* request, requirement; **requerir** require; JUR summons

requesón *m* cottage cheese

requisar *Arg, Chi* MIL requisition; **requisito** *m* requirement

res *f L.Am.* bull; **carne** *f* **de ~** beef; **~es** cattle *pl*

resaca *f* MAR undertow; *de beber* hangover

resaltar 1 *v/t* highlight, stress **2** *v/i* ARQUI jut out; *fig* stand out

resbaladizo slippery; *fig* tricky; **resbalar** slide; *fig* slip (up)

rescatar rescue, save; **rescate** *m de peligro* rescue; *en secuestro* ransom

rescindir cancel; *contrato* terminate

resentido resentful; **resentimiento** *m* resentment; **resentirse** get upset; *de rendimiento, calidad* suffer

reseña *f de libro etc* review

reserva 1 *f* reservation; **~ natural** nature reserve; **sin ~s** without reservation; **2** *m/f* DEP reserve; **reservado 1** *adj* reserved **2** *m* private room; **reservar** (*guardar*) set aside, put by; *billete* reserve

resfriado 1 *adj*: **estar ~** have a cold **2** *m* cold; **resfriarse** catch (a) cold

resguardar protect (**de** from); **resguardo** *m* COM counterfoil

residencia *f* residence; **~ de ancianos** *o* **para la tercera edad** retirement home; **residir** reside; **~ en** *fig* lie in; **residuo** *m* residue; **~s** waste

resignación *f* actitud resignation; **resignarse** resign o.s. (**a** to)

resina *f* resin

resistencia *f* resistance; ELEC, TÉC resistor; **resistente** (*fuerte*) strong, tough; **~ al calor** heat-resistant; **~ al fuego** fireproof; **resistir**

1 v/i resist; (*aguantar*) hold out **2** v/t *tentación* resist; *frío, dolor etc* stand, bear; **resistirse** be reluctant (**a** to)

resolución f *actitud* determination; *de problema* solution (**de** to); JUR ruling; **resolver** *problema* solve; **resolverse** decide (**a** to; *por* on)

resonancia f TÉC resonance; **tener ~** have an impact; **resonar** boom

resorte m spring

respaldar back, support; **respaldo** m *de silla* back; *fig* backing, support

respectivo respective; **respecto** m: **al ~** on the matter; **con ~ a** regarding

respetable respectable; **respetar** respect; **respeto** m respect; **respetuoso** respectful

respiración f breathing; **estar con ~ asistida** MED be on a respirator; **respirar** breathe; **respiro** m *fig* breather, break

resplandecer shine, gleam; **resplandor** m shine, gleam

responder 1 v/t answer **2** v/i: **~ a** answer, reply to; MED respond to; *descripción* fit, match; (*ser debido a*) be due to

responsabilidad f responsibility; **responsable 1** adj responsible (**de** for) **2** m/f person responsible (**de** for)

respuesta f (*contestación*) reply, answer; *fig* response

restablecer re-establish; **restablecerse** recover; **restablecimiento** m re-establishment; *de enfermo* recovery

restante 1 adj remaining **2** m/fpl: **los / las ~s** the rest pl, the remainder pl; **restar 1** v/t subtract; **~ importancia** a play down the importance of **2** v/i remain, be left

restaurante m restaurant

restaurar restore

restitución f restitution; *de confianza, calma* restoration; *en cargo* reinstatement; **restituir** restore; *en cargo* reinstate

resto m rest, remainder; **los ~s mortales** the (mortal) remains

restricción f restriction; **restringir** restrict, limit

resuelto 1 part ☞ **resolver 2** adj decisive, resolute

resultado m result; **sin ~** without success; **resultar** turn out; **~ caro** turn out to be expensive

resumen m summary; **en ~** in short; **resumir** summarize

resurrección f REL resurrection

retablo m altarpiece

retaguardia f MIL rearguard

retal m remnant

retama f BOT broom

retar challenge; *Rpl* (*regañar*) scold, tell off

retardar delay; **retardarse** be late

retención f MED retention; *de*

persona detention; **~ fiscal** tax deduction; **retener** *dinero etc* withhold, deduct; *persona* detain

retina *f* ANAT retina

retirada *f* MIL retreat, withdrawal; **retirar** take away, remove; *acusación, dinero* withdraw; **retirarse** MIL withdraw; **retiro** *m lugar* retreat

reto *m* challenge; *Rpl (regañina)* scolding

retocar FOT retouch, touch up; *(acabar)* put the finishing touches to

retorcer twist; **retorcerse** writhe

retorno *m* return

retractar retract, withdraw

retransmisión *f* RAD, TV transmission, broadcast; **retransmitir** transmit, broadcast

retrasado 1 *part* ☞ **retrasar 2** *adj* tren, entrega late; *con trabajo, pagos* behind; **está ~ en clase** he's lagging behind in class; **~ mental** mentally handicapped; **retrasar 1** *v/t* hold up; *reloj* put back; *reunión* postpone, put back **2** *v/i* de reloj lose time; *en los estudios* be behind; **retrasarse** *(atrasarse)* be late; *de reloj* lose time; *con trabajo, pagos* get behind; **retraso** *m* delay; **ir con ~** be late

retratar FOT take a picture of; *fig* depict; **retrato** *m* picture; **~-robot** composite photo, E-

Fit®

retrete *m* bathroom

retrovisor *m* AUTO rear-view mirror; **~ exterior** wing mirror

retumbar boom

reuma, reúma *m* MED rheumatism

reunificación *f* POL reunification; **reunificar** reunify, reunite

reunión *f* meeting; *de amigos* get-together; **reunir** *personas* bring together; *requisitos* meet; *datos* gather (together); **reunirse** meet up, get together; COM meet

revalorizar revalue

revancha *f* revenge

revelado *m* development; **revelar** FOT develop

reventa *f* resale

reventar 1 *v/i* burst; **lleno a ~** full to bursting **2** *v/t puerta etc* break down; **reventón** *m* AUTO blowout

reverencia *f* reverence; *saludo: de hombre* bow; *de mujer* curtsy

reversible *ropa* reversible; **reverso** *m* reverse, back

revés *m* setback; *tenis* backhand; **al o del ~** back to front; *con el interior fuera* inside out

revestimiento *m* TÉC covering, coating; **revestir** TÉC cover **(de)** with); **~ gravedad** be serious

revisar check, inspect; **revisión** *f* check, inspection; AU-

TO service; **~ técnica** road-worthiness test, Br MOT (test); **~ médica** check-up; **revisor** m, **~a** f FERR (ticket) inspector

revista f magazine; **pasar ~ a** MIL inspect, review; fig review; **revistero** m magazine rack

revocar pared render; JUR revoke

revolución f revolution; **revolucionar** revolutionize

revolver 1 v/t GASTR stir; estómago turn; (desordenar) mess up **2** v/i rummage (**en** in)

revólver m revolver

revuelo m stir

revuelta f uprising

rey m king

rezar 1 v/t oración say **2** v/i pray; de texto say

ribera f shore, bank

ribete m trimming, edging; **~s** fig elements

rico 1 adj rich; comida delicious; Br niño cute, sweet **2** m rich man; **nuevo ~** nouveau riche

ridículo 1 adj ridiculous **2** m ridicule; **hacer el ~, quedar en ~** make a fool of o.s.

riego 1 vb ► **regar 2** m AGR irrigation; **~ sanguíneo** blood flow

riel m FERR rail; **~ para cortinas** curtain rail

rienda f rein; **dar ~ suelta a** give free rein to

riesgo m risk; **correr el ~** run the risk (**de** of); **agencia** f **de calificación de ~s** FIN rating agency; **riesgoso** L.Am. risky

rifa f raffle

rifle m rifle

rigidez f rigidity; de carácter inflexibility; fig strictness; **rígido** rigid; carácter inflexible; fig strict; **rigor** m rigor, Br rigour; **riguroso** rigorous, harsh

rima f rhyme; **rimar** rhyme

rímel m mascara

rincón m corner; **rinconera** f corner unit

rinoceronte m ZO rhinoceros, rhino

riña f quarrel, fight

riñón m ANAT kidney

riñonera f fanny pack, Br bum bag

río 1 m river; **~ abajo / arriba** down / up river **2** vb ► **reír**

riqueza f wealth

risa f laugh; **~s** laughter; **dar ~** be funny; **morirse de ~** laugh o.s. laughing; **tomar algo a ~** treat sth as a joke

risueño cheerful

ritmo m rhythm; de desarrollo rate, pace

rito m rite; **ritual** m/adj ritual

rival m/f rival; **rivalizar: ~ con** rival

rizado curly; **rizar** curl; **rizo** m curl

roaming m IT roaming

robar persona, banco rob; objeto steal; naipe take

roble m BOT oak

robo m robbery; **en casa** burglary

robot m robot; **~ de cocina** food processor

robusto robust, sturdy

roca f rock

rociar spray; **rocío** m dew

rodaja f slice

rodaje m de película shooting, filming; **rodar** 1 v/i roll; de coche, travel (**a** at); **sin rumbo fijo** wander 2 v/t película shoot

rodear surround; **rodeo** m detour; con caballos y vaqueros cattle; **andarse con ~s** beat about the bush; **hablar sin ~s** not beat about the bush

rodilla f knee; **de ~s** kneeling, on one's knees; **hincarse** or **ponerse de ~s** kneel (down)

roedor m rodent; **roer** gnaw; fig eat into

rogar ask for; (implorar) beg for, plead for; **hacerse de ~** play hard to get

rojo 1 adj red; **al ~ vivo** red hot 2 m color red 3 m, -a f POL red, commie F

rollo m FOT roll; fig F drag F; **buen / mal ~** F good / bad atmosphere

románico m/adj Romanesque; **romano** 1 adj Roman 2 m, -a f Roman; **romántico** 1 adj romantic 2 m, -a f romantic

romería f procession

romper 1 v/t break; (hacer añicos) smash; tela, papel tear 2 v/i break; **~ a** start to; **~ con alguien** break up with s.o.

ron m rum

roncar snore

ronco hoarse; **quedarse ~** go hoarse

ronda f round

ronquera f hoarseness

ropa f clothes pl; **~ de cama** bedclothes pl; **~ interior** underwear; **~ íntima** L.Am. underwear; **ropero** m closet, Br wardrobe

rosa 1 adj pink 2 f BOT rose; **rosado** 1 adj pink; vino rosé 2 m rosé; **rosario** m REL rosary; fig string

rosbif m GASTR roast beef

rosca f TÉC thread; GASTR F pastry similar to a donut

rostro m face

rotación f rotation

roto 1 part v romper 2 adj pierna etc broken; (hecho añicos) smashed; tela, papel torn 3 m, -a f Chi one of the urban poor

rotonda f traffic circle, Br roundabout

rotulador m fiber-tip, Br fibre-tip, felt-tip; **rotular** label; **rótulo** m sign

rotura f breakage; **una ~ de cadera** MED a broken hip

rozar 1 v/t rub; (tocar ligeramente) brush; fig touch on 2 v/i rub

rubeola, rubéola f MED German measles sg

rubí m ruby

rubio blond; **tabaco ~** Virgin-

ia tobacco
rudo rough
rueda f wheel; **~ dentada** cogwheel; **~ de prensa** press conference; **~ de recambio** spare wheel
ruedo m TAUR bullring
ruego 1 vb ⇒ **rogar 2** m request
rufián m rogue
ruido m noise; **mucho ~ y pocas nueces** all talk and no action; **ruidoso** noisy
ruina f ruin; **llevar a alguien a la ~** fig bankrupt s.o.
ruiseñor m ZO nightingale
ruleta f roulette
rulo m roller
Rumania Romania; **rumano**

1 adj Romanian **2** m, **-a** f Romanian **3** m idioma Romanian
rumbo m course; **tomar ~ a** head for; **perder el ~** fig lose one's way
rumor m rumor, Br rumour
ruptura f **de relaciones** breaking off; de pareja break-up
rural 1 adj rural **2** m Rpl station wagon, Br estate car; **-es** Méx (rural) police
Rusia Russia; **ruso 1** adj Russian **2** m, **-a** f Russian **3** m idioma Russian
rústico rustic
ruta f route
rutina f routine; **rutinari(** routine atr

S

S.A. (= **sociedad anónima**) inc. (= incorporated), Br plc (= public limited company)
sábado m Saturday
sabana f savanna(h)
sábana f sheet; **~ ajustable** fitted sheet
saber 1 v/t know (**de** about); **~ hacer algo** know how to do sth, be able to do sth; **hacer ~ algo a alguien** let s.o. know sth; **¡qué sé yo!** who knows?; **que yo sepa** as far as I know **2** v/i taste (**a** of); **me sabe mal** fig it upsets me **3** m knowledge, learning; **sabido** well-

known
sabio 1 adj wise; (sensato sensible **2** m, **-a** f wise person; (experto) expert
sable m saber, Br sabre
sabor m flavor, Br flavou taste; **saborear** savor, Br sa vour; fig relish
sabotaje m sabotage; **sabo tear** sabotage
sabroso tasty; fig juicy L.Am. (agradable) nice
sacacorchos m inv cork screw; **sacapuntas** m in pencil sharpener
sacar v/t take out; manch take out, remove; informa ción get; disco, libro brin

out; *lengua* stick out; *fotocopias* make; **~ a alguien a bailar** ask s.o. to dance; **~ algo en claro** (*entender*) make sense of sth; **~ de paseo** take for a walk

sacarina f saccharin(e)

sacerdote m priest

saco m sack; *L.Am.* jacket; **~ de dormir** sleeping bag

sacramento m sacrament

sacrificar sacrifice; (*matar*) slaughter; **sacrificio** m sacrifice; **sacrilegio** m sacrilege; **sacristán** m sexton; **sacristía** f vestry

sacudida f shake, jolt; ELEC shock; **sacudir** *tb* fig shake; F *niño* beat

sagaz shrewd, sharp

Sagitario m/f inv ASTR Sagittarius

sagrado sacred, holy

sal 1 f salt; **~ común** cooking salt **2** vb → **salir**

sala f room, hall; **~ de cine** screen; JUR court room; **~ de chat** chat room; **~ de embarque** AVIA departure lounge; **~ de espera** waiting room; **~ de estar** living room; **~ de fiestas** night club; **~ de sesiones** o **de juntas** boardroom

salado salted; (*con demasiada sal*) salty; (*no dulce*) savory, *Br* savoury; fig funny, witty; *C.Am., Chi, Rpl* F pric(e)y F

salar 1 v/t add salt to, salt; *para conservar* salt **2** m Arg salt mine

salario m salary

salchicha f sausage; **salchichón** m type of spiced sausage

saldar *disputa* settle; *deuda* settle, pay; *géneros* sell off; **saldo** m COM balance; (*resultado*) result; **~ acreedor** credit balance; **~ deudor** debit balance; **de ~** reduced, on sale

salero m salt cellar; fig wit

salida f exit, way out; TRANSP departure; *de carrera* start; **~ de emergencia** emergency exit

saliente projecting, protruding; *presidente* outgoing

salir leave, go out; (*aparecer*) appear, come out; INFOR log on o off; **~ de** (*ir fuera de*) leave, go out of; (*venir fuera de*) leave, come out of; **~ a alguien** take after s.o.; **~ a 1000 dólares** cost 1000 dollars; **~ bien / mal** turn out well / badly; **no me salió el trabajo** I didn't get the job; **~ con alguien** date s.o.; **~ perdiendo** end up losing; **salirse de** *líquido* overflow; (*dejar*) leave; **~ con la suya** get what one wants

saliva f saliva; **tragar ~** hold one's tongue

salmo m psalm

salmón m ZO salmon

salón m living room; **~ de actos** auditorium, hall; **~ de baile** dance hall; **~ de belle-**

za beauty salon

salpicar splash, spatter (**con** with); *fig* sprinkle, pepper

salsa f GASTR sauce; *baile* salsa; **en su ~** *fig* in one's element; **salsera** f sauce boat

saltar 1 v/i jump, leap; **~ a la vista** *fig* be obvious; **~ sobre** pounce on; **~ a la comba** jump rope, *Br* skip **2** v/t *valla* jump

salto m leap, jump; **~ de agua** waterfall; **~ de altura** high jump; **~ de longitud** broad jump, *Br* long jump; **~ mortal** somersault

salubridad f *L.Am.* health; **Salubridad** *L.Am.* Department of Health

salud f health; **¡(a tu) ~!** cheers!; **saludable** healthy; **saludar** say hello to, greet; MIL salute; **saludo** m greeting; MIL salute; **~s en carta** best wishes

salvación f REL salvation; **salvador** m REL savior, *Br* saviour

salvadoreño 1 *adj* Salvador(e)an **2** m, -a f Salvador(e)an

salvaje 1 *adj* wild; (*bruto*) brutal **2** m/f savage

salvamento m rescue; **buque de ~** lifeboat; **salvar** save; *obstáculo* get over; **salvapantallas** m *inv* INFOR screensaver; **salvavidas** m *inv* life belt

salvia f BOT sage

salvo 1 *adj:* **estar a ~** be safe (and sound); **ponerse a ~**

reach safety **2** *adv* & *prp* except, save

San Saint

sanar 1 v/t cure **2** v/i *de persona* get well, recover; *de herida* heal; **sanatorio** m sanitarium, clinic

sanción f JUR penalty, sanction; **sancionar** penalize; (*multar*) fine

sandalia f sandal

sandía f watermelon

saneamiento m cleaning up; COM restructuring; **sanear** clean up; COM restructure

sangrar v/t & v/i bleed; **sangre** f blood; **~ fría** *fig* coolness; **a ~ fría** *fig* in cold blood; **sangría** f GASTR sangria; **sangriento** bloody

sanidad f health; **sano** healthy; **~ y salvo** safe and well; **cortar por lo ~** take drastic measures

santiguarse cross o.s., make the sign of the cross

santo 1 *adj* holy **2** m saint; **~ y seña** F password; **¿a ~ de qué?** F what on earth for?; **santuario** m *fig* sanctuary

sapo m ZO toad

saque m *en tenis* serve; **~ de banda** *in fútbol* throw-in; **~ de esquina** corner (kick); **tener buen ~** F have a big appetite; **saquear** sack, ransack

sarampión m MED measles

sarcasmo m sarcasm

sarcástico sarcastic

sardina f sardine; **como ~**

en lata like sardines

sargento *m* sergeant

sarna *f* MED scabies *sg*

sarro *m* tartar

sartén *f* frying pan

sastre *m* tailor; **sastrería** *f* tailoring; (*taller*) tailor's shop

satélite *m* satellite; **ciudad ~** satellite town

sátira *f* satire; **satírico 1** *adj* satirical **2** *m*, -a *f* satirist

satisfacción *f* satisfaction; **satisfacer** satisfy; *requisito, exigencia tb* meet; *deuda* settle, pay off; **satisfactorio** satisfactory; **satisfecho 1** *part* ☞ **satisfacer 2** *adj* satisfied; (*lleno*) full; **darse por ~** be satisfied (**con** with)

~auce *m* BOT willow; **~ llorón** weeping willow

~aúco *m* BOT elder

~audí *m/f & adj* Saudi; **saudita** *m/f* Saudi

~auna *f* sauna

~azonar GASTR season

~cooter *m* motor scooter

~e ◇ complemento indirecto: a él (to) him; *a ella* (to) her; *a usted, ustedes* (to) you; *a ellos* (to) them; **~ lo daré** I will give it to him / her / you / them ◇ *reflexivo:* con él himself; con ella herself; *cosa* itself; con usted yourself; con ustedes yourselves; con ellos themselves; **~ vistió** he got dressed, he dressed himself; **se lavó las manos** she washed her hands; **~**

abrazaron they hugged each other **~ cree** it is thought; **~ habla español** Spanish spoken

sebo *m* grease, fat

secador *m*: **~ (de pelo)** hair dryer; **secadora** *f* dryer; **secar, secarse** dry

sección *f* section

seco dry; *fig: persona* curt, brusque; **parar en ~** stop dead

secretaria *f* secretary; **~ de dirección** executive secretary; **secretaría** *f* secretary's office; *de organización* secretariat; **secretario** *m tb* POL secretary; **secreto 1** *adj* secret **2** *m* secret; **un ~ a voces** an open secret

secta *f* sect

sector *m* sector

secuela *f* MED after-effect

secuestrar *barco, avión* hijack; *persona* abduct, kidnap; **secuestro** *m de barco, avión* hijacking; *de persona* abduction, kidnapping; **~ aéreo** hijacking

secular secular, lay

secundario secondary

sed *f tb fig* thirst; **tener ~** be thirsty

seda *f* silk

sedante *m* sedative

sede *f de organización* headquarters; *de acontecimiento* site; **~ social** head office

sediento thirsty; **estar ~ de** *fig* thirst for

seducción f seduction; (*atracción*) attraction; **seducir** seduce; (*atraer*) attract; (*cautivar*) captivate, charm; **seductor 1** adj seductive; (*atractivo*) attractive; *oferta* tempting **2** m seducer; **seductora** f seductress

segadora f reaper, harvester; **segar** reap, harvest

seguida f: **en ~** at once, immediately; **seguido 1** adj consecutive, successive; *ir todo ~* go straight on **2** adv L.Am. often, frequently; **seguir 1** v/t follow **2** v/i continue, carry on; *sigue enfadado conmigo* he's still angry with me

según 1 prp according to **2** adv it depends

segundo m/adj second

seguridad f safety; *contra crimen* security; (*certeza*) certainty; *Seguridad Social Esp* Welfare, *Br* Social Security; **seguro 1** adj safe; (*estable*) steady; (*cierto*) sure; *es ~* (*cierto*) it's a certainty; *~ de sí mismo* self-confident, sure of o.s. **2** adv for sure **3** m COM insurance; *de puerta, coche* lock; L.Am. (*imperdible*) safety pin; *poner el ~* lock the door; *ir sobre ~* be on the safe side

seis six

seísmo m earthquake

selección f selection; *~ nacional* DEP national team; **seleccionar** choose, select;

selecto select

sellar seal; *sello* m stamp; *fig* hallmark; *~ discográfico* (record) label

selva f (*bosque*) forest; (*jungla*) jungle; *~ tropical* tropical rain forest

semáforo m traffic light

semana f week; *Semana Santa* Holy Week, Easter; **semanal** weekly; **semanario** m weekly

sembradora f seed drill; *mujer* sower; **sembrar** sow; *fig, pánico etc* spread

semejante 1 adj similar; *jamás he oído ~ tontería* I've never heard such nonsense **2** m human being, fellow creature

semen m BIO semen

semestre m six-month period; EDU semester

semicírculo m semicircle

semicorchea f MÚS sixteenth note, *Br* semiquaver

semifinal f DEP semifinal

semilla f seed

seminario m seminary

sémola f semolina

senado m senate; **senador** m, *~a* f senator

sencillez f simplicity; **sencillo 1** adj simple **2** m L.Am. small change

senda f path, track; **sendero** m path, track

senil senile

seno m tb fig bosom; *~s* breasts

sensación f feeling, sensa

tion; **causar ~** *fig* cause a sensation; **sensacional** sensational

sensato sensible

sensibilidad *f* feeling; (*emotividad*) sensitivity; **sensible** sensitive; (*apreciable*) appreciable, noticeable; **sensual** sensual; **sensualidad** *f* sensuality

sentado sitting, seated; **dar por ~** *fig* take for granted, assume; **sentar 1** *v/t fig* establish, create **2** *v/i:* **~ bien a alguien** *de comida* agree with s.o.; **le sienta bien esa chaqueta** that jacket suits her; **sentarse** sit down

sentencia *f* JUR sentence

sentido *m* sense; (*significado*) meaning; **~ común** common sense; **~ del humor** sense of humor *o* Br humour; **perder / recobrar el ~** lose / regain consciousness

sentimental emotional; **ser ~** be sentimental; **sentimiento** *m* feeling; **lo acompaño en el ~** my condolences

sentir 1 *m* feeling, opinion **2** *v/t* feel; (*percibir*) sense; **lo siento** I'm sorry

seña *f* gesture, sign; **~s** address; **hacer ~** wave

señal *f* signal; *fig* sign, trace; COM deposit; **en ~ de** as a token of; **señalar** indicate, point out

señor 1 *m* gentleman, man; *trato* sir; *escrito* Mr; **el ~ López** Mr López; **los ~es Ló-**

pez Mr and Mrs López; **señora** *f* lady, woman; *trato* ma'am; Br madam; *escrito* Mrs, Ms; **la ~ López** Mrs López; **mi ~** my wife; **~s y señores** ladies and gentlemen; **señorita** *f* young lady, young woman; *tratamiento* miss; *escrito* Miss; **la ~ López** Ms López, Miss López

Señor *m* Lord

separación *f* separation; **~ de bienes** JUR division of property; **separado** separated; **por ~** separately; **separar** separate; **separarse** separate, split up F; **separatismo** *m* separatism; **separatista** *m/f* & *adj* separatist

sepia *f* ZO cuttlefish

septiembre *m* September

séptimo seventh

sepulcro *m* tomb; **sepultar** bury; **sepultura** *f* burial; (*tumba*) tomb; **dar ~ a alguien** bury s.o.

sequía *f* drought

séquito *m* retinue, entourage

ser 1 *v/i* be; **es de Juan** it's Juan's, it belongs to Juan; **a no ~ que** unless; **¡eso es!** exactly!, that's right!; **es de esperar** it's to be hoped; **¿cuánto es?** how much is it?; **¿qué es de ti?** how's life?, how's things?; **o sea** in other words **2** *m* being

Serbia Serbia; **serbio 1** *adj* Serb(ian) **2** *m, -a f* Serb **3** *m idioma* Serbian

serenidad *f* calmness, serenity; **sereno 1** *m*: *dormir al ~* sleep outdoors **2** *adj* calm, serene

serial *m* TV, RAD series *sg*

serie *f* series *sg*; *fuera de ~* out of this world

seriedad *f* seriousness; **serio** serious; (*responsable*) reliable; *en ~* seriously

sermón *m* sermon

seropositivo MED HIV positive

serpentina *f* streamer; **serpiente** *f* ZO snake; *~ de cascabel* rattlesnake

serrar *v/t* saw; **serrín** *m* sawdust; **serrucho** *m* handsaw

servicio *m* service; *~s* restroom, *Br* toilets; *~ militar* military service; *~ de atención al cliente* customer service; *estar de ~* be on duty; *~ en línea* IT online service; **servidor** *m* INFOR server; **servidumbre** *f* (*criados*) servants *pl*; (*condición*) servitude; **servil** servile; **servilleta** *f* napkin, serviette; **servir 1** *v/t* serve **2** *v/i* be of use; *¿para qué sirve esto?* what is this (used) for?; *no ~ de nada* be no use at all; **servirse** help o.s.; *comida* help oneself to

sésamo *m* sesame

sesenta sixty

sesión *f* session; *en cine, teatro* show, performance

seso *m* ANAT brain; *fig* brains *pl*, sense

seta *f* BOT mushroom; *vene-nosa* toadstool

setenta seventy

seto *m* hedge

seudónimo *m* pseudonym

severo severe

sexismo *m* sexism; **sexista** *m/f & adj* sexist; **sexo** *m* sex

sexto sixth

sexual sexual; **sexualidad** *f* sexuality

sí 1 *adv* yes **2** *pron tercera persona*: *singular masculino* himself; *femenino* herself; *cosa, animal* itself; *pl* themselves; *usted* yourself; *ustedes* yourselves; *por ~ solo* by himself / itself, on his / its own

si if; *~ no* if not; *como ~* as if; *por ~* in case; *me pregunto si vendrá* I wonder whether he'll come

SIDA *m* (= *síndrome de inmunidad deficiente adquirida*) Aids (= acquired immune deficiency syndrome)

sidra *f* cider

siembra *f* sowing

siempre always; *~ que* providing that, as long as; *lo de ~* the same old story; *para ~* for ever

sien *f* ANAT temple

sierra *f* saw; GEOG mountain range

siesta *f* siesta, nap; *dormir la ~* have a siesta *o* nap

siete seven

sífilis *f* MED syphilis

sifón *m* TÉC siphon

sigla f abbreviation, acronym

siglo m century; **hace~s o un ~ que no le veo** fig I haven't seen him in a long long time

significado m meaning; **significar** mean, signify; **significativo** meaningful, significant

signo m sign; **~ de admiración** exclamation mark; **~ de interrogación** question mark; **~ de puntuación** punctuation mark

siguiente 1 adj next, following **2** pron next (one)

sílaba f syllable

silbar whistle; **silbato** m whistle; **silbido** m whistle

silenciador m AUTO muffler, Br silencer; **silenciar** silence; **silencio** m silence; **silencioso** silent

silla f chair; **~ de montar** saddle; **~ de ruedas** wheelchair; **sillón** m armchair, easy chair

silueta f silhouette

silvestre wild

simbólico symbolic; **simbolismo** m symbolism; **simbolizar** symbolize; **símbolo** m symbol

simétrico symmetrical

similar similar

simpatía f warmth, friendliness; **simpático** nice, lik(e)able

simple 1 adj simple; (*mero*) ordinary **2** m simpleton; **simplicidad** f simplicity;-

simplificar simplify; **simplista** simplistic

simulación f simulation; **simulacro** m (*cosa falsa*) pretense, Br pretence, sham; (*simulación*) simulation; **~ de incendio** fire drill; **simulador** m simulator; **simular** simulate

simultáneo simultaneous

sin without; **~ que** without; **~ preguntar** without asking

sinceridad f sincerity; **sincero** sincere

sindical union atr; **sindicato** m (labor o Br trade) union

sinfonía f MÚS symphony

singular 1 adj singular; fig outstanding, extraordinary **2** m GRAM singular

siniestro 1 adj sinister **2** m accident; (*catástrofe*) disaster

sino 1 m fate **2** conj but; (*salvo*) except

síntesis f inv synthesis; (*resumen*) summary; **sintético** synthetic

síntoma m symptom

sinvergüenza m/f swine; **¡qué ~!** (*descarado*) what a nerve!

siquiera: ni ~ not even; **~ bebe algo** L.Am. at least have a drink

sirena f siren

sirvienta f maid; **sirviente** m servant

sistema m system; **~ operativo** operating system; **sistemático** systematic

sitiar surround, lay siege to;

sitio *m* place; (*espacio*) room; **en ningún ~** nowhere; **~ web** website; **situación** *f* situation; **situado** situated; **estar ~** be situated; **bien ~** *fig* in a good position; **situar** situate, put; **situarse** be

slalom *m* slalom

sobaco *m* armpit

soberbio proud, arrogant; *fig* superb

sobornar bribe; **soborno** *m* bribe

sobra *f* surplus, excess; **hay de ~** there's more than enough; **~s** leftovers; **sobrar**: **sobra comida** there's food left over; **sobrado 1** *adj* **estar** *o* **andar ~ de algo** have plenty of sth; **no andar muy ~ de algo** not have much sth **2** *adv* easily; **te conozco ~** I know you well enough; **sobrante** remaining, left over

sobre 1 *m* envelope **2** *prp* on; **~ esto** about this; **~ las tres** about three o'clock; **~ todo** above all, especially

sobrecargar overload

sobreestimar overestimate

sobremanera exceedingly

sobremesa f: **de ~** afternoon *atr*

sobrenombre *m* nickname

sobresaliente outstanding, excellent

sobrevivir survive

sobrina *f* niece; **sobrino** *m* nephew

sobrio sober; *comida, decoración* simple; (*moderado*) restrained

socarrón sarcastic, snide *F*

social social; **socialismo** *m* socialism; **socialista** *m/f* & *adj* socialist

sociedad *f* society; **~ anónima** public corporation, *Br* public limited company; **~ de consumo** consumer society

socio *m*, **-a** *f* de club etc member; COM partner

sociología *f* sociology

socorrer help, assist; **socorro** *m* help, assistance; **¡~!** help!

soda *f* soda (water)

sodio *m* sodium

soez *f* crude, coarse

sofá *m* sofa; **sofá-cama** *m* sofa bed

sofisticación *f* sophistication; **sofisticado** sophisticated

sofocar suffocate; *incendio* put out

soga *f* rope

soja *f* soy, *Br* soya

sol *m* sun; **hace ~** it's sunny; **tomar el ~** sunbathe

solamente only

solar *m* vacant lot

solario, solárium *m* solarium

soldado *m/f* soldier

soldar weld, solder

soleado sunny

soledad *f* solitude, loneliness

solemne solemn; **solemnidad** *f* solemnity; **de ~** extremely

soler: **~ hacer algo** usually do sth; **suele venir temprano** he usually comes early; **solía visitarme** he used to visit me

solicitante m/f applicant; solicitar request; *empleo, beca* apply for; solícito attentive; solicitud f application, request

solidario supportive, understanding

solidez f solidity; *fig* strength; sólido solid; *fig* sound

solista m/f soloist

solitaria ZO tapeworm; solitario **1** adj solitary; *lugar* lonely **2** m solitaire; Br patience; **actuó en ~** he acted alone

sollozar sob; sollozo m sob

sólo only, just

solo single; **estar ~** be alone; **sentirse ~** feel lonely; **un ~ día** a single day; **a solas** alone, by o.s.; **por sí ~** by o.s.

solomillo m GASTR sirloin

soltar let go of; *(librar)* release, let go; *olor* give off

soltera f single *o* unmarried woman; soltero **1** adj single, not married **2** m bachelor, unmarried man; solterona f *desp* old maid

soltura f fluency, ease

soluble soluble; solución f solution; solucionar solve

solvente solvent

sombra f shadow; **a la ~ de un árbol** in the shade of a tree; **a la ~ de** *fig* under the protection of; **~ de ojos** eye shadow

sombrero m hat

sombrilla f sunshade, beach umbrella

sombrío *fig* somber, Br sombre

someter subject; **~ algo a votación** put sth to the vote

somier m bed base

somnífero m sleeping pill

somnolencia f sleepiness; somnoliento sleepy

son **1** m sound; **al ~ de** to the sound of **2** vb ☞ **ser**

sonar ring out; **~ a** sound like; **me suena esa voz** I know that voice

sonda f MED catheter; **~ espacial** space probe; sondear *fig* survey, poll; sondeo m: **~ (de opinión)** survey, (opinion) poll

sonido m sound

sonreír smile; sonrisa f smile

sonrojar: **~ a alguien** make s.o. blush; sonrojarse blush; sonrojo m blush

soñar dream (**con** about)

soñoliento sleepy

sopa f soup; sopera f soup tureen

soplar **1** v/i *del viento* blow **2** v/t *vela* blow out; *polvo* blow away; **~ algo a la policía** tip the police off about sth; soplo m: **en un ~** F in an instant; soplón m F informer

soportable bearable; soportar *fig* put up with, bear; **no puedo ~ a José** I can't stand José; soporte m sup-

port, stand; **~ lógico** INFOR
software; **~ físico** INFOR
hardware

soprano MÚS *m/f* soprano

sorber sip

sorbete *m* sorbet; *C.Am.* ice
cream

sorbo *m* sip

sordera *f* deafness

sordo 1 *adj* deaf **2** *m*, -a *f* deaf
person; **hacerse el ~** turn a
deaf ear; **sordomudo 1** *adj*
deaf and dumb **2** *m*, -a *f*
deaf-mute

soroche *m* *Pe, Bol* altitude
sickness

sorprendente surprising;
sorprender surprise; **sorpresa** *f* surprise; **de o por
~** by surprise

sortear draw lots for;
obstáculo get around; **sorteo**
m (*lotería*) lottery, (prize)
draw

sortija *f* ring

sosiego *m* calm, quiet

soso 1 *adj* tasteless, insipid;
fig dull **2** *m*, -a *f* stick-in-
the-mud F

sospecha *f* suspicion; **sospechar 1** *v/t* suspect **2** *v/i*
be suspicious; **~ de alguien**
suspect someone; **sospechoso 1** *adj* suspicious **2**
m, -a *f* suspect

sostén *m* brassiere, bra; *fig*
pillar, mainstay; **sostener**
familia support; *opinión* hold

sota *f naipes* jack

sótano *m* basement

su, sus *de él* his; *de ella* her; *de*
cosa its; *de usted, ustedes*
your; *de ellos* their; *de uno*
one's

suave soft, smooth; *sabor, licor* mild; **suavizante** *m de
pelo, ropa* conditioner; **suavizar** *tb fig* soften

subasta *f* auction; **sacar a ~**
put up for auction; **subastar**
auction (off)

subcontratar subcontract,
outsource

súbdito *m* subject

subestimar underestimate

subida *f* rise; **subido: ~ de tono** *fig* risqué, racy; **subir 1**
v/t cuesta, escalera go up,
climb; *objeto* raise, lift; *intereses, precio* raise **2** *v/i para
indicar acercamiento* come
up; *para indicar alejamiento*
go up; *de precio* rise, go up; *a
un tren, autobús* get on; *a
un coche* get in

súbito: de ~ suddenly, all of a
sudden

subjetivo subjective

subjuntivo *m* GRAM subjunctive

sublevar 1 *v/t* incite to revolt;
fig infuriate, get angry

sublime sublime, lofty

submarinismo *m* scuba diving; **submarino 1** *adj* underwater **2** *m* submarine

subnormal subnormal

subordinado 1 *adj* subordinate **2** *m*, -a *f* subordinate

subrayar *tb fig* underline

subsidio *m* welfare; *Br* benefit; **~ de paro** *o* **desempleo**

unemployment compensation o Br benefit

subsistencia f subsistence, survival; *de pobreza, tradición* persistence; **subsistir** live, survive; *de pobreza, tradición* live on, persist

subsuelo m subsoil; *Rpl en edificio* basement

subterráneo 1 adj underground **2** m L.Am. subway, Br underground

subtítulo m subtitle

suburbio m slum area

subvención f subsidy

suceder happen, occur; **~ a** follow; **¿qué sucede?** what's going on?; **sucesión** f succession; **sucesivo** successive; **en lo ~** from now on; **suceso** m event; **sucesor** m, **-a** f successor

suciedad f dirt; **sucio** tb fig dirty

sucumbir succumb, give in

sucursal f COM branch

sudadera f sweatshirt; **sudar** sweat

Sudáfrica South Africa; **sudafricano 1** adj South African **2** m, **-a** f South African; **Sudamérica** South America; **sudamericano 1** adj South American **2** m, **-a** f South American; **sudeste** m southeast; **sudoeste** m southwest

sudor m sweat; **sudoroso** sweaty

Suecia Sweden; **sueco 1** adj Swedish **2** m, **-a** f Swede **3**

m idioma Swedish

suegra f mother-in-law; **suegro** m father-in-law

suela f de zapato sole

sueldo m salary

suelo m en casa floor; *en el exterior* earth, ground; AGR soil; **estar por los ~s** F be at rock bottom F

suelto 1 adj loose, free; **un pendiente ~** a single earring; **andar ~** be at large **2** m loose change

sueño m *(estado de dormir)* sleep; *(fantasía, imagen mental)* dream; **tener ~** be sleepy

suero m MED saline solution; *sanguíneo* blood serum

suerte f luck; **por ~** luckily; **echar a ~s** toss for, draw lots for; **probar ~** try one's luck

suéter m sweater

suficiente 1 adj enough, sufficient **2** m EDU pass

sufrir *v/t fig* suffer, put up with **2** *v/i* suffer (**de** from)

sugerencia f suggestion; **sugerir** suggest

suicida 1 adj suicidal **2** m/f suicide victim; **suicidarse** commit suicide; **suicidio** m suicide

Suiza Switzerland; **suizo 1** adj Swiss **2** m, **-a** f Swiss **3** m GASTR sugar topped bun

sujetador m brassiere; bra; **sujetar** hold (down), keep in place; *(sostener)* hold; **sujeto 1** adj secure **2** m individual; GRAM subject

suma f sum; **en ~** in short; **su-**

mamente extremely; **sumar 1** v/t add; **5 y 6 suman 11** 5 and 6 make 11 **2** v/i add up; **sumario** m summary; JUR indictment; **sumarse: ~ a** join

sumergir submerge

sumidero m drain

suministrar supply, provide; **suministro** m supply

sumisión f submission; **sumiso** submissive

sumo supreme; **con ~ cuidado** with the utmost care; **a lo ~** at the most

suntuoso sumptuous

superar persona beat; límite go beyond, exceed; obstáculo overcome, surmount

superávit m surplus

superficial superficial, shallow; **superficie** f surface

superfluo superfluous

superior 1 adj upper; en jerarquía superior; **ser ~ a** be superior to **2** m superior; **superioridad** f superiority

supermercado m supermarket

supersónico supersonic

superstición f superstition; **supersticioso** superstitious

suplementario supplementary; **suplemento** m supplement

suplente m/f substitute, stand-in

suplicar cosa plead for, beg for; persona beg

suplicio m fig torment, ordeal

suponer suppose, assume

suposición f supposition

supositorio m MED suppository

supremacía f supremacy; **supremo** supreme

supresión f suppression; de impuesto, ley abolition; de restricción lifting; de servicio withdrawal; **suprimir** suppress; ley, impuesto abolish; restricción lift; servicio withdraw; puesto de trabajo cut

supuesto 1 part ☞ **suponer 2** adj supposed, alleged; **por ~** of course **3** m assumption

supurar weep, ooze

sur m south

surafricano ☞ **sudafricano**

suramericano ☞ **sudamericano**

surcar sail

surco m AGR furrow

surf(ing) m surfing; **surfista** m/f surfer

surgimiento m emergence; **surgir** fig emerge; de problema come up; de agua spout

surtido 1 adj assorted; **bien ~** COM well stocked **2** m assortment, range; **surtidor** m: **~ de gasolina** o **de nafta** gas pump, Br petrol pump; **surtir 1** v/t supply; **~ efecto** have the desired effect **2** v/i spout

susceptible touchy; **ser ~ de mejora** leave room for improvement

suscitar arouse; polémica generate; escándalo provoke

suscribir subscribe to; **suscripción** *f* subscription; **suscriptor** *m*, **~a** *f* subscriber

suspender 1 *v/t empleado, alumno* suspend; *objeto* hang; *reunión* adjourn; *examen* **2** *v/i* EDU fail; **suspensión** *f* suspension; **suspenso 1** *adj alumnos* **~s** students who have failed; **en ~** suspended **2** *m* fail

suspicacia *f* suspicion; **suspicaz** suspicious

suspirar sigh; **~ por algo** yearn for sth, long for sth; **suspiro** *m* sigh

sustancia *f* substance; **sustancial** substantial; **sustantivo** *m* GRAM noun

sustituir **~ X por Y** replace X with Y, substitute Y for X; **sustituto** *m* substitute

susto *m* fright, scare; **dar o pegar un ~ a alguien** give s.o. a fright

sustraer subtract, take away; *(robar)* steal

susurrar whisper; **susurro** *m* whisper

sutil *fig* subtle; **sutileza** *f fig* subtlety

sutura *f* MED suture

suyo, suya *de él* his; *de ella* hers; *de usted, ustedes* yours; *de ellos* theirs; **los ~s** his / her etc folks, his / her etc family; **salirse con la -a** get one's own way

T

tabaco *m* tobacco

tábano *m* ZO horsefly

taberna *f* bar

tabique *m* partition

tabla *f de madera* board, plank; PINT panel; *(cuadro)* table; **~ de planchar** ironing board; **~ de surf** surfboard; **acabar o quedar en ~s** end in a tie

tablado *m en un acto* platform; *de escenario* stage

tablero *m* board, plank; *de juego* board; **~ de mandos o de instrumentos** AUTO dashboard; **tableta** *f* IT tablet; **ordenador** *m* **~**, *L.Am.*

computadora *f* **~** tablet computer; **PC** *m* **~** tablet PC; **~ de chocolate** chocolate bar

taburete *m* stool

tacaño 1 *adj* F miserly **2** *m*, **-a** *f* F miser

tachar cross out

tácito tacit

taco *m* F *(palabrota)* swear word; *L.Am.* heel; GASTR taco *(filled tortilla)*

tacón *m de zapato* heel; **zapatos de ~** high-heeled shoes

táctica *f* tactics *pl*

tacto *m* (sense of) touch; *fig* tact, discretion

tafetán m taffeta

tajada f GASTR slice; **agarrar una ~** F get drunk; **tajante** categorical

tal 1 adj such; **no dije ~ cosa** I said no such thing; **un ~ Lucas** someone called Lucas **2** adv: **~ como** such as; **dejó la habitación ~ cual la encontró** she left the room just as she found it; **~ para cual** two of a kind; **~ vez** maybe, perhaps; **¿qué ~?** how's it going?; **¿que ~ la película?** what was the movie like?; **con ~ de que** + subj as long as

taladradora f drill; **taladrar** drill; **taladro** m drill

talento m talent

talla f size; (estatura) height; C.Am. (mentira) lie; **dar la ~** fig make the grade; **tallar** carve; **piedra preciosa** cut

tallarín m noodle

talle m waist

taller m workshop; **~ mecánico** AUTO repair shop; **~ de reparaciones** repair shop

tallo m BOT stalk, stem

talón m ANAT heel; COM stub; **pisar los talones a alguien** be hot on s.o.'s heels; **talonario** m: **~ de cheques** check book, Br cheque book

tamaño 1 adj: **~ problema** such a great problem **2** m size

tambalearse stagger, lurch; de coche sway

también also, too, as well; **yo ~** me too

tambor m drum; persona drummer

tamiz m sieve

tampoco neither; **él ~ va** he's not going either

tampón m tampon; de tinta ink-pad

tan so; **~... como...** as ... as ...; **~ sólo** merely

tanda f series sg, batch; (turno) shift; L.Am. (commercial) break; **~ de penaltis** DEP penalty shootout

tanque m tb MIL tank

tanto 1 pron so much; **igual cantidad** as much; **un ~ a** little; **~s** so many pl; **igual número** as many; **tienes ~** you have so much; **a las -as de la noche** in the small hours **2** adv so much; **igual cantidad** as much; periodo **as long**; **~ mejor** so much the better; **no es para ~** it's not such a big deal; **estar al ~** be informed (de about); **por lo ~** therefore, so **3** m point; **~ por ciento** percentage

tapa f lid; **~ dura** hardback

tapacubos m inv AUTO hubcap

tapadera f lid; fig front; **tapar** cover; recipiente put the lid on

tapete m tablecloth; **poner algo sobre el ~** bring sth up for discussion

tapia f wall; **más sordo que una ~** as deaf as a post

tapicero m, -a f upholsterer; **tapiz** m tapestry; **tapizar** upholster

tapón m top, cap; de baño plug; de tráfico traffic jam; **taponar** block; herida swab

taquigrafía f shorthand; **taquigrafiar** take down in shorthand; **taquígrafo** m, -a f stenographer, shorthand writer

taquilla f ticket office; TEA box-office; C.Am. (bar) small bar

taquímetro m tachometer

tara f defect; COM tare

tarántula f ZO tarantula

tardanza f delay; **tardar** take a long time; tardamos dos horas we were two hours overdue o late; ¡no tardes! don't be late; a más ~ at the latest; ¿cuánto se tarda ...? how long does it take to ...?; **tarde 1** adv late; ~ o temprano sooner or later **2** f hasta las 5 ó 6 afternoon; desde las 5 ó 6 evening; ¡buenas ~s! good afternoon / evening; por la ~ in the afternoon / evening; de ~ en ~ from time to time; **tardío** late

tardo slow

tarea f task, job; ~s domésticas housework

tarifa f rate; de tren fare; ~ plana flat rate

tarima f platform; suelo de ~ wooden floor

tarjeta f card; ~ amarilla DEP yellow card; ~ de crédito credit card; ~ de débito debit card; ~ de embarque AVIA boarding card; ~ de sonido INFOR sound card; ~ de visita (business) card; ~ gráfica INFOR graphics card; ~ inteligente smart card; ~ postal postcard; ~ roja DEP red card; ~ telefónica phonecard

tarro m jar; P (cabeza) head

tarta f cake; plana tart; ~ helada ice-cream cake

tartamudear stutter, stammer

tarugo m F blockhead F

tasa f rate; (impuesto) tax; ~ de desempleo o paro unemployment rate; **tasar** fix a price for; (valorar) assess

tasca f F bar

tatuaje m tattoo

taurino bullfighting atr; **Tauro** m/f inv ASTR Taurus; **tauromaquia** f bullfighting

taxi m cab, taxi; **taxista** m/f cab o taxi driver

taza f cup; del wáter bowl

te directo you; indirecto (to) you; reflexivo yourself

té m tea

tea f torch

teatral fig theatrical; **teatro** m tb fig theater, Br theatre

tebeo m children's comic

techo m ceiling; (tejado) roof; ~ solar AUTO sun-roof; los sin ~ the homeless; **tocar** ~ fig peak

tecla f key; **teclado** m MÚS,

INFOR keyboard; **teclear**
key; **teclista** m/f INFOR keyboarder; MÚS keyboard player

técnica f technique; **técnico**
1 adj technical **2** m/f technician; de televisor, lavadora etc
repairman; **tecnología** f
technology; **alta ~** hi-tech;
~ punta state-of-the-art
technology, leading-edge
technology

tedio m tedium

teja f roof tile; **a toca ~** in hard
cash; **tejado** m roof

tejano m adj Texan; of Texas
Texas **2** m, -a f Texan; **Tejas**
Texas; **tejanos** mpl jeans

tejer v/t weave; (hacer punto)
knit; F **intriga** devise **2** v/i
L.Am. F plot, scheme; **tejido**
m fabric; ANAT tissue

tejón m ZO badger

tela f fabric, material; **~ de**
araña spiderweb; **poner en**
~ de juicio call into question; **hay ~ para rato** F
there's a lot to be done

telar m loom; **telaraña** f spiderweb

teleadicto, m -a f F couch potato F, teleaddict F

telecomedia f sitcom

telecomunicaciones fpl telecommunications

telediario m TV (television)
news sg

teledirigido remote-con-
trolled

teleférico m cable car

telefonear call, phone; **tele-**

fónico (tele)phone atr; **telé-**
fono m (tele)phone; **~**
inalámbrico cordless
(phone); **~ móvil** cell
(phone), Br mobile (phone)
~ con cámara camera phone

telenovela m L.Am. (phone)
message

telenovela f soap (opera)

telescopio m telescope

telesilla f chair lift

telespectador m, **~a** f (television) viewer

telesquí m drag lift

teletexto m teletext

teletrabajo m teleworking

teletrabajador, **~a** f tele-
worker

televidente m/f (television)
viewer; **televisión** f televisión; **~ por cable** cable (televisión); **~ de pago** pay-per
view television; **~ vía satéli**
te satellite television; **televi-**
sivo television atr; **televisor**
m TV, television (set)

telón m TEA curtain; **el ~ de**
acero POL the Iron Curtain
~ de fondo fig backdrop
background

tema m subject, topic; MÚS; de
novela theme

temblar tremble, shake; de
frío shiver; **temblor** m trembling, shaking; de frío shivering; L.Am. (terremoto)
earthquake; **~ de tierra** earth
tremor; **tembloroso** trembling, shaking; de frío shiver
ing

temer be afraid of; **temerse**

be afraid; **~ lo peor** fear the worst

temerario rash, reckless; **temeridad** *f* rashness, recklessness

temeroso fearful, frightened; **temor** *m* fear

temperamento *m* temperament; **temperante** *Méx* teetotal

temperatura *f* temperature

tempestad *f* storm; **tempestuoso** *tb fig* stormy

templado warm; *clima* temperate; *fig* moderate; **templar** *ira, nervios* calm

templo *m* temple

temporada *f* season; **una ~ a** time, some time; **temporal 1** *adj* temporary **2** *m* storm; **temprano** early

tenacidad *f* tenacity; **tenaz** determined, tenacious; **tenaza** *f* pincer, claw; **~s** pincers; *para las uñas* pliers

tendedero *m* clotheshorse

tendencia *f* tendency; *(corriente)* trend; **tendencioso** tendentious

tender 1 *v/t ropa* hang out; *cable* lay; **le tendió la mano** he held out his hand to her **2** *v/i:* **~ a** tend to

tendón *m* ANAT tendon

tenebroso dark, gloomy

tenedor *m* fork

tener have; **~ 10 años** be 10 (years old); **~ un metro de ancho / largo** be one meter wide / long; **~ por** consider to be; **tengo que madrugar**

I must get up early, I have to *o* I've got to get up early; **tenerse** stand up; *fig* stand firm; **se tiene por atractivo** he thinks he's attractive

tenia *f* ZO tapeworm

teniente *m/f* MIL lieutenant

tenis *m* tennis; **~ de mesa** table tennis; **tenista** *m/f* tennis player

tenor *m* MÚS tenor; **a ~ de** along the lines of

tensión *f* tension; ELEC voltage; MED blood pressure; **tenso** tense; *cuerda* taut

tentación *f* temptation; **tentador** tempting; **tentar** tempt, entice

tentativa *f* attempt

tenue faint

teñir dye; *fig* tinge

teología *f* theology

teoría *f* theory; **en ~** in theory; **teórico 1** *adj* theoretical **2** *m,* **-a** *f* theorist

terapeuta *m/f* therapist; **terapéutico** therapeutic; **terapia** *f* therapy

tercer third; **Tercer Mundo** Third World; **tercero** *m/adj* third; **tercio** *m* third

terciopelo *m* velvet

terco stubborn

termal thermal

termas *fpl* hot springs

terminación *f* GRAM ending; **terminal 1** *m* INFOR terminal **2** *f* AVIA terminal; **~ de autobuses** bus terminal; **terminar 1** *v/t* end, finish **2** *v/i* end, finish; *(parar)* stop; **tér-**

mino *m* end, conclusion; (*palabra*) term; **~ municipal** municipal area; **por ~ medio** on average; **poner ~ a algo** put an end to sth

termo *m* thermos® (flask)

termómetro *m* thermometer; **termostato** *m* thermostat; **ternera** *f* calf; GASTR veal; **ternero** *m* calf

terno *m* C Sur suit

ternura *f* tenderness

terraplén *m* embankment; **terrateniente** *m/f* landowner

terraza *f* terrace; (*balcón*) balcony; (*café*) sidewalk *o* Br pavement café

terremoto *m* earthquake

terreno *m* land; *fig* field; **un ~** a plot *o* piece of land; **~ de juego** DEP field

terrestre *animal* land *atr*; *transporte* surface *atr*; **la atmósfera ~** the earth's atmosphere

terrible terrible, awful

territorio *m* territory

terrón *m* lump; **~ de azúcar** sugar lump

terror *m* terror; **terrorismo** *m* terrorism; **terrorista 1** *adj* terrorist *atr* **2** *m/f* terrorist; **~ suicida** suicide bomber

terso smooth

tertulia *f* TV debate, round table discussion

tesis *f inv* thesis

tesorería *f oficio* post of treasurer; *oficina* treasury; (*activo disponible*) liquid assets *pl*

testaferro *m* front man

testamento *m* JUR will

testarudo stubborn

testículo *m* ANAT testicle

testificar 1 *v/t* (*probar, mostrar*) be proof of; **~ que** JUR testify that, give evidence that **2** *v/i* testify, give evidence; **testigo 1** *m/f* JUR witness; **~ de cargo** witness for the prosecution; **~ ocular** *o* **presencial** eye witness **2** *m* DEP baton

testimoniar testify; **testimonio** *m* testimony, evidence

teta *f* F boob F; ZO teat, nipple

tétanos *m* MED tetanus

tetera *f* teapot

tétrico gloomy

textil 1 *adj* textile *atr* **2** *mpl*: **~es** textiles

texto *m* text; **textual** textual

textura *f* texture

tez *f* complexion

ti you; *reflexivo* yourself

tía *f* aunt; F (*chica*) girl, chick F

tibia *f* ANAT tibia

tibio *tb fig* lukewarm

tiburón *m* ZO, *fig* F shark

ticket *m* (sales) receipt

tiempo *m* time; (*clima*) weather; GRAM tense; **~ real** INFOR real time; **a ~** in time; **a un ~, al mismo ~** at the same time; **antes de ~ llegar** ahead of time, early; *celebrar* too soon; **con ~** in good time, early; **hace buen / mal ~** the weather's fine / bad

tienda *f* store, shop; **~ de campaña** tent; **ir de ~s** go shopping

tierno soft; *carne* tender; *pan* fresh

tierra *f* land; *materia* soil, earth; *(patria)* native land; **la Tierra** the earth; **~ firme** dry land, terra firma; **echar por ~** ruin, wreck

tieso stiff, rigid

tiesto *m* flowerpot

tifus *m* MED typhus

tigre *m* ZO tiger; *L.Am.* puma; *L.Am.* (*leopardo*) jaguar

tijeras *fpl* scissors

tila *f* lime blossom tea

tildar: **~ a alguien de** *fig* brand s.o. as

tilde *f* accent; *en* ñ tilde

tilo *m* BOT lime (tree)

timador *m*, **~a** *f* cheat; **timar** cheat

timbal *m* MÚS kettle drum

timbre *m* de puerta bell; *Méx* (postage) stamp

timidez *f* shyness, timidity; **tímido** shy, timid

timo *m* confidence trick, swindle

timón *m* MAR, AVIA rudder; **timonel** MAR **1** *m* helmsman **2** *f* helmswoman

tímpano *m* ANAT eardrum

tina *f* large jar; *L.Am.* (*bañera*) (bath)tub

tinerfeño *m /* from Tenerife

tinieblas *fpl* darkness

tinta *f* ink; **de buena ~** *fig* on good authority; **medias ~s** *fig* half measures; **tinte** *m*

dye; *fig* veneer, gloss

tinto: *vino* **~** red wine

tintorería *f* dry cleaner

tío *m* uncle; *F (tipo)* guy F; *apelativo* pal F

tiovivo *m* carousel, merry-go-round

típico typical (*de* of); **tipo** *m* type, kind; F *persona* guy F; COM rate; **~ de cambio** exchange rate; **~ de interés** interest rate; **tener buen ~** be well built; *de mujer* have a good figure

tipografía *f* typography

tíquet, tiquete *m* L.Am. receipt

tira *f* strip; **la ~ de** F loads of F; **~ y afloja** *fig* give and take

tirada *f* TIP print run; **de una ~** in one go; **estar ~** F (*fácil*) be a piece of cake F

tirador *m* shot, marksman; *de puerta* handle; **tiradores** *mpl* Arg suspenders, Br braces

tiranía *f* tyranny; **tiránico** tyrannical; **tiranizar** tyrannize; **tirano 1** *adj* tyrannical **2** *m*, **-a** *f* tyrant

tirante 1 *adj* taut; *fig* tense **2** *m* strap; **~s** suspenders, Br braces; **tirantez** *f* fig tension

tirar 1 *v/t* throw; *edificio*, *persona* knock down; *(volcar)* knock over; *basura*, *dinero* throw away; TIP print; F *en examen* fail F *v/i* attract; *(disparar)* shoot; **~a** tend toward; **~ de algo** pull sth; **ir tirando** F get by, manage; **ti-**

rarse throw o.s.; F *tiempo* spend

tirita f MED Band-Aid®, Br plaster

tiritar shiver

tiro m shot; ~ *al blanco* target practice; *al* ~ CSur F right away; *de* ~*s largos* F dressed up; *ni a* ~ F for love nor money

tiroides m ANAT thyroid (gland)

tirón m tug, jerk; *de un* ~ at a stretch, without a break

tiroteo m shooting

tisana f herbal tea

títere m tb fig puppet; *no dejar* ~ *con cabeza* F spare no one

titiritero m, -a f acrobat

titubear waver, hesitate

titular de periódico headline; título m title; *universitario* degree; JUR title; COM bond; *tener muchos* ~s be highly qualified; *a* ~ *de* as; ~*s de crédito* credits

tiza f chalk

toalla f towel; **toallero** m towel rail

tobillo m ankle

tobogán m slide

tocadiscos m inv record player

tocado: *estar* ~ fig F be crazy

tocador m dressing-table

tocante: *en lo* ~ *a...* with regard to ...

tocar 1 v/t touch; MÚS play 2 v/i L.Am. *a la puerta* knock (on the door); L.Am. (*sonar* la campanita*) ring the doorbell; *te toca jugar* it's your turn

tocino m bacon

tocólogo m, -a f obstetrician

todavía still, yet; ~ *no ha llegado* he still hasn't come, he hasn't come yet; ~ *no* not yet

todo 1 adj all; ~*s los domingos* every Sunday; *-a la clase* the whole o the entire class 2 adv all; *estaba* ~ *sucio* it was all dirty; *con* ~ all the same; *del* ~ entirely, absolutely 3 pron all, everything; pl everybody, everyone; *ir a por* ~*s* go all out

todoterreno m AUTO off-road o all-terrain vehicle

toldo m awning; L.Am. Indian hut

tolerable tolerable; **tolerancia** f tolerance; **tolerante** tolerant; **tolerar** tolerate

toma f FOT shot, take; ~ *de conciencia* realization; ~ *de corriente* outlet, Br socket; ~ *de posesión* POL taking office; **tomar 1** v/t take; *bebida, comida* have; ~ *la con alguien* F have it in for s.o. F; ~ *el sol* sunbathe; *¡toma!* here (you are); *tomar y daca* give and take 2 v/i L.Am. (*beber*) drink; ~ *a por la derecha* turn right, take a right

tomate m tomato

tomavistas m inv movie camera

tomillo m BOT thyme

tomo m volume, tome

tonel *m* barrel, cask; **tonelada** *f peso* ton; **tonelaje** *m* tonnage

tónica *f* tonic; **tónico** *m* MED tonic; **tono** *m* MÚS, MED, PINT tone

tontería *f fig* stupid *o* dumb F thing; **~s** nonsense; **tonto 1** *adj* silly, foolish 2 *m*, -**a** *f* fool, idiot; **hacer el ~** play the fool; **hacerse el ~** act dumb F

toparse: ~ **con alguien** bump into s.o., run into s.o.

tope *m* limit; *pieza* stop; *Méx en la calle* speed bump; **pasarlo a ~** F have a great time

tópico *m* cliché, platitude

topo *m* ZO mole

topográfico topographic(al)

toque *m*: ~ **de queda** MIL, *fig* curfew; **dar los últimos** (~**s a** to) put the finishing touches (*a* to)

torbellino *m* whirlwind

torcer 1 *v/t* twist; (*doblar*) bend; (*girar*) turn 2 *v/i* turn; ~ **a la derecha** turn right; **torcerse** twist, bend; *fig* go wrong; ~ **un pie** sprain one's ankle; **torcido** twisted, bent

tordo *m pájaro* thrush; *caballo* dapple-gray, *Br* dapple-grey

torear 1 *v/i* fight bulls 2 *v/t* fight; *fig* dodge, sidestep; **toreo** *m* bullfighting; **torero** *m* bullfighter

tormenta *f* storm; **tormento** *m* torture

torneo *m* competition, tournament

tornillo *m* screw; **con tuerca** bolt; **le falta un ~** F he's got a screw loose F

torniquete *m* turnstile; MED tourniquet

torno *m de alfarería* wheel; **en ~** a around, about

toro *m* bull; **ir a los ~s** go to a bullfight

torpe clumsy; (*tonto*) dense, dim

torpedo *m* MIL torpedo

torpeza *f* clumsiness; (*necedad*) stupidity

torre *f* tower; ~ **de control** AVIA control tower

torrencial torrential; **torrente** *m fig* avalanche, flood

tórrido torrid

torsión *f* twisting; TÉC torsion, torque

torta *f* cake; *plana* tart; F (*bofetada*) slap

tortilla *f* omelet, *Br* omelette; *L.Am.* tortilla

tórtola *f* ZO turtledove

tortuga *f* ZO tortoise; *marina* turtle; **a paso de ~** *fig* at a snail's pace

tortuoso *fig* tortuous

tortura *f tb fig* torture; **torturar** torture

tos *f* cough

tosco *fig* rough, coarse

toser cough

tostada *f* piece of toast; **tostador** *m* toaster; **tostar** toast; *café* toast; *al sol* tan

total 1 *adj* total; **en ~** in total 2 *m* total; **totalidad** *f* totality

tóxico toxic; **toxicómano** *m*,

-a f drug addict

tozudo obstinate

traba f obstacle; **poner ~s** raise objections; **sin ~s** without a hitch

trabajador 1 adj hard-working **2** m, ~a f worker; ~ **eventual** casual worker; **trabajar 1** v/i work **2** v/t work; tema, músculos work on; **trabajo** m work; ~ **en equipo** team work; ~ **a tiempo parcial** part-time work; **trabajoso** hard, laborious

trabar amistad strike up

tracción f TÉC traction; ~ **delantera / trasera** front / rear-wheel drive

tractor m tractor

tradición f tradition; **tradicional** traditional

traducción f translation; **traducir** translate; **traductor** m, ~a f translator

traer bring; de periódico carry; ~ **consigo** involve, entail

traficante m dealer; **traficar** deal (**en** in); **tráfico** m traffic; ~ **de drogas** drug traffic; **en pequeña escala** drug dealing

tragaluz m skylight; **tragaperras** f inv slot machine

tragar swallow; **no lo trago** I can't stand him

tragedia f tragedy; **trágico** tragic

trago m mouthful; F bebida drink; **de un ~** in one gulp; **pasar un mal ~** fig have a hard time

traición f treachery, betrayal; **traicionar** betray; **traidor 1** adj treacherous **2** m, ~a f traitor

traje 1 m suit; ~ **de baño** swimsuit **2** vb → **traer**

trajín m hustle and bustle

trama f (tema) plot; **tramar** complot hatch

tramitación f processing; **tramitar** documento: de persona apply for; de banco etc process; **trámite** m formality

trampa f trap; (truco) scam F, trick; **hacer ~** cheat

trampolín m diving board

tramposo m, ~a f cheat, crook

trance m (momento difícil) tough time; **en ~ de médium** in a trance

tranquilidad f calm, quietness; **tranquilizar:** ~ **a alguien** calm s.o. down; **tranquilo** calm, quiet; **¡~!** don't worry; **déjame** ~ leave me alone; **quedarse tan** ~ not bat an eyelid

transacción f COM deal, transaction

transatlántico 1 adj transatlantic **2** m liner

transbordador m ferry; ~ **espacial** space shuttle; **transbordo** m: **hacer ~** TRANSP transfer, change

transcripción f transcription

transcurrir de tiempo pass, go by; **transcurso** m course; de tiempo passing

transeúnte m/f passer-by

transferencia f COM transfer

transferible transferable; **transferir** transfer

transformación f transformation; **transformador** m ELEC transformer; **transformar** transform

transfusión f: ~ **de sangre** blood transfusion

transgénico genetically modified, GM

transgredir infringe; **transgresión** f infringement, transgression

transición f transition

transigente accommodating; **transigir** compromise, make concessions

transistor m transistor

transitable passable; **transitar** de persona walk; de vehículo travel (**por** along)

transitivo GRAM transitive

tránsito m COM transit; L.Am. (circulación) traffic

transmisión f transmission; ~ **de datos** data transmission; **enfermedad de ~ sexual** sexually transmitted disease; **transmitir** spread; RAD, TV broadcast, transmit

transparencia f para proyectar transparency, slide; **transparente** transparent

transpirar perspire

transportar transport; **transporte** m transport; **transportista** m/f haulage contractor

transversal transverse, cross atr

tranvía m streetcar, Br tram

trapecio m trapeze

trapo m viejo rag; para limpiar cloth; ~**s** F clothes

tráquea f ANAT windpipe, trachea

tras en el espacio behind; en el tiempo after

trascendental, **trascendente** momentous; en filosofía transcendental

trasero 1 adj rear atr, back atr **2** m F butt F

trasfondo m background; fig undercurrent

trasladar move; trabajador transfer; **trasladarse** move (**a** to); **se traslada** Méx: en negocio under new management; **traslado** m move; de trabajador transfer; ~ **al aeropuerto** airport transfer

traslucirse be visible; fig be evident, show

trasnochador m night owl; **trasnochar** (acostarse tarde) go to bed late, stay up late; (no dormir) stay up all night; L.Am. (pernoctar) stay the night

traspapelar mislay

traspasar (atravesar) go through; COM transfer; **traspaso** m COM transfer

trasplantar AGR, MED transplant; **trasplante** m AGR, MED transplant

trastero m lumber room; **trasto** m desp piece of junk; persona good-for-nothing

trastornar upset; (molestar) inconvenience; **trastorno** m inconvenience; MED disorder

trata f trade

tratado m esp POL treaty

tratamiento m treatment; ~ **de datos / textos** data / word processing; **tratar** 1 v/t treat; (manejar) handle; (dirigirse a) address (**de** as); **gente** come into contact with; **tema** deal with 2 v/i: ~ **con alguien** deal with s.o.; ~ **de** (intentar) try to; **tratarse**: **¿de qué se trata?** what's it about?; **trato** m treatment; COM deal; **malos ~s** abuse; **tener ~ con alguien** have dealings with s.o.; **¡~ hecho!** it's a deal; **tratante** m/f dealer, trader

trauma m trauma; **traumatismo** m MED trauma, injury; **traumático** traumatic

través m: **a ~ de** through; **travesaño** m en fútbol crossbar; **travesía** f crossing

travesti m transvestite

travesura f bit of mischief, prank; **travieso** niño mischievous

trayecto m journey; **10 dólares por ~** 10 dollars each way; **trayectoria** f fig course, path

trazado m acción drawing; (diseño) plan, design; de camino route; **trazar** (dibujar) draw; ruta plot, trace; (describir) outline, describe; **trazo** m line

trece thirteen

trecho m stretch, distance

tregua f truce, cease-fire; **sir** ~ relentlessly

treinta thirty

trekking m SP trekking; **bici cleta** f **de trekking** trekking bike; **bota** f **de trekking** trekking boot; **zapato** n **de trekking** trekking shoe

tremendo awful, dreadful éxito, alegría tremendous

tren m FERR train; ~ **de lava do** car wash; **vivir a todo ~** live in style; **estar como un** ~ F be absolutely gorgeous

trenza f braid, Br plait; **tren** zar plait; pelo braid, Br plai

trepar climb (**a** up), scale (a sth)

trepidar vibrate, shake

tres three

tresillo m living-room suite Br three-piece suite

triangular triangular; **trián gulo** m triangle

tribu f tribe

tribuna f grandstand

tribunal m court

tributario 1 adj COM tax atr **?** m tributary; **tributo** m trib ute; (impuesto) tax

triciclo m tricycle

tricolor tricolor, Br tricolou

trigo m wheat

trilladora f thresher; **trilla** AGR thresh

trimestral quarterly; **trimes** tre m quarter; escolar semes ter, Br term

trinchar GASTR carve

trinchera f MIL trench

trineo *m* sled, sleigh
trinidad *f* REL trinity
tripa *f* F belly F, gut F
triple triple; *el ~ que el año pasado* three times as much as last year
trípode *m* tripod
tripulación *f* AVIA, MAR crew; tripular crew, man
triste sad; tristeza *f* sadness
triturar grind
triunfador **1** *adj* winning **2** *m*, ~*a f* winner, victor; triunfar triumph, win; triunfo *m* triumph, victory; *en naipes* trump
trivial trivial; trivialidad *f* triviality
trofeo *m* trophy
trombón *m* MÚS trombone
trompa **1** *adj* F wasted F **2** *f* MÚS horn; ZO trunk
trompeta *f* MÚS trumpet; trompetista *m/f* MÚS trumpeter
trompo *m* spinning top
tronar thunder
tronco *m* trunk; *cortado* log; *dormir como un ~* sleep like a log
trono *m* throne
tropa *f* MIL ordinary soldier; ~*s* troops
tropezar trip, stumble
tropical tropical; trópico *m* tropic
tropiezo *m* fig setback
trote *m* trot
trozo *m* piece
trucha *f* ZO trout
truco *m* trick; *coger el ~ a*

algo F get the hang of sth F
trueno *m* thunder
trueque *m* barter
trufa *f* BOT truffle
tu, tus your
tú you
tuberculosis *f* MED tuberculosis, TB
tubería *f* pipe; tubo *m* tube; ~ *de escape* AUTO exhaust (pipe); *por un ~* F an enormous amount
tuerca *f* TÉC nut
tuétano *m*: *hasta los ~s* fig through and through
tulipán *m* BOT tulip
tumba *f* tomb, grave
tumbar knock down; tumbona *f* (sun) lounger
tumor *m* MED tumor, Br tumour
tumulto *m* uproar; tumultuoso uproarious
tuna *f* Méx fruta prickly pear
tunecino **1** *adj* Tunisian **2** *m*, -*a f* Tunisian
túnel *m* tunnel; ~ *de lavado* car wash
Túnez *país* Tunisia; *ciudad* Tunis
turbar (*emocionar*) upset; *paz* disturb; (*avergonzar*) embarrass
turbina *f* turbine
turbio cloudy, murky; *fig* shady, murky
turbulencia *f* turbulence; turbulento turbulent
turco **1** *adj* Turkish **2** *m*, -*a f* Turk **3** *m idioma* Turkish
turismo *m* tourism; *automóvil*

sedan, Br saloon (car); **turista** m/f tourist

turnarse take it in turns; **turno** m turn; **~ de noche** night shift; **por ~s** in turns

turquesa f turquoise; **azul ~** turquoise

Turquía Turkey

turrón m nougat

tutear address as 'tu'

tutela f guardianship; cargo tutorship

tutor m, **-a** f EDU tutor

tuyo, tuya yours; **los tuyos** your folks, your family

twitter v/i, v/t IT tweet; IT twitter

U

u (instead of **o** before words starting with o) or

ubicación f L.Am. location; (localización) finding; **ubicado** located, situated; **ubicar** L.Am. place, put; (localizar) locate

ubre f udder

Ud. ☞ **usted**

Uds. ☞ **ustedes**

úlcera f MED ulcer

ulterior subsequent

últimamente lately; **ultimar** finalize; L.Am. (rematar) finish off; **último** last; (más reciente) latest; **piso top** atr; **-as noticias** latest news sg; **por ~** finally

ultraje m outrage; (insulto) insult

ultramar m: **de ~** overseas, foreign

ultrasonido m ultrasound

ulular de viento howl; de búho hoot

umbral m fig threshold

un, una a; antes de vocal y h muda an; **~os coches / pá-**

jaros some cars / birds; **~os cuantos** a few, some; **-as mil pesetas** about a thousand pesetas

unánime unanimous

ungüento m ointment

únicamente only; **único** only; (sin par) unique; **hijo ~** only child; **lo ~ que...** the only thing that ...

unidad f MIL, MAT unit; (cohesión) unity; **~ de cuidados intensivos, ~ de vigilancia intensiva** MED intensive care unit; **~ de disco** INFOR disk drive; **unido** united; familia close-knit; **unificar** unify

uniformar fig standardize; **uniforme 1** adj uniform; superficie even **2** m uniform

unión f union; **Unión Europea** European Union

unir join; personas unite; características combine (con with); ciudades link; **unirse** join together; **~ a** join

universal universal

universidad f university; **~ a distancia** university correspondence school, Br Open University; **universitario 1** adj university atr m, -a f (estudiante) university student

universo m universe

uno 1 pron one; **es la -a** it's one o'clock; **me lo dijo; me a uno** someone o somebody told me; **~ a ~, ~ por ~, de ~ en ~** one by one **2** m one; **el de enero** January first, the first of January

untar spread

uña f ANAT nail; ZO claw; **ser ~ y carne** personas be extremely close

uranio m uranium

urbanismo m city planning, Br town planning; **urbanización** f (urban) development; (colonia) housing development, Br housing estate; **urbanizar** terreno develop; **urbano** (urban); (cortés) courteous; **guardia ~** local police officer

urgencia f urgency; (prisa) haste; MED emergency; **~s** emergency room, Br casualty; **urgente** urgent

urinario m urinal

urna f urn; **~ electoral** ballot box

urólogo m MED urologist

urraca f ZO magpie

Uruguay Uruguay; **uruguayo 1** adj Uruguayan **2** m, -a f Uruguayan

usanza f usage, custom; **usado** (gastado) worn; (de segunda mano) second hand; **usar 1** v/t use; ropa, gafas wear **2** v/i: **listo para ~** ready to use; **uso** m use; (costumbre) custom; **en buen ~** still in use

USB m IT USB; **cable m ~** USB cable; (llave f de) **memoria f ~** USB drive, USB stick

usted you; **~es** you; **de ~/~es** your; **es de ~/~es** it's yours

usual common, usual

usuario m, -a f user; **~ final** end user; **cuenta f de ~** IT user account; **identidad f de ~** IT user ID, user identification; **nombre m de ~** IT user name

usura f usury

utensilio m tool; **de cocina** utensil; **~s** equipment; **~s de pesca** fishing tackle

útero m ANAT uterus

útil 1 adj useful **2** m tool; **~es de pesca** fishing tackle; **utilidad** f usefulness; **utilitario 1** adj functional, utilitarian **2** m AUTO compact; **utilizar** use

utopía f utopia; **utópico** utopian

uva f BOT grape; **estar de mala ~** F be in a foul mood; **tener mala ~** F be a nasty piece of work F

úvula f ANAT uvula

vaca f cow; GASTR beef; **~ marina** manatee, sea cow

vacaciones fpl vacation, Br holiday; **de ~** on vacation, Br on holiday

vacante 1 adj vacant, empty **2** f job opening, position, Br tb vacancy; **cubrir una ~** fill a position; **vaciar** empty

vacío 1 adj empty **2** m FÍS vacuum; fig espacio void; **~ de poder** power vacuum; **~ legal** loophole; **dejar un ~** fig leave a gap; **envasado al ~** vacuum-packed; **hacer el ~ a alguien** fig ostracize s.o.

vacuna f vaccine; **vacunación** f vaccination; **vacunar** vaccinate

vacuno bovine; **ganado ~** cattle pl

vado m ford; **en la calle** entrance ramp

vagabundo 1 adj perro stray **2** m, **-a** f hobo, Br tramp; **vagar** wander

vagina f ANAT vagina

vago (holgazán) lazy; (indefinido) vague; **hacer el ~** laze around

vagón m de carga wagon; de pasajeros car, Br coach; **~ restaurante** dining car, Br tb restaurant car

vaho m (aliento) breath; (vapor) steam

vaina f BOT pod; S.Am. F (molestia) drag F

vainilla f vanilla

vaivén m to-and-fro; **vaivenes** fig ups and downs

vajilla f dishes pl; **juego** dinner service, set of dishes

vale m voucher, coupon; **~ de regalo** gift certificate, Br gift token; **valer 1** v/t be worth; (costar) cost **2** v/i be billete, carné be valid; (estar permitido) be allowed; (tener valor) be worth; (servir) be of use; **no ~ para algo** be no good at sth; **vale más caro** it's more expensive; **más vale...** it's better to ...; **más te vale...** you'd better ...; **¡vale!** okay, sure; **valerse** manage (by o.s.); **~ de** make use of

validez f validity; **válido** valid

valija f (maleta) bag, suitcase, Br tb case

valioso valuable

valla f fence; DEP, fig hurdle; **~ publicitaria** billboard, Br hoarding; **carrera de ~** DEP hurdles; **vallar** fence in

valle m valley

valor m value; (valentía) courage; **~ añadido**, L.Am. **~ agregado** added value; **objetos de ~** valuables; **~es** COM securities; **valorar** value ue (**en** at)

vals *m* waltz

válvula *f* ANAT, ELEC valve; ~
de escape *fig* safety valve

vampiresa *f* vamp, femme
fatale; **vampiro** *m fig* vampire

vanagloriarse boast (**de**
about), brag (**de** about)

vandálico destructive; **vandalismo** *m* vandalism;
vándalo *m*, **-a** *f* vandal

vanguardia *f* MIL vanguard;
de ~ *fig* avant-garde

vanidad *f* vanity; **vanidoso**
conceited, vain; **vano** futile,
vain; **en** ~ in vain

vapor *m* vapor, *Br* vapour *de
agua* steam; **cocinar al** ~
steam; **vaporizador** *m* spray,
vaporizer **vaporizar** vaporize

vaquero 1 *adj* tela denim;
pantalones ~**s** jeans 2 *m*
cowboy, cowhand; ~(**s**) *pantalones* jeans

vara *f* stick; TÉC rod; (*bastón
de mando*) staff

variable variable; *tiempo*
changeable; **variación** *f* variation; **variado** varied; **variante** *f* variant; **variar** vary;
para ~ for a change

varicela *f* MED chickenpox

variedad *f* variety; ~**es**
vaudeville, *Br* variety

vario varied; **variopinto** varied, diverse; **varios** several,
various

varón *m* man, male; **varonil**
manly, virile

vasija *f* container, vessel; **vaso** *m* glass; ANAT vessel

vástago *m* BOT shoot; TÉC
rod

vasto vast

vatio *m* ELEC watt

Vd. ☞ **usted**

Vds. ☞ **ustedes**

vecinal neighborhood *atr*, *Br*
neighbourhood *atr*; **vecindad** *f Méx* poor area; **vecindario** *m* neighborhood, *Br*
neighbourhood; **vecino** 1
adj neighboring, *Br* neighbouring 2 *m*, **-a** *f* neighbor,
Br neighbour

veda *f en caza* closed season;
vedar ban, prohibit

vega *f* plain

vegetación *f* vegetation; **vegetal** 1 *adj* vegetable, plant
atr 2 *m* vegetable; **vegetar**
fig vegetate; **vegetariano** 1
adj vegetarian 2 *m*, **-a** *f* vegetarian

vehemencia *f* vehemence;
vehemente vehement

vehículo *m tb fig* vehicle; MED
carrier

veinte *m/adj* twenty

vejación *f* humiliation

vejez *f* old age

vejiga *f* ANAT bladder

vela *f para alumbrar* candle;
DEP sailing; *de barco* sail; **a
toda** ~ F flat out F; *pasar
la noche en* ~ stay up all
night; **velada** *f evening*; **velar**: ~ *por algo* look after
sth; **velero** *m* MAR sailing
ship

veleta 1 f weathervane **2** m/f fig weathercock

vello m (body) hair

velo m veil

velocidad f speed; (marcha) gear; **velocímetro** m speedometer; **velocista** m/f DEP sprinter

velódromo m velodrome

veloz fast, speedy

vena f ANAT vein; **estar en ∼** F be on form

venado m ZO deer

vencedor 1 adj winning **2** m, **∼a** f winner; **vencer 1** v/t defeat; fig (superar) overcome **2** v/i win; COM de plazo etc expire; **vencimiento** m expiration, Br expiry; de bono maturity

venda f bandage; **vendaje** m MED dressing; **vendar** MED bandage, dress; **∼ los ojos a alguien** blindfold s.o.

vendedor m, **∼a** f seller; vender sell; fig (traicionar) betray; **se vende** for sale

vendimia f grape harvest

veneno m poison; **venenoso** poisonous

venerar venerate, worship

venezolano 1 adj Venezuelan **2** m, **∼a** f Venezuelan; **Venezuela** Venezuela

venganza f vengeance, revenge; **vengarse** take revenge (**de** on; **por** for); **vengativo** vengeful

venidero future

venir come; **∼ bien** be convenient; **∼ mal** be inconvenient;

viene a ser lo mismo it comes down to the same thing; **el año que viene** next year; **¡venga!** come on; **¿a qué viene eso?** why do you say that?

venta f sale; **∼ por correo** o **por catálogo** mail order; **∼ al detalle** o **al por menor** retail; **en ∼** for sale

ventaja f advantage; DEP en carrera, partido lead; **ventajoso** advantageous

ventana f window; **∼ de la nariz** nostril; **ventanilla** f AVIA, AUTO, FERR window; MAR porthole

ventilación f ventilation; **ventilador** m fan; **ventilar** air; fig: problema talk over

ventoso windy

ver 1 v/t see; televisión watch; JUR pleito hear; L.Am. (mirar) look at; **está por ∼** it remains to be seen; **no puede verla** fig he can't stand the sight of her; **no tiene nada que ∼ con** it doesn't have anything to do with; **¡a ∼!** let's see; **¡hay que ∼!** would you believe it!; **ya veremos** we'll see **2** v/i L.Am. (mirar) look

veraneante m/f vacationer, Br holidaymaker; **veranear** spend the summer vacation o Br holidays; **veraneo** m summer vacation o Br holidays; **ir de ∼** go on one's summer vacation o Br holidays; **verano** m summer

vez

veras f: **de ~** really, truly
verbal GRAM verbal
verbena f (*fiesta*) party
verbo m GRAM verb
verdad f truth; **a decir ~** to tell
the truth; **de ~** real, proper;
no te gusta, ¿~? you don't
like it, do you?; **vas a venir,
¿~?** you're coming, aren't
you?; **es ~** it's true, it's the
truth; **verdadero** true; (*cierto*) real
verde 1 adj green; **fruta** un-
ripe; F **chiste** blue; **viejo ~**
dirty old man; **poner ~ a alguien** F criticize s.o. **2** m
green; **los ~s** POL the
Greens
verdugo m executioner
verdura f: **~(s)** (*hortalizas*)
greens pl, (green) vegetables
pl
vereda f S.Am. sidewalk, Br
pavement
veredicto m JUR, fig verdict
vergonzoso disgraceful,
shameful; (*tímido*) shy; **vergüenza** f shame; (*escándalo*)
disgrace; **me da ~** I'm embarrassed
verídico true
verificación f verification;
verificar verify
verja f railing; (*puerta*) iron
gate
vermú, vermut m vermouth
verruga f wart
versado well-versed (*en* in)
versátil fickle; *artista* versatile
versión f version; **en ~ original** *película* original lan-

guage version
verso m verse
vértebra f ANAT vertebra
vertedero m dump, tip; **verter** dump; (*derramar*) spill;
fig: *opinión* voice
vertical vertical
vertiente f L.Am. (*cuesta*)
slope; (*lado*) side
vertiginoso dizzy; (*rápido*)
frantic; **vértigo** m MED vertigo; **darle a alguien ~** make
s.o. dizzy
vesícula f blister; **~ biliar**
ANAT gall-bladder
vestíbulo m de casa hall; **de
edificio público** lobby
vestido m dress; L.Am. de
hombre suit
vestigio m vestige, trace
vestir 1 v/t dress; (*llevar puesto*) wear **2** v/i dress; **~ de negro** wear black, dress in
black; **vestirse** get dressed;
(*disfrazarse*) dress up; **~ de
algo** wear sth
veterano 1 adj veteran; (*experimentado*) experienced **2** m,
-a f veteran
veterinario 1 adj veterinary **2**
m, -a f veterinarian, vet
vez f time; **a la ~** at the same
time; **a su ~** for his / her
part; **de ~ en cuando** from
time to time; **en ~ de** instead
of; **érase una ~** once upon a
time, there was; **otra ~** again;
tal ~ perhaps, maybe; **una ~**
once; **a veces** sometimes;
muchas veces (*con frecuencia*) often; **hacer las veces**

de de objeto serve as; *de persona* act as

vía 1 f FERR track; ~ *estrecha* FERR narrow gauge; *darle ~ libre a alguien* give s.o. a free hand; *por ~ aérea* by air; *en ~s de* fig in the process of **2** prp via

viable viable, feasible

viaducto m viaduct

viajante m/f sales rep; **viajar** travel; **viaje** m trip, journey; *sus ~s por...* his travels in ...; ~ *organizado* package tour; ~ *de ida* outward journey; ~ *de ida y vuelta* round trip; ~ *de novios* honeymoon; ~ *de vuelta* return journey; **viajero** m, -a f traveler, Br traveller

viario road atr; *educación -a* instruction in road safety

víbora f tb fig viper

vibración f vibration; **vibrar** vibrate

vicepresidente m, -a f POL vice-president; COM vice-president, Br deputy chairman

viceversa: *y* ~ and vice versa

vicio m vice; *pasarlo de ~* F have a great time F; **vicioso** vicious; (*corrompido*) depraved

víctima f victim

victoria f victory; *cantar ~* claim victory; **victorioso** victorious

vid f vine

vida f life; *de por ~* for life; *en mi ~* never (in my life); *ga-*

narse la ~ earn a living; ~ *mía* my love

vidente m/f seer, clairvoyant

vídeo m video; **videocámara** f video camera; **videoca-s(s)et(t)e** m video cassette; **videollamada** f IT, TELEC video call; **videoteca** f video library; **videoteléfono** m videophone

vidriera f L.Am. store o Br shop window; window atr; **vidrio** m, -a f glazier; **vidrio** m L.Am. glass; (*ventana*) window

viejo **1** adj old **2** m old man; *mis ~s* F my folks F

viento m wind; *hacer* ~ be windy; *proclamar a los cuatro ~s* fig shout from the rooftops

vientre m belly

viernes m inv Friday; **Viernes Santo** Good Friday

viga f beam, girder

vigente *legislación* in force

vigilancia f watchfulness, vigilance; **vigilante 1** adj watchful, vigilant **2** m L.Am. policeman; ~ *nocturno* night watchman; ~ *jurado* security guard; **vigilar 1** v/i keep watch **2** v/t watch; *a un preso* guard

vigor m vigor, Br vigour; *en ~* in force; **vigoroso** vigorous

vil vile, despicable

villa f town

villancico m Christmas carol

vilo: *en* ~ in the air; fig in suspense

vinagre *m* vinegar; **vinagrera** *f* vinegar bottle; *S.Am.* (*indigestión*) indigestion; **~s** cruet

vínculo *m* link; *fig* (*relación*) tie, bond

vino **1** *m* wine; **~ blanco** white wine; **~ de mesa** table wine; **~ tinto** red wine **2** *vb* → **venir**

viña *f* vineyard; **viñedo** *m* vineyard

viola *f* MÚS viola

violación *f* violence; *de derechos* violation; **violar** rape

violencia *f* violence; **violento** violent; (*embarazoso*) embarrassing; *persona* embarrassed

violeta **1** *f* BOT violet **2** *m/adj* violet

violín *m* violin; **violinista** *m/f* violinist; **violonc(h)elo** *m* cello

viraje *m* MAR tack; AVIA bank; AUTO swerve; *fig* change of direction; **virar** MAR, AVIA turn

virgen **1** *adj* virgin; *cinta* blank; *lana* **~** pure new wool **2** *f* virgin

Virgo *m/f inv* ASTR Virgo

viril virile, manly; **virilidad** *f* virility; manliness; *edad* manhood

virtud *f* virtue; **en ~ de** by virtue of; **virtuoso 1** *adj* virtuous **2** *m*, -a *f* virtuoso

viruela *f* MED smallpox

virulento *adj* virulent

virus *m inv* MED virus; **~ informático** computer virus

visa *f* L.Am. visa; **visado** *m*

visa

vísceras *fpl* guts, entrails

visera *f* de gorra peak; *de casco* visor

visibilidad *f* visibility; **visible** visible; *fig* obvious

visillo *m* sheer, Br net curtain

visión *f* vision, sight; *fig* vision; (*opinión*) view; **tener ~ de futuro** be forward looking

visita *f* visit; **~ a domicilio** house call; **~ guiada** guided tour; **visitante 1** *adj* visiting; DEP away **2** *m/f* visitor; **visitar** visit

visón *m* ZO mink

visor *m* FOT viewfinder; *en arma de fuego* sight

víspera *f* eve; **en ~s de** on the eve of

vista *f* (eye)sight; JUR hearing; **~ cansada** MED tired eyes; **a la ~** COM at sight; **a primera ~** at first sight; **con ~s a** with a view to; **en ~ de** in view of; **hasta la ~** bye!, see you!; **tener ~ para algo** fig have a good eye for sth; **volver la ~ atrás** *tb* fig look back; **vistazo** *m* look; **echar un ~ a** take a (quick) look at

visto **1** *part* *vb* → **ver 2** *adj*: **está bien** it's the done thing; **está mal** it's not the done thing; **está ~ que** it's obvious that; **por lo ~** apparently **3** *m* check(mark), Br tick; **dar el ~ bueno** give one's approval; **vistoso** eye-catching

vital vital; *persona* lively; **vitalidad** *f* vitality, liveliness

vitamina *f* vitamin

viticultor *m*, **~a** *f* wine grower; **viticultura** *f* wine-growing

vitrina *f* display cabinet; *L.Am.* shop window

viuda *f* widow; **viudo 1** *adj* widowed **2** *m* widower; **quedarse ~** be widowed

vivaz bright, sharp

vivencia *f* experience

víveres *mpl* provisions

vivienda *f* housing; (*casa*) house

vivir 1 *v/t* live through, experience **2** *v/i* live; **~ de algo** live on sth; **vivo** alive; *color* bright; *ritmo* lively; *fig* F sharp, smart

Vizcaya Biscay; **Golfo de ~** Bay of Biscay

vocablo *m* word; **vocabulario** *m* vocabulary

vocación *f* vocation

vocal 1 *m/f* member **2** *f* vowel

vocero *m*, **-a** *f esp L.Am.* spokesperson

volante 1 *adj* flying **2** *m* AUTO steering wheel; *de vestido* flounce; MED referral (slip); **volar 1** *v/i* fly; *fig* vanish **2** *v/t* fly; *edificio* blow up

volcán *m* volcano; **volcánico** volcanic

volcar 1 *v/t* knock over; (*vaciar*) empty; *barco, coche* overturn **2** *v/i de coche, barco* overturn

voleibol *m* volleyball

voltaje *m* ELEC voltage; **voltio** *m* ELEC volt

volumen *m* volume; **voluminoso** bulky; *vientre* ample; *historial* lengthy

voluntad *f* will; **buena / mala ~** good / ill will; **voluntario 1** *adj* volunteer **2** *m*, **-a** *f* volunteer

voluptuoso voluptuous

volver 1 *v/t página, mirada etc* turn (**a** to; **hacia** toward); **~ loco** drive crazy **2** *v/i* return; **~ a hacer algo** do sth again; **volverse** turn around; **~ loco** go crazy

vomitar 1 *v/t* throw up; *lava* hurl, throw out **2** *v/i* throw up, be sick; **tengo ganas de ~** I feel nauseous, *Br* I feel sick; **vómito** *m* vomit

voraz voracious; *incendio* fierce

vos *sg Rpl, C.Am., Ven* you

vosotros, vosotras *pl* you

votar vote; **voto** *m* vote; **~ en blanco** spoiled ballot paper

voz *f* voice; *fig* rumor, *Br* rumour; **a media ~** in a hushed voice; **a ~ en grito** at the top of one's voice; **en ~ alta** aloud; **en ~ baja** in a low voice; **correr la ~** spread the word; **no tener ~ ni voto** *fig* not have a say; **~ en off** voice-over

vuelo 1 *vb* ☞ **volar 2** *m* flight; **~ chárter** charter flight; **~ nacional** domestic flight; **al ~** coger, cazar in mid-air; **una falda con ~** a full skirt

vuelta *f* return; *en carrera* lap;

~ de carnero *L.Am.* half-somersault; **~ al mundo** round-the-world trip; **a la ~** on the way back; **a la ~ de la esquina** *fig* just around the corner; **dar la ~ llave** *etc* turn; **dar media ~** turn around; **dar una ~** go for a walk

vuestro 1 *adj* your **2** *pron* yours
vulcanizar vulcanize
vulgar vulgar, common; *abundante* common
vulnerable vulnerable; **vulnerar** violate; *fig* damage

W

walkman® *m* personal stereo, walkman®
wáter *m* bathroom, toilet
Wi-Fi *m o f* IT wi-fi; **hotspot** *m*

Wi-Fi wireless hotspot
windsurf(ing) *m* windsurfing; **windsurfista** *m/f* windsurfer

X

xenofobia *f* xenophobia; **xenófobo 1** *adj* xenophobic **2**
m, **-a** *f* xenophobe
xilófono *m* MÚS xylophone

Y

y and
ya already; *(ahora mismo)* now; **¡~!** *incredulidad* oh, yeah!, sure!; *comprensión* I know; *asenso* OK, sure; *al terminar* finished!, done!; **~ no vive aquí** he doesn't live here any more, he no longer lives here; **~ que** since, as; **~ lo sé** I know; **~... ~...** either ... or ...
yacer lie; **yacimiento** *m* MIN deposit
yanqui *m/f* Yankee

yate *m* yacht
yaya *f* grandma; **yayo** *m* grandpa
yegua *f* ZO mare
yema *f* yolk; **~ del dedo** fingertip
yerba *f* *L.Am.* grass; **~ mate** maté
yerno *m* son-in-law
yeso *m* plaster
yo I; **soy ~** it's me; **~ que tú** if I were you
yodo *m* iodine
yogur *m* yog(h)urt
yugo *m* yoke

yunque *m* anvil
yunta *f* yoke, team

yute *m* jute
yuyo *m* *L.Am.* weed

Z

zafiro *m* sapphire
zambullida *f* dive; **zambullirse** dive (**en** into); *fig* throw o.s. (**en** into)
zamparse F wolf down F
zanahoria *f* carrot
zanco *m* stilt
zancudo *m* *L.Am.* mosquito
zángano *m* ZO drone; *fig* F lazybones *sg*
zanja *f* ditch; **zanjar** *fig* *problemas* settle; *dificultades* overcome
zapatería *f* shoe store, shoe shop; **zapatero** *m*, -*a* *f* shoemaker; ~ **remendón** shoe mender; **zapatilla** *f* slipper; *de deporte* sneaker, *Br* trainer; **zapato** *m* shoe
Zaragoza Saragossa
zarpa *f* paw
zarpar MAR set sail (**para** for)
zarza *f* BOT bramble; **zarzamora** *f* BOT blackberry
zarzuela *f* type of operetta
zigzag *m* zigzag

zinc *m* zinc
zócalo *m* baseboard, *Br* skirting board
zodíaco, zodiaco *m* zodiac
zona *f* area, zone
zonzo *L.Am.* F stupid
zoo *m* zoo; **zoología** *f* zoology; **zoológico 1** *adj* zoological **2** *m* zoo
zorra *f* ZO vixen; P whore P; **zorro 1** *adj* sly, crafty **2** *m* ZO fox; *fig* old fox
zorzal *m* ZO thrush
zozobrar MAR overturn; *fig* go under
zueco *m* clog
zumbar 1 *v/i* buzz **2** *v/t golpe, bofetada* give
zumo *m* juice
zurcir *calcetines* darn; *chaqueta, pantalones* patch
zurdo 1 *adj* left-handed **2** *m, f* left-hander
zurra *f* TÉC tanning; *fig* F hiding F; **zurrar** TÉC tan; ~ **a alguien** F tan s.o.'s hide F

A

abandon [ə'bændən] abandonar

abbreviate [ə'bri:vieit] abreviar; **abbreviation** abreviatura f

abduct [əb'dʌkt] raptar

ability [ə'biləti] capacidad f, habilidad f

able ['eibl] (*skillful*) capaz, hábil; **be ~ to** poder

abnormal [æb'nɔ:rml] anormal

aboard [ə'bɔ:rd] **1** *prep* a bordo de **2** *adv* a bordo

abolish [ə'bɑ:liʃ] abolir; **abolition** abolición f

abort [ə'bɔ:rt] cancelar; **abortion** aborto m (*provocado*); **have an ~** abortar; **abortive** fallido

about [ə'baut] **1** *prep* (*concerning*) acerca de, sobre; **what's it ~?** *of book* ¿de qué trata? **2** *adv* (*roughly*) más o menos; **be ~ to** (*be going to*) estar a punto de

above [ə'bʌv] **1** *prep* por encima de; **~ all** sobre todo **2** *adv*: **on the floor ~** en el piso de arriba

abrasive [ə'breisiv] *personality* abrasivo

abreast [ə'brest] de frente, en fondo; **keep ~ of** mantenerse al tanto de

abridge [ə'bridʒ] abreviar

abroad [ə'brɔ:d] *live* en el extranjero; *go* al extranjero

abrupt [ə'brʌpt] brusco

abscess ['æbsis] absceso m

absence ['æbsəns] *of person* ausencia f; (*lack*) falta f; **absent** ausente; **absentee** ausente m/f; **absenteeism** absentismo m; **absent-minded** despistado, distraído

absolute ['æbsəlu:t] *power* absoluto; *idiot* completo; *mess* total; **absolution** REL absolución f; **absolve** absolver

absorb [əb'sɔ:rb] absorber; **absorbent** absorbente; **absorbent cotton** algodón m hidrófilo; **absorbing** absorbente

abstain [əb'stein] *in vote* abstenerse; **abstention** *in vote* abstención f

abstract ['æbstrækt] abstracto

absurd [əb'sɜ:rd] absurdo; **absurdity** lo absurdo

abundance [ə'bʌndəns] abundancia f; **abundant** abundante

abuse[1] [ə'bju:s] n (*insults*) insultos mpl; (*child*) ~ malos tratos mpl a menores; *sexual* agresión f sexual a menores

abuse[2] [ə'bju:z] v/t abusar de; *verbally* insultar

abysmal [ə'bizml] F (*very*

bad) desastroso F

academic [ækə'demɪk] **1** n
académico(-a) m(f), profe-
sor(a) m(f) **2** adj académico; **academy** academia f

accelerate [ək'seləreɪt] acelerar; **acceleration** aceleración f; **accelerator** acelerador m

accent ['æksənt] acento m;
(emphasis) énfasis m; **accentuate** acentuar

accept [ək'sept] aceptar; **acceptable** aceptable; **acceptance** aceptación f

access ['ækses] **1** n acceso m
2 v/t also COMPUT acceder a;
accessible accesible

accessory [ək'sesərɪ] *for
wearing* accesorio m; LAW
cómplice m/f

accident ['æksɪdənt] accidente m; **by ~** por casualidad;
accidental accidental; **acci-
dentally** sin querer

acclimate, **acclimatize**
[ə'klaɪmət,   ə'klaɪmətaɪz]
aclimatarse

accommodate [ə'kɑːmədeɪt]
alojar; *needs* hacer frente a;
accommodations aloja-
miento m

accompaniment [ə'kʌmpə-
nɪmənt] MUS acompaña-
miento m; **accompany** *also*
MUS acompañar

accomplice [ə'kʌmplɪs] cómplice m/f

accomplished [ə'kʌmplɪʃt]
consumado; **accomplish-
ment** *of task* realización f;

(talent) habilidad f; *(achievement)* logro m

accord [ə'kɔːrd] acuerdo m;
of one's own ~ de motu propio

accordance [ə'kɔːrdəns]: **in ~
with** de acuerdo con

according [ə'kɔːrdɪŋ]: **~ to** (según); **accordingly** *(consequently)* por consiguiente;
(appropriately) como corresponde

account [ə'kaʊnt] *financial*
cuenta f; *(report)* relato m,
descripción f; **give an ~ of**
relatar, describir; **on no ~**
de ninguna manera; **on ~
of** a causa de; **take sth into
~** tener algo en cuenta; **ac-
countable** responsable (**to**
ante); **accountant** contable
m/f, L.Am. contador(a)
m(f); **accounts** contabilidad f

accumulate [ə'kjuːmjʊleɪt] **1**
v/t acumular **2** v/i acumularse; **accumulation** acumulación f

accuracy ['ækjʊrəsɪ] precisión f; **accurate** preciso; **ac-
curately** con precisión

accusation [ækjuː'zeɪʃn]
acusación f; **accuse:** **~ s.o.
of sth** acusar a alguien de algo; **accused** LAW acusa-
do(-a) m(f); **accusing** acusa-
dor

accustom [ə'kʌstəm]: **get
~ed to** acostumbrarse a

ace [eɪs] *in cards* as m; *(in tennis: shot)* ace m

ache [eɪk] **1** n dolor m **2** v/i doler

achieve [əˈtʃiːv] conseguir, lograr; **achievement** logro m

acid [ˈæsɪd] ácido m

acknowledge [əkˈnɑːlɪdʒ] reconocer; **~ receipt of** acusar recibo de; **acknowledg(e)-ment** reconocimiento m

acoustics [əˈkuːstɪks] acústica f

acquaint [əˈkweɪnt] fml: **be ~ed with** conocer; **acquaint-ance** person conocido(-a) m(f)

acquire [əˈkwaɪr] adquirir; **acquisition** adquisición f

acquit [əˈkwɪt] LAW absolver; **acquittal** LAW absolución f

acre [ˈeɪkər] acre m (4.047m²)

across [əˈkrɔːs] **1** prep al otro lado de; **sail ~ the Atlantic** cruzar el Atlántico **2** adv de un lado a otro; **10 m ~** 10 m de ancho

act [ækt] **1** v/i THEA actuar **2** n (deed), of play acto m; in vaudeville número m; (law) ley f

action [ˈækʃn] acción f; **take ~** actuar

active [ˈæktɪv] activo; party member en activo; **activist** POL activista m/f; **activity** actividad f

actor [ˈæktər] actor m

actress [ˈæktrɪs] actriz f

actual [ˈæktʃʊəl] verdadero, real; **actually** en realidad

acute [əˈkjuːt] pain agudo; sense muy fino

AD [eɪˈdiː] (= anno Domini) D.C. (= después de Cristo)

ad [æd] ☞ advertisement

adamant [ˈædəmənt] firme

adapt [əˈdæpt] **1** v/t adaptar **2** v/i of person adaptarse; **adaptability** adaptabilidad f; **adaptable** adaptable; **adaptation** of play etc adaptación f; **adapter** electrical adaptador m

add [æd] **1** v/t añadir; MATH sumar **2** v/i of person sumar

◆ **add on** sumar

◆ **add up 1** v/t sumar **2** v/i fig cuadrar

addict [ˈædɪkt] adicto(-a) m(f); **drug ~** drogadicto(-a) m(f); **addicted** adicto; **ad-diction** adicción f; **addictive** adictivo

addition [əˈdɪʃn] MATH suma f; to list, company incorporación f; **in ~** además (**to** de); **additional** adicional; **additive** aditivo m; **add-on** extra m, accesorio m

address [əˈdres] **1** n dirección f **2** v/t letter dirigir; audience dirigirse a; **addressee** destinatario(-a) m(f)

adequate [ˈædɪkwət] suficiente; (satisfactory) aceptable; **adequately** suficientemente; (satisfactorily) aceptablemente

◆ **adhere to** surface adherirse a; rules cumplir

adhesive [ədˈhiːsɪv] adhesivo m

adjacent [əˈdʒeɪsnt] adyacen-

te
adjective ['ædʒɪktɪv] adjetivo m
adjoining [ə'dʒɔɪnɪŋ] contiguo
adjourn [ə'dʒɜːrn] *of meeting* aplazar; **adjournment** aplazamiento m
adjust [ə'dʒʌst] ajustar, regular; **adjustable** ajustable; **adjustment** ajuste m; *psychological* adaptación f
ad lib [æd'lɪb] **1** adj improvisado **2** v/i improvisar
administer [əd'mɪnɪstər] administrar; **administration** administración f; **administrative** administrativo; **administrator** administrador(a) m(f)
admirable ['ædmərəbl] admirable; **admiration** admiración f; **admire** admirar; **admirer** admirador(a) m(f)
admiring de admiración; **admiringly** con admiración
admissible [əd'mɪsəbl] admisible; **admission** (*confession*) confesión f; ~ **free** entrada gratis; **admit** *to place* dejar entrar; *to organization* admitir; *to hospital* ingresar; (*confess*) confesar; (*accept*) admitir; **admittance** admisión f; **no** ~ prohibido el paso
adolescence [ædə'lesns] adolescencia f; **adolescent 1** n adolescente m/f **2** adj de adolescente

adopt [ə'dɑːpt] adoptar; **adoption** adopción f
adorable [ə'dɔːrəbl] encantador; **adoration** adoración f; **adore** adorar
adrenalin [ə'drenəlɪn] adrenalina f
adult ['ædʌlt] **1** n adulto(-a) m(f) **2** adj adulto; **adultery** adulterio m
advance [əd'væns] **1** n *money* adelanto m; *in science, MIL* avance m; **in** ~ con antelación; *get money* por adelantado **2** v/i MIL avanzar; (*make progress*) avanzar, progresar **3** v/t *theory* presentar; *money* adelantar; *knowledge, cause* hacer avanzar; **advanced** avanzado
advantage [əd'væntɪdʒ] ventaja f; **take** ~ **of** aprovecharse de; **advantageous** ventajoso
adventure [əd'ventʃər] aventura f; **adventurous** aventurero; *investment* arriesgado
adverb ['ædvɜːrb] adverbio m
adversary ['ædvərseri] adversario(-a) m(f)
adverse ['ædvɜːrs] adverso
advertise ['ædvərtaɪz] **1** v/t anunciar **2** v/i anunciarse, poner un anuncio; **advertisement** anuncio m; **advertiser** anunciante m/f; **advertising** publicidad f
advice [əd'vaɪs] consejo m; **some** ~ un consejo; **advisable** aconsejable; **advise** aconsejar; *government* ase-

sorar

advocate ['ædvəkeit] abogar por

aerial ['eriəl] Br antena f; **aerial photograph** fotografía f aérea

aerobics [e'roubiks] aerobic m

aerodynamic [eroudai'næmik] aerodinámico

aeroplane ['erouplein] Br avión m

aerosol ['erəsɑːl] aerosol m

aesthetic Br ☞ **esthetic**

affair [ə'fer] (matter) asunto m; (love ~) aventura f, lío m

affection [ə'fekʃn] afecto m; **affectionate** afectuoso; **affectionately** con afecto

affirmative [ə'fɜːrmətiv] afirmativo

affluence ['æfluəns] prosperidad f; **affluent** próspero

afford [ə'fɔːrd] permitirse

afloat [ə'flout] boat a flote

afraid [ə'freid] **be ~** tener miedo (**of** de); **I'm ~** expressing regret me temo

afresh [ə'freʃ] de nuevo

Africa ['æfrikə] África; **African 1** adj africano **2** n africano(-a) m(f); **African-American 1** adj afroamericano **2** n afroamericano(-a) m(f)

after ['æftər] **1** prep después de; **it's ten ~ two** son las dos y diez **2** adv (afterward) después; **the day ~** el día siguiente

afternoon [æftər'nuːn] tarde f; **good ~** buenas tardes

'after sales service servicio m posventa; **aftershave** after shave m; **afterward** después

again [ə'gein] otra vez; **I never saw him ~** no lo volví a ver

against [ə'genst] contra

age [eidʒ] **1** n edad f; (era) era f; **she's 5 years of ~** tiene 5 años **2** v/i envejecer; **aged: ~ 16** con 16 años de edad; **age group** grupo m de edades; **age limit** límite m de edad

agency ['eidʒənsi] agencia f

agenda [ə'dʒendə] orden m del día

agent ['eidʒənt] agente m/f

aggravate ['ægrəveit] agravar; (annoy) molestar

aggression [ə'greʃn] agresividad f; **aggressive** agresivo; **aggressively** agresivamente

aghast [ə'gæst] horrorizado

agile ['ædʒəl] ágil; **agility** agilidad f

agitated ['ædʒiteitid] agitado; **agitation** agitación f; **agitator** agitador(a) m(f)

agnostic [æg'nɑːstik] agnóstico(-a) m(f)

ago [ə'gou] **two days ~** hace dos días; **long ~** hace mucho tiempo

agonize ['ægənaiz] atormentarse (**over** por); **agonizing pain** atroz; **wait** angustioso; **agony** agonía f

agree [ə'griː] **1** v/i estar de acuerdo; of figures coincidir;

(reach agreement) ponerse de acuerdo **2** *v/t price* acordar; **agreeable** *(pleasant)* agradable; **agreement** acuerdo *m*

agricultural [əgrɪˈkʌltʃərəl] agrícola; **agriculture** agricultura *f*

ahead [əˈhed] delante; *movement* adelante; *in race* por delante; **be ~ of** estar por delante de; **plan ~** planear con antelación

aid [eɪd] **1** *n* ayuda *f* **2** *v/t* ayudar

aide [eɪd] asistente *m/f*

Aids [eɪdz] sida *m*

ailing [ˈeɪlɪŋ] *economy* débil

ailment [ˈeɪlmənt] achaque *m*

aim [eɪm] **1** *n (objective)* objetivo *m* **2** *v/i in shooting* apuntar; **~ to do sth** tener como intención hacer algo **3** *v/t*: **be ~ed at** *of remark* estar dirigido a; *of gun* estar apuntando a; **aimless** sin objetivos

air [er] **1** *n* aire *m*; **by ~** *travel* en avión; *send mail* por correo aéreo; **in the open ~** al aire libre **2** *v/t room, views* airear; **airbag** airbag *m*; **air-conditioned** con aire acondicionado, climatizado; **air-conditioning** aire *m* acondicionado; **aircraft** avión *m*; **aircraft carrier** portaaviones *m inv*; **air force** fuerza *f* aérea; **air hostess** azafata *f*, *L.Am.* aeromoza *f*; **airline** línea *f* aérea; **airliner** avión *m* de pasajeros; **airmail: by**

~ por correo aéreo; **airplane** avión *m*; **airport** aeropuerto *m*; **air terminal** terminal *f* aérea; **air-traffic controller** controlador(a) *m(f)* del tráfico aéreo

aisle [aɪl] pasillo *m*

ajar [əˈdʒɑːr] **be ~** estar entreabierto

alarm [əˈlɑːrm] **1** *n* alarma *f* **2** *v/t* alarmar; **alarming** alarmante; **alarmingly** de forma alarmante

album [ˈælbəm] álbum *m*

alcohol [ˈælkəhɑːl] alcohol *m*; **alcoholic 1** *n* alcohólico(-a) *m(f)* **2** *adj* alcohólico

alert [əˈlɜːrt] **1** *n signal* alerta *f* **2** *v/t* alertar **3** *adj* alerta

alibi [ˈælɪbaɪ] coartada *f*

alien [ˈeɪlɪən] **1** *n* extranjero(-a) *m(f)*; *from space* extraterrestre *m/f* **2** *adj* extraño; **alienate** alienar

align [əˈlaɪn] alinear

alike [əˈlaɪk] **1** *adj*: **be ~** parecerse **2** *adv* igual; **old and young ~** viejos y jóvenes sin distinción

alimony [ˈælɪmənɪ] pensión *f* alimenticia

alive [əˈlaɪv]: **be ~** estar vivo

all [ɔːl] **1** *adj* todo(s) **2** *pron* todo; **~ of us / them** todos nosotros / ellos; **for ~ I know** por lo que sé **3** *adv*: **~ at once** *(suddenly)* de repente; *(at the same time)* a la vez; **~ but** *(except)* todos menos; *(nearly)* casi; **~ the better** mucho mejor; **they're not at ~ alike** no

amateurish

se parecen en nada; **not at ~!**
¡en absoluto!; **two ~** SP empate a dos

allegation [ælɪˈɡeɪʃn] acusación f; **allege** alegar; **alleged**
presunto; **allegedly** presun-
tamente

allegiance [əˈliːdʒəns] lealtad
f

allergic [əˈlɜːrdʒɪk] alérgico

alleviate [əˈliːvɪeɪt] aliviar

alley [ˈælɪ] callejón m

alliance [əˈlaɪəns] alianza f

allocate [ˈæləkeɪt] asignar; **al-
location** asignación f

allot [əˈlɑːt] asignar

allow [əˈlaʊ] (permit) permitir;
(calculate for) calcular

◆ **allow for** tener en cuenta

allowance [əˈlaʊəns] (money)
asignación f; (pocket money)
paga f

alloy [ˈælɔɪ] aleación f

all-'purpose multiuso; **all-
round** completo

◆ **allude to** [əˈluːd] aludir a

alluring [əˈlʊrɪŋ] atractivo

all-wheel 'drive tracción f
a las cuatro ruedas

ally [ˈælaɪ] aliado(-a) m(f)

almond [ˈɑːmənd] almendra f

almost [ˈɔːlməʊst] casi

alone [əˈləʊn] solo

along [əˈlɒŋ] **1** prep (situated
beside) a lo largo de; **walk
~ this path** sigue por esta calle **2** adv: **would you like to
come ~?** ¿te gustaría venir
con nosotros?; **~ with** junto
con; **all ~** (all the time) todo
el tiempo

alongside [əlɒŋˈsaɪd] (in cooperation with) junto a; (parallel to) al lado de

aloof [əˈluːf] distante

aloud [əˈlaʊd] en voz alta

alphabet [ˈælfəbet] alfabeto
m; **alphabetical** alfabético

already [ɔːlˈredɪ] ya

alright [ɔːlˈraɪt] (not hurt, in
working order) bien; **that's
~** (don't mention it) de nada;
(I don't mind) no importa

altar [ˈɔːltər] altar m

alter [ˈɔːltər] alterar; **alteration** alteración f

alternate 1 v/i [ˈɔːltərneɪt] alternar **2** [ˈɔːltərnət] adj alterno

alternative [ɔːltˈɜːrnətɪv] **1** n
alternativa f **2** adj alternativo; **alternatively** si no

although [ɔːlˈðəʊ] aunque, si
bien

altitude [ˈæltɪtuːd] altitud f; of
mountain altura f

altogether [ɔːltəˈɡeðər] (completely) completamente; (in
all) en total

altruism [ˈæltruːɪzm] altruis-
mo m; **altruistic** altruista

aluminium [æljʊˈmɪnɪəm] Br,
aluminum [əˈluːmənəm] aluminio m

always [ˈɔːlweɪz] siempre

a.m. [ˈeɪem] (= ante meridiem) a.m.; **at 11 ~** a las 11
de la mañana

amass [əˈmæs] acumular

amateur [ˈæmətʃʊr] unskilled
aficionado(-a) m(f); SP amateur m/f; **amateurish** pej

chapucero

amaze [ə'meɪz] asombrar; **amazed** asombrado; **amazement** asombro *m*; **amazing** asombroso; F (*very good*) alucinante F; **amazingly** increíblemente

Amazon ['æməzən] *the* ~ el Amazonas

ambassador [æm'bæsədər] embajador(a) *m(f)*

amber ['æmbər] ámbar

ambience ['æmbɪəns] ambiente *m*

ambiguity [æmbɪ'gjuːətɪ] ambigüedad *f*; **ambiguous** ambiguo

ambition [æm'bɪʃn] *also pej* ambición *f*; **ambitious** ambicioso

ambivalent [æm'bɪvələnt] ambivalente

amble ['æmbl] deambular

ambulance ['æmbjələns] ambulancia *f*

ambush ['æmbʊʃ] **1** *n* emboscada *f* **2** *v/t* tender una emboscada a

amend [ə'mend] enmendar; **amendment** enmienda *f*; **amends**: **make** ~ **for** compensar

amenities [ə'miːnətiz] servicios *mpl*

America [ə'merɪkə] *continent* América; *USA* Estados *mpl* Unidos; **American 1** *adj North American* estadounidense **2** *n North American* estadounidense *m/f*

amicable ['æmɪkəbl] amisto-

so; **amicably** amistosamente

ammunition [æmju'nɪʃn] munición *f*

amnesia [æm'niːzɪə] amnesia *f*

amnesty ['æmnəstɪ] amnistía *f*

among(st) [ə'mʌŋ(st)] entre

amoral [eɪ'mɔːrəl] amoral

amount [ə'maʊnt] cantidad *f*
♦ **amount to** ascender a

amphibian [æm'fɪbɪən] anfibio *m*

ample ['æmpl] abundante

amplifier ['æmplɪfaɪr] amplificador *m*; **amplify** amplificar

amputate ['æmpjʊteɪt] amputar; **amputation** amputación *f*

amuse [ə'mjuːz] (*make laugh*) divertir; (*entertain*) entretener; **amusement** (*merriment*) diversión *f*; (*entertainment*) entretenimiento *m*; **amusement park** parque *m* de atracciones; **amusing** divertido

an [æn] ☞ **a**

anaemia *Br* ☞ **anemia**

anaesthetic *Br* ☞ **anesthetic**

analog ['ænəlɒg] analógico; **analogy** analogía *f*

analysis [ə'næləsɪs] análisis *m inv*; PSYCH psicoanálisis *m inv*; **analyst** analista *m/f*; PSYCH psicoanalista *m/f*; **analytical** analítico; **analyze** analizar; PSYCH psicoanalizar

anarchy ['ænərkɪ] anarquía *f*

ancestor ['ænsestər] antepasado(-a) *m(f)*

anchor ['æŋkər] **1** *n* NAUT ancla *f*; TV presentador(a) *m(f)* **2** *v/i* NAUT anclar

ancient ['eɪnʃənt] antiguo

and [ænd] y

Andean ['ændɪən] andino; **Andes:** *the ~* los Andes

anemia [ə'niːmɪə] anemia *f*; **anemic** anémico

anesthetic [ænəs'θetɪk] anestesia *f*

angel ['eɪndʒl] ángel *m*

anger ['æŋgər] **1** *n* enfado *m* **2** *v/t* enfadar

angle ['æŋgl] ángulo *m*

angry ['æŋgrɪ] enfadado

animal ['ænɪml] animal *m*

animated ['ænɪmeɪtɪd] animado; **animated cartoon** dibujos *mpl* animados; **animation** animación *f*

animosity [ænɪ'mɑːsətɪ] animosidad *f*

ankle ['æŋkl] tobillo *m*

annex ['æneks] **1** *n building* edificio *m* anexo **2** *v/t state* anexionar

annihilate [ə'naɪəleɪt] aniquilar; **annihilation** aniquilación *f*

anniversary [ænɪ'vɜːrsərɪ] aniversario *m*

announce [ə'naʊns] anunciar; **announcement** anuncio *m*; **announcer** TV, RAD presentador(a) *m(f)*

annoy [ə'nɔɪ] irritar; **annoyance** (*anger*) irritación *f*; (*nuisance*) molestia *f*; annoying irritante

annual ['ænʊəl] anual

annul [ə'nʌl] anular; **annulment** anulación *f*

anonymous [ə'nɑːnɪməs] anónimo

anorexia [ænə'reksɪə] anorexia *f*

another [ə'nʌðər] **1** *adj* otro **2** *pron* otro(-a) *m(f)*; *they helped one* ~ se ayudaron (el uno al otro)

answer ['ænsər] **1** *n respuesta f*, contestación *f*; *to problem* solución *f* **2** *v/t* responder, contestar; **answerphone** contestador *m*

ant [ænt] hormiga *f*

antagonism [æn'tægənɪzm] antagonismo *m*; **antagonistic** hostil; **antagonize** antagonizar, enfadar

Antarctic [ænt'ɑːrktɪk]: *the ~* el Antártico

antenatal [æntɪ'neɪtl] prenatal

antenna [æn'tenə] antena *f*

antibiotic [æntɪbaɪ'ɑːtɪk] antibiótico *m*

anticipate [æn'tɪsɪpeɪt] esperar, prever; **anticipation** expectativa *f*, previsión *f*

antics ['æntɪks] payasadas *fpl*

antidote ['æntɪdoʊt] antídoto *m*

antifreeze ['æntɪfriːz] anticongelante *m*

antipathy [æn'tɪpəθɪ] antipatía *f*

antiquated ['æntɪkweɪtɪd] anticuado

antique [æn'ti:k] antigüedad *f*

antiseptic [ænti'septik] **1** *adj* antiséptico **2** *n* antiséptico *m*

antisocial [ænti'souʃl] antisocial, poco sociable

antivirus program [ænti-'vairəs] COMPUT antivirus *m inv*

anxiety [æŋ'zaiəti] ansiedad *f*; **anxious** preocupado; (*eager*) ansioso

any ['eni] **1** *adj*: *are there ~ glasses?* ¿hay vasos?; *there isn't ~ bread* no hay pan; *have you ~ idea at all?* ¿tienes alguna idea?; *no matter which* cualquier(a) **2** *pron* alguno(-a); *there isn't ~ left* no queda

anybody ['enibɔːdɪ] alguien; *no matter who* cualquiera; *there wasn't ~ there* no había nadie allí

anyhow ['enihau] en todo caso, de todos modos

anyone ['eniwʌn] ☞ **anybody**

anything ['eniθɪŋ] algo; *with negatives* nada; *I didn't hear ~* no oí nada; *~ but* todo menos

anyway ['eniwei] ☞ **anyhow**

anywhere ['eniweir] en alguna parte; *I can't find it ~* no lo encuentro por ninguna parte

apart [ə'pɑːrt] aparte; *~ from* aparte de

apartment [ə'pɑːrtmənt] apartamento *m*, Span piso *m*; **apartment block** bloque *m* de apartamentos *or* Span piso

ape [eip] simio *m*

aperitif [ə'periti:f] aperitivo *m*

apologize [ə'pɑːlədʒaiz] disculparse; **apology** disculpa *f*

app [æp] IT app *f*, aplicación *f*

appalling [ə'pɔːlɪŋ] horroroso

apparatus [æpə'reitəs] aparatos *mpl*

apparent [ə'pærənt] aparente, evidente; **apparently** al parecer, por lo visto

appeal [ə'piːl] (*charm*) atractivo *m*; *for funds etc* llamamiento *m*; LAW apelación *f*

◆ **appeal for** solicitar
◆ **appeal to** (*be attractive to*) atraer a

appealing [ə'piːlɪŋ] *idea, offer* atractivo

appear [ə'pɪr] aparecer; *in court* comparecer; (*seem*) parecer; **appearance** aparición *f*; *in court* comparecencia *f*; (*look*) apariencia *f*, aspecto *m*

appendicitis [əpendi'saitis] apendicitis *f*

appendix [ə'pendiks] MED, *of book* apéndice *m*

appetite ['æpitait] *also fig* apetito *m*; **appetizer** aperitivo *m*; **appetizing** apetitoso

applaud [ə'plɔːd] aplaudir; **applause** aplauso *m*

apple ['æpl] manzana *f*

appliance [ə'plaiəns] aparato *m*; *household* electrodoméstico *m*

applicable [ə'plɪkəbl] aplicable; **applicant** solicitante *m/f*; **application** for job etc solicitud *f*; **apply 1** *v/t* rules, ointment aplicar **2** *v/i* of rule, law aplicarse

◆ **apply for** job, passport solicitar; university solicitar el ingreso en

◆ **apply to** (contact) dirigirse a; (affect) aplicarse a

appoint [ə'pɔɪnt] to position nombrar; **appointment** to position nombramiento *m*; meeting cita *f*

appraisal [ə'preɪz(ə)l] evaluación *f*

appreciable [ə'priːʃəbl] apreciable; **appreciate 1** *v/t* (value) apreciar; (be grateful for) agradecer; (acknowledge) ser consciente de **2** *v/i* FIN revalorizarse; **appreciative** agradecido

apprehensive [æprɪ'hensɪv] aprensivo, temeroso

approach [ə'proʊtʃ] **1** *n* aproximación *f*; (proposal) propuesta *f*; to problem enfoque *m* **2** *v/t* (get near to) aproximarse a; (contact) ponerse en contacto con; problem enfocar; **approachable** accesible

appropriate [ə'proʊprɪət] apropiado, adecuado

approval [ə'pruːvl] aprobación *f*; **approve 1** *v/i*: **my parents don't ~** a mis padres no les parece bien **2** *v/t* apro-

bar

approximate [ə'prɑːksɪmət] aproximado; **approximately** aproximadamente

apricot ['eɪprɪkɑːt] albaricoque *m*, LAm. damasco *m*

April ['eɪprəl] abril *m*

apt [æpt] remark oportuno; **aptitude** aptitud *f*

aquarium [ə'kweriəm] acuario *m*

Arab ['ærəb] **1** adj árabe **2** *n* árabe *m/f*; **Arabic 1** adj árabe **2** *n* árabe *m*

arbitrary ['ɑːrbɪtrɪ] arbitrario

arbitrate ['ɑːrbɪtreɪt] arbitrar; **arbitration** arbitraje *m*

arch [ɑːrtʃ] arco *m*

archaeology Br ☞ **archeology**

archaic [ɑːr'keɪɪk] arcaico

archeological [ɑːrkɪə'lɑːdʒɪkl] arqueológico; **archeologist** arqueólogo(-a) *m(f)*; **archeology** arqueología *f*

architect ['ɑːrkɪtekt] arquitecto(-a) *m(f)*; **architectural** arquitectónico; **architecture** arquitectura *f*

archives ['ɑːrkaɪvz] archivos *mpl*

Arctic ['ɑːrktɪk]: **the ~** el Ártico

ardent ['ɑːrdənt] ardiente

arduous ['ɑːrdjʊəs] arduo

area ['erɪə] área *f*; *f*; **area code** TELEC prefijo *m*

arena [ə'riːnə] SP estadio *m*

Argentina [ɑːrdʒən'tiːnə] Argentina *f*; **Argentinian 1** adj argentino 2 *n* argentino(-a) *m(f)*

arguably ['ɑːrgjuəblɪ] posiblemente; **argue** discutir; (*reason*) argumentar; **argument** discusión *f*; (*reasoning*) argumento *m*

arid ['ærɪd] *land* árido

arise [ə'raɪz] *of situation* surgir

arithmetic [ə'rɪθmətɪk] aritmética *f*

arm¹ [ɑːrm] *n* brazo *m*

arm² [ɑːrm] *v/t* armar

armaments ['ɑːrməmənts] armamento *m*

armchair ['ɑːrmtʃer] sillón *m*

armed [ɑːrmd] armado; **armed forces** fuerzas *fpl* armadas; **armed robbery** atraco *m* a mano armada

'**armpit** sobaco *m*

arms [ɑːrmz] (*weapons*) armas *fpl*

army ['ɑːrmɪ] ejército *m*

around [ə'raund] **1** *prep* (*enclosing*) alrededor de; **it's ~ the corner** está a la vuelta de la esquina **2** *adv* (*in the area*) por ahí; (*encircling*) alrededor; (*roughly*) alrededor de; (*with expressions of time*) en torno a

arouse [ə'rauz] despertar; *sexually* excitar

arrange [ə'reɪndʒ] (*put in order*) ordenar; *flowers, music* arreglar; *meeting etc* organizar; *time and place* acordar; **I've ~d to meet her** he quedado con ella; **arrangement**

(*plan*) plan *m*, preparativo *m*; (*agreement*) acuerdo *m*; (*layout*) disposición *f*; *of flowers, music* arreglo *m*

arrears [ə'rɪrz] atrasos *mpl*

arrest [ə'rest] **1** *n* detención *f*, arresto *m* **2** *v/t* detener, arrestar

arrival [ə'raɪvl] llegada *f*; **arrive** llegar

◆ **arrive** at llegar a

arrogance ['ærəgəns] arrogancia *f*; **arrogant** arrogante

arrow ['ærəu] flecha *f*

arson ['ɑːrsn] incendio *m* provocado

art [ɑːrt] arte *m*

artery ['ɑːrtərɪ] arteria *f*

art gallery museo *m*; *private* galería *f* de arte

arthritis [ɑːr'θraɪtɪs] artritis *f*

artichoke ['ɑːrtɪtʃəuk] alcachofa *f*, *L.Am.* alcaucil *m*

article ['ɑːrtɪkl] artículo *m*

articulate [ɑːr'tɪkjulət] *person* elocuente

artificial [ɑːrtɪ'fɪʃl] artificial

artillery [ɑːr'tɪlərɪ] artillería *f*

artist ['ɑːrtɪst] artista *m/f*; **artistic** artístico

'**arts degree** licenciatura *f* en letras

as [æz] **1** *conj* (*while, when*) cuando; (*because, like*) como; **~ if** como si; **~ usual** como de costumbre **2** *adv* como; **~ high ...** tan alto como...; **~ much ~ that?** ¿tanto? **3** *prep* como; **work ~ a teacher** trabajar como profesor; **~ for** por lo que respecta a;

from or *of* a partir de

ash [æʃ] ceniza *f*

ashamed [əˈʃeɪmd] avergonzado, *L.Am.* apenado

'ash can cubo *m* de la basura

ashore [əˈʃɔːr] en tierra; **go ~** desembarcar

ashtray [ˈæʃtreɪ] cenicero *m*

Asia [ˈeɪʃə] Asia; **Asian** **1** *adj* asiático **2** *n* asiático(-a) *m(f)*; **Asian American** norteamericano(-a) *m(f)* de origen asiático

aside [əˈsaɪd] a un lado

ask [æsk] *person* preguntar; *question* hacer; (*invite*) invitar; *favor* pedir; **~ s.o. for sth** pedir algo a alguien

◆ **ask after** *person* preguntar por

◆ **ask for** pedir

◆ **ask out** invitar a salir

asleep [əˈsliːp] dormido; **fall ~** dormirse

asparagus [əˈspærəɡəs] espárragos *mpl*

aspect [ˈæspekt] aspecto *m*

aspiration [æspəˈreɪʃn] aspiración *f*

aspirin [ˈæsprɪn] aspirina *f*

ass¹ [æs] (*idiot*) burro(-a) *m(f)*

ass² [æs] P (*butt*) culo P

assassin [əˈsæsɪn] asesino(-a) *m(f)*; **assassinate** asesinar; **assassination** asesinato *m*

assault [əˈsɔːlt] **1** *n* agresión *f*; (*attack*) ataque *m* **2** *v/t* atacar, agredir

assemble [əˈsembl] **1** *v/t parts* montar **2** *v/i of people* reunirse; **assembly** *of parts* montaje *m*; POL asamblea *f*; **assembly line** cadena *f* de montaje

assent [əˈsent] asentir

assertive [əˈsɜːrtɪv] *person* seguro y firme

assess [əˈses] *situation* evaluar; *value* valorar; **assessment** evaluación *f*

asset [ˈæset] FIN activo *m*; *fig* ventaja *f*

assign [əˈsaɪn] asignar; **assignment** (*task*) trabajo *m*

assimilate [əˈsɪmɪleɪt] asimilar; *in group* integrar

assist [əˈsɪst] ayudar; **assistance** ayuda *f*, asistencia *f*; **assistant** ayudante *m/f*; **assistant manager** subdirector(a) *m(f)*

associate [əˈsoʊʃieɪt] **1** *v/t* asociar **2** *v/i*: **~ with** relacionarse con **3** *n* colega *m/f*; **association** asociación *f*

assortment [əˈsɔːrtmənt] *of food* surtido *m*; *of people* diversidad *f*

assume [əˈsuːm] (*suppose*) suponer; **assumption** suposición *f*

assurance [əˈʃʊrəns] garantía *f*; (*confidence*) seguridad *f*; **assure** (*reassure*) asegurar

asthma [ˈæsmə] asma *f*

astonish [əˈstɑːnɪʃ] asombrar; **astonishing** asombroso; **astonishment** asombro *m*

astound [əˈstaʊnd] pasmar

astride [ə'straɪd] a horcajadas sobre

astrology [ə'strɑːlədʒɪ] astrología f

astronaut ['æstrənɔːt] astronauta m/f

astronomer [ə'strɑːnəmər] astrónomo(-a) m(f); **astronomical** price *adj* astronómico; **astronomy** astronomía f

astute [ə'stuːt] astuto, sagaz

asylum [ə'saɪləm] asilo m; **mental** manicomio m

at [æt] *with places* en; ~ *Joe's house* en casa de Joe; ~ *the door* a la puerta; ~ *10 dollars* a 10 dólares; ~ *the age of 18* a los 18 años; ~ *5 o'clock* a las 5; *be good* ~ *sth* ser bueno haciendo algo

atheist ['eɪθiɪst] ateo(-a) m(f)

athlete ['æθliːt] atleta m/f; **athletic** atlético; **athletics** atletismo m

Atlantic [ət'læntɪk]: *the* ~ el Atlántico

atlas ['ætləs] atlas m inv

ATM [eɪtiː'em] (= *automatic teller machine*) cajero m automático

atmosphere ['ætmɒsfɪr] atmósfera f; (*ambience*) ambiente m

atom ['ætəm] átomo m; **atomic** atómico

atone [ə'toʊn]: ~ *for* expiar

atrocious [ə'troʊʃəs] atroz; **atrocity** atrocidad f

at-'seat TV televisor en el respaldo del asiento

attach [ə'tætʃ] sujetar, fijar;

importance atribuir; **attachment** *to e-mail* archivo m adjunto

attack [ə'tæk] **1** n ataque m **2** v/t atacar

attempt [ə'tempt] **1** n intento m **2** v/t intentar

attend [ə'tend] acudir a

♦ **attend to** ocuparse de

attendance [ə'tendəns] asistencia f; **attendant** *in museum etc* vigilante m/f

attention [ə'tenʃn] atención f; *pay* ~ prestar atención; **attentive** atento

attic ['ætɪk] ático m

attitude ['ætɪtjuːd] actitud f

attorney [ə'tɜːrni] abogado(-a) m(f)

attract [ə'trækt] atraer; **attraction** atracción f; **attractive** atractivo

auction ['ɔːkʃn] subasta f, *L.Am.* remate m

audacity [ɔː'dæsətɪ] audacia f

audible ['ɔːdəbl] audible

audience ['ɔːdɪəns] público m; *TV* audiencia f

audio ['ɔːdɪoʊ] de audio; **audio guide, audioguide** audioguía f; **audiovisual** audiovisual

audit ['ɔːdɪt] **1** n auditoría f **2** v/t auditar; *course* asistir de oyente a

audition [ɔː'dɪʃn] **1** n audición f **2** v/i hacer una prueba

auditor ['ɔːdɪtər] FIN auditor(a) m(f)

auditorium [ɔːdɪ'tɔːrɪəm] *of theater etc* auditorio m

August [ˈɔːgəst] agosto *m*

aunt [ænt] tía *f*

au pair [ouˈpeɪr] au pair *m/f*

aura [ˈɔːrə] aura *f*

auspicious [ɔːˈspɪʃəs] propicio

austere [ɔːˈstɪr] austero; **austerity** austeridad *f*

Australia [ɒˈstreɪlɪə] Australia; **Australian 1** *adj* australiano **2** *n* australiano(-a) *m(f)*

Austria [ˈɒstrɪə] Austria; **Austrian 1** *adj* austriaco **2** *n* austriaco(-a) *m(f)*

authentic [ɔːˈθentɪk] auténtico; **authenticity** autenticidad *f*

author [ˈɔːθər] escritor(a) *m(f)*; *of text* autor(a) *m(f)*

authoritarian [əθɔːrɪˈterɪən] autoritario; **authoritative** autorizado; **authority** autoridad *f*; *(permission)* autorización *f*; **authorization** autorización *f*; **authorize** autorizar

autistic [ɔːˈtɪstɪk] autista

autobiography [ɔːtəbaɪˈɑːgrəfɪ] autobiografía *f*

autocratic [ɔːtəˈkrætɪk] autocrático

autograph [ˈɔːtəgræf] autógrafo *m*

automate [ˈɔːtəmeɪt] automatizar; **automatic 1** *adj* automático **2** *n* *car* (coche *m*) automático *m*; **automatically** automáticamente; **automation** automatización

automobile [ˈɔːtəmoʊbiːl] automóvil *m*, coche *m*, *L.Am.* carro *m*, *Rpl* auto *m*; **automobile industry** industria *f* automovilística

autonomous [ɔːˈtɑːnəməs] autónomo

autopilot [ˈɔːtoʊpaɪlət] piloto *m* automático

autopsy [ˈɔːtɑːpsɪ] autopsia *f*

autumn [ˈɔːtəm] *Br* otoño *m*

auxiliary [ɔːgˈzɪljərɪ] auxiliar

available [əˈveɪləbl] disponible

avalanche [ˈævəlænʃ] avalancha *f*, alud *m*

avenue [ˈævənuː] avenida *f*, *fig* camino *m*

average [ˈævərɪdʒ] **1** *adj* medio; *(mediocre)* regular **2** *n* promedio *m*, media *f*; **on ~** como promedio, de media ◆ **average out at** salir a

averse [əˈvɜːrs]: **not be ~ to** no ser reacio a; **aversion** aversión *f*

avid [ˈævɪd] ávido

avocado [ɑːvəˈkɑːdoʊ] aguacate *m*, *S.Am.* palta *f*

avoid [əˈvɔɪd] evitar

await [əˈweɪt] aguardar, esperar

awake [əˈweɪk] despierto

award [əˈwɔːrd] **1** *n* (*prize*) premio *m* **2** *v/t* *prize, damages* conceder; **awards ceremony** ceremonia *f* de entrega de premios

aware [əˈwer]: **be ~ of sth** ser consciente de algo; **become ~ of sth** darse cuenta de algo; **awareness** conciencia f

away [əˈweɪ]: **look ~** mirar hacia otra parte; **it's 5 miles ~** está a 5 millas; **take sth ~ from s.o.** quitar algo a alguien; **be ~** estar fuera; **~ game** SP partido m fuera de casa

awesome [ˈɔːsəm] F aluci-

nante F; **awful** horrible

awkward [ˈɔːkwəd] (clumsy) torpe; (difficult) difícil; (embarrassing) embarazoso; **feel ~** sentirse incómodo

ax, Br **axe** [æks] **1** n hacha f **2** v/t project suprimir; budget, job recortar

axle [ˈæksl] eje m

B

baby [ˈbeɪbɪ] bebé m; **baby-sit** hacer de Span canguro or L.Am. babysitter

bachelor [ˈbætʃələr] soltero m

back [bæk] **1** n of person, clothes espalda f; of car, bus, house parte f trasera; of paper, book dorso m; of drawer fondo m; of chair respaldo m; SP defensa m/f; **in ~** in store en la trastienda; **in the ~ (of the car)** atrás (del coche); **~ to front** del revés **2** adj trasero **3** adv atrás; **give sth ~ to s.o.** devolver algo a alguien; **she'll be ~ tomorrow** volverá mañana **4** v/t (support) apoyar; horse apostar por

◆ **back down** echarse atrás

◆ **back out** of commitment echarse atrás

◆ **back up 1** v/t (support) respaldar; file hacer una copia de seguridad de **2** v/i in car dar marcha atrás

'**backache** dolor m de espal-

da; **backbone** columna f vertebral; **backdate: ~d to** ... con efecto retroactivo a partir del...; **backdoor** puerta f trasera; **backer: the ~s of the movie** las personas que financiaron la película; **background** fondo m; of person origen m; of situation contexto m; **backhand** in tennis revés m; **backing** (support) apoyo m; MUS acompañamiento m; **backing group** grupo m de acompañamiento; **backlash** reacción f violenta; **backlog** acumulación f; **backpack** mochila f; **backpacker** mochilero(-a) m(f); **back seat** asiento m trasero; **back streets** callejuelas fpl poorer part zonas fpl deprimidas; **backstroke** SP espalda f; **backtrack** volver atrás; **backup** (support) apoyo m for police refuerzos mpl; COMPUT copia f de segudad; **backyard** jardín *m* trasero

bacon ['beɪkn] tocino *m*, *Span* bacon *m*

bacteria [bæk'tɪrɪə] bacterias *fpl*

bad [bæd] malo; *before singular masculine noun* mal; *headache etc* fuerte; *mistake, accident* grave; **that's really too ~** (*shame*) es una verdadera pena

badge [bædʒ] insignia *f*; *of policeman* placa *f*

bad 'language palabrotas *fpl*; **badly injured** gravemente; *damaged* seriamente; *work* mal; **he ~ needs ...** necesita urgentemente ...

badminton ['bædmɪntən] bádminton *m*

bad-tempered [bæd'tempərd] malhumorado

baffle ['bæfl] confundir

bag [bæg] bolsa *f*; *for school* cartera *f*; (*purse*) bolso *m*, *S.Am.* cartera *f*

baggage ['bægɪdʒ] equipaje *m*; **baggage check** consigna *f*

baggy ['bægɪ] ancho

bail [beɪl] LAW libertad *f* bajo fianza; (*money*) fianza *f*; **on ~** bajo fianza

bait [beɪt] cebo *m*

bake [beɪk] hornear; **baked potato** *Span* patata *f* or *L.Am.* papa *f* asada (*con piel*); **baker** panadero(-a) *m(f)*; **bakery** panadería *f*

balance ['bæləns] **1** *n* equilibrio *m*; (*remainder*) resto *m*; *of bank account* saldo *m* **2** *v/t* poner en equilibrio **3** *v/i* mantener en equilibrio; *of accounts* cuadrar; **balanced** (*fair*) objetivo; *diet, personality* equilibrado; **balance sheet** balance *m*

balcony ['bælkənɪ] balcón *m*; *in theater* anfiteatro *m*

bald [bɔːld] calvo; **balding** medio calvo

ball [bɔːl] pelota *f*; *football size* balón *m*, pelota *f*; *billiard-ball size* bola *f*

ballad ['bæləd] balada *f*

ballet [bæˈleɪ] ballet *m*; **ballet dancer** bailarín(-ina) *m(f)*

'ball game (*baseball*) partido *m* de béisbol

ballistic missile [bəˈlɪstɪk] misil *m* balístico

balloon [bəˈluːn] globo *m*

ballot ['bælət] **1** *n* voto *m* **2** *v/t members* consultar por votación; **ballot box** urna *f*; **ballot paper** papeleta *f*

'ballpark (*baseball*) campo *m* de béisbol; **ballpark figure** F cifra *f* aproximada; **ballpoint** (**pen**) bolígrafo *m*, *Mex* pluma *f*, *Rpl* birome *m*

balls [bɔːlz] V huevos *mpl* V

bamboo [bæmˈbuː] bambú *m*

ban [bæn] **1** *n* prohibición *f* **2** *v/t* prohibir

banal [bəˈnæl] banal

banana [bəˈnænə] plátano *m*, *Rpl* banana *f*

band [bænd] banda f; *pop* grupo m

bandage ['bændɪdʒ] **1** n vendaje m **2** v/t vendar

'Band-Aid® *Span* tirita f, *L.Am.* curita f

bandit ['bændɪt] bandido m

bandy ['bændɪ] *legs* arqueado

bang [bæŋ] **1** n *noise* estruendo m; (*blow*) golpe m **2** v/t *door* cerrar de un portazo; (*hit*) golpear

bangle ['bæŋgl] brazalete m

bangs [bæŋz] flequillo m

banisters ['bænɪstərz] barandilla f

banjo ['bændʒoʊ] banjo m

bank¹ [bæŋk] *of river* orilla f

bank² [bæŋk] FIN banco m

♦ bank on contar con

'bank account cuenta f (bancaria); banker banquero m; banker's card tarjeta f bancaria; banking banca f; bank loan préstamo m bancario; bank manager director(a) m(f) de banco; bank rate tipo m de interés bancario; bankroll financiar; bankrupt en bancarrota o quiebra; *go* → quebrar; bankruptcy quiebra f, bancarrota f

banner ['bænər] pancarta f

banquet ['bæŋkwɪt] banquete m

baptism ['bæptɪzm] bautismo m; baptize bautizar

bar¹ [bɑːr] n *of iron* barra f; *of chocolate* tableta f; *for drinks* bar m; (*counter*) barra f

bar² [bɑːr] v/t *from premises* prohibir la entrada a

barbaric [bɑːr'bærɪk] brutal

barbecue ['bɑːrbɪkjuː] **1** n barbacoa f **2** v/t cocinar en la barbacoa

barbed wire [bɑːrbd] alambre f de espino

barber ['bɑːrbər] barbero m

'bar code código m de barras

bare [ber] *skin* desnudo; *room* vacío; *floor* descubierto; barefoot descalzo; bare-headed sin sombrero; barely apenas

bargain ['bɑːrgɪn] **1** n (*deal*) trato m; (*good buy*) ganga f **2** v/i regatear

barge [bɑːrdʒ] NAUT barcaza f

♦ barge into *person* tropezarse con; *room* irrumpir en

baritone ['bærɪtoʊn] barítono m

bark¹ [bɑːrk] **1** n *of dog* ladrido m **2** v/i ladrar

bark² [bɑːrk] n *of tree* corteza f

barn [bɑːrn] granero m

barometer [bə'rɑːmɪtər] *also fig* barómetro m

barracks ['bærəks] MIL cuartel m

barrel ['bærəl] tonel m, barril m

barren ['bærən] *land* yermo

barrette [bə'ret] pasador m

barricade [bærɪ'keɪd] barricada f

barrier ['bærɪər] barrera f

'bar tender camarero(-a) m(f), *L.Am.* mesero(-a) m(f), *Rpl* mozo(-a) m(f)

barter ['bɑːrtər] **1** n trueque m **2** v/t trocar (**for** por)

base [beɪs] **1** n base f **2** v/t basar (**on** en); baseball béisbol m; ball pelota f de béisbol; **baseball** ['beɪsbɔːl] n baseball gorra f de béisbol; **baseboard** rodapié m; **basement** of house sótano m

basic ['beɪsɪk] (rudimentary) básico; room sencillo; skills elemental; (fundamental) fundamental; **basically** básicamente

basin ['beɪsn] for washing barreño m; in bathroom lavabo m

basis ['beɪsɪs] base f

bask [bæsk] tomar el sol

basket ['bæskɪt] cesta f; in basketball canasta f; **basketball** ['bæskɪtbɔːl] n; ball balón m or pelota f de baloncesto game baloncesto m, L.Am. básquetbol m; ball balón m or pelota f de baloncesto

Basque [bæsk] **1** adj vasco **2** n person vasco(-a) m(f); language vasco m

bass [beɪs] bajo m; instrument contrabajo m

bastard ['bæstərd] P cabrón (-ona) m(f) P

bat¹ [bæt] **1** n baseball bate m; table tennis pala f **2** v/i in baseball batear

bat² [bæt] (animal) murciélago m

batch [bætʃ] of students tanda f; of bread hornada f; of products lote m

bath [bæθ] baño m

bathe [beɪð] bañarse

'**bathrobe** albornoz m; **bathroom** cuarto m de baño; (toilet) servicio m, L.Am. baño m; **bath towel** toalla f de baño; **bathtub** bañera f

batter ['bætər] asa f; in baseball bateador(a) m(f); **battered** maltratado

battery ['bætərɪ] pila f; in computer, car batería f

battle ['bætl] **1** n batalla f **2** v/i against illness etc luchar; **battleship** acorazado m

bawl [bɔːl] (shout) gritar, vociferar; (weep) berrear

bay [beɪ] (inlet) bahía f

BC [biː'siː] (= **before Christ**) A.C. (= antes de Cristo)

be [biː] ◊ permanent characteristics, profession, nationality ser; position, temporary condition estar; **there is, there are** hay; ◊ **has the mailman been?** ¿ha venido el cartero?; **I've never been to Japan** no he estado en Japón; ◊ tags: **that's right, isn't it?** eso es, ¿no?; **she's Chinese, isn't she?** es china, ¿verdad? ◊ passive: **he was arrested** fue detenido, lo detuvieron

beach [biːtʃ] playa f; **beachwear** ropa f playera

beads [biːdz] cuentas fpl

beak [biːk] pico m

beam [biːm] **1** n in ceiling etc viga f **2** v/i (smile) sonreír de oreja a oreja

bean [biːn] judía f, alubia f,

L.Am. frijol *m*, *S.Am.* poroto *m*

bear¹ [ber] *n animal* oso(-a) *m(f)*

bear² [ber] *v/t weight* resistir; *costs* correr con; *(tolerate)* soportar; **bearable** soportable

beard [bɪrd] barba *f*

beat [biːt] **1** *n of heart* latido *m*; *of music* ritmo *m* **2** *v/i of heart* latir; *of rain* golpear **3** *v/t in competition* derrotar, ganar *a*; *(hit)* pegar *a*; *(pound)* golpear

♦ **beat up** dar una paliza a

beaten ['biːtən]: **off the ~ track** retirado; **beating** *physical* paliza *f*; **beat-up** F destartalado F

beautiful ['bjuːtɪfl] bonito, precioso, F guapo; *name, taste, meal* delicioso, *L.Am.* rico; *vacation* estupendo; **beautifully** *cooked, done* perfectamente; **beauty** belleza *f*

beaver ['biːvər] castor *m*

because [bɪ'kɑːz] porque; **~ of** debido a, a causa de

become [bɪ'kʌm] hacerse, volverse; *it became clear that ...* quedó claro que...; *what's ~ of her?* ¿qué fue de ella?; **becoming** favorecedor

bed [bed] cama *f*; *of flowers* macizo *m*; *of sea* fondo *m*; *of river* cauce *m*; **go to ~** ir a la cama; **bedding** ropa *f* de cama; **bedridden**: *be ~* estar postrado en cama; **bedroom**

dormitorio *m*, *L.Am.* cuarto *m*; **bedtime** hora *f* de irse a la cama

bee [biː] abeja *f*

beech [biːtʃ] haya *f*

beef [biːf] carne *f* de vaca; **beefburger** hamburguesa *f*

beep [biːp] **1** *n* pitido *m* **2** *v/i* pitar

beer [bɪr] cerveza *f*

beet [biːt] remolacha *f*

beetle ['biːtl] escarabajo *m*

before [bɪ'fɔːr] **1** *prep* antes de **2** *adv* antes; *I've seen this movie ~* ya he visto esta película; **the week ~** la semana anterior **3** *conj* antes de que; **beforehand** de antemano

befriend [bɪ'frend] hacerse amigo de

beg [beg] **1** *v/i* mendigar, pedir **2** *v/t*: **~ s.o. to do sth** suplicar a alguien que haga algo; **beggar** mendigo(-a) *m(f)*

begin [bɪ'gɪn] empezar, comenzar (**to do** a hacer); **beginner** principiante *m/f*; **beginning** principio *m*, comienzo *m*; *(origin)* origen *m*

behalf [bɪ'hɑːf]: **on ~ of** en nombre de

behave [bɪ'heɪv] comportarse, portarse; **~ (yourself)!** ¡pórtate bien!; **behavior**, *Br* **behaviour** comportamiento *m*, conducta *f*

behind [bɪ'haɪnd] **1** *prep* detrás de; *be ~ ...* *(responsible)* estar detrás de...; *(support)* respaldar... **2** *adv* (*at* *the back*) detrás; **leave sth ~** dejarse algo

beige [beiʒ] beige, *Span* beis

being ['bi:ɪŋ] ser *m*

belated [bɪ'leitɪd] tardío

belch [beltʃ] **1** *n* eructo *m* **2** *v/i* eructar

Belgian ['beldʒən] **1** *adj* belga **2** *n* belga *m/f*; **Belgium** Bélgica

belief [bɪ'li:f] creencia *f*; **believe** creer

◆ **believe in** creer en

believer [bɪ'li:vər] REL creyente *m/f*; *fig* partidario(-a) *m(f)* (*in* de)

Belize [be'li:z] Belice

bell [bel] timbre *m*; *of church* campana *f*; **bellhop** botones *m inv*

belligerent [bɪ'lɪdʒərənt] beligerante

bellow ['belou] bramar

belly ['beli] estómago *m*; *fat* barriga *f*; *of animal* panza *f*

◆ **belong to** pertenecer a

belongings [bɪ'lɔːɪŋz] pertenencias *fpl*

beloved [bɪ'lʌvɪd] querido

below [bɪ'lou] **1** *prep* debajo de; *in amount, level* por debajo de **2** *adv* abajo; *in text* más abajo; **10 degrees ~** 10 grados bajo cero

belt [belt] cinturón *m*

benchmark ['bentʃmɑːrk] punto *m* de referencia

bend [bend] **1** *n* curva *f* **2** *v/t* doblar **3** *v/i* torcer, girar; *of person* agacharse

◆ **bend down** agacharse

beneath [bɪ'ni:θ] **1** *prep* debajo de **2** *adv* abajo

benefactor ['benɪfæktər] benefactor(a) *m(f)*

beneficial [benɪ'fɪʃl] beneficioso

benefit ['benɪfɪt] **1** *n* beneficio *m* **2** *v/t* beneficiar **3** *v/i* beneficiarse

benevolent [bɪ'nevələnt] benevolente

benign [bɪ'naɪn] agradable; MED benigno

bequeath [bɪ'kwi:ð] *also fig* legar; **bequest** legado *m*

beret [bə'rei] boina *f*

berry ['beri] baya *f*

berth [bɜːrθ] *on ship* litera *f*; *on train* camarote *m*; *for ship* amarradero *m*

beside [bɪ'saɪd] al lado de; **be ~ o.s.** estar fuera de sí; **that's ~ the point** eso no tiene nada que ver

besides [bɪ'saɪdz] **1** *adv* además **2** *prep* (*apart from*) además de

best [best] **1** *adj & adv* mejor; **which did you like ~?** ¿cuál te gustó más? **2** *n*: **do one's ~** hacer todo lo posible; **the ~** el / la mejor; **all the ~!** ¡que te vaya bien!; best before date fecha *f* de caducidad; **best man** *at wedding* padrino *m*

bet [bet] **1** *n* apuesta *f* **2** *v/t & v/i* apostar; **you ~!** ¡ya lo creo!

betray [bɪ'treɪ] traicionar; *husband, wife* engañar; be-

trayal traición f; *of husband, wife* engaño m

better ['betər] **1** *adj & adv* mejor; **get ~** mejorar; **I'd really ~ not** mejor no; **I like her ~** me gusta más ella; **better-off** (*wealthier*) más rico

between [bɪ'twiːn] entre

beware [bɪ'wer]: **~ of** tener cuidado con

bewilder [bɪ'wɪldər] desconcertar; **bewilderment** desconcierto m

beyond [bɪ'jɑːnd] más allá de

bias ['baɪəs] *against* prejuicio m; *in favor* favoritismo m; **bias(s)ed** parcial

Bible ['baɪbl] Biblia f; **biblical** bíblico

bicentennial [baɪsen'teniəl] bicentenario m

bicker ['bɪkər] reñir, discutir

bicycle ['baɪsɪkl] bicicleta f

bid [bɪd] **1** *n at auction* puja f; (*attempt*) intento m **2** *v/i at auction* pujar; **bidder** postor(a) m(f)

biennial [baɪ'eniəl] bienal

big [bɪg] **1** *adj* grande; *before singular nouns* gran; **my ~ brother / sister** mi hermano / hermana mayor **2** *adv*: **talk ~** alardear

bigamist ['bɪgəmɪst] bígamo(-a) m(f)

'bighead creído(-a) m(f) F

bigot ['bɪgət] fanático(-a) m(f), intolerante m/f

bike [baɪk] F bici f; *motorbike* moto f F; **biker** motero(-a) m(f)

bikini [bɪ'kiːni] biquini m

bilingual [baɪ'lɪŋgwəl] bilingüe

bill [bɪl] *for gas, electricity* factura f; (*money*) billete m; POL proyecto m de ley; (*poster*) cartel m; *Br in restaurant etc* cuenta f; **billboard** valla f publicitaria; **billfold** cartera f, billetera f

billion ['bɪljən] mil millones mpl, millardo m

bin [bɪn] cubo m

bind [baɪnd] (*connect*) unir; (*tie*) atar; LAW obligar; **binding** *agreement* vinculante

binoculars [bɪ'nɑːkjʊlərz] prismáticos mpl

biodegradable [baɪoʊdɪ'greɪdəbl] biodegradable

biographer [baɪ'ɑːgrəfər] biógrafo(-a) m(f); **biography** biografía f

biological [baɪoʊ'lɑːdʒɪkl] biológico; **biology** biología f

bird [bɜːrd] ave f, pájaro m

biro® ['baɪroʊ] *Br* bolígrafo m, *Mex* pluma f, *Rpl* birome m

birth [bɜːrθ] nacimiento m; (*labor*) parto m; **give ~ to child** dar a luz; *of animal* parir; **date of ~** fecha f de nacimiento; **birth certificate** partida f de nacimiento; **birth control** control m de natalidad; **birthday** cumpleaños m inv; **happy ~!** ¡feliz cumpleaños!

biscuit ['bɪskɪt] bollo m, panecillo m; *Br* galleta f

bisexual ['baɪsekʃuəl] **1** f

bisexual **2** n bisexual m/f

bishop ['bɪʃəp] obispo m

bit [bɪt] (piece) trozo m; (part)
parte f; of puzzle pieza f;
COMPUT bit m; **a ~ of** (a little)
un poco de

bitch [bɪtʃ] **1** n of dog perra f; F
woman zorra f F **2** v/i F (complain) quejarse

bite [baɪt] **1** n of dog mordisco
m; of mosquito, snake picadura f; of food bocado m **2**
v/t & v/i of dog morder; of
mosquito, flea, snake picar

bitter ['bɪtər] amargo; person
resentido

black [blæk] **1** adj negro; coffee solo; tea sin leche **2** n (color) negro m; (person) negro(-a) m(f) neg
◆ **black out** (faint) perder el
conocimiento

'blackboard pizarra f, encerado m; **black coffee** café
m solo; **black economy** economía f sumergida; **black
eye** ojo m morado; **blacklist**
lista f negra; **blackmail 1** n
chantaje m **2** v/t chantajear;
black market mercado m
negro; **blackness** oscuridad
f; **blackout** ELEC apagón m;
MED desmayo m

bladder ['blædər] vejiga f

blade [bleɪd] hoja f; of propeller pala f; of grass brizna f

blame [bleɪm] **1** n culpa f **2** v/t
culpar

bland [blænd] smile insulso;
food insípido

blank [blæŋk] **1** adj (not writ-
ten on) en blanco; tape virgen; look inexpresivo **2** n
(empty space) espacio m en
blanco; **blank check**, Br
blank cheque cheque m en
blanco

blanket ['blæŋkɪt] manta f,
L.Am. frazada f

blast [blæst] **1** n (explosion)
explosión f; (gust) ráfaga f
2 v/t tunnel abrir (con explosivos); rock volar; **~!** F ¡mecachis! F; **blast-off** despegue m

blatant ['bleɪtənt] descarado

blaze [bleɪz] **1** n (fire) incendio m **2** v/i of fire arder

blazer ['bleɪzər] americana f

bleach [bliːtʃ] **1** n for clothes
lejía f; for hair decolorante
m **2** v/t hair aclarar, desteñir

bleak [bliːk] countryside inhóspito; weather desapacible; future desolador

bleary-eyed ['blɪraɪd] con
ojos de sueño

bleat [bliːt] of sheep balar

bleed [bliːd] sangrar; **bleeding** hemorragia f

bleep [bliːp] **1** n pitido m **2** v/i
pitar

blemish ['blemɪʃ] imperfección f

blend [blend] **1** n of coffee etc
mezcla f; fig combinación f **2**
v/t mezclar; **blender**
machine licuadora f

bless [bles] bendecir; **~ you!**
in response to sneeze ¡Jesús!;
blessing bendición f

blind [blaɪnd] **1** adj ciego; cor-

ner sin visibilidad **2** *v/t of sun* cegar; **blind alley** callejón *m* sin salida; **blind date** cita *f* a ciegas; **blindfold 1** *n* venda *f* **2** *v/t* vendar los ojos a; *blind light* cegador; *headache* terrible; **blindly** a ciegas; *fig* ciegamente; **blind spot** *in road* punto *m* sin visibilidad; *in driving mirror* ángulo *m* muerto

blink [blɪŋk] parpadear

blizzard ['blɪzərd] ventisca *f*

bloc [blɑːk] POL bloque *m*

block [blɑːk] **1** *n* bloque *m*; *buildings* manzana *f*, L.Am. cuadra *f*; *(blockage)* bloqueo *m* **2** *v/t* bloquear; *sink* atascar; **blockage** obstrucción *f*; **blockbuster** gran éxito *m*; **block letters** letras *fpl* mayúsculas

blond [blɑːnd] rubio; **blonde** *woman* rubia *f*

blood [blʌd] sangre *f*; **blood donor** donante *m/f* de sangre; **blood group** grupo *m* sanguíneo; **blood poisoning** septicemia *f*; **blood pressure** tensión *f* (arterial); **blood sample** muestra *f* de sangre; **bloodshed** derramamiento *m* de sangre; **bloodshot** enrojecido; **bloodstained** ensangrentado; **blood test** análisis *m* inv de sangre; **bloodthirsty** sanguinario; *movie* macabro

bloom [bluːm] *also fig* florecer

blossom ['blɑːsəm] **1** *n* flores

fpl **2** *v/i also fig* florecer

blot [blɑːt] mancha *f*

◆ **blot out** borrar; *sun, view* ocultar

blouse [blauz] blusa *f*

blow¹ [bloʊ] *n* golpe *m*

blow² [bloʊ] **1** *v/t smoke* exhalar; *whistle* tocar **2** *v/i of wind, person* soplar; *of whistle* sonar; *of fuse* fundirse; *of tire* reventarse

◆ **blow out 1** *v/t candle* apagar **2** *v/i of candle* apagarse

◆ **blow over 1** *v/t* derribar **2** *v/i* derrumbarse; *of storm* amainar; *of argument* calmarse

◆ **blow up 1** *v/t with explosives* volar; *balloon* hinchar; *photograph* ampliar **2** *v/i* explotar

'blow-dry secar *(con secador)*; **blowout** *of tire* reventón *m*

blue [bluː] azul; F *movie* porno *inv* F; **blueberry** arándano *m*; **blue chip** puntero, de primera fila; **blues** MUS blues *m inv*; **have the ~** estar deprimido

bluff [blʌf] **1** *n (deception)* farol *m* **2** *v/i ir* de farol

blunder ['blʌndər] error *m* de bulto

blunt [blʌnt] *pencil* sin punta; *knife* desafilado; *person* franco; **bluntly** francamente

blur [blɜːr] **1** *n* imagen *f* desenfocada **2** *v/t* desdibujar

◆ **blurt out** [blɜːrt] soltar

blush [blʌʃ] **1** *n* rubor *m* **2** *v/i* ruborizarse; **blusher** cos-

metic colorete *m*

blustery ['blʌstərɪ] tempestuoso

BO [biː'oʊ] (= *body odor*) olor *m* corporal

board [bɔːrd] **1** *n* tablón *m*, tabla *f*; *for game* tablero *m*; *for notices* tablón *m*; **~ (of directors)** consejo *m* de administración; **on ~** a bordo **2** *v/t airplane* etc embarcar; *train* subir a **3** *v/i of passengers* embarcar

◆ **board up** cubrir con tablas

boarder ['bɔːrdər] *in house* huésped *m/f*; **board game** juego *m* de mesa; **boarding card** tarjeta *f* de embarque; **boarding school** internado *m*; **board meeting** reunión *f* del consejo de administración; **board room** sala *f* de reuniones *or* juntas

boast [boʊst] **1** *n* presunción *f* **2** *v/i* presumir (**about** de)

boat [boʊt] barco *m*; *small, for leisure* barca *f*

bodily ['bɑːdɪlɪ] **1** *adj* corporal; *needs* físico; *function* fisiológico **2** *adv* en volandas; *body* cuerpo *m*; *dead* cadáver *m*; **bodyguard** guardaespaldas *m*; **bodywork** MOT carrocería *f*

bogus ['boʊɡəs] falso

boil[1] [bɔɪl] *n* (*swelling*) forúnculo

boil[2] [bɔɪl] **1** *v/t* hervir; *egg, vegetables* cocer **2** *v/i* hervir

◆ **boil down to** reducirse a

boiler ['bɔɪlər] caldera *f*

boisterous ['bɔɪstərəs] escandaloso

bold [boʊld] **1** *adj* valiente, audaz; *text* en negrita **2** *n print* negrita *f*

Bolivia [bə'lɪvɪə] Bolivia; **Bolivian 1** *adj* boliviano **2** *n* boliviano(-a) *m(f)*

bolster ['boʊlstər] *confidence* reforzar

bolt [boʊlt] **1** *n don door* cerrojo *m*; *with nut* perno *m* **2** *adv*: **~ upright** erguido **3** *v/t* (*fix with bolts*) atornillar; *close* cerrar con cerrojo **4** *v/i* (*run off*) fugarse

bomb [bɑːm] **1** *n* bomba *f* **2** *v/t* MIL bombardear; *of terrorist* poner una bomba en; **bombard** *also fig* bombardear; **bomb attack** atentado *m* con bomba; **bomber** bombardero *m*; *terrorist* terrorista *m/f* (*que pone bombas*); **bomb scare** amenaza *f* de bomba; **bombshell** *fig*: *news* bomba *f*

bond [bɑːnd] **1** *n* (*tie*) unión *f*; FIN bono *m* **2** *v/i of glue* adherirse

bone [boʊn] hueso *m*; *of fish* espina *f*

bonnet ['bɑːnɪt] *Br of car* capó *m*

bonus ['boʊnəs] *money* plus *m*, bonificación *f*; (*extra*) ventaja *f* adicional

boob [buːb] **1** *n* (*breast*) teta *f* P

booboo ['buːbuː] F metedura *f* de pata

book [bʊk] **1** *n* libro *m* **2** *v/t* reservar; *of policeman* multar; **bookcase** estantería f, librería f; **booked up** lleno, completo; *person* ocupado; **bookie** F corredor(a) m(f) de apuestas; **booking** reserva f; **bookkeeper** tenedor(a) m(f) de libros; **bookkeeping** contabilidad f; **booklet** folleto m; **bookmaker** corredor(a) m(f) de apuestas; **books** *(accounts)* contabilidad f; **bookseller** librero(-a) m(f); **bookstore** librería f

boom¹ [buːm] **1** n boom m **2** v/i *of business* experimentar un boom

boom² [buːm] n *noise* estruendo m

boost [buːst] **1** n impulso m **2** v/t estimular; *morale* levantar

boot [buːt] bota f; Br *of car* maletero m, C.Am., Mex cajuela f, Rpl baúl m

◆ **boot up** COMPUT arrancar

booth [buːð] *at market* cabina f; *at exhibition* puesto m, stand m

border ['bɔːrdər] **1** n frontera f; *(edge)* borde m **2** v/t *country* limitar con

◆ **border on** limitar con; *(be almost)* rayar en

bore¹ [bɔːr] v/t *hole* taladrar

bore² [bɔːr] **1** n *person* pesado(-a) m(f) **2** v/t aburrir

bored [bɔːrd] aburrido; **boredom** aburrimiento m; **boring** aburrido

born [bɔːrn]: **be ~** nacer

borrow ['bɑːrou] tomar prestado

bosom ['buzm] pecho m

boss [bɑːs] jefe(-a) m(f)

◆ **boss around** dar órdenes a

bossy ['bɑːsɪ] mandón

botanical [bə'tænɪkl] botánico

botch [bɑːtʃ] arruinar

both [bouθ] **1** *adj & pron* ambos, los dos; **~ of them** ambos, los dos **2** *adv*: **~ my mother and I** tanto mi madre como yo

bother ['bɑːðər] **1** n molestias fpl **2** v/t *(disturb)* molestar; *(worry)* preocupar

bottle ['bɑːtl] botella f; *for baby* biberón m

◆ **bottle up** *feelings* reprimir

'bottle bank contenedor m de vidrio; **bottled water** agua f embotellada; **bottleneck** embotellamiento m; *in production* cuello m de botella; **bottle-opener** abrebotellas m inv

bottom ['bɑːtəm] **1** *adj* inferior; *of drawer* de abajo **2** n *of case, garden* fondo m; *of hill, page* pie m; *of pile* parte f inferior; *(underside)* parte f de abajo; *of street* final m; *(buttocks)* trasero m

◆ **bottom out** tocar fondo

bottom 'line *financial* saldo m final; *(real issue)* realidad f

boulder ['bouldər] roca f redondeada

bounce [bauns] **1** v/t *ball* botar **2** v/i of ball (re)botar; of rain rebotar; of check ser rechazado; **bouncer** portero m, gorila m

bound¹ [baʊnd] adj: **he's ~ to ...** (sure to) seguro que ...

bound² [baʊnd] v/i: **be ~ for** of ship llevar destino a

bound³ [baʊnd] n (jump) salto m

boundary ['baʊndərɪ] límite m; of countries frontera f

bouquet [buːˈkeɪ] ramo m

bourbon ['bɜːrbən] bourbon m

bout [baʊt] MED ataque m; in boxing combate m

bow¹ [baʊ] **1** n as greeting reverencia f **2** v/i saludar con la cabeza **3** v/t head inclinar

bow² [bəʊ] n (knot) lazo m; MUS, for archery arco m

bow³ [baʊ] n of ship proa f

bowels ['baʊəlz] entrañas fpl

bowl¹ [bəʊl] n for rice etc cuenco m; for soup plato m sopero; for salad ensaladera f; for washing barreño m

bowl² [bəʊl] **1** n (ball) bola f **2** v/i in bowling lanzar la bola

bowling ['bəʊlɪŋ] bolos mpl; **bowling alley** bolera f

bow tie [bəʊ] pajarita f

box¹ [bɑːks] n caja f, on form casilla f

box² [bɑːks] v/i boxear

boxer ['bɑːksər] boxeador(a) m(f); **boxing** boxeo m; **boxing glove** guante m de boxeo; **boxing match** combate m de boxeo

'**box number** at post office apartado m de correos; **box office** taquilla f, L.Am. boletería f

boy [bɔɪ] niño m, chico m

boycott ['bɔɪkɑːt] **1** n boicot m **2** v/t boicotear

'**boyfriend** novio m

bra [brɑː] sujetador m

bracelet ['breɪslɪt] pulsera f

bracket ['brækɪt] for shelf escuadra f

brag [bræg] fanfarronear

braid [breɪd] in hair trenza f; trimming trenzado m

braille [breɪl] braille m

brain [breɪn] cerebro m; **brainless** F estúpido; **brains** (intelligence) inteligencia f; **brain surgeon** neurocirujano(-a) m(f); **brain tumor**, Br **brain tumour** tumor m cerebral; **brainwash** lavar el cerebro a

brake [breɪk] **1** n freno m **2** v/i frenar

branch [bræntʃ] of tree rama f; of company sucursal f

brand [brænd] **1** n marca f **2** v/t: **be ~ed a liar** ser tildado de mentiroso; **brand image** imagen f de marca

brandish ['brændɪʃ] blandir

brand '**leader** marca f líder del mercado; **brand name** nombre m comercial; **brand-new** nuevo, flamante

brandy ['brændɪ] brandy m

brassière [brəˈzɪr] sujetador m, sostén m

brat [bræt] *pej* niñato(-a) *m(f)*

brave [breɪv] valiente, valeroso; **bravery** valentía *f*, valor *m*

brawl [brɔ:l] **1** *n* pelea *f* **2** *v/i* pelearse

Brazil [brə'zɪl] Brasil; **Brazilian 1** *adj* brasileño **2** *n* brasileño(-a) *m(f)*

breach [bri:tʃ] (*violation*) infracción *f m*; *in party* ruptura *f*; **breach of contract** incumplimiento *m* de contrato

bread [bred] pan *m*

breadth [bredθ] ancho *m*; *of knowledge* amplitud *f*

'breadwinner: **be the ~** ser el que gana el pan

break [breɪk] **1** *n* fractura *f*, rotura *f*; (*rest*) descanso *m* **2** *v/t also promise* romper; *rules, law* violar; *news* dar; *record* batir **3** *v/i* romperse; *of news* saltar; *of storm* estallar

◆ **break down 1** *v/i of vehicle* averiarse, estropearse; *of machine* estropearse; *of talks* romperse; *in tears* romper a llorar; *mentally* venirse abajo **2** *v/t door* derribar; *figures* desglosar

◆ **break even** cubrir gastos

◆ **break in** (*interrupt*) interrumpir; *of burglar* entrar

◆ **break up 1** *v/t into parts* descomponer; *fight* poner fin a **2** *v/i of ice* romperse; *of couple, band* separarse; *of meeting* terminar

breakable ['breɪkəbl] rompible, frágil; **breakage** rotura

f; **breakdown** *of vehicle, machine* avería *f*; *of talks* ruptura *f*; (*nervous*) crisis *f inv* nerviosa; *of figures* desglose *m*

breakfast ['brekfəst] desayuno *m*; **have ~** desayunar

'break-in entrada *f* (*mediante la fuerza*); *robbery* robo *m*; **breaking news** TV noticias *fpl* de última hora; **some breaking news** una noticia de última hora; **breakthrough** *in negotiations* paso *m* adelante; *of technology* avance *m*; **breakup** *of partnership* ruptura *f*, separación *f*

breast [brest] pecho *m*; **breastfeed** amamantar; **breaststroke** braza *f*

breath [breθ] respiración *f*; **be out of ~** estar sin respiración

breathe [bri:ð] respirar

◆ **breathe in** aspirar, inspirar

◆ **breathe out** espirar

breathing ['bri:ðɪŋ] respiración *f*

breathtaking ['breθteɪkɪŋ] impresionante

breed [bri:d] **1** *n* raza *f* **2** *v/t* criar; *plants* cultivar; *fig* causar **3** *v/i of animals* reproducirse; **breeding** *of animals* cría *f*; *of person* educación *f*

breeze [bri:z] brisa *f*; **breezy** ventoso

brew [bru:] **1** *v/t beer* elaborar **2** *v/i of storm* avecinarse; *of trouble* fraguarse; **brewery** fábrica *f* de cerveza

bribe [braɪb] **1** *n* soborno *m*,

Mex mordida *f*, *S.Am.* coima
f **2** *v/t* sobornar; bribery soborno *m*, *Mex* mordida *f*, *S.Am.* coima *f*

brick [brɪk] ladrillo *m*

bride [braɪd] novia *f* (*en boda*); **bridegroom** novio *m* (*en boda*); **bridesmaid** dama *f* de honor

bridge [brɪdʒ] **1** *n also* NAUT puente *m* **2** *v/t gap* superar

bridle [braɪdl] brida *f*

brief[1] [briːf] *adj* breve, corto

brief[2] [briːf] **1** *n* (*mission*) misión *f* **2** *v/t:* ~ *s.o.* **on sth** informar a alguien de algo

'**briefcase** maletín *m*; **briefing** reunión *f* informativa; **briefly** brevemente, (*in few words*) en pocas palabras, (*to sum up*) en resumen; **briefs** *for women* bragas *fpl*; *for men* calzoncillos *mpl*

bright [braɪt] *color* vivo; *smile* radiante, (*sunny*) luminoso; (*intelligent*) inteligente; **brightly** *shine* intensamente, *smile* alegremente

brilliance [ˈbrɪljəns] *of person* genialidad *f*; *of color* resplandor *m*; **brilliant** *sunshine etc* resplandeciente, (*very good*) genial, (*very intelligent*) brillante

brim [brɪm] *of container* borde *m*; *of hat* ala *f*

bring [brɪŋ] traer

◆ **bring back** (*return*) devolver; (*re-introduce*) reinstaurar; *memories* traer

◆ **bring down** *government* derrocar; *airplane* derribar; *price* reducir

◆ **bring on** *illness* provocar

◆ **bring out** *product* sacar

◆ **bring up** *child* criar; *subject* mencionar; (*vomit*) vomitar

brink [brɪŋk] borde *m*

brisk [brɪsk] *person* enérgico; *walk* rápido; *trade* animado

bristles [ˈbrɪslz] *on chin* pelos *mpl*; *of brush* cerdas *fpl*

Britain [ˈbrɪtn] Gran Bretaña *f*; **British 1** *adj* británico **2** *npl:* **the** ~ los británicos

brittle [ˈbrɪtl] frágil

broach [broʊtʃ] broche *m*

broad [brɔːd] **1** *adj* ancho; *smile* amplio; (*general*) general **2** *n* F (*woman*) tía *f* ; **in ~ daylight** a plena luz del día; **broadcast 1** *n* emisión *f* **2** *v/t* emitir; **broadcaster** presentador(a) *m(f)*; **broadjump** salto *m* de longitud; **broad in general**; **broadminded** tolerante, abierto

broccoli [ˈbrɑːkəlɪ] brécol *m*, brócoli *m*

brochure [ˈbroʊʃər] folleto *m*

broil [brɔɪl] asar a la parrilla; **broiler** *on stove* parrilla *f*; *chicken* pollo *m* (*para asar*)

broke [broʊk] F: **be** ~ estar sin blanca F; *long-term* estar arruinado; **broken** *adj* roto; *home* deshecho; **broker** corredor(a) *m(f)*

bronchitis [brɑːŋˈkaɪtɪs] bronquitis *f*

bronze [brɑːnz] bronce *m*

brooch [broʊtʃ] *Br* broche *m*

brothel ['brɒ:θl] burdel *m*

brother ['brʌðər] hermano *m*; **brother-in-law** cuñado *m*; **brotherly** fraternal

brow [brau] (*forehead*) frente *f*; *of hill* cima *f*

brown [braun] **1** *n* marrón *m*, *L.Am.* color *m* café **2** *adj* marrón; *eyes, hair* castaño; (*tanned*) moreno; **brownie** (*cake*) pastel *m* de chocolate y nueces; **brown paper bag** bolsa *f* de cartón

browse [brauz] *in store* echar una ojeada; COMPUT navegar; **browser** COMPUT navegador *m*

bruise [bru:z] magulladura *f*, cardenal *f*; *on fruit* maca *f*

brunette [bru:'net] morena *f*

brush [brʌʃ] **1** *n* cepillo *m*; *conflict* roce **2** *v/t* cepillar; (*touch lightly*) rozar

◆ **brush aside** hacer caso omiso a

◆ **brush up** repasar

brusque [brusk] brusco

brutal ['bru:tl] brutal; **brutality** brutalidad *f*; **brutally** brutalmente; **brute** bestia *m/f*

bubble ['bʌbl] burbuja *f*

buck[1] [bʌk] *n* F (*dollar*) dólar *m*

buck[2] [bʌk] *v/i of horse* corcovear

bucket ['bʌkɪt] cubo *m*

buckle[1] ['bʌkl] **1** *n* hebilla *f* **2** *v/t belt* abrochar

buckle[2] ['bʌkl] *v/i of metal* combarse

buddy ['bʌdɪ] F amigo(-a) *m(f)*

budge [bʌdʒ] **1** *v/t* mover **2** *v/i* moverse

budget ['bʌdʒɪt] presupuesto *m*

buff [bʌf] aficionado(-a) *m(f)*

buffalo ['bʌfələu] búfalo *m*

buffet ['bufeɪ] *meal* bufé *m*

bug [bʌg] **1** *n insect* bicho *m*; *virus* virus *m inv*; (*for spying*) micrófono *m* oculto; COMPUT error *m* **2** *v/t room* colocar un micrófono en; F (*annoy*) fastidiar F

buggy ['bʌgɪ] *for baby* silla *f* de paseo

build [bɪld] **1** *n of person* constitución *f* **2** *v/t* construir

◆ **build up 1** *v/t strength* aumentar; *relationship* fortalecer **2** *v/i of dirt* acumularse; *of pressure etc* aumentar

builder ['bɪldər] albañil *m/f*; *company* constructora *f*; **building** edificio *m*; *activity* construcción *f*; **building site** obra *f*; **building society** *Br* caja *f* de ahorros; **building trade** industria *f* de la construcción; **build-up** acumulación *f*; **after all the ~** *publicity* después de tantas expectativas; **built-in** *cupboard* empotrado; *flash* incorporado

bulge [bʌldʒ] **1** *n* bulto *m* **2** *v/i of wall* abombarse

bulky ['bʌlkɪ] voluminoso

bull [bul] *animal* toro *m*; **bulldozer** bulldozer *m*

bullet ['bʊlɪt] bala f

bulletin ['bʊlɪtɪn] boletín m; **bulletin board** tablón m de anuncios

'**bullet-proof** antibalas inv

'**bull fight** corrida f de toros; **bull fighter** torero(-a) m(f); **bull fighting** tauromaquia f, los toros; **bull ring** plaza f de toros; **bull's-eye** diana f, blanco m; **bullshit** n V Span gilipollez f V, L.Am. pendejada f V

bully ['bʊlɪ] **1** n matón(-ona) m(f); child abusón(-ona) m(f) **2** v/t intimidar; **bullying** intimidación f

bum [bʌm] **F 1** n (tramp) vagabundo(-a) m(f); (worthless person) inútil m/f **2** v/t cigarette etc gorronear

bump [bʌmp] **1** n (swelling) chichón m; on road bache m **2** v/t golpear; **bumper** MOT parachoques m inv; **bumpy** con baches; flight movido

bunch [bʌntʃ] of people grupo m; of keys manojo m; of flowers ramo m; of grapes racimo m; **thanks a ~** iron no sabes lo que te lo agradezco

bungle ['bʌŋgl] echar a perder

bunk [bʌŋk] litera f

buoy [bɔɪ] NAUT boya f; **buoyant** optimista; economy boyante

burden ['bɜːrdn] **1** n also fig carga f **2** v/t: **~ s.o. with sth** fig cargar a alguien con

algo

bureau ['bjʊroʊ] (chest of drawers) cómoda f; (office) departamento m, oficina f; **bureaucrat** burócrata m/f; **bureaucratic** burocrático

burger ['bɜːrgər] hamburguesa f

burglar ['bɜːrglər] ladrón (-ona) m(f); **burglar alarm** alarma f antirrobo; **burglarize** robar; **burglary** robo m

burial ['berɪəl] entierro m

burn [bɜːrn] **1** n quemadura f **2** v/t quemar **3** v/i quemarse ♦ **burn down 1** v/t incendiar **2** v/i incendiarse

burp [bɜːrp] **1** n eructo m **2** v/i eructar

burst [bɜːrst] **1** n in pipe rotura f **2** adj tire reventado **3** v/t & v/i reventar; **~ into tears** echarse a llorar; **~ out laughing** echarse a reír

bus [bʌs] local autobús m, Mex camión m, Arg colectivo m, C.Am. guagua f; long distance autobús m, Span autocar m

bush [bʊʃ] plant arbusto m; **bushy** beard espeso

business ['bɪznɪs] negocios mpl; (company) empresa f; (sector) sector m; (affair, matter) asunto m; as subject of study empresariales fpl; **on ~** de negocios; **mind your own ~!** ¡no te metas en lo que no te importa!; **business card** tarjeta f de visita; **business class** clase f ejecutiva; **businesslike** eficiente; **businessman** hombre *m* de negocios; **business meeting** reunión *f* de negocios; **business school** escuela *f* de negocios; **business studies** empresariales *mpl*; **business trip** viaje *m* de negocios; **businesswoman** mujer *f* de negocios, ejecutiva *f*

bust¹ [bʌst] *n of woman* busto *m*

bust² [bʌst] *adj* F *(broken)* escacharrado F

'**bus station** estación *f* de autobuses; **bus stop** parada *f* de autobús

'**bust-up** F corte *m* F; **busty** pechugona

busy ['bɪzɪ] *adj* ocupado; *full of people* abarrotado; *restaurant etc: making money* ajetreado; **busybody** metomentodo *m/f*

but [bʌt] **1** *conj* pero **2** *prep: all ~ him* todos excepto él; *the last ~ one* el penúltimo; *~ for you* si no hubiera sido por ti

butcher ['bʊtʃər] carnice-

ro(-a) *m(f)*

butt [bʌt] **1** *n of cigarette* colilla *f*; F *(buttocks)* trasero *m* F **2** *v/t of bull* embestir

butter ['bʌtər] mantequilla *f*; **butterfly** mariposa *f*

buttocks ['bʌtəks] nalgas *fpl*

button ['bʌtn] botón *m*; *(badge)* chapa *f*

buy [baɪ] comprar

◆ **buy out** COM comprar la parte de

buyer ['baɪr] comprador(a) *m(f)*

buzz [bʌz] **1** *n* zumbido *m* **2** *v/i of insect* zumbar; **buzzer** timbre *m*

by [baɪ] *to show agent* por; *(near, next to)* al lado de, junto a; *(no later than)* no más tarde de; *mode of transport* en; **~ day** de día; **~ bus** en autobús; **~ my watch** en mi reloj; *a play ~ ...* una obra de...; *~ o.s. without company* solo

bye(-bye) [baɪ] adiós

'**bypass** circunvalación *f*; MED bypass *m*; **by-product** subproducto *m*; **bystander** transeúnte *m/f*

C

cab [kæb] taxi *m*; *of truck* cabina *f*; **cab driver** taxista *m/f*

cabin ['kæbɪn] *of plane* cabina *f*; *of ship* camarote *m*; **cabin attendant** auxiliar *m/f* de vuelo; **cabin crew** personal

m de a bordo

cabinet ['kæbɪnɪt] armario *m*; POL gabinete *m*

cable ['keɪbl] cable *m*; **cable car** teleférico *m*; **cable television** televisión *f* por cable

'cab stand parada f de taxis

cactus ['kæktəs] cactus m inv

cadaver [kə'dævər] cadáver m

caddie ['kædı] in golf caddie m/f

Caesarean Br ☞ **Cesarean**

café ['kæfeı] café m; cafetería cafetería f, cantina f

caffeine ['kæfiːn] cafeína f

cage [keıdʒ] jaula f; **cagey** cauteloso

cake [keık] tarta f; small pastel m

calculate ['kælkjʊleıt] calcular; **calculating** calculador; **calculation** cálculo m; **calculator** calculadora f

calendar ['kælındər] calendario m

calf¹ [kæf] of cow ternero(-a) m(f)

calf² [kæf] of leg pantorrilla f

caliber, Br **calibre** ['kælıbər] of gun calibre m

call [kɔːl] **1** n llamada f; (demand) llamamiento m **2** v/t also TELEC llamar; meeting convocar; **be ~ ed ...** llamarse... **3** v/ii also TELEC llamar; (visit) pasarse

◆ **call back 1** v/t (phone again) volver a llamar; (return call) devolver la llamada; (summon) hacer volver **2** v/ii on phone volver a llamar; (make another visit) volver a pasar

◆ **call for** (collect) pasar a recoger; (demand) pedir, exigir; (require) requerir

◆ **call off** cancelar

caller ['kɔːlər] on phone persona f que llama; (visitor) visitante m/f

calm [kɑːm] **1** adj tranquilo; weather apacible **2** n calma f

◆ **calm down** v/t calmar **2** v/ii calmarse

calmly ['kɑːmlı] con calma, tranquilamente

calorie ['kælərı] caloría f

camcorder ['kæmkɔːrdər] videocámara f

camera ['kæmərə] cámara f; **cameraman** cámara m, camarógrafo m; **camera phone** teléfono m con cámara

camouflage ['kæməflɑːʒ] **1** n camuflaje m **2** v/t camuflar

camp [kæmp] **1** n campamento m **2** v/ii acampar

campaign [kæm'peın] **1** n campaña f **2** v/ii hacer campaña (**for** a favor de)

camper ['kæmpər] campista m/f; vehicle autocaravana f; **camping** campada f; on campsite camping m; **campsite** camping m

campus ['kæmpəs] campus m

can¹ [kæn] v/aux poder; **~ you swim?** ¿sabes nadar?; **~ you hear me?** ¿me oyes?; **~ I have a beer?** ¿me pones una cerveza?

can² [kæn] n container: lata f

Canada ['kænədə] Canadá; **Canadian 1** adj canadiense **2** n canadiense m/f

canal [kə'næl] waterway canal

m

Canary Islands, Canaries [kəˈneriːz]: **the ~** las Islas Canarias

cancel [ˈkænsl] cancelar; **cancellation** cancelación *f*

cancer [ˈkænsər] cáncer *m*

candid [ˈkændɪd] sincero

candidacy [ˈkændɪdəsɪ] candidatura *f*; **candidate** candidato(-a) *m(f)*

candle [ˈkændl] vela *f*

candor, *Br* **candour** [ˈkændər] sinceridad *f*

candy [ˈkændɪ] *(sweet)* caramelo *m*; *(sweets)* dulces *mpl*

cane [keɪn] caña *f*

canister [ˈkænɪstər] bote *m*

canned [kænd] enlatado, en lata; *(recorded)* grabado

cannot [ˈkænɒt] ☞ **can not**

canny [ˈkænɪ] *(astute)* astuto

canoe [kəˈnuː] canoa *f*, piragua *f*

'can opener abrelatas *m inv*

can't [kænt] ☞ **= can not**

canteen [kænˈtiːn] *in plant* cantina *f*, cafetería *f*

canvas [ˈkænvəs] *for painting* lienzo *m*; *material* lona *f*

canyon [ˈkænjən] cañón *m*

cap [kæp] *hat* gorro *m*; *with peak* gorra *f*

capability [keɪpəˈbɪlətɪ] capacidad *f*; **capable** capaz

capacity capacidad *f*; *of engine* cilindrada *f*

capital [ˈkæpɪtl] *city* capital *f*; *letter* mayúscula *f*; *money* capital *m*; **capitalism** capitalismo *m*; **capitalist 1** *adj* capitalista **2** *n* capitalista *m/f*;

capital punishment pena *f* capital

capsize [kæpˈsaɪz] volcar

capsule [ˈkæpsəl] cápsula *f*

captain [ˈkæptɪn] capitán (-ana) *m(f)*; *of aircraft* comandante *m/f*

caption [ˈkæpʃn] pie *m* de foto

captivate [ˈkæptɪveɪt] cautivar; **captive 1** *adj* prisionero **2** *n* prisionero(-a) *m(f)*; **captivity** cautividad *f*; **capture 1** *n of city* toma *f*; *of criminal, animal* captura *f* **2** *v/t person, animal* capturar; *city, building* tomar; *market share* ganar

car [kɑːr] coche *m*, *L.Am.* carro *m*, *Rpl* auto *m*; *of train* vagón *m*; **by ~** en coche; **car bomb attack** atentado *m* con coche bomba

carbon monoxide [kɑːrbənmənˈɒksaɪd] monóxido *m* de carbono

carburetor, carburetor [kɑːrbʊˈretər] carburador *m*

carcass [ˈkɑːrkəs] cadáver *m*

card [kɑːrd] tarjeta *f*; *(post~)* (tarjeta *f*) postal *f*; *(playing ~)* carta *f*, naipe *m*; **cardboard** cartón *m*

cardiac [ˈkɑːrdɪæk] cardíaco

cardinal [ˈkɑːrdɪnl] REL cardenal *m*

care [ker] **1** *n* cuidado *m*; *medical* asistencia *f* médica; *(worry)* preocupación *f*; **care of** ☞ **c/o**, **take ~** *(be cautious)* tener cuidado; ***take ~ of*** cuidar; (*deal with*) ocuparse de **2** *v/i* preocuparse; ***I don't ~!*** ¡me da igual!

◆ **care about** preocuparse por

◆ **care for** (*look after*) cuidar

career [kəˈrɪr] carrera *f*

careful [ˈkerfl] cuidadoso; ***be ~*** tener cuidado; **carefully** con cuidado; *worded etc* cuidadosamente; **careless** descuidado; **carelessly** descuidadamente

caress [kəˈres] acariciar

ˈcar ferry ferry *m*, transbordador *m*

cargo [ˈkɑːrgoʊ] cargamento *m*

Caribbean [kəˈɪbiən]: ***the ~*** el Caribe

caricature [ˈkærɪkətʃər] caricatura *f*

carnival [ˈkɑːrnɪvl] feria *f*

carpenter [ˈkɑːrpɪntər] carpintero(-a) *m(f)*

carpet [ˈkɑːrpɪt] alfombra *f*

ˈcar phone teléfono *m* de coche; **carpool** *compartir el vehículo para ir al trabajo*; **car rental** alquiler *m* de automóviles

carrier [ˈkærɪər] *company* transportista *m*; *airline* línea *f* aérea; *of disease* portador(a) *m(f)*

carrot [ˈkærət] zanahoria *f*

carry [ˈkærɪ] **1** *v/t* llevar; *disease* ser portador de; *of ship, bus etc* transportar **2** *v/i of sound* oírse

◆ **carry on 1** *v/i* continuar **2** *v/t business* efectuar

◆ **carry out** *survey etc* llevar a cabo

car sharing coches *mpl* compartidos

cart [kɑːrt] carro *m*; *for shopping* carrito *m*

carton [ˈkɑːrtn] caja *f* de cartón; *for milk, cigarettes* cartón *m*

cartoon [kɑːrˈtuːn] tira *f* cómica; *on TV* dibujos *mpl* animados

carve [kɑːrv] *meat* trinchar; *wood* tallar

case[1] [keɪs] *container* funda *f*; *of wine etc* caja *f*; *Br* (*suitcase*) maleta *f*

case[2] [keɪs] *instance, criminal*, MED caso *m*; LAW causa *f*; ***in ~ ...*** por si…; ***in any ~*** en cualquier caso

cash [kæʃ] **1** *n* efectivo *m* **2** *v/t check* hacer efectivo; **cash desk** caja *f*; **cash flow** flujo *m* de caja, cash-flow *m*; **cashier** *in store etc* cajero(-a) *m(f)*; **cashpoint** *Br* cajero *m* automático; **cash register** caja *f* registradora

casino [kəˈsiːnoʊ] casino *m*

casket [ˈkæskɪt] (*coffin*) ataúd *m*

casserole [ˈkæsəroʊl] *meal* guiso *m*; *container* cacerola *f*

cassette [kəˈset] cinta *f*, casete *f*; **cassette player, cassette recorder** casete *m*

cast [kæst] **1** *n of play* reparto *m*; (*mold*) molde *m* **2** *v/t* *doubt* proyectar; *metal* fundir

Castilian [kæs'tɪliən] castellano

cast 'iron hierro *m* fundido

castle ['kæsl] castillo *m*

casual ['kæʒʊəl] (*chance*) casual; (*offhand*) despreocupado; (*not formal*) informal; **casually** *dressed* de manera informal; *say* a la ligera; **casualty** víctima *f*

cat [kæt] gato *m*

Catalan ['kætəlæn] catalán

catalog, *Br* catalogue ['kætəlɔːg] catálogo *m*

catalyst ['kætəlɪst] catalizador *m*

catastrophe [kə'tæstrəfɪ] catástrofe *f*; **catastrophic** catastrófico

catch [kætʃ] **1** *n* parada *f* (*sin que la pelota toque el suelo*); *of fish* captura *f*, (*lock*) cierre *m*; (*problem*) pega *f* **2** *v/t ball* agarrar, *Span* coger; *animal* atrapar; *escapee* capturar; (*get on: bus, train*) tomar, *Span* coger; (*not miss: bus, train*) alcanzar, *Span* coger; *fish* pescar; *illness* agarrar, *Span* coger; **catching** *also fig* contagioso; **catchy** pegadizo

categoric [kætə'gɑːrɪk] categórico; **category** categoría *f*

caterer ['keɪtərər] hostelero(-a) *m(f)*

cathedral [kə'θiːdrl] catedral *f*

Catholic ['kæθəlɪk] **1** *adj* católico **2** *n* católico(-a) *m(f)*; **Catholicism** catolicismo *m*

cattle ['kætl] ganado *m*

cause [kɔːz] **1** *n* causa *f*; (*grounds*) motivo *m* **2** *v/t* causar, provocar

caution ['kɔːʃn] **1** *n* precaución *f* **2** *v/t* (*warn*) prevenir; **cautious** cauto, prudente; **cautiously** cautelosamente

cave [keɪv] cueva *f*

cavity ['kævətɪ] caries *f inv*

CD [siː'diː] (= *compact disc*) CD *m* (= disco *m* compacto); **CD player** (reproductor *m* de) CD *m*; **CD-ROM** CD-ROM *m*

cease [siːs] **1** *v/i* cesar **2** *v/t* suspender; **cease-fire** alto *m* el fuego

ceiling ['siːlɪŋ] techo *m*; (*limit*) tope *m*

celebrate ['selɪbreɪt] **1** *v/i*: *let's ~ with a bottle of champagne* celebrémoslo con una botella de champán **2** *v/t* celebrar; **celebrated** célebre; **celebration** celebración *f*; **celebrity** celebridad *f*

cell [sel] *in prison, spreadsheet* celda *f*; BIO célula *f*

cellar ['selər] sótano *m*; *for wine* bodega *f*

cello ['tʃeloʊ] violonchelo *m*

cell phone, cellular phone ['seljələr] (teléfono *m*) móvil *m*, *L.Am.* (teléfono *m*) celular *m*

cement [sɪ'ment] cemento *m*

cemetery ['semətrɪ] cementerio *m*

chance

censor ['sensər] censor(a)
m(f)

census ['sensəs] censo m

cent [sent] céntimo m

centenary [sen'ti:nərɪ] centenario m

center ['sentər] 1 n centro m 2
v/t centrar

centigrade ['sentɪgreɪd] centígrado m

centimeter ['sentɪmi:tər],
Br centimetre
['sentɪmi:tər] centímetro m

central ['sentrəl] central; location, apartment céntrico;
Central America Centro-
américa, América Central;
Central American 1 adj centroamericano, de (la) América f Central 2 n centroame-
ricano(-a) m(f); central
heating calefacción f central; centralize centralizar;
central locking MOT cierre
m centralizado

centre Br ☞ center

century ['sentʃərɪ] siglo m

CEO [si:i:'ou] (= Chief Executive Officer) consejero(-a)
m(f) delegado

ceramic [sɪ'ræmɪk] de cerámica

cereal ['sɪrɪəl] cereal m; for
breakfast cereales mpl

ceremonial [serɪ'mounɪəl] 1
adj ceremonial 2 n ceremonial m; ceremony ceremo-
nia f

certain ['sɜːrtn] (sure) seguro;
(particular) cierto; certainly
(definitely) claramente; (of
course) por supuesto; certainty (confidence) certeza
f; (inevitability) seguridad f

certificate [sər'tɪfɪkət] (qualification) título m; (official paper) certificado m

certified public accountant
['sɜːrtɪfaɪd] censor(a) m(f)
jurado de cuentas; certify
certificar

Cesarean [sɪ'zerɪən] cesárea f

CFO [si:ef'ou] (= Chief Financial Officer) director(a)
m(f) financiero(a)

chain [tʃeɪn] 1 n also of hotels
etc cadena f 2 v/t encadenar

chair [tʃer] 1 n silla f; (arm-)
sillón m; at university cátedra
f 2 v/t meeting presidir; chair
lift telesilla f; chairman presidente m; chairmanship
presidencia f; chairperson
presidente(-a) m(f)

chalk [tʃɔːk] tiza f; in soil creta
f

challenge ['tʃælɪndʒ] 1 n (difficulty) desafío m; in competition ataque m 2 v/t desafiar;
(call into question) cuestionar; challenger aspirante
m/f; challenging job estimulante

Chamber of 'Commerce
Cámara f de Comercio

champagne [ʃæm'peɪn]
champán m

champion ['tʃæmpɪən] 1 n SP
campeón(-ona) m(f) 2 v/t
cause abanderar; championship campeonato m

chance [tʃæns] posibilidad f;
(opportunity) oportunidad f;

(*luck*) casualidad *f*; **by ~** por casualidad; **take a ~** correr el riesgo

change [tʃeɪndʒ] **1** *n* cambio *m*; (*small coins*) suelto *m*; *from purchase* cambio *m*, *L.Am.* vuelto *m*; **for a ~** para variar **2** *v/t* cambiar **3** *v/i* cambiar; (*put on different clothes*) cambiarse; (*take different train / bus*) hacer transbordo; **changeover** transición *f* (**to** a); **changing room** *m* vestuario *m*; *in shop* probador *m*

channel ['tʃænl] canal *m*

chant [tʃænt] **1** *n* REL canto *m*; *of fans* cántico *m*; *of demonstrators* consigna *f* **2** *v/i* gritar **3** *v/t* corear

chaos ['keɪɒs] caos *m*, **chaotic** caótico

chapel ['tʃæpl] capilla *f*

chapter ['tʃæptər] capítulo *m*

character ['kærɪktər] carácter *m*; *person, in book* personaje *m*; **characteristic 1** *n* característica *f* **2** *adj* característico; (*be typical of*) caracterizar; (*describe*) describir

charge [tʃɑːrdʒ] **1** *n* (*fee*) tarifa *f*; LAW acusación *f*; **free of ~** gratis; **be in ~** estar a cargo **2** *v/t sum of money* cobrar; (*put on account*) pagar con tarjeta; LAW acusar (**with** de); *battery* cargar **3** *v/i* (*attack*) cargar; **charge account** cuenta *f* de crédito; **charge card** tarjeta *f* de compra

charitable ['tʃærɪtəbl] de caridad; *person* caritativo; **charity** caridad *f*; *organization* entidad *f* benéfica

charm [tʃɑːrm] **1** *n* encanto *m*; *on bracelet etc* colgante *m* **2** *v/t* (*delight*) encantar; **charming** encantador

charred [tʃɑːrd] carbonizado

chart [tʃɑːrt] gráfico *m*; (*map*) carta *f* de navegación; **charter flight** ['tʃɑːrtər] vuelo *m* chárter

chase [tʃeɪs] **1** *n* persecución *f* **2** *v/t* perseguir

◆ **chase away** ahuyentar

chassis ['ʃæsɪ] *of car* chasis *m inv*

chat [tʃæt] **1** *n* charla *f* **2** *v/i* charlar; **chatline** *party line f*; *for male* sala *f* de chat

chatter ['tʃætər] **1** *n* cháchara *f* **2** *v/i talk* parlotear; *of teeth* castañetear

chauffeur ['ʃoʊfər] chófer *m*, *L.Am.* chofer *m*

chauvinist ['ʃoʊvɪnɪst] (*male ~*) machista *m*

cheap [tʃiːp] barato; (*nasty*) chabacano; (*mean*) tacaño

cheat [tʃiːt] **1** *n* (*person*) tramposo(-a) *m(f)* **2** *v/t* engañar **3** *v/i in exam* copiar; *in cards etc* hacer trampa

check[1] [tʃek] **1** *adj shirt* a cuadros **2** *n* cuadro *m*

check[2] [tʃek] FIN cheque *m*; *in restaurant etc* cuenta *f*

check[3] [tʃek] **1** *n to verify* comprobación *f* **2** *v/t* (*verify*) comprobar; *machinery* inspeccionar; **with a ~mark** poner un tic en; *coat* dejar en el guardarropa **3** *v/i* comprobar

◆ **check in** *at airport* facturar; *at hotel* registrarse

◆ **check out 1** *v/i of hotel* dejar el hotel **2** *v/t (look into)* investigar; *club etc* probar

◆ **check up on** investigar

◆ **checkbook** talonario *m* de cheques, *L.Am.* chequera *f*;
checked *material* a cuadros;
checkered ['tʃekərd] *shirt* a cuadros; *career* accidentado

check-in (counter) mostrador *m* de facturación;
checking account cuenta *f* corriente; **checklist** lista *f* de verificación; **check mark** tic *m*; **check-out** caja *f*;
checkpoint control *m*;
checkroom *for coats* guardarropa *m*; *for baggage* consigna *f*; **checkup** revisión *f* (médica)

cheek [tʃiːk] ANAT mejilla *f*

cheer [tʃɪr] **1** *n* ovación *f* **2** *v/t* ovacionar **3** *v/i* lanzar vítores

◆ **cheer up 1** *v/i* animarse **2** *v/t* animar

cheerful ['tʃɪrfəl] alegre;
cheering vítores *mpl*;
cheerleader animadora *f*

cheese [tʃiːz] queso *m*

chef [ʃef] chef *m*, jefe *m* de cocina

chemical ['kemɪkl] **1** *adj* químico **2** *n* producto *m* químico; **chemist** *in laboratory* químico(-a) *m(f)*; *Br dis-*

pensing farmacéutico(-a) *m(f)*; **chemistry** química *f*

chemotherapy [kiːmou'θerəpɪ] quimioterapia *f*

cheque [tʃek] *Br* ☞ **check²**

chess [tʃes] ajedrez *m*

chest [tʃest] pecho *m*; *box* cofre *m*

chew [tʃuː] mascar, masticar; *of dog, rats* mordisquear;
chewing gum chicle *m*

chick [tʃɪk] pollito *m*; *young bird* polluelo *m*; F *girl* nena *f* F

chicken ['tʃɪkɪn] **1** *n* gallina *f*; *food* pollo *m*

chief [tʃiːf] **1** *n* jefe(-a) *m(f)* **2** *adj* principal; **chiefly** principalmente

child [tʃaɪld] niño(-a) *m(f)*;
childhood infancia *f*; **childish** *pej* infantil; **childlike** infantil

children ['tʃɪldrən] *pl* ☞ **child**

Chile ['tʃɪlɪ] Chile; **Chilean 1** *adj* chileno **2** *n* chileno(-a) *m(f)*

chill(i) (pepper) chile *m*, *Span* guindilla *f*

◆ **chill out** P relajarse; *(calm down)* tranquilizarse

chilly ['tʃɪlɪ] *also fig* fresco

chimney ['tʃɪmnɪ] chimenea *f*

chin [tʃɪn] barbilla *f*

China ['tʃaɪnə] China

china ['tʃaɪnə] porcelana *f*

Chinese [tʃaɪ'niːz] **1** *adj* chino **2** *n (language)* chino *m*; *(person)* chino(-a) *m(f)*

chip [tʃɪp] **1** *n damage* mella *f*; *in gambling* ficha *f*; **~s** patatas *fpl* fritas **2** *v/t* (*damage*) mellar; **chipmunk** ardilla *f* listada

chisel ['tʃɪzl] *for stone* cincel *m*; *for wood* formón *m*

chlorine ['klɔːriːn] cloro *m*

chocolate ['tʃɑːkələt] chocolate *m*

choice [tʃɔɪs] **1** *n* elección *f*; (*selection*) selección *f*; **I had no ~** no tuve alternativa **2** *adj* (*top quality*) selecto

choir [kwaɪr] coro *m*

choke [tʃouk] **1** *v/i* ahogarse **2** *v/t* estrangular

cholesterol [kə'lestərɔːl] colesterol *m*

choose [tʃuːz] elegir, escoger; **choosey** F exigente

chop [tʃɑːp] **1** *n meat* chuleta *f* **2** *v/t wood* cortar; *meat* trocear; *vegetables* picar

◆ **chop down** *tree* talar

chore [tʃɔːr] tarea *f*

choreography [kɔːri'ɑːɡrəfi] coreografía *f*

chorus ['kɔːrəs] *singers* coro *m*; *of song* estribillo *m*

Christ [kraɪst] Cristo

christen ['krɪsn] bautizar

Christian ['krɪstʃən] **1** *n* cristiano(-a) *m(f)* **2** *adj* cristiano; **Christianity** cristianismo *m*

Christmas ['krɪsməs] Navidad(es) *f(pl)*; **Merry ~!** ¡Feliz Navidad!; **Christmas card** crismas *m inv*; **Christmas Day** día *m* de Navidad; **Christmas Eve** Nochebuena *f*; **Christmas present** re-

galo *m* de Navidad; **Christmas tree** árbol *m* de Navidad

chronic ['krɑːnɪk] crónico

chubby ['tʃʌbɪ] rechoncho

chuck [tʃʌk] F tirar

chuckle ['tʃʌkl] **1** *n* risita *f* **2** *v/i* reírse por lo bajo

chunk [tʃʌŋk] trozo *m*

church ['tʃɜːrtʃ] iglesia *f*; **church service** oficio *m* religioso; **churchyard** cementerio *m* (al lado de iglesia)

chute [ʃuːt] rampa *f*; *for garbage* colector *m* de basura

cigar [sɪ'ɡɑːr] puro *m*

cigarette [sɪɡə'ret] cigarrillo *m*; **cigarette lighter** encendedor *m*

cinema ['sɪnɪmə] *Br* cine *m*

circle ['sɜːrkl] **1** *n* círculo *m* **2** *v/i of plane* volar en círculo

circuit ['sɜːrkɪt] circuito *m*; (*lap*) vuelta *f*; **circuit board** COMPUT placa *f* or tarjeta *f* de circuitos

circular ['sɜːrkjələr] **1** *n* circular *f* **2** *adj* circular; **circulate 1** *v/i* circular **2** *v/t memo* hacer circular; **circulation** circulación *f*; *of newspaper* tirada *f*

circumstances ['sɜːrkəmstənsɪz] circunstancias *fpl*; *financial* situación *f* económica

circus ['sɜːrkəs] circo *m*

cistern ['sɪstərn] cisterna *f*

citizen ['sɪtɪzn] ciudadano(-a) *m(f)*; **citizenship** ciudadanía *f*

city ['sɪtɪ] ciudad f; **city center, **Br** city centre** centro m de la ciudad; **city hall** ayuntamiento m

civic ['sɪvɪk] cívico

civil ['sɪvl] civil; (*polite*) cortés; **civil ceremony** ceremonia f civil; **civil engineer** ingeniero(-a) m(f) civil; **civilian** civil m/f; **civilization** civilización f; **civilize** civilizar; **civil rights** derechos mpl civiles; **civil servant** funcionario(-a) m(f); **civil service** administración f pública; **civil war** guerra f civil

claim [kleɪm] **1** n (*request*) reclamación f (**for** de); (*assertion*) afirmación f **2** v/t (*ask for as a right*) reclamar; (*assert*) afirmar; *lost property* reclamar; **claimant** reclamante m/f

clam [klæm] almeja f

clammy ['klæmɪ] húmedo

clamp [klæmp] *fastener* abrazadera f

◆ **clamp down** actuar contundentemente (**on** contra)

clandestine [klæn'destɪn] clandestino

clap [klæp] (*applaud*) aplaudir

clarification [klærɪfɪ'keɪʃn] aclaración f; **clarify** aclarar; **clarity** claridad f

clash [klæʃ] **1** n choque m **2** v/i chocar; *of colors* desentonar; *of events* coincidir

clasp [klɑːsp] **1** n broche m **2** v/t *in hand* estrechar

class [klæs] **1** n clase f **2** v/t

clasificar (**as** como)

classic ['klæsɪk] **1** adj clásico **2** n clásico m; **classical** clásico; **classification** clasificación f; **classified** *information* reservado; **classified ad** anuncio m por palabras; **classify** clasificar; **classroom** clase f, aula f; **classy** F con clase

clause [klɔːz] cláusula f

claustrophobia [klɔːstrə'fəʊbɪə] claustrofobia f

claw [klɔː] garra f; *of lobster* pinza f

clay [kleɪ] arcilla f

clean [kliːn] **1** adj limpio **2** adv F (*completely*) completamente **3** v/t limpiar

cleaner ['kliːnə] *person* limpiador(a) m(f); (*dry*) ~ tintorería f

cleanse [klenz] *skin* limpiar; **cleanser** *for skin* loción f limpiadora

clear [klɪr] **1** adj claro; *sky* despejado; *water* transparente; *conscience* limpio **2** v/t *roads etc* despejar; (*acquit*) absolver; (*authorize*) autorizar **3** v/i *of mist* despejarse

◆ **clear out 1** v/t *closet* ordenar, limpiar **2** v/i marcharse

◆ **clear up 1** v/i ordenar; *of weather* despejarse; *of illness* desaparecer **2** v/t (*tidy*) ordenar; *problem* aclarar

clearance ['klɪrəns] *space* espacio m; (*authorization*) autorización f; **clearance sale**

liquidación f; **clearing** claro m; **clearly** claramente

cleavage ['kli:vɪdʒ] escote m

clench [klentʃ] apretar

clergy ['klɜːrdʒɪ] clero m; **clergyman** clérigo m

clerk [klɜːrk] oficinista m/f; in store dependiente(-a) m/f

clever ['klevər] listo; idea, gadget ingenioso

click [klɪk] **1** n COMPUT clic m **2** v/i hacer clic

♦ **click on** COMPUT hacer clic en

client ['klaɪənt] cliente m/f; clientele clientela f

climate ['klaɪmət] also fig clima m; **climate catastrophe** catástrofe f climática; **climate change** cambio m climático

climax ['klaɪmæks] clímax m

climb [klaɪm] **1** n up mountain ascensión f **2** v/t & v/i subir; **climber** person escalador(a) m/f; L.Am. andinista m/f

clinch [klɪntʃ] deal cerrar

cling [klɪŋ] of clothes pegarse al cuerpo

♦ **cling to** aferrarse a

clingy ['klɪŋɪ] person pegajoso

clinic ['klɪnɪk] clínica f; **clinical** clínico

clip¹ [klɪp] **1** n fastener clip m **2** v/t: ~ **sth to sth** sujetar algo a algo

clip² [klɪp] **1** n extract fragmento m **2** v/t hair, grass cortar; **clipping** from press recorte m

clock [klɑːk] reloj m; **clock**

radio radio m despertador; **clockwise** en el sentido de las agujas del reloj

clone [kloun] **1** n clon m **2** v/t clonar; **cloning** clonación f

close¹ [klous] adv cerca; ~ **to the school** cerca del colegio; adj family cercano; friend íntimo; **be ~ to s.o.** emotionally estar muy unido a alguien

close² [klouz] v/t cerrar

closed-circuit 'television circuito m cerrado de televisión; **close-knit** muy unido; **closely** watch atentamente; cooperate de cerca

closet ['klɑːzɪt] armario m

close-up ['klousʌp] primer plano m

closing date ['klouzɪŋ] fecha f límite

closure ['klouʒər] cierre m

clot [klɑːt] **1** n of blood coágulo m **2** v/i coagularse

cloth [klɑːθ] tela f, tejido m; for cleaning trapo m

clothes [klouðz] ropa f; **clothing** ropa f

cloud [klaud] nube f; **cloudless** despejado; **cloudy** nublado

clout [klaut] fig influencia f

clove of garlic [klouv] diente m de ajo

clown [klaun] also fig payaso m

club [klʌb] palo m; organization club m

clue [kluː] pista f

clumsiness ['klʌmzɪnɪs] torpeza f; **clumsy** torpe

cluster ['klʌstər] grupo m

clutch [klʌtʃ] **1** n MOT embrague m **2** v/t agarrar
◆ **clutch at** agarrarse a

Co. (= **Company**) Cía. (= Compañía f)

c/o (= **care of**) en el domicilio de

coach [koutʃ] **1** n (trainer) entrenador(a) m(f); Br (bus) autobús m **2** v/t footballer entrenar; singer preparar; **coaching** entrenamiento m

coagulate [kou'ægjuleit] of blood coagularse

coal [koul] carbón m

coalition [kouə'lɪʃn] coalición f

coalmine mina f de carbón

coarse [kɔːrs] áspero; hair, (vulgar) basto; **coarsely** (vulgarly) de manera grosera

coast [koust] costa f; **coastal** costero; **coastguard** servicio m de guardacostas; person guardacostas m/f inv; **coastline** litoral m, costa f

coat [kout] **1** n chaqueta f, L.Am. saco m; (over-) abrigo m; of animal pelaje m; of paint capa f **2** v/t (cover) cubrir (**with** de); **coathanger** percha f; **coating** capa f

coax [kouks] persuadir

cocaine [kə'keɪn] cocaína f

cock [kɑːk] chicken gallo m; any male bird macho m; **cockpit** of plane cabina f; **cockroach** cucaracha f; **cocktail** cóctel m

cocoa ['koukou] cacao m

coconut ['koukənʌt] coco m; **coconut palm** cocotero m

code [koud] código m; **in ~** cifrado

coeducational [kouedu'keiʃnl] mixto

coerce [kou'ɜːrs] coaccionar

coexist [kouɪg'zɪst] coexistir; **coexistence** coexistencia f

coffee ['kɑːfi] café m; **coffee maker** cafetera f (para preparar); **coffee pot** cafetera f (para servir); **coffee shop** café m

cohabit [kou'hæbɪt] cohabitar

coherent [kou'hɪrənt] coherente

coil [kɔɪl] **1** n of rope rollo m; of snake anillo m **2** v/t: **~ (up)** enrollar

coin [kɔɪn] moneda f

coincide [kouɪn'saɪd] coincidir; **coincidence** coincidencia f

Coke® [kouk] Coca-Cola® f

cold [kould] **1** adj frío; **I'm ~** tengo frío; **it's ~** of weather hace frío **2** n frío m; MED resfriado m; **cold-blooded** de sangre fría; murder a sangre fría; **coldly** fríamente, con frialdad; **coldness** frialdad f; **cold sore** calentura f

collaborate [kə'læbəreit] colaborar (**on** en); **collaboration** colaboración f; **collaborator** colaborador(a) m(f); with enemy colaboracionista m/f

collapse [kə'læps] desplomarse; **collapsible** plegable

collar ['kɑːlər] cuello m; for dog collar m

colleague ['kɑːliːg] colega m/f

collect [kə'lekt] **1** v/t recoger; as hobby coleccionar **2** v/i (gather together) reunirse; **collect call** llamada f a cobro revertido; **collection** colección f; in church colecta f; **collective** colectivo; **collector** coleccionista m/f

college ['kɑːlɪdʒ] universidad f

collide [kə'laɪd] chocar, colisionar; **collision** choque m, colisión f

Colombia [kə'lʌmbɪə] Colombia; **Colombian 1** adj colombiano **2** n colombiano(-a) m(f)

colon ['koʊlən] punctuation dos puntos mpl

colonel ['kɜːrnl] coronel m

colonial [kə'loʊnɪəl] colonial; **colonize** colonizar; **colony** colonia f

color ['kʌlər] color m f; **colorblind** daltónico; **colored** person de color; **colorful** lleno de colores; account colorido

colossal [kə'lɑːsl] colosal

colour Br → **color**

colt [koʊlt] potro m

Columbus [kə'lʌmbəs] Colón m

column ['kɑːləm] columna f; **columnist** columnista m/f

coma ['koʊmə] coma m

comb [koʊm] **1** n peine m **2** v/t hair, area peinar; **~ one's hair** peinarse

combat ['kɑːmbæt] **1** n combate m **2** v/t combatir

combination [kɑːmbɪ'neɪʃn] combinación f; **combine 1** v/t combinar; ingredients mezclar **2** v/i combinarse

come [kʌm] venir
◆ **come across** (find) encontrar
◆ **come along** (come too) venir; (turn up) aparecer; (progress) marchar
◆ **come back** volver
◆ **come down 1** v/i bajar; of rain, snow caer **2** v/t: **come down the stairs** bajar las escaleras
◆ **come for** (attack) atacar; (collect: thing) venir a por; (collect: person) venir a buscar a
◆ **come forward** presentarse
◆ **come from** (travel) venir de; (originate) ser de
◆ **come in** entrar; of train llegar; of tide subir
◆ **come in for** criticism recibir
◆ **come off** of handle etc soltarse; of paint etc quitarse
◆ **come out** salir; of book publicarse; of stain irse
◆ **come to 1** v/t place llegar a; of hair, water llegar hasta **2** v/i (regain consciousness) volver en sí
◆ **come up** subir; of sun salir
'**comeback** regreso m

comedian [kə'mi:dɪən] humorista *m/f*; *pej* payaso(-a) *m(f)*; comedy comedia *f*

comfort ['kʌmfət] 1 *n* comodidad *f*, confort *m*; (*consolation*) consuelo *m* 2 *v/t* consolar; comfortable cómodo

comic ['kɒmɪk] 1 *n to read* cómic *m*; (*comedian*) cómico(-a) *m(f)* 2 *adj* cómico; comical cómico; comic book cómic *m*; comics tiras *fpl* cómicas; comic strip tira *f* cómica

comma ['kɒmə] coma *f*

command [kə'mænd] 1 *n* orden *f* 2 *v/t* ordenar, mandar

commandeer [kəmən'dɪr] requisar

commander [kə'mændər] comandante *m/f*; commander-in-chief comandante *m/f* en jefe

commemorate [kə'meməreɪt] conmemorar

commence [kə'mens] comenzar

commendable [kə'mendəbl] encomiable; commendation *for bravery* mención *f*

comment ['kɒment] 1 *n* comentario *m* 2 *v/i* hacer comentarios (*on* sobre); commentary comentarios *mpl*; commentator comentarista *m/f*

commerce ['kɒmɜːrs] comercio *m*; commercial 1 *adj* comercial 2 *n* (*ad*) anuncio *m* (publicitario); commercial break pausa *f* publi-

citaria; commercialize comercializar

commission [kə'mɪʃn] (*payment*, *committee*) comisión *f*; (*job*) encargo *m*

commit [kə'mɪt] *crime* cometer; *money* comprometer; commitment compromiso *m* (*to* con); committee comité *m*

commodity [kə'mɒdɪtɪ] *raw material* producto *m* básico; *product* bien *m* de consumo

common ['kɒmən] común; have sth in ~ tener algo en común; commonly comúnmente; common sense sentido *m* común

commotion [kə'moʊʃn] alboroto *m*

communal [kə'mjuːnl] comunal

communicate [kə'mjuːnɪkeɪt] 1 *v/i* comunicarse 2 *v/t* comunicar; communication comunicación *f*; communicative comunicativo

Communion [kə'mjuːnjən] REL comunión *f*

Communism ['kɒmjʊnɪzəm] comunismo *m*; Communist 1 *adj* comunista 2 *n* comunista *m/f*

community [kə'mjuːnətɪ] comunidad *f*

commute [kə'mjuːt] *v/i* viajar al trabajo 2 *v/t* LAW conmutar

compact 1 [kəm'pækt] *adj* compacto 2 ['kɒmpækt] *n*

MOT utilitario *m*; **companion** [kəm'pænjən] compañero(-a) *m(f)*

company ['kʌmpəni] compañía *f*; COM *also* empresa *f*

comparable ['kɑːmpərəbl] comparable; **comparative** *adj* relativo; *study* comparado; **compare** comparar; **comparison** comparación *f*

compartment [kəm'pɑːrtmənt] compartimento *m*

compass ['kʌmpəs] brújula *f*; *for geometry* compás *m*

compassion [kəm'pæʃn] compasión *f*; **compassionate** compasivo

compatibility [kəmpætə'bɪlɪtɪ] compatibilidad *f*; **compatible** compatible

compel [kəm'pel] obligar

compensate ['kɑːmpənseɪt] **1** *v/t* compensar **2** *v/i*: **~ for** compensar; **compensation** (*money*) indemnización *f*; (*reward*, *comfort*) compensación *f*

compete [kəm'piːt] competir (**for** por)

competence ['kɑːmpɪtəns] competencia *f*; **competent** competente

competition [kɑːmpə'tɪʃn] (*contest*) concurso *m*; SP competición *f*; (*competitors*) competencia *f*; **competitive** competitivo; **competitiveness** COM competitividad *f*; *of person* espíritu *m* competitivo; **competitor** *in con-*

test concursante *m/f*; SP competidor(a) *m(f)*, contrincante *m/f*; COM competidor(a) *m(f)*

complacent [kəm'pleɪsənt] complaciente

complain [kəm'pleɪn] quejarse; **complaint** queja *f*; MED dolencia *f*

complementary [kɑːmplɪ'mentərɪ] complementario

complete [kəm'pliːt] **1** *adj* (*total*) absoluto, total; (*full*) completo; (*finished*) finalizado **2** *v/t task*, *building etc* finalizar; *course* completar; *form* rellenar; **completely** completamente; **completion** finalización *f*

complex ['kɑːmpleks] **1** *adj* complejo **2** *n also* PSYCH complejo *m*; **complexion** *facial* tez *f*; **complexity** complejidad *f*

compliance [kəm'plaɪəns] cumplimiento *m* (**with** de)

complicate ['kɑːmplɪkeɪt] complicar; **complicated** complicado; **complication** complicación *f*

complimentary [kɑːmplɪ'mentərɪ] elogioso; (*free*) de regalo, gratis

comply [kəm'plaɪ] cumplir; **~ with** cumplir

component [kəm'poʊnənt] pieza *f*, componente *m*

compose [kəm'poʊz] *also* MUS componer; **composed** (*calm*) sereno; **composer**

MUS compositor(a) *m(f)*; **composition** *also* MUS composición *f*; **composure** compostura *f*

compound ['kɑːmpaʊnd] *chemical* compuesto *m*

comprehend [kɑːmprɪ'hend] comprender; **comprehension** comprensión *f*; **comprehensive** detallado

compress [kəm'pres] comprimir; *information* condensar

comprise [kəm'praɪz] comprender; **be ~d of** constar de

compromise ['kɑːmprəmaɪz] **1** *n* solución *f* negociada **2** *v/i* transigir, efectuar concesiones **3** *v/t principles* traicionar; *(jeopardize)* poner en peligro

compulsion [kəm'pʌlʃn] PSYCH compulsión *f*; **compulsive** *behavior* compulsivo; *reading* absorbente; **compulsory** obligatorio

computer [kəm'pjuːtər] *Span* ordenador *m*, *L.Am.* computadora *f*; **computer game** juego *m* de *Span* ordenador *or L.Am.* computadora; **computerize** informatizar, *L.Am.* computarizar; **computer science** informática *f*, *L.Am.* computación *f*; **computing** informática *f*, *L.Am.* computación *f*

comrade ['kɑːmreɪd] compañero(-a) *m(f)*; POL camarada *m/f*; **comradeship** camaradería *f*

conceal [kən'siːl] ocultar; **concealment** ocultación *f*

conceit [kən'siːt] engreimiento; **conceited** engreído

conceivable [kən'siːvəbl] concebible; **conceive** *v/i of woman* concebir

concentrate ['kɑːnsəntreɪt] *v/i* concentrarse **2** *v/t energies* concentrar; **concentration** concentración *f*

concept ['kɑːnsept] concepto *m*; **conception** *of child* concepción *f*

concern [kən'sɜːrn] **1** *n* (*anxiety, care*) preocupación *f*; (*business*) asunto *m*; (*company*) empresa *f* **2** *v/t* (*involve*) concernir; (*worry*) preocupar; **concerned** preocupado (**about** por); (*involved*) en cuestión; **concerning** en relación con

concert ['kɑːnsərt] concierto *m*; **concerted** concertado

concession [kən'seʃn] concesión *f*

concise [kən'saɪs] conciso

conclude [kən'kluːd] concluir (**from** de); **conclusion** conclusión *f*; **conclusive** concluyente

concrete ['kɑːŋkriːt] **1** *adj* concreto **2** *n* hormigón *m*, *L.Am.* concreto *m*

concussion [kən'kʌʃn] conmoción *f* cerebral

condemn [kən'dem] condenar; **condemnation** condena *f*

condescend [kɑːndɪ'send]:

he ~ed to speak to me se dignó a hablarme; **condescending** condescendiente

condition [kənˈdɪʃn] **1** *n* (*state*) condiciones *fpl; of health* estado *m; illness* enfermedad *f; (requirement, term)* condición *f* **2** *v/t* PSYCH condicionar; **conditioning** PSYCH condicionamiento *m*

condo [ˈkɑːndoʊ] F apartamento *m, Span* piso *m; building* bloque de apartamentos

condolences [kənˈdoʊlənsɪz] condolencias *fpl*

condom [ˈkɑːndəm] condón *m*, preservativo *m*

condominium [kɑːndəˈmɪnɪəm] ☞ **condo**

condone [kənˈdoʊn] justificar

conduct [ˈkɑːndʌkt] **1** *n* conducta *f* **2** [kənˈdʌkt] *v/t (carry out)* realizar, hacer; ELEC conducir; MUS dirigir; **conducted tour** visita *f* guiada; **conductor** MUS director(a) *m(f)* de orquesta; *on train* revisor(-a) *m(f)*

cone [koʊn] cono *m; for ice cream* cucurucho *m; of pine tree* piña *f*

conference [ˈkɑːnfərəns] congreso *m; discussion* conferencia *f;* **conference room** sala *f* de conferencias

confess [kənˈfes] **1** *v/t* confesar **2** *v/i* confesar; REL confesarse; **confession** confesión *f*

confide [kənˈfaɪd] **1** *v/t* confiar **2** *v/i:* ~ *in s.o.* confiarse

a alguien; **confidence** confianza *f;* **confident** *(self-assured)* seguro de sí mismo; *(convinced)* seguro; **confidential** confidencial; **confidently** con seguridad

confine [kənˈfaɪn] *(imprison)* confinar, recluir; *(restrict)* limitar; **confined** *space* limitado

confirm [kənˈfɜːrm] confirmar; **confirmation** confirmación *f*

confiscate [ˈkɑːnfɪskeɪt] confiscar

conflict 1 [ˈkɑːnflɪkt] *n* conflicto *m* **2** [kənˈflɪkt] *v/i* chocar

confront [kənˈfrʌnt] hacer frente a; **confrontation** confrontación *f*

confuse [kənˈfjuːz] confundir; **confused** *person* confundido; *situation* confuso; **confusing** confuso; **confusion** confusión *f*

congestion [kənˈdʒestʃn] congestión *f*

congratulate [kənˈgrætʃʊleɪt] felicitar; **congratulations** felicitaciones *fpl*

congregate [ˈkɑːngrɪgeɪt] congregarse; **congregation** REL congregación *f*

Congress [ˈkɑːngres] congreso *m;* **Congressional** del Congreso; **Congressman** congresista *m;* **Congresswoman** congresista *f*

conjecture [kənˈdʒektʃər] conjetura *f*

con man ['kɑ:mæn] F timador *m* F

connect [kə'nekt] conectar; (*link*) relacionar, vincular; *to power supply* enchufar; **connected: be well-~** estar bien relacionado; **be ~ with** estar relacionado con; **connection** conexión *f*; (*personal contact*) contacto *m*

connoisseur [kɑnə'sɜ:r] entendido(-a) *m(f)*

conquer ['kɑ:ŋkər] conquistar; *fear etc* vencer; **conqueror** conquistador(a) *m(f)*; **conquest** conquista *f*

conscience ['kɑ:nʃəns] conciencia *f*; **conscientious** concienzudo; **conscientiousness** aplicación *f*

conscious ['kɑ:nʃəs] consciente; **consciously** conscientemente; **consciousness** conciencia *f*

consecutive [kən'sekjʊtɪv] consecutivo

consensus [kən'sensəs] consenso *m*

consent [kən'sent] **1** *n* consentimiento *m* **2** *v/i* consentir (*to* en)

consequence ['kɑ:nsɪkwəns] consecuencia *f*; **consequently** por consiguiente

conservation [kɑ:nsər'veɪʃn] conservación *f*; **conservationist** ecologista *m/f*; **conservative** conservador; *estimate* prudente; **conserve 1** *n* (*jam*) compota *f* **2** *v/t* conservar

consider [kən'sɪdər] considerar; (*show regard for*) mostrar consideración por; **considerable** considerable; **considerably** considerablemente; **considerate** considerado; **considerately** con consideración; **consideration** consideración *f*; (*factor*) factor *m*; **take sth into ~** tomar algo en consideración

♦ **consist of** [kən'sɪst] consistir en

consistency [kən'sɪstənsɪ] (*texture*) consistencia *f*; (*unchangingness*) coherencia *f*; *of player* regularidad *f*; **consistent** *person* coherente; *improvement* constante

consolidate [kən'sɑ:lɪdeɪt] consolidar

conspicuous [kən'spɪkjʊəs] llamativo

conspiracy [kən'spɪrəsɪ] conspiración *f*; **conspirator** conspirador(a) *m(f)*; **conspire** conspirar

constant ['kɑ:nstənt] constante; **constantly** constantemente

constipated ['kɑ:nstɪpeɪtɪd] estreñido; **constipation** estreñimiento *m*

constitute ['kɑ:nstɪtu:t] constituir; **constitution** constitución *f*; **constitutional** POL constitucional

constraint [kən'streɪnt] restricción *f*, límite *m*

construct [kən'strʌkt] construir; **construction** construcción f; **constructive** constructivo

consul ['kɑːnsl] cónsul m/f; **consulate** consulado m

consult [kənˈsʌlt] consultar; **consultancy** company consultoría f; (advice) asesoramiento m; **consultant** asesor(a) m(f), consultor(a) m(f); **consultation** consulta f

consume [kənˈsuːm] consumir; **consumer** consumidor(a) m(f); **consumer confidence** confianza f del consumidor; **consumption** consumo m

contact ['kɑːntækt] **1** n contacto m **2** v/t contactar con; **contact lens** lentes fpl de contacto, Span lentillas fpl

contagious [kənˈteɪdʒəs] contagioso

contain [kənˈteɪn] contener; **container** recipiente m; COM contenedor m

contaminate [kənˈtæmɪneɪt] contaminar; **contamination** contaminación f

contemporary [kənˈtempərərɪ] **1** adj contemporáneo **2** n contemporáneo(-a) m(f)

contempt [kənˈtempt] desprecio m; **contemptible** despreciable; **contemptuous** despectivo

contender [kənˈtendər] contendiente m/f; against champion aspirante m/f

content[1] ['kɑːntent] n contenido m

content[2] [kənˈtent] **1** adj satisfecho **2** v/t: ~ **o.s. with** contentarse con; **contented** satisfecho; **contentment** satisfacción f

contents ['kɑːntents] contenido m

contest[1] ['kɑːntest] n (competition) concurso m; (struggle) lucha f

contest[2] [kənˈtest] v/t leadership presentarse como candidato a; decision, will impugnar

contestant [kənˈtestənt] concursante m/f; in sport competidor(a) m(f)

context ['kɑːntekst] contexto m

continent ['kɑːntɪnənt] continente m; **continental** continental

continual [kənˈtɪnjʊəl] continuo; **continually** continuamente; **continuation** continuación f; **continue** continuar; **continuous** continuo; **continuously** continuamente

contort [kənˈtɔːrt] face contraer; body contorsionar

contraception [kɑːntrəˈsepʃn] anticoncepción f; **contraceptive** anticonceptivo m

contract[1] ['kɑːntrækt] n contrato m

contract[2] [kənˈtrækt] **1** v/i (shrink) contraerse **2** v/t illness contraer

contractor [kənˈtræktər] contratista *m/f*; **contractual** [kən'træktuəl] contractual

contradict [kɑːntrə'dɪkt] *statement* desmentir; *person* contradecir; **contradiction** contradicción *f*; **contradictory** contradictorio

contrary[1] ['kɑːntrərɪ] **1** *adj* contrario; **~ to** al contrario de **2** *n*: **on the ~** al contrario

contrary[2] [kən'treri] *adj* (*perverse*) difícil

contrast ['kɑːntræst] **1** *n* contraste *m* **2** *v/t* & *v/i* contrastar; **contrasting** opuesto

contravene [kɑːntrə'viːn] contravenir

contribute [kən'trɪbjuːt] **1** *v/i* contribuir (**to** a) **2** *v/t* *money, suggestion* contribuir con, aportar; **contribution** contribución *f*; *to political party, church* donación *f*; **contributor** *of money* donante *m/f*; *to magazine* colaborador(a) *m(f)*

control [kən'trəʊl] **1** *n* control *m*; **be in ~ of** controlar **2** *v/t* controlar

controversial [kɑːntrə'vɜːrʃl] polémico, controvertido; **controversy** polémica *f*, controversia *f*

convenience [kən'viːnɪəns] conveniencia *f*; **convenience store** tienda *f* de barrio; **convenient** conveniente; *time* oportuno

convent ['kɑːnvənt] convento *m*

convention [kən'venʃn] con-

vención *f*; (*meeting*) congreso *m*; **conventional** convencional

conversation [kɑːnvər'seɪʃn] conversación *f*; **conversational** coloquial

conversion [kən'vɜːrʃn] conversión *f*; **convert 1** *n* converso(-a) *m(f)* (**to** a) **2** *v/t* convertir; **convertible** *car* descapotable *m*

convey [kən'veɪ] (*transmit*) transmitir; (*carry*) transportar; **conveyor belt** cinta *f* transportadora

convict 1 ['kɑːnvɪkt] *n* convicto(-a) *m(f)* **2** [kən'vɪkt] *v/t* LAW: **~ s.o. of sth** declarar a alguien culpable de algo; **conviction** LAW condena *f*; (*belief*) convicción *f*

convince [kən'vɪns] convencer

convoy ['kɑːnvɔɪ] convoy *m*

cook [kʊk] **1** *n* cocinero(-a) *m(f)* **2** *v/t* & *v/i* cocinar; **cookbook** libro *m* de cocina; **cookery** cocina *f*; **cookie** galleta *f*; **cooking** cocina *f*

cool [kuːl] **1** *n*: **keep one's ~** F mantener la calma **2** *adj* fresco; *drink* frío; (*calm*) tranquilo; (*unfriendly*) frío; F (*great*) *Span* guay *P*, *L.Am.* chévere *P*, *Mex* padre *P*, *Rpl* copante *P* **3** *v/i* enfriarse; *of tempers* calmarse **4** *v/t*: **~ it** F cálmate

♦ **cool down** **1** *v/i* enfriarse; *of weather* refrescar; *of tempers* calmarse **2** *v/t* *food* enfriar; *fig* calmar

cooperate [kouˈɑːpəreɪt] cooperar; cooperation coopera-
ción f; cooperative (helpful) cooperativo

coordinate [kouˈɔːrdɪnɪt]
coordinar; coordination coordinación f

cop [kɑːp] F poli m/f F

cope [koup] arreglárselas; ~
with poder con

copier [ˈkɑːpɪər] machine fotocopiadora f

copper [ˈkɑːpər] cobre m

copy [ˈkɑːpɪ] 1 n copia f; of
book ejemplar m 2 v/t copiar

cord [kɔːrd] (string) cuerda f,
cordel m; (cable) cable m

cordon [ˈkɔːrdn] cordón m

cords [kɔːrdz] pantalo-
nes mpl de pana

core [kɔːr] 1 n of fruit corazón
m; of party núcleo m 2 adj issue central

cork [kɔːrk] corcho m; cork-
screw sacacorchos m inv

corn [kɔːrn] grain maíz m

corner [ˈkɔːrnər] 1 n of page,
street esquina f; of room rincón m; on road curva f; in
soccer córner m, saque m
de esquina 2 v/t person arrinconar; ~ a market monopo-
lizar un mercado 3 v/i of
driver, car girar

coronary [ˈkɑːrənerɪ] 1 adj
coronario 2 n infarto de
miocardio

coroner [ˈkɑːrənər] oficial encargado de investigar muertes
sospechosas

corporal [ˈkɔːrpərəl] cabo

m/f; corporal punishment
castigo m corporal

corporate [ˈkɔːrpərət] COM
corporativo, de empresa;
corporation (business) sociedad f anónima

corpse [kɔːrps] cadáver m

corral [kəˈræl] corral m

correct [kəˈrekt] 1 adj correcto; time exacto 2 v/t corregir;
correction corrección f;
correctly correctamente

correspond [kɑːrɪˈspɑːnd]
(match) corresponderse;
correspondence corres-
pondencia f; correspond-
ent (reporter) corresponsal
m/f

corridor [ˈkɔːrɪdər] pasillo m

corroborate [kəˈrɑːbəreɪt]
corroborar

corrosion [kəˈrouʒn] corrosión f

corrupt [kəˈrʌpt] 1 adj corrupto; COMPUT corrompido
2 v/t corromper; (bribe) sobornar; corruption corrupción f

cosmetic [kɑːzˈmetɪk] cosmético; fig superficial; cosmetics cosméticos mpl;
cosmetic surgery cirugía f
estética

cosmopolitan [kɑːzməˈpɑː-
lɪtən] cosmopolita

cost [kɑːst] 1 n also fig costo
m, Span coste m 2 v/t costar;
project estimar el costo de;
how much does it ~
¿cuánto cuesta?

Costa Rica [kɑːstəˈriːkə] Cos-

ta Rica; **Costa Rican 1** *adj*
costarricense **2** *n* costarricense *m/f*

'**cost driver** COM, FIN generador *m* de costes; **cost-effective** rentable; **cost of living** costo *m* or *Span* coste *m* de la vida

costume ['kɑːstuːm] *for actor* traje *m*

cosy *Br* ☞ **cozy**

cot [kɑːt] *(camp-bed)* catre *m*

cottage ['kɑːtɪdʒ] casa *f* de campo, casita *f*

cotton ['kɑːtn] **1** *n* algodón *m* **2** *adj* de algodón; **cotton candy** algodón *m* dulce; **cotton wool** *Br* algodón *m* (hidrófilo)

couch [kaʊtʃ] sofá *m*; **couch potato** F teleadicto(-a) *m(f)* F

cough [kɑːf] **1** *n* tos *f* **2** *v/i* toser; *to get attention* carraspear; **cough medicine** jarabe *m* para la tos

could [kʊd]: **~ I have my key?**
¿me podría dar la llave?; **~ you help me?** ¿me podrías ayudar?; **you ~ be right** puede que tengas razón; **you ~ have warned me!** ¡me podías haber avisado!

council ['kaʊnsl] consejo *m*; **councilor** concejal(a) *m(f)*

'**counsel** ['kaʊnsl] **1** *n (advice)* consejo *m*; *(lawyer)* abogado(-a) *m(f)* **2** *v/t (advise)* aconsejar; *person* ofrecer apoyo psicológico a; **counseling**, *Br* **counselling** apo-

yo *m* psicológico; **counsellor** *Br*, **counselor** *of student* orientador(a) *m(f)*; LAW abogado(-a) *m(f)*

count [kaʊnt] **1** *n* cuenta *f*; *(action of ~ing)* recuento *m* **2** *v/t & v/i* contar

♦ **count on** contar con

countdown cuenta *f* atrás

counter ['kaʊntər] *in shop* mostrador *m*; *in café* barra *f*; *in game* ficha *f*

'**counteract** contrarrestar; **counter-attack 1** *n* contraataque *m* **2** *v/i* contraatacar; **counterclockwise** en sentido contrario al de las agujas del reloj; **counterespionage** contraespionaje *m*; **counterfeit 1** *v/t* falsificar **2** *adj* falso; **counterpart** *(person)* homólogo(-a) *m(f)*; **counterproductive** contraproducente

countless ['kaʊntlɪs] incontables

country ['kʌntrɪ] país *m*; *as opposed to town* campo *m*

county ['kaʊntɪ] condado *m*

coup [kuː] POL golpe *m* (de Estado); *fig* golpe *m* de efecto

couple ['kʌpl] pareja *f*; **a ~ of** un par de

courage ['kʌrɪdʒ] valor *m*, coraje *m*; **courageous** valiente

courier ['kʊrɪr] mensajero(-a) *m(f)*; *with tourist party* guía *m/f*

course [kɔːrs] *(lessons)* curso

m; *of meal* plato m; *of ship, plane* rumbo m; *for horse race* circuito m; *for golf* campo m; *for marathon* recorrido m; **of ~** por supuesto

court ['kɔːrt] LAW tribunal m; (*courthouse*) palacio m de justicia; SP pista f, cancha f; **court case** proceso m, causa f

courtesy ['kɜːrtəsɪ] cortesía f

'**courthouse** palacio m de justicia; **courtroom** sala f de juicios; **courtyard** patio m

cousin ['kʌzn] primo(-a) m(f)

cover ['kʌvər] **1** n *protective* funda f; *of book, magazine* portada f; (*shelter*) protección f; (*insurance*) cobertura f **2** v/t cubrir

♦ **cover up 1** v/t cubrir; *scandal* encubrir **2** v/i disimular

coverage ['kʌvərɪdʒ] by *media* cobertura f informativa

covert ['kouvɜːrt] encubierto

'**cover-up** encubrimiento m

cow [kau] vaca f

coward ['kauərd] cobarde m/f; **cowardice** cobardía f

'**cowboy** vaquero m

co-worker ['kouwɜːrkər] compañero(a) m(f) de trabajo

cozy ['kouzɪ] *room* acogedor; *job* cómodo

crab [kræb] cangrejo m

crack [kræk] **1** n grieta f; *in cup* raja f; (*joke*) chiste m (*malo*) **2** v/t *cup* rajar; *nut*

cascar; *code* descifrar; F (*solve*) resolver **3** v/i rajarse;

crack (**cocaine**) crack m;

cracked *cup* rajado; **cracker** *to eat* galleta f salada

cradle ['kreɪdl] cuna f

craft[1] [kræft] NAUT embarcación f

craft[2] [kræft] (*skill*) arte m; (*trade*) oficio m; **craftsman** artesano m; **crafty** astuto

crag [kræg] *rock* peñasco m

cram [kræm] embutir

cramps [kræmps] calambre m; **stomach ~** retorcijón m

crane [kreɪn] **1** n *machine* grúa f **2** v/t: **~ one's neck** estirar el cuello

crank [kræŋk] *person* maniático(-a) m(f); **cranky** (*bad-tempered*) gruñón

crap [kræp] P mierda f P; (*nonsense*) *Span* gilipolleces fpl P, *L.Am.* pendejadas fpl P, *Rpl* boludeces fpl P

crash [kræʃ] **1** n *noise* estruendo m; *accident* accidente m; COM quiebra f, crac m; COMPUT bloqueo m **2** v/i *of car, airplane* estrellarse (**into** con); *of market* hundirse; COMPUT bloquearse **3** v/i *car* estrellar; **crash course** curso m intensivo; **crash diet** dieta f drástica; **crash helmet** casco m protector; **crash-land** realizar un aterrizaje forzoso

crate [kreɪt] caja f

crater ['kreɪtər] cráter m

crave [kreɪv] ansiar; **craving**

ansia f m

crawl [krɔːl] **1** n in swimming crol m **2** v/i on floor arrastrarse; of baby andar a gatas; (move slowly) avanzar lentamente

crayon ['kreɪən] lápiz m de color

craze [kreɪz] locura f (**for** de); **crazy** loco

creak [kriːk] of hinge chirriar; of floor, shoes crujir; **creaky** que chirría; floor, shoes que cruje

cream [kriːm] n for skin crema f; for coffee, cake nata f **2** adj crema

crease [kriːs] **1** n arruga f; deliberate raya f **2** v/t arrugar

create [kriː'eɪt] crear; **creation** creación f; **creative** creativo; **creator** creador(a) m(f) f

creature ['kriːtʃər] criatura f

credibility [kredə'bɪlətɪ] credibilidad f; **credible** creíble

credit ['kredɪt] crédito m; **creditable** estimable; **credit card** tarjeta f de crédito; **credit limit** límite m de crédito; **creditor** acreedor(a) m(f); **creditworthy** solvente

creep [kriːp] **1** n pej asqueroso(-a) m(f) **2** v/i moverse sigilosamente; **creepy** F espeluznante F

cremate [krɪ'meɪt] incinerar; **cremation** incineración f

crest [krest] of hill cima f; of bird cresta f

crevice ['krevɪs] grieta f

crew [kruː] tripulación f; **crew cut** rapado m

crib [krɪb] for baby cuna f

crime [kraɪm] delito m; serious, also fig crimen m; **criminal 1** n delincuente m/f, criminal m/f **2** adj criminal; (LAW: not civil) penal; (shameful) vergonzoso; act delictivo

crimson ['krɪmzn] carmesí

cripple ['krɪpl] **1** n inválido(-a) m(f) **2** v/t person dejar inválido; fig paralizar

crisis ['kraɪsɪs] crisis f inv

crisp [krɪsp] weather fresco; lettuce crujiente; dollar bill flamante; **crisps** Br patatas fpl fritas, L.Am papas fpl fritas

criterion [kraɪ'tɪərɪən] criterio m

critic ['krɪtɪk] crítico(-a) m(f); **critical** crítico; moment decisivo; **criticism** crítica f; **criticize** criticar

crocodile ['krɒkədaɪl] cocodrilo m

crony ['krəʊnɪ] F amiguete m/f F

crook [krʊk] ladrón (-ona) m(f); dishonest trader granuja m/f; **crooked** torcido; (dishonest) deshonesto

crop [krɒp] **1** n also fig cosecha f; plant grown cultivo m **2** v/t hair cortar; photo recortar

◆ **crop up** salir

cross [krɒs] **1** adj (angry) enfadado **2** n cruz f **3** v/t (go across) cruzar; **~ o.s.** REL

santiguarse **4** v/i (*go across*)
cruzar; *of lines* cruzarse
◆ **cross off** tachar
'crosscheck n comprobación f **2** v/t comprobar;
cross-examine interrogar;
cross-eyed bizco; **crossing**
NAUT travesía f; **crossroads**
also fig encrucijada f;
cross-walk paso m de peatones;
crossword (*puzzle*) crucigrama m
crotch [krɒtʃ] entrepierna f
crouch [kraʊtʃ] agacharse
crowd [kraʊd] multitud f, muchedumbre f; *at sports event*
público m; **crowded** abarrotado (*with* de)
crown [kraʊn] corona f
crucial ['kruːʃl] crucial
crucifix ['kruːsɪfɪks] crucifijo
m; **crucifixion** crucifixión
f; **crucify** *also* fig crucificar
crude [kruːd] **1** *adj* (*vulgar*)
grosero; (*unsophisticated*)
primitivo **2** n: ~ (*oil*) crudo
m
cruel ['kruːəl] cruel (*to* con);
cruelty crueldad f
cruise [kruːz] **1** n crucero m **2**
v/i *of people* hacer un crucero; *of car* ir a la velocidad de
crucero; *of plane* volar
crumb [krʌm] miga f
crumble ['krʌmbl] *of bread*
desmigajarse; *of stonework*
desmenuzarse; fig: *of opposition* desmoronarse
crumple ['krʌmpl] (*crease*)
arrugar
crush [krʌʃ] **1** n (*crowd*) muchedumbre f **2** v/t aplastar;
(*crease*) arrugar
crust [krʌst] *on bread* corteza
f
crutch [krʌtʃ] *walking aid* muleta f
cry [kraɪ] **1** n (*call*) grito m **2**
v/i (*weep*) llorar
◆ **cry out** gritar
cryptic ['krɪptɪk] críptico
crystal ['krɪstl] cristal m
cu [siːjuː] *in texting* A2
(*adiós*)
Cuba ['kjuːbə] Cuba; **Cuban**
1 *adj* cubano **2** n cubano(-a)
m(f)
cube [kjuːb] cubo m; **cubic**
cúbico
cubicle ['kjuːbɪkl] (*changing*
room) cubículo m
cuddle ['kʌdl] abrazar
cue [kjuː] *for actor etc* pie m;
for pool taco m
cuff [kʌf] *of shirt* puño m; *of*
pants vuelta f; (*blow*) cachete m
culminate ['kʌlmɪneɪt] culminar (*in* en); **culmination** culminación f
culprit ['kʌlprɪt] culpable
m/f
cult [kʌlt] (*sect*) secta f
cultivate ['kʌltɪveɪt] *also* fig
cultivar; **cultivated** *person*
culto; **cultivation** *of land*
cultivo m
cultural ['kʌltʃərəl] cultural;
culture cultura f; **cultured**
culto
cumulative ['kjuːmjʊlətɪv]
acumulativo

cunning [ˈkʌnɪŋ] **1** n astucia f **2** adj astuto

cup [kʌp] taza f; trophy copa f

cupboard [ˈkʌbərd] armario m

curb [kɜːrb] **1** n of street bordillo m; on powers etc freno m **2** v/t frenar

cure [kjʊr] **1** n MED cura f **2** v/t MED, meat curar

curiosity [kjʊriˈɑːsəti] curiosidad f; curioso curioso

curl [kɜːrl] **1** n in hair rizo m; of smoke voluta f **2** v/t hair rizar; (wind) enroscar **3** v/i of hair rizarse; of paper ondularse

◆ **curl up** acurrucarse

curly [ˈkɜːrlɪ] hair rizado; tail enroscado

currency [ˈkʌrənsɪ] money moneda f; **foreign ~** divisas fpl; current **1** n in sea, ELEC corriente f **2** adj actual; **current affairs** la actualidad

curse [kɜːrs] **1** n (spell) maldición f; (swearword) palabrota f **2** v/t maldecir **3** v/i (swear) decir palabrotas

cursor [ˈkɜːrsər] COMPUT cursor m

cursory [ˈkɜːrsərɪ] superficial

curt [kɜːrt] brusco, seco

curtain [ˈkɜːrtn] cortina f; THEA telón m

curve [kɜːrv] **1** n curva f **2** v/i curvarse

cushion [ˈkʊʃn] **1** n cojín m **2** v/t blow, fall amortiguar

custody [ˈkʌstədɪ] of children custodia f; **in ~** LAW detenido

custom [ˈkʌstəm] costumbre f; COM clientela f; **customer** cliente(-a) m(f); **customer service** atención f al cliente

customs [ˈkʌstəmz] aduana f; **customs officer** funcionario(-a) m(f) de aduanas

cut [kʌt] **1** n (reduction) recorte m (**in** de) **2** v/t cortar; (reduce) recortar; hours acortar; **get one's hair ~** cortarse el pelo

◆ **cut down 1** v/t tree talar, cortar **2** v/i in expenses gastar menos; in smoking fumar menos

◆ **cut off** cortar; (isolate) aislar

◆ **cut up** trocear

cutback recorte m

cute [kjuːt] guapo, lindo; (clever) listo

cut-off date fecha f límite; **cut-price** rebajado; store de productos rebajados; **cut-throat** competition despiadado; **cutting 1** n from newspaper recorte m **2** adj remark hiriente

cyber ... [ˈsaɪbər] ciber...

cycle [ˈsaɪkl] **1** n bicicleta f; of events ciclo m **2** v/i ir en bicicleta; **cycling** ciclismo m; **cyclist** ciclista m/f

cylinder [ˈsɪlɪndər] cilindro m; **cylindrical** cilíndrico

cynic [ˈsɪnɪk] escéptico(-a) m(f); **cynical** escéptico; **cynicism** escepticismo m

Czech [tʃek] **1** adj checo; **the ~**

Republic la República Checa **2** n person checo(-a) m(f);

language checho m

D

DA [diːˈeɪ] (= **district attorney**) fiscal m/f (del distrito)

◆ **dabble in** ['dæbl] ser aficionado a

dad [dæd] talking to him papá m; talking about him padre m

daily ['deɪlɪ] **1** n (paper) diario m **2** adj diario

'**dairy products** productos mpl lácteos

dam [dæm] **1** n for water presa f **2** v/t river embalsar

damage ['dæmɪdʒ] **1** n daños mpl; to reputation etc daño m **2** v/t also fig dañar; **damages** LAW daños mpl y perjuicios; **damaging** perjudicial

damn [dæm] **F 1** int ¡mecachis! **F 2** adj maldito **F 3** adv muy; **damning** evidence condenatorio; report crítico

damp [dæmp] húmedo

dance [dæns] **1** n baile m **2** v/i bailar; **dancer** bailarín (-ina) m(f); **dancing** baile m

Dane [deɪn] danés(-esa) m(f)

danger ['deɪndʒər] peligro m; **dangerous** peligroso

dangle ['dæŋgl] **1** v/t balancear **2** v/i colgar

Danish ['deɪnɪʃ] **1** adj danés **2** n language danés m; **Danish** (pastry) pastel m de hojaldre (dulce)

dare [der] atreverse; ~ **to do** sth atreverse a hacer algo; ~ **s.o. to do sth** desafiar a alguien para que haga algo; **daring** atrevido

dark [dɑːrk] **1** n oscuridad f **2** adj oscuro; **dark glasses** gafas fpl oscuras, L.Am. lentes fpl oscuras; **darkness** oscuridad f

darling ['dɑːrlɪŋ] cielo m

dart [dɑːrt] **1** n for throwing dardo m **2** v/i lanzarse

dash [dæʃ] **1** n punctuation raya f; (small amount) chorrito m **2** v/i correr **3** v/t hopes frustrar; **dashboard** salpicadero m

data ['deɪtə] datos mpl; **database** base f de datos

date[1] [deɪt] fruit dátil m

date[2] [deɪt] fecha f; (meeting) cita f; (person) pareja f; **out of** ~ clothes pasado de moda; passport caducado; **up to** ~ al día; dated anticuado

daughter ['dɔːtər] hija f. **daughter-in-law** nuera f

dawn [dɔːn] amanecer m, alba f; fig albores mpl

day [deɪ] día m; **the** ~ **after** el día siguiente; **the** ~ **after tomorrow** pasado mañana; **the** ~ **before** el día anterior; **the** ~ **before yesterday** anteayer; **in those** ~s en aque-

331

llos tiempos; **the other ~** (*recently*) el otro día; **daybreak** amanecer *m*, alba *f*; **daydream 1** *n* fantasía *f* **2** *v/i* soñar despierto; **daylight** luz *f* del día; **day spa** centro *m* de salud

dazed [deɪzd] aturdido

dazzle ['dæzl] *also fig* deslumbrar

dead [ded] **1** adj muerto; *battery* agotado; *light bulb* fundido; *place* muerto **F 2** *adv* F (*very*) tela de F; **~ beat, ~ tired** hecho polvo **3** *npl*: **the ~** los muertos; **dead end** *street* callejón *m* sin salida; **dead heat** empate *m*; **deadline** fecha *f* tope; *for newspaper* hora *f* de cierre; **meet a ~** cumplir un plazo; **deadlock** *in talks* punto *m* muerto; **deadly** *mortal*

deaf [def] sordo; **deafening** ensordecedor; **deafness** sordera *f*

deal [diːl] **1** *n* acuerdo *m*; **a great ~** mucho(s) **2** *v/t cards* repartir

◆ **deal in** COM comerciar con

◆ **deal with** *tratar; situation* hacer frente a; *customer, applications* encargarse de; (*do business with*) hacer negocios con

dealer ['diːlər] comerciante *m/f*; (*drug ~*) traficante *m/f*; **dealing** (*drug ~*) tráfico *m*; **dealings** (*business ~*) tratos *mpl*

dear [dɪr] querido; (*expensive*)

caro; *Dear Sir* Muy Sr. Mío

death [deθ] muerte *f*; **death toll** saldo *m* de víctimas mortales

debatable [dɪ'beɪtəbl] discutible; **debate 1** *n* debate *m* **2** *v/t & v/i* debatir

debit ['debɪt] **1** *n* cargo *m* **2** *v/t account* cargar en; *amount* cargar; **debit card** tarjeta *f* de débito

debris [də'briː] *nsg of building* escombros *mpl*; *of airplane* restos *mpl*

debt [det] deuda *f*; **be in ~** estar endeudado; **debtor** deudor(-a) *m(f)*

debug [diː'bʌg] COMPUT depurar

decade ['dekeɪd] década *f*

decadent ['dekədənt] decadente

decaffeinated [dɪ'kæfɪneɪtɪd] descafeinado

decay [dɪ'keɪ] **1** *n of plant* putrefacción *f*; *of civilization* declive *m*; *in teeth* caries *f inv* **2** *v/i of plant* pudrirse; *of civilization* decaer; *of teeth* cariarse

deceased [dɪ'siːst]: **the ~** el difunto / la difunta

deceit [dɪ'siːt] engaño *m*, mentira *f*; **deceitful** mentiroso; **deceive** engañar

December [dɪ'sembər] diciembre *m*

decency ['diːsənsɪ] decencia *f*; **decent** decente

deception [dɪ'sepʃn] engaño *m*; **deceptive** engañoso

decide [dɪ'saɪd] decidir; **de-cided** (*definite*) tajante

decimal ['desɪml] decimal *m*

decipher [dɪ'saɪfər] descifrar

decision [dɪ'sɪʒn] decisión *f*; **decisive** decidido; (*crucial*) decisivo

deck [dek] *of ship* cubierta *f*; *of cards* baraja *f*

declaration [dekləˈreɪʃn] declaración *f*; **declare** declarar

decline [dɪ'klaɪn] **1** *n* descenso *m*; *in standards* caída *f*; *in health* empeoramiento *m* **2** *v/t invitation* declinar **3** *v/i* (*refuse*) rehusar; (*decrease*) declinar; *of health* empeorar

decode [diːˈkoʊd] descodificar

décor ['deɪkɔːr] decoración *f*

decorate ['dekəreɪt] *with paint* pintar; *with paper* empapelar; (*adorn*) decorar; *soldier* condecorar; **decoration** *paint* pintado *m*; *paper* empapelado *m*; (*ornament*) decoración *f*; **decorator** (*interior ~*) decorador(a) *m(f)*

decoy ['diːkɔɪ] señuelo *m*

decrease 1 [ˈdiːkriːs] *n* disminución *f* (*in* de) **2** [dɪˈkriːs] *v/t & v/i* disminuir

dedicate ['dedɪkeɪt] *book* dedicar; **dedicated** dedicado; **dedication** dedicación *f*; *in book* dedicatoria *f*

deduce [dɪ'djuːs] deducir

deduct [dɪ'dʌkt] descontar; **deduction** deducción *f*

deed [diːd] (*act*) acción *f*, obra *f*; LAW escritura *f*

deep [diːp] profundo; *color* intenso; **deepen 1** *v/t* profundizar **2** *v/i* hacerse más profundo; *of mystery* agudizarse; **deep freeze** congelador *m*

deer [dɪr] ciervo *m*

deface [dɪ'feɪs] desfigurar

defamation [defəˈmeɪʃn] difamación *f*; **defamatory** difamatorio

defeat [dɪ'fiːt] **1** *n* derrota *f* **2** *v/t* derrotar

defect ['diːfekt] defecto *m*; **defective** defectuoso

de'fence *Br* ☞ **defense**

defend [dɪ'fend] defender; **defendant** acusado(-a) *m(f)*; *in civil case* demandado(-a) *m(f)*; **defense** defensa *f*; **defenseless** indefenso; **Defense Secretary** POL ministro(-a) *m(f)* de Defensa; *in USA* secretario *m* de Defensa; **defensive 1** *n*: **go on the ~** ponerse a la defensiva **2** *adj* defensivo

defer [dɪ'fɜːr] (*postpone*) aplazar, diferir

defiance [dɪ'faɪəns] desafío *m*; **defiant** desafiante

deficiency [dɪ'fɪʃənsɪ] deficiencia *f*

deficit ['defɪsɪt] déficit *m*

define [dɪ'faɪn] definir

definite ['defɪnɪt] definitivo; *improvement* claro; (*certain*) seguro; **definitely** con certeza, sin lugar a dudas

definition [defɪ'nɪʃn] definición *f*

deformity [dɪ'fɔːrmɪtɪ] deformidad *f*

defrost [diː'frɒst] descongelar

defuse [diː'fjuːz] *bomb* desactivar; *situation* calmar

defy [dɪ'faɪ] desafiar

degrading [dɪ'greɪdɪŋ] degradante

degree [dɪ'griː] grado *m; from university* título *m*

dehydrated [diːhaɪ'dreɪtɪd] deshidratado

deign [deɪn]: **~ to** dignarse a

dejected [dɪ'dʒektɪd] abatido, desanimado

delay [dɪ'leɪ] **1** *n* retraso *m* **2** *v/t* retrasar; **be ~ed** llevar retraso **3** *v/i* retrasarse

delegate ['delɪgeɪt] **1** *n* delegado(-a) *m(f)* **2** ['delɪbərət] *v/t task* delegar; *person* delegar en; **delegation** delegación *f*

delete [dɪ'liːt] borrar; (*cross out*) tachar; **deletion** borrado *m*

deliberate 1 [dɪ'lɪbərət] *adj* deliberado **2** [dɪ'lɪbəreɪt] *v/i* deliberar; **deliberately** deliberadamente

delicate ['delɪkət] delicado; *health* frágil

delicatessen [delɪkə'tesn] tienda de productos alimenticios de calidad

delicious [dɪ'lɪʃəs] delicioso

delight [dɪ'laɪt] placer *m*; **delighted** encantado; **delightful** encantador

deliver [dɪ'lɪvər] entregar, repartir; *message* dar; *baby* dar

a luz; *speech* pronunciar; **delivery** entrega *f*, reparto *m; of baby* parto *m*; **delivery date** fecha *f* de entrega

de luxe [də'lʌks] de lujo

demand [dɪ'mænd] **1** *n* exigencia *f; by union* reivindicación *f*, COM demanda *f; in ~* solicitado **2** *v/t* exigir; (*require*) requerir; **demanding** *job* que exige mucho; *person* exigente

demo ['deməu] (*protest*) manifestación *f; of video etc* maqueta *f*

democracy [dɪ'mɒkrəsɪ] democracia *f*; **democrat** demócrata *m/f*; **democratic** democrático

demolish [dɪ'mɒlɪʃ] demoler; *argument* destruir; **demolition** demolición *f; of argument* destrucción *f*

demonstrate ['demənstreɪt] **1** *v/t* demostrar **2** *v/i politically* manifestarse; **demonstration** demostración *f*; (*protest*) manifestación *f*; **demonstrator** (*protester*) manifestante *m/f*

demoralized [dɪ'mɒrəlaɪzd] desmoralizado; **demoralizing** desmoralizador

demote [diː'məut] degradar

den [den] (*study*) estudio *m*

denial [dɪ'naɪəl] *of accusation* negación *f; of request* denegación *f*

denim ['denɪm] tela *f* vaquera

Denmark ['denmɑːrk] Dinamarca

denomination [dɪnɑ:m-ɪ'neɪʃn] *of money* valor *m*; *religious* confesión *f*

dense [dens] denso; *foliage* espeso; *crowd* compacto; **density** *of population* densidad *f*

dent [dent] **1** *n* abolladura *f* **2** *v/t* abollar

dental ['dentl] dental

dented ['dentɪd] abollado

dentist ['dentɪst] dentista *m/f*; **dentures** dentadura *f* postiza

Denver boot ['denvər] cepo *m*

deny [dɪ'naɪ] *charge* negar; *right, request* denegar

deodorant [di:'oʊdərənt] desodorante *m*

department [dɪ'pɑ:rtmənt] departamento *m*; *of government* ministerio *m*; **Department of State** Ministerio *m* de Asuntos Exteriores; **department store** grandes almacenes *mpl*

departure [dɪ'pɑ:rtʃər] salida *f*; *from job* marcha *f*; *(deviation)* desviación *f*; **departure lounge** sala *f* de embarque; **departure time** hora *f* de salida

depend [dɪ'pend] depender; **that ~s** depende; **dependence** dependencia *f*

depict [dɪ'pɪkt] describir

deplorable [dɪ'plɔ:rəbl] deplorable; **deplore** deplorar

deploy [dɪ'plɔɪ] *(use)* utilizar; *(position)* desplegar

deport [dɪ'pɔ:rt] deportar; **deportation** deportación *f*

deposit [dɪ'pɑ:zɪt] **1** *n* depósito *m*; *of coal* yacimiento *m* **2** *v/t money* depositar, *Span* ingresar; *(put down)* depositar; **deposition** LAW declaración *f*

depot ['di:poʊ] *for storage* depósito *m*

depreciation [dɪpri:ʃɪ'eɪʃn] FIN depreciación *f*

depress [dɪ'pres] *person* deprimir; **depressed** deprimido; **depressing** deprimente; **depression** depresión *f*; *meteorological* borrasca *f*

deprivation [deprɪ'veɪʃn] privación *f*; **deprive** privar; **deprived** desfavorecido

depth [depθ] profundidad *f*; *of color* intensidad *f*; **in ~** en profundidad

deputy ['depjʊti] segundo(-a) *m(f)*

derail [dɪ'reɪl]: **be ~ed** descarrilar

derelict ['derəlɪkt] en ruinas

deride [dɪ'raɪd] ridiculizar, mofarse de; **derision** burla *f*, mofa *f*; **derisory** irrisorio

derivative [dɪ'rɪvətɪv] poco original; **derive** obtener; **be ~d from** *of word* derivar(se) de

dermatologist [dɜ:rmə'tɑ:lədʒɪst] dermatólogo(-a) *m(f)*

derogatory [dɪ'rɑ:gətɔ:ri] despectivo

descendant [dɪ'sendənt] descendiente *m/f*; **descent** descenso *m*; *(ancestry)* ascendencia *f*

describe [dɪˈskraɪb] describir; **description** descripción *f*

desegregate [diːˈsegrəget] acabar con la segregación racial en

desert[1] [ˈdezərt] *n* desierto *m*

desert[2] [dɪˈzɜːrt] **1** *v/t* abandonar **2** *v/i of soldier* desertar; **deserted** desierto; **deserter** MIL desertor(a) *m(f)*; **desertion** abandono *m*; MIL deserción *f*

deserve [dɪˈzɜːrv] merecer

design [dɪˈzaɪn] **1** *n* diseño *m*; *(pattern)* motivo **2** *v/t* diseñar

designate [ˈdezɪɡneɪt] *person* designar; *area* declarar

designer [dɪˈzaɪnər] diseñador(a) *m(f)*; **designer clothes** ropa *f* de diseño

desirable [dɪˈzaɪrəbl] deseable; *house* apetecible; **desire** deseo *m*

desk [desk] *in classroom* pupitre *m*; *in office* mesa *f*; *in hotel* recepción *f*; **desk clerk** recepcionista *m/f*; **desktop publishing** autoedición *f*

desolate [ˈdesələt] *place* desolado

despair [dɪˈsper] **1** *n* desesperación *f*; *in* ~ desesperado **2** *v/i* desesperarse; **desperate** desesperado; **be** ~ **for sth** necesitar algo desesperadamente; **desperation** desesperación *f*

despicable [dɪsˈpɪkəbl] despreciable; **despise** despreciar

despite [dɪˈspaɪt] a pesar de

dessert [dɪˈzɜːrt] postre *m*

destination [destɪˈneɪʃn] destino *m*

destroy [dɪˈstrɔɪ] destruir; **destroyer** NAUT destructor *m*; **destruction** destrucción *f*; **destructive** destructivo; *child* revoltoso

detach [dɪˈtætʃ] separar, soltar; **detached** *(objective)* distanciado; **detachment** *(objectivity)* distancia *f*

detail [ˈdiːteɪl] detalle *m*; **detailed** detallado

detain [dɪˈteɪn] *(hold back)* entretener; *as prisoner* detener; **detainee** detenido(-a) *m(f)*

detect [dɪˈtekt] percibir; *of device* detectar; **detection** *of criminal* descubrimiento *m*; *of smoke etc* detección *f*; **detective** detective *m/f*; **detector** detector *m*

détente [ˈdeɪtɑːnt] POL distensión *f*

deter [dɪˈtɜːr] disuadir

detergent [dɪˈtɜːrdʒənt] detergente *m*

deteriorate [dɪˈtɪriəreɪt] deteriorarse; *of weather* empeorar

determination [dɪtɜːrmɪˈneɪʃn] determinación *f*; **determine** *(establish)* determinar; **determined** resuelto, decidido

detest [dɪ'test] detestar; **detestable** detestable

detour ['diːtʊr] rodeo *m*; (*diversion*) desvío *m*

devaluation [diːvæljuˈeɪʃn] devaluación *f*; **devalue** devaluar

devastate ['devəsteɪt] devastar; *fig: person* asolar

develop [dɪ'veləp] **1** *v/t film* revelar; *site* urbanizar; *business* desarrollar; (*improve on*) perfeccionar; *illness* contraer **2** *v/i* (*grow*) desarrollarse; *developing country* país *m* en vías de desarrollo; *development of film* revelado *m*; *of site* urbanización *f*; *of business, country* desarrollo *m*; (*event*) acontecimiento *m*; (*improving*) perfeccionamiento *m*

device [dɪ'vaɪs] *tool* aparato *m*, dispositivo *m*

devil ['devl] *also fig* diablo *m*

devise [dɪ'vaɪz] idear

devote [dɪ'vəʊt] dedicar (**to** a); **devoted** *son etc* afectuoso; **devotion** devoción *f*

devour [dɪ'vaʊər] devorar

devout [dɪ'vaʊt] devoto

diabetes [daɪə'biːtiːz] *nsg* diabetes *f*; **diabetic** diabético(-a) *m(f)*

diagnose ['daɪəgnəʊz] diagnosticar; **diagnosis** diagnóstico *m*

diagonal [daɪ'ægənl] diagonal; **diagonally** diagonalmente, en diagonal

diagram ['daɪəgræm] diagrama *m*

dial ['daɪl] **1** *n of clock* esfera *f*; *of instrument* cuadrante *m* **2** *v/t & v/i* TELEC marcar

dialog, *Br* **dialogue** ['daɪəlɒg] diálogo *m*

'dial tone tono *m* de marcar

diameter [daɪ'æmɪtər] diámetro *m*

diamond ['daɪmənd] diamante *m*; *shape* rombo *m*

diaper ['daɪpər] pañal *m*

diaphragm ['daɪəfræm] diafragma *m*

diarrhea, *Br* **diarrhoea** [daɪə'riːə] diarrea *f*

diary ['daɪrɪ] diario *m*; *for appointments* agenda *f*

dice [daɪs] dado *m*; *pl* dados *mpl*

dictate [dɪk'teɪt] dictar; **dictator** POL dictador(a) *m(f)*; **dictatorship** dictadura *f*

dictionary ['dɪkʃənerɪ] diccionario *m*

die [daɪ] morir

◆ **die down** *of storm* amainar; *of excitement* calmarse

◆ **die out** desaparecer

diet ['daɪət] **1** *n* dieta *f* **2** *v/i* hacer dieta

differ ['dɪfər] ser distinto; (*disagree*) discrepar; **difference** diferencia *f*; **different** diferente, distinto (**from** de); **differently** de manera diferente

difficult ['dɪfɪkəlt] difícil; **difficulty** dificultad *f*

dig [dɪg] cavar

digest [daɪ'dʒest] *also fig* digerir; **digestion** digestión *f*

digit ['dɪdʒɪt] dígito *m*; **digital** digital; **digital camera** cámara *f* digital; **digital photo** foto *f* digital

dignified ['dɪgnɪfaɪd] digno; **dignity** dignidad *f*

dilapidated [dɪ'læpɪdeɪtɪd] destartalado

dilemma [dɪ'lemə] dilema *m*

dilute [daɪ'luːt] diluir

dim [dɪm] **1** *adj room* oscuro; *light* tenue; *outline* borroso; (*stupid*) tonto **2** *v/i of lights* atenuarse

dime [daɪm] moneda de diez centavos

dimension [daɪ'menʃn] dimensión *f*

diminish [dɪ'mɪnɪʃ] disminuir

din [dɪn] estruendo *m*

dine [daɪn] *fml* cenar

dinghy ['dɪŋɪ] *small yacht* bote *m* de vela; *rubber boat* lancha *f* neumática

dining car ['daɪnɪŋ] RAIL coche *m* comedor; **dining room** comedor *m*

dinner ['dɪnər] cena *f*; *at midday* comida *f*; (*formal*) cena *f* de gala; **dinner party** cena *f*

dip [dɪp] **1** *n for food* salsa *f*; (*slope*) inclinación *f*; (*depression*) hondonada *f* **2** *v/i of road* bajar

diploma [dɪ'pləʊmə] diploma *m*

diplomacy [dɪ'pləʊməsɪ] diplomacia *f*; **diplomat** diplomático(-a) *m(f)*; **diplo-matic** diplomático

direct [daɪ'rekt] **1** *adj* directo **2** *v/t* dirigir; **direction** dirección *f*; **~s** *to a place* indicaciones *fpl*; (*instructions*) instrucciones *fpl*; *for medicine* posología *f*; *to a place* indicazioni *fpl*; *for use* istruzioni *fpl*; **directly** (*straight*) directamente; (*soon*) pronto; (*immediately*) ahora mismo; **director** director(a) *m(f)*; **directory** directorio *m*; TELEC guía *f* telefónica

dirt [dɜːrt] suciedad *f*; **dirty 1** *adj* sucio; (*pornographic*) pornográfico **2** *v/t* ensuciar

disability [dɪsə'bɪlətɪ] discapacidad *f*; **disabled** discapacitado

disadvantage [dɪsəd'væntɪdʒ] desventaja *f*; **disadvantaged** desfavorecido

disagree [dɪsə'griː] no estar de acuerdo; **disagreeable** desagradable; **disagreement** desacuerdo *m*; (*argument*) discusión *f*

disappear [dɪsə'pɪr] desaparecer; **disappearance** desaparición *f*

disappoint [dɪsə'pɔɪnt] desilusionar, decepcionar; **disappointing** decepcionante; **disappointment** desilusión *f*, decepción *f*

disapproval [dɪsə'pruːvl] desaprobación *f*; **disapprove** desaprobar, estar en contra; **disapproving** desaprobatorio

disarm [dɪs'ɑːrm] desarmar; **disarmament** desarme *m*

disaster [dɪ'zæstər] desastre *m*; **disastrous** desastroso

disband [dɪs'bænd] **1** *v/t* disolver **2** *v/i* disolverse

disbelief [dɪsbə'liːf] incredulidad *f*

disc [dɪsk] (CD) compact *m* (disc)

discard [dɪs'kɑːrd] desechar; *boyfriend* deshacerse de

disciplinary [dɪsɪ'plɪnərɪ] disciplinario; **discipline** disciplina *f*

'disc jockey disc jockey *m/f*, *Span* pinchadiscos *m/f inv*

disclaim [dɪs'kleɪm] negar

disclose [dɪs'kloʊs] revelar

disco ['dɪskoʊ] discoteca *f*

discomfort [dɪs'kʌmfərt] (*pain*) molestia *f*; (*embarrassment*) incomodidad *f*

disconcert [dɪskən'sɜːrt] desconcertar

disconnect [dɪskə'nekt] desconectar

discontent [dɪskən'tent] descontento *m*

discontinue [dɪskən'tɪnjuː] *product* dejar de producir; *bus service* suspender

discotheque ['dɪskətek] discoteca *f*

discount ['dɪskaʊnt] descuento *m*

discourage [dɪs'kʌrɪdʒ] (*dissuade*) disuadir (**from** de); (*dishearten*) desanimar

discover [dɪs'kʌvər] descubrir; **discovery** descubri-

miento *m*

discredit [dɪs'kredɪt] desacreditar

discreet [dɪ'skriːt] discreto

discrepancy [dɪ'skrepənsɪ] discrepancia *f*

discretion [dɪ'skreʃn] discreción *f*

discriminate [dɪ'skrɪmɪneɪt] discriminar (**against** contra); **discriminating** entendido; **discrimination** *sexual etc* discriminación *f*

discuss [dɪ'skʌs] discutir; *of article* analizar; **discussion** discusión *f*

disease [dɪ'ziːz] enfermedad *f*

disembark [dɪsəm'bɑːrk] desembarcar

disentangle [dɪsən'tæŋgl] desenredar

disfigure [dɪs'fɪgər] desfigurar

disgrace [dɪs'greɪs] **1** *n* vergüenza *f* **2** *v/t* deshonrar; **disgraceful** vergonzoso

disguise [dɪs'gaɪz] **1** *n* disfraz *m* **2** *v/t voice etc* cambiar; *fear, anxiety* disfrazar

disgust [dɪs'gʌst] **1** *n* asco *m* repugnancia *f* **2** *v/t* dar asco, repugnar; **disgusting** asqueroso, repugnante

dish [dɪʃ] plato *m*

disheartening [dɪs'hɑːrtnɪŋ] descorazonador

dishonest [dɪs'ɑːnɪst] deshonesto; **dishonesty** deshonestidad *f*

dishonor [dɪs'ɑːnər] deshonra f; **dishonorable** deshonroso; **dishonour** etc Br **dishonor** etc

disillusion [dɪsɪ'luːʒn] desilusionar; **disillusionment** desilusión f

disinfect [dɪsɪn'fekt] desinfectar; **disinfectant** desinfectante m

disinherit [dɪsɪn'herɪt] desheredar

disintegrate [dɪs'ɪntəgreɪt] desintegrarse; of marriage deshacerse

disjointed [dɪs'dʒɔɪntɪd] deshilvanado

disk [dɪsk] also COMPUT disco m; **disk drive** COMPUT unidad f de disco; **diskette** disquete m

dislike [dɪs'laɪk] **1** n antipatía f **2** v/t: **I ~ him** no me gusta

dislocate ['dɪsləkeɪt] dislocar

disloyal [dɪs'lɔɪəl] desleal

dismal ['dɪzməl] weather horroroso; prospect negro; person (sad) triste; person (negative) negativo; failure estrepitoso

dismantle [dɪs'mæntl] desmantelar

dismay [dɪs'meɪ] (alarm) consternación f; (disappointment) desánimo m

dismiss [dɪs'mɪs] worker despedir; suggestion rechazar; idea descartar; **dismissal** of worker despido m

disobedience [dɪsə'biːdɪəns] desobediencia f; **disobedient** desobediente; **disobey**

desobedecer

disorganized [dɪs'ɔːrgənaɪzd] desorganizado

disoriented [dɪs'ɔːrɪəntɪd] desorientado

disparaging [dɪ'spærɪdʒɪŋ] despreciativo

disparity [dɪ'spærətɪ] disparidad f

dispassionate [dɪ'spæʃənət] desapasionado

dispatch [dɪ'spætʃ] (send) enviar

disperse [dɪ'spɜːrs] of crowd dispersarse; of mist disiparse

display [dɪ'spleɪ] **1** n muestra f; in store window objetos mpl expuestos; COMPUT pantalla f **2** v/t emotion mostrar; for sale exponer; COMPUT visualizar

displease [dɪs'pliːz] desagradar; **displeasure** desagrado m

disposable [dɪ'spouzəbl] desechable; **disposal** eliminación f; **put sth at s.o.'s ~** poner algo a disposición de alguien

◆ **dispose** [dɪ'spouz] (get rid of) deshacerse de

disprove [dɪs'pruːv] refutar

dispute [dɪ'spjuːt] **1** n disputa f; industrial conflicto m laboral **2** v/t discutir; (fight over) disputarse

disqualification [dɪskwɑːlɪfɪ'keɪʃn] descalificación f; **disqualify** descalificar

disregard [dɪsrə'gɑːrd] **1** n indiferencia f **2** v/t no tener en cuenta

disreputable [dɪs'repjutəbl] poco respetable

disrespect [dɪsrə'spekt] falta f de respeto; **disrespectful** irrespetuoso

disrupt [dɪs'rʌpt] *train service* alterar; *meeting, class* interrumpir; **disruption** of *train service* alteración f; of *meeting, class* interrupción f

dissatisfaction [dɪssætɪs'fækʃn] insatisfacción f; **dissatisfied** insatisfecho

dissident ['dɪsɪdənt] disidente m/f

dissolve [dɪ'zɑːlv] **1** v/t disolver **2** v/i disolverse

distance ['dɪstəns] distancia f; **in the ~** en la lejanía; **distant** distante

distaste [dɪs'teɪst] desagrado m; **distasteful** desagradable

distinct [dɪs'tɪŋkt] (*clear*) claro; (*different*) distinto; **distinctive** característico; **distinctly** claramente, con claridad; (*decidedly*) verdaderamente

distinguish [dɪ'stɪŋgwɪʃ] distinguir (**between** entre); **distinguished** distinguido

distort [dɪ'stɔːrt] distorsionar

distract [dɪ'strækt] distraer; **distraught** [dɪ'strɔːt] angustiado, consternado

distress [dɪ'stres] **1** n sufrimiento m **2** v/t (*upset*) angustiar; **distressing** angustiante

distribute [dɪ'strɪbjuːt] distri-

buir; **distribution** distribución f; **distributor** COM distribuidor(a) m(f)

district ['dɪstrɪkt] zona f (*neighborhood*) barrio m; **district attorney** fiscal m/f del distrito

distrust [dɪs'trʌst] **1** n desconfianza f

disturb [dɪ'stɜːrb] (*interrupt*) molestar; (*upset*) preocupar; **disturbance** (*interruption*) molestia f; **~s** (*civil unrest*) disturbios mpl; **disturbed** preocupado; *mentally* perturbado; **disturbing** inquietante

disused [dɪs'juːzd] abandonado

ditch [dɪtʃ] **1** n zanja f **2** v/t plan abandonar

dive [daɪv] **1** n salto m de cabeza; *underwater* inmersión f; of *plane* descenso m en picado; F *bar etc* antro m **F 2** v/i tirarse de cabeza; of *plane* descender en picado; *diver un derwater* buceador(a) m(f)

diverge [daɪ'vɜːrdʒ] bifurcarse

diversification [daɪvɜːrsɪfɪ keɪʃn] COM diversificación f; **diversify** COM diversificarse

diversion [daɪ'vɜːrʃn] for *traffic* desvío m; *to distract attention* distracción f; **divert** desviar

divide [dɪ'vaɪd] dividir

dividend ['dɪvɪdend] FIN dividendo *m*

diving ['daɪvɪŋ] *from board* salto *m* de trampolín; (*scuba ~*) buceo *m*; **diving board** trampolín *m*

division [dɪ'vɪʒn] división *f*

divorce [dɪ'vɔːrs] **1** *n* divorcio *m* **2** *v/t* divorciarse de **3** *v/i* divorciarse; **divorced** divorciado; **divorcee** divorciado(-a) *m(f)*

divulge [daɪ'vʌldʒ] divulgar

DIY [diːaɪ'waɪ] (= *do it yourself*) bricolaje *m*

dizziness ['dɪzɪnɪs] mareo *m*; **dizzy** mareado

DJ ['diːdʒeɪ] (= *disc jockey*) disc jockey *m/f*, *Span* pinchadiscos *m/f inv*

DNA [diːen'eɪ] (= *deoxyribonucleic acid*) AND *m* (= ácido *m* desoxirribonucleico)

do [duː] **1** *v/t* hacer; *100 mph etc* ir a; *~ one's hair* arreglarse el pelo **2** *v/i*: *that'll ~ nicely* eso bastará; *that will ~!* ¡ya vale!; *~ well* de business ir bien; *he's ~ing well* le van bien las cosas; *well done!* (*congratulations!*) ¡bien hecho!; *how ~ you ~?* encantado de conocerle

◆ **do away with** abolir
◆ **do up** (*renovate*) renovar; *coat* abrochar; *laces* atarse
◆ **do with**: *I could do with ...* no me vendría mal...
◆ **do without** pasar sin

docile ['dəʊsail] dócil

dock[1] [dɒk] **1** *n* NAUT muelle *m* **2** *v/i of ship* atracar; *of spaceship* acoplarse

dock[2] [dɒk] *n* LAW banquillo *m* (de los acusados)

doctor ['dɒktər] médico *m*; *form of address* doctor *m*; **doctorate** doctorado *m*

doctrine ['dɒktrɪn] doctrina *f*

document ['dɒkjumənt] documento *m*; **documentary** documental *m*; **documentation** documentación *f*

dodge [dɒdʒ] *blow, person* esquivar; *question* eludir

dog [dɒːg] **1** *n* perro(-a) *m(f)* **2** *v/t of bad luck* perseguir

dogma ['dɒːgmə] dogma *m*; **dogmatic** dogmático

'dog tag MIL chapa *f* de identificación; **dog-tired** F hecho polvo F

do-it-yourself [duːɪtjər'self] bricolaje *m*

doldrums ['dəʊldrəmz]: *be in the ~ of economy* estar en un bache; *of person* estar deprimido

doll [dɒːl] *toy* muñeca *f*; F *woman* muñeca *f* F

dollar ['dɒːlər] dólar *m*

dolphin ['dɒːlfɪn] delfín *m*

dome [dəʊm] cúpula *f*

domestic [də'mestɪk] **1** *adj chores* doméstico; *news, policy* nacional **2** *n* empleado(-a) *m(f)* del hogar; **domestic flight** vuelo *m* nacional

dominant ['dɒːmɪnənt] dominante; **dominate** dominar; **domination** dominación *f*;

domineering dominante
donate ['dəʊneɪt] donar; **do-nation** donación f
dongle ['dɒŋgl] IT dongle m, mochila f
donkey ['dɒŋkɪ] burro m
donor ['dəʊnə] donante m/f
donut ['dəʊnʌt] dónut m
doom [duːm] (fate) destino m; (ruin) fatalidad f; **doomed project** condenado al fracaso
door [dɔː] puerta f; **doorbell** timbre m; **doorman** portero m; **doorway** puerta f
dope [dəʊp] (drugs) droga f; F (idiot) lelo(-a) m(f)
dormant ['dɔːmənt] volcano inactivo
dormitory ['dɔːmɪtɔːrɪ] (hall of residence) residencia f de estudiantes; Br dormitorio m (colectivo)
dose [dəʊs] dosis f inv
dot [dɒt] punto m
double ['dʌbl] **1** n person doble m/f **2** adj doble **3** v/t doblar **4** v/i doblarse; **double bed** cama f de matrimonio; **doublecheck** volver a comprobar; **double click** COMPUT hacer doble clic (on en); **doublecross** engañar; **double park** aparcar en doble fila; **double room** habitación f doble; **doubles** in tennis dobles mpl
doubt [daʊt] **1** n duda f; (uncertainty) dudas fpl; **no ~** (probably) sin duda **2** v/t dudar; **doubtful** look dubitativo; **be ~** of person tener du-

das; **doubtless** sin duda
dough [dəʊ] masa f
dove [dʌv] also fig paloma f
down [daʊn] **1** adv (downward) (hacia) abajo; **~ there** allá abajo; **$200 ~** (as deposit) una entrada de 200 dólares **~ south** hacia el sur; **be ~** o price haber bajado; of numbers haber descendido; (not working) no funcionar; **~** (depressed) estar deprimido **2** prep: **run ~ the stairs** bajar las escaleras corriendo **walk ~ the street** andar por la calle; **down-and-out** vagabundo(-a) m(f); **download** COMPUT **1** v/t descargar, bajar **2** n descarga f **downmarket** Br barato **down payment** entrada f **downplay** quitar importancia a; **downpour** chaparrón m; **downscale** barato **downside** (disadvantage) desventaja f; **downsize** car reducir el tamaño de; company reajustar la plantilla de; **downstairs** en el piso de abajo; **I ran ~** bajé corriendo; **downtown 1** n centro m **2** adj del centro **3** adj live en el centro; go al centro **doze** [dəʊz] echar una cabezada
dozen ['dʌzn] docena f
draft [drɑːft] **1** n of air corriente f; of document borrador m; MIL reclutamiento m; **~ beer** cerveza f de barril **2** v/t document redactar un bo

          drink

rrador de; MIL reclutar; **draft dodger** prófugo(-a) *m(f)*; **draftsman** delineante *m/f*

drag [dræg] **1** *v/t (pull)* arrastrar; *(search)* dragar **2** *v/i of movie* ser pesado

drain [dreɪn] **1** *n pipe* sumidero *m*; *under street* alcantarilla *f* **2** *v/t water, vegetables* escurrir; *land* drenar; *tank, oil* vaciar; *person* agotar; **drainage** *(drains)* desagües *mpl*; *of water from soil* drenaje *m*; **drainpipe** tubo *m* de desagüe

drama ['drɑːmə] drama *m*; *(excitement)* dramatismo *m*; **dramatic** dramático *m*; *scenery* espectacular; **dramatist** dramaturgo(-a) *m(f)*; **dramatize** *also fig* dramatizar

drapes [dreɪps] cortinas *fpl*

drastic ['dræstɪk] drástico

draught [dræft] *Br* ☞ **draft**

draw [drɔː] **1** *n in game* empate *m*; *in lottery* sorteo *m*; *(attraction)* atracción *f* **2** *v/t picture* dibujar; *curtain* correr; *in lottery* sortear; *knife* sacar; *(attract)* atraer; *(lead)* llevar; *from bank account* sacar **3** *v/i in game* empatar; *of train* dibujar
◆ **draw back 1** *v/i (recoil)* echarse atrás **2** *v/t (pull back)* retirar
◆ **draw out** *v/t* sacar
◆ **draw up 1** *v/t document* redactar; *chair* acercar **2** *v/i of vehicle* parar

drawback desventaja *f*

drawer [drɔːr] *of desk* cajón *m*

drawing ['drɔːɪŋ] dibujo *m*

drawl [drɔːl] acento *m* arrastrado

dread [dred] tener pavor a; **dreadful** horrible

dream [driːm] **1** *n* sueño *m* **2** *v/i* soñar
◆ **dream up** inventar

dreary ['drɪrɪ] triste

dress [dres] **1** *n for woman* vestido *m*; *(clothing)* traje *m* **2** *v/t person* vestir; *wound* vendar; **get ~ed** vestirse **3** *v/i* vestirse
◆ **dress up** vestirse elegante; *(wear a disguise)* disfrazarse (**as** de)

dress circle piso *m* principal; **dresser** *(dressing table)* tocador *m*; *in kitchen* aparador *m*; **dressing** *for salad* aliño *m*, *Span* arreglo *m*; *for wound* vendaje *m*; **dress rehearsal** ensayo *m* general

dribble ['drɪbl] *of baby* babear; *of water* gotear; SP driblar

dried [draɪd] *fruit etc* seco; **drier** ['draɪr] ☞ **dryer**

drift [drɪft] *of snow* amontonarse; *of ship* ir a la deriva; *(go off course)* desviarse del rumbo; *of person* vagar; **drifter** vagabundo(-a) *m(f)*

drill [drɪl] **1** *n tool* taladro *m*; *exercise* simulacro *m*; MIL instrucción *f* **2** *v/t hole* taladrar **3** *v/i for oil* hacer perforaciones; MIL entrenar

drily ['draɪlɪ] *say* secamente

drink [drɪŋk] **1** *n* bebida *f* **2** *v/t* beber **3** *v/i* beber, *L.Am.* to-

mar; **drinkable** potable;
drinker bebedor(a) *m(f)*;
drinking water agua *f* potable

drip [drɪp] **1** *n* gota *f*; MED gotero *m* **2** *v/i* gotear

drive [draɪv] **1** *n* (en coche); (*energy*) energía *f*; COMPUT unidad *f*; (*campaign*) campaña *f* **2** *v/t vehicle* conducir, *L.Am.* manejar; (*own*) tener; (*take in car*) llevar (en coche); TECH impulsar **3** *v/i* conducir, *L.Am.* manejar

'**drive-in** *movie theater* autocine *m*

drivel ['drɪvl] tonterías *fpl*

driver ['draɪvər] conductor(a) *m(f)*; COMPUT controlador *m*; **driver's license** carné *m* de conducir; **drivethru** *restaurante* / *banco etc* en el que se atiende al cliente sin que salga del coche; **driveway** camino *m* de entrada

drizzle ['drɪzl] **1** *n* llovizna *f* **2** *v/i* lloviznar

drop [drɑːp] **1** *n* gota *f*; *in price, temperature* caída *f* **2** *v/t object* dejar caer; *person from car* dejar; *person from team* excluir; (*stop seeing*) abandonar; *charges etc* retirar; (*give up*) dejar **3** *v/i* caer; *of wind* amainar

♦ **drop in** pasar a visitar

♦ **drop off 1** *v/t person* dejar; (*deliver*) llevar **2** *v/i* (*fall asleep*) dormirse; (*decline*)

disminuir

♦ **drop out** (*withdraw*) retirarse; *drop out of schoo* abandonar el colegio

drought [draʊt] sequía *f*

drown [draʊn] ahogarse

drug [drʌg] *n* droga *f* **2** *v/* drogar; **drug addict** drogadicto(-a) *m(f)*; **drug deale** traficante *m/f* (de drogas)

druggist farmacéutico(-a *m(f)*; **drugstore** *tienda* e la que se venden medicinas cosméticos, periódicos y que a veces tiene un bar; **drug trafficking** tráfico *m* de drogas

drum [drʌm] MUS tambor *m container* barril *m*; **~s in band** batería *f*; **drumstick** MUS baqueta *f*

drunk [drʌŋk] **1** *n* borracho(-a) *m(f)* **2** *adj* borracho **get ~** emborracharse; **drunk driving** conducción *f* baj los efectos del alcohol

dry [draɪ] **1** *adj* seco *2 v/t & v/* secar; **dryclean** limpiar en seco; **dry cleaner** tintorerí *f*; **dryer** *machine* secadora *f*

dual ['duːəl] doble

dub [dʌb] *movie* doblar

dubious ['duːbɪəs] dudoso (*having doubts*) dudoso

duck [dʌk] *n* pato *m*, pata *f* **2** *v/i* agacharse

dud [dʌd] F (*false bill*) billete *m* falso

due [duː] debido; *payment now ~* el pago se debe hace efectivo ahora

dull [dʌl] *weather* gris; *sound, pain* sordo; *(boring)* aburrido, soso

duly ['duːlɪ] *(as expected)* tal y como se esperaba; *(properly)* debidamente

dumb [dʌm] *(mute)* mudo; F *(stupid)* estúpido

dump [dʌmp] **1** *n for garbage* vertedero *m*; *(unpleasant place)* lugar *m* de mala muerte **2** *v/t (deposit)* dejar; *(dispose of)* deshacerse de; *waste* verter

dune [duːn] duna *f*

duplex (apartment) ['duːpleks] dúplex *m*

duplicate 1 *n* ['duːplɪkət] duplicado *m*

durable ['dʊrəbl] duradero

during ['dʊrɪŋ] durante

dusk [dʌsk] crepúsculo *m*

dust [dʌst] **1** *n* polvo *m* **2** *v/t* quitar el polvo a; **duster** trapo *m* del polvo; **dustpan** recogedor *m*; **dusty** polvoriento

Dutch [dʌtʃ] holandés; **Dutchman** holandés *m*; **Dutchwoman** holandesa *f*

duty ['duːtɪ] deber *m*; *(task)* tarea *f*; *on goods* impuesto *m*; **be on** ~ estar de servicio; **duty-free** libre de impuestos

DVD [diːviː'diː] (= *digital versatile disk*) DVD *m*; **DVD-ROM** DVD-ROM *m*

dwarf [dwɔːrf] **1** *n* enano *m* **2** *v/t* empequeñecer

dwindle ['dwɪndl] menguar

dye [daɪ] tinte *m* 2 *v/t* teñir

dying ['daɪɪŋ] moribundo; *tradition etc* en vías de desaparición

dynamic [daɪ'næmɪk] dinámico; **dynamism** dinamismo *m*

dynasty ['daɪnəstɪ] dinastía *f*

dyslexic [dɪs'leksɪk] **1** *adj* disléxico **2** *n* disléxico(-a) *m(f)*

E

each [iːtʃ] **1** *adj* cada **2** *adv*: **he gave us one** ~ nos dio una a cada uno; **they're $1.50** ~ valen 1.50 dólares cada uno **3** *pron* cada uno; ~ **other** el uno al otro; **we love** ~ **other** nos queremos

eager ['iːgər] ansioso; **eagerly** ansiosamente; **eagerness** entusiasmo *m*

eagle ['iːgl] águila *f*; **eagle-eyed** con vista de lince

ear[1] [ɪr] oreja *f*

ear[2] [ɪr] *of corn* espiga *f*

earache dolor *m* de oídos

early ['ɜːrlɪ] **1** *adj (not late)* temprano; *(ahead of time)* anticipado; *(farther back in time)* primero; *(in the near future)* pronto; *music* antiguo **2** *adv (not late)* pronto, temprano; *(ahead of time)* antes de tiempo; **early bird** madrugador(a) *m(f)*

earmark ['ɪrmɑːrk] destinar

earn [ɜːrn] *salary* ganar; *interest* devengar; *holiday, drink etc* ganarse

earnest ['ɜːrnɪst] serio

earnings ['ɜːrnɪŋz] ganancias *fpl*

'**earphones** auriculares *mpl*; **earring** pendiente *m*

earth [ɜːrθ] tierra *f*; **earthenware** loza *f*; **earthly** terrenal; **it's no ~ use** F no sirve para nada; **earthquake** terremoto *m*; **earth-shattering** extraordinario

ease [iːz] **1** *n* facilidad *f*; *feel at ~* sentirse cómodo **2** *v/t* (*relieve*) aliviar

easel ['iːzl] caballete *m*

easily ['iːzəlɪ] fácilmente; (*by far*) con diferencia

east [iːst] **1** *n* este *m* **2** *adj* oriental, este; *wind* del este **3** *adv* *travel* hacia el este

Easter ['iːstər] Pascua *f*; *period* Semana *f* Santa; **Easter Day** Domingo *m* de Resurrección; **Easter egg** huevo *m* de pascua

easterly ['iːstərlɪ] del este

Easter 'Monday Lunes *m* Santo

eastern ['iːstərn] del este; (*oriental*) oriental; **easterner** habitante de la costa este estadounidense

Easter 'Sunday Domingo *m* de Resurrección

eastward ['iːstwərd] hacia el este

easy ['iːzɪ] fácil; (*relaxed*) tranquilo; *easy chair* sillón *m*; *easy-going* tratable

eat [iːt] comer

◆ **eat out** comer fuera

eatable ['iːtəbl] comestible

eavesdrop ['iːvzdrɑːp] escuchar a escondidas (*on s.o.* alguien)

ebb [eb] *of tide* bajar

e-bike ['iːbaɪk] bicicleta *f* eléctrica; **e-book** libro *m* electrónico; **e-book reader** IT lector *m* de libros electrónicos; **e-business** comercio *m* electrónico

eccentric [ɪk'sentrɪk] **1** *adj* excéntrico **2** *n* excéntrico(-a) *m(f)*; **eccentricity** excentricidad *f*

echo ['ekou] **1** *n* eco *m* **2** *v/t* resonar **3** *v/t* *words* repetir; *views* mostrar acuerdo con

eclipse [ɪ'klɪps] **1** *n* eclipse *m* **2** *v/t* *fig* eclipsar

ecological [iːkə'lɑːdʒɪkl] ecológico; **ecologically** ecológicamente; **ecologically friendly** ecológico; **ecologist** ecologista *m/f*; **ecology** ecología *f*

economic [iːkə'nɑːmɪk] económico; **economical** (*cheap*) económico; (*thrifty*) cuidadoso; **economics** economía *f*; *financial aspects* aspecto *m* económico; **economist** economista *m/f*; **economize** economizar

◆ **economize on** economizar, ahorrar

economy [ɪ'kɑːnəmɪ] econo-

mía f; (saving) ahorro m;
economy class clase f turista

ecosystem ['iːkoʊsɪstm] eco-
sistema m; **ecotourism** eco-
turismo m

ecstasy ['ekstəsɪ] éxtasis m;
ecstatic extasiado

Ecuador ['ekwədɔːr] Ecuador; **Ecuadorean 1** adj ecuatoriano **2** n ecuatoriano(-a)
m(f)

eczema ['eksmə] eczema f

edge [edʒ] **1** n of knife filo m;
of table, road, cliff borde m;
on ~ tenso **2** v/i (move slowly)
acercarse despacio; **edge-**
wise: **I couldn't get a word
in ~** no me dejó decir una
palabra; **edgy** tenso

edible ['edɪbl] comestible

edit ['edɪt] text corregir; book
editar; newspaper dirigir; TV
program montar; **edition**
edición f; **editor** of text, book
editor(a) m(f); of newspaper
director(a) m(f); of TV program montador(a) m(f); **editorial 1** adj editorial **2** n in
newspaper editorial m

educate ['edʒəkeɪt] child educar; consumers concienciar;
educated culto; **education**
educación f; **educational**
educativo; (informative) instructivo

eerie ['ɪrɪ] escalofriante

effect [ɪ'fekt] efecto m; **effective** efectivo; (striking) impresionante

effeminate [ɪ'femɪnət] afemi-

nado

efficiency [ɪ'fɪʃənsɪ] of person
eficiencia f; of machine rendimiento m; of system eficacia f; in motel cuarto m con
cocina; **efficient** person eficiente; machine de buen rendimiento; method eficaz; **efficiently** eficientemente

effort ['efərt] esfuerzo m;
effortless fácil

e.g. [iː'dʒiː] p. ej.

egg [eg] huevo m; **egghead**
F cerebrito(-a) m(f) F; **eggplant**
berenjena f

ego ['iːgoʊ] PSYCH ego m;
(self-esteem) amor m propio;
egocentric egocéntrico;
egoism egoísmo m; **egoist**
egoísta m/f

eiderdown ['aɪdərdaʊn] quilt
edredón m

eight [eɪt] ocho; **eighteen**
dieciocho; **eighteenth** decimoctavo; **eighth** octavo;
eightieth octogésimo;
eighty ochenta

either ['aɪðər] **1** adj & pron
cualquiera de los dos; with
negative constructions ninguno de los dos; (both) cada,
ambos **2** adv tampoco; **I
won't go ~** yo tampoco iré
3 conj: **~ ... or** choice o...
o; with negative constructions
ni... ni

eject [ɪ'dʒekt] **1** v/t expulsar **2**
v/i from plane eyectarse

◆ **eke out** [iːk] (make last) hacer durar; **~ a living** ganarse

la vida a duras penas
el [el] ferrocarril *m* elevado
elaborate 1 [ɪˈlæbərət] *adj* elaborado **2** [ɪˈlæbəreɪt] *v/t* elaborar **3** [ɪˈlæbəreɪt] *v/i* dar detalles
elapse [ɪˈlæps] pasar
elastic [ɪˈlæstɪk] **1** *adj* elástico **2** *n* elástico *m*; **elasticated** elástico
elated [ɪˈleɪtɪd] eufórico; **elation** euforia *f*
elbow [ˈelboʊ] codo *m*
elder [ˈeldər] **1** *adj* mayor **2** *n* mayor *m/f*; **elderly 1** *adj* mayor **2** *npl*: **the ~** las personas mayores; **eldest 1** *adj* mayor **2** *n* mayor *m/f*
elect [ɪˈlekt] elegir; **elected** elegido; **election** elección *f*; **election campaign** campaña *f* electoral; **election day** día *m* de las elecciones; **electorate** electorado *m*
electric [ɪˈlektrɪk] eléctrico; *fig* atmosphere electrizado; **electrical** eléctrico; **electric chair** silla *f* eléctrica; **electrician** electricista *m/f*; **electricity** electricidad *f*; **electrify** electrificar; *fig* electrizar
electrocute [ɪˈlektrəkjuːt] electrocutar
electron [ɪˈlektrɑːn] electrón *m*; **electronic** electrónico; **electronics** electrónica *f*
elegance [ˈelɪɡəns] elegancia *f*; **elegant** elegante
element [ˈelɪmənt] elemento *m*; **elementary** (*rudimentary*) elemental; **elementary**

school escuela *f* primaria
elephant [ˈelɪfənt] elefante *m*
elevate [ˈelɪveɪt] elevar; **elevated railroad** ferrocarril *m* elevado; **elevation** (*altitude*) altura *f*; **elevator** ascensor *m*
eleven [ɪˈlevn] once; **eleventh** undécimo
eligible [ˈelɪdʒəbl] que reúne los requisitos; **be ~ to do sth** tener derecho a hacer algo
eliminate [ɪˈlɪmɪneɪt] eliminar; *poverty* acabar con; (*rule out*) descartar; **elimination** eliminación *f*
elite [eɪˈliːt] **1** *n* élite *f* **2** *adj* de élite
eloquence [ˈeləkwəns] elocuencia *f*; **eloquent** elocuente
El Salvador [elˈsælvədɔːr] El Salvador
else [els]: *anything ~?* ¿algo más?; *nothing ~* nada más; *no one ~* nadie más; *every one ~ is going* todos (los demás) van; *someone ~* otra persona; *something ~* algo más; *let's go somewhere ~* vamos a otro sitio; *or ~* sí no; elsewhere en otro sitio
elude [ɪˈluːd] (*escape from*) escapar de; (*avoid*) evitar; **elusive** evasivo
emaciated [ɪˈmeɪsɪeɪtɪd] demacrado
e-mail [ˈiːmeɪl] **1** *n* correo *m* electrónico **2** *v/t person* mandar un correo electrónico a

e-mail address dirección *f* electrónica

emancipation [ɪmænsɪ'peɪʃn] emancipación *f*

embalm [ɪm'bɑːm] embalsamar

embankment [ɪm'bæŋkmənt] *of river* dique *m*; RAIL terraplén *m*

embargo [em'bɑːrgoʊ] embargo *m*

embark [ɪm'bɑːrk] embarcar

embarrass [ɪm'bærəs] avergonzar; **embarrassed** avergonzado; **embarrassing** embarazoso; **embarrassment** embarazo *m*

embassy ['embəsɪ] embajada *f*

embezzle [ɪm'bezl] malversar; **embezzlement** malversación *f*

emblem ['embləm] emblema *m*

embodiment [ɪm'bɑːdɪmənt] personificación *f*; **embody** personificar

embrace [ɪm'breɪs] **1** *n* abrazo *m* **2** *v/t (hug)* abrazar; *(take in)* abarcar **3** *v/i of two people* abrazarse

embroider [ɪm'brɔɪdər] bordar; *fig* adornar

embryo ['embrɪoʊ] embrión *m*; **embryonic** *fig* embrionario

emerald ['emərəld] esmeralda *f*

emerge [ɪ'mɜːrdʒ] emerger, salir; *of truth* aflorar

emergency [ɪ'mɜːrdʒənsɪ]

emergencia *f*; **emergency exit** salida *f* de emergencia; **emergency landing** aterrizaje *m* forzoso; **emergency services** servicios *mpl* de urgencia

emigrate ['emɪgreɪt] emigrar; **emigration** emigración *f*

Eminence ['emɪnəns] REL: *His* ~ Su Eminencia; **eminent** eminente

emission [ɪ'mɪʃn] *of gases* emisión *f*; **emit** emitir; *heat, odor* desprender

emotion [ɪ'moʊʃn] emoción *f*; **emotional** *problems* sentimental; *(full of emotion)* emotivo

emphasis ['emfəsɪs] *in word* acento *m*; *fig* énfasis *m*; **emphasize** *syllable* acentuar; *fig* hacer hincapié en; **emphatic** enfático

empire ['empaɪr] imperio *m*

employ [ɪm'plɔɪ] emplear; **employee** empleado(-a) *m(f)*; **employer** empresario(-a) *m(f)*; **employment** empleo *m*; *(work)* trabajo *m*

emptiness ['emptɪnɪs] vacío *m*; **empty 1** *adj* vacío *m* **2** *v/t drawer, pockets* vaciar; *glass, bottle* acabar **3** *v/i of room, street* vaciarse

emulate ['emjʊleɪt] emular

enable [ɪ'neɪbl] permitir

enchanting [ɪn'tʃæntɪŋ] encantador

encircle [ɪn'sɜːrkl] rodear

enclose [ɪn'kloʊz] *in letter* ad-

juntar; *area* rodear; **enclosure** *with letter* documento
m adjunto

encore ['ɑːŋkɔːr] bis *m*

encounter [ɪn'kaʊntər] **1** *n*
encuentro *m* **2** *v/t person* encontrarse con; *problem, resistance* tropezar con

encourage [ɪn'kʌrɪdʒ] animar; *violence* fomentar; **encouragement** ánimo *m*; **en-
couraging** alentador

encyclopedia [ɪsaɪklə'piːdɪə]
enciclopedia *f*

end [end] **1** *n of journey,
month* final *m*; *(extremity)* extremo *m*; *(conclusion, purpose)* fin *m*; **in the ~** al final
2 *v/t* & *v/i* terminar
♦ **end up** acabar

endanger [ɪn'deɪndʒər] poner
en peligro; **endangered
species** especie *f* en peligro
de extinción

endeavor, *Br* **endeavour** [ɪn'-
devər] **1** *n* esfuerzo *m* **2** *v/t*
procurar

endemic [ɪn'demɪk] endémi-
co

ending ['endɪŋ] final *m*;
GRAM terminación *f*; **endless** interminable

endorse [ɪn'dɔːrs] apoyar;
product representar; **en-
dorsement** apoyo *m*; *of
product* representación *f*

end 'product producto *m* final

endurance [ɪn'dʊrəns] resistencia *f*; **endure 1** *v/t* resistir
2 *v/i (last)* durar; **enduring**

duradero

enemy ['enəmɪ] enemigo(-a)
m(f)

energetic [enər'dʒetɪk] enérgico; **energy** energía *f*; **energy efficiency** eficiencia *f*
energética; **energy supply**
suministro *m* de energía

enforce [ɪn'fɔːrs] hacer cumplir

engage [ɪn'geɪdʒ] **1** *v/t (hire)*
contratar **2** *v/i* TECH engranar; **engaged** *to be married*
prometido; *Br* TELEC ocupado; **get ~** prometerse; **engagement** compromiso *m*;
MIL combate *m*; **engagement ring** anillo *m* de compromiso

engine ['endʒɪn] motor *m*;
engineer ingeniero(-a)
m(f); NAUT, RAIL maquinista
m/f; **engineering** ingeniería
f

England ['ɪŋglənd] Inglaterra; **English 1** *adj* inglés
(-esa) **2** *n language* inglés
m; **the ~** los ingleses; **Englishman** inglés *m*; **Englishwoman** inglesa *f*

engrave [ɪn'greɪv] grabar; **engraving** grabado *m*

engrossed [ɪn'groʊst] absor-
to (*in* en)

engulf [ɪn'gʌlf] devorar

enhance [ɪn'hæns] realzar

enigma [ɪ'nɪgmə] enigma *m*

enjoy [ɪn'dʒɔɪ] disfrutar; **~
o.s.** divertirse; **~ (your
meal)!** ¡que aproveche!; **enjoyable** agradable; **enjoy-**

ment diversión *f*

enlarge [ɪnˈlɑːrdʒ] ampliar; **enlargement** ampliación *f*

enlighten [ɪnˈlaɪtn] educar

enlist [ɪnˈlɪst] MIL alistarse

enmity [ˈenmətɪ] enemistad *f*

enormous [ɪˈnɔːrməs] enorme; *satisfaction, patience* inmenso

enough [ɪˈnʌf] **1** *adj & pron* suficiente, bastante; **will $50 be ~?** ¿llegará con 50 dólares?; **that's ~!** ¡ya basta! **2** *adv* suficientemente, bastante; **big ~** suficientemente *or* bastante grande

enquire [ɪnˈkwaɪr] ☞ **inquire**

enroll, *Br* **enrol** [ɪnˈroʊl] matricularse

en suite [ˈɑːnswiːt]: **~ bathroom** baño *m* privado

ensure [ɪnˈʃʊər] asegurar

entail [ɪnˈteɪl] conllevar

entangle [ɪnˈtæŋɡl] *in rope* enredar

enter [ˈentər] **1** *v/t room, house* entrar en; *competition* participar en; COMPUT introducir **2** *v/i* entrar; THEA entrar en escena; *in competition* inscribirse **3** *n* COMPUT intro *m*

enterprise [ˈentərpraɪz] *(initiative)* iniciativa *f*; *(venture)* empresa *f*; **enterprising** con iniciativa

entertain [entərˈteɪn] *(amuse)* entretener; *(consider)* considerar; **entertainer** artista *m/f*; **entertaining** entretenido; **entertainment** entretenimiento *m*

---

enthusiasm [ɪnˈθuːzɪæzm] entusiasmo *m*; **enthusiast** entusiasta *m/f*; **enthusiastic** entusiasta; **enthusiastically** con entusiasmo

entire [ɪnˈtaɪr] entero; **entirely** completamente

entitle [ɪnˈtaɪtld]: **~ s.o. to sth** dar derecho a alguien a algo; **be ~d to** tener derecho a

entrance [ˈentrəns] entrada *f*

entranced [ɪnˈtrænst] encantado

'entrance exam(ination) examen *m* de acceso

entrant [ˈentrənt] participante *m/f*

entrepreneur [ɑːntrəprəˈnɜːr] empresario(-a) *m(f)*; **entrepreneurial** empresarial

entrust [ɪnˈtrʌst] confiar

entry [ˈentrɪ] entrada *f*; *for competition* inscripción *f*; **entryphone** portero *m* automático

envelop [ɪnˈveləp] cubrir

envelope [ˈenvəloʊp] sobre *m*

enviable [ˈenviəbl] envidiable; **envious** envidioso

environment [ɪnˈvaɪrənmənt] *(nature)* medio *m* ambiente; *(surroundings)* entorno *m*, ambiente *m*; **environmental** medioambiental; **environmentalist** ecologista *m/f*; **environmentally friendly** ecológico; **environs** alrededores *mpl*

envisage [ɪnˈvɪzɪdʒ] imaginar

envoy [ˈenvɔɪ] enviado(-a) *m(f)*

envy ['envɪ] **1** n envidia f **2** v/t envidiar

epic ['epɪk] **1** n epopeya f **2** adj journey épico

epicenter, Br **epicentre** ['epɪsentər] epicentro m

epidemic [epɪ'demɪk] epidemia f

episode ['epɪsoud] episodio m

epitaph ['epɪtæf] epitafio m

equal ['iːkwl] **1** adj igual **2** n igual m/f **3** v/t with numbers equivaler; (be as good as) igualar; **be ~ to** a task estar capacitado para; **equality** igualdad f; **equalize 1** v/t igualar **2** v/i Br SP empatar; **equalizer** Br SP gol m del empate; **equally** igualmente; share, divide en partes iguales; **equal rights** igualdad f de derechos

equation [ɪ'kweɪʒn] MATH ecuación f

equator [ɪ'kweɪtər] ecuador m

equip [ɪ'kwɪp] equipar; **equipment** equipo m

equity ['ekwətɪ] FIN acciones fpl ordinarias

equivalent [ɪ'kwɪvələnt] **1** adj equivalente **2** n equivalente m

era ['ɪrə] era f

eradicate [ɪ'rædɪkeɪt] erradicar

erase [ɪ'reɪz] borrar

erect [ɪ'rekt] **1** adj erguido **2** v/t levantar, erigir; **erection** construcción f; of penis erec-

ción f

ergonomic [ɜːrgou'nɑːmɪk] ergonómico

erode [ɪ'roud] also fig erosionar; **erosion** erosión f

errand ['erənd] recado m

erratic [ɪ'rætɪk] irregular; course errático

error ['erər] error m

erupt [ɪ'rʌpt] of volcano entrar en erupción; of violence brotar; of person explotar; **eruption** of volcano erupción f; of violence brote m

escalate ['eskəleɪt] intensificarse; **escalation** intensificación f; **escalator** escalera f mecánica

escape [ɪ'skeɪp] **1** n fuga f **2** v/i of prisoner, animal, gas escaparse

escort 1 ['eskɔːrt] n acompañante m/f; (guard) escolta m/f **2** [ɪ'skɔːrt] v/t escoltar socially acompañar

especially [ɪ'speʃlɪ] especialmente

espionage ['espɪənɑːʒ] espionaje m

espresso (coffee) [es'presou] café m exprés

essay ['eseɪ] creative redacción f; factual trabajo m

essential [ɪ'senʃl] esencial

establish [ɪ'stæblɪʃ] company fundar; (create, determine) establecer; **establishment** firm, shop etc establecimiento m

estate [ɪ'steɪt] land finca f; of dead person patrimonio m

esthetic [ɪs'θetɪk] estético

estimate ['estɪmət] **1** *n* estimación *f*; *for job* presupuesto *m* **2** *v/t* estimar

estuary ['estʃʊərɪ] estuario *m*

etc [et'setrə] etc

eternal [ɪ'tɜːrnl] eterno; **eternity** eternidad *f*

ethical ['eθɪkl] ético; **ethics** ética *f*

ethnic ['eθnɪk] étnico

EU [iː'juː] (= *European Union*) UE *f* (= Unión *f* Europea); **EU citizenship** ciudadanía *f* europea, ciudadanía *f* de la Unión Europea

euphemism ['juːfəmɪzm] eufemismo *m*

euro ['jʊərəʊ] euro *m*

Europe ['jʊərəp] Europa; **European 1** *adj* europeo **2** *n* europeo(-a) *m(f)*

euthanasia [juːθə'neɪʒɪə] eutanasia *f*

evacuate [ɪ'vækjʊeɪt] evacuar

evade [ɪ'veɪd] evadir

evaluate [ɪ'væljʊeɪt] evaluar; **evaluation** evaluación *f*

evaporate [ɪ'væpəreɪt] evaporarse; *of confidence* desvanecerse; **evaporation** evaporación *f*

evasion [ɪ'veɪʒn] evasión *f*; **evasive** evasivo

eve [iːv] víspera *f*

even [iːvn] **1** *adj* (*regular*) regular; (*level*) llano; *number* par; (*distribution*) igualado; **I'll get ~ with him** me las pa-

garé **2** *adv* incluso; **~ bigger** incluso *or* aún mayor; **not ~** ni siquiera; **~ so** aun así; **~ if** aunque **3** *v/t*: **~ the score** igualar el marcador

evening ['iːvnɪŋ] tarde *f*; *after dark* noche *f*; **in the ~** por la tarde / noche; **yesterday ~** anoche *f*; **good~** buenas noches; **evening class** clase *f* nocturna; **evening dress** *for woman* traje *f* de noche; *for man* traje *f* de etiqueta

evenly ['iːvnlɪ] (*regularly*) regularmente

event [ɪ'vent] acontecimiento *m*; SP prueba *f*; **eventful** agitado, lleno de incidentes

eventually [ɪ'ventʃʊəlɪ] finalmente

ever ['evər]: **have you ~ been to Colombia?** ¿has estado alguna vez en Colombia?; **for ~** siempre; **~ since** desde entonces; **~ since I've known him** desde que lo conozco; **everlasting** *love* eterno

every ['evrɪ] cada; **I see him ~ day** le veo todos los días; **everybody ☞ everyone**; **everyday** cotidiano; **everyone** todo el mundo; **everything** todo; **everywhere** en *or* por todos sitios; (*wherever*) dondequiera que

evict [ɪ'vɪkt] desahuciar

evidence ['evɪdəns] prueba(s) *f(pl)*; **give ~** prestar declaración; **evident** evidente; **evidently** (*clearly*) evidentemente; (*apparently*) aparentemente, al parecer

evil ['iːvl] **1** *adj* malo **2** *n* mal *m*

evolution [iːvə'luːʃn] evolución *f*; **evolve** evolucionar

ex [eks] (*former wife, husband*) ex *m/f* F

exact [ɪɡ'zækt] exacto; **exacting** exigente; *task* duro; **exactly** exactamente

exaggerate [ɪɡ'zædʒəreɪt] exagerar; **exaggeration** exageración *f*

exam [ɪɡ'zæm] examen *m*; **examination** examen *m*; *of patient* reconocimiento *m*; **examine** examinar; *patient* reconocer

example [ɪɡ'zæmpl] ejemplo *m*; **for ~** por ejemplo

excavate ['ekskəveɪt] excavar; **excavation** excavación *f*

exceed [ɪk'siːd] (*be more than*) exceder; (*go beyond*) sobrepasar; **exceedingly** sumamente

excel [ɪk'sel] **1** *v/i* sobresalir (**at** en) **2** *v/t*: **~ o.s.** superarse a sí mismo; **excellence** excelencia *f*; **excellent** excelente

except [ɪk'sept] excepto; **~ for** a excepción de; **exception** excepción *f*; **exceptional** excepcional

excerpt ['eksɜːrpt] extracto *m*

excess [ɪk'ses] **1** *n* exceso *m* **2** *adj* excedente; **excessive** excesivo

exchange [ɪks'tʃeɪndʒ] **1** *n* intercambio *m* **2** *v/t* cambiar; **exchange rate** FIN tipo *m*

de cambio

excite [ɪk'saɪt] (*make enthusiastic*) entusiasmar; **excited** emocionado, excitado; **get ~ (about)** emocionarse *or* excitarse (con); **excitement** emoción *f*, excitación *f*; **exciting** emocionante, excitante

exclaim [ɪk'skleɪm] exclamar; **exclamation** exclamación *f*; **exclamation point** signo *m* de admiración

exclude [ɪk'skluːd] excluir; *possibility* descartar; **excluding** exceptuando; **exclusive** exclusivo

excuse 1 [ɪk'skjuːs] *n* excusa *f* **2** [ɪk'skjuːz] *v/t* (*forgive*) excusar, perdonar; (*allow to leave*) disculpar; **~ me** perdone

ex-di'rectory Br: **be ~** no aparecer en la guía telefónica

execute ['eksɪkjuːt] *criminal, plan* ejecutar; **execution** *of criminal, plan* ejecución *f*; **executive** ejecutivo(-a) *m(f)*

exempt [ɪg'zempt] exento

exercise ['eksərsaɪz] **1** *n* ejercicio *m* **2** *v/t muscle* ejercitar; *dog* pasear; *caution* proceder con **3** *v/i* hacer ejercicio

exhale [eks'heɪl] exhalar

exhaust [ɪg'zɔːst] **1** *n* fumes gases *mpl* de la combustión; *pipe* tubo *m* de escape **2** *v/t* (*tire*) cansar; (*use up*) agotar; **exhausted** (*tired*) agotado; **exhausting** agotador; **ex-**

haustion agotamiento *m*; **exhaustive** exhaustivo

exhibit [ɪg'zɪbɪt] **1** *n* objeto *m* expuesto **2** *v/t of gallery* exhibir; *of artist* exponer; *(give evidence of)* mostrar; **exhibition** exposición *f*; *of bad behavior, skill* exhibición *f*

exhilarating [ɪg'zɪləreɪtɪŋ] estimulante

exile ['eksaɪl] **1** *n* exilio *m*; *person* exiliado(-a) *m(f)* **2** *v/t* exiliar

exist [ɪg'zɪst] existir; **~ on** subsistir a base de; **existence** existencia *f*; **be in ~** existir; **existing** existente

exit ['eksɪt] **1** *n* salida *f* **2** *v/i* COMPUT salir

exonerate [ɪg'zɑːnəreɪt] exonerar de

exotic [ɪg'zɑːtɪk] exótico

expand [ɪk'spænd] **1** *v/t* expandir **2** *v/i* expandirse; *of metal* dilatarse; **expanse** extensión *f*; **expansion** expansión *f*; *of metal* dilatación *f*

expect [ɪk'spekt] **1** *v/t* esperar; *(suppose)* suponer, imaginar(se); *(demand)* exigir **2** *v/i*: **be ~ing** *(be pregnant)* estar en estado; **I ~ so** creo que sí; **expectant mother** futura madre *f*; **expectation** expectativa *f*

expedition [ekspɪ'dɪʃn] expedición *f*

expel [ɪk'spel] expulsar

expendable [ɪk'spendəbl] prescindible

expenditure [ɪk'spendɪtʃər]

gasto *m*

expense [ɪk'spens] gasto *m*; **expenses** gastos *mpl*; **expensive** caro

experience [ɪk'spɪrɪəns] **1** *n* experiencia *f* **2** *v/t* experimentar; **experienced** experimentado

experiment [ɪk'sperɪmənt] **1** *n* experimento *m* **2** *v/i* experimentar; **experimental** experimental

expert ['ekspɜːrt] **1** *adj* experto **2** *n* experto(-a) *m(f)*; **expertise** destreza *f*

expiration date [ekspɪ'reɪʃn] fecha *f* de caducidad; **expire** caducar; **expiry** *of contract* vencimiento *m*; *of passport* caducidad *f*; **expiry date** *Br* fecha *f* de caducidad

explain [ɪk'spleɪn] explicar; **explanation** explicación *f*; **explanatory** explicativo

explicit [ɪk'splɪsɪt] explícito

explode [ɪk'sploʊd] **1** *v/i of bomb* explotar **2** *v/t bomb* hacer explotar

exploit[1] ['eksplɔɪt] *n* hazaña *f*

exploit[2] [ɪk'splɔɪt] *v/t person, resources* explotar

exploitation [eksplɔɪ'teɪʃn] explotación *f*

exploration [eksplə'reɪʃn] exploración *f*; **explore** *country etc* explorar; *possibility* estudiar; **explorer** explorador(a) *m(f)*

explosion [ɪk'sploʊʒn] explosión *f*; **explosive** explosivo *m*

export ['ekspɔːrt] **1** n exportación f; *item* producto m de exportación; **~s** exportaciones fpl **2** v/t also COMPUT exportar; **exporter** exportador(a) m(f)

expose [ɪk'spəʊz] (*uncover*) exponer; *scandal* sacar a la luz; *exposure* exposición f; PHOT foto(grafía)

express [ɪk'spres] **1** adj (*fast*) rápido; (*explicit*) expreso m **2** n *train* expreso m **3** v/t expresar; *expression voiced* muestra f; *phrase, on face* expresión f; **expressive** expresivo; **expressly** *state* expresamente; *forbid* terminantemente; **expressway** autopista f

expulsion [ɪk'spʌlʃn] expulsión f

extend [ɪk'stend] **1** v/t *house* ampliar; *runway, path* alargar; *contract* prorrogar **2** v/i *of garden etc* llegar; **extension** *to house* ampliación f; *of contract* prórroga f; TELEC extensión f; **extensive** *damage* cuantioso; *knowledge* considerable; *search* intenso, amplio; **extent** alcance m; **to a certain ~** hasta cierto punto

exterior [ɪk'stɪrɪər] **1** adj exterior **2** n exterior m

exterminate [ɪk'stɜːrmɪneɪt] exterminar

external [ɪk'stɜːrnl] exterior, externo

extinct [ɪk'stɪŋkt] *species* ex-

tinguido; **extinction** *of species* extinción f; **extinguish** extinguir, apagar; *cigarette* apagar; **extinguisher** extintor m

extortion [ɪk'stɔːrʃn] extorsión f

extra ['ekstrə] **1** n extra m **2** adj extra; **be~** (*cost more*) pagarse aparte **3** adv super

extra 'time Br SP prórroga f

extract¹ ['ekstrækt] n extracto m

extract² [ɪk'strækt] v/t sacar; *oil, tooth* extraer; *information* sonsacar; **extraction** *of oil, tooth* extracción f

extradite ['ekstrədaɪt] extraditar; **extradition** extradición f

extramarital [ekstrə'mærɪtl] extramarital

extraordinary [ɪk'strɔːrdɪnerɪ] extraordinario

extravagance [ɪk'strævəgəns] *with money* despilfarro m; *of claim etc* extravagancia f; **extravagant** *with money* despilfarrador; *claim* extravagante

extreme [ɪk'striːm] **1** n extremo m **2** adj extremo; *views* extremista; **extremely** extremadamente; **extremist** extremista m/f

extrovert ['ekstrəvɜːrt] **1** adj extrovertido **2** n extrovertido(-a) m(f)

exuberant [ɪg'zuːbərənt] exuberante

eye [aɪ] **1** n ojo m **2** v/t mirar;

eye-catching llamativo; **eyeglasses** gafas *fpl*, *L.Am.* anteojos *mpl*, *L.Am.* lentes *mpl*; **eyeliner** lápiz *m* de ojos; **eyeshadow** sombra *f* de ojos; **eyesight** vista *f*; **eyewitness** testigo *m/f* ocular

F

°**abric** ['fæbrɪk] tejido *m*
°**abulous** ['fæbjuləs] fabuloso, estupendo
°**açade** [fə'sɑːd] fachada *f*
°**ace** [feɪs] **1** *n* cara *f* **2** *v/t* (*be opposite*) estar enfrente de; (*confront*) enfrentarse a
◆ **face up to** hacer frente a
°**acebook** ['feɪsbʊk] *v/t* IT: ~ **sb** agregar a alguien a tu lista de amigos en Facebook
facecloth toallita *f*; **facelift** lifting *m*
°**acial** ['feɪʃl] limpieza *f* de cutis
°**acilitate** [fə'sɪlɪteɪt] facilitar; **facilities** instalaciones *fpl*
°**act** [fækt] hecho *m*; **in ~, as a matter of ~** de hecho
°**action** ['fækʃn] facción *f*
°**actor** ['fæktər] factor *m*
°**aculty** ['fækəltɪ] facultad *f*
°**ad** [fæd] moda *f*
°**ade** [feɪd] *of colors* desteñirse; *of memories* desvanecerse; **faded** *color* desteñido, descolorido
°**ag** [fæg] F (*homosexual*) maricón *m* F
°**ail** [feɪl] **1** *v/i* fracasar **2** *v/t* *exam* suspender; **failing** fallo *m*; **failure** fracaso *m*; *in exam* suspenso *m*

faint [feɪnt] **1** *adj* line, smile tenue; *smell, noise* casi imperceptible **2** *v/i* desmayarse; **faintly** levemente
fair[1] [fer] *n* COM feria *f*
fair[2] [fer] *adj* hair rubio; *complexion* claro; (*just*) justo
fairly ['ferlɪ] treat justamente, con justicia; (*quite*) bastante; **fairness** *of treatment* imparcialidad *f*
faith [feɪθ] fe *f*; **faithful** fiel; **faithfully** religiosamente
fake [feɪk] **1** *n* falsificación *f* **2** *adj* falso **3** *v/t* (*forge*) falsificar; (*feign*) fingir
fall[1] [fɔːl] *n* season otoño *m*
fall[2] [fɔːl] **1** *v/i* of person caerse **2** *n* caída *f*
◆ **fall behind** retrasarse
◆ **fall for** *person* enamorarse de; (*be deceived by*) dejarse engañar por
◆ **fall through** *of plans* venirse abajo
fallible ['fæləbl] falible
false [fɔːls] falso; **false start** *in race* salida *f* nula; **false teeth** dentadura *f* postiza; **falsify** falsificar
fame [feɪm] fama *f*
familiar [fə'mɪljər] familiar; **be ~ with sth** estar familiari-

zado con algo; **familiarity with** subject etc familiaridad f; **familiarize: ~ o.s. with** familiarizarse con

family ['fæmlɪ] familia f; **family doctor** médico m/f de familia; **family planning** planificación f familiar; **family tree** árbol m genealógico

famine ['fæmɪn] hambruna f

famous ['feɪməs] famoso

fan¹ [fæn] n (supporter) seguidor(a) m(f); of singer, band admirador(a) m(f), fan m/f

fan² [fæn] **1** n electric ventilador m; handheld abanico m **2** v/t abanicar

fanatical [fə'nætɪkl] fanático; **fanaticism** fanatismo m

fantasize ['fæntəsaɪz] fantasear (**about** sobre); **fantastic** (very good) fantástico; (very big) inmenso; **fantasy** fantasía f

fanzine ['fænziːn] fanzine m

far [fɑːr] lejos; (much) mucho; **~ bigger** mucho más grande; **how ~ is it to …?** ¿a cuánto está…?; **as ~ as the corner** hasta la esquina

farce [fɑːrs] farsa f

fare [fer] (price) tarifa f; actual money dinero m

Far 'East Lejano Oriente m

farewell [fer'wel] despedida f

farfetched [fɑːr'fetʃt] inverosímil, exagerado

farm [fɑːrm] granja f; **farmer** granjero(a) m(f); **farming** agricultura f; **farmworker** trabajador(a) m(f) del campo; farmyard corral m

'far-off lejano; **farsighted** previsor; optically hipermétrope; **farther** más lejos; **farthest** más lejos

fascinate ['fæsɪneɪt] fascinar; **fascinating** fascinante; **fascination** fascinación f

fascism ['fæʃɪzm] fascismo m; **fascist 1** n fascista m/f **2** adj fascista

fashion ['fæʃn] moda f; (manner) modo m, manera f; **out of ~** pasado de moda; **fashionable** de moda; **fashionably** dressed a la moda; **fashion-conscious** que sigue la moda; **fashion designer** modisto(-a) m(f); **fashion show** desfile f de moda

fast¹ [fæst] **1** adj rápido; **be ~** of clock ir adelantado **2** adv rápido; **~ asleep** profundamente dormido

fast² [fæst] n not eating ayuno m

fasten ['fæsn] **1** v/t lid cerrar (poniendo el cierre); dress abrochar **2** v/i of dress etc abrocharse; **fastener** for dress, lid cierre f

fast food comida f rápida; **fast lane** carril f rápido; **fast train** rápido m

fat [fæt] **1** adj **2** n on meat, for baking grasa f

fatal ['feɪtl] illness mortal; error fatal; **fatality** víctima f mortal; **fatally** mortalmente

fate [feɪt] destino m

'fat-free sin grasas

father ['fɑːðər] padre *m*; **fatherhood** paternidad *f*; **father-in-law** suegro *m*; **fatherly** paternal

fatigue [fə'tiːg] fatiga *f*

fatten ['fætn] *animal* engordar; **fatty** *adj* graso **2** *n* F (*person*) gordinflón (-ona) *m(f)* F

faucet ['fɔːsɪt] *Span* grifo *m*, *L.Am.* llave *f*

fault [fɔːlt] (*defect*) fallo *m*; **it's your ~** es culpa tuya; **faultless** impecable; **faulty** defectuoso

favor ['feɪvər] **1** *n favor m* **2** *v/t* (*prefer*) preferir; **favorable** favorable; **favorite 1** *n* favorito(-a) *m(f)*; *food* comida *f* favorita **2** *adj* favorito; **favoritism** favoritismo *m*; **favour** *Br* **favor**

fax [fæks] **1** *n* fax **2** *v/t* enviar por fax

fear [fɪr] **1** *n* miedo *m*, temor *m* **2** *v/t* temer; **fearless** valiente; **fearlessly** sin miedo

feasibility study [fiːzə'bɪlətɪ] estudio *m* de viabilidad; **feasible** factible, viable

feast [fiːst] banquete *m*

feat [fiːt] hazaña *f*, proeza *f*

feather ['feðər] pluma *f*

feature ['fiːtʃər] *on face* rasgo *m*, facción *f*; *of city, building, style* característica *f*; *article in paper* reportaje *m*; **feature film** largometraje *m*

February ['febrʊərɪ] febrero *m*

federal ['fedərəl] federal; **federation** federación *f*

fed up F harto, hasta las narices F

fee [fiː] honorarios *mpl*; *for entrance* entrada *f*; *for membership* cuota *f*

feeble ['fiːbl] *person, laugh* débil; *attempt* flojo; *excuse* pobre

feed [fiːd] alimentar, dar de comer a; **feedback** reacción *f*

feel [fiːl] **1** *v/t* (*touch*) tocar; (*sense*) sentir; (*think*) creer, pensar **2** *v/i*: **it ~s like silk** tiene la textura de la seda; **do you ~ like a drink?** ¿te apetece una bebida?

◆ **feel up to** sentirse con fuerzas para

feeler ['fiːlər] *of insect* antena *f*; **feeling** sentimiento *m*; (*sense*) sensación *f*

fellow 'citizen conciudadano(-a) *m(f)*

felony ['felənɪ] delito *m* grave

felt [felt] fieltro *m*; **felt tip** rotulador *m*

female ['fiːmeɪl] **1** *adj* hembra; *relating to people* femenino **2** *n* hembra *f*; *person* mujer *f*

feminine ['femɪnɪn] **1** *adj* femenino **2** *n* GRAM femenino *m*; **feminism** feminismo *m*; **feminist 1** *n* feminista *m/f* **2** *adj* feminista

fence [fens] cerca *f*, valla *f*

fender ['fendər] MOT aleta *f*

fermentation [fɜːrmen'teɪʃn]

fermentación f

ferocious [fəˈrouʃəs] feroz

ferry [ˈferɪ] ferry m, transbordador m

fertile [ˈfɜːtaɪl] fértil; **fertility** fertilidad f; **fertilize** fertilizar; **fertilizer** for soil fertilizante m

fervent [ˈfɜːrvənt] ferviente

fester [ˈfestər] of wound enconarse

festival [ˈfestɪvl] festival m; **festive** festivo; **festivities** fpl celebraciones fpl

fetal [ˈfiːtl] fetal

fetch [fetʃ] person recoger; thing traer, ir a buscar; price alcanzar

fetus [ˈfiːtəs] feto m

feud [fjuːd] enemistad f

fever [ˈfiːvər] fiebre f; **feverish** con fiebre; excitement febril

few [fjuː] **1** adj pocos; a ~ unos pocos **2** pron pocos(-as); **quite a ~** bastantes; **fewer** menos

fiancé [fɪˈɑːnseɪ] prometido m, novio m; **fiancée** prometida f, novia f

fiber [ˈfaɪbər] fibra f; **fiberglass** fibra f de vidrio; **fiber optics** tecnología f de la fibra óptica

fibre Br ☞ **fiber**

fickle [ˈfɪkl] inconstante

fiction [ˈfɪkʃn] literatura f de ficción; (made-up story) ficción f; **fictional** de ficción; **fictitious** ficticio

fiddle [ˈfɪdl] **1** n violín m **2** v/i:

~ **around with** enredar con **3** v/t accounts, result amañar

fidgety [ˈfɪdʒɪtɪ] inquieto

field [fiːld] campo m; for sport campo m, L.Am. cancha f; (competitors in race) participantes mpl; **fielder** in baseball fildeador(-a) m(f)

fierce [fɪrs] feroz; storm violento; **fiercely** ferozmente

fiery [ˈfaɪrɪ] fogoso, ardiente

fifteen [fɪfˈtiːn] quince; **fifteenth** decimoquinto; **fifth** quinto; **fiftieth** quincuagésimo; **fifty** cincuenta; **fifty-fifty** a medias

fight [faɪt] **1** n lucha f, pelea f; (argument) pelea f; for survival etc lucha f, in boxing combate m **2** v/t enemy, person luchar contra, pelear contra; injustice luchar contra **3** v/i luchar, pelear; (argue) pelearse; **fighter** combatiente m/f; (boxer) púgil m; airplane caza m; **fighting** peleas fpl; MIL luchas fpl

figure [ˈfɪɡər] **1** n figura f; (digit) cifra f **2** v/t F (think) imaginarse, pensar

◆ **figure on** F (plan) pensar

◆ **figure out** entender; calculation resolver

file[1] [faɪl] **1** n of documents expediente m; COMPUT archivo m, fichero m **2** v/t archivar

file[2] [faɪl] n for wood etc lima f; **'file cabinet** archivador m

fill [fɪl] llenar; tooth empastar, L.Am. emplomar; prescription despachar

◆ **fill in** *form, hole* rellenar

◆ **fill out** 1 *v/t form* rellenar 2 *v/i* (*get fatter*) engordar

illet ['fɪlɪt] filete *m*

illing ['fɪlɪŋ] 1 *n in sandwich* relleno *m*; *in tooth* empaste *m*, L.Am. emplomadura *f* 2 *adj*: **be ~** *of food* llenar mucho; **filling station** estación *f* de servicio

ilm [fɪlm] 1 *n* (*movie*) película *f* 2 *v/t* filmar; **film-maker** cineasta *m/f*; **film star** estrella *f* de cine

ilter ['fɪltər] 1 *n* filtro *m* 2 *v/t* filtrar

ilth [fɪlθ] suciedad *f*; *filthy* sucio; *language etc* obsceno

inal ['faɪnl] 1 *adj* último; *decision* final, definitivo 2 *n SP* final *m*; **finale** final *m*; **finalist** finalista *m/f*; **finalize** ultimar; **finally** finalmente

inance ['faɪnæns] 1 *n* finanzas *fpl* 2 *v/t* financiar; **financial** financiero; **financially** económicamente; **financier** financiero(-a) *m(f)*

ind [faɪnd] encontrar

◆ **find out** descubrir

indings ['faɪndɪŋz] *of report* conclusiones *fpl*

ine¹ [faɪn] *adj day* bueno; *wine, performance, city* excelente; *distinction, line* fino

ine² [faɪn] 1 *n* multa *f* 2 *v/t* multar, poner una multa a

inger ['fɪŋgər] 1 *n* dedo *m* 2 *v/t* tocar; **fingerprint** huella *f* digital *or* dactilar

finicky ['fɪnɪkɪ] *person* quisquilloso; *design* enrevesado

finish ['fɪnɪʃ] 1 *v/t* & *v/i* acabar, terminar 2 *n of product* acabado *m*; *of race* final *f*

◆ **finish with** *boyfriend etc* cortar con

Finland ['fɪnlənd] Finlandia *f*; **Finn** finlandés(-esa) *m(f)*; **Finnish** 1 *adj* finlandés 2 *n language* finés *m*

fire [faɪr] *n* fuego *m*; *electric, gas* estufa *f*; (*blaze*) incendio *m*; (*bonfire, campfire etc*) hoguera *f*; **be on** ~ estar ardiendo; **set** ~ **to sth** prender fuego a algo 2 *v/i* (*shoot*) disparar (**at** a) 3 *v/t* F (*dismiss*) despedir; **fire alarm** alarma *f* contra incendios; **firearm** arma *f* de fuego; **firecracker** petardo *m*; **fire department** (cuerpo *m* de) bomberos *mpl*; **fire engine** coche *m* de bomberos; **fire escape** salida *f* de incendios; **fire extinguisher** extintor *m*; **fire fighter** bombero (-a) *m(f)*; **fireplace** chimenea *f*, hogar *m*; **fire station** parque *m* de bomberos; **fire truck** coche *m* de bomberos; **fireworks** fuegos *mpl* artificiales

firm¹ [fɜːrm] *adj* firme

firm² [fɜːrm] *n com* empresa *f*

first [fɜːrst] 1 *adj* & *adv* primero; **at** ~ al principio 2 *n* primero(-a) *m(f)*; **first aid** primeros *mpl* auxilios; **first class** 1 *adj ticket, seat* de primera (clase); (*very good*) excelente **2** *adv travel* en primera (clase); **first floor** planta *f* baja, *Br* primer piso *m*; **First Lady** primera dama *f*; **firstly** en primer lugar; **first name** nombre *m* (de pila); **first night** estreno *m*; **first-rate** excelente

fiscal ['fɪskl] fiscal; **fiscal year** año *m* fiscal

fish [fɪʃ] **1** *n* pez *m*; *to eat* pescado *m* **2** *v/i* pescar; **fisherman** pescador *m*; **fishing** pesca *f*; **fishing boat** (barco *m*) pesquero *m*; **fish stick** palito *m* de pescado; **fishy** F (*suspicious*) sospechoso

fist [fɪst] puño *m*

fit¹ [fɪt] *n* MED ataque *m*

fit² [fɪt] *adj* en forma; *morally* adecuado

fit³ [fɪt] **1** *v/t* (*attach*) colocar; *these pants don't ~ me any more* estos pantalones ya no me entran **2** *v/i of clothes* quedar bien

fitness ['fɪtnɪs] *physical* buena forma *f*; **fitting** apropiado; **fittings** equipamiento *m*

five [faɪv] cinco

fix [fɪks] **1** *n* (*solution*) solución *f* **2** *v/t* (*attach*) fijar; (*repair*) reparar; *meeting etc* organizar; *lunch* preparar; *dishonestly*: *match etc* amañar; **fixed** fijo; **fixings** guarnición *f*

flab [flæb] *on body* grasa *f*; **flabby** *muscles etc* fofo

flag¹ [flæg] *n* bandera *f*

flag² [flæg] *v/i* (*tire*) desfalle-

cer

flagpole asta *f* (de bandera)

flagrant ['fleɪgrənt] flagrante

flair [fler] (*talent*) don *m*

flake [fleɪk] *of snow* copo *m*; *of skin* escama *f*; *of plaster* desconchón *m*

flamboyant [flæm'bɔɪənt] extravagante; **flamboyantly** extravagantemente

flame [fleɪm] llama *f*

flamenco [flə'meŋkoʊ] flamenco *m*; **flamenco dancer** bailaor(a) *m(f)*

flammable ['flæməbl] inflamable

flank [flæŋk] **1** *n of horse etc* costado *m*; MIL flanco *m* **2** *v/t* flanquear

flap [flæp] **1** *n of envelope, pocket* solapa *f*; *of table* hoja *f* **2** *v/t wings* batir **3** *v/i of flag etc* ondear

◆ **flare up** [fler] *of violence* estallar; *of illness* exacerbarse; *of fire* llamear; (*get very angry*) estallar

flash [flæʃ] **1** *n of light* destello *m*; PHOT flash *m*; *in a ~* F en un abrir y cerrar de ojos; *a ~ of lightning* un relámpago **2** *v/i of light* destellar; *a ~ of lightning* un relámpago **flashback** flash-back *m*; **flashlight** linterna *f*, PHOT flash *m*; **flashy** *pej* ostentoso, chillón

flask [flæsk] (*hip ~*) petaca *f*

flat¹ [flæt] **1** *adj* llano, plano; *beer* sin gas; *battery* descargado; *tire* deshinchado; *shoes* bajo; MUS bemol **2** *adv* MUS demasiado bajo **3** n (~ tire) pinchazo m

flat² [flæt] n Br apartamento m, Span piso m

flatly ['flætlɪ] deny rotundamente; flat rate tarifa f única; **flatten** land, road allanar, aplanar; by bombing, demolition arrasar

flatter ['flætər] halagar; **flatterer** adulador(a) m(f); **flattering** comments halagador; color, clothes favorecedor; **flattery** halagos mpl

flavor ['fleɪvər] **1** n sabor m **2** v/t food condimentar; **flavoring** aromatizante m; **flavour** Br ► **flavor**

flaw [flɔː] defecto m, fallo m; **flawless** impecable

flee [fliː] escapar, huir

fleet [fliːt] NAUT, of vehicles flota f

fleeting ['fliːtɪŋ] visit etc fugaz

flesh [fleʃ] carne f; of fruit pulpa f

flex [fleks] muscles flexionar; **flexibility** flexibilidad f; **flexible** flexible; **flextime** horario m flexible

flicker ['flɪkər] parpadear

flier [flaɪr] (circular) folleto m

flight [flaɪt] in airplane vuelo m; (fleeing) huida f; ~ **(of stairs)** tramo m (de escaleras); **flight attendant** auxiliar m/f de vuelo; **flight path** ruta f de vuelo; **flight recorder** caja f negra; **flight time** departure hora f del vuelo; duration duración f

del vuelo; **flighty** inconstante

flimsy ['flɪmzɪ] furniture endeble; dress, material débil; excuse pobre

flinch [flɪntʃ] encogerse

flipper ['flɪpər] aleta f

flirt [flɜːrt] **1** v/i flirtear, coquetear **2** n ligón (-ona) m(f); **flirtatious** coqueto

float [flout] also FIN flotar

flock [flɑːk] **1** n of sheep rebaño m **2** v/i acudir en masa

flood [flʌd] **1** n inundación f **2** v/t of river inundar; **flooding** inundaciones fpl; **floodlight** foco m; **flood waters** crecida f

floor [flɔːr] suelo m; (story) piso m

flop [flɑːp] v/i dejarse caer; F (fail) pinchar **F 2** n F (failure) pinchazo m F; **floppy (disk)** disquete m

florist ['flɔːrɪst] florista m/f

flour [flaʊr] harina f

flourish ['flʌrɪʃ] of plant crecer rápidamente; fig florecer; **flourishing** business, trade floreciente

flow [floʊ] **1** v/i fluir **2** n flujo m; **flowchart** diagrama m de flujo

flower [flaʊr] **1** n flor f **2** v/i florecer

flu [fluː] gripe f

fluctuate ['flʌktjʊeɪt] fluctuar; **fluctuation** fluctuación f

fluency ['fluːənsɪ] in a language fluidez f; **fluent: he**

speaks ~ Spanish habla español con soltura; **fluently** *speak, write* con soltura

fluid [fluːɪd] fluido *m*

flunk [flʌŋk] F *subject* suspender, *Span* catear F

flush [flʌʃ] **1** *v/t:* ~ **the toilet** tirar de la cadena **2** *v/i (go red)* ruborizarse

flutter ['flʌtər] *of wings* aletear; *of flag* ondear; *of heart* latir con fuerza

fly[1] [flaɪ] *n insect* mosca *f*

fly[2] [flaɪ] *n on pants* bragueta *f*

fly[3] [flaɪ] **1** *v/i volar; of flag* ondear **2** *v/t airplane* pilotar; *airline* volar con; *(transport by air)* enviar por avión

◆ **fly past** *of time* volar

flying ['flaɪɪŋ] volar *m*

foam [foum] *on liquid* espuma *f;* **foam rubber** gomaespuma *f*

focus ['foukəs] foco *m*

◆ **focus on** concentrarse en; PHOT enfocar

fodder ['fɑːdər] forraje *m*

fog [fɑːg] niebla *f;* **foggy** neblinoso, con niebla

foil[1] [fɔɪl] *n papel m* de aluminio

foil[2] [fɔɪl] *v/t (thwart)* frustrar

fold [fould] **1** *v/t paper etc* doblar; ~ *one's arms* cruzarse de brazos **2** *v/i of business* quebrar **3** *n in cloth etc* pliegue *m*

◆ **fold up 1** *v/t* plegar **2** *v/i of chair, table* plegarse

folder ['fouldər] *for documents,* COMPUT carpeta *f;*

folding plegable

foliage ['foulɪdʒ] follaje *m*

folk [fouk] *(people)* gente *f;* **folk music** música *f* folk *or* popular; **folk singer** cantante *m/f* de folk

follow ['fɑːlou] **1** *v/t* seguir; *(understand)* entender **2** *v/i logically* deducirse

◆ **follow up** *inquiry* hacer el seguimiento de; **follower** seguidor(a) *m(f);* **following 1** *adj* siguiente **2** *n people* seguidores(-as) *mpl (fpl);* **the** ~ lo siguiente

fond [fɑːnd] cariñoso; *memory* entrañable; *he's ~ of travel* le gusta viajar; **I'm very ~ of him** le tengo mucho cariño

fondle ['fɑːndl] acariciar

fondness ['fɑːndnɪs] *for s.o.* cariño *m* (**for** por); *for wine, food* afición *f*

font [fɑːnt] *for printing* tipo *m; in church* pila *f* bautismal

food [fuːd] comida *f;* **food poisoning** intoxicación *f* alimentaria

fool [fuːl] **1** *n* tonto(-a) *m(f),* idiota *m/f* **2** *v/t* engañar; **foolhardy** temerario; **foolish** tonto; **foolproof** infalible

foot [fut] *also measurement* pie *m; of animal* pata *f;* **put one's ~ in it** F meter la pata F; **footage** secuencias *fpl;* **football** *Br (soccer)* fútbol *m; American* fútbol *m* americano; *ball* balón *m or* pelota f (de fútbol); **football player** American style jugador(a) m(f) de fútbol americano; Br in soccer jugador(a) m(f) de fútbol, futbolista m/f; **foothills** estribaciones fpl; **footnote** nota f a pie de página; **footpath** sendero m; **footprint** pisada f; **footstep** paso m

'or [fɔːr] purpose, destination para; (in exchange for) por; **what is this ~?** ¿para qué sirve esto?; **what ~?** ¿para qué?; **I bought it ~ $25** lo compré por 5 dólares; **~ three days** durante tres días; **please get it done ~ Monday** por favor tenlo listo (para) el lunes; **I walked ~ a mile** caminé una milla; **~ ~ the idea** estoy a favor de la idea

'orbid [fərˈbɪd] prohibir; **forbidden** person, prohibido; **forbidding** person, look amenazador; prospect intimidador

'orce [fɔːrs] **1** n fuerza f; **come into ~** of law etc entrar en vigor **2** v/t door, lock forzar; **~ s.o. to do sth** forzar a alguien a hacer algo; **forced** forzado; **forced landing** aterrizaje m forzoso; **forceful** argument poderoso; speaker vigoroso; character enérgico

orceps [ˈfɔːrseps] MED fórceps m inv

orcibly [ˈfɔːrsəblɪ] por la fuerza

oreboding [fərˈboʊdɪŋ] pre-

monición f; **forecast 1** n pronóstico m **2** v/t pronosticar; **forefathers** ancestros mpl; **forefinger** (dedo m) índice m; **foreground** primer plano m; **forehead** frente f

foreign [ˈfɑːrən] extranjero; **foreign affairs** asuntos mpl exteriores; **foreign body** cuerpo m extraño; **foreign currency** divisa f extranjera; **foreigner** extranjero(-a) m(f); **foreign exchange** divisas f

foreman capataz m; **foremost** principal

forensic medicine [fəˈrensɪk] medicina f forense; **forensic scientist** forense m/f

'forerunner predecesor(a) m(f); **foresee** prever; **foresight** previsión f

forest [ˈfɑːrɪst] bosque m; **forestry** silvicultura f

fore'tell predecir

forever [fəˈrevər] siempre

forfeit [ˈfɔːrfɪt] (lose) perder; (give up) renunciar a

forge [fɔːrdʒ] falsificar; **forgery** falsificación f

forget [fərˈget] olvidar; **forgetful** olvidadizo

forgive [fərˈgɪv] perdonar; **forgiveness** perdón m

fork [fɔːrk] for eating tenedor m; for garden horca f; in road bifurcación f

form [fɔːrm] **1** n (shape) forma f; document formulario m, impreso m **2** v/t in clay etc moldear; *friendship* establecer; *opinion* formarse; *(constitute)* formar **3** *v/i (take shape, develop)* formarse; **formal** formal; *recognition etc* oficial; *dress* de etiqueta; **formality** formalidad *f*; **formally** *speak* formalmente; *recognized* oficialmente

format ['fɔːrmæt] **1** *v/t text* formatear **2** *n* of paper, program etc formato *m*

formation [fɔːr'meɪʃn] formación *f*

former ['fɔːrmər] antiguo; *the* **~** el primero; **formerly** antiguamente

formidable ['fɔːrmɪdəbl] *personality* formidable; *opponent, task* terrible

formula ['fɔːrmjʊlə] fórmula *f*

fort [fɔːrt] MIL fuerte *m*

forthcoming ['fɔːrθkʌmɪŋ] *(future)* próximo; *personality* comunicativo

'**forthright** directo

fortieth ['fɔːrtɪɪθ] cuadragésimo

fortnight ['fɔːrtnaɪt] *Br* quincena *f*

fortress ['fɔːrtrɪs] MIL fortaleza *f*

fortunate ['fɔːrtʃnət] afortunado; **fortunately** afortunadamente; **fortune** fortuna *f*

forty ['fɔːrtɪ] cuarenta

forward ['fɔːrwərd] **1** *adv* hacia delante **2** *adj pej: person* atrevido **3** *n* SP delantero(-a) *m(f)* **4** *v/t letter* reexpedir; **forward-looking** con visión

de futuro

fossil ['fɑːsəl] fósil *m*

foster ['fɔːstər] *child* acoger; *attitude, belief* fomentar

foul [faʊl] **1** *n* SP falta *f* **2** *adj smell* asqueroso; *weather* terrible **3** *v/t* SP hacer (una) falta a

found [faʊnd] *school etc* fundar; **foundation** *of theory etc* fundamento *m*; *(organization)* fundación *f*; **foundations** *of building* cimientos *mpl*; **founder** fundador(a) *m(f)*

fountain ['faʊntn] fuente *f*

four [fɔːr] cuatro; **four-star** *hotel etc* de cuatro estrellas; **fourteen** catorce; **fourteenth** decimocuarto; **fourth** cuarto; **four-wheel drive** MOT todoterreno *m*

fox [fɑːks] **1** *n* zorro *m* **2** *v/t (puzzle)* dejar perplejo

foyer ['fɔɪər] vestíbulo *m*

fraction ['frækʃn] fracción *f*; **fractionally** ligeramente

fracture ['fræktʃər] **1** *n* fractura *f* **2** *v/t* fracturar

fragile ['frædʒaɪl] frágil

fragment ['frægmənt] fragmento *m*

fragrance ['freɪgrəns] fragancia *f*; **fragrant** fragante

frail [freɪl] frágil, delicado

frame [freɪm] **1** *n* of picture window marco *m*; of eyeglasses montura *f*; of bicycle cuadro *m*; *v/t picture* enmarcar; F *person* tender una trampa a; **framework** estructura f; *for agreement* marco m

France [fræns] Francia f

franchise [ˈfræntʃaɪz] *for business* franquicia f

frank [fræŋk] franco; **frankly** francamente; **frankness** franqueza f

frantic [ˈfræntɪk] frenético

fraternal [frəˈtɜːrnl] fraternal

fraud [frɔːd] fraude m; *person* impostor(a) m(f); **fraudulent** fraudulento

frayed [freɪd] *cuffs* deshilachado

freak [friːk] **1** *n event* fenómeno m anormal; *two-headed animal etc* monstruo m; F *strange person* bicho m raro F **2** *adj storm etc* anormal

free [friː] **1** *adj* libre; *no cost* gratis, gratuito **2** *v/t prisoners* liberar; **freedom** libertad f; **free enterprise** empresa f libre; **free kick** golpe m franco; **freelance** autónomo, free-lance; **freely** *admit* libremente; **free speech** libertad f de expresión; **freeway** autopista f

freeze [friːz] **1** *v/t food, wages, video* congelar **2** *v/i of water* congelarse; **freeze-dried** liofilizado; **freezer** congelador m; **freezing 1** *adj* muy frío **2** *n*: **10 degrees below** ~ diez grados bajo cero

freight [freɪt] flete m; *costs* flete m; **freighter** *ship* carguero m; *airplane* avión m de carga

French [frentʃ] **1** *adj* francés **2** *n language* francés m; *the* ~ los franceses; **French fries** *Span* patatas fpl *or L.Am.* papas fpl fritas; **Frenchman** francés m; **Frenchwoman** francesa f

frenzied [ˈfrenzɪd] frenético; *mob* desenfrenado; **frenzy** frenesí m

frequency [ˈfriːkwənsɪ] *also* RAD frecuencia f

frequent¹ [ˈfriːkwənt] *adj* frecuente

frequent² [frɪˈkwent] *v/t bar* frecuentar

frequently [ˈfriːkwəntlɪ] con frecuencia

fresh [freʃ] *fresco; start* nuevo; *(impertinent)* descarado; **fresh air** aire m fresco

♦ **freshen up 1** *v/i* refrescarse **2** *v/t paintwork etc* renovar

freshly [ˈfreʃlɪ] recién; **freshman** estudiante m/f de primer año; **freshwater** de agua dulce

fret [fret] **1** *v/i* inquietarse **2** *n of guitar* traste m

friction [ˈfrɪkʃn] PHYS rozamiento m; *between people* fricción f

Friday [ˈfraɪdeɪ] viernes m inv

fridge [frɪdʒ] nevera f, frigorífico m

friend [frend] amigo(-a) m(f); **friendliness** simpatía f; **friendly** agradable; *person also* simpático; *argument, relations* amistoso; **friendship** amistad f

fries [fraiz] *Span* patatas *fpl or L.Am.* papas *fpl* fritas

fright [frait] susto *m*; **frighten** asustar; **be ~ed of** tener miedo de; **frightening** aterrador; espantoso

frill [fril] *on dress etc* volante *m*; *(fancy extra)* extra *m*

fringe [frindʒ] *on dress etc* flecos *mpl*; *Br in hair* flequillo *m*; *(edge)* margen *m*; **fringe benefits** ventajas *fpl* adicionales

frisk [frisk] cachear

◆ **fritter away** ['fritər] *time* desperdiciar; *fortune* despilfarrar

frivolity [frɪ'vɑːlətɪ] frivolidad *f*; **frivolous** frívolo

frizzy ['frɪzɪ] *hair* crespo

frog [frɑːg] rana *f*

'frogman hombre *m* rana

from [frɑːm] *in time* desde; *in space* de, desde; **~ 9 to 5** de 9 a 5; **~ today** a partir de hoy; **here to there** de *or* desde aquí hasta allí; **we drove here ~ Las Vegas** vinimos en coche desde Las Vegas; **a letter ~ Jo** una carta de Jo; **I am ~ New Jersey** soy de Nueva Jersey

front [frʌnt] **1** *n of building, book* portada *f*; *(cover organization)* tapadera *f*; MIL, *of weather* frente *m*; *in distance*; *in a race* en cabeza; **in ~ of** delante de **2** *adj wheel, seat* delantero **3** *v/t TV program*

presentar; **front door** puerta *f* principal

frontier [frʌn'tɪr] frontera *f*; *of science* límite *m*

front 'line MIL línea *f* del frente; **front page** *of newspaper* portada *f*; **front-wheel 'drive** tracción *f* delantera

frost [frɔːst] escarcha *f*; **frostbite** congelación *f*; **frosting** *on cake* glaseado *m*; **frosty** *weather* gélido; *welcome* glacial

froth [frɔːθ] espuma *f*

frown [fraun] fruncir el ceño

frozen ['frouzn] *ground, food* congelado

fruit [fruːt] fruta *f*; **fruitful** *discussions etc* fructífero; **fruit juice** *Span* zumo *m or L.Am.* jugo *m* de fruta; **fruit salad** macedonia *f*

frustrate ['frʌstreit] frustrar; **frustrating** frustrante; **frustration** frustración *f*

fry [frai] freír; **frypan** sartén *f*

fuck [fʌk] V *Span* follar con V, *L.Am.* coger V; **~!** *~!* ¡joder!

fuel ['fjuːəl] **1** *n* combustible *m* **2** *v/t fig* avivar

fugitive ['fjuːdʒətɪv] fugitivo(-a) *m(f)*

fulfill, *Br* **fulfil** [ful'fɪl] *dream, task* realizar; *contract* cumplir; **fulfillment**, *Br* **fulfilment** *of contract etc* cumplimiento *m*; *moral, spiritual* satisfacción *f*

full [ful] lleno; *account, schedule* completo; *life* pleno; **pay**

fuzzy

in ~ pagar al contado; **full moon** luna *f* llena; **full stop** *Br* punto *m*; **full-time** *worker*, *job* a tiempo completo; **fully** completamente; *describe* en detalle

fumble ['fʌmbl] *ball* dejar caer

fumes [fjuːmz] humos *mpl*

fun [fʌn] **1** *n* diversión *f*; **for** ~ para divertirse; **it was great** ~ fue muy divertido **2** *adj* F *person, game* divertido

function ['fʌŋkʃn] **1** *n* función *f*; *(reception etc)* acto *m* **2** *v/i* funcionar; ~ **as** hacer de; **functional** funcional

fund [fʌnd] **1** *n* fondo *m* **2** *v/t project etc* financiar

fundamental [fʌndə'mentl] fundamental; *(crucial)* esencial; **fundamentalist** fundamentalista *m/f*; **fundamentally** fundamentalmente

funding ['fʌndɪŋ] *(money)* fondos *mpl*, financiación *f*

funeral ['fjuːnərəl] funeral *m*; **funeral home** funeraria *f*

fungus ['fʌŋgəs] hongos *mpl*

funnies ['fʌnɪz] F sección *f* de humor; **funnily** *(oddly)* de modo extraño; *(comically)* de forma divertida; ~

enough curiosamente; **funny** *(comical)* divertido, gracioso; *(odd)* curioso, raro

fur [fɜːr] piel *f*

furious ['fjʊriəs] furioso; *effort* febril

furnace ['fɜːrnɪs] horno *m*

furnish ['fɜːrnɪʃ] *room* amueblar; *(supply)* suministrar; **furniture** mobiliario *m*, muebles *mpl*

further ['fɜːrðər] **1** *adj* adicional; *(more distant)* más lejano **2** *adv walk, drive* más lejos **3** *v/t cause etc* promover; **furthermore** es más

furtive ['fɜːrtɪv] furtivo

fury ['fjʊri] furia *f*, ira *f*

fuse [fjuːz] **1** *n* ELEC fusible *m* **2** *v/i* ELEC fundirse **3** *v/t* ELEC fundir; **fusebox** caja *f* de fusibles

fusion ['fjuːʒn] fusión *f*

fuss [fʌs] escándalo *m*; **fussy** *person* quisquilloso; *design etc* recargado

futile ['fjuːtl] inútil, vano; **futility** inutilidad *f*

future ['fjuːtʃər] **1** *n* futuro *m* **2** *adj* futuro; **futuristic** *design* futurista

fuzzy ['fʌzi] *hair* crespo; *(out of focus)* borroso

G

gadget ['gædʒɪt] artilugio *m*, chisme *m*

gag [gæg] **1** *n over mouth* mordaza *f*; (*joke*) chiste *m* **2** *v/t also fig* amordazar

gain [geɪn] (*acquire*) ganar; *victory* obtener

gala ['gɑːlə] gala *f*

galaxy ['gæləksɪ] galaxia *f*

gale [geɪl] vendaval *m*

gallery ['gælərɪ] *for art* museo *m*; *private* galería de arte; *in theater* galería *f*

gallon ['gælən] galón *m* (*0,785 litros, en GB 0,546*)

gallop ['gæləp] galopar

gamble ['gæmbl] jugar; **gambler** jugador(a) *m(f)*; **gambling** juego *m*

game [geɪm] partido *m*; *children's, in tennis* juego *m*

gang [gæŋ] *of criminals* banda *f*; *of friends* cuadrilla *f*; **gangster** gánster *m*; **gangway** pasarela *f*

gap [gæp] *in wall* hueco *m*; *for parking, in figures* espacio *m*; *in time* intervalo *m*; *in conversation* interrupción *f*

gape [geɪp] *of person* mirar boquiabierto; **gaping** *hole* enorme

garage [gə'rɑːʒ] *for parking* garaje *m*; *for repairs* taller *m*; *Br for gas* gasolinera *f*

garbage ['gɑːbɪdʒ] *also fig* basura *f*; *fig* (*nonsense*) ton-

terías *fpl*; **garbage can** cubo *m* de la basura; *in street* papelera *f*; **garbage truck** camión *m* de la basura

garbled ['gɑːbld] *message* confuso

garden ['gɑːrdn] jardín *m*; **gardening** jardinería *f*

garish ['geərɪʃ] *color* chillón; *design* estridente

garlic ['gɑːrlɪk] ajo *m*

garment ['gɑːrmənt] prenda *f* (de vestir)

garnish ['gɑːrnɪʃ] guarnecer

gas [gæs] gas *m*; (*gasoline*) gasolina *f*, *Rpl* nafta *f*

gash [gæʃ] corte *m* profundo

gasket ['gæskɪt] junta *f*

gasoline ['gæsəliːn] gasolina *f*, *Rpl* nafta *f*

gasp [gæsp] **1** *n* grito *m* apagado **2** *v/i* lanzar un grito apagado

'**gas pedal** acelerador *m*; **gas pump** surtidor *m* (de gasolina); **gas station** gasolinera *f*, *S.Am.* bomba

gate [geɪt] *of house, at airport* puerta *f*; *made of iron* verja *f*

gateway *also fig* entrada *f*

gather [gæ] **1** *v/t facts* reunir; **~ speed** ganar velocidad **2** *v/i of crowd* reunirse; **gathering** grupo *m* de personas

gaudy ['gɔːdɪ] chillón

gauge [geɪdʒ] **1** *n* indicador *m* **2** *v/t pressure* medir, calcular *opinion* estimar

gaunt [gɔːnt] demacrado

gawky ['gɔːkɪ] desgarbado

gawp [gɔːp] F mirar boquiabierto

gay [geɪ] gay

gaze [geɪz] **1** *n* mirada *f* **2** *v/i* mirar fijamente

gear [gɪr] (*equipment*) equipo *m*; *in vehicle* marcha *f*; **gearbox** MOT caja *f* de cambios; **gear shift** MOT palanca *f* de cambios

gel [dʒel] *for hair* gomina *f*; *for shower* gel *m*

gem [dʒem] gema *f*; *fig* (*book etc*) joya *f*; (*person*) cielo *m*

gender ['dʒendər] género *m*

gene [dʒiːn] gen *m*

general ['dʒenərəl] **1** *n* MIL general *m* **2** *adj* general; **generalization** generalización *f*; **generalize** generalizar; **generally** generalmente, por lo general; **~ speaking** en términos generales

generate ['dʒenəreɪt] generar; *feeling* provocar; **generation** generación *f*; **generator** generador *m*

generosity [dʒenə'rɑːsətɪ] generosidad *f*; **generous** generoso

genetic [dʒɪ'netɪk] genético; **genetically** genéticamente; **~ modified** transgénico; **~ engineered** transgénico; **genetic engineering** ingeniería *f* genética; **genetic fingerprint** identificación *f* genética; **genetics** genética *f*

genial ['dʒiːnjəl] afable

genitals ['dʒenɪtlz] genitales *mpl*

genius ['dʒiːnjəs] genio *m*

genocide ['dʒenəsaɪd] genocidio *m*

gentle ['dʒentl] *person* tierno, delicado; *touch, detergent, breeze* suave; *slope* poco inclinado; **gentleman** caballero *m*; **gentleness** *of person* ternura *f*, delicadeza *f*; *of touch, detergent, breeze* suavidad *f*; **gently** con delicadeza

genuine ['dʒenʊɪn] *antique* genuino, auténtico; (*sincere*) sincero; **genuinely** realmente, de verdad

geographical [dʒɪə'græfɪkl] geográfico; **geography** geografía *f*

geological [dʒɪə'lɑːdʒɪkl] geológico; **geologist** geólogo(-a) *m(f)*; **geology** geología *f*

geometric, geometrical [dʒɪə'metrɪk(l)] geométrico; **geometry** geometría *f*

geriatric [dʒerɪ'ætrɪk] **1** *adj* geriátrico **2** *n* anciano(-a) *m(f)*

germ [dʒɜːrm] *also fig* germen *m*

German ['dʒɜːrmən] **1** *adj* alemán **2** *n person* alemán (-ana) *m(f)*; *language* alemán *m*; **German shepherd** pastor *m* alemán; **Germany** Alemania

gesture ['dʒestʃər] *also fig* gesto *m*

get [get] (*obtain*) conseguir; (*buy*) comprar; (*fetch*) traer; (*receive: letter, knowledge, respect*) recibir; (*catch: bus, train etc*) tomar, *Span* coger; (*understand*) entender; ~ **home** llegar a casa; ~ *tired* cansarse; ~ *the TV fixed* hacer que arreglen la televisión; ~ **one's hair cut** cortarse el pelo; ~ *s.o. to do sth* hacer que alguien haga algo; ~ *to do sth* (*have opportunity*) llegar a hacer algo; ~ *sth ready* preparar algo; ~ *going* (*leave*) marcharse, irse; **have got** tener; **have got to** tener que; *I have got to see him* tengo que verlo; ~ *to know* llegar a conocer

◆ **get at** (*criticize*) meterse con; (*mean*) querer decir

◆ **get by** (*pass*) pasar; *financially* arreglárselas

◆ **get down 1** *v/i from ladder etc* bajarse (**from** de); (*duck etc*) agacharse **2** *v/t* (*depress*) desanimar

◆ **get in 1** *v/i* (*arrive*) llegar; *to car* subir(se) **2** *v/t to suitcase etc* meter

◆ **get into** *house* entrar en; *car* subir(se) en; *a computer system* introducirse en

◆ **get off 1** *v/i from bus etc* bajarse; (*finish work*) salir; (*not be punished*) librarse **2** *v/t* (*remove*) quitar; *clothes* quitarse

◆ **get on 1** *v/i to bike, bus* montarse, subirse; (*be friendly*) llevarse bien; (*advance: of time*) hacerse tarde; (*become old*) hacerse mayor; (*make progress*) progresar **2** *v/t: get on the bus* montarse en el autobús

◆ **get out 1** *v/i of car, prison etc* salir; *get out!* ¡vete!, ¡fuera de aquí! **2** *v/t nail etc* sacar, extraer; *stain* quitar; *gun, pen* sacar

◆ **get through** *on telephone* conectarse

◆ **get up 1** *v/i* levantarse **2** *v/t* (*climb*) subir

'getaway *from robbery* fuga *f*; **get-together** reunión *f*

ghastly ['gæstli] terrible

ghetto ['getou] gueto *m*

ghost [goust] fantasma *m*; **ghostly** fantasmal

ghoul [gu:l] macabro(-a) *m(f)*

giant ['dʒaɪənt] **1** *n* gigante *m* **2** *adj* gigantesco, gigante

gibberish ['dʒɪbərɪʃ] F memeces *fpl* F

gibe [dʒaɪb] pulla *f*

giddiness ['gɪdɪnɪs] mareo *m*; **giddy** mareado

gift [gɪft] regalo *m*; *talent* don *m*; **gift certificate** vale *m* de regalo; **gifted** con talento; **giftwrap** envolver para regalo

gig [gɪg] F concierto *m*

gigabyte ['gɪgəbaɪt] COMPUT gigabyte *m*

gigantic [dʒaɪ'gæntɪk] gigantesco

jiggle ['gɪgl] **1** v/i soltar risitas **2** n risita f

jimmick ['gɪmɪk] truco m

jin [dʒɪn] ginebra f; **~ and tonic** gin-tonic m

jipsy ['dʒɪpsɪ] gitano(-a) m(f)

jirder ['gɜːrdər] viga f

jirl [gɜːrl] chica f; **(young)** ~ niña f, chica f; **girlfriend** of boy novia f; of girl amiga f; **girlish** de niñas

jist [dʒɪst] esencia f

jive [gɪv] dar; as present regalar; (supply) proporcionar; cry, groan soltar

◆ **give away** as present regalar; (betray) traicionar

◆ **give back** devolver

◆ **give in 1** v/i (surrender) rendirse **2** v/t (hand in) entregar

◆ **give onto** (open onto) dar a

◆ **give out 1** v/t leaflets etc repartir **2** v/i of supplies, strength agotarse

◆ **give up 1** v/t smoking etc dejar de **2** v/i (stop making effort) rendirse

◆ **give way** of bridge etc hundirse

jive-and-'take toma m y daca

jizmo ['gɪzmoʊ] F cacharro m

jlad [glæd] contento; **gladly** con mucho gusto

jlamor ['glæmər] atractivo m, glamour m; **glamorize** hacer atractivo; **glamorous** atrac-

tivo, glamoroso; **glamour** Br ☞ **glamor**

glance [glæns] **1** n ojeada f **2** v/i echar una ojeada

gland [glænd] glándula f

glare [gler] **1** n of sun, lights resplandor m **2** v/i of lights resplandecer

◆ **glare at** mirar con furia a

glaring ['glerɪŋ] mistake garrafal

glass [glæs] vidrio m; for drink vaso m; **glasses** gafas fpl, L.Am. lentes mpl, L.Am. anteojos mpl

glazed [gleɪzd] look vidrioso

gleam [gliːm] **1** n resplandor m **2** v/i resplandecer

glee [gliː] júbilo m, regocijo m; **gleeful** jubiloso

glib [glɪb] fácil; **glibly** con labia

glide [glaɪd] of bird, plane planear; of piece of furniture deslizarse; **glider** planeador m; **gliding** sport vuelo m sin motor

glimpse [glɪmps] **1** n vistazo m **2** v/t vislumbrar

glint [glɪnt] **1** n destello m; in eyes centelleo m **2** v/i of light destellar; of eyes centellear

glisten ['glɪsn] relucir

glitter ['glɪtər] destellar

gloat [gloʊt] regodearse

◆ **gloat over** regodearse de

global ['gloʊbl] global; **globalization** COM globalización f; **global warming** calentamiento m global; **globe** globo m; (model of earth) globo *m* terráqueo

gloom [glu:m] (*darkness*) tinieblas *fpl*; *mood* abatimiento *m*; **gloomy** *room* tenebroso; *mood, person* abatido

glorious ['glɔ:rɪəs] *weather* espléndido; *victory* glorioso; **glory** gloria *f*

gloss [glɑs] (*shine*) lustre *m*; (*general explanation*) glosa *f*; **glossary** glosario *m*; **glossy 1** *adj paper* satinado **2** *n magazine* revista *f* en color

glove [glʌv] guante *m*; **glove compartment** guantera *f*

glow [gləʊ] **1** *n* resplandor *m*, brillo *m*; *in cheeks* rubor *m* **2** *v/i* resplandecer, brillar; *of cheeks* ruborizarse; **glowing** *description* entusiasta

glucose ['glu:kəʊs] glucosa *f*

glue [glu:] **1** *n* pegamento *m*, cola *f* **2** *v/t* pegar, encolar

glum [glʌm] sombrío, triste

glut [glʌt] exceso *m*, superabundancia *f*

gluten gluten *m*; **gluten-free** sin gluten

glutton ['glʌtən] glotón(-ona) *m(f)*

gnaw [nɔ:] *bone* roer

go [gəʊ] ir (**to** a); (*leave*) irse, marcharse; (*work, function*) funcionar; (*come out: of stain etc*) irse; (*cease: of pain etc*) pasarse; (*match: of colors etc*) ir bien, pegar; ~ **shopping** ir de compras; **hamburger to** ~ hamburguesa para llevar

◆ **go away** *of person* irse, marcharse; *of rain, pain, clouds* desaparecer

◆ **go back** (*return*) volver; (*date back*) remontarse

◆ **go by** *of car, time* pasar

◆ **go down** bajar; *of sun* ponerse

◆ **go in** *to room, house* entrar; *of sun* ocultarse; (*fit: of part etc*) ir, encajar

◆ **go off** (*leave*) marcharse; *of bomb* explotar; *of gun* dispararse; *of alarm* saltar; *Br of milk etc* echarse a perder

◆ **go on** (*continue*) continuar; (*happen*) pasar

◆ **go out** *of person* salir; *of light, fire* apagarse

◆ **go over** (*check*) examinar

◆ **go through** *illness, hard times* atravesar; (*check*) revisar; (*read through*) estudiar

◆ **go under** (*sink*) hundirse; *of company* ir a la quiebra

◆ **go up** subir

◆ **go without 1** *v/t food* pasar sin **2** *v/i* pasar privaciones

'go-ahead 1 *n luz f verde* **2** *adj* dinámico

goal [gəʊl] *SP target* portería *f*, *L.Am.* arco *m*; *SP point* gol *m*; (*objective*) objetivo *m*, meta *f*; **goalkeeper** portero(-a) *m(f)*, *L.Am.* arquero(-a) *m(f)*; **goal kick** saque *m* de puerta; **goalpost** poste

goat [gəʊt] cabra *f*

gobble ['gɑ:bl] engullir

gobbledygook ['gɑːbldɪguːk] F jerigonza f F

go-between intermediario(-a) m(f)

god [gɑːd] dios m; **thank God!** ¡gracias a Dios!; **godchild** ahijado(-a) m(f); **godfather** also in mafia padrino m; **godmother** madrina f

gofer ['goufər] F recadero(-a) m(f)

goggles ['gɑːglz] gafas fpl

goings-on [gouɪŋz'ɑːn] actividades fpl

gold [gould] **1** n oro m **2** adj de oro; **golden** dorado; **golden wedding** bodas fpl de oro; **gold medal** medalla f de oro; **gold mine** fig mina f

golf [gɑːlf] golf m; **golf ball** pelota f de golf; **golf club** organization club m de golf; stick palo m de golf; **golf course** campo m de golf; **golfer** golfista m/f

good [gud] bueno; **goodbye** adiós; **good-for-nothing** inútil m/f; **Good Friday** Viernes m inv Santo; **good-humored**, Br **good-humoured** jovial, afable; **good-looking** guapo; **good-natured** bondadoso; **goodness** moral bondad f; of fruit etc valor m nutritivo; **goods** COM mercancías fpl; **goodwill** buena voluntad f

goof [guːf] F meter la pata F

goose [guːs] ganso m, oca f; **goose bumps** carne f de gallina

gorgeous ['gɔːrdʒəs] weather maravilloso; dress, hair precioso; woman, man buenísimo; smell estupendo

gospel ['gɑːspl] evangelio m

gossip ['gɑːsɪp] **1** n cotilleo m; person cotilla m/f **2** v/i cotillear; **gossip column** ecos mpl de sociedad

gourmet ['gurmeɪ] gourmet m/f

govern ['gʌvərn] gobernar; **government** gobierno m; **governor** gobernador(a) m(f)

gown [gaun] long dress vestido m; wedding dress traje m; of academic, judge toga f; of surgeon bata f

grab [græb] agarrar; food tomar

grace [greɪs] of dancer etc gracia f; **say** ~ bendecir la mesa; **graceful** elegante; **gracious** person amable; style elegante

grade [greɪd] **1** n quality grado m; EDU curso m; (mark) nota f **2** v/t clasificar; **grade crossing** paso m a nivel; **grade school** escuela f primaria

gradient ['greɪdɪənt] pendiente f

gradual ['grædʒuəl] gradual; **gradually** gradualmente, poco a poco

graduate 1 ['grædʒuət] n licenciado(-a) m(f); from high school bachiller m/f **2** ['grædʒueɪt] v/i from univer-

sity licenciarse, *L.Am.* egresarse; *from high school* sacar el bachillerato; **graduation** graduación *f*

graffiti [grə'fi:ti] graffiti *m*

grain [greɪn] grano *m; in wood* veta *f*

gram [græm] gramo *m*

grammar ['græmər] gramática *f;* **grammatical** gramatical

grand [grænd] **1** *adj* grandioso; F (*very good*) estupendo, genial **2** *n* F ($1000) mil dólares; **grandchild** nieto(-a) *m(f);* **granddaughter** nieta *f;* **grandeur** grandiosidad *f;* **grandfather** abuelo *m;* **grand jury** jurado *m* de acusación, gran jurado; **grandmother** abuela *f;* **grandparents** abuelos *mpl;* **grand piano** piano *m* de cola; **grandson** nieto *m*

granite ['grænɪt] granito *m*

grant [grænt] **1** *n money* subvención *f* **2** *v/t* conceder

granule ['grænju:l] gránulo *m*

grape [greɪp] uva *f;* **grapefruit** pomelo *m, L.Am.* toronja *f*

graph [græf] gráfico *m,* gráfica *f;* **graphic 1** *adj* (*vivid*) gráfico **2** *n* COMPUT gráfico *m*

◆ **grapple with** ['græpl] *attacker* forcejear con; *problem etc* enfrentarse a

grasp [græsp] **1** *n physical* asimiento *m; mental* comprensión *f* **2** *v/t physically* agarrar;

(*understand*) comprender

grass [græs] hierba *f;* **grasshopper** saltamontes *m inv;* **grass roots** *people* bases *fpl;* **grassy** lleno de hierba

grate[^1] [greɪt] *n metal* parrilla *f,* reja *f*

grate[^2] [greɪt] **1** *v/t in cooking* rallar **2** *v/i of sound* rechinar

grateful ['greɪtfʊl] agradecido; **gratefully** con agradecimiento

gratify ['grætɪfaɪ] satisfacer

grating ['greɪtɪŋ] **1** *n* reja *f* **2** *adj sound, voice* chirriante

gratitude ['grætɪtu:d] gratitud *f*

grave[^1] [greɪv] *n* tumba *f*

grave[^2] [greɪv] *adj* grave

gravel ['grævl] gravilla *f*

gravestone lápida *f,* **graveyard** cementerio *m*

gravity ['grævɪtɪ] PHYS gravedad *f*

gray [greɪ] gris; **gray-haired** canoso

graze[^1] [greɪz] *v/i of cow etc* pastar, pacer

graze[^2] [greɪz] **1** *v/t arm etc* rozar **2** *n* rozadura *f*

grease [gri:s] grasa *f;* **greasy** *food, hands, plate* grasiento; *hair, skin* graso

great [greɪt] grande, *before singular noun* gran; F (*very good*) estupendo, genial F; **Great Britain** Gran Bretaña; **greatly** muy; **greatness** grandeza *f*

Greece [gri:s] Grecia

greed [gri:d] *for money* codi-

cia *f*; **for food** glotonería *f*;
greedily *con* codicia; *eat*
con glotonería; **greedy for**
food glotón; **for money** codicioso

Greek [griːk] **1** *adj* griego **2** *n*
griego(-a) *m(f)*; *language*
griego *m*

green [griːn] verde; *environ-*
mentally also ecologista;
green beans judías *fpl* verdes, *L.Am.* porotos *mpl* verdes, *Mex* ejotes *mpl*; **green**
belt cinturón *m* verde;
green card (*work permit*)
permiso *m* de trabajo;
greenhouse effect efecto
m invernadero; **greens** verduras *f*

greet [griːt] saludar; **greeting**
saludo *m*

grenade [grɪ'neɪd] granada *f*

grey *Br* → **gray**

grid [grɪd] reja *f*, rejilla *f*; **grid-**
iron SP *campo de fútbol*
americano; **gridlock** *in traffic*
paralización *f* del tráfico

grief [griːf] dolor *m*, aflicción
f; **grief-stricken** afligido;
grievance queja *f*; **grieve**
sufrir; **~ for s.o.** llorar por alguien

grill [grɪl] **1** *n* *on window* reja *f*
2 *v/t* (*interrogate*) interrogar

grille [grɪl] reja *f*

grim [grɪm] *face* severo; *pro-*
spects desolador; *surround-*
ings lúgubre

grimace ['grɪməs] gesto *m*,
mueca *f*

grime [graɪm] mugre *f*; **grimy**

mugriento

grin [grɪn] **1** *n* sonrisa *f* (am-
plia) **2** *v/i* sonreír abiertamente

grind [graɪnd] *coffee* moler;
meat picar

grip [grɪp] agarrar; **gripping**
apasionante

gristle ['grɪsl] cartílago *m*

grit [grɪt] **1** *n* (*dirt*) arenilla *f*;
for roads gravilla *f* **2** *v/t*: **~**
one's teeth apretar los dientes; **gritty** F *movie etc* duro F

groan [grəʊn] **1** *n* gemido *m* **2**
v/i gemir

groceries ['grəʊsərɪz] comestibles *mpl*; **grocery store**
tienda *f* de comestibles *or*
Mex abarrotes

groggy ['grɒgɪ] F grogui F

groin [grɔɪn] ANAT ingle *f*

groom [gruːm] **1** *n* *for bride*
novio *m*; *for horse* mozo *m*
de cuadra **2** *v/t* *horse* almo-
hazar; (*train, prepare*) preparar

groove [gruːv] ranura *f*

grope [grəʊp] *v/i* **in the dark**
caminar a tientas **2** *v/t* *sexu-*
ally manosear

gross [grəʊs] (*coarse, vulgar*)
grosero; *exaggeration* tremendo; *error* craso; FIN bruto

ground [graʊnd] **1** *n* suelo *m*;
(*reason*) motivo *m*; ELEC tierra *f* **2** *v/t* ELEC conectar a
tierra; **grounding** *in subject*
fundamento *m*; **groundless**
infundado; **ground meat**
carne *f* picada; **groundwork**

group   378

trabajos *mpl* preliminares
group [gruːp] **1** *n* grupo *m* **2**
v/t agrupar; **groupie** F grupi
f F

grouse [graʊs] **1** *n* F queja *f* **2**
v/i F quejarse, refunfuñar
grovel ['grɒvl] *fig* arrastrarse
grow [groʊ] **1** *v/i* crecer; ~
old / tired envejecer / cansarse **2** *v/t flowers* cultivar
◆ **grow up** crecer
growl [graʊl] **1** *n* gruñido *m* **2**
v/i gruñir
'**grown-up 1** *n* adulto(-a)
m(f) **2** *adj* maduro
growth [groʊθ] crecimiento
m; *(increase)* incremento *m*;
MED bulto *m*
grudge [grʌdʒ] rencor *m*;
grudging rencoroso; **grudgingly** de mala gana
grueling, *Br* **gruelling**
['gruːəlɪŋ] agotador
gruff [grʌf] seco, brusco
grumble ['grʌmbl] murmurar; **grumbler** quejica *m/f*
grunt [grʌnt] **1** *n* gruñido *m* **2**
v/i gruñir
guarantee [gærən'tiː] **1** *n* garantía *f* **2** *v/t* garantizar;
guarantor garante *m/f*
guard [gɑːrd] **1** *n (security* ~)
guardia *m/f*, guarda *m/f*;
MIL guardia *f*; *in prison* guardián (-ana) *m(f)* **2** *v/t* guardar; **guard dog** perro *m*
guardián; **guarded** *reply*
cauteloso; **guardian** LAW tu-
tor(a) *m(f)*
Guatemala [gwætə'mɑːlə]
Guatemala; **Guatemalan 1**

adj guatemalteco **2** *n* guate-
malteco(-a) *m(f)*
guerrilla [gə'rɪlə] guerrille-
ro(-a) *m(f)*; **guerrilla warfare** guerra *f* de guerrillas
guess [ges] **1** *n* conjetura *f*,
suposición *f* **2** *v/t the answer*
adivinar; *I ~ so* me imagino
que sí **3** *v/i* adivinar; **guess-
work** conjeturas *fpl*
guest [gest] invitado(-a)
m(f); **guestroom** habitación
f para invitados
guidance ['gaɪdəns] orientación *f*; **guide 1** *n person* guía
m/f; *book* guía *f* **2** *v/t* guiar;
guidebook guía *f*; **guided
missile** misil *m* teledirigido;
guided tour visita *f* guiada;
guidelines directrices *fpl*
guilt [gɪlt] culpa *f*, culpabilidad *f*; LAW culpabilidad *f*;
guilty *also* LAW culpable
guinea pig ['gɪnɪpɪg] *also fig*
conejillo *m* de Indias
guitar [gɪ'tɑːr] guitarra *f*; **guitarist** guitarrista *m/f*
gulf [gʌlf] golfo *m*; *fig* abismo
m; **Gulf of Mexico** Golfo *m*
de México
gull [gʌl] *bird* gaviota *f*
gullet ['gʌlɪt] ANAT esófago *m*
gullible ['gʌlɪbl] crédulo
gulp [gʌlp] **1** *n of water etc* trago *m* **2** *v/i in surprise* tragar
saliva
◆ **gulp down** *drink* tragar;
food engullir
gum[1] [gʌm] *in mouth* encía *f*
gum[2] [gʌm] *(glue)* pegamento
m, cola *f*; *(chewing* ~) chicle

m

gun [gʌn] pistola *f*; *rifle* rifle *m*; *cannon* cañón *m*
◆ **gun down** matar a tiros
gunfire disparos *mpl*; **gunman** hombre *m* armado; **gunshot** disparo *m*; **gunshot wound** herida *f* de bala
gurgle ['gɜːrgl] *of baby* gorjear; *of drain* gorgotear
guru ['guːruː] *fig* gurú *m*
gush [gʌʃ] *of liquid* manar
gusto ['gʌstoʊ] entusiasmo *m*
gusty ['gʌstɪ] con viento racheado
gut [gʌt] **1** *n* intestino *f*; F *(stomach)* tripa *f* F **2** *v/t* *(de-*

stroy) destruir; **guts** F *(courage)* agallas *fpl* F; **gutsy** F *(brave)* valiente, con muchas agallas F
gutter ['gʌtər] *on sidewalk* cuneta *f*; *on roof* canal *m*
guy [gaɪ] F tipo *m* F, *Span* tío *m* F
guzzle ['gʌzl] tragar; *drink* engullir
gym [dʒɪm] gimnasio *m*; **gymnast** gimnasta *m/f*; **gymnastics** gimnasia *f*
gynecology, *Br* **gynaecology** [gaɪnɪ'kɑːlədʒɪ] ginecología *f*
gypsy ['dʒɪpsɪ] gitano(-a) *m(f)*

H

habit ['hæbɪt] hábito *m*, costumbre *f*
habitable ['hæbɪtəbl] habitable; **habitat** hábitat *m*
habitual [hə'bɪtʃuəl] habitual
hacker ['hækər] COMPUT pirata *m/f* informático(-a)
hackneyed ['hæknɪd] manido
haemorrhage *Br* ☞ **hemorrhage**
haggard ['hægərd] demacrado
haggle ['hægl] regatear
hail [heɪl] granizo *m*
hair [her] pelo *m*, cabello *m*; *single* pelo *m*; *(body ~)* vello *m*; **hairbrush** cepillo *m*; **haircut** corte *m* de pelo;

have a ~ cortarse el pelo; **hairdo** peinado *m*; **hairdresser** peluquero(-a) *m(f)*; **hairdryer** secador *m* (de pelo); **hairpin** horquilla *f*; **hairpin curve** curva *f* muy cerrada; **hair-raising** espeluznante; **hair remover** depilatorio *m*; **hair-splitting** sutilezas *fpl*; **hairstyle** peinado *m*; **hairstylist** estilista *m/f*, peluquero(-a) *m(f)*; **hairy** *arm, animal* peludo; F *(frightening)* espeluznante
half [hæf] **1** *n* mitad *f*; **~ past ten**, **~ after ten** las diez y media; **~ an hour** media hora **2** *adj* medio **3** *adv* a medias;

half-hearted desganado;
half time SP descanso m;
halfway 1 adj stage, point intermedio **2** adv a mitad de
camino

hall [hɔːl] large room sala f;
(hallway) vestíbulo m

Halloween [hæləʊ'wiːn] víspera de Todos los Santos

halo ['heɪləʊ] halo m

halt [hɔːlt] **1** v/i detenerse **2** v/t
detener **3** n alto m

halve [hæv] input, costs reducir a la mitad; apple partir
por la mitad

ham [hæm] jamón m; **hamburger** hamburguesa f

hammer ['hæmər] **1** n martillo m **2** v/i: ~ **at the door** golpear la puerta

hammock ['hæmək] hamaca f

hamper[1] ['hæmpər] n for food
cesta f

hamper[2] ['hæmpər] v/t (obstruct) estorbar, obstaculizar

hand [hænd] mano f; of clock
manecilla f; (worker) brazo
m; **at** ~, **to** ~ a mano; **on
the one** ~ ..., **on the other**
~ por una parte..., por otra
parte; **on your right** ~ a mano derecha; **give s.o. a** ~
echar una mano a alguien
◆ **hand down** transmitir
◆ **hand out** repartir
◆ **hand over** entregar

handbag Br bolso m, L.Am.
cartera f; **hand baggage**
equipaje m de mano; **handcuff** esposar; **handcuffs** esposas fpl

handicap ['hændɪkæp] desventaja f; **handicapped** physically minusválido

handkerchief ['hæŋkərtʃɪf]
pañuelo m

handle ['hændl] **1** n of door
manilla f; of suitcase asa f;
of pan, knife mango m **2** v/t
goods, person manejar; case,
deal llevar; **handlebars** manillar m, L.Am. manubrio m

hand luggage equipaje m de
mano; **handmade** hecho a
mano; **hands-free** manos libres; **handshake** apretón m
de manos

handsome ['hænsəm] guapo,
atractivo

handwriting ['hændraɪtɪŋ] caligrafía f;
handwritten escrito a mano; **handy** device práctico

hang [hæŋ] colgar
◆ **hang on** (wait) esperar
◆ **hang up** TELEC colgar

hangar ['hæŋər] hangar m

hanger ['hæŋər] for clothes
percha f

hang glider person piloto m
de ala delta; device ala f delta; **hang gliding** ala f delta; **hangover** resaca f

hankie, hanky ['hæŋkɪ] F pañuelo m

haphazard [hæp'hæzərd] descuidado

happen ['hæpn] ocurrir, pasar

happily ['hæpɪlɪ] alegremente; (luckily) afortunadamente; **happiness** felicidad f;
happy feliz, contento; coincidence afortunado; **happy-**

have

go-lucky despreocupado

harass [ha'ræs] acosar; *enemy* asediar, hostigar; **harassed** agobiado; **harassment** acoso *m*

harbor, *Br* **harbour** ['ha:rbər] **1** *n* puerto *m* **2** *v/t criminal* proteger; *grudge* albergar

hard [ha:rd] **1** *adj* duro; *(difficult)* difícil; *facts, evidence* real **2** *adv hit, rain* fuerte; *work* duro; *try* ~ esforzarse; **hard-back** libro *m* de tapas duras; **hard-boiled** *egg* duro; **hard copy** copia *f* impresa; **hard core** *(pornography)* porno *m* duro; **hard currency** divisa *f* fuerte; **hard disk** disco *m* duro; **harden 1** *v/t* endurecer **2** *v/i of glue, attitude* endurecerse; **hard hat** casco *m*; *(construction worker)* obrero(-a) *m(f)* (de la construcción); **hardheaded** pragmático; **hardhearted** insensible; **hard line** línea *f* dura; **hardliner** partidario(-a) *m(f)* de la línea dura; **hardly** ['ha:rdlɪ] apenas

hardness ['ha:rdnɪs] dureza *f*; *(difficulty)* dificultad *f*; **hardship** penuria *f*, privación *f*; **hardware** ferretería *f*; COMPUT hardware *m*; **hardware store** ferretería *f*; **hard-working** trabajador; **hardy** resistente

harm [ha:rm] **1** *n* daño *m* **2** *v/t* hacer daño a, dañar; **harmful** dañino, perjudicial; **harmless** inofensivo; *fun* inocente

harmonious [ha:r'moʊnɪəs] armonioso; **harmonize** armonizar; **harmony** MUS, *fig* armonía *f*

harsh [ha:rʃ] *words* duro, severo; *color* chillón; *light* potente; **harshly** con dureza

harvest ['ha:rvɪst] cosecha *f*

hash browns [hæʃ] *Span* patatas *fpl* al *L.Am.* papas *fpl* fritas; **hash mark** almohadilla *f*, *el signo* '#'

haste [heɪst] prisa *f*; **hastily** precipitadamente; **hasty** precipitado

hat [hæt] sombrero *m*

hatch [hætʃ] *for serving* trampilla *f*; *on ship* escotilla *f*

◆ **hatch out** *of eggs* romperse; *of chicks* salir del cascarón

hatchet ['hætʃɪt] hacha *f*

hate [heɪt] **1** *n* odio *m* **2** *v/t* odiar; **hatred** odio *m*

haul [hɔ:l] **1** *n of fish* captura *f*; *from robbery* botín *m* **2** *v/t* *(pull)* arrastrar; **haulage** transporte *m*

haunch [hɔ:ntʃ] *of person* trasero *m*; *of animal* pierna *f*

haunt [hɔ:nt] **1** *n* lugar *m* favorito **2** *v/t*: *this place is* ~*ed* en este lugar hay fantasmas

Havana [hə'vænə] La Habana

have [hæv] **1** *v/t (own)* tener; *breakfast, lunch* tomar; *can I* ~ *a coffee?* ¿me da un café?; ~ *(got) to* tener que; *I'll* ~ *it repaired* haré que lo arreglen; *I had my hair cut*

me corté el pelo; **2** v/aux
(past tense): **I ~ eaten** he comido

◆ **have on** (wear) llevar puesto

haven ['heɪvn] fig refugio m

hawk [hɔːk] also fig halcón m

hay [heɪ] heno m; **hay fever**
fiebre f del heno

hazard ['hæzərd] peligro m;
hazard lights MOT luces
fpl de emergencia; **hazardous** peligroso

haze [heɪz] neblina f; **hazy**
image, memories vago

he [hiː] él; **~ is a doctor** es médico

head [hed] **1** n cabeza f; (boss,
leader) jefe(-a) m(f); Br: of
school director(a) m(f); on
beer espuma f **2** v/t (lead) estar a la cabeza de; ball cabecear

◆ **head for** dirigirse hacia

'**headache** dolor m de cabeza; **headband** cinta f para
la cabeza; **header** in soccer
cabezazo m; in document encabezamiento m; **headhunter**
COM cazatalentos m/f inv;
heading in list encabezamiento m; **headlamp** faro
m; **headline** in newspaper titular m; **head office** of company central f; **head-on 1**
adv crash de frente **2** adj
crash frontal; **headphones**
auriculares mpl; **headquarters** sede f; of army cuartel
m general; **headrest** reposacabezas f inv; **headroom** un-

der bridge gálibo m; in car espacio m vertical; **headscarf**
pañuelo m (para la cabeza);
headstrong cabezudo;
head waiter maître m;
heady wine etc que se sube
a la cabeza

heal [hiːl] curar

health [helθ] salud f; **health
food store** tienda f de comida integral; **health insurance** seguro m de enfermedad; **healthy** person sano;
food, lifestyle saludable;
economy saneado

heap [hiːp] montón m

hear [hɪr] oír

◆ **hear from** (have news
from) tener noticias de

hearing ['hɪrɪŋ] oído m; LAW
vista f; **hearing aid** audífono
m

hearse [hɜːrs] coche m fúnebre

heart [hɑːrt] also fig corazón
m; of problem meollo m;
know sth by ~ saber algo
de memoria; **heart attack**
infarto m; **heartbreaking**
desgarrador; **heartbroken**
descorazonado; **heartburn**
acidez f (de estómago)

hearth [hɑːrθ] chimenea f

heartless ['hɑːrtlɪs] despiadado; **hearty** appetite voraz;
meal copioso; person cordial

heat [hiːt] calor m

◆ **heat up** calentar

heated ['hiːtɪd] pool climatizado; discussion acalorado;

heater in room estufa f;

heating calefacción f; heatproof resistente al calor; heatwave ola f de calor

heave [hi:v] (lift) subir

heaven ['hevn] cielo m; heavenly F divino F

heavy ['hevɪ] pesado; cold, rain, accent fuerte; smoker empedernido; loss of life grande; bleeding abundante; heavy-duty resistente; heavyweight SP de los pesos pesados

hectic ['hektɪk] frenético

hedge [hedʒ] seto m

heel [hi:l] talón m; of shoe tacón m; heel bar zapatería f

hefty ['heftɪ] weight pesado; person robusto

height [haɪt] altura f; heighten tension intensificar

heir [er] heredero m; heiress heredera f

helicopter ['helɪkɒptər] helicóptero m

hell [hel] infierno m; **what the ~ are you doing?** F ¿qué demonios estás haciendo? F: **go to ~!** F ¡vete a paseo!

hello [hə'ləʊ] hola; TELEC ¿sí?, Span ¿diga?, S. Am. ¿aló?, Rpl ¿oigo?, Mex ¿bueno?

helmet ['helmɪt] casco m

help [help] **1** n ayuda f **2** v/t ayudar; **just ~ yourself to** food toma lo que quieras; **I can't ~ it** no puedo evitarlo; helper ayudante m/f; helpful advice útil; person servicial; helping of food ración

f; helpless (unable to cope) indefenso; (powerless) impotente; helplessness impotencia f

hem [hem] of dress etc dobladillo m

hemisphere ['hemɪsfɪr] hemisferio m

'hemline bajo m

hemorrhage ['hemərɪdʒ] **1** n hemorragia f **2** v/i sangrar

hen [hen] gallina f; hen party despedida f de soltera

hepatitis [hepə'taɪtɪs] hepatitis f

her [hɜːr] **1** adj su **2** pron direct object la; indirect object le; after prep ella; **I know ~** la conozco; **I gave ~ the keys** le di las llaves; **I sold it to ~** se lo vendí; **this is for ~** esto es para ella; **it's ~** es ella

herb [ɜːrb] hierba f; herb(al) tea infusión f

herd [hɜːrd] rebaño m

here [hɪr] aquí; **over ~** aquí; **~'s to you!** as toast ¡a tu salud!; **~ you are** giving sth ¡aquí tienes!

hereditary [hə'redɪterɪ] hereditario; heredity herencia f; heritage patrimonio m

hero ['hɪrəʊ] héroe m; heroic heroico; heroically heroicamente

heroin ['herəʊɪn] heroína f

heroine ['herəʊɪn] heroína f

heroism ['herəʊɪzm] heroísmo m

herpes ['hɜːrpiːz] herpes m

hers [hɜːrz] el suyo, la suya

that ticket is ~ esa entrada es suya; *a cousin of* ~ un primo suyo

herself [hɜːrˈself] *reflexive* se; *emphatic* ella misma; *she hurt* ~ se hizo daño

hesitant [ˈhezɪtənt] indeciso; **hesitantly** con indecisión; **hesitate** dudar, vacilar; **hesitation** vacilación *f*

heterosexual [hetərouˈsekʃuəl] heterosexual

hi [haɪ] ¡hola!

hibernate [ˈhaɪbərneɪt] hibernar

hiccup [ˈhɪkʌp] hipo *m*; (*minor problem*) tropiezo *m*

hidden [ˈhɪdn] oculto

hide¹ [haɪd] **1** *v/t* esconder **2** *v/i* esconderse

hide² [haɪd] *n of animal* piel *f*

'hide-and-seek escondite *m*; **hideaway** escondite *m*

hideous [ˈhɪdɪəs] horrendo; *person* repugnante

hiding [ˈhaɪdɪŋ] (*beating*) paliza *f*; **hiding place** escondite *m*

hierarchy [ˈhaɪrɑːrkɪ] jerarquía *f*

high [haɪ] **1** *adj* alto; *wind* fuerte; (*on drugs*) colocado P **2** *n* MOT directa *f*; *in statistics* máximo *m*; EDU escuela *f* secundaria, *Span* instituto *m*; **highbrow** intelectual; **highchair** trona *f*; **high-class** de categoría; **high-frequency** de alta frecuencia; **high-grade** de calidad superior; **high-handed** des-

pótico; **high-heeled** de tacón alto; **high jump** salto *m* de altura; **high-level** de alto nivel; **highlight 1** *n* (*main event*) momento *m* cumbre; *in hair* reflejo *m* **2** *v/t with pen* resaltar; COMPUT seleccionar, resaltar; **highlighter** *pen* fluorescente *m*; **highly** *desirable, likely* muy; **think** ~ *of s.o.* tener una buena opinión de alguien; **high performance** *drill, battery* de alto rendimiento; **high-pitched** agudo; **high point** *of career* punto *m* culminante; **high-powered** *engine* potente; *intellectual* de alto(s) vuelo(s); **high pressure** *weather* altas presiones *fpl*; **high-pressure** TECH a gran presión; *salesman* agresivo; *lifestyle* muy estresante; **high school** escuela *f* secundaria, *Span* instituto *m*; **high-strung** muy nervioso; **high tech 1** *n* alta *f* tecnología **2** *adj* de alta tecnología; **highway** autopista *f*

hijack [ˈhaɪdʒæk] **1** *v/t* secuestrar **2** *n* secuestro *m*; **hijacker** secuestrador(a) *m(f)*

hike¹ [haɪk] **1** *n* caminata *f* **2** *v/i* caminar

hike² [haɪk] *n in prices* subida *f*

hiker [ˈhaɪkər] senderista *m/f*; **hiking** senderismo *m*

hilarious [hɪˈlerɪəs] divertidísimo, graciosísimo

ill [hɪl] colina f; *(slope)* cuesta f; **hillside** ladera f; **hilltop** cumbre f; **hilly** con colinas

ilt [hɪlt] puño m

im [hɪm] *direct object* lo; *indirect object* le; *after prep* él; **I know ~** lo conozco; **I gave ~ the keys** le di las llaves; **I sold it to ~** se lo vendí; **this is for ~** esto es para él; **it's ~** es él; **himself** *reflexive* se; *emphatic* él mismo; **he hurt ~** se hizo daño

hinder ['hɪndər] obstaculizar; **~ s.o. from doing sth** impedir a alguien hacer algo; **hindrance** obstáculo m

hinge [hɪndʒ] bisagra f

hint [hɪnt] *(clue)* pista f; *(piece of advice)* consejo m; *(suggestion)* indirecta f; *of red, sadness* rastro m

hip [hɪp] cadera f; **hip pocket** bolsillo m trasero

hire [haɪr] alquilar

his [hɪz] **1** *adj* su **2** *pron* el suyo, la suya; **that ticket is ~** esa entrada es suya; **a cousin of ~** un primo suyo

Hispanic [hɪ'spænɪk] **1** *n* hispano(-a) m(f) **2** *adj* hispano, hispánico

hiss [hɪs] silbar

historian [hɪ'stɔːrɪən] historiador(a) m(f); **historic** histórico; **historical** histórico; **history** historia f

hit [hɪt] **1** *v/t* golpear; *(collide with)* chocar contra **2** *n* *(blow)* golpe m; MUS, *(success)* éxito m; *on website* ac-

ceso m

hitch [hɪtʃ] **1** *n (problem)* contratiempo m **2** *v/t (fix)* enganchar; **hitchhike** hacer autoestop; **hitchhiker** autoestopista m/f

'hi-tech [haɪ'tek] **1** *n* alta tecnología f **2** *adj* de alta tecnología

'hitman asesino m a sueldo; **hit-or-miss** a la buena ventura

HIV [eɪtʃaɪ'viː] *(= human immunodeficiency virus)* VIH m *(= virus m inv de la inmunodeficiencia humana)*

hive [haɪv] *for bees* colmena f

HIV-'positive seropositivo

hoard [hɔːrd] **1** *n* reserva f **2** *v/t* hacer acopio de; *money* acumular

hoarse [hɔːrs] ronco

hoax [houks] bulo m, engaño m

hobble ['hɑːbl] cojear

hobby ['hɑːbɪ] hobby m

hobo ['houbou] F vagabundo(-a) m(f)

hockey ['hɑːkɪ] *(ice ~)* hockey m sobre hielo

hog [hɑːg] *(pig)* cerdo m, L.Am. chancho m

hoist [hɔɪst] **1** *n* montacargas m inv; *manual* elevador m **2** *v/t (lift)* levantar; *flag* izar

hold [hould] **1** *v/t in hand* llevar; *(support, keep in place)* sostener; *passport, license* tener; *prisoner* retener; *(contain)* contener; *post* ocupar; **~ the line, please** espere, por favor **2** *n in ship, plane* bodega *f*; **take ~ of sth** agarrar algo

◆ **hold back** crowds contener; facts guardar

◆ **hold out 1** *v/t* hand tender; prospect ofrecer **2** *v/i* of supply durar; (survive) resistir

◆ **hold up** hand levantar; bank etc atracar; (make late) retrasar

holder ['houldər] (container) receptáculo *m*; of passport, ticket etc titular *m/f*; of record poseedor(a) *m(f)*; **holding company** holding *m*; **hold-up** (robbery) atraco *m*; (delay) retraso *m*

hole [houl] agujero *m*; in ground hoyo *m*

holiday ['hɑːlɪdeɪ] día *m* de fiesta; *Br*: period vacaciones *fpl*

Holland ['hɑːlənd] Holanda

hollow ['hɑːləʊ] hueco; cheeks hundido; promise vacío

holocaust ['hɑːləkɔːst] holocausto *m*

hologram ['hɑːləɡræm] holograma *m*

holster ['houlstər] pistolera *f*

holy ['houlɪ] santo; **Holy Spirit** Espíritu *m* Santo

home [houm] **1** *n* casa *f*; (native country) tierra *f*; for old people residencia *f*; *at ~ also* SP en casa; (in country) en mi / su / nuestra tierra; *make yourself at ~* ponte cómodo **2** *adv* a casa; *go ~* ir a casa; *to country* ir a

mi / tu / su tierra; *to town, part of country* ir a mi / tu / su ciudad; **home address** domicilio *m*; **home banking** telebanca *f*, banca *f* electrónica; **homecoming** vuelta *f* a casa; **home computer** *Span* ordenador *m*, *L.Am.* computadora *f* doméstica; **home game** partido *m* en casa; **homeless 1** *adj* sin casa; **the ~** los sin casa; **homeloving** hogareño; **homely** (homeloving) hogareño; (not good-looking) feúcho; **homemade** casero; **home page** página *f* inicial; **homesick** nostálgico; **be ~** tener morriña; **home town** ciudad *f* natal; **homeward** *to own house* a casa; *to own country* a mi / tu / su país; **homework** EDU deberes *mpl*

homicide ['hɑːmɪsaɪd] homicidio *m*; department brigada *f* de homicidios

homophobia [hɑːmə'foubiə] homofobia *f*

homosexual [hɑːmə'sekʃuəl] **1** *adj* homosexual **2** *n* homosexual *m/f*

Honduran [hɑːn'durən] **1** *adj* hondureño **2** *n* hondureño(-a) *m(f)*; **Honduras** Honduras

honest ['ɑːnɪst] honrado; **honestly** honradamente; *¡*desde luego!; **honesty** honradez *f*

honey ['hʌnɪ] miel *f*; F (darling

ling) cariño m; **honeymoon** luna f de miel

honk [hɑːŋk] **horn** tocar

honor ['ɑːnər] **1** n honor m **2** v/t honrar; **honorable** honorable; honour Br ☞ **honor**

hood [hʊd] over head capucha f; over cooker campana f extractora; MOT capó m; F (gangster) matón(-ona) m(f)

hook [hʊk] gancho m; for coat etc colgador m; for fishing anzuelo m; **off the ~** TELEC descolgado; **hooked** enganchado (**on** a); **hooker** F fulana f

hoot [huːt] **1** v/t horn tocar **2** v/i of car dar bocinazos; of owl ulular

hop [hɑːp] saltar

hope [həʊp] **1** n esperanza f **2** v/i esperar; **I ~ so** eso espero **3** v/t: **I ~ you like it** espero que te guste; **hopeful** prometedor; **hopefully** say, wait esperanzadamente; **~ ...** (let's hope) esperemos que...; **hopeless** position desesperado; (useless: person) inútil

horizon [həˈraɪzn] horizonte m; **horizontal** horizontal

hormone ['hɔːrməʊn] hormona f

horn [hɔːrn] of animal cuerno m; MOT bocina f

hornet ['hɔːrnɪt] avispón m

horny ['hɔːrnɪ] F sexually cachondo F

horrible ['hɔːrɪbl] horrible; person muy antipático; hor-

rify horrorizar; **horrifying** horroroso; **horror** horror m

horse [hɔːrs] caballo m; **horse race** carrera f de caballos; **horseshoe** herradura f

horticulture ['hɔːrtɪkʌltʃər] horticultura f

hose [həʊz] manguera f

hospitable [haːˈspɪtəbl] hospitalario

hospital ['haːspɪtl] hospital m; **hospitality** hospitalidad f

host [həʊst] at party anfitrión m; of TV program presentador(a) m(f)

hostage ['haːstɪdʒ] rehén m; **hostage taker** persona que toma rehenes

hostel ['haːstl] for students residencia f; (youth ~) albergue m

hostess ['həʊstɪs] at party anfitriona f; on airplane azafata f; in bar cabaretera f

hostile ['haːstl] hostil; **hostility** hostilidad f; **hostilities** hostilidades

hot [haːt] caliente; weather caluroso; (spicy) picante; **it's ~** of weather hace calor; **I'm ~** tengo calor; **hot dog** perrito m caliente

hotel [həʊˈtel] hotel m

hour [aʊr] hora f

house [haʊs] casa f; **housebreaking** allanamiento m de morada; **household** hogar m; **household name** nombre m conocido; **housekeeper** ama f de llaves;

House of Representatives
Cámara *f* de Representantes; **housewarming (party)** fiesta *f* de estreno de una casa; **housewife** ama *f* de casa; **housework** tareas *fpl* domésticas; **housing** vivienda *f*; TECH cubierta *f*

hovel ['hɒvl] chabola *f*

hover ['hɒvər] *of bird* cernerse; *of helicopter* permanecer inmóvil en el aire

how [haʊ] cómo; ~ *are you?* ¿cómo estás?; ~ *about …?* ¿qué te parece…?; ~ *about a drink?* ¿te apetece tomar algo?; ~ *much?* ¿cuánto?; ~ *much is it?* *cost* ¿cuánto vale or cuesta?; ~ *many?* ¿cuántos?; ~ *often?* ¿con qué frecuencia?; ~ *sad!* ¡qué triste!; **however** sin embargo, ~ *big they are* independientemente de lo grandes que sean

howl [haʊl] *of dog* aullido *m*; *of pain* alarido *m*; *with laughter* risotada *f*

hub [hʌb] *of wheel* cubo *m*; **hubcap** tapacubos *m inv*

◆ **huddle together** ['hʌdl] apiñarse, acurrucarse

hug [hʌg] abrazar

huge [hju:dʒ] enorme

hull [hʌl] *of ship* casco *m*

hum [hʌm] tararear; *of machine* zumbar

human ['hju:mən] **1** *n* humano *m* **2** *adj* humano; **human being** ser *m* humano

humane [hju:'meɪn] humano

humanitarian [hju:mænɪ'teriən] humanitario

humanity [hju:'mænətɪ] humanidad *f*; **human race** raza *f* humana; **human resources** recursos *mpl* humanos

humble ['hʌmbl] humilde

humdrum ['hʌmdrʌm] monótono, anodino

humid ['hju:mɪd] húmedo; **humidifier** humidificador *m*; **humidity** humedad *f*

humiliate [hju:'mɪlɪeɪt] humillar; **humiliating** humillante; **humiliation** humillación *f*; **humility** humildad *f*

humor ['hju:mər] humor *m*; **humorous** gracioso; **humour** *Br* ☞ **humor**

hunch [hʌntʃ] *(idea)* presentimiento *m*, corazonada *f*

hundred ['hʌndrəd] cien *m*; *a ~ and one* ciento uno; *two ~* doscientos; **hundredth** centésimo

hunger ['hʌŋgər] hambre *f*

hung-over: *be* ~ tener resaca

hungry ['hʌŋgrɪ] hambriento; *I'm* ~ tengo hambre

hunk [hʌŋk] cacho *m*; F *man* cachas *m inv* F

hunt [hʌnt] **1** *n* caza *f* 2 *v/t* caza; **hunter** cazador(a) *m(f)*; **hunting** caza *f*

hurdle ['hɜːrdl] SP valla *f*; *fig* obstáculo *m*

hurl [hɜːrl] lanzar

hurray [hʊ'reɪ] ¡hurra!

hurricane ['hʌrɪkən] huracán *m*

hurried ['hʌrɪd] apresurado; **hurry** 1 *n* prisa *f*; *be in a ~* tener prisa 2 *v/i* darse prisa
◆ **hurry up** 1 *v/i* darse prisa; *hurry up!* ¡date prisa! 2 *v/t* meter prisa a

hurt [hɜːrt] 1 *v/i* doler 2 *v/t* hacer daño a; *emotionally* herir; *I've ~ my hand* me he hecho daño en la mano

husband ['hʌzbənd] marido *m*

hush [hʌʃ] silencio *m*
◆ **hush up** *scandal etc* acallar

husky ['hʌskɪ] *voice* áspero

hut [hʌt] cabaña *f*; *workman's* cobertizo *m*

hybrid ['haɪbrɪd] híbrido *m*

hydrant ['haɪdrənt] hidrante *m* de incendios

hydraulic [haɪ'drɔːlɪk] hidráulico

hydroelectric [haɪdrəʊɪ'lektrɪk] hidroeléctrico

hydrogen ['haɪdrədʒən] hidrógeno *m*

hygiene ['haɪdʒiːn] higiene *f*; **hygienic** higiénico

hymn [hɪm] himno *m*

hype [haɪp] bombo *m*

hyperactive [haɪpər'æktɪv] hiperactivo; **hypersensitive** hipersensible; **hypertext** COMPUT hipertexto *m*

hypnosis [hɪp'nəʊsɪs] hipnosis *f*; **hypnotize** hipnotizar

hypocrisy [hɪ'pɑːkrəsɪ] hipocresía *f*; **hypocrite** hipócrita *m/f*; **hypocritical** hipócrita

hypothesis [haɪ'pɑːθəsɪs] hipótesis *f inv*; **hypothetical** hipotético

hysterectomy [hɪstə'rektəmɪ] histerectomía *f*

hysteria [hɪ'stɪrɪə] histeria *f*; **hysterical** histérico; F (*very funny*) tronchante F; **hysterics** ataque *f* de histeria; (*laughter*) ataque *f* de risa

I

[aɪ] yo; *~ am a student* soy estudiante

ice [aɪs] hielo *m*; **icebox** nevera *f*, *Rpl* heladera *f*; **ice cream** helado *m*; **ice cube** cubito *m* de hielo; **iced** *drink* helado; **ice hockey** hockey *m* sobre hielo; **ice rink** pista *f* de hielo; **ice skate** patín *m* de cuchilla; **ice skating** patinaje *m* sobre hielo

icon ['aɪkɑːn] *also* COMPUT icono *m*

icy ['aɪsɪ] *road* con hielo; *surface* helado; *welcome* frío

ID [aɪ'diː] (= *identity*) documentación *f*

idea [aɪ'diːə] idea *f*; **ideal** ideal; **idealistic** idealista

identical [aɪ'dentɪkl] idéntico; **identification** identificación *f*; *papers etc* documentación *f*; **identify** identificar; **identity** identidad *f*; *~ card* carné *m* de identidad

ideological [aɪdɪə'lɒːdʒɪkl] ideológico; **ideology** ideología *f*

idiomatic [ɪdɪə'mætɪk] *natural* natural

idiot ['ɪdɪət] idiota *m/f*; **idiotic** idiota

idle ['aɪdl] **1** *adj not working* desocupado; (*lazy*) vago; *threat* vano; *machinery* inactivo **2** *v/i of engine* funcionar al ralentí

idol ['aɪdl] ídolo *m*; **idolize** idolatrar

if [ɪf] si

ignite [ɪg'naɪt] inflamar; **ignition** *in car* encendido *m*; ~ **key** llave *m* de contacto

ignorance ['ɪgnərəns] ignorancia *f*; **ignorant** ignorante; (*rude*) maleducado; **ignore** ignorar; COMPUT omitir

ill [ɪl] enfermo; *fall ~*, *be taken ~* caer enfermo

illegal [ɪ'liːgl] ilegal

illegible [ɪ'ledʒəbl] ilegible

illegitimate [ɪlɪ'dʒɪtɪmət] *child* ilegítimo

illicit [ɪ'lɪsɪt] ilícito

illiterate [ɪ'lɪtərət] analfabeto

illness ['ɪlnɪs] enfermedad *f*

illogical [ɪ'lɒːdʒɪkl] ilógico

illtreat maltratar

illuminating [ɪ'luːmɪneɪtɪŋ] *remarks* iluminador

illusion [ɪ'luːʒn] ilusión *f*

illustrate ['ɪləstreɪt] ilustrar; **illustration** ilustración *f*; **illustrator** ilustrador(a) *m(f)*

image ['ɪmɪdʒ] imagen *f*

imaginary [ɪ'mædʒɪnərɪ] imaginario; **imagination** imaginación *f*; **imaginative** imaginativo; **imagine** imaginar, imaginarse; *you're imagining things* son imaginaciones tuyas

IMF [aɪem'ef] (= *International Monetary Fund*) FMI *m* (= Fondo *m* Monetario Internacional)

imitate ['ɪmɪteɪt] imitar; **imitation** imitación *f*

immaculate [ɪ'mækjʊlət] inmaculado

immature [ɪmə'tʃʊər] inmaduro

immediate [ɪ'miːdɪət] inmediato; **immediately** inmediatamente

immense [ɪ'mens] inmenso

immerse [ɪ'mɜːrs] sumergir

immigrant ['ɪmɪgrənt] inmigrante *m/f*; **immigrate** inmigrar; **immigration** inmigración *f*

imminent ['ɪmɪnənt] inminente

immobilize [ɪ'moʊbɪlaɪz] *factory* paralizar; *person, car* inmovilizar

immoderate [ɪ'mɑːdərət] desmedido, exagerado

immoral [ɪ'mɔːrəl] inmoral; **immorality** inmoralidad *f*

immortal [ɪ'mɔːrtl] inmortal; **immortality** inmortalidad *f*

immune [ɪ'mjuːn] *to illness* inmune; *from ruling* con inmunidad; **immune system** MED sistema *m* inmunológico;

immunity inmunidad *f*

impact ['ɪmpækt] impacto *m*

impair [ɪm'per] dañar

impartial [ɪm'pɑːrʃl] imparcial

impassable [ɪm'pæsəbl] *road* intransitable

impassioned [ɪm'pæʃnd] *speech, plea* apasionado

impatience [ɪm'peɪʃəns] impaciencia *f*; **impatient** impaciente; **impatiently** impacientemente

impeccable [ɪm'pekəbl] impecable

impede [ɪm'piːd] dificultar; **impediment** *in speech* defecto *m* del habla

impending [ɪm'pendɪŋ] inminente

imperative [ɪm'perətɪv] **1** *adj* imprescindible **2** *n* GRAM imperativo *m*

imperfect [ɪm'pɜːrfekt] **1** *adj* imperfecto **2** *n* GRAM imperfecto *m*

impersonal [ɪm'pɜːrsənl] impersonal; **impersonate** *as a joke* imitar; *illegally* hacerse pasar por

impertinence [ɪm'pɜːrtɪnəns] impertinencia *f*; **impertinent** impertinente

impervious [ɪm'pɜːrvɪəs]: ~ **to** inmune a

impetuous [ɪm'petʃʊəs] impetuoso

impetus ['ɪmpɪtəs] *of campaign etc* ímpetu *m*

implement 1 ['ɪmplɪmənt] *n* utensilio *m* **2** [ˈɪmplɪment]

v/t poner en práctica

implicate ['ɪmplɪkeɪt] implicar; **implication** consecuencia *f*

implore [ɪm'plɔːr] implorar

imply [ɪm'plaɪ] implicar

impolite [ɪmpə'laɪt] maleducado

import ['ɪmpɔːrt] **1** *n* importación *f* **2** *v/t* importar

importance [ɪm'pɔːrtəns] importancia *f*; **important** importante

importer [ɪm'pɔːrtər] importador(a) *m(f)*

impose [ɪm'pəʊz] *tax* imponer; **imposing** imponente

impossibility [ɪmpɑːsɪ'bɪlɪti] imposibilidad *f*; **impossible** imposible

impotence ['ɪmpətəns] impotencia *f*; **impotent** impotente

impractical [ɪm'præktɪkəl] poco práctico

impress [ɪm'pres] impresionar; **impression** impresión *f*; *(impersonation)* imitación *f*; **impressive** impresionante

imprint ['ɪmprɪnt] *of credit card* impresión *f*

imprison [ɪm'prɪzn] encarcelar; **imprisonment** encarcelamiento *m*

improbable [ɪm'prɑːbəbl] improbable

improve [ɪm'pruːv] mejorar; **improvement** mejora *f*, mejoría *f*

improvise ['ɪmprəvaɪz] improvisar

impudent ['ɪmpjʊdənt] insolente, desvergonzado

impulse ['ɪmpʌls] impulso *m*; impulsivo

in [ɪn] **1** *prep* en; ~ *two hours from now* dentro de dos horas; *(over period of)* en dos horas; ~ *the morning* por la mañana; ~ *yellow* de amarillo; ~ *crossing the road (while)* al cruzar la calle; ~ *agreeing to this (by virtue of)* al expresar acuerdo con esto; *one* ~ *ten* uno de cada diez **2** *adv* dentro; *is he* ~*?* at home ¿está en casa?; ~ *here* aquí dentro **3** *adj (fashionable)* de moda

inability [ɪnə'bɪlɪtɪ] incapacidad *f*

inaccurate [ɪn'ækjʊrət] inexacto

inadequate [ɪn'ædɪkwət] insuficiente

inadvisable [ɪnəd'vaɪzəbl] poco aconsejable

inanimate [ɪn'ænɪmət] inanimado

inappropriate [ɪnə'prəʊprɪət] inadecuado, improcedente; *choice* inapropiado

inaudible [ɪn'ɔːdəbl] inaudible

inaugural [ɪ'nɔːgjʊrəl] *speech* inaugural; **inaugurate** inaugurar

inborn ['ɪnbɔːn] innato

Inc. (= *Incorporated*) S.A. (= sociedad *f* anónima)

incalculable [ɪn'kælkjʊləbl] *damage* incalculable

incapable [ɪn'keɪpəbl]] incapaz

incentive [ɪn'sentɪv] incentivo *m*

incessant [ɪn'sesnt] incesante; **incessantly** incesantemente

incest ['ɪnsest] incesto *m*

inch [ɪntʃ] pulgada *f*

incident ['ɪnsɪdənt] incidente *m*; **incidental** sin importancia; ~ *expenses* gastos *mpl* varios; **incidentally** a propósito

incision [ɪn'sɪʒn] incisión *f*; **incisive** incisivo

incite [ɪn'saɪt] incitar

inclination [ɪnklɪ'neɪʃn] inclinación *f*

inclose ☞ **enclose**

include [ɪn'kluːd] incluir; **including** incluyendo; **inclusive** *1 adj price* total, global **2** *prep*: ~ *of* incluyendo, incluido **3** *adv*: *from Monday to Thursday* ~ de lunes a jueves, ambos inclusive; *$1000* ~ 1.000 dólares todo incluido

incoherent [ɪnkəʊ'hɪrənt] incoherente

income ['ɪnkəm] ingresos *mpl*; **income tax** impuesto *m* sobre la renta

incomparable [ɪn'kɑːmpərəbl] incomparable

incompatibility [ɪnkəmpætɪ'bɪlɪtɪ] incompatibilidad *f*; **incompatible** incompatible

incompetence [ɪn'kɑːm

pitəns] incompetencia f; **incompetent** incompetente

incomplete [ɪnkəm'pliːt] incompleto

incomprehensible [ɪnkɒmprɪ'hensɪbl] incomprensible

inconceivable [ɪnkən'siːvəbl] inconcebible

inconsiderate [ɪnkən'sɪdərət] desconsiderado

inconsistent [ɪnkən'sɪstənt] incoherente, inconsecuente; *player* irregular

inconspicuous [ɪnkən'spɪkjʊəs] discreto

inconvenience [ɪnkən'viːnɪəns] inconveniencia f; **inconvenient** inconveniente

incorporate [ɪn'kɔːrpəreɪt] incorporar

incorrect [ɪnkə'rekt] incorrecto

increase 1 [ɪn'kriːs] *v/t & v/i* aumentar **2** ['ɪnkriːs] *n* aumento *m*; **increasing** creciente; **increasingly** cada vez más

incredible [ɪn'kredɪbl] increíble

incur [ɪn'kɜːr] *costs* incurrir en; *debts* contraer; *anger* provocar

incurable [ɪn'kjʊərəbl] incurable

indecent [ɪn'diːsnt] indecente

indecisive [ɪndɪ'saɪsɪv] indeciso; **indecisiveness** indecisión f

indeed [ɪn'diːd] (*in fact*) ciertamente,   efectivamente;

yes, agreeing ciertamente, en efecto

indefinable [ɪndɪ'faɪnəbl] indefinible

indefinite [ɪn'defɪnɪt] indefinido; **indefinitely** indefinidamente

indelicate [ɪn'delɪkət] poco delicado

independence [ɪndɪ'pendəns] independencia f; **Independence Day** Día m de la Independencia; **independent** independiente

indescribable [ɪndɪ'skraɪbəbl] indescriptible

index ['ɪndeks] *for book* índice m

India ['ɪndɪə] (la) India; **Indian 1** *adj neg* indio **2** *n from India* indio(-a) *m(f)*, hindú *m/f*; *neg: native American* indio(-a) *m(f) neg*

indicate ['ɪndɪkeɪt] **1** *v/t* indicar **2** *v/i Br when driving* poner el intermitente; **indication** indicio m

indict [ɪn'daɪt] acusar

indifference [ɪn'dɪfrəns] indiferencia f; **indifferent** indiferente; (*mediocre*) mediocre

indigestion [ɪndɪ'dʒestʃn] indigestión f

indignant [ɪn'dɪgnənt] indignado; **indignation** indignación f

indirect [ɪndɪ'rekt] indirecto; **indirectly** indirectamente

indiscreet [ɪndɪ'skriːt] indiscreto

indiscriminate [ɪndɪˈskrɪmɪnət] indiscriminado

indispensable [ɪndɪˈspensəbl] indispensable

indisposed [ɪndɪˈspəʊzd] (*not well*) indispuesto

indisputable [ɪndɪˈspjuːtəbl] indiscutible

indistinct [ɪndɪˈstɪŋkt] indistinto, impreciso

indistinguishable [ɪndɪˈstɪŋgwɪʃəbl] indistinguible

individual [ɪndɪˈvɪdʒʊəl] **1** *n* individuo *m* **2** *adj* individual; **individually** individualmente

indoctrinate [ɪnˈdɒktrɪneɪt] adoctrinar

Indonesia [ɪndəˈniːziə] Indonesia; **Indonesian 1** *adj* indonesio **2** *n* person indonesio(-a) *m(f)*

indoor [ˈɪndɔːr] *activities* de interior; *sport* de pista cubierta; *arena* cubierto; **indoors** dentro

indorse ☞ **endorse**

indulgent [ɪnˈdʌldʒənt] indulgente

industrial [ɪnˈdʌstrɪəl] industrial; **industrial dispute** conflicto *m* laboral; **industrialist** industrial *m/f*; **industrious** trabajador, aplicado; **industry** industria *f*

ineffective [ɪnɪˈfektɪv] ineficaz

inefficient [ɪnɪˈfɪʃənt] ineficiente

inept [ɪˈnept] inepto

inequality [ɪnɪˈkwɒlɪtɪ] desigualdad *f*

inescapable [ɪnɪˈskeɪpəbl] inevitable

inevitable [ɪnˈevɪtəbl] inevitable; **inevitably** inevitablemente

inexcusable [ɪnɪksˈkjuːzəbl] inexcusable

inexhaustible [ɪnɪgzɔːstəbl] *supply* inagotable

inexpensive [ɪnɪkˈspensɪv] barato, económico

inexperienced [ɪnɪkspɪrɪənst] inexperto

inexplicable [ɪnɪkˈsplɪkəbl] inexplicable

infallible [ɪnˈfælɪbl] infalible

infamous [ˈɪnfəməs] infame

infancy [ˈɪnfənsɪ] infancia *f*; **infant** bebé *m*; **infantile** *pej* infantil

infantry [ˈɪnfəntrɪ] infantería *f*

infect [ɪnˈfekt] infectar; **infection** infección *f*; **infectious** infeccioso; *laughter* contagioso

infer [ɪnˈfɜːr] inferir (*from* de)

inferior [ɪnˈfɪərɪər] inferior (*to* a); **inferiority** inferioridad *f*; **inferiority complex** complejo *m* de inferioridad

infertile [ɪnˈfɜːtɪl] *woman, plant* estéril; *soil* estéril, yermo; **infertility** esterilidad *f*

infidelity [ɪnfɪˈdelɪtɪ] infidelidad *f*

infinite [ˈɪnfɪnət] infinito; **infinitive** infinitivo *m*; **infinity** infinidad *f*

inflammable [ɪnˈflæməbl] inflamable; **inflammation** MED inflamación f

inflatable [ɪnˈfleɪtəbl] *dinghy* hinchable, inflable; **inflate** *tire, dinghy* hinchar, inflar; *economy* inflar; **inflation** inflación *f*; **inflationary** inflacionario, inflacionista

inflexible [ɪnˈfleksɪbl] inflexible

inflict [ɪnˈflɪkt] infligir (**on** a)

influence [ˈɪnfluəns] **1** *n* influencia *f* **2** *v/t* influir en, influenciar; **influential** influyente

inform [ɪnˈfɔːrm] **1** *v/t* informar **2** *v/i*: **~ on s.o.** delatar a alguien

informal [ɪnˈfɔːrml] informal; **informality** informalidad *f*

informant [ɪnˈfɔːrmənt] confidente *m/f*; **information** información *f*; **information technology** tecnologías *fpl* de la información; **informative** informativo; **informer** confidente *m/f*

infra-red [ˈɪnfrəˈred] infrarrojo

infrastructure [ˈɪnfrətrʌktʃər] infraestructura *f*

infrequent [ɪnˈfriːkwənt] poco frecuente

infuriate [ɪnˈfjʊrieɪt] enfurecer, exasperar; **infuriating** exasperante

ingenious [ɪnˈdʒiːniəs] ingenioso

ingot [ˈɪŋɡət] lingote *m*

ingratitude [ɪnˈɡrætɪtuːd] in-

gratitud *f*

ingredient [ɪnˈɡriːdiənt] *also fig* ingrediente *m*

inhabit [ɪnˈhæbɪt] habitar; **inhabitant** habitante *m/f*

inhale [ɪnˈheɪl] **1** *v/t* inhalar **2** *v/i when smoking* tragarse el humo

inherit [ɪnˈherɪt] heredar; **inheritance** herencia *f*

inhibited [ɪnˈhɪbɪtɪd] inhibido, cohibido; **inhibition** inhibición *f*

inhospitable [ɪnhɑːˈspɪtəbl] *person* inhospitalario; *city, climate* inhóspito

inhuman [ɪnˈhjuːmən] inhumano

initial [ɪˈnɪʃl] **1** *adj* inicial **2** *n* inicial *f* **3** *v/t (write ~s on)* poner las iniciales en; **initially** inicialmente; **initiate** iniciar; **initiation** iniciación *f*, inicio *m*; **initiative** iniciativa *f*

inject [ɪnˈdʒekt] inyectar; **injection** inyección *f*

injure [ˈɪndʒər] lesionar; **injury** lesión *f*; *wound* herida *f*

injustice [ɪnˈdʒʌstɪs] injusticia *f*

ink [ɪŋk] tinta *f*

inland [ˈɪnlənd] interior; *mail* nacional

in-laws [ˈɪnlɔːz] familia *f* política

inmate [ˈɪnmeɪt] *of prison* recluso(-a) *m(f)*; *of mental hospital* paciente *m/f*

inn [ɪn] posada *f*, mesón *m*

innate [ɪˈneɪt] innato

inner [ˈɪnər] interior

innocence ['ɪnəsəns] inocencia f; **innocent** inocente

innocuous [ɪ'nɒkjʊəs] inocuo

innovation [ɪnə'veɪʃn] innovación f; **innovative** innovador; **innovator** innovador(a) m(f)

inoculate [ɪ'nɒkjʊleɪt] inocular; **inoculation** inoculación f

inoffensive [ɪnə'fensɪv] inofensivo

'in-patient paciente m/f interno(-a)

input ['ɪnpʊt] **1** n into project etc contribución f; COMPUT entrada f **2** v/t into project etc contribuir; COMPUT introducir

inquest ['ɪnkwest] investigación f (into sobre)

inquire [ɪn'kwaɪr] preguntar; **inquiry** consulta f, pregunta f; into rail crash etc investigación f

inquisitive [ɪn'kwɪzətɪv] curioso, inquisitivo

insane [ɪn'seɪn] person loco, demente; idea descabellado

insanitary [ɪn'sænɪterɪ] antihigiénico

insanity [ɪn'sænɪtɪ] locura f, demencia f

inscription [ɪn'skrɪpʃn] inscripción f

insect ['ɪnsekt] insecto m; **insecticide** insecticida f

insecure [ɪnsɪ'kjʊr] inseguro; **insecurity** inseguridad f

insensitive [ɪn'sensɪtɪv] insensible

insert 1 ['ɪnsɜːrt] n in magazine etc encarte m **2** [ɪn'sɜːrt] v/t introducir, meter; extra text insertar

inside 1 [ɪn'saɪd] n interior m; ~ out del revés **2** prep dentro de; ~ of 2 hours dentro de 2 horas; ~ stay, remain dentro; go, carry adentro; we went ~ entramos **3** adj: ~ information información f confidencial; ~ lane SP calle f de dentro; **inside pocket** bolsillo m interior; **insider** persona con acceso a información confidencial; **insider trading** FIN uso m de información privilegiada; **insides** (stomach) tripas fpl

insignificant [ɪnsɪg'nɪfɪkənt] insignificante

insincere [ɪnsɪn'sɪr] poco sincero, falso; **insincerity** falta f de sinceridad

insinuate [ɪn'sɪnʊeɪt] (imply) insinuar

insist [ɪn'sɪst] insistir (on en); **insistent** insistente

insolent ['ɪnsələnt] insolente

insolvent [ɪn'sɑːlvənt] insolvente

insomnia [ɪn'sɑːmnɪə] insomnio m

inspect [ɪn'spekt] inspeccionar; **inspection** inspección f; **inspector** in factory inspector(a) m(f)

inspiration [ɪnspə'reɪʃn] inspiración f; **inspire** respect etc inspirar

nstability [ɪnstə'bɪlɪtɪ] **ines-tabilidad** f

nstall [ɪn'stɔːl] instalar; **in-stallation** instalación f; **in-stallment,** Br **instalment** of story etc episodio m; payment plazo m; **installment plan** compra f a plazos

nstance ['ɪnstəns] ejemplo m; **for ~** por ejemplo

nstant ['ɪnstənt] **1** adj instantáneo **2** n instante m; **instantaneous** instantáneo; **instant coffee** café m instantáneo; **instantly** al instante

nstead [ɪn'sted]: **would you like coffee ~?** ¿preferiría mejor café?; **~ of me** en mi lugar; **~ of going** en vez de ir, en lugar de ir

nstinct ['ɪnstɪŋkt] instinto m; **instinctive** instintivo

nstitute ['ɪnstɪtuːt] **1** n instituto m **2** v/t new law establecer; inquiry iniciar; **institution** institución f; (setting up) iniciación f

nstruct [ɪn'strʌkt] (order) dar instrucciones a; (teach) instruir; **instruction** instrucción f; **instructive** instructivo; **instructor** instructor(a) m(f)

nstrument ['ɪnstrəmənt] instrumento m

nsubordinate [ɪnsə'bɔːrdɪnət] insubordinado

nsufficient [ɪnsə'fɪʃnt] insuficiente

nsulate ['ɪnsəleɪt] aislar; **in-sulation** aislamiento m

insulin ['ɪnsəlɪn] insulina f

insult 1 ['ɪnsʌlt] n insulto m **2** [ɪn'sʌlt] v/t insultar

insurance [ɪn'ʃʊrəns] seguro m; **insurance company** compañía f de seguros, aseguradora f; **insurance policy** póliza f de seguros; **insurance premium** prima f (del seguro); **insure** asegurar

insurmountable [ɪnsər'maʊntəbl] insuperable

intact [ɪn'tækt] intacto

integrate ['ɪntɪgreɪt] integrar (into en); **integrity** (honesty) integridad f; **a man of ~** un hombre íntegro

intellect ['ɪntəlekt] intelecto m; **intellectual 1** adj intelectual **2** n intelectual m/f

intelligence [ɪn'telɪdʒəns] inteligencia f; (information) información f secreta; **intelligent** inteligente

intelligible [ɪn'telɪdʒəbl] inteligible

intend [ɪn'tend]: **~ to do sth** tener la intención de hacer algo

intense [ɪn'tens] intenso; personality serio; **intensify** v/t intensificar **2** v/i intensificarse; **intensity** intensidad f; **intensive** intensivo; **intensive care** cuidados mpl intensivos

intention [ɪn'tenʃn] intención f; **intentional** intencionado; **intentionally** a propósito,

adrede
interaction [ɪntərˈækʃn] interacción f; **interactive** interactivo
intercept [ɪntərˈsept] interceptar
interchange [ˈɪntərtʃeɪndʒ] of highways nudo m vial; **interchangeable** intercambiable
intercom [ˈɪntərkɑːm] interfono m; for front door portero m automático
intercourse [ˈɪntərkɔːrs] sexual coito m
interdependent [ɪntərdɪˈpendənt] interdependiente
interest [ˈɪntrəst] **1** n also FIN interés m **2** v/t interesar; **interested** interesado; **interesting** interesante; **interest rate** tipo m de interés
interface [ˈɪntərfeɪs] **1** n interface m, interfaz f **2** v/i relacionarse
interfere [ɪntərˈfɪr] interferir; **interference** intromisión f; on radio interferencia f
interior [ɪnˈtɪrɪər] **1** adj interior **2** n interior m; **interior design** interiorismo m; **interior designer** interiorista m/f
interlude [ˈɪntərluːd] at theater, concert intermedio m; (period) intervalo m
intermediary [ɪntərˈmiːdɪərɪ] intermediario; **intermediate** intermedio m
intermission [ɪntərˈmɪʃn] in theater intermedio m
internal [ɪnˈtɜːrnl] interno; internally internamente; **Internal Revenue (Service)** Hacienda f, Span Agencia f Tributaria
international [ɪntərˈnæʃnl] internacional; **internationally** internacionalmente
Internet [ˈɪntərnet] Internet f; **on the ~** en Internet
interpret [ɪnˈtɜːrprɪt] interpretar; **interpretation** interpretación f; **interpreter** intérprete m/f
interrogate [ɪnˈterəgeɪt] interrogar; **interrogation** interrogación f; **interrogator** interrogador(a) m(f)
interrupt [ɪntərˈrʌpt] interrumpir; **interruption** interrupción f
intersect [ɪntərˈsekt] **1** v/t cruzar **2** v/i cruzarse; **intersection** of roads intersección f
interstate [ˈɪntərsteɪt] autopista f interestatal
interval [ˈɪntərvl] intervalo m; in theater intermedio m
intervene [ɪntərˈviːn] intervenir; **intervention** intervención f
interview [ˈɪntərvjuː] **1** n entrevista f **2** v/t entrevistar; **interviewer** entrevistador(a) m(f)
intimate [ˈɪntɪmət] íntimo
intimidate [ɪnˈtɪmɪdeɪt] intimidar; **intimidation** intimidación f
into [ˈɪntʊ] en; *translate ~ English* traducir al inglés; *he's ~ classical music* F

(*likes*) le gusta *or* Span le va mucho la música clásica; **he's ~ local politics** F (*is involved with*) está muy metido en el mundillo de la política local

ntolerable [ɪn'tɑːlərəbl] intolerable; **intolerant** intolerante

ntoxicated [ɪn'tɑːksɪkeɪtɪd] ebrio, embriagado

ntravenous [ɪntrə'viːnəs] intravenoso

ntricate ['ɪntrɪkət] intrincado

ntrigue 1 ['ɪntriːg] *n* intriga *f* **2** [ɪn'triːg] *v/t* intrigar; **intriguing** intrigante

ntroduce [ɪntrə'duːs] presentar; *new technique etc* introducir; **introduction** *to person* presentación *f*; *to a new food, sport etc* iniciación *f*; *in book, of new techniques etc* introducción *f*

ntrude [ɪn'truːd] molestar; **intruder** intruso(-a) *m(f)*; **intrusion** intromisión *f*

ntuition [ɪntuː'ɪʃn] intuición *f*

nvade [ɪn'veɪd] invadir

nvalid¹ [ɪn'vælɪd] *adj* nulo

nvalid² ['ɪnvəlɪd] *n* MED minusválido(-a) *m(f)*

nvalidate [ɪn'vælɪdeɪt] invalidar

nvaluable [ɪn'væljʊbl] inestimable

nvariably [ɪn'veɪriəbli] (*always*) invariablemente

nvasion [ɪn'veɪʒn] invasión *f*

nvent [ɪn'vent] inventar; **in-**

vention *action* invención *f*; *thing invented* invento *m*; **inventive** inventivo; **inventor** inventor(a) *m(f)*

inventory ['ɪnvəntɔːrɪ] inventario *m*

invert [ɪn'vɜːrt] invertir

invest [ɪn'vest] invertir

investigate [ɪn'vestɪgeɪt] investigar; **investigation** investigación *f*

investment [ɪn'vestmənt] inversión *f*; **investor** inversor(a) *m(f)*

invincible [ɪn'vɪnsəbl] invencible

invisible [ɪn'vɪzɪbl] invisible

invitation [ɪnvɪ'teɪʃn] invitación *f*; **invite** invitar

invoice ['ɪnvɔɪs] **1** *n* factura *f* **2** *v/t customer* enviar la factura a

involuntary [ɪn'vɑːləntərɪ] involuntario

involve [ɪn'vɑːlv] *work, expense* involucrar, entrañar; **what does it ~?** ¿en qué consiste?; **involved** (*complex*) complicado; **involvement** *in project, crime* participación *f*, intervención *f*

invulnerable [ɪn'vʌlnərəbl] invulnerable

inward ['ɪnwərd] **1** *adj feeling, smile* interior **2** *adv* hacia dentro; **inwardly** por dentro

IP [aɪ'piː] IT *IP f*; **IP address** IT dirección *f* IP

IQ [aɪ'kjuː] (= *intelligence quotient*) cociente *m* intelectual

Iran [ɪ'rɑːn] Irán; **Iranian 1** *adj* iraní **2** *n* iraní *m/f*

Iraq [ɪ'rɑːk] Iraq, Irak; **Iraqi 1** *adj* iraquí **2** *n* iraquí *m/f*

Ireland ['aɪrlənd] Irlanda; **Irish** irlandés

iron ['aɪərn] **1** *n* hierro *m*; *for clothes* plancha *f* **2** *v/t* planchar

ironic(al) [aɪ'rɒnɪk(l)] irónico

'ironing board tabla *f* de planchar

irony ['aɪrənɪ] ironía *f*

irrational [ɪ'ræʃənl] irracional

irreconcilable [ɪrekən'saɪləbl] irreconciliable

irregular [ɪ'reɡjʊlər] irregular

irrelevant [ɪ'reləvənt] irrelevante

irreplaceable [ɪrɪ'pleɪsəbl] irreemplazable

irrepressible [ɪrɪ'presəbl] *sense of humor* incontenible; *person* irreprimible

irresistible [ɪrɪ'zɪstəbl] irresistible

irresponsible [ɪrɪ'spɑːnsəbl] irresponsable

irreverent [ɪ'revərənt] irreverente

irrevocable [ɪ'revəkəbl] irrevocable

irrigate ['ɪrɪɡeɪt] regar; **irrigation** [ɪrɪ'ɡeɪʃn] riego *m*

irritable ['ɪrɪtəbl] irritable; **irritate** irritar; **irritating** irritante; **irritation** irritación *f*

Islam ['ɪzlɑːm] (el) Islam; **Islamic** islámico

island ['aɪlənd] isla *f*

isolate ['aɪsəleɪt] aislar; **isolated** aislado; **isolation** aislamiento *m*

ISP [aɪes'piː] (= *Internet service provider*) proveedor *m* de (acceso a) Internet

Israel ['ɪzreɪl] Israel; **Israeli 1** *adj* israelí **2** *n person* israelí *m/f*

issue ['ɪʃuː] **1** *n* (*matter*) tema *m*, asunto *m*; *of magazine* número *m* **2** *v/t coins* emitir; *passport etc* expedir; *warning* dar

IT [aɪ'tiː] (= *information technology*) tecnologías *fpl* de la información

it [ɪt] *as object* lo *m*, la *f*; *what color is ~? - ~ is red* ¿de qué color es? - es rojo; *~'s raining* llueve; *~'s me / him* soy yo / es él; *that's ~!* (*that's right*) ¡eso es!; (*finished*) ¡ya está!

Italian [ɪ'tæljən] **1** *adj* italiano **2** *n person* italiano(-a) *m(f)*; *language* italiano *m*

italics [ɪ'tælɪks] cursiva *f*

Italy ['ɪtəlɪ] Italia

itch [ɪtʃ] **1** *n* picor *m* **2** *v/i* picar

item ['aɪtəm] artículo *m*; *or agenda* punto *m*; *of news* noticia *f*; **itemize** *invoice* detallar

itinerary [aɪ'tɪnərərɪ] itinerario *m*

its [ɪts] su

it's [ɪts] ☞ *it is*; *it has*

itself [ɪt'self] *reflexive* se; *by ~* (*alone, automatically*) solo

J

jab [dʒæb] clavar

jack [dʒæk] MOT gato *m*; *in cards* jota *f*

jacket [ˈdʒækɪt] chaqueta *f*; *of book* sobrecubierta *f*

jackpot gordo *m*

jagged [ˈdʒægɪd] accidentado

jaguar [ˈdʒægʊər] jaguar *m*

jail [dʒeɪl] cárcel *f*

jam¹ [dʒæm] *n for bread* mermelada *f*

jam² [dʒæm] **1** *n* mot atasco *m*; F *(difficulty)* aprieto *m* **2** *v/t (ram)* meter, embutir; *(cause to stick)* atascar **3** *v/i (stick)* atascarse

janitor [ˈdʒænɪtər] portero(-a) *m(f)*

January [ˈdʒænʊeri] enero *m*

Japan [dʒəˈpæn] Japón; **Japanese 1** *adj* japonés **2** *n* japonés(-esa) *m(f)*; *language* japonés *m*; **the ~** los japoneses

jar¹ [dʒɑːr] *container* tarro *m*

jargon [ˈdʒɑːrgən] jerga *f*

jaw [dʒɔː] mandíbula *f*

jaywalker [ˈdʒeɪwɔːkər] peatón(-ona) *m(f)* imprudente

jazz [dʒæz] jazz *m*

jealous [ˈdʒeləs] celoso; **jealousy** celos *mpl*; *of possessions* envidia *f*

jeans [dʒiːnz] vaqueros *mpl*, jeans *mpl*

jeep [dʒiːp] jeep *m*

jeer [dʒɪr] **1** *n* abucheo *m* **2** *v/i* abuchear

Jello® [ˈdʒeloʊ] gelatina *f*

jelly [ˈdʒeli] mermelada *f*; **jellyfish** medusa *f*

jeopardize [ˈdʒepərdaɪz] poner en peligro

jerk¹ [dʒɜːrk] **1** *n* sacudida *f* **2** *v/t* dar un tirón a

jerk² [dʒɜːrk] *n* F imbécil *m/f*, *Span* gilipollas *m/f inv*

jerky [ˈdʒɜːrkɪ] brusco

Jesus [ˈdʒiːzəs] Jesús

jet [dʒet] *(airplane)* reactor *m*; *of water* chorro *m*; *(nozzle)* boquilla *f*; **jetlag** desfase *m* horario, jet lag *m*

jettison [ˈdʒetɪsn] tirar por la borda

jetty [ˈdʒeti] malecón *m*

Jew [dʒuː] judío(-a) *m(f)*

jewel [ˈdʒuːəl] *also fig* joya *f*; **jeweler** *Br* **jeweller** joyero(-a) *m(f)*; **jewellery** *Br*, **jewelry** joyas *fpl*

Jewish [ˈdʒuːɪʃ] judío

jigsaw [ˈdʒɪgsɔː] rompecabezas *m inv*, puzzle *m*

jilt [dʒɪlt] dejar plantado

jingle [ˈdʒɪŋgl] **1** *n song* melodía *f* publicitaria **2** *v/i of keys, coins* tintinear

jinx [dʒɪŋks] gafe *m*; **there's a ~ on this project** este proyecto está gafado

jittery [ˈdʒɪtəri] F nervioso

job [dʒɑːb] trabajo *m*; **jobless** desempleado, *Span* parado jockey ['dʒɑːkɪ] jockey m/f

jog [dʒɑːg] as exercise hacer jogging or footing; jogger persona f que hace jogging or footing; jogging: go ~ ir a hacer jogging or footing

john [dʒɑːn] P (toilet) baño m, váter m

join [dʒɔɪn] 1 n juntura f v/i of roads, rivers juntarse; (become a member) hacerse socio 3 v/t (connect) unir; person unirse a; club hacerse socio de; of road desembocar en

◆ join in participar

joint [dʒɔɪnt] ANAT articulación f; in woodwork junta f; of meat pieza f; joint account cuenta f conjunta; joint venture empresa f conjunta

joke [dʒəʊk] 1 n chiste m; (practical ~) broma f 2 v/i bromear; joker bromista m/f; in cards comodín m; jokingly en broma

jostle ['dʒɑːsl] empujar

journal ['dʒɜːrnl] (magazine) revista f; (diary) diario m; journalism periodismo m; journalist periodista m/f

journey ['dʒɜːrnɪ] viaje m

joy [dʒɔɪ] alegría f, gozo m

jubilant ['dʒuːbɪlənt] jubiloso; jubilation júbilo m

judge [dʒʌdʒ] 1 n juez m/f v/t juzgar; (estimate) calcular 3 v/i juzgar; judg(e)ment LAW fallo m; (opinion) juicio m; Judg(e)ment Day Día m

del Juicio Final

judicial [dʒuːˈdɪʃl] judicial

juggle [dʒʌgl] also fig hacer malabarismos con

juice [dʒuːs] Span zumo m, L.Am. jugo m; juicy also fig jugoso

July [dʒʊˈlaɪ] julio m

jumbo (jet) ['dʒʌmbəʊ] jumbo m; jumbo(-sized) gigante

jump [dʒʌmp] 1 n salto m; (increase) incremento m, subida f 2 v/i saltar; (increase) dispararse 3 v/t fence etc saltar; F (attack) asaltar; ~ the lights saltarse el semáforo

◆ jump at opportunity no dejar escapar

jumper ['dʒʌmpər] dress pichi m; jumpy nervioso

June [dʒuːn] junio m

jungle ['dʒʌŋgl] selva f, jungla f

junior ['dʒuːnjər] 1 adj de rango inferior; (younger) más joven 2 n in rank subalterno(-a) m(f); junior high escuela f secundaria (para alumnos de entre 12 y 14 años)

junk [dʒʌŋk] trastos mpl; junk food comida f basura; junkie F drogata m/f F; junk mail propaganda f postal

jurisdiction [dʒʊrɪsˈdɪkʃn] jurisdicción f

juror ['dʒʊrər] miembro m del jurado; jury jurado m

just [dʒʌst] 1 adj cause justo 2 adv (barely) justo; (exactly) justo, justamente; (only) sólo, solamente; *have ~ done sth* acabar de hacer algo; ~ *about* (*almost*) casi; *I was ~ about to leave when ...* estaba a punto de salir cuando...; ~ *now* (*at the moment*) ahora mismo; *I saw her ~ now* a few moments ago te acabo de ver

justice ['dʒʌstɪs] justicia *f*
justifiable [dʒʌstɪ'faɪəbl] justificable; **justifiably** justifi-

cadamente; **justification** justificación *f*; **justify** *also text* justificar

justly ['dʒʌstlɪ] (*fairly*) con justicia; (*rightly*) con razón
◆ **jut out** ['dʒʌt] sobresalir

juvenile ['dʒuːvənl] *crime* juvenil; *court* de menores; *pej* infantil; **juvenile delinquent** delincuente *m/f* juvenil

K

k [keɪ] (= *kilobyte*) k (= *kilobyte m*); (= *thousand*) mil
keel [kiːl] NAUT quilla *f*
keen [kiːn] *interest* gran
keep [kiːp] **1** *v/t* guardar; (*not lose*) conservar; (*detain*) entretener; *family* mantener; *animals* tener, criar; ~ *trying!* ¡sigue intentándolo!; *don't ~ interrupting!* ¡deja de interrumpirme!; ~ *sth from s.o.* ocultar algo a alguien **2** *v/i of food, milk* aguantar; ~ *calm!* ¡tranquilízate!
◆ **keep back** (*hold in check*) contener; *information* ocultar
◆ **keep down** *voice* bajar; *costs etc* reducir; *food* retener
◆ **keep to** *path* seguir; *rules* cumplir, respetar
◆ **keep up 1** *v/i when walking, running etc* seguir el ritmo

(*with* de) **2** *v/t pace* seguir, mantener; *payments* estar al corriente de; *bridge, pants* sujetar

keepsake recuerdo *m*
kennel ['kenl] caseta *f* del perro; **kennels** residencia *f* canina

kerosene ['kerəsiːn] queroseno *m*
ketchup ['ketʃʌp] ketchup *m*
kettle ['ketl] hervidor *m*
key [kiː] **1** *n* llave *f*; *on keyboard, piano* tecla *f*; *of piece of music* clave *f*; *on map* leyenda *f* **2** *adj* (*vital*) clave **3** *v/t* & *v/i* COMPUT teclear
◆ **key in** *data* teclear

keyboard COMPUT, MUS teclado *m*; **keyboarder** COMPUT operador(a) *m(f)*, teclista *m/f*; **keycard** tarjeta *f* (de hotel); **keyed-up** nervioso; **keyring** llavero *m*

kick [kɪk] **1** *n* patada *f* **2** *v/t* dar

una patada a; F *habit* dejar **3**
v/i of horse cocear
◆ **kick around** *ball* dar patadas a; F *(discuss)* comentar
◆ **kick off** comenzar, sacar de centro; F *(start)* empezar
◆ **kick out** *of bar, company* echar; *of country* expulsar
'kickback F *(bribe)* soborno *m*; **kickoff** SP saque *m*
kid [kɪd] F **1** *n (child)* crío *m* F, niño *m* **2** *v/t* tomar el pelo a F **3** *v/i* bromear
kidnap ['kɪdnæp] secuestrar; **kidnapper** secuestrador *m*; **kidnapping** secuestro *m*
kidney ['kɪdnɪ] ANAT riñón *m*; *in cooking* riñones *mpl*
kill [kɪl] matar; **killer** *(murderer)* asesino *m*; **killing** asesinato *m*
kiln [kɪln] horno *m*
kilo ['kiːloʊ] kilo *m*; **kilobyte** kilobyte *m*; **kilogram** kilogramo *m* F; **kilometer**, *Br* **kilometre** kilómetro *m*
kind[1] [kaɪnd] *adj* amable
kind[2] [kaɪnd] *n (sort)* tipo *m*; *(make, brand)* marca *f*; **~ of** ... *sad, lonely etc* un poco...
kind-hearted [kaɪnd'hɑ:rtɪd] agradable, amable; **kindly** amable, amablemente; **kindness** amabilidad *f*
king [kɪŋ] rey *m*; **kingdom** reino *m*
kinky ['kɪŋkɪ] F vicioso
kiosk ['kiːɑːsk] quiosco *m*
kiss [kɪs] **1** *n* beso *m* **2** *v/t* besar **3** *v/i* besarse
kit [kɪt] *(equipment)* equipo *m*

kitchen ['kɪtʃɪn] cocina *f*
kitten ['kɪtn] gatito *m*
kitty ['kɪtɪ] *money* fondo *m*
klutz [klʌts] F *(clumsy person)* manazas *m* F
knack [næk] habilidad *f*
knee [niː] rodilla *f*; **kneecap** rótula *f*
kneel [niːl] arrodillarse
knee-length hasta la rodilla
knife [naɪf] *for food* cuchillo *m*; *carried outside* navaja *f*
knit [nɪt] **1** *v/t* tejer **2** *v/i* tricotar; **knitwear** prendas *fpl* de punto
knob [nɑːb] *on door* pomo *m*; *on drawer* tirador *m*; *of butter* nuez *f*
knock [nɑːk] **1** *n* golpe *m* **2** *v/t (hit)* golpear; F *(criticize)* criticar **3** *v/i on door* llamar
◆ **knock down** *of car* atropellar; *building* tirar; *object* tirar al suelo; F *(reduce price of)* rebajar
◆ **knock out** dejar K.O.; *of medicine* dejar para el arrastre F; *power lines etc* destruir; *(eliminate)* eliminar
◆ **knock over** tirar; *of car* atropellar
knockout ['nɑːkaʊt] K.O. *m*
knot [nɑːt] **1** *n* nudo *m* **2** *v/t* anudar
know [noʊ] **1** *v/t* saber; *person, place* conocer; *(recognize)* reconocer **2** *v/i* saber; **I don't ~** (lo) sé; **knowhow** pericia *f*; **knowing** cómplice; **knowingly** deliberadamente; *smile etc* con complicidad

landmark

know-it-all F sabiondo F;
knowledge conocimiento
m; *to the best of my* ~ por
lo que sé
knuckle ['nʌkl] nudillo *m*
Koran [kə'ræn] Corán *m*

Korea [kə'riːə] Corea; **Korean**
1 *adj* coreano **2** *n* coreano(a)
m(f); *language* coreano *m*
kosher ['kəʊʃər] REL kosher;
F legal F
kudos ['kjuːdɑːs] prestigio *m*

L

lab [læb] laboratorio *m*
label ['leɪbl] **1** *n* etiqueta *f* **2** *v/t*
etiquetar
labor ['leɪbər] trabajo *m*; *in*
pregnancy parto *m*
laboratory ['læbrətɔːrɪ] laboratorio *m*
labored ['leɪbərd] *style, speech*
elaborado; **laborer** obre-
ro(-a) *m(f)*; **laborious** labo-
rioso; **labor union** sindicato
m; **labour** Br ☞ **labor**
lace [leɪs] encaje *m*; *for shoe*
cordón *m*
lack [læk] **1** *n* falta *f*, carencia *f*
2 *v/t* carecer de; *he ~s confi-*
dence le falta confianza
lacquer ['lækər] laca *f*
lactose lactosa *f*; **lactose in-**
tolerance MED intolerancia
f a la lactosa; **lactose-free**
sin lactosa
ladder ['lædər] escalera *f* (de
mano)
laden ['leɪdn] cargado (*with*
de)
ladies room ['leɪdiːz] servicio *m*
de señoras
lady ['leɪdɪ] señora *f*; **ladybug**
mariquita *f*; **ladylike** femenino

lager ['lɑːgər] Br cerveza *f* rubia
laidback [leɪd'bæk] tranquilo,
despreocupado
lake [leɪk] lago *m*
lamb [læm] cordero *m*
lame [leɪm] cojo; *excuse* pobre
laminated ['læmɪneɪtɪd] lami-
nado; *paper* plastificado *m*
lamp [læmp] lámpara *f*; **lamp-**
post farola *f*; **lampshade**
pantalla *f* (de lámpara)
land [lænd] **1** *n* tierra *f*; *by* ~
por tierra **2** *v/t airplane* aterrizar; *job* conseguir **3** *v/i*
of airplane aterrizar; *of ball*
caer; **landing** *of airplane* aterrizaje *m*; *of staircase* rellano
m; **landing strip** pista *f* de
aterrizaje; **landlady** *of hostel*
etc dueña *f*; *of rented room*
casera *f*; Br: *of bar* patrona
f; **landline** TELEC número
m fijo; *I'll call you later on*
the ~ te llamo luego al fijo;
landline number número
m de teléfono fijo; **landlord**
of hostel etc dueño *m*; *of*
rented room casero *m*; Br:
of bar patrón *m*; **landmark**
punto *m* de referencia; *fig*

hito m; **land owner** terrateniente m/f; **landscape 1** n (also painting) paisaje m **2** adv print en formato apaisado; **landslide** corrimiento m de tierras; **landslide victory** victoria f arrolladora

lane [leɪn] in country camino m; (alley) callejón m; MOT carril m

language [ˈlæŋgwɪdʒ] lenguaje m; of nation idioma m, lengua f; **language lab** laboratorio m de idiomas

lap¹ [læp] of track vuelta f

lap² [læp] of water chapoteo m

lap³ [læp] of person regazo m

lapel [ləˈpel] solapa f

lapse [læps] **1** n (mistake) desliz m; of time lapso m **2** v/i of membership vencer

laptop [ˈlæptɑːp] COMPUT ordenador m portátil, L.Am. computadora f portátil

larceny [ˈlɑːrsənɪ] latrocinio m

larder [ˈlɑːrdər] despensa f

large [lɑːrdʒ] grande; (mainly) en gran parte, principalmente

laryngitis [lærɪnˈdʒaɪtɪs] laringitis f

laser [ˈleɪzər] láser m; **laser printer** impresora f láser

lash¹ [læʃ] v/t with whip azotar

lash² [læʃ] n (eyelash) pestaña f

last¹ [læst] **1** adj in series último; (preceding) anterior; ~ **Friday** el viernes pasado; ~ **night** anoche **2** adv at ~

por fin, al fin

last² [læst] v/i durar; **lasting** duradero; **lastly** por último

late [leɪt] **1** adj: be ~ of person, bus etc llegar tarde; **it's** ~ es tarde; **be** ~ of day arrive, leave tarde; **lately** últimamente, recientemente; **later** más tarde; **latest** último

Latin A'merica Latinoamérica, América Latina; **Latin American 1** n latinoamericano(-a) m(f) **2** adj latinoamericano

Latino [læˈtiːnou] **1** adj latino **2** n latino(-a)

latitude [ˈlætɪtuːd] latitud f; (freedom) libertad f

latter [ˈlætər] último

laugh [læf] **1** n risa f **2** v/i reírse

◆ **laugh at** reírse de

laughter [ˈlæftər] risas fpl

launch [lɔːntʃ] **1** n small boat lancha f; of ship botadura f; of rocket, product lanzamiento m **2** v/t rocket, product lanzar; ship botar

launder [ˈlɔːndər] clothes lavar (y planchar); money blanquear; **laundromat** lavandería f; **laundry** place lavadero m; dirty clothes ropa f sucia; clean clothes ropa f lavada

lavatory [ˈlævətɔːrɪ] place cuarto m de baño, lavabo m; equipment retrete m

lavish [ˈlævɪʃ] espléndido

law [lɔː] ley f; subject derecho m; **be against the** ~ estar

leave

prohibido; **law-abiding** respetuoso con la ley; **law court** juzgado *m*; **lawful** legal; *wife* legítimo; **lawless** sin ley

awn [lɔːn] césped *m*; **lawn mower** cortacésped *m*

lawsuit pleito *m*; **lawyer** abogado(-a) *m(f)*

ax [læks] poco estricto

axative [ˈlæksətɪv] laxante *m*

ay [leɪ] (*put down*) dejar, poner; *eggs* poner; **V** *sexually* tirarse a **V**

◆ **lay off** *workers* despedir

◆ **lay out** *objects* colocar; *page* diseñar, maquetar

ayer [ˈleɪə] estrato *m*; *of soil, paint* capa *f*

layman laico *m*

lay-out diseño *m*

azy [ˈleɪzɪ] *person* holgazán, perezoso; *day* ocioso

b (= *pound*) libra *f* (de peso)

ead[1] [liːd] **1** *v/t procession* ir al frente de; *company* dirigir; (*guide, take*) conducir **2** *v/i in race, competition* ir en cabeza; (*provide leadership*) tener el mando

ead[2] [liːd] *n for dog* correa *f*

ead[3] [led] *n substance* plomo *m*; **leaded** gas con plomo

eader [ˈliːdə] líder *m*; **leadership** liderazgo *m*

ead-free [ˈledfriː] gas sin plomo

eading [ˈliːdɪŋ] *runner* en cabeza; *company, product* puntero; **leading-edge** *company* en la vanguardia; *technology*

de vanguardia

leaf [liːf] hoja *f*

◆ **leaf through** hojear

leaflet [ˈliːflət] folleto *m*

league [liːg] liga *f*

leak [liːk] **1** *n in roof* gotera *f*; *in pipe* agujero *m*; *of air, gas* fuga *f*; *of information* filtración *f* **2** *v/i of boat* hacer agua; *of pipe* tener un agujero; *of liquid, gas* escaparse

lean[1] [liːn] **1** *v/i* estar inclinado; **~ against sth** apoyarse en algo **2** *v/t* apoyar

lean[2] [liːn] *adj meat* magro

leap [liːp] **1** *n* salto *m* **2** *v/i* saltar; **leap year** año *m* bisiesto

learn [lɜːn] **1** *v/t* aprender **2** *v/i* aprender; **~ about** (*hear about*) enterarse de; **learner** estudiante *m/f*; **learning** (*knowledge*) conocimientos *mpl*; *act* aprendizaje *m*

lease [liːs] **1** *n* arrendamiento *m* **2** *v/t* arrendar

◆ **lease out** arrendar

leash [liːʃ] *for dog* correa *f*

least [liːst] **1** *adj* (*slightest*) menor **2** *adv* menos **3** *n* lo menos; **at ~** por lo menos

leather [ˈleðə] **1** *n* piel *f*, cuero *m* **2** *adj* de piel, de cuero

leave [liːv] **1** *n* (*vacation*) permiso *m* **2** *v/t city, place* marcharse de, irse de; *person, food, memory,* (*forget*) dejar; **~ s.o. / sth alone** dejar a alguien / algo en paz; **be left** quedar **3** *v/i of person* marcharse, irse; *of plane, train, bus* salir

◆ **leave behind** *intentionally* dejar; *(forget)* dejarse

◆ **leave out** omitir; *(not put away)* no guardar

leaving party ['liːvɪŋ] fiesta *f* de despedida

lecture ['lektʃər] **1** *n* clase *f*; *to general public* conferencia *f* **2** *v/i at university* dar clases (**in** de); **lecturer** profesor(a) *m(f)*

ledge [ledʒ] *of window* alféizar *f*; *on rock face* saliente *m*; **ledger** COM libro *m* mayor

left [left] **1** *adj* izquierdo **2** *n also* POL izquierda *f*; **on** / **to the ~** a la izquierda **3** *adv turn, look* a la izquierda; **left-hand** de la izquierda; **left-handed** zurdo; **left luggage (office)** *Br* consigna *f*; **left-overs** *food* sobras *fpl*; **left-wing** POL izquierdista, de izquierdas

leg [leg] *of person* pierna *f*; *of animal, table* pata *f*

legacy ['legəsɪ] legado *m*

legal ['liːgl] legal; **legal adviser** asesor(a) *m(f)* jurídico(-a); **legality** legalidad *f*; **legalize** legalizar

legend ['ledʒənd] leyenda *f*; **legendary** legendario

legible ['ledʒəbl] legible

legislate ['ledʒɪsleɪt] legislar; **legislation** legislación *f*; **legislative** legislativo; **legislature** POL legislativo *m*

legitimate [lɪ'dʒɪtɪmət] legítimo

'leg room espacio *m* para las piernas

leisure ['liːʒər] ocio *m*; **leisurely** tranquilo, relajado

lemon ['lemən] limón *m*; **lemonade** limonada *f*

lend [lend] prestar

length [leŋθ] longitud *f*; *(piece: of material etc)* pedazo *m*; **at ~** *describe* detalladamente; *(finally)* finalmente; **lengthen** alargar; **lengthy** largo

lenient ['liːnɪənt] indulgente, poco severo

lens [lenz] *of camera* objetivo *m*, lente *f*; *of eyeglasses* cristal *m*; *of eye* cristalino *m*; *(contact ~)* lente *m* de contacto, *Span* lentilla *f*

Lent [lent] REL Cuaresma *f*

leotard ['liːoʊtɑːrd] malla *f*

lesbian ['lezbɪən] **1** *n* lesbiana *f* **2** *adj* lésbico, lesbiano

less [les] menos; **~ than $200** menos de 200 dólares; **lessen** disminuir

lesson ['lesn] lección *f*

let [let] *(allow)* dejar, permitir; *Br house* alquilar; **~ me go!** ¡déjame!; **~'s go** vamos; **~'s stay** vaquedémonos; **~ go of sth** soltar algo

◆ **let down** *hair* soltarse; *blinds* bajar; *(disappoint)* decepcionar

◆ **let in** *to house* dejar pasar

◆ **let out** *from room, building* dejar salir; *jacket etc* agrandar; *groan* soltar; *Br room* alquilar, *Mex* rentar

◆ **let up** (*stop*) amainar

lethal ['liːθl] letal

lethargic [lɪ'θɑːrdʒɪk] aletargado; **lethargy** sopor *m*

letter ['letər] *of alphabet* letra *f*; *in mail* carta *f*; **letterbox** *Br* buzón *m*; **letterhead** (*heading*) membrete *m*; (*headed paper*) papel *m* con membrete

lettuce ['letɪs] lechuga *f*

leukemia [luː'kiːmɪə] leucemia *f*

level ['levl] **1** *adj surface* nivelado, llano; *in competition* igualado **2** *n* nivel *m*; **on the ~** F (*honest*) honrado; **level-headed** ecuánime

lever ['levər] palanca *f*; **leverage** apalancamiento *m*; (*influence*) influencia *f*

◆ **levy** ['levɪ] *taxes* imponer

liability [laɪə'bɪlətɪ] responsabilidad *f*; (*likeliness*) propensión *f* (*to* a); **liable** responsable (*for* de); **be ~ to** (*likely*) ser propenso a

◆ **liaise with** [lɪ'eɪz] actuar de enlace con

liaison [lɪ'eɪzɑːn] (*contacts*) contacto *m*, enlace *m*

liar [laɪr] mentiroso(-a) *m(f)*

libel ['laɪbl] **1** *n* calumnia *f* **2** *v/t* calumniar

liberal ['lɪbərəl] liberal; *portion etc* abundante

liberate ['lɪbəreɪt] liberar; **liberated** liberado; **liberation** liberación *f*; **liberty** libertad *f*

librarian [laɪ'breriən] bibliotecario(-a) *m(f)*; **library** biblioteca *f*

Libya ['lɪbɪə] Libia; **Libyan 1** *adj* libio **2** *n* libio(-a) *m(f)*

licence *Br* **license** *n*

license ['laɪsns] **1** *n* permiso *m*, licencia *f* **2** *v/t* autorizar; **license number** (número *m* de) matrícula *f*; **license plate** *of car* (placa *f* de) matrícula *f*

lick [lɪk] lamer

lid [lɪd] (*top*) tapa *f*

lie¹ [laɪ] **1** *n* (*untruth*) mentira *f* **2** *v/i* mentir

lie² [laɪ] *v/i of person* estar tumbado; *of object* estar; (*be situated*) estar, encontrarse

◆ **lie down** tumbarse

lieutenant [luː'tenənt] teniente *m/f*

life [laɪf] vida *f*; **life expectancy** esperanza *f* de vida; **lifeguard** socorrista *m/f*; **life imprisonment** cadena *f* perpetua; **life insurance** seguro *m* de vida; **life jacket** chaleco *m* salvavidas; **lifeless** sin vida; **lifelike** realista; **lifelong** de toda la vida; **lifesized** de tamaño natural; **life support** máquina *f* de respiración asistida; **lifethreatening** que puede ser mortal; **lifetime** vida *f*; **in my ~** durante mi vida

lift [lɪft] **1** *v/t* levantar **2** *v/i of fog* disiparse **3** *n Br* (*elevator*) ascensor *m*; **give s.o. a ~** llevar a alguien (en coche); **lift-**

off *of rocket* despegue *m*
ligament ['lɪgəmənt] ligamento *m*
light¹ [laɪt] **1** *n* luz *f*; *do you
have a ~?* ¿tienes fuego? **2**
v/t fire, cigarette encender; *(illuminate)* iluminar **3** *adj col-
or, sky* claro; *room* luminoso
light² [laɪt] *adj (not heavy)* ligero
♦ **light up 1** *v/t* iluminar **2** *v/i
(start to smoke)* encender un
cigarrillo
'**light bulb** bombilla *f*
lighten¹ ['laɪtn] *color* aclarar
lighten² ['laɪtn] *load* aligerar
lighter ['laɪtər] *for cigarettes*
encendedor *m*, *Span* meche-
ro *m*; **light-headed** mareado; **lighting** iluminación *f*;
lightness *of room, color* claridad *f*; *in weight* ligereza *f*;
lightning: *a flash of ~* un
relámpago; **lightweight** *in
boxing* peso *m* ligero; **light
year** año *m* luz
like¹ [laɪk] **1** *prep* como; *what
is she~?* ¿cómo es?; *it's not
~ him* (*not his character*) no
es su estilo **2** *conj* como; *...
I said* como dije
like² [laɪk] *v/t: I ~ it / her* me
gusta; *I would ~ ...* querría
...; *I would ~ ...* me gustaría...; *would you ~ ...?*
¿querrías...?; *she ~s to
swim* le gusta nadar; *if you
~* si quieres
likeable ['laɪkəbl] simpático;
likelihood probabilidad *f*;
likely probable; **likeness**

(resemblance) parecido *m*;
likewise igualmente; **liking**
afición *f* (**for** a)
limb [lɪm] miembro *m*
lime¹ [laɪm] *fruit, tree* lima *f*
lime² [laɪm] *substance* cal *f*
limit ['lɪmɪt] **1** *n* límite *m* **2** *v/t*
limitar; **limitation** limitación
f; **limited company** *Br* sociedad *f* limitada
limousine ['lɪməziːn] limusi-
na *f*
limp¹ [lɪmp] *adj* flojo
limp² [lɪmp] *n: he has a ~* co-
jea
line¹ [laɪn] *n* línea *f*; *of trees* fila *f*; *of people* fila *f*, cola *f*;
the ~ is busy está ocupado,
Span está comunicando;
stand in ~ hacer cola
line² [laɪn] *v/t with lining* fo-
rrar
linear ['lɪnɪər] lineal
linen ['lɪnɪn] *material* lino *m*;
(sheets etc) ropa *f* blanca
liner ['laɪnər] *ship* transatlántico *m*
linesman ['laɪnzmən] *SP* juez
m de línea, linier *m*
linger ['lɪŋgər] *of person* entretenerse; *of pain* persistir
lingerie ['lænʒəriː] lencería *f*
linguist ['lɪŋgwɪst] lingüista
m/f; **linguistic** lingüístico *c*
lining ['laɪnɪŋ] *of clothes* forro
m; *of brakes, pipe* revestimiento *m*
link [lɪŋk] **1** *n* conexión *f*; *between countries* vínculo *m*;
in chain eslabón *m*; *in Internet* enlace *m* **2** *v/t* conectar

lion ['laɪən] león *m*
lip [lɪp] labio *m*
liposuction ['lɪpoʊsʌkʃn] liposucción *f*
lipread leer los labios; **lipstick** barra *f* de labios
liqueur [lɪ'kjʊr] licor *m*
liquid ['lɪkwɪd] **1** *n* líquido *m* **2** *adj* líquido; **liquidate** *assets* liquidar; F (*kill*) cepillarse *f*; **liquidation** liquidación *f*; **go into ~** ir a la quiebra; **liquidity** FIN liquidez *f*; **liquidize** licuar; **liquidizer** licuadora *f*
liquor ['lɪkər] bebida *f* alcohólica; **liquor store** tienda *f* de bebidas alcohólicas
isp [lɪsp] **1** *n* ceceo *m* **2** *v/i* cecear
ist [lɪst] **1** *n* lista *f* **2** *v/t* enumerar
isten ['lɪsn] escuchar
◆ **listen to** escuchar
istener ['lɪsnər] *to radio* oyente *m/f*
istless ['lɪstlɪs] apático
iter ['liːtər] litro *m*
iteral ['lɪtərəl] literal; **literally** literalmente
iterary ['lɪtərerɪ] literario; **literature** literatura *f*; *about product* folletos *mpl*
itre *Br* ➞ **liter**
itter ['lɪtər] basura *f*; *of animal* camada *f*
ittle ['lɪtl] **1** *adj* pequeño **2** *n* poco *m*; **a ~ wine** un poco de vino **3** *adv* poco; **a ~ bigger** un poco más grande
ive¹ [lɪv] *v/i* vivir

◆ **live up to** *expectations* responder a; *reputation* estar a la altura de
live² [laɪv] *adj broadcast* en directo; *ammunition* real; *wire* con corriente
livelihood ['laɪvlɪhʊd] vida *f*, sustento *m*; **liveliness** vivacidad *f*; *of debate* lo animado; **lively** animado
liver ['lɪvər] hígado *m*
livestock ['laɪvstɑːk] ganado *m*
livid ['lɪvɪd] (*angry*) enfurecido, furioso
living ['lɪvɪŋ] **1** *adj* vivo **2** *n* vida *f*; **living room** sala *f* de estar, salón *m*
lizard ['lɪzərd] lagarto *m*
load [loʊd] **1** *n* carga *f* **2** *v/t car, truck, gun* cargar; *camera* poner el carrete a; *software* cargar (en memoria)
loaf [loʊf] pan *m*
◆ **loaf around** F gandulear F
loafer ['loʊfər] *shoe* mocasín *m*
loan [loʊn] **1** *n* préstamo *m*; **on ~** prestado **2** *v/t* prestar
loathe [loʊð] detestar, aborrecer; **loathing** odio *m*, aborrecimiento *m*
lobby ['lɑːbɪ] *in hotel, theater* vestíbulo *m*; POL lobby *m*
lobe [loʊb] *of ear* lóbulo *m*
lobster ['lɑːbstər] langosta *f*
local ['loʊkl] **1** *adj* local **2** *n* **are you a ~?** ¿eres de aquí?; **local call** TELEC llamada *f* local; **local elections** elecciones *fpl* municipales; **local**

government administración f municipal; **locality** localidad f; **localize** localizar; **locally** live, work cerca, en la zona; **local time** hora f local

locate [loʊˈkeɪt] new factory etc emplazar, ubicar; (identify position of) situar; **be** ~**d** encontrarse; **location** (siting) emplazamiento m; (identifying position of) localización f; **on** ~ movie en exteriores

lock¹ [lɑːk] n of hair mechón m

lock² [lɑːk] **1** n on door cerradura f **2** v/t door cerrar (con llave)

♦ **lock up** in prison encerrar

locker [ˈlɑːkər] taquilla f; **locker room** vestuario m

locust [ˈloʊkəst] langosta f

lodge [lɑːdʒ] **1** v/t complaint presentar **2** v/i of bullet alojarse

lofty [ˈlɑːftɪ] elevado

log [lɑːg] wood tronco m; written record registro m

♦ **log in** entrar

♦ **log off** salir

♦ **log on** entrar (**to** a)

♦ **log off** salir

'log cabin cabaña f

logic [ˈlɑːdʒɪk] lógica f; **logical** lógico; **logically** lógicamente

logistics [ləˈdʒɪstɪks] logística f

logo [ˈloʊgoʊ] logotipo m

loiter [ˈlɔɪtər] holgazanear

lollipop [ˈlɑːlɪpɑːp] piruleta f

London [ˈlʌndən] Londres

loneliness [ˈloʊnlɪnɪs] soledad f; **lonely** person solo; place solitario; **loner** solitario(-a) m(f)

long¹ [lɔːŋ] **1** adj largo **2** adv mucho tiempo; **that was** ~ **ago** eso fue hace mucho tiempo; **how** ~ **will it take?** ¿cuánto se tarda?; **we can't wait any** ~ no podemos esperar más tiempo; **so** ~ **as** (provided) siempre que ; **so** ~**!** ¡hasta la vista!

long² [lɔːŋ] v/i: ~ **for sth** home echar en falta algo; change anhelar algo; **be** ~**ing to do sth** anhelar hacer algo

long-distance race de fondo; flight, call de larga distancia; **longevity** longevidad f; **longing** anhelo m; **longitude** longitud f; **long jump** salto m de longitud; **long-range** missile de largo alcance; forecast a largo plazo; **long-sleeved** de manga larga; **long-standing** antiguo; **long-term** a largo plazo

loo [luː] Br F baño m

look [lʊk] **1** n (appearance) aspecto m; (glance) mirada f; ~**s** (beauty) atractivo m, guapura f **2** v/i mirar; (search) buscar; (seem) parecer

♦ **look after** children cuidar (de); property proteger

♦ **look ahead** fig mirar hacia el futuro

♦ **look around 1** v/i mirar **2** v/t museum, city dar un

loyalty

vuelta por
◆ **look at** mirar; (*examine*) estudiar; (*consider*) considerar
◆ **look back** mirar atrás
◆ **look down on** mirar por encima del hombro a
◆ **look for** buscar
◆ **look into** (*investigate*) investigar
◆ **look onto** *garden etc* dar a
◆ **look out** *through window etc* mirar; (*pay attention*) tener cuidado
◆ **look over** *translation* revisar; *house* inspeccionar
◆ **look through** *magazine, notes* echar un vistazo a
◆ **look up 1** *v/i from paper etc* levantar la mirada; (*improve*) mejorar **2** *v/t word, phone number* buscar; (*visit*) visitar
◆ **look up to** (*respect*) admirar

'lookout *person* centinela *m*
loop [luːp] bucle *m*; **loophole** *in law etc* vacío *m* legal
loose [luːs] *connection, clothes* suelto; *morals* disoluto; *wording* impreciso; **loosely worded** vagamente; **loosen** aflojar
op-sided [luːpˈsaɪdɪd] torcido
Lord [lɔːrd] (*God*) Señor *m*
orry [ˈlɒrɪ] *Br* camión *m*
ose [luːz] **1** *v/t perder; (*of clock*) retrasarse; **loser** perdedor(-a) *m(f)*; **F** *in life* fracasado(-a) *m(f)*
oss [lɒs] pérdida *f*
ost [lɒst] perdido; **lost-and-**found, *Br* **lost property** (**office**) oficina *f* de objetos perdidos
lot [lɒt]: **a ~ (of)**, **~s (of)** mucho, muchos; **a ~ easier** mucho más fácil
lotion [ˈləʊʃn] loción *f*
lottery [ˈlɒtərɪ] lotería *f*
loud [laʊd] fuerte; *color* chillón; **loudspeaker** altavoz *m*, *L.Am.* altoparlante *m*
louse [laʊs] piojo *m*; **lousy** **F** asqueroso
lout [laʊt] gamberro *m*
lovable [ˈlʌvəbl] adorable, encantador; **love 1** *n amor m*; *in tennis* nada *f*; **fall in ~** enamorarse (**with** de); **make ~** hacer el amor **2** *v/t* amar; **love affair** aventura *f* amorosa; **lovely** *face, hair, color, tune* precioso, lindo; *person, character* encantador; *holiday, weather, meal* estupendo; **lover** amante *m/f*; **loving** cariñoso; **lovingly** con cariño
low [ləʊ] **1** *adj bajo* **2** *n in weather* zona *f* de bajas presiones; *in statistics* mínimo *m*; **lowbrow** poco intelectual; **low-calorie** bajo en calorías; **low-cut** escotado; **lower** *to the ground, hemline, price* bajar; *flag* arriar; *pressure* reducir; **low-fat** de bajo contenido graso; **lowkey** discreto
loyal [ˈlɔɪəl] leal (**to** a); **loyally** lealmente; **loyalty** lealtad *f* (**to** a)

Ltd (= *limited*) S.L. (= sociedad *f* limitada)
lubricant ['lu:brıkənt] lubricante *m*; **lubricate** lubricar; **lubrication** lubricación *f*
lucid ['lu:sıd] lúcido
luck [lʌk] suerte *f*; **good ~!** ¡buena suerte!; **luckily** por suerte; **lucky** *person, coincidence* afortunado; *day, number* de la suerte; **you were ~** tuviste suerte!
lucrative ['lu:krətıv] lucrativo
ludicrous ['lu:dıkrəs] ridículo
lug [lʌg] arrastrar
luggage ['lʌgıdʒ] equipaje *m*
lukewarm ['lu:kwɔ:rm] tibio; *reception* indiferente
lull [lʌl] *in storm, fighting* tregua *f*; *in conversation* pausa *f*
lumber ['lʌmbər] (*timber*) madera *f*
luminous ['lu:mınəs] luminoso
lump [lʌmp] *of sugar, earth* terrón *m*; (*swelling*) bulto *m*; **lump sum** pago *m* único;

lumpy *liquid, sauce* grumoso; *mattress* lleno de bultos
lunacy ['lu:nəsı] locura *f*
lunar ['lu:nər] lunar
lunatic ['lu:nətık] lunático(-a) *m(f)*
lunch [lʌntʃ] almuerzo *m*, comida *f*; **have ~** almorzar, comer; **lunch box** fiambrera *f*; **lunch break** pausa *f* para el almuerzo; **lunchtime** hora *f* del almuerzo
lung [lʌŋ] pulmón *m*
lurch [lɜ:rtʃ] *of drunk* tambalearse; *of ship* dar sacudidas
lure [lʊr] **1** *n* atractivo **m 2** *v/t* atraer
lurk [lɜ:rk] *of person* estar oculto
lush [lʌʃ] *vegetation* exuberante
lust [lʌst] lujuria *f*
luxurious [lʌg'ʒʊrıəs] lujoso; **luxuriously** lujosamente; **luxury 1** *n* lujo **m 2** *adj* de lujo
lynch [lıntʃ] linchar
lyrics ['lırıks] letra *f*

M

ma'am [mæm] señora *f*
machine [mə'ʃi:n] máquina *f*; **machine gun** ametralladora *f*; **machinery** maquinaria *f*
machismo [mə'kızmou] machismo *m*
macho ['mætʃou] macho
macro ['mækrou] COMPUT macro *m*

mad [mæd] (*insane*) loco; F (*angry*) enfadado; **madden** (*infuriate*) sacar de quici; **maddening** exasperante; **madhouse** *fig* casa *f* de locos; **madman** loco *m*; **madness** locura *f*
Madonna [mə'dɑ:nə] madona *f*

Mafia ['mɑːfɪə]: **the ~** la mafia

magazine [mægə'ziːn] *printed* revista *f*

Magi ['meɪdʒaɪ] REL: **the ~** los Reyes Magos

nagic ['mædʒɪk] **1** *n* magia *f* **2** *adj* mágico; *magical* mágico; **magician** *performer* mago(-a) *m(f)*

nagnet ['mægnɪt] imán *m*; **magnetic** magnético; *fig*: *personality* cautivador; **magnetism** *of person* magnetismo *m*

magnificence [mæg'nɪfɪsəns] magnificencia *f*; **magnificent** magnífico

magnify ['mægnɪfaɪ] aumentar; *difficulties* exagerar; **magnifying glass** lupa *f*

magnitude ['mægnɪtuːd] magnitud *f*

naid [meɪd] *(servant)* criada *f*; *in hotel* camarera *f*

naiden name ['meɪdn] apellido *m* de soltera

nail [meɪl] **1** *n* correo *m* **2** *v/t letter* enviar (por correo); **mailbox** *also* COMPUT buzón *m*; **mailing list** lista *f* de direcciones; **mailman** cartero *m*; **mailshot** mailing *m*

naim [meɪm] mutilar

nain [meɪn] principal; **main course** plato *m* principal; **mainframe** *Span* ordenador *m* central, *L.Am.* computadora *f* central; **mainly** principalmente; **main road** carretera *f* general; **main street** calle *f* principal

maintain [meɪn'teɪn] mantener; **maintenance** mantenimiento *m*

majestic [mə'dʒestɪk] majestuoso

major ['meɪdʒər] **1** *adj (significant)* importante, principal **2** *n* MIL comandante *m*
♦ **major in** especializarse en

majority [mə'dʒɑːrətɪ] *also* POL mayoría *f*

make [meɪk] **1** *n (brand)* marca *f* **2** *v/t* hacer; *cars* fabricar, producir; *movie* rodar; *speech* pronunciar; *decision* tomar; *(earn)* ganar; MATH hacer; **two and two ~ four** dos y dos son cuatro; **~ s.o. do sth** *(force to)* obligar a alguien a hacer algo; *(cause to)* hacer que alguien haga algo; **~ s.o. happy / angry** hacer feliz / enfadar a alguien; **~ it** *(catch bus, train)* llegar a tiempo; *(come)* ir; *(succeed)* tener éxito; *(survive)* sobrevivir; **what time do you ~ it?** ¿qué hora llevas?; **~ do with** conformarse con; **what do you ~ of it?** ¿qué piensas?
♦ **make out** *list* hacer, elaborar; *check* extender; *(see)* distinguir; *(imply)* pretender
♦ **make up 1** *v/i of woman, actor* maquillarse; *after quarrel* reconciliarse **2** *v/t story* inventar; *face* maquillar; *(constitute)* suponer, formar
♦ **make up for** compensar por

'make-believe ficción *f*, fantasía *f*

maker ['meɪkər] (*manufacturer*) fabricante *m*; **makeshift** improvisado; **make-up** (*cosmetics*) maquillaje *m*

maladjusted [mælə'dʒʌstɪd] inadaptado

male [meɪl] **1** *adj* masculino; *animal* macho **2** *n* man hombre *m*, varón *m*; *animal*, *bird* macho *m*; **male chauvinism** machismo *m*; **male chauvinist pig** machista *m*

malevolent [mə'levələnt] malévolo

malfunction [mæl'fʌŋkʃn] **1** *n* fallo *m* (**in** de) **2** *v/i* fallar

malice ['mælɪs] malicia *f*; **malicious** malicioso

malignant [mə'lɪɡnənt] *tumor* maligno

mall [mɔːl] (*shopping* ∼) centro *m* comercial

malnutrition [mælnuː'trɪʃn] desnutrición *f*

maltreat [mæl'triːt] maltratar; **maltreatment** maltrato *m*

mammal ['mæml] mamífero *m*

man [mæn] **1** *n* hombre *m*; (*humanity*) el hombre; *in checkers* ficha *f* **2** *v/t telephones*, *front desk* atender; *spacecraft* tripular

manage ['mænɪdʒ] **1** *v/t business* dirigir; *money* gestionar; *suitcase* poder con; ∼ **to** ... conseguir... **2** *v/i* (*cope*) arreglárselas; **manageable** (*easy to handle*) ma-

nejable; (*feasible*) factible; **management** (*managing*) gestión *f*, administración *f*; (*managers*) dirección *f*; **management consultant** consultor(a) *m(f)* en administración de empresas; **manager** *of hotel*, *company* director(a) *m(f)*; *of shop*, *restaurant* encargado(a) *m(f)*; **managerial** de gestión **managing director** director(a) *m(f)* gerente

mandate ['mændeɪt] (*authority*) mandato *m*; (*task*) tarea *f* **mandatory** obligatorio

maneuver [mə'nuːvər] **1** *n* maniobra *f* **2** *v/t* maniobrar

mangle ['mæŋɡl] (*crush*) destrozar

manhandle ['mænhændl] mover a la fuerza

manhood ['mænhʊd] madurez *f*; (*virility*) virilidad *f*; **manhunt** persecución *f*

mania ['meɪnɪə] (*craze*) pasión *f*; **maniac** F chiflado(-a *m(f)* F

manicure ['mænɪkjʊr] manicura *f*

manifest ['mænɪfest] **1** *adj* manifiesto **2** *v/t* manifestar

manipulate [mə'nɪpjəleɪt] *person*, *bones* manipular; **manipulation of** *person*, *bones* manipulación *f*; **manipulator** manipulador

man'kind la humanidad; **manly** (*brave*) de hombres; (*strong*) varonil; **man-made** *materials* sintético; *structur-*

artificial

manner ['mænər] *of doing sth* manera *f*, modo *m*; *(attitude)* actitud *f*; **manners** modales *mpl*; **good** / **bad** ~ buena / mala educación

manoeuvre *Br* ☞ **maneuver**

manpower *(workers)* mano *f* de obra; *for other tasks* recursos *mpl* humanos

manual ['mænjuəl] **1** *adj* manual **2** *n* manual *m*; **manually** a mano

manufacture [mænju'fæktʃər] **1** *n* fabricación *f* **2** *v/t equipment* fabricar; **manufacturer** fabricante *m*; **manufacturing** *industry* manufacturero

manuscript ['mænjuskrɪpt] manuscrito *m*

many ['menɪ] **1** *adj* muchos; **take** ~ **as apples as you like** toma todas las manzanas que quieras; **too** ~ **problems** demasiados problemas **2** *pron* muchos; **a great** ~, **a good** ~ muchos; **how** ~ **do you need?** ¿cuántos necesitas?; **as** ~ **as 200** hasta 200

map [mæp] mapa *m*

maple ['meɪpl] arce *m*

mar [mɑːr] empañar

marathon ['mærəθən] *race* maratón *m or f*

marble ['mɑːrbl] *material* mármol *m*

March [mɑːrtʃ] marzo *m*

march [mɑːrtʃ] **1** *n* marcha *f* **2** *v/i* marchar; **marcher** manifestante *m/f*

Mardi Gras ['mɑːrdɪɡrɑː] martes *m inv* de Carnaval

margin ['mɑːrdʒɪn] *also* COM margen *m*; **marginal** *(slight)* marginal; **marginally** *(slightly)* ligeramente

marihuana, **marijuana** [mærɪ'hwɑːnə] marihuana *f*

marina [mə'riːnə] puerto *m* deportivo

marine [mə'riːn] **1** *adj* marino **2** *n* MIL marine *m/f*, infante *m/f* de marina

marital ['mærɪtl] marital; **marital status** estado *m* civil

maritime ['mærɪtaɪm] marítimo

mark [mɑːrk] **1** *n* señal *f*, marca *f*; *(stain)* marca *f*, mancha *f*; *(sign, token)* signo *m*, señal *f*; *(trace)* señal *f*; *Br* EDU nota *f* **2** *v/t* *(stain)* manchar; *Br* EDU calificar; *(indicate, commemorate)* marcar **3** *v/i* *fabric* mancharse; **marked** *(definite)* marcado, notable; **marker** *(highlighter)* rotulador *m*

market ['mɑːrkɪt] **1** *n* mercado *m*; *(stock* ~*)* bolsa *f* **2** *v/t* comercializar; **marketable** comercializable; **market economy** economía *f* de mercado; **marketing** marketing *m*; **market leader** líder *m* del mercado; **marketplace** *in town* plaza *f* del mercado; *for commodities* mercado *m*; **market research** investigación *f* de mercado; **market share** cuo-

ta f de mercado
mark-up ['mɑːrkʌp] margen m

marriage ['mærɪdʒ] matrimonio m; *event* boda f; **marriage certificate** certificado m de matrimonio; **married** casado m; **be ~ to ...** estar casado con...; **married life** vida f matrimonial; **marry** casarse con; *of priest* casar; **get married** casarse

marsh [mɑːrʃ] *Br* pantano m, ciénaga f

marshal ['mɑːrʃl] *in police* jefe(-a) m(f) de policía; *in security service* miembro m del servicio de seguridad

martial 'law ley f marcial

martyr ['mɑːrtər] mártir m/f

marvel ['mɑːrvl] maravilla f; **marvelous**, *Br* **marvellous** maravilloso

Marxism ['mɑːrksɪzm] marxismo m; **Marxist 1** *adj* marxista **2** n marxista m/f

mascara [mæ'skærə] rímel m

mascot ['mæskɒt] mascota f

masculine ['mæskjʊlɪn] masculino; **masculinity** (*virility*) masculinidad f

mash [mæʃ] hacer puré de, majar

mask [mæsk] **1** n máscara f; *to cover mouth, nose* mascarilla f **2** v/t *feelings* enmascarar

masochism ['mæsəkɪzm] masoquismo m; **masochist** masoquista m/f

mass¹ [mæs] **1** n (*great amount*) gran cantidad f;

(*body*) masa f; **~es of** F un montón de F **2** v/i concentrarse

mass² [mæs] n REL misa f

massacre ['mæsəkər] **1** n masacre f, matanza f; F *in sport* paliza f **2** v/t masacrar; F *in sport* dar una paliza a

massage ['mæsɑːʒ] **1** n masaje m **2** v/t dar un masaje en; *figures* maquillar

massive ['mæsɪv] enorme *heart attack* muy grave

mass 'media medios mpl de comunicación; **mass-produce** fabricar en serie; **mass production** fabricación f en serie

mast [mæst] *of ship* mástil m; *for radio signal* torre f

master ['mæstər] **1** n *of dog* dueño m, amo m; *of ship* patrón m **2** v/t *skill* dominar; **master bedroom** dormitorio m principal; **master key** llave f maestra; **masterly** magistral; **mastermind 1** n cerebro m **2** v/t dirigir, organizar; **masterpiece** obra f maestra; **master's (degree)** máster m; **mastery** dominio m

mat [mæt] *for floor* estera f; *for table* salvamanteles m inv

match¹ [mætʃ] n *for cigarette* cerilla f, fósforo m

match² [mætʃ] **1** n SP partido m; *in chess* partida f **2** v/t (*be the same as*) coincidir con; (*be in harmony with*) hacer juego con; (*equal*) igua-

lar **3** *v/i of colors* hacer juego;
matching a juego; **match
stick** cerilla *f*, fósforo *m*
mate [meɪt] *n of animal* pareja *f*; NAUT oficial *m/f* **2** *v/i*
aparearse
material [məˈtɪrɪəl] **1** *n* (*fabric*) tejido *m*; (*substance*) material *m* **2** *adj* material;
materialism materialismo *m*;
materialist materialista
m/f; **materialistic** materialista; **materialize** (*appear*)
aparecer; (*come into existence*) hacerse realidad
maternal [məˈtɜːrnl] maternal; **maternity** maternidad
f; **maternity leave** baja *f*
por maternidad
math [mæθ] matemáticas *fpl*;
mathematical matemático;
mathematician matemático(-a) *m(f)*
maths *Br* **math**
matinée [ˈmætɪneɪ] sesión *f* de
tarde
matriarch [ˈmeɪtrɪɑːrk] matriarca *f*
matrimony [ˈmætrəmoʊnɪ]
matrimonio *m*
matt [mæt] mate
matter [ˈmætər] **1** *n* (*affair*)
asunto *m*; PHYS materia *f*;
what's the ~? ¿qué pasa? **2**
v/i importar; **it doesn't ~**
no importa; **matter-of-fact**
tranquilo
mattress [ˈmætrɪs] colchón *m*
mature [məˈtʃʊr] **1** *adj* maduro
2 *v/i of person* madurar; *of insurance policy* vencer; **matu-**

rity madurez *f*
maximize [ˈmæksɪmaɪz] maximizar; **maximum 1** *adj*
máximo **2** *n* máximo *m*
May [meɪ] mayo *m*
may [meɪ] *v/aux* ◇ *possibility*:
it ~ rain puede que llueva;
you ~ be right puede que
tengas razón; *it ~ not happen* puede que no ocurra
◇ *permission* poder; **~ I
help?** ¿puedo ayudar
maybe [ˈmeɪbɪ] quizás, tal
vez
mayo, mayonnaise [ˈmeɪoʊ,
meɪəˈneɪz] mayonesa *f*
mayor [mer] alcalde *m*
maze [meɪz] laberinto *m*
MB (= **megabyte**) MB (= megabyte *m*)
MBA [embiˈeɪ] (= **Master of
Business Administration**)
MBA *m* (= Máster en Administración de Empresas)
MD [emˈdiː] (= **Doctor of Medicine**) Doctor(a) *m(f)* en
Medicina; (= **managing director**) director(a) *m(f)* gerente
me [miː] *object* me; *after prep*
mí; *he knows ~* me conoce;
he sold it to ~ me lo vendió;
this is for ~ esto es para mí;
with ~ conmigo; *it's ~* soy yo;
taller than ~ más alto que yo
meadow [ˈmedoʊ] prado *m*
meager, *Br* **meagre** [ˈmiːgər]
escaso, exiguo
meal [miːl] comida *f*
mean[1] [miːn] *adj with money*
tacaño; (*nasty*) malo, cruel

mean² [mi:n] v/t (intend to say)
querer decir; (signify) querer
decir, significar; **be ~t for** ser
para; of remark ir dirigido a;
meaning of word significado
m; **meaningful** (comprehen-
sible) con sentido; (constructive), glance significativo;
meaningless sin sentido

means [mi:nz] financial medios mpl; (way) medio m;
by all ~ (certainly) por supuesto; **by ~ of** mediante

meantime ['mi:ntaɪm] mientras tanto

measles ['mi:zlz] sarampión
m

measure ['meʒər] **1** n (step)
medida f **2** v/t & v/i medir
♦ **measure up** estar a la altura (**to** de)

measurement ['meʒərmənt]
medida f; **measuring tape**
cinta f métrica

meat [mi:t] carne f; **meatball**
albóndiga f

mechanic [mɪ'kænɪk] mecá-
nico(-a) m(f); **mechanical**
also fig mecánico; **mechanical engineer** ingeniero(-a)
m(f) industrial; **mechani-
cally** also fig mecánicamen-
te; **mechanism** mecanismo
m; **mechanize** mecanizar

medal ['medl] medalla f;
medalist, Br **medallist** medallista m/f

meddle ['medl] entrometerse

media ['mi:dɪə]: **the ~** los medios de comunicación; **me-
dia coverage** cobertura f in-

formativa

median strip [mi:dɪən'strɪp]
mediana f

'**media studies** ciencias fpl
de la información

mediate ['mi:dɪeɪt] mediar;
mediation mediación f; **mediator** mediador(a) m(f)

medical ['medɪkl] **1** adj médico **2** n reconocimiento m
médico; **medicated** medicinal; **medication** medicamento m, medicina f; **medicinal** medicinal; **medicine
science** medicina f; (medication) medicina f, medica-
mento m

medieval [medɪ'i:vl] medieval

mediocre [mi:dɪ'oʊkər] mediocre; **mediocrity** of work
etc, person mediocridad f

meditate ['medɪteɪt] meditar
meditation meditación f

Mediterranean [medɪtə'reɪ-
nɪən] **1** adj mediterráneo **2**
n: **the ~** el Mediterráneo

medium ['mi:dɪəm] **1** adj (average) medio; steak a punto **2**
n size talla f media; (means)
medio m; (spiritualist) medium m/f

medley ['medlɪ] (assortment)
mezcla f

meet [mi:t] **1** v/t by appointment encontrarse con, reunirse con; by chance, of eyes
encontrarse con; (get to
know) conocer; (collect) ir a
buscar; in competition enfrentarse con; (satisfy) satis-

facer **2** v/i encontrarse; *in competition* enfrentarse; *of committee etc* reunirse **3** n SP reunión f; *meeting by chance* encuentro m; *in business* reunión f

megabyte ['megəbaɪt] COMPUT megabyte m

mellow ['meləʊ] **1** adj suave **2** v/i *of person* suavizarse, sosegarse

melodious [mɪ'ləʊdɪəs] melodioso

melodramatic [melədrə'mætɪk] melodramático

melody ['melədɪ] melodía f

melon ['melən] melón m

melt [melt] **1** v/i fundirse, derretirse **2** v/t fundir, derretir; **melting pot** fig crisol m

member ['membər] miembro m; **Member of Congress** diputado(-a) m(f); **membership** afiliación f; *number of members* número m de miembros

membrane ['membreɪn] membrana f

memento [me'mentəʊ] recuerdo m

memo ['meməʊ] nota f

memoirs ['memwɑːrz] memorias fpl

memorable ['memərəbl] memorable

memorial [mɪ'mɔːrɪəl] **1** adj conmemorativo **2** n monumento m conmemorativo; **Memorial Day** Día m de los Caídos

memorize ['meməraɪz] me-

morizar; **memory** (*recollection*) recuerdo m; (*power of recollection*), COMPUT memoria f

men [men] pl ☞ **man**

menace ['menɪs] **1** n amenaza f; *person* peligro m **2** v/t amenazar; **menacing** amenazador

mend [mend] reparar; *clothes* coser, remendar; *shoes* remendar

menial ['miːnɪəl] ingrato, penoso

menopause ['menəpɔːz] menopausia f

men's room servicio m de caballeros

menstruate ['menstrʊeɪt] menstruar

mental ['mentl] mental; F (*crazy*) chiflado F, pirado F; **mental hospital** hospital m psiquiátrico; **mental illness** enfermedad f mental; **mentality** mentalidad f; **mentally** mentalmente

mention ['menʃn] **1** n mención f **2** v/t mencionar; **don't ~ it** (*you're welcome*) no hay de qué

mentor ['mentɔːr] mentor(a) m(f)

menu ['menuː] *for food*, COMPUT menú m

mercenary ['mɜːrsɪnərɪ] **1** adj mercenario **2** n MIL mercenario(-a) m(f)

merchandise ['mɜːrtʃəndaɪz] mercancías fpl, L.Am. mercadería f merchant ['mɜːrtʃənt] comerciante m/f

merciful ['mɜːrsɪfəl] compasivo, piadoso; **mercifully** (thankfully) afortunadamente; **merciless** despiadado; **mercy** clemencia f, compasión f

mere [mɪr] mero, simple; **merely** meramente, simplemente

merge [mɜːrdʒ] of two lines etc juntarse, unirse; of companies fusionarse; **merger** COM fusión f

merit ['merɪt] **1** n (worth) mérito m; (advantage) ventaja f **2** v/t merecer

mesh [meʃ] malla f

mess [mes] (untidiness) desorden m; (trouble) lío m

message ['mesɪdʒ] also of movie etc mensaje m

messenger ['mesɪndʒər] (courier) mensajero(-a) m(f)

messy ['mesɪ] room, person desordenado; job sucio; divorce desagradable

metabolism [mə'tæbəlɪzm] metabolismo m

metal ['metl] **1** n metal m **2** adj metálico; **metallic** metálico

metaphor ['metəfər] metáfora f

meteor ['miːtɪər] meteoro m; **meteoric** fig meteórico; **meteorite** meteorito m

meteorological [miːtɪrə'lɑːdʒɪkl] meteorológico; **meteorologist** meteorólogo(-a) m(f); **meteorology** meteorología f

meter[1] ['miːtər] for gas, electricity contador m; (parking ~) parquímetro m

meter[2] ['miːtər] unit of length metro m

method ['meθəd] método m **methodical** metódico

meticulous [mə'tɪkjʊləs] meticuloso, minucioso

metre Br ☞ **meter[2]**

metropolis [mɪ'trɑːpəlɪs] metrópolis f inv; **metropolitan** metropolitano

mew [mjuː] ☞ **miaow**

Mexican ['meksɪkən] **1** adj mexicano, mejicano **2** n mexicano(-a) m(f), mejicano(-a) m(f); **Mexico** México, Méjico; **Mexico City** Ciudad f de México, Méx México, Mex el Distrito Federal, Mex el D.F.

miaow [mjaʊ] **1** n maullido m **2** v/i maullar

mice [maɪs] ☞ **mouse**

microchip microchip m; **microclimate** microclima m; **microcosm** microcosmos m inv; **microorganism** microorganismo m; **microphone** micrófono m; **microprocessor** microprocesador m; **microscope** microscopio m; **microscopic** microscópico; **microwave** oven microondas m inv

midday [mɪd'deɪ] mediodía m

middle ['mɪdl] **1** adj del medio **2** n medio m; **be in the ~ of** doing sth estar ocupado haciendo algo; **middle-aged** de mediana edad; **middle-class** de clase media; **middle class(es)** clases *fpl* medias; **Middle East** Oriente *m* Medio; **middleman** intermediario *m*; **middle name** segundo nombre *m*; **middleweight** *boxer* peso *m* medio *m*; no lo podías haber dicho!; **midfielder** [mɪdˈfiːldər] centrocampista *m/f*

midget [ˈmɪdʒɪt] en miniatura

midnight [ˈmɪdnaɪt] medianoche *f*; **midsummer** pleno verano *m*; **midweek** a mitad de semana; **Midwest** Medio Oeste *m* (de Estados Unidos); **midwife** comadrona *f*; **midwinter** pleno invierno *m*

night[1] [naɪt] *v/aux* poder, ser posible que; **I ~ be late** puede *or* es posible que llegue tarde; **you ~ have told me!** ¡me lo podías haber dicho!

might[2] [maɪt] *n* (*power*) poder *m*, fuerza *f*

mighty [ˈmaɪtɪ] **1** *adj* poderoso **2** *adv* F (*extremely*) muy, cantidad de F

migraine [ˈmiːɡreɪn] migraña *f*

migrant worker [ˈmaɪɡrənt] trabajador(a) *m(f)* itinerante; **migrate** emigrar; **migration** emigración *f*

mike [maɪk] F micro *m* F

mild [maɪld] *weather* apacible; *cheese, voice* suave; *curry etc* no muy picante; **mildly** *say sth* con suavidad; *spicy* ligeramente; **mildness** of weath-

er, *voice* suavidad *f*

mile [maɪl] milla *f*; **milestone** *fig* hito *m*

militant [ˈmɪlɪtənt] **1** *adj* militante **2** *n* militante *m/f*

military [ˈmɪlɪterɪ] **1** *adj* militar **2** *n*: **the ~** el ejército, las fuerzas armadas

militia [mɪˈlɪʃə] milicia *f*

milk [mɪlk] **1** *n* leche *f* **2** *v/t* ordeñar; **milk chocolate** chocolate *m* con leche; **milkshake** batido *m*

mill [mɪl] *for grain* molino *m*; *for textiles* fábrica *f* de tejidos

millennium [mɪˈlenɪəm] milenio *m*

milligram [ˈmɪlɪɡræm] miligramo *m*

millimeter, Br millimetre [ˈmɪlɪmiːtər] milímetro *m*

million [ˈmɪljən] millón *m*; **millionaire** millonario(-a) *m(f)*

mime [maɪm] representar con gestos

mimic [ˈmɪmɪk] **1** *n* imitador(a) *m(f)* **2** *v/t* imitar

mince [mɪns] picar

mind [maɪnd] **1** *n* mente *f*; **bear** *or* **keep sth in ~** recordar algo; **change one's ~** cambiar de opinión; **make up one's ~** decidirse; **have something on one's ~** tener algo en la cabeza; **keep one's ~ on sth** concentrarse en algo **2** *v/t* (*look after*) cuidar (de); (*heed*) prestar atención a; **I don't ~ what we do** no me importa lo que haga-

mos; *do you ~ if I smoke?*
¿le importa que fume? **3**
v/i: **never** *~!* ¡no importa!; *I
don't ~* no me importa, me
da igual; **mind-boggling** increíble; **mindless** *violence*
gratuito

mine[1] [maɪn] *pron* el mío, la
mía; *that book is ~* eso libro
es mío; *a cousin of ~* un primo mío

mine[2] [maɪn] *n for coal etc* mina *f*

mine[3] [maɪn] **1** *n (explosive)*
mina *f* **2** *v/t* minar

'minefield MIL campo *m* de
minas; *fig* campo *m* minado;
miner minero(-a) *m(f)*

mineral ['mɪnərəl] mineral *m*;
mineral water agua *f* mineral

'minesweeper NAUT draga-
minas *m inv*

mingle ['mɪŋgl] *of sounds etc*
mezclarse; *at party* alternar

mini ['mɪni] *skirt* minifalda *f*

miniature ['mɪnɪtʃər] en miniatura

minimal ['mɪnɪməl] mínimo;
minimalism minimalismo
m; **minimize** minimizar;
minimum 1 *adj* mínimo **2**
n mínimo *m*

mining ['maɪnɪŋ] minería *f*

'miniskirt minifalda *f*

minister ['mɪnɪstər] POL mi-
nistro(-a) *m(f)*; REL minis-
tro(-a) *m(f)*, pastor(-a)
m(f); **ministerial** ministerial

'minivan monovolumen *m*

mink [mɪŋk] visón *m*; *coat*

abrigo *m* de visón

minor ['maɪnər] **1** *adj problem,*
setback menor, pequeño; *op-*
eration, argument de poca
importancia; *aches and pains*
leve **2** *n* LAW menor *m/f* de
edad; **minority** minoría *f*

mint [mɪnt] *herb* menta *f*;
chocolate pastilla *f* de chocolate con sabor a menta; *hard*
candy caramelo *m* de menta

minus ['maɪnəs] **1** *n (~ sign)*
(signo *m* de) menos *m* **2** *prep*
menos

minuscule ['mɪnəskjuːl] minúsculo

minute[1] ['mɪnɪt] *n of time* minuto *m*

minute[2] [maɪ'nuːt] *adj (tiny)*
diminuto, minúsculo;
(detailed) minucioso

'minute hand ['mɪnɪt] minu-
tero *m*

minutely [maɪ'njuːtlɪ] *in detail*
minuciosamente; *(very*
slightly) mínimamente

minutes ['mɪnɪts] *of meeting*
acta(s) *f(pl)*

miracle ['mɪrəkl] milagro *m*;
miraculous milagroso; **mi-**
raculously milagrosamente

mirror ['mɪrər] **1** *n* espejo *m*;
MOT (espejo *m*) retrovisor
m **2** *v/t* reflejar

misanthropist [mɪ'zænθrə-
pɪst] misántropo(-a) *m(f)*

misbehave [mɪsbə'heɪv] portarse mal; **misbehaviour**, *Br*
misbehavior mal comportamiento *m*

miscalculate [mɪs'kælkjuː-

lett] calcular mal; **miscalculation** error *m* de cálculo

miscarriage ['mɪskærɪdʒ] MED aborto *m* (espontáneo)

miscellaneous [mɪsə'leɪnɪəs] diverso

mischief ['mɪstʃɪf] (*naughtiness*) travesura *f*, trastada *f*; **mischievous** (*naughty*) travieso; (*malicious*) malicioso

misconception [mɪskən'sepʃn] idea *f* equivocada

misconduct [mɪs'kɑːndʌkt] mala conducta *f*

misconstrue [mɪskən'struː] malinterpretar

misdemeanor, *Br* **misdemeanour** [mɪsdə'miːnər] falta *f*, delito *m* menor

miserable ['mɪzrəbl] (*unhappy*) triste, infeliz; *weather, performance* horroroso

miserly ['maɪzərlɪ] *person* avaro

misery ['mɪzərɪ] (*unhappiness*) tristeza *f*, infelicidad *f*; (*wretchedness*) miseria *f*

misfire [mɪs'faɪr] *of joke, scheme* salir mal

misfit ['mɪsfɪt] *in society* inadaptado(-a) *m(f)*

misfortune [mɪs'fɔːrtʃən] desgracia *f*

misguided [mɪs'gaɪdɪd] *person* equivocado; *attempt, plan* desacertado

mishandle [mɪs'hændl] *situation* llevar mal

misinform [mɪsɪn'fɔːrm] informar mal

misinterpret [mɪsɪn'tɜːrprɪt]

malinterpretar; **misinterpretation** mala interpretación *f*

misjudge [mɪs'dʒʌdʒ] *person, situation* juzgar mal

mislay [mɪs'leɪ] perder

mislead [mɪs'liːd] engañar; **misleading** engañoso

mismanage [mɪs'mænɪdʒ] gestionar mal; **mismanagement** mala gestión *f*

misprint ['mɪsprɪnt] errata *f*

mispronounce [mɪsprə'naʊns] pronunciar mal; **mispronunciation** pronunciación *f* incorrecta

misread [mɪs'riːd] *word, figures* leer mal; *situation* malinterpretar

misrepresent [mɪsreprɪ'zent] deformar, tergiversar

miss¹ [mɪs]: *Miss Smith* la señorita Smith; *~!* ¡señorita!

miss² [mɪs] **1** *n* SP fallo *m* **2** *v/t target* no dar en; *emotionally* echar de menos; *bus, train* perder; (*not notice*) pasar por alto; (*not be present at*) perderse; *~ a class* faltar a una clase **3** *v/i* fallar

misshapen [mɪs'ʃeɪpən] deforme

missile ['mɪsəl] misil *m*; (*sth thrown*) arma *f* arrojadiza

missing ['mɪsɪŋ] desaparecido; *be ~ of person, plane* haber desaparecido

mission ['mɪʃn] *task* misión *f*; *people* delegación *f*

misspell [mɪs'spel] escribir incorrectamente

mist [mɪst] neblina *f*

mistake [mɪ'steɪk] **1** *n* error *m*, equivocación *f*; **make a** ~ cometer un error, equivocarse; *v/t* confundir; **~ X for Y** confundir X con Y; **mistaken** erróneo, equivocado; **be** ~ estar equivocado

mister ['mɪstər] ☞ **Mr**

mistress ['mɪstrɪs] lover amante *f*, querida *f*; *of servant* ama *f*; *of dog* dueña *f*, ama *f*

mistrust [mɪs'trʌst] **1** *n* desconfianza *f* (**of** en) **2** *v/t* desconfiar de

misunderstand [mɪsʌndər'stænd] entender mal; **misunderstanding** (*mistake*) malentendido *m*; (*argument*) desacuerdo *m*

misuse 1 [mɪs'ju:s] *n* uso *m* indebido **2** [mɪs'ju:z] *v/t* usar indebidamente

mitigating circumstances ['mɪtɪgeɪtɪŋ] circunstancias *fpl* atenuantes

mitt [mɪt] *in baseball* guante *m* de béisbol; **mitten** mitón *m*

mix [mɪks] **1** *n* (*mixture*) mezcla *f*; *cooking*: ready to use preparado *m* **2** *v/t* mezclar; *cement* preparar **3** *v/i socially* relacionarse

◆ **mix up** (*confuse*) confundir (**with** con); (*put in wrong order*) revolver, desordenar; **be mixed up in** estar metido en

mixed [mɪkst] *feelings* contradictorio; *reviews* variado;

mixer *for food* batidora *f*; *drink* refresco *m* (*para mezclar con bebida alcohólica*); **mixture** mezcla *f*; *medicine* preparado *m*; **mix-up** confusión *f*

moan [moʊn] **1** *n of pain* gemido *m* **2** *v/i in pain* gemir

mob [mɑːb] **1** *n* muchedumbre *f* **2** *v/t* asediar, acosar

mobile ['moʊbəl] **1** *adj person* con movilidad; (*that can be moved*) móvil **2** *n* móvil *m*; **mobile home** casa *f* caravana; **mobile phone** *Br* teléfono *m* móvil; **mobility** movilidad *f*

mobster ['mɑːbstər] gángster *m*

mock [mɑːk] **1** *adj* fingido, simulado **2** *v/t* burlarse de

mode [moʊd] (*form*), COMPUT modo *m*

model ['mɑːdl] **1** *adj employee*, *husband* modélico, modelo **2** *n miniature* maqueta *f*, modelo *m*; (*pattern*) modelo *m*; (*fashion* ~) modelo *m/f* **3** *v/i for designer* trabajar de modelo; *for artist, photographer* posar

modem ['moʊdem] módem *m*

moderate 1 ['mɑːdərət] *adj* moderado **2** ['mɑːdərət] *n* POL moderado(-a) *m(f)* **3** ['mɑːdəreɪt] *v/t* moderar; **moderately** medianamente, razonablemente; **moderation** moderación *f*

modern ['mɑːdn] moderno; **modernization** modernización f; **modernize 1** v/t modernizar **2** v/i of business, country modernizarse

modest ['mɑ:dɪst] modesto; **modesty** modestia f

modification [mɑ:dɪfɪ'keɪʃn] modificación f; **modify** modificar

module ['mɑ:du:l] módulo m

moist [mɔɪst] húmedo; **moisten** humedecer; **moisture** humedad f; **moisturizer** for skin crema f hidratante

molasses [mə'læsɪz] melaza f

mold[1] [mould] n on food moho m

mold[2] [mould] **1** n molde m **2** v/t clay, character moldear

moldy ['mouldɪ] food mohoso

molecule ['mɑ:lɪkju:l] molécula f

molest [mə'lest] child, woman abusar sexualmente de

mollycoddle ['mɑ:lɪkɑ:dl] F mimar, consentir

molten ['moultən] fundido

mom [mɑ:m] F mamá f

moment ['moumənt] momento m; **at the ~** en estos momentos, ahora mismo; **momentarily** (for a moment) momentáneamente; (in a moment) de un momento a otro; **momentary** momentáneo; **momentous** trascendental, muy importante

momentum [mə'mentəm] impulso m

monarch ['mɑ:nərk] monarca m/f

monastery ['mɑ:nəsterɪ] monasterio m; **monastic** monástico

Monday ['mʌndeɪ] lunes m inv

monetary ['mʌnɪterɪ] monetario

money ['mʌnɪ] dinero m; **money belt** faltriquera f; **money market** mercado m monetario; **money order** giro m postal

mongrel ['mʌŋɡrəl] perro m cruzado

monitor ['mɑ:nɪtər] **1** n COMPUT monitor m **2** v/t controlar

monk [mʌŋk] monje m

monkey ['mʌŋkɪ] mono m; F child diablillo m F; **monkey wrench** llave f inglesa

monolog, Br **monologue** ['mɑ:nəlɑ:ɡ] monólogo m

monopolize [mə'nɑ:pəlaɪz] monopolizar; **monopoly** monopolio m

monotonous [mə'nɑ:tənəs] monótono; **monotony** monotonía f

monster ['mɑ:nstər] monstruo m; **monstrosity** monstruosidad f

month [mʌnθ] mes m; **monthly 1** adj mensual **2** adv mensualmente **3** n magazine revista f mensual

monument ['mɑ:nʊmənt] monumento m

mood [mu:d] (frame of mind) humor m; (bad ~) mal humor m; of meeting, country atmósfera f; **moody** temperamental; (bad-tempered) malhumorado

moon [muːn] luna f; **moonlight** luz f de luna; **moonlit** iluminado por la luna

moor [mur] boat atracar

moose [muːs] alce m americano

mop [maːp] **1** n for floor fregona f; for dishes estropajo m (con mango) **2** v/t floor fregar; face limpiar

moral ['mɔːrəl] **1** adj moral; person, behavior moralista **2** n of story moraleja f; **~s** moral f, moralidad f

morale [mə'ræl] moral f

morality [mə'rælətɪ] moralidad f

morbid ['mɔːrbɪd] morboso

more [mɔːr] **1** adj más; **there are no ~ eggs** no quedan huevos; **some ~ tea?** ¿más té?; **~ and ~ students** cada vez más estudiantes **2** adv más; **~ important** más importante; **~ and ~** cada vez más; **~ or less** más o menos; **once ~** una vez más; **than $100 ~** más de 100 dólares; **he earns ~ than I do** gana más que yo; **I don't live there any ~** ya no vivo allí **3** pron más; **a little ~** un poco más; **moreover** además

morgue [mɔːrg] depósito m de cadáveres

morning ['mɔːrnɪŋ] mañana f; **in the ~** por la mañana; **tomorrow ~** mañana por la

mañana; **good~** buenos días

moron ['mɔːraːn] F imbécil m/f F, subnormal m/f F

morphine ['mɔːrfiːn] morfina f

mortal ['mɔːrtl] **1** adj mortal **2** n mortal m/f; **mortality** mortalidad f

mortar ['mɔːrtər] MIL, cemento mortero m

mortgage ['mɔːrɡɪdʒ] **1** n hipoteca f **2** v/t hipotecar

mosaic [mou'zeɪɪk] mosaico m

Moscow ['maːskau] Moscú

Moslem ['muzlɪm] **1** adj musulmán **2** n musulmán(-ana) m(f)

mosque [maːsk] mezquita f

mosquito [maːs'kiːtou] mosquito m

moss [maːs] musgo m

most [moust] **1** adj la mayoría de **2** adv (very) muy, sumamente; **the ~ beautiful** el más hermoso; **that's the one I like ~** ése es el que más me gusta; **~ of all** sobre todo **3** pron la mayoría; **~ of her novels** la mayoría de sus novelas; **at (the) ~** como mucho; **make the ~ of** aprovechar al máximo; **mostly** principalmente, sobre todo

motel [mou'tel] motel m

moth [maːθ] mariposa f nocturna; (clothes ~) polilla f

mother ['mʌðər] **1** n madre f **2** v/t mimar; **motherhood** maternidad f; **Mothering Sunday** ☞ **Mother's Day**; moth-

er-in-law suegra *f*; **motherly** maternal; **Mother's Day** Día *m* de la Madre; **mother tongue** lengua *f* materna

motif [mou'ti:f] motivo *m*

motion ['mouʃn] (*movement*) movimiento *m*; (*proposal*) moción *f*; **motionless** inmóvil

motivate ['moutɪveɪt] *person* motivar; **motivation** motivación *f*; **motive** motivo *m*

motor ['moutər] motor *m*; **motorbike** moto *f*; **motorcycle** motocicleta *f*; **motorcyclist** motociclista *m/f*; **motor home** autocaravana *f*; **motor mechanic** mecánico(-a) *m(f)* (de automóviles); **motor racing** carreras *fpl* de coches; **motor vehicle** vehículo *m* de motor

motto ['mɑːtou] lema *m*

mould *etc Br* ☞ **mold** *etc*

mound [maund] montículo *m*

mount [maunt] **1** *n* (*mountain*) monte *m*; (*horse*) montura *f* **2** *v/t steps* subir; *horse, bicycle* montar en; *campaign, photo* montar **3** *v/i* aumentar, crecer

◆ **mount up** acumularse

mountain ['mauntɪn] montaña *f*; **mountaineer** montañero(-a) *m(f)*, alpinista *m/f*, *L.Am.* andinista *m/f*; **mountaineering** montañismo *m*, alpinismo *m*, *L.Am.* andinismo *m*; **mountainous** montañoso

mourn [mɔːrn] llorar; **mourn**er doliente *m/f*; **mournful** *voice, face* triste

mouse [maus] (*pl* **mice** [mais]) *also* COMPUT ratón *m*; **mouse mat** alfombrilla *f*

moustache ☞ **mustache**

mouth [mauθ] boca *f*; *of river* desembocadura *f*; **mouthful** *of food* bocado *m*; *of drink* trago *m*; **mouthpiece** *of instrument* boquilla *f*; (*spokesperson*) portavoz *m/f*; **mouthwash** enjuague *m* bucal; **mouthwatering** apetitoso

move [muːv] **1** *n in chess, checkers* movimiento *m*; (*step, action*) paso *m*; (*change of house*) mudanza *f* **2** *v/t object* mover; (*transfer*) trasladar; *emotionally* conmover; **~ house** mudarse de casa **3** *v/i* moverse; (*transfer*) trasladarse

◆ **move around** *in room* andar; *from place to place* trasladarse, mudarse

◆ **move in** *to house, neighborhood* mudarse; *to office* trasladarse

movement ['muːvmənt] *also organization,* MUS movimiento *m*; **movers** firm empresa *f* de mudanzas; (*men*) empleados *mpl* de una empresa de mudanzas

movie ['muːvɪ] película *f*; **go to a ~ / the ~s** ir al cine; **moviegoer** aficionado(-a) *m/f* al cine; **movie theater** cine *m*, sala *f* de cine

moving ['muːvɪŋ] movible;
emotionally conmovedor

mow [moʊ] *grass* cortar;
mower cortacésped *m*

mph [empiːˈeɪtʃ] (= *miles per hour*) millas *fpl* por hora

Mr ['mɪstər] Sr.

Mrs ['mɪsɪz] Sra.

Ms [mɪz] Sra. (*casada o no casada*)

much [mʌtʃ] **1** *adj* mucho; **~ money** tanto dinero; **as ~ ... as ...** tanto... como **2** *adv* mucho; **too large** demasiado grande; **very ~** mucho; **thank you very ~** muchas gracias; **I love you very ~** te quiero muchísimo; **too ~** demasiado **3** *pron* mucho; **what did she say? – nothing ~** ¿qué dijo? – no demasiado; **as ~ as ...** tanto... como...

mud [mʌd] barro *m*

muddle ['mʌdl] **1** *n* lío *m* **2** *v/t person* liar

muddy ['mʌdɪ] embarrado

muffin ['mʌfɪn] magdalena *f*

muffle ['mʌfl] ahogar, amortiguar; **muffler** MOT silenciador *m*

mug¹ [mʌg] *n* taza *f*; F (*face*) jeta *f* F, Span careto *m* F

mug² [mʌg] *v/t* (*attack*) atracar

mugger ['mʌgər] atracador(a) *m(f)*; **mugging** atraco *m*; **muggy** bochornoso

mule [mjuːl] *animal* mulo(-a) *m(f)*; (*slipper*) pantufla *f*

multicultural [mʌltɪˈkʌltʃərəl]

multicultural; **multilatera**
POL multilateral; **multime**
dia 1 *n* multimedia *f* **2** *ad*
multimedia; **multinationa**
1 *adj* multinacional **2** *n*
COM multinacional *f*

multiple ['mʌltɪpl] múltiple
multiple sclerosis esclero
sis *f* múltiple

multiplex ['mʌltɪpleks] *movi*
theater (cine *m*) multisalas *n*
inv, multicine *m*

multiplication [mʌltɪplɪ
keɪʃn] multiplicación *f*; **mul**
tiply 1 *v/t* multiplicar **2** *v*
multiplicarse

multi-tasking [mʌltiˈtæskɪŋ
multitarea *f*

mumble ['mʌmbl] **1** *n* mur
mullo *m* **2** *v/t* farfullar **3** *v*
hablar entre dientes

munch [mʌntʃ] mascar

municipal [mjuːˈnɪsɪpl] mu
nicipal

mural ['mjʊrəl] mural *m*

murder ['mɜːrdər] **1** *n* asesi
nato *m* **2** *v/t person* asesinar
matar; *song* destrozar; **mur**
derer asesino(-a) *m(f)*

murky ['mɜːrkɪ] *water* turbio
oscuro; *fig* turbio

murmur ['mɜːrmər] **1** *n* mur
mullo *m* **2** *v/t* murmurar

muscle ['mʌsl] músculo *m*
muscular *pain* muscular;
person musculoso

museum [mjuːˈzɪəm] museo

mushroom ['mʌʃrʊm] **1** *n* se
ta *f*, hongo *m*; (*button ~*
champiñón *m* **2** *v/i* crece

rápidamente

music ['mjuːzɪk] música *f*; *in written form* partitura *f*; **musical 1** *adj* musical; *person* con talento para la música **2** *n* musical *m*; **musician** músico(-a) *m(f)*

mussel ['mʌsl] mejillón *m*

must [mʌst] *v/aux ◇ necessity* tener que, deber; *I ~ be on time* tengo que *or* debo llegar a la hora; *I ~n't be late* no tengo que llegar tarde, no debo llegar tarde ◇ *probability* deber de; *it ~ be about 6 o'clock* deben de ser las seis

mustache [məˈstæʃ] bigote *m*

mustard ['mʌstərd] mostaza *f*

musty ['mʌstɪ] *room* que huele a humedad; *smell* a humedad

mutilate ['mjuːtɪleɪt] mutilar

mutiny ['mjuːtɪnɪ] **1** *n* motín *m* **2** *v/i* amotinarse

mutter ['mʌtər] murmurar

mutual ['mjuːtʃʊəl] mutuo

muzzle ['mʌzl] **1** *n of animal* hocico *m*; *for dog* bozal *m* **2** *v/t* poner un bozal a; *~ the press* amordazar a la prensa

my [maɪ] mi; **myself** *reflexive* me; *emphatic* yo mismo(-a); *I hurt ~* me hizo daño

mysterious [mɪˈstɪrɪəs] misterioso; **mysteriously** misteriosamente; **mystery** misterio *m*; **mystify** dejar perplejo

myth [mɪθ] *also fig* mito *m*; **mythical** mítico

N

nag [næg] *of person* dar la lata; **nagging** *person* quejica; *doubt* persistente; *pain* continuo

nail [neɪl] *for wood* clavo *m*; *on finger, toe* uña *f*; **nail polish** esmalte *m* de uñas; **nail polish remover** quitaesmaltes *m inv*

naive [naɪˈiːv] ingenuo

naked ['neɪkɪd] desnudo

name [neɪm] **1** *n* nombre *m*; *what's your ~?* ¿cómo te llamas? **2** *v/t* llamar; **namely** a saber; **namesake** tocayo(-a)

dad

mutilate ['mjuːtɪleɪt] mutilar

m(f), homónimo(-a) *m(f)*

nanny ['nænɪ] niñera *f*

nap [næp] cabezada *f*

napkin ['næpkɪn] *(table ~)* servilleta *f*; *(sanitary ~)* compresa *f*

narcotic [naːrˈkɑːtɪk] narcótico *m*, estupefaciente *m*

narrate [nəˈreɪt] narrar; **narrative 1** *n (story)* narración *f* **2** *adj poem, style* narrativo; **narrator** narrador(a) *m(f)*

narrow ['næroʊ] estrecho; *views, mind* cerrado; **narrowly** *win* por poco; **nar-**

row-minded cerrado

nasty ['næstı] *person, smell* desagradable; *thing to say* malintencionado; *weather* horrible; *cut, wound* feo; *disease* serio

nation ['neɪʃn] nación *f*; **national 1** *adj* nacional **2** *n* ciudadano(-a) *m(f)*; **national anthem** himno *m* nacional; **national debt** deuda *f* pública; **nationalism** nacionalismo *m*; **nationality** nacionalidad *f*; **nationalize** *industry etc* nacionalizar

native ['neɪtɪv] **1** *adj* nativo **2** *n* nativo(-a) *m(f)*, natural *m/f*; *tribesman* nativo(-a) *m(f)*, indígena *m/f*; **Native American** indio(-a) *m (f)* americano(-a)

NATO ['neɪtoʊ] (= **North Atlantic Treaty Organization**) OTAN *f* (= Organización *f* del Tratado del Atlántico Norte)

natural ['nætʃrəl] natural; **naturalist** naturalista *m/f*; **naturalize**: *become ~d* naturalizarse, nacionalizarse; **naturally** *(of course)* naturalmente; *behave, speak* con naturalidad; *(by nature)* por naturaleza

nature naturaleza *f*; **nature reserve** reserva *f* natural

naughty ['nɔːtɪ] travieso, malo; *photograph, word etc* picante

nausea ['nɔːzɪə] náusea *f*; **nauseate** dar náuseas a;

nauseating *smell, taste* nauseabundo; *person* repugnante; **nauseous** nauseabundo; **feel ~** tener náuseas

nautical ['nɔːtɪkl] náutico

naval ['neɪvl] naval

navel ['neɪvl] ombligo *m*

navigate ['nævɪgeɪt] navegar; *in car* hacer de copiloto; **navigation** navegación *f*; *in car* direcciones *fpl*; **navigator** *on ship* oficial *m* de derrota; *in airplane* navegante *m/f*; *in car* copiloto *m/f*

navy ['neɪvɪ] armada *f*, marina *f* (de guerra); **navy blue 1** *n* azul *m* marino **2** *adj* azul marino

near [nɪr] **1** *adv* cerca **2** *prep* cerca de **3** *adj* cercano, próximo; **nearby** cerca; **nearly** casi; **near-sighted** miope

neat [niːt] ordenado; *whiskey* solo, seco; *solution* ingenioso; F *(terrific)* genial F

necessarily ['nesəserɪlɪ] necesariamente; **necessary** necesario, preciso; **necessity** necesidad *f*

neck [nek] cuello *m*; **necklace** collar *m*; **neckline** *of dress* escote *m*; **necktie** corbata *f*

née [neɪ] de soltera

need [niːd] **1** *n* necesidad *f*; *if ~ be* si fuera necesario **2** *v/t* necesitar; *you don't ~ wait* no hace falta que esperes; *I ~ to talk to you* necesito hablar contigo

needle ['niːdl] aguja *f*; **nee-**

dlework costura f

needy ['niːdɪ] necesitado

negative ['negǝtɪv] negativo

neglect [nɪ'glekt] **1** n abandono m, descuido m **2** v/t abandonar, health descuidar, garden, health descuidar, destender; **neglected** garden abandonado, descuidado; author olvidado

negligence ['neglɪdʒǝns] negligencia f; **negligent** negligente; **negligible** amount insignificante

negotiable [nɪ'gouʃǝbl] negociable; **negotiate 1** v/i negociar **2** v/t deal negociar; obstacles franquear, salvar; bend in road tomar; **negotiation** negociación f; **negotiator** negociador(a) m(f)

neighbor ['neɪbǝr] vecino(-a) m(f); **neighborhood** vecindario m, barrio m; **neighboring** house, state vecino, colindante; **neighborly** amable

neighbour etc Br ☞ **neighbor** etc

neither ['niːðǝr] **1** adj ninguno; ~ **applicant** ninguno de los candidatos **2** pron ninguno(-a) m(f); **3** adv: ~ ... **nor** ... ni ... ni ... **4** conj: ~ **do I** yo tampoco; ~ **can I** yo tampoco

neon light ['niːɑːn] luz f de neón

nephew ['nefjuː] sobrino m

nerve [nɜːrv] nervio m; (courage) valor m; (impudence) descaro m; **nerve-racking** angustioso, exasperante;

---

nervous nervioso; **nervous breakdown** crisis f inv nerviosa; **nervousness** nervosismo m; **nervy** (fresh) descarado

nest [nest] nido m

net¹ [net] n red f; **the ~** COMPUT la Red; **on the ~** en Internet

net² [net] adj price, weight neto

nettle ['netl] ortiga f

network of contacts, cells, COMPUT red f

neurologist [nuː'rɑːlǝdʒɪst] neurólogo(-a) m(f)

neurosis [nuː'rousɪs] neurosis f inv; **neurotic** neurótico

neuter ['nuːtǝr] animal castrar; **neutral 1** adj country neutral; color neutro **2** n gear punto m muerto; **neutrality** neutralidad f; **neutralize** neutralizar

never ['nevǝr] nunca; **you're ~ going to believe this** no te vas a creer esto; **nevertheless** sin embargo, no obstante

new [nuː] nuevo; **newborn** recién nacido; **newcomer** recién llegado(-a) m(f); **newly** (recently) recientemente, recién; **newly-weds** recién casados mpl

news [nuːz] also RAD noticias fpl; on TV noticias fpl, telediario m; on TV noticias fpl, telediario m; on radio noticias fpl; **newscaster** TV presentador(a) m(f) de informativos; **news flash** flash *m* informativo; **newspaper** periódico *m*; **newsreader** TV *etc* presentador(a) *m(f)* de informativos; **news report** reportaje *m*; **newsstand** quiosco *m*; **newsvendor** vendedor(a) *m(f)* de periódicos

'**New Year** año *m* nuevo; *Happy* ~*!* ¡Feliz Año Nuevo!; **New Year's Day** Día *m* de Año Nuevo; **New Year's Eve** Nochevieja *f*; **New York** 1 *n:* ~ (**City**) Nueva York 2 *adj* neoyorquino; **New Yorker** neoyorquino(-a) *m(f)*; **New Zealand** ['zi:lənd] Nueva Zelanda; **New Zealander** neozelandés(-esa) *m(f)*

next [nekst] 1 *adj in time* próximo, siguiente; *in space* siguiente 2 *adv* luego, después; ~ *to* (*beside*) al lado de; (*in comparison with*) en comparación con; **next-door** 1 *adj neighbor* de al lado 2 *adv live* al lado; **next of kin** pariente *m* más cercano

nibble ['nɪbl] mordisquear

Nicaragua [nɪkə'ræɡwə] Nicaragua; **Nicaraguan** 1 *adj* nicaragüense 2 *n* nicaragüense *m/f*

nice [naɪs] *trip, house, hair* bonito, *L.Am.* lindo; *person* agradable, simpático; *weather* bueno, agradable; *meal, food* bueno, rico; **nicely** *written, presented* bien; (*pleasantly*) amablemente

niche [niːʃ] *in market* hueco *m*, nicho *m*; (*special position*) hueco *m*

nick [nɪk] (*cut*) muesca *f*, mella *f*

nickel ['nɪkl] níquel *m*; (*coin*) moneda de cinco centavos

'**nickname** apodo *m*, mote *m*

niece [niːs] sobrina *f*

night [naɪt] noche *f*; *tomorrow* ~ mañana por la noche; **11 o'clock at** ~ las 11 de la noche; *during the* ~ por la noche; *good* ~ buenas noches; **nightcap** *drink* copa *f* (*tomada antes de ir a dormir*); **nightclub** club *m* nocturno, discoteca *f*; **nightdress** camisón *m*; **night flight** vuelo *m* nocturno; **nightlife** vida *f* nocturna; **nightly** todas las noches; **nightmare** *also fig* pesadilla *f*; **night porter** portero *m* de noche; **night school** escuela *f* nocturna; **night shift** turno *m* de noche; **nightshirt** camisa *f* de dormir; **nightspot** local *m* nocturno; **nighttime:** *at* ~, *in the* ~ por la noche

nimble ['nɪmbl] ágil

nine [naɪn] nueve; **nineteen** diecinueve; **nineteenth** decimonoveno; **ninetieth** nonagésimo; **ninety** noventa; **ninth** noveno

nip [nɪp] (*pinch*) pellizco *m*; (*bite*) mordisco *m*

nipple ['nɪpl] pezón *m*

no [nəʊ] 1 *adv* no 2 *adj*: *there's* ~ *coffee left* no queda café; **I have ~ money** no tengo dinero; **I'm ~ expert** no soy un experto; **~ smoking** prohibido fumar

noble ['nəʊbl] noble

nobody ['nəʊbədɪ] nadie

no-brainer [nəʊ'breɪnə] juego *m* de niños; **the math test was a ~** la prueba de matemáticas estaba chupada

nod [nɒd] **1** *n* movimiento *m* de la cabeza **2** *v/i* asentir con la cabeza

noise [nɔɪz] ruido *m*; **noisy** ruidoso

nominal ['nɒmɪnl] simbólico

nominate ['nɒmɪneɪt] (*appoint*) nombrar; **nomination** nombramiento *m*; (*proposal*) nominación *f*; **nominee** candidato(-a) *m(f)*

nonalco'holic sin alcohol

noncommissioned officer ['nɒnkəmɪʃnd] suboficial *m/f*

noncom'mittal [nɒnkə'mɪtl] evasivo

nondescript ['nɒndɪskrɪpt] anodino

none [nʌn]: **~ of the students** ninguno de los estudiantes; **~ of the water** nada del agua; **there are ~ left** no queda ninguno; **there is ~ left** no queda nada

nonentity [nɒn'entɪtɪ] nulidad *f*

none'xistent inexistente

non'fiction no ficción *f*

noninter'ference no intervención *f*

noninter'vention no intervención *f*

no-'nonsense *approach* directo

non'payment impago *m*

nonpol'luting que no contamina

non'resident no residente *m/f*

nonsense ['nɒnsəns] disparate *m*, tontería *f*

non'smoker no fumador(a) *m(f)*

non'standard no estándar

non'stop 1 *adj flight* directo, sin escalas; *chatter* ininterrumpido **2** *adv travel* directamente; *chatter* sin parar

non'union no sindicado

non'violence no violencia *f*; **nonviolent** no violento

noodles ['nuːdlz] tallarines *mpl* (chinos)

noon [nuːn] mediodía *m*

'no-one ☞ **nobody**

noose [nuːs] lazo *m* corredizo

nor [nɔːr] ni; **~ do I** yo tampoco, ni yo

norm [nɔːrm] norma *f*; **normal** normal; **normality** normalidad *f*; **normally** normalmente

north [nɔːrθ] **1** *n* norte *m* **2** *adj* norte **3** *adv travel* al norte; **North America** América del Norte, Norteamérica; **North American 1** *n* norteamericano(-a) *m(f)* **2** *adj* norteamericano; **northeast** nordeste *m*, noreste *m*; **northerly** norte, del norte;

northern norteño, del norte;
northerner norteño(-a)
m(f); **North Korea** Corea
del Norte; **North Korean 1**
adj norcoreano **2** n norco-
reano(-a) m(f); **North Pole**
Polo m Norte; **northward**
travel hacia el norte; **northwest** noroeste m

Norway ['nɔːrweɪ] Noruega;
Norwegian 1 adj noruego
2 n person noruego(-a)
m(f); language noruego m

nose [nouz] nariz m; of animal
hocico m
◆ **nose around** F husmear

nostalgia [naːˈstældʒə] nostalgia f; **nostalgic** nostálgico

nostril ['naːstrəl] ventana f de
la nariz

nosy ['nouzɪ] F entrometido

not [naːt] no; ~ **this one, that
one** éste no, ése; ~ **now** ahora no; ~ **for me, thanks** para
mí no, gracias; **I don't know**
no lo sé; **he didn't help** no
ayudó

notable ['noutəbl] notable

notch [naːtʃ] muesca f, mella
f

note [nout] written, MUS nota
f; **notebook** cuaderno m, libreta f; COMPUT Span ordenador m portátil, L.Am.
computadora f portátil; **not-
ed** destacado; **notepad** bloc
m de notas; **notepaper** papel m de carta

nothing ['nʌθɪŋ] nada; ~ **but**
sólo; ~ **much** no mucho;

for ~ (for free) gratis; (for
no reason) por nada

notice ['noutɪs] **1** n on bulletin
board cartel m, letrero m;
(advance warning) aviso m;
in newspaper anuncio m; **at
short** ~ con poca antelación;
until further ~ hasta nuevo
aviso; **hand in one's** ~ to employer presentar la dimisión;
take no ~ of no hacer caso
de **2** v/t notar, fijarse en; **noticeable** apreciable, evidente

notify ['noutɪfaɪ] notificar, informar

notion ['noʊʃn] noción f, idea
f

notorious [nouˈtɔːrɪəs] de
mala fama

noun [naun] nombre m, sustantivo m

nourishing ['nʌrɪʃɪŋ] nutritivo; **nourishment** alimento
m, alimentación f

novel [naːvl] novela f; **novelist** novelista m/f; **novelty**
(being new) lo novedoso;
(sth new) novedad f

November [nouˈvembər] noviembre m

novice ['naːvɪs] principiante
m/f

now [nau] ahora; ~ **and again,**
~ **and then** de vez en cuando; **by** ~ ya; **nowadays** hoy
en día

nowhere ['nouwer] en ningún
lugar; **it's** ~ **near finished** no
está acabado ni mucho me-
nos; **he was** ~ **to be seen**

no se le veía en ninguna parte

nuclear ['nu:kliər] nuclear; **nuclear energy** energía f nuclear; **nuclear power** energía f nuclear; POL potencia f nuclear; **nuclear power station** central f nuclear; **nuclear reactor** reactor m nuclear

nude [nu:d] **1** adj desnudo **2** n painting desnudo m

nudge [nʌdʒ] dar un toque con el codo a; parked car dar un empujoncito a

nudist ['nu:dist] nudista m/f

nuisance ['nu:sns] incordio m, molestia f; **make a ~ of o.s.** dar la lata

null and 'void [nʌl] nulo y sin efecto

numb [nʌm] entumecido; emotionally insensible

number ['nʌmbər] **1** n núme-

ro m **2** v/t (put a ~ on) numerar

numeral ['nu:mərəl] número m

numerous ['nu:mərəs] numeroso

nun [nʌn] monja f

nurse [nɜːrs] enfermero(-a) m(f); for plants vivero m; **nursery** guardería f; **nursery rhyme** canción f infantil; **nursery school** parvulario m, jardín m de infancia; **nursing** enfermería f; **nursing home** for old people residencia f

nut [nʌt] nuez f; for bolt tuerca f; **nutcrackers** cascanueces m inv

nutrient ['nu:triənt] nutriente m; **nutrition** nutrición f; **nutritious** nutritivo

nuts [nʌts] F (crazy) chalado F, pirado F

O

oar [ɔːr] remo m

oasis [ou'eisis] also fig oasis m inv

oath [ouθ] LAW, (swearword) juramento m

oatmeal harina f de avena

obedience [ou'bi:diəns] obediencia f; **obedient** obediente; **obediently** obedientemente

obese [ou'bi:s] obeso; **obesity** obesidad f

obey [ou'bei] obedecer

obituary [ə'bituəri] necrología f, obituario m

object[1] ['a:bdʒikt] n also gram objeto m; (aim) objetivo m

object[2] [əb'dʒekt] v/i oponerse

objection [əb'dʒekʃn] objeción f; **objectionable** (unpleasant) desagradable; **objective 1** adj objetivo **2** n objetivo m; **objectively** objetivamente; **objectivity** objetividad *f*

obligation [ɑːblɪˈgeɪʃn] obligación *f*; **obligatory** obligatorio; **obliging** atento, servicial

oblique [əˈbliːk] **1** *adj reference* indirecto **2** *n in punctuation* barra *f* inclinada

obliterate [əˈblɪtəreɪt] *city* arrasar; *memory* borrar

oblivion [əˈblɪvɪən] olvido *m*

oblong [ˈɑːblɒŋ] rectangular

obscene [ɑːbˈsiːn] obsceno; *salary, poverty* escandaloso; **obscenity** obscenidad *f*

obscure [əbˈskjʊr] oscuro; **obscurity** oscuridad *f*

observant [əbˈzɜːrvnt] observador; **observation** observación *f*; **observe** observar; **observer** observador(a) *m(f)*

obsess [ɑːbˈses] obsesionar; **obsession** obsesión *f*

obsolete [ˈɑːbsəliːt] obsoleto

obstacle [ˈɑːbstəkl] obstáculo *m*

obstetrician [ɑːbstəˈtrɪʃn] obstetra *m/f*, tocólogo(-a) *m(f)*; **obstetrics** obstetricia *f*, tocología *f*

obstinacy [ˈɑːbstɪnəsɪ] obstinación *f*; **obstinate** obstinado

obstruct [əbˈstrʌkt] *road* obstruir; *investigation, police* obstaculizar; **obstruction** *on road etc* obstrucción *f*; **obstructive** *behavior* obstruccionista

obtain [əbˈteɪn] obtener, lo-

grar; **obtainable** *products* disponible

obtuse [əbˈtuːs] *fig* duro de mollera

obvious [ˈɑːbvɪəs] obvio, evidente; **obviously** obviamente

occasion [əˈkeɪʒn] ocasión *f*; **occasional** ocasional, esporádico; **occasionally** ocasionalmente

occupant [ˈɑːkjʊpənt] ocupante *m/f*; **occupation** ocupación *f*; **occupy** ocupar

occur [əˈkɜːr] ocurrir, suceder; **occurrence** acontecimiento *m*

ocean [ˈoʊʃn] océano *m*

o'clock [əˈklɑːk]: *at five* ~ a las cinco

October [ɑːkˈtoʊbər] octubre *m*

odd [ɑːd] *(strange)* raro, extraño; *(not even)* impar

odometer [oʊˈdɑːmətər] cuentakilómetros *m inv*

odor, *Br* **odour** [ˈoʊdər] olor *m*

of [ɑːv] de; *the name* ~ *the street / hotel* el nombre de la calle / del hotel; *five minutes* ~ *twelve* las doce menos cinco, *L.Am* cinco para los doce; *die* ~ *cancer* morir de cáncer; *love* ~ *money* amor por el dinero

off [ɑːf] **1** *prep:* ~ *the main road (away from)* apartado de la carretera principal; *(leading off)* saliendo de la carretera principal; *$20* ~

the price una rebaja en el precio de 20 dólares; **he's ~ his food** no come nada, está desganado **2** *adv*: **be ~** *of light, TV, machine* estar apagado; *of brake, lid, top* no estar puesto; *not at work* faltar; *on vacation* estar de vacaciones; *canceled* estar cancelado; **we're ~ tomorrow** leaving nos vamos mañana; **take a day ~** tomarse un día de fiesta; **it's 3 miles ~** está a tres millas de distancia; **it's a long way ~** *in distance* está muy lejos; *in future* todavía queda mucho tiempo **3** *adj*: **the ~ switch** el interruptor de apagado

offence *Br* **offense**

offend [əˈfend] *(insult)* ofender; **offender** LAW delincuente *m/f*; **offense** LAW delito *m*; **take ~ at sth** ofenderse por algo; **offensive 1** *adj behavior, remark* ofensivo; *smell* repugnante **2** *n* (MIL: *attack*) ofensiva *f*

offer [ˈɒːfər] **1** *n* oferta *f* **2** *v/t* ofrecer

off'hand *attitude* brusco

office [ˈɒːfɪs] *building* oficina *f*; *room* oficina *f*, despacho *m*; *position* cargo *m*; **officer** MIL oficial *m/f*; *in police* agente *m/f*; **official 1** *adj* oficial **2** *n* funcionario(-a) *m(f)*; **officially** oficialmente; **officious** entrometido

off-line *work* fuera de línea; **go ~** desconectarse

'offpeak *rates* en horas valle, fuera de las horas punta

'off-season temporada *f* baja

'offset *losses* compensar

'offshore *drilling rig* cercano a la costa; *investment* en el exterior

'offside SP fuera de juego

'offspring *of person* vástagos *mpl*, hijos *mpl*; *of animal* crías *fpl*

off-the-'record confidencial

often [ˈɒːfn] a menudo, frecuentemente

oil [ɔɪl] **1** *n* aceite *m*; *petroleum* petróleo *m* **2** *v/t hinges, bearings* engrasar; **oil change** cambio *m* del aceite; **oil company** compañía *f* petrolera; **oilfield** yacimiento *m* petrolífero; **oil painting** óleo *m*; **oil refinery** refinería *f* de petróleo; **oil rig** plataforma *f* petrolífera; **oil slick** marea *f* negra; **oil tanker** petrolero *m*; **oil well** pozo *m* petrolífero; **oily** grasiento

ointment [ˈɔɪntmənt] ungüento *m*, pomada *f*

ok [ouˈkeɪ]: **can I? – ~** ¿puedo? – de acuerdo *or* Span vale; **is it ~ with you if …?** ¿te parecería bien si…?; **are you ~?** *(well, not hurt)* ¿estás bien?

old [ould] viejo; *(previous)* anterior, antiguo; **how ~ is he?** ¿cuántos años tiene?; **old age** vejez *f*; **old-fashioned** anticuado

olive [ˈɑːlɪv] aceituna *f*, oliva

f; **olive oil** aceite *m* de oliva
Olympic 'Games [ə'lɪmpɪk]
Juegos *mpl* Olímpicos
omelet *Br* **omelette** ['ɒmlɪt]
tortilla *f* (francesa)
ominous ['ɒmɪnəs] siniestro
omission [oʊ'mɪʃn] omisión
f; **omit** omitir
on [ɒn] **1** *prep* en; **~ the table**
en la mesa; **~ TV** en la televisión; **~ Sunday** el domingo;
~ the 1st of ... el uno de...;
this is ~ me (*I'm paying*) invito yo; **have you any money ~ you?** ¿llevas dinero encima?; **~ his arrival** cuando llegue; **~ hearing this** al escuchar esto **2** *adv*: **be ~** (*of light, TV, computer etc*) estar encendido or L.Am. prendido; (*of brake, lid*) estar puesto; *of meeting etc*: *be scheduled to happen* haber sido acordado; **what's ~ tonight?** *on TV etc* ¿qué dan or *Span* ponen esta noche?; (*what's planned?*) ¿qué planes hay para esta noche?; **with his hat ~** con el sombrero puesto; **you're ~** (*I accept*) trato hecho; **~ you go** (*go ahead*) adelante; **talk ~** seguir hablando; **and so ~** etcétera; **~ and ~ talk etc** sin parar **3** *adj*: **the ~ switch** el interruptor de encendido
once [wʌns] **1** *adv* (*one time, formerly*) una vez; **~ again,
~ more** una vez más; **at ~** (*immediately*) de inmediato **2** *conj* una vez que; **~ you have**

finished una vez que hayas acabado
one [wʌn] **1** *n number* uno *m* **2** *adj* un(a); (*any*) uno(-a) **3** *pron* uno(-a); **which ~?** ¿cuál?; **~ by ~** uno por uno; **we help ~ another** nos ayudamos mutuamente; **what can ~ say?** ¿qué puede de uno decir?; **the little ~s** los pequeños; **I for ~** yo personalmente; **what can ~ say?** ¿qué puede uno decir?; **one-parent family** familia *f* monoparental; **oneself** uno(-a) mismo(-a) *m(f)*; **do sth by ~** hacer algo sin ayuda; **look after ~** cuidarse; **be by ~** estar solo; **one-way street** calle *f* de sentido único; **one-way ticket** billete *m* de ida
onion ['ʌnjən] cebolla *f*
'on-line en línea; **go ~ to** conectarse a; **on-line banking** banca *f* electrónica; **on-line dating** encuentros *mpl* online; **on-line service** IT servicio *m* en línea; **on-line shopping** compras *fpl* online
onlooker ['ɒnlʊkər] espectador(a) *m(f)*, curioso(-a) *m(f)*
only ['oʊnlɪ] **1** *adv* sólo, solamente; **not ~ ... but ... also** no sólo... sino también... **2** *adj* único
'onset comienzo *m*
on-the-job 'training formación *f* continua

opaque [ou'peɪk] opaco

open ['oupən] **1** *adj also honest* abierto; ***in the ~ air*** al aire libre **2** *v/i* abrir **3** *v/i* of door, shop abrir; of flower abrirse; **open-air** meeting, concert al aire libre; *pool* descubierto; **open day** jornada *f* de puertas abiertas; **open-ended** contract etc abierto; **opening** in wall etc abertura *f*; of film, novel etc comienzo *m*; (job) puesto *m* vacante; **openly** (honestly, frankly) abiertamente; **open-minded** de mentalidad abierta; **open ticket** billete *m* abierto

opera ['ɑ:pərə] ópera *f*; **opera house** (teatro *m* de la) ópera *f*; **opera singer** cantante *m/f* de ópera

operate ['ɑ:pəreɪt] **1** *v/i* operar; of machine funcionar (**on** con) **2** *v/t* machine manejar

◆ **operate on** MED operar

operating room MED quirófano *m*; **operating system** COMPUT sistema *m* operativo; **operation** MED operación *f*; of machine manejo *m*; **operator** TELEC operador(a) *m(f)*; of machine operario(-a) *m(f)*; (tour ~) operador *m* turístico

opinion [ə'pɪnjən] opinión *f*; **opinion poll** encuesta *f* de opinión

opponent [ə'pounənt] oponente *m/f*, adversario(-a) *m(f)*

opportunist [ɑ:pər'tu:nɪst] oportunista *m/f*; **opportunity** oportunidad *f*

oppose [ə'pouz] oponerse a; **be ~d to ...** estar en contra de ...

opposite ['ɑ:pəzɪt] **1** *adj* contrario; *views, meaning* opuesto **2** *adv* enfrente; ***the house*** *~* la casa de enfrente **3** *prep* enfrente de; **opposite number** homólogo(-a) *m(f)*

opposition [ɑ:pə'zɪʃn] to plan, POL oposición *f*

oppress [ə'pres] *the people* oprimir; **oppressive** *rule* opresor; *weather* agobiante

optician [ɑ:p'tɪʃn] óptico(-a) *m(f)*

optimism ['ɑ:ptɪmɪzm] optimismo *m*; **optimist** optimista *m/f*; **optimistic** optimista; **optimistically** con optimismo

optimum ['ɑ:ptɪməm] óptimo

option ['ɑ:pʃn] opción *f*; **optional** optativo

or [ɔːr] o; before a word beginning with the letter o u

oral ['ɔːrəl] oral; *hygiene* bucal

orange ['ɔːrɪndʒ] **1** *adj* naranja **2** *n* fruit naranja *f*; color naranja *m*; **orange juice** Span zumo *m* or L.Am. jugo *m* de naranja

orator ['ɔːrətər] orador(a) *m(f)*

orbit ['ɔːrbɪt] **1** *n* of earth órbita *f* **2** *v/t* the earth girar alrededor de

orchard ['ɔːrtʃərd] huerta *f*

(de frutales)

orchestra ['ɔːrkɪstrə] orquesta f

orchid ['ɔːrkɪd] orquídea f

ordain [ɔːr'deɪn] ordenar

ordeal [ɔːr'diːl] calvario m, experiencia f penosa

order ['ɔːrdər] **1** n (command, sequence) orden m; for goods pedido m; **an ~ of fries** unas patatas fritas; **in ~ to** para; **out of ~** (not functioning) estropeado; (not in sequence) desordenado **2** v/t (put in sequence, proper layout) ordenar; goods, meal pedir; ~ **s.o. to do sth** ordenar a alguien hacer algo or que haga algo **3** v/i in restaurant pedir; **orderly 1** adj lifestyle ordenado, metódico **2** n in hospital celador(a) m(f)

ordinarily [ɔːrdɪ'nerɪlɪ] (as a rule) normalmente; **ordinary** común, común

ore [ɔːr] mineral m, mena f

organ ['ɔːrɡən] ANAT, MUS órgano m; **organic** food ecológico, biológico; fertilizer orgánico; **organically** grown ecológicamente, biológicamente; **organism** organismo m

organization [ɔːrɡənaɪ'zeɪʃn] organización f; **organize** organizar; **organizer** person organizador(a) m(f)

orient ['ɔːrɪent] (direct) orientar; **Oriental** oriental

origin ['ɑːrɪdʒɪn] origen m; **original 1** adj original **2** n

painting etc original m; **originality** originalidad f; **originally** originalmente; **originate 1** v/t idea crear **2** v/i of idea, belief originarse; of family proceder

ornamental [ɔːrnə'mentl] ornamental

ornate [ɔːr'neɪt] recargado

orphan ['ɔːrfn] huérfano(-a) m(f)

orthodox ['ɔːrθədɑːks] ortodoxo

orthopedic [ɔːrθə'piːdɪk] ortopédico

ostensibly [ɑː'stensəblɪ] aparentemente

ostentatious [ɑːsten'teɪʃəs] ostentoso

ostracize ['ɑːstrəsaɪz] condenar al ostracismo

other ['ʌðər] **1** adj otro; **the ~ day** (recently) el otro día; **every ~ day** cada dos días **2** n: **the ~** el otro; **the ~s** los otros

otherwise ['ʌðərwaɪz] **1** conj si no **2** adv (differently) de manera diferente

ought [ɔːt]: **I / you ~ to know** debo / debes saberlo; **you ~ to have done it** deberías haberlo hecho

ounce [aʊns] onza f

our [aʊr] nuestro(-a)

ours [aʊrz] el nuestro, la nuestra; **that book is ~** ese libro es nuestro; **a friend of ~** un amigo nuestro; **ourselves** reflexive nos; emphatic nosotros mismos mpl, nosotras mismas fpl; **we hurt**

~ **nos hicimos daño**
oust [aʊst] *from office* derrocar

out [aʊt]: **be ~** *of light, fire* estar apagado; *of flower* estar en flor; *(not at home), of sun* haber salido; *of calculations* estar equivocado; *(be published)* haber sido publicado; *(no longer in competition)* estar eliminado; *(no longer in fashion)* estar pasado de moda; **~ here in Dallas** aquí en Dallas; **(get) ~!** ¡vete!; **(get) ~ of my room!** ¡fuera de mi habitación!; **that's ~!** *(out of the question)* ¡eso es imposible!; **he's ~ to win** *(fully intends to)* va a por la victoria

'outbreak estallido *m*
'outcast paria *m/f*
'outcome resultado *m*
'outcry protesta *f*
out'dated anticuado
out'do superar
out'door *toilet, life* al aire libre; **out'doors** fuera
outer ['aʊtər] *wall etc* exterior
'outfit *(clothes)* traje *m*, conjunto *m*; *(company, organization)* grupo *m*
out'last durar más que
'outlet *of pipe* desagüe *m*; *for sales* punto *m* de venta; ELEC enchufe *m*
'outline 1 *n of person, building etc* perfil *m*, contorno *m*; *of plan, novel* resumen *m* **2** *v/t plans etc* resumir
out'live sobrevivir a

out'number superar en número
out of ◇ *motion* fuera de; **run ~ the house** salir corriendo de la casa; ◇ *position*: **100 miles ~ Detroit** a 100 millas de Detroit ◇ *cause* por; **~ curiosity** por curiosidad ◇ *without*: **we're ~ gas** no nos queda gasolina ◇ *from a group* de cada **2 ~ 10** 2 de cada 10
out-of-'date anticuado, desfasado
'output 1 *n of factory* producción *f*; COMPUT salida *f* **2** *v/t (produce)* producir
'outrage 1 *n feeling* indignación *f*; *act* ultraje *m* **2** *v/t* indignar, ultrajar; **outrageous** *acts* atroz; *prices* escandaloso
out'right 1 *adj winner* absoluto **2** *adv win* completamente; *kill* en el acto
'outset principio *m*
out'shine eclipsar
'outside 1 *adj wall* exterior; *lane* de fuera **2** *adv sit, go* fuera **3** *prep* fuera de; *(apart from)* aparte de **4** *n of building, case etc* exterior *m*
out'size *clothing* de talla especial
'outskirts afueras *fpl*
out'smart ☞ **outwit**
'outsource subcontratar
out'standing *quality* destacado; *writer, athlete* excepcio-

nal; FIN pendiente

outstretched ['autstretʃt] *hands* extendido

outward ['autwəd] *appearance* externo; **~ journey** viaje *m* de ida; **outwardly** aparentemente

out'weigh pesar más que

out'wit mostrarse más listo que

oval ['ouvl] oval, ovalado

oven ['ʌvn] horno *m*

over ['ouvər] **1** *prep* (*above*) sobre, encima de; (*across*) al otro lado de; (*more than*) más de; (*during*) durante; **she walked ~ the street** cruzó la calle; **travel all ~ Brazil** viajar por todo Brasil; **we're ~ the worst** lo peor ya ha pasado; **~ and above** además de 2 **2** *adv*: **be ~** (*finished*) haber acabado; **there were just 6 ~** sólo quedaban seis; **~ in Japan** allá en Japón; **~ here / there** por aquí / allá; **it hurts all ~** me duele por todas partes; **painted white all ~** pintado todo de blanco; **it's all ~** se ha acabado; **~ and ~ again** una y otra vez; **do sth ~** (*again*) volver a hacer algo; **overall** (*in general*) en general; **overalls** *Span* mono *m*, *L.Am.* overol *m*

over'awe intimidar

over'balance perder el equilibrio

over'bearing dominante

'overcast *day* nublado; *sky* cubierto

over'charge *customer* cobrar de más a

'overcoat abrigo *m*

over'come *difficulties* superar, vencer

over'crowded *train* atestado; *city* superpoblado

over'do (*exaggerate*) exagerar; *in cooking* recocer, cocinar demasiado; **over'done** *meat* demasiado hecho

'overdose sobredosis *f inv*

'overdraft descubierto *m*; **over'draw** *account* dejar al descubierto

over'dressed demasiado trajeado

over'estimate sobreestimar

over'expose sobreexponer

'overflow¹ *n pipe* desagüe *m*, rebosadero *m*

over'flow² *v/i of water* desbordarse

over'haul revisar

'overhead 1 *adj lights, railway* elevado **2** *n* FIN gastos *mpl* generales

over'hear oír por casualidad

over'heated recalentado

overjoyed [ouvər'dʒɔɪd] contentísimo, encantado

'overland 1 *adj route* terrestre **2** *adv travel* por tierra

over'lap *of tiles etc* solaparse; *of periods of time* coincidir; *of theories* tener puntos en común

over'load sobrecargar

over'look *of tall building etc* dominar; (*not see*) pasar por alto

overly ['ouvərli] excesivamente, demasiado

overnight *travel* por la noche; *fig change etc* de la noche a la mañana

overpass paso *m* elevado

over'power *physically* dominar

overpriced [ouvər'praist] demasiado caro

overrated [ouvə'reitid] sobrevalorado

over'ride anular; **overriding** *concern* primordial

over'rule *decision* anular

over'seas 1 *adv live, work* en el extranjero; *go* al extranjero **2** *adj* extranjero

over'see supervisar

over'shadow *fig* eclipsar

oversight descuido *m*

over'sleep quedarse dormido

over'state exagerar; **overstatement** exageración *f*

over'take *in work, development* adelantarse a; *Br MOT* adelantar

over'throw[1] *v/t* derrocar

overthrow[2] *n* derrocamiento *m*

'overtime 1 *n SP:* **in ~** en la prórroga **2** *adv:* **work ~** hacer horas extras

over'turn 1 *v/t vehicle* volcar; *object* dar la vuelta a; *government* derribar **2** *v/i of vehicle* volcar

'overview visión *f* general

overwhelming [ouvər'welmɪŋ] *feeling* abrumador; *majority* aplastante

over'work 1 *n* exceso *m* de trabajo **2** *v/i* trabajar en exceso

owe [ou] deber; **owing to** debido a

owl [aul] búho *m*

own[1] [oun] *v/t* poseer

own[2] [oun] **1** *adj* propio; **2** *pron:* **an apartment of my ~** mi propio apartamento; **on my ~** yo solo

◆ **own up** confesar

owner ['ounər] dueño(-a) *m(f)*, propietario(-a) *m(f)*; **ownership** propiedad *f*

oxygen ['ɑːksɪdʒən] oxígeno *m*

oyster ['ɔɪstər] ostra *f*

ozone ['ouzoun] ozono *m*; **ozone layer** capa *f* de ozono

P

'PA [piː'eɪ] (= *personal assistant*) secretario(-a) *m(f)* personal

pace [peɪs] (*step*) paso *m*; (*speed*) ritmo *m*; **pacemaker**

MED marcapasos *m inv*; SP liebre *f*

Pacific [pə'sɪfɪk]: **the ~ (Ocean)** el (Océano) Pacífico

pacifier ['pæsɪfaɪər] *for baby* chupete *m*; **pacifism** pacifismo *m*; **pacifist** pacifista *m/f*; **pacify** tranquilizar; *country* pacificar

pack [pæk] **1** *n* (*back~*) mochila *f*; *of food, cigarettes* paquete *m* **2** *v/t item of clothing etc* meter en la maleta; *goods* empaquetar; *groceries* meter en una bolsa; ~ **one's bag** hacer la bolsa **3** *v/i* hacer la maleta; **package 1** *n* paquete *m* **2** *v/t in packs* embalar; *idea* presentar; **packaging** *of product* embalaje *m*; *of idea* presentación *f*; **packet** paquete *m*

pact [pækt] pacto *m*

pad¹ [pæd] **1** *n for protection* almohadilla *f*; *for absorbing liquid* compresa *f*; *for writing* bloc *m* **2** *v/t with material* acolchar; *speech, report* meter paja en

pad² [pæd] *v/i* (*move quietly*) caminar silenciosamente

padding ['pædɪŋ] *material* relleno *m*; *in speech etc* paja *f*

paddle ['pædəl] **1** *n for canoe* canalete *m*, remo *m* **2** *v/i in canoe* remar; *in water* chapotear

paddock ['pædək] potrero *m*

page¹ [peɪdʒ] *n of book* página *f*

page² [peɪdʒ] *v/t* (*call*) llamar; *by PA* llamar por megafonía; *by beeper* llamar por el buscapersonas *or Span* busca

pager ['peɪdʒər] buscaperso-

nas *m inv*, *Span* busca *m*

paid employment [peɪd] empleo *m* remunerado

pain [peɪn] dolor *m*; **be in ~** sentir dolor; **painful** dolorido; *blow, condition, subject* doloroso; (*laborious*) difícil; **painfully** (*extremely, acutely*) extremadamente; **painkiller** analgésico *m*; **painless** indoloro; **painstaking** meticuloso

paint [peɪnt] **1** *n* pintura *f* **2** *v/t* pintar; **paintbrush** *large* brocha *f*; *small* pincel *m*; **painter** (*decorator*) pintor(a) *m(f)* (de brocha gorda); *artist* pintor/a *m(f)*; **painting** *activity* pintura *f*; *picture* cuadro *m*; **paintwork** pintura *f*

pair [per] *of shoes etc* par *m*; *of people, animals* pareja *f*; **a ~ of pants** unos pantalones

pajamas [pə'dʒɑːməz] pijama *m*

Pakistan [pɑːkɪ'stɑːn] Paquistán, Pakistán; **Pakistani 1** *n* paquistaní *m/f*, pakistaní *m/f* **2** *adj* paquistaní, pakistaní

pal [pæl] F (*friend*) amigo(-a) *m(f)*, *Span* colega *m/f* F

palace ['pælɪs] palacio *m*

palate ['pælət] paladar *m*

palatial [pə'leɪʃl] palaciego

pale [peɪl] *person* pálido; **she went ~** palideció

Palestine ['pæləstaɪn] ~ Palestina; **Palestinian 1** *n* palestino(-a) *m(f)* **2** *adj* palestino

pallet ['pælɪt] palé *m*

pallor ['pælər] palidez *f*

palm [pɑːm] *of hand* palma *f*; **palm tree** palmera *f*

paltry ['pɔːltrɪ] miserable

pamper ['pæmpər] mimar

pamphlet ['pæmflɪt] *for information* folleto *m*, *political* panfleto *m*

pan [pæn] *for cooking* cacerola *f*; *for frying* sartén *f*

Panama ['pænəmɑː] Panamá; **Panama Canal: the** ~ el Canal de Panamá; **Panama City** Ciudad *f* de Panamá; **Panamanian 1** *adj* panameño **2** *n* panameño(-a) *m(f)*

pancake ['pænkeɪk] crepe *m*, *L.Am.* panqueque *m*

pane [peɪn] *of glass* hoja *f*

panel ['pænl] panel *m*; *people* grupo *m*, panel *m*; **paneling**, *Br* **panelling** paneles *mpl*

panic ['pænɪk] **1** *n* pánico *m* **2** *v/i* se preso del pánico; **panic-stricken** preso del pánico

panorama [pænə'rɑːmə] panorama *m*; **panoramic** panorámico

pant [pænt] jadear

panties ['pæntɪz] *Span* bragas *fpl*, *L.Am.* calzones *mpl*

pantihose ['pæntɪhəʊz] → **pantyhose**

pants [pænts] pantalones *mpl*

pantyhose ['pæntɪhəʊz] medias *fpl*, pantis *mpl*

papal ['peɪpl] papal

paparazzi [pæpə'rætsi] paparazzi *mfpl*

paper ['peɪpər] **1** *n* papel *m*; *(news-~)* periódico *m*; *academic* estudio *m*; *at confer-*

ence ponencia *f*; *(examination* ~) examen *m*; ~**s** *(documents)* documentos *mpl*; *(of vehicle, identity* ~**s)** papeles *mpl*, documentación *f* **2** *adj* de papel **3** *v/t room* empapelar; **paperback** libro *m* en rústica; **paper clip** clip *m*; **paperwork** papeleo *m*

parachute ['pærəʃuːt] **1** *n* paracaídas *m inv* **2** *v/i* saltar en paracaídas **3** *v/t troops, supplies* lanzar en paracaídas

parade [pə'reɪd] **1** *n* procesión desfile *m* **2** *v/i* desfilar; *(walk about)* pasearse

paradise ['pærədaɪs] paraíso *m*

paradox ['pærədɑːks] paradoja *f*; **paradoxical** paradójico; **paradoxically** paradójicamente

paragraph ['pærəgræf] párrafo *m*

Paraguay ['pærəgwaɪ] Paraguay; **Paraguayan 1** *adj* paraguayo **2** *n* paraguayo(-a) *m(f)*

parallel ['pærəlel] **1** *n* paralela *f*, GEOG paralelo *m*; *fig* paralelismo *m* **2** *adj also fig* paralelo **3** *v/t (match)* equipararse a

paralysis [pə'ræləsɪs] parálisis *f*; **paralyze** *also fig* paralizar

paramedic [pærə'medɪk] auxiliar *m/f* sanitario(-a)

parameter [pə'ræmɪtər] parámetro *m*

paramilitary [pærə'mɪlɪterɪ] **1**

adj paramilitar **2** *n* paramilitar *m/f*

paranoia [pærə'nɔɪə] paranoia *f*; **paranoid** paranoico *m*

paraphrase ['pærəfreɪz] parafrasear

parasite ['pærəsaɪt] *also fig* parásito *m*

parasol ['pærəsɒl] sombrilla *f*

parcel ['pɑːrsl] paquete *m*

pardon ['pɑːrdn] **1** *n* LAW indulto *m*; **I beg your ~?** (*what did you say?*) ¿cómo ha dicho?; **I beg your ~** (*I'm sorry*) discúlpeme **2** *v/t* perdonar; LAW indultar; **~ me?** ¿perdón?

parent ['perənt] *father* padre *m*; *mother* madre *f*; **my ~s** mis padres; **parental** de los padres; **parent company** empresa *f* matriz; **parent-teacher association** asociación *f* de padres y profesores

parish ['pærɪʃ] parroquia *f*

park[1] [pɑːrk] *n* parque *m*

park[2] [pɑːrk] *v/t & v/i* MOT estacionar, *Span* aparcar; **parking** MOT estacionamiento *m*, *Span* aparcamiento *m*; **parking brake** freno *m* de mano; **parking garage** párking *m*, *Span* aparcamiento *m*; **parking lot** estacionamiento *m*, *Span* aparcamiento *m* (*al aire libre*); **parking meter** parquímetro *m*; **parking ticket** multa *f* de estacionamiento

parliament ['pɑːrləmənt] parlamento *m*

parole [pə'roʊl] **1** *n* libertad *f* condicional **2** *v/t* poner en libertad condicional

parrot ['pærət] loro *m*

part [pɑːrt] **1** *n* parte *f*; *of machine* pieza *f* (de repuesto); *in movie* papel *m*; *in hair* raya *f*; **take ~** tomar parte en **2** *adv* (*partly*) en parte **3** *v/i* separar; **partial** (*incomplete*) parcial; **partially** parcialmente

participant [pɑːr'tɪsɪpənt] participante *m/f*; **participate** participar; **participation** participación *f*

particular [pər'tɪkjələr] (*specific*) particular, concreto; (*demanding*) exigente; *about friends etc* selectivo; *pej* especial, quisquilloso; **particularly** particularmente

partition [pɑːr'tɪʃn] (*screen*) tabique *m*; *of country* partición *f*, división *f*

partly ['pɑːrtlɪ] en parte

partner ['pɑːrtnər] COM socio(-a) *m(f)*; *in relationship* compañero(-a) *m(f)*; *in tennis, dancing* pareja *f*; **partnership** COM sociedad *f*; *in particular activity* colaboración *f*

'part-time *n* tiempo parcial

party ['pɑːrtɪ] **1** *n* (*celebration*) fiesta *f*; POL partido *m*; (*group of people*) grupo *m* **2** *v/i* F salir de marcha F

pass [pæs] **1** *n for entry*, SP pase *m*; *in mountains* desfiladero *m* **2** *v/t* (*hand*) pasar; (*go past*) pasar por delante de; (*overtake*) adelantar; (*go beyond*) sobrepasar; (*approve*) aprobar **3** *v/i of time* pasar; *in exam* aprobar; (*go away*) pasarse

♦ **pass away** *euph* fallecer, pasar a mejor vida

♦ **pass on 1** *v/t information, book* pasar **2** *v/i* (*euph: die*) fallecer, pasar a mejor vida

♦ **pass out** (*faint*) desmayarse

♦ **pass up** *opportunity* dejar pasar

passable ['pæsəbl] *road* transitable; (*acceptable*) aceptable

passage ['pæsɪdʒ] (*corridor*) pasillo *m*; *from book* pasaje *m*; *of time* paso *m*

passenger ['pæsɪndʒər] pasajero(-a) *m(f)*

passer-by [pæsər'baɪ] transeúnte *m/f*

passion ['pæʃn] pasión *f*; **passionate** *lover* apasionado; (*fervent*) fervoroso

passive ['pæsɪv] **1** *adj* pasivo **2** *n* GRAM (voz *f*) pasiva *f*; **passive smoking** (el) fumar pasivamente

passport pasaporte *m*; **passport control** control *m* de pasaportes; **password** contraseña *f*

past [pæst] **1** *adj* (*former*) pasado; **the ~ few days** los últimos días **2** *n* pasado **3** *prep in position* después de; **it's**

half ~ two son las dos y media **4** *adv:* **run / walk ~** pasar

pasta ['pæstə] pasta *f*

paste [peɪst] **1** *n* (*adhesive*) cola *f* **2** *v/t* (*stick*) pegar

pastime ['pæstaɪm] pasatiempo *m*

past par'ticiple GRAM participio *m* pasado

pastry ['peɪstrɪ] *for pie* masa *f*; *small cake* pastel *m*

'past tense GRAM (tiempo *m*) pasado *m*

pasty ['peɪstɪ] *face* pálido

pat [pæt] **1** *n* palmadita *f* **2** *v/t* dar palmaditas a

patch [pætʃ] **1** *n on clothing* parche *m*; (*area*) mancha *f*; **a bad ~** *of time* un mal momento, una mala racha **2** *v/t clothing* remendar

♦ **patch up** (*repair*) hacer un remiendo a, arreglar a medias; *quarrel* solucionar

patchy ['pætʃɪ] *quality* desigual; *work* irregular

patent ['peɪtnt] **1** *adj* patente, evidente **2** *n for invention* patente *f* **3** *v/t invention* patentar

paternal [pə'tɜːrnl] *relative* paterno; *pride, love* paternal; **paternalism** paternalismo *m*; **paternalistic** paternalista; **paternity** paternidad *f*

path [pæθ] *also fig* camino *m*

pathetic [pə'θetɪk] *invoking pity* patético; F (*very bad*) lamentable F

pathological [pæθə'lɑːdʒɪkl] patológico

patience ['peɪʃns] paciencia *f*;
patient 1 *n* paciente *m/f* **2**
adj paciente; **patiently** pacientemente

patio ['pætɪoʊ] *Br* patio *m*

patriot ['peɪtrɪət] patriota
m/f; **patriotic** patriótico; **patriotism** patriotismo *m*

patrol [pə'troʊl] **1** *n* patrulla *f*
2 *v/t streets, border* patrullar;
patrol car coche *m* patrulla;
patrolman policía *m*, patrullero *m*; **patrol wagon** furgón *m* policial

patron ['peɪtrən] *of store,
movie theater* cliente *m/f*; *of
artist, charity etc* patrocinador(a) *m(f)*; **patronize** *person* tratar con condescendencia; **patronizing** condescendiente; **patron saint** santo(-a) *m(f)* patrón(-ona),
patrón(-ona) *m(f)*

pattern ['pætərn] *on fabric* estampado *m*; *for sewing* diseño *m*; (*model*) modelo *m*; *in
behavior, events* pauta *f*

paunch [pɔːntʃ] barriga *f*

pause [pɔːz] **1** *n* pausa *f* **2** *v/i*
parar; *when speaking* hacer
una pausa **3** *v/t tape* poner
en pausa

pave [peɪv] *with concrete* pavimentar; *with slabs* adoquinar; **pavement** (*roadway*)
calzada *f*; *Br* (*sidewalk*) acera *f*

paw [pɔː] **1** *n of animal* pata *f*;
F (*hand*) pezuña *f* F **2** *v/t*
sobar F

pawn [pɔːn] *in chess* peón *m*;

fig títere *m*

pay [peɪ] **1** *n* paga *f*, sueldo *m*
2 *v/t* pagar; **~ attention** prestar atención **3** *v/i* pagar; (*be
profitable*) ser rentable; **~
for purchase** pagar
♦ **pay back** *person* devolver
el dinero a; *loan* devolver
♦ **pay off 1** *v/t debt* liquidar;
(*bribe*) sobornar **2** *v/i* (*be
profitable*) valer la pena
♦ **pay up** pagar

payable ['peɪəbl] pagadero;
pay check, *Br* **pay cheque**
cheque *m* del sueldo; **payday** día *m* de paga; **payee**
beneficiario(-a) *m(f)*; **payment** pago *m*; **pay phone** teléfono *m* público

PC [piː'siː] (= *personal computer*) PC *m*, *Span* ordenador *m* or *L.Am.* computadora personal; (= *politically
correct*) políticamente correcto

pea [piː] *Span* guisante *m*,
L.Am. arveja *f*, *Mex* chícharo *m*

peace [piːs] paz *f*; (*quietness*)
tranquilidad; **peaceful** tranquilo; *demonstration* pacífico; **peacefully** pacíficamente

peach [piːtʃ] *fruit* melocotón
m, *L.Am.* durazno *m*; *tree*
melocotonero *m*, *L.Am.* duraznero *m*

peak [piːk] **1** *n of mountain* cima *f*; *mountain* pico *m*; *fig*
clímax *m* **2** *v/i* alcanzar el
máximo; **peak hours** horas

fpl punta
peanut ['piːnʌt] cacahuete m, L.Am. maní m, Mex cacahuate m; **get paid ~s** F cobrar una miseria F; **peanut butter** crema f de cacahuete
pear [per] pera f
pearl [pɜːrl] perla f
pecan ['piːkən] pacana f
peck [pek] **1** n bite picotazo m; kiss besito m **2** v/t bite picotear; kiss dar un besito a
peculiar [pɪ'kjuːljər] (strange) raro; **peculiarity** rareza f; (special feature) peculiaridad f
pedal ['pedl] **1** n of bike pedal m **2** v/t pedalear; (cycle) recorrer en bicicleta
pedestrian [pɪ'destrɪən] peatón(-ona) m(f)
pediatric [piːdɪ'ætrɪk] pediátrico; **pediatrician** pediatra m/f; **pediatrics** pediatría f
pedicure ['pedɪkjʊr] pedicura f
pedigree ['pedɪgriː] **1** n of animal pedigrí; of person linaje m **2** adj con pedigrí
pee [piː] F hacer pis F
peek [piːk] **1** n ojeada f **2** v/i echar una ojeada
peel [piːl] **1** n piel f **2** v/t fruit, vegetables pelar **3** v/i of nose, shoulders pelarse; of paint levantarse
peep [piːp] *☞* **peek**; **peephole** mirilla f
peer[1] [pɪr] n (equal) igual m
peer[2] [pɪr] v/i mirar
peg [peg] for hat, coat percha

f; for tent clavija f; **off the ~** de confección
pejorative [pɪ'dʒɑːrətɪv] peyorativo
pellet ['pelɪt] pelotita f; (bullet) perdigón m
pen[1] [pen] (ballpoint ~) bolígrafo m
pen[2] [pen] (enclosure) corral m
pen[3] [pen] *☞* **penitentiary**
penalize ['piːnəlaɪz] penalizar
penalty ['penltɪ] sanción f; SP penalti m; **penalty area** SP área f de castigo; **penalty clause** LAW cláusula f de penalización; **penalty kick** (lanzamiento m de) penalti m
pencil ['pensl] lápiz m; **pencil sharpener** sacapuntas m inv
pendant ['pendənt] necklace colgante m
penetrate ['penɪtreɪt] (pierce) penetrar; market penetrar en; **penetration** penetración f; of defenses incursión f; of market entrada f
penguin ['peŋgwɪn] pingüino m
penicillin [penɪ'sɪlɪn] penicilina f
peninsula [pə'nɪnsʊlə] península f
penitence ['penɪtəns] (remorse) arrepentimiento m; **penitentiary** prisión f, cárcel f
'pen name seudónimo m
pennant ['penənt] banderín f

penniless ['penɪlɪs] sin un centavo

'pen pal amigo(-a) *m(f)* por correspondencia

pension ['penʃn] pensión *f*
◆ **pension off** jubilar

pensive ['pensɪv] pensativo

Pentagon ['pentəgɑːn]: *the* ~ el Pentágono

pentathlon [pen'tæθlən] pentatlón *m*

penthouse ['penthaus] ático *m* (*de lujo*)

pent-up ['pentʌp] reprimido

penultimate [pe'nʌltɪmət] penúltimo

people ['piːpl] gente *f*; (*individuals*) personas *fpl*; (*race, tribe*) pueblo *m*; *the* ~ (*citizens*) pueblo *m*, los ciudadanos; ~ *say* ... se dice que...

pepper ['pepər] *spice* pimienta *f*; *vegetable* pimiento *m*; **peppermint** *candy* caramelo *m* de menta

per [pɜːr] por; ~ *annum* al año, por año

perceive [pər'siːv] percibir; (*view, interpret*) interpretar

percent [pər'sent] por ciento; **percentage** porcentaje *m*, tanto *m* por ciento

perceptible [pər'septəbl] perceptible; **perceptibly** visiblemente; **perception** *through senses* percepción *f*; *of situation* apreciación *f*; (*insight*) perspicacia *f*; **perceptive** perceptivo

percolate ['pɜːrkəleɪt] *of coffee* filtrarse; **percolator** cafetera *f* de filtro

perfect 1 ['pɜːrfɪkt] *n* GRAM pretérito *m* perfecto **2** ['pɜːrfɪkt] *adj* perfecto **3** [pər'fekt] *v/t* perfeccionar; **perfection** perfección *f*; **perfectionist** perfeccionista *m/f*; **perfectly** perfectamente; (*totally*) completamente

perforated ['pɜːrfəreɪtɪd] *line* perforado

perform [pər'fɔːrm] **1** *v/t* (*carry out*) realizar; *of actors etc* interpretar **2** *v/i of actor, musician, dancer* actuar; *of machine* funcionar; **performance** *by actor etc* actuación *f*, interpretación *f*; *of play* representación *f*; *of employee* rendimiento *m*; *of official, company, in sport* actuación *f*; *of machine* rendimiento *m*; **performer** intérprete *m/f*

perfume ['pɜːrfjuːm] perfume *m*

perfunctory [pər'fʌŋktərɪ] superficial

perhaps [pər'hæps] quizá(s), tal vez

peril ['perəl] peligro *m*

perimeter [pə'rɪmɪtər] perímetro *m*

period ['pɪrɪəd] período *m*, período *m*; (*menstruation*) período *m*, regla *f*; *punctuation mark* punto *m*; **periodic** periódico; **periodical** publicación *f* periódica

peripheral [pə'rɪfərəl] **1** *adj* (*not crucial*) secundario **2** *n* COMPUT periférico *m*; periphery periferia f

perish ['perɪʃ] *of rubber* estropearse; *of person* perecer; **perishable** *food* perecedero

perjure ['pɜːrdʒər]: **~ o.s.** perjurar; **perjury** perjurio m

perm [pɜːrm] **1** *n* permanente *f* **2** *v/t* hacer la permanente

permanent ['pɜːrmənənt] permanente; **permanently** permanentemente

permeate ['pɜːrmɪeɪt] impregnar

permissible [pər'mɪsəbl] permisible; **permission** permiso *m*; **permissive** permisivo; **permit 1** *n* licencia *f* **2** *v/t* permitir

perpendicular [pɜːrpən'dɪkjʊlər] perpendicular

perpetual [pər'petʃʊəl] perpetuo; *interruptions* continuo; **perpetually** constantemente

perplex [pər'pleks] dejar perplejo; **perplexity** perplejidad *f*

persecute ['pɜːrsɪkjuːt] perseguir; *(hound)* acosar; **persecution** persecución *f*; *(harassment)* acoso *m*; **persecutor** perseguidor(a) *m(f)*

perseverance [pɜːrsɪ'vɪrəns] perseverancia *f*; **persevere** perseverar

persist [pər'sɪst] persistir; **persistent** *person, questions* perseverante; *rain, unemployment etc* persistente; **persistently** *(continually)*

constantemente

person ['pɜːrsn] persona *f*; **personal** *(private)* personal; *life* privado; **personal computer** *Span* ordenador *m* personal, *L.Am.* computadora *f* personal; **personality** personalidad *f*; **personally** *(for my part)* personalmente; *(in person)* en persona; **personal organizer** organizador *m* personal; **personal stereo** walkman *m* ®; **personify** *of person* personificar

personnel [pɜːrsə'nel] personal *m*

perspective [pər'spektɪv] *in art* perspectiva *f*; **get sth into ~** poner algo en perspectiva

perspiration [pɜːrspɪ'reɪʃn] sudor *m*, transpiración *f*; **perspire** sudar, transpirar

persuade [pər'sweɪd] persuadir; **persuasion** persuasión *f*; **persuasive** persuasivo

perturb [pər'tɜːrb] perturbar; **perturbing** perturbador

Peru [pə'ruː] Perú; **Peruvian 1** *adj* peruano **2** *n* peruano(-a) *m(f)*

pervasive [pər'veɪsɪv] *influence, ideas* dominante

perversion [pər'vɜːrʃn] *sexual* perversión *f*; **pervert** *sexual* pervertido(-a) *m(f)*

pessimism ['pesɪmɪzm] pesimismo *m*; **pessimist** pesimista *m/f*; **pessimistic** pesimista

pest [pest] plaga *f*; F *person*

tostón *m* F

pester ['pestər] acosar; ~ *s.o. to do sth* dar la lata a alguien para que haga algo

pesticide ['pestisaid] pesticida *f*

pet [pet] **1** *n animal m* doméstico; *(favorite)* preferido(-a) *m(f)* **2** *adj* preferido **3** *v/t an animal* acariciar **4** *v/i of couple* magrearse F

petite [pə'ti:t] chiquito(-a); *size* menudo

petition [pə'tɪʃn] petición *f*

petrify ['petrɪfaɪ] dejar petrificado

petrochemical [petrou'kemɪkl] petroquímico

petrol ['petrl] *Br* gasolina *f*, *Arg* nafta *f*

petroleum [pɪ'trouliəm] petróleo *m*

petting ['petɪŋ] magreo *m* F

petty ['petɪ] *person, behavior* mezquino; *details* sin importancia

pew [pju:] banco *m (de iglesia)*

pharmaceutical [fɑ:rmə'su:tɪkl] farmacéutico; **pharmaceuticals** fármacos *mpl*

pharmacist ['fɑ:rməsɪst] *in store* farmacéutico(-a) *m(f)*; **pharmacy** *store* farmacia *f*

phase [feiz] fase *f*

phenomenal [fɪ'nɑ:mɪnl] fenomenal; **phenomenon** fenómeno *m*

philanthropic [fɪlən'θrɑ:pɪk] filantrópico; **philanthropist** filántropo(-a) *m(f)*; **philanthropy** filantropía *f*

Philippines ['fɪlɪpi:nz]: *the ~* las Filipinas

philosopher [fɪ'lɑ:səfər] filósofo(-a) *m(f)*; **philosophical** filosófico; **philosophy** filosofía *f*

phobia ['foubɪə] fobia *f*

phone [foun] **1** *n* teléfono *m* **2** *v/t* llamar (por teléfono) a **3** *v/i* llamar (por teléfono); **phone book** guía *f* (de teléfonos); **phone booth** cabina *f* (de teléfonos); **phonecall** llamada *f* (telefónica); **phone card** tarjeta *f* telefónica; **phone number** número *m* de teléfono

photo ['foutou] foto *f*; **photocopier** fotocopiadora *f*; **photocopy 1** *n* fotocopia *f* **2** *v/t* fotocopiar; **photogenic** fotogénico; **photograph 1** *n* fotografía *f* **2** *v/t* fotografiar; **photographer** fotógrafo(-a) *m(f)*; **photography** fotografía *f*

phrase [freiz] **1** *n* frase *f* **2** *v/t* expresar

physical ['fɪzɪkl] **1** *adj* físico **2** *n* MED reconocimiento *m* médico; **physically** físicamente

physician [fɪ'zɪʃn] médico(-a) *m(f)*

physicist ['fɪzɪsɪst] físico(-a) *m(f)*; **physics** física *f*

physiotherapist [fɪziou'θerəpɪst] fisioterapeuta *m/f*; **physiotherapy** fisioterapia *f*

physique [fɪ'zi:k] físico *m*

pianist ['pɪənɪst] pianista *m/f*

piano piano *m*

pick [pɪk] (*choose*) escoger, elegir; *flowers, fruit* recoger

♦ **pick up** *v/t* recoger, *Span* coger; *habit* adquirir, *Span* coger; *illness* contraer, *Span* coger; *telephone* descolgar; *language, skill* aprender; (*buy*) comprar; *sexually* ligar con 2 *v/i* (*improve*) mejorar

picket ['pɪkɪt] **1** *n of strikers* piquete *m* **2** *v/t* hacer piquete delante de

pickpocket carterista *m/f*

pick-up (**truck**) ['pɪkʌp] camioneta *f*

picky ['pɪkɪ] F tiquismiquis *f*

picnic ['pɪknɪk] **1** *n* picnic *m* **2** *v/i* ir de picnic

picture ['pɪktʃər] **1** *n* (*photo*) fotografía *f*; (*painting*) cuadro *m*; (*illustration*) dibujo *m*; (*movie*) película *f*; *on TV* imagen *f* **2** *v/t* imaginar

picturesque [pɪktʃə'resk] pintoresco

pie [paɪ] pastel *m*

piece [piːs] (*fragment*) fragmento *m*; (*component, in game*) pieza *f*; **a ~ of advice** un consejo; **take to ~s** desmontar

♦ **piece together** *broken plate* recomponer; *evidence* reconstruir

pier [pɪr] *Br at seaside* malecón *m*

pierce [pɪrs] (*penetrate*) perforar; *ears* agujerear; **piercing** *scream* desgarrador; *gaze* penetrante; *wind* cortante

pig [pɪɡ] *also fig* cerdo *m*; *greedy* glotón(-a) *m(f)*

pigeon ['pɪdʒɪn] paloma *f*; **pigeonhole** casillero *m*

pigheaded [pɪɡ'hedɪd] F cabezota F; **pigpen** *also fig* pocilga *f*

pile [paɪl] montón *m*, pila *f*

♦ **pile up** *v/i of work, bills* acumularse **2** *v/t* amontonar

pile-up ['paɪlʌp] MOT choque *m* múltiple

pill [pɪl] pastilla *f*; **be on the ~** tomar la píldora

pillar ['pɪlər] pilar *m*

pillow ['pɪloʊ] almohada *f*; **pillowcase** funda *f* de almohada

pilot ['paɪlət] **1** *n of airplane* piloto *m/f*; *for ship* práctico *m* **2** *v/t airplane* pilotar

pimp [pɪmp] proxeneta *m*, *Span* chulo *m*

pimple ['pɪmpl] grano *m*

PIN [pɪn] (= *personal identification number*) PIN *m* (= número *m* de identificación personal)

pin [pɪn] **1** *n for sewing* alfiler *m*; *in bowling* bolo *m*; (*badge*) pin *m*; ELEC clavija *f* **2** *v/t* (*hold down*) mantener; (*attach*) sujetar

♦ **pin up** *notice* sujetar con chinchetas

pincers ['pɪnsərz] *of crab* pinzas *fpl*; *tool* tenazas *fpl*

pinch [pɪntʃ] **1** *n* pellizco *m*; *of salt etc* pizca *f* **2** *v/t* pellizcar **3** *v/i of shoes* apretar

pine [paɪn] *tree, wood* pino *m*;

pineapple piña f, L.Am. ananá(s) f

pink [pɪŋk] rosa

pinnacle ['pɪnəkl] fig cima f

pinpoint determinar; **pins and needles** hormigueo m; **pin-up** modelo m/f de revista

pioneer [paɪə'nɪr] **1** n pionero(-a) m(f) **2** v/t ser pionero en; **pioneering** work pionero

pious ['paɪəs] piadoso

pip [pɪp] Br of fruit pepita f

pipe [paɪp] **1** n tubería f; for smoking pipa f; **2** v/t conducir por tuberías; **pipeline** for oil oleoducto m; for gas gasoducto m

pirate ['paɪrət] **1** n pirata m/f **2** v/t software piratear

pissed [pɪst] P (annoyed) cabreado P; Br P (drunk) borracho, pedo P

pistol ['pɪstl] pistola f

piston ['pɪstən] pistón m

pit [pɪt] (hole) hoyo m; (coal mine) mina f; of fruit hueso m

pitch¹ [pɪtʃ] n MUS tono m

pitch² [pɪtʃ] **1** v/i in baseball lanzar la pelota v/t SP tent montar; ball lanzar

pitcher¹ ['pɪtʃər] baseball player lanzador(a) m(f), pítcher m/f

pitcher² ['pɪtʃər] container jarra f

pitfall ['pɪtfɔːl] dificultad f

pitiful ['pɪtɪfəl] sight lastimoso; excuse, attempt lamentable; **pitiless** despiadado

pittance ['pɪtns] miseria f

pity ['pɪtɪ] **1** n pena f, lástima f; **what a ~!** ¡qué pena! **2** v/t person compadecerse de

pizza ['piːtsə] pizza f

placard ['plækɑːrd] pancarta f

place [pleɪs] **1** n sitio m, lugar m; in race, competition puesto m; (seat) sitio m; **at my / his ~** en mi / su casa; **in ~ of** en lugar de; **take ~** tener lugar **2** v/t (put) poner, colocar; order hacer

placid ['plæsɪd] apacible

plagiarism ['pleɪdʒərɪzm] plagio m; **plagiarize** plagiar

plain¹ [pleɪn] n llanura f

plain² [pleɪn] adj (clear, obvious) claro; (not fancy) simple; (not pretty) feíllo; (not patterned) liso; (blunt) directo **2** adv verdaderamente; **plainly** (clearly) evidentemente; (bluntly) directamente; (simply) con sencillez; **plain spoken** directo

plaintive ['pleɪntɪv] quejumbroso

plan [plæn] **1** n plan m; (drawing) plano m **2** v/t planear; (design) hacer los planos de **3** v/i hacer planes

plane¹ [pleɪn] (airplane) avión m

plane² [pleɪn] tool cepillo m

planet ['plænɪt] planeta f

plank [plæŋk] of wood tablón m; fig: of policy punto m

planning ['plænɪŋ] planificación f

plant¹ [plænt] **1** n planta f **2** v/t

plantar

plant² [plænt] *n* (*factory*) fábrica *f*, planta *f*; (*equipment*) maquinaria *f*

plantation [plæn'teɪʃn] plantación *f*

plaque [plæk] *on wall, teeth* placa *f*

plaster ['plɑːstər] **1** *n* yeso *m* **2** *v/t* enyesar

plastic ['plæstɪk] **1** *n* plástico *m* **2** *adj* (*made of ~*) de plástico; **plastic** (*money*) tarjetas *fpl* de pago; **plastic surgeon** cirujano(-a) *m(f)* plástico(-a); **plastic surgery** cirugía *f* estética

plate [pleɪt] plato *m*; *of metal* chapa *f*

plateau ['plætəʊ] meseta *f*

platform ['plætfɔːrm] (*stage*) plataforma *f*; *of railroad station* andén *m*; *fig: political* programa *m*

platinum ['plætɪnəm] **1** *n* platino *m* **2** *adj* de platino

platonic [plə'tɒnɪk] platónico

platoon [plə'tuːn] *of soldiers* sección *f*

plausible ['plɔːzəbl] plausible

play [pleɪ] **1** *n* juego *m*; *in theater, on TV* obra *f* (de teatro) **2** *v/i* jugar; *of musician* tocar **3** *v/t* MUS tocar; *game* jugar; *tennis, football* jugar a; *opponent* jugar contra; (*perform: Macbeth etc*) representar; *particular role* interpretar

♦ **play around** F (*be unfaithful*) acostarse con otras per-

sonas

♦ **play down** quitar importancia a

player ['pleɪər] SP jugador(a) *m(f)*; (*musician*) intérprete *m/f*; (*actor*) actor *m*, actriz *f*; **playful** *punch etc* de broma; **playground** zona *f* de juegos; **playing card** carta *f*; **playwright** autor(a) *m(f)*

plaza ['plɑːzə] *for shopping* centro *m* comercial

plc [piːel'siː] *Br* (*= public limited company*) S.A. *f* (*= sociedad f anónima*)

plea [pliː] súplica *f*

plead [pliːd]: *~ guilty / not guilty* declararse culpable / inocente; *~ with* suplicar

pleasant ['pleznt] agradable

please [pliːz] **1** *adv* por favor; *~ do* claro que sí, por supuesto **2** *v/t* complacer; *~ yourself!* ¡haz lo que quieras!; **pleased** contento; (*satisfied*) satisfecho; *~ to meet you* encantado de conocerle; **pleasing** agradable; **pleasure** satisfacción *f*; *as opposed to work* placer *m*; *with ~* faltaría más

pleat [pliːt] *in skirt* tabla *f*

pledge [pledʒ] **1** *n* (*promise*) promesa *f*; (*guarantee*) compromiso *m*; (*money*) donación *f*; *Pledge of Allegiance* juramento de lealtad a la bandera estadounidense **2** *v/t* (*promise*) prometer; (*guarantee*) comprometerse; *money*

donar
plentiful ['plentɪfəl] abundante; **plenty** abundancia *f*; **~ of books / food** muchos libros / mucha comida
pliable ['plaɪəbl] flexible
pliers ['plaɪərz] alicates *mpl*
plight [plaɪt] situación *f* difícil
plod [plɑːd] (*walk*) arrastrarse
plot[1] [plɑːt] *n* (*land*) terreno *m*
plot[2] [plɑːt] **1** *n* (*conspiracy*) complot *m*, conjura *f*; *of novel* argumento *m* **2** *v/t* tramar **3** *v/i* conspirar
plotter ['plɑːtər] conspirador(a) *m(f)*; COMPUT plóter *m*
plow, *Br* **plough** [plaʊ] **1** *n* arado *m* **2** *v/t* & *v/i* arar
♦ **plow back** *profits* reinvertir
pluck [plʌk] *eyebrows* depilar; *chicken* desplumar
plug [plʌg] **1** *n* for sink, bath tapón *m*; *electrical* enchufe *m*; (*spark* ~) bujía *f* **2** *v/t* hole tapar; *new book etc* hacer publicidad de
♦ **plug in** enchufar
plumage ['pluːmɪdʒ] plumaje *m*
plumber ['plʌmər] *Span* fontanero(-a) *m(f)*, *L.Am.* plomero(-a) *m(f)*; **plumbing** *pipes* tuberías *fpl*
plummet ['plʌmɪt] caer en picado
plump [plʌmp] rellenito
plunge [plʌndʒ] **1** *n* salto *m*; *in prices* caída *f* **2** *v/i* precipitar-

se; *of prices* caer en picado **3** *v/t* hundir; (*into water*) sumergir; **plunging** *neckline* escotado
plural ['plʊərəl] plural *m*
plus [plʌs] **1** *prep* más **2** *adj* más de **3** *n symbol* signo *m* más; (*advantage*) ventaja *f* **4** *conj* (*moreover, in addition*) además
plush [plʌʃ] lujoso
plywood ['plaɪwʊd] madera *f* contrachapada
PM [piː'em] *Br* (= *Prime Minister*) Primer(a) *m(f)* Ministro(a)
p.m. [piː'em] (= *post meridiem*) p.m.; *at 2 ~* a las 2 de la tarde; *at 11 ~* a las 11 de la noche
pneumonia [nuː'moʊnɪə] pulmonía *f*, neumonía *f*
poach[1] [poʊtʃ] *cook* hervir
poach[2] [poʊtʃ] (*hunt*) cazar furtivamente; *fish* pescar furtivamente
poached egg [poʊtʃt'eg] huevo *m* escalfado
P.O. Box [piː'oʊbɑːks] apartado *m* de correos
pocket ['pɑːkɪt] **1** *n* bolsillo *m* **2** *adj* radio, dictionary de bolsillo **3** *v/t* meter en el bolsillo; **pocketbook** (*purse*) bolso *m*; (*billfold*) cartera *f*; *book* libro *m* de bolsillo; **pocket calculator** calculadora *f* de bolsillo
podium ['poʊdɪəm] podio *m*
poem ['poʊɪm] poema *m*; **poet** poeta *m/f*, poetisa *f*;

459

polystyrene

ic poético; **poetry** poesía f

poignant ['pɔɪnjənt] conmovedor

point [pɔɪnt] **1** n of pencil, knife punta f; in competition punto m; (purpose) objetivo m; (moment) momento m; in decimals coma f; **what's the ~ of telling him?** ¿qué se consigue diciéndoselo?; **that's beside the ~** eso no viene a cuento; **be on the ~** of estar a punto de; **get to the ~** ir al grano **2** v/i señalar con el dedo
♦ **point out** sights indicar; advantages etc destacar
♦ **point to** señalar con el dedo; fig (indicate) indicar

pointed ['pɔɪntɪd] remark mordaz; **pointer** for teacher puntero m; (hint) consejo m; (sign, indication) indicador m; **pointless** inútil; **point of view** punto m de vista

poise [pɔɪz] confianza f; **poised** person con aplomo

poison ['pɔɪzn] **1** n veneno m **2** v/t envenenar; **poisonous** venenoso

poke [pouk] **1** n empujón m **2** v/t (prod) empujar; (stick) clavar
♦ **poke around** F husmear

poker ['poukər] game póquer m

polar ['poulər] polar

pole[1] [poul] for support poste m; for tent, pushing things palo m

pole[2] [poul] of earth polo m

police [pə'liːs] policía f; **police car** coche m de policía; **policeman** policía m; **police state** estado m policial; **police station** comisaría f (de policía); **policewoman** (mujer f) policía f

policy[1] ['paːlɪsɪ] política f

policy[2] ['paːlɪsɪ] (insurance ~) póliza f

polio ['pouliou] polio f

polish ['paːlɪʃ] **1** n abrillantador m; (nail ~) esmalte m de uñas **2** v/t dar brillo a; speech pulir; **polished** performance brillante

polite [pə'laɪt] educado; **politely** educadamente; **politeness** educación f

political [pə'lɪtɪkl] político; **politically correct** políticamente correcto; **politician** político(-a) m(f); **politics** política f

poll [poul] **1** n (survey) encuesta f, sondeo m; **go to the ~s** (vote) acudir a las urnas **2** v/t people sondear; votes obtener

pollen ['paːlən] polen m

pollster ['poulstər] encuestador(a) m(f)

pollutant [pə'luːtənt] contaminante m; **pollute** contaminar; **pollution** contaminación f

'polo shirt polo m

polyester [paːlɪ'estər] poliéster m

polystyrene [paːlɪ'staɪriːn]

poliestireno *m*
polyunsaturated [pɑː-
lɪʌn'sætʃəreɪtɪd] poliinsatu-
rado
pond [pɑːnd] estanque *m*
pontiff ['pɑːntɪf] pontífice *m*
pony ['pəʊnɪ] poni *m*; **pony-
tail** coleta *f*
pool[1] [puːl] *n* (*swimming* ∼)
piscina *f*, *L.Am.* pileta *f*,
Mex alberca *f*; *of water, blood*
charco *m*
pool[2] [puːl] *n game* billar *m*
americano
pool[3] [puːl] **1** *n* (*common
fund*) bote *m*, fondo *m* común **2** *v/t resources* juntar
'**pool hall** sala *f* de billares
'**pool table** mesa *f* de billar
americano
poop [puːp] F caca *f* F
pooped [puːpt] F hecho polvo
F
poor [pʊr] **1** *adj* pobre; (*not
good*) mediocre, malo **2**
npl: **the** ∼ los pobres; **poorly**
mal
pop[1] [pɑːp] MUS pop *m*
pop[2] [pɑːp] F (*father*) papá *m*
F
'**popcorn** palomitas *fpl* de
maíz
pope [pəʊp] papa *m*
Popsicle® ['pɑːpsɪkl] polo *m*
(*helado*)
popular ['pɑːpjʊlər] popular;
popularity popularidad *f*
populate ['pɑːpjʊleɪt] poblar;
population población *f*
porch [pɔːrtʃ] porche *m*
pork [pɔːrk] cerdo *m*

porn [pɔːrn] F porno *m* F;
pornographic pornográfico; **pornography** pornografía *f*
port[1] [pɔːrt] *n* puerto *m*
port[2] [pɔːrt] *adj* (*left-hand*) a
babor
portable ['pɔːrtəbl] **1** *adj*
portátil **2** *n* COMPUT portátil
m; *TV* televisión *f* portátil
porter ['pɔːrtər] *for luggage*
mozo(-a) *m(f)*
portion ['pɔːrʃn] parte *f*; *of
food* ración *f*
portrait ['pɔːrtreɪt] **1** *n* retrato
m **2** *adv print* en formato vertical; **portray** *of artist* retratar; *of actor* interpretar; *of
author* describir
Portugal ['pɔːrtʃʊgl] Portugal;
Portuguese 1 *adj* portugués
2 *n person* portugués(-esa)
m(f); *language* portugués *m*
pose [pəʊz] **1** *n* (*pretense*) pose *f* **2** *v/i for artist* posar **3** *v/t
problem, threat* representar
position [pə'zɪʃn] **1** *n* posición *f*; (*stance, point of view*)
postura *f*; (*job*) puesto *m* **2** *v/t*
situar, colocar
positive ['pɑːzətɪv] positivo;
positively (*decidedly*) verdaderamente; (*definitely*) claramente
possess [pə'zes] poseer;
possession posesión *f*;
possessive posesivo
possibility [pɑːsə'bɪlətɪ] posibilidad *f*; **possible** posible;
possibly (*perhaps*) puede
ser, quizás

post¹ [pəʊst] **1** n of wood, metal poste m **2** v/t notice pegar; *on bulletin board* poner; *profits* presentar

post² [pəʊst] **1** n (*place of duty*) puesto m **2** v/t *soldier, employee* destinar; *guards* apostar

post³ [pəʊst] *Br* **1** n (*mail*) correo m **2** v/t *letter* echar al correo

postage ['pəʊstɪdʒ] franqueo m; **postage stamp** *fml* sello m, *L.Am.* estampilla f, *Mex* timbre m; **postal** postal; **postcard** (tarjeta f) postal f; **postdate** posfechar

poster ['pəʊstər] póster m, *L.Am.* afiche m

postgraduate ['pəʊstɡrædʒʊət] posgraduado(-a) m(f)

posthumous ['pɑːstʊməs] póstumo

posting ['pəʊstɪŋ] (*assignment*) destino m

postmark matasellos m inv

post-mortem [pəʊst'mɔːrtəm] autopsia f

post office oficina f de correos

postpone [pəʊst'pəʊn] posponer, aplazar; **postponement** aplazamiento m

pot¹ [pɑːt] *for cooking* olla f; *for coffee* cafetera f; *for tea* tetera f; *for plant* maceta f

pot² [pɑːt] F (*marijuana*) maría f F

potato [pə'teɪtəʊ] *Span* patata f, *L.Am.* papa f; **potato chips**, *Br* **potato crisps**

Span patatas fpl fritas, *L.Am.* papas fpl fritas

potent ['pəʊtənt] potente

potential [pə'tenʃl] **1** adj potencial **2** n potencial m; **potentially** potencialmente

pothole ['pɑːthəʊl] *in road* bache m

potter ['pɑːtər] alfarero(-a) m(f); **pottery** alfarería f

pouch [paʊtʃ] *bag* bolsa f; *for mail* saca f

poultry ['pəʊltrɪ] *birds* aves fpl de corral; *meat* carne f de ave

pound¹ [paʊnd] n *weight* libra f (453.6 gr)

pound² [paʊnd] n *for strays* perrera f; *for cars* depósito m

pound³ [paʊnd] v/i *of heart* palpitar con fuerza

pour [pɔːr] v/t *into a container* verter; (*spill*) derramar **2** v/i: **it's ~ing (with rain)** está lloviendo a cántaros

◆ **pour out** *liquid* servir; *troubles* contar

poverty ['pɑːvərtɪ] pobreza f

powder ['paʊdər] **1** n polvo m; *for face* polvos mpl **2** v/t *face* empolvar

power ['paʊər] (*strength*) fuerza f; *of engine* potencia f; (*authority*) poder m; (*energy*) energía f; (*electricity*) electricidad f; **power cut** apagón m; **power failure** apagón m; **powerful** poderoso; *car* potente; *drug* fuerte; **powerless** impotente; **power line** línea f de conducción eléctrica; **power outage** apagón m; **power station** central f eléctrica; **power steering** dirección f asistida

PR [pi:'ɑ:r] (= **public relations**) relaciones fpl públicas

practical ['præktɪkl] práctico; *layout* funcional; **practically** de manera práctica; (*almost*) prácticamente

practice ['præktɪs] **1** n práctica f; (*rehearsal*) ensayo m; (*custom*) costumbre f **2** v/i practicar; *of musician* ensayar; *of footballer* entrenarse **3** v/t practicar; *law, medicine* ejercer

practise Br ☞ **practice** v/i & v/t

prairie ['preri] pradera f

praise [preɪz] **1** n elogio m, alabanza f **2** v/t elogiar; **praiseworthy** elogiable

pray [preɪ] rezar; **prayer** oración f

preach [pri:tʃ] **1** v/i predicar; (*moralize*) sermonear **2** v/t *sermon* predicar; **preacher** predicador(a) m(f)

precaution [prɪ'kɔ:ʃn] precaución f; **precautionary** *measure* preventivo

precede [prɪ'si:d] preceder; (*walk in front of*) ir delante de; **precedent** precedente m; **preceding** anterior

precious ['preʃəs] preciado; *gem* precioso

precise [prɪ'saɪs] preciso; **precisely** exactamente; **pre-**

cision precisión f

preconceived ['pri:kənsi:vd] *idea* preconcebido

precondition [pri:kən'dɪʃn] condición f previa

predator ['predətər] *animal* depredador(a) m(f); **predatory** depredador

predecessor ['pri:dɪsesər] *in job* predecesor(a) m(f); *machine* modelo m anterior

predicament [prɪ'dɪkəmənt] apuro m

predict [prɪ'dɪkt] predecir, pronosticar; **prediction** predicción f, pronóstico m

predominant [prɪ'dɑ:mɪnənt] predominante; **predominantly** predominantemente

prefabricated [pri:'fæbrɪkeɪtɪd] prefabricado

preface ['prefɪs] prólogo m, prefacio m

prefer [prɪ'fɜ:r] preferir; **preferable** preferible; **preferably** preferentemente; **preference** preferencia f; **preferential** preferencial

pregnancy ['pregnənsɪ] embarazo m; **pregnant** embarazada; *animal* preñada

prehistoric [pri:hɪs'tɑ:rɪk] prehistórico

prejudice ['predʒʊdɪs] **1** n prejuicio m **2** v/t *person* predisponer, influir; *chances* perjudicar; **prejudiced** parcial, predispuesto

preliminary [prɪ'lɪmɪnərɪ] preliminar

premarital [pri:'mærɪtl] prematrimonial

premature ['pri:mətʊr] prematuro

premier ['premɪr] (*Prime Minister*) primer(a) ministro(-a) *m(f)*

première ['premɪr] estreno *m*

premises ['premɪsɪz] local *m*

premium ['pri:mɪəm] *in insurance* prima *f*

prenatal [pri:'neɪtl] prenatal

preoccupied [pri:'ɒkjʊpaɪd] preocupado

preparation [prepə'reɪʃn] preparación *f*; **~s** preparativos *mpl*; **prepare 1** *v/t* preparar; **be ~d to do sth** *be willing* estar dispuesto a hacer algo **2** *v/i* prepararse

preposition [prepə'zɪʃn] preposición *f*

prerequisite [pri:'rekwɪzɪt] requisito *m* previo

prescribe [prɪ'skraɪb] MED recetar; **prescription** MED receta *f*

presence ['prezns] presencia *f*

present¹ ['preznt] **1** *adj* (*current*) actual; **be ~** estar presente **2** *n*: **the ~** *also* gram el presente

present² ['preznt] *n* (*gift*) regalo *m*

present³ [prɪ'zent] *v/t* presentar; *award* entregar

presentation [prezn'teɪʃn] presentación *f*; **present-day** actual; **presenter** presentador(a) *m(f)*; **presently** (*at the moment*) actualmente; (*soon*) pronto

preservative [prɪ'zɜ:rvətɪv] conservante *m*; **preserve 1** *n* (*domain*) dominio *m* **2** *v/t standards, peace etc* mantener; *food, wood* conservar

preside [prɪ'zaɪd] presidir; **presidency** presidencia *f*; **president** presidente(-a) *m(f)*; **presidential** presidencial

press [pres] **1** *n*: **the ~** la prensa *f* **2** *v/t button* pulsar, presionar; (*urge*) presionar; (*squeeze*) apretar; *clothes* planchar; **pressing** urgente; **pressure 1** *n* presión *f* **2** *v/t* presionar

prestige [pre'sti:ʒ] prestigio *m*; **prestigious** prestigioso

presumably [prɪ'zu:məblɪ] presumiblemente; **presume** suponer; **presumption** *of innocence, guilt* presunción *f*

presuppose [pri:sə'pəʊs] presuponer

pre-tax ['pri:tæks] antes de impuestos

pretence *Br* ☞ **pretense**

pretend [prɪ'tend] **1** *v/t* fingir, hacer como si; *claim* pretender **2** *v/i* fingir; **pretense** farsa *f*; **pretentious** pretencioso

pretext ['pri:tekst] pretexto *m*

pretty ['prɪtɪ] **1** *adj village, house, fabric etc* bonito, lindo; *child, woman* guapo, lindo **2** *adv* (*quite*) bastante

prevail [prɪ'veɪl] (*triumph*)

prevalecer; **prevailing** predominante

prevent [prɪ'vent] impedir, evitar; **prevention** prevención f; **preventive** preventivo

preview ['priːvjuː] **1** n of movie etc preestreno m **2** v/t hacer la presentación previa de

previous ['priːvɪəs] anterior, previo; **previously** anteriormente, antes

prey [preɪ] presa f

price [praɪs] **1** n precio m **2** v/t COM poner precio a; **priceless** que no tiene precio

prick[1] [prɪk] **1** n pain punzada f **2** v/t (jab) pinchar

prick[2] [prɪk] n V (penis) polla f V, carajo m V; V person Span gilipollas m inv V, L.Am. pendejo m V

prickle ['prɪkl] on plant espina f; **prickly** beard, plant que pincha; (irritable) irritable

pride [praɪd] in person, achievement orgullo m; (self-respect) amor m propio

priest [priːst] sacerdote m; (parish ~) cura m

primarily [praɪ'merɪlɪ] principalmente; **primary 1** adj principal **2** n POL elecciones fpl primarias

prime 'minister primer(a) ministro m(f)

primitive ['prɪmɪtɪv] primitivo

prince [prɪns] príncipe m; **princess** princesa f

principal ['prɪnsəpl] **1** adj

principal 2 n of school director(a) m(f); of university rector(a) m(f); **principally** principalmente

principle ['prɪnsəpl] principio m; on ~ por principios; in ~ en principio

print [prɪnt] **1** n in book etc letra f; (photograph) grabado m; out of ~ agotado **2** v/t imprimir; (use block capitals) escribir en mayúsculas; **printer** person impresor(a) m(f); machine impresora f; company imprenta f; **printout** copia f impresa

prior [praɪr] **1** adj previo **2** prep: ~ **to** antes de

prioritize [praɪ'ɔːrətaɪz] (put in order of priority) ordenar atendiendo a las prioridades; (give priority to) dar prioridad a; **priority** prioridad f

prison ['prɪzn] prisión f, cárcel f; **prisoner** prisionero(-a) m(f); **take s.o.** ~ hacer prisionero a alguien; **prisoner of war** prisionero(-a) m(f) de guerra

privacy ['prɪvəsɪ] intimidad f; **private 1** adj privado **2** n MIL soldado m/f raso; **privately** (in private) en privado; with one other a solas; (inwardly) para sí

privilege ['prɪvəlɪdʒ] (special treatment) privilegio m; (honor) honor m; **privileged** privilegiado

prize [praɪz] **1** n premio m **2**

v/t apreciar, valorar; **prize-winner** premiado(-a) *m(f)*; **prizewinning** premiado

probability [prɑːbə'bɪlətɪ] probabilidad *f*; **probable** probable; **probably** probablemente

probation [prə'beɪʃn] *in job* período *m* de prueba; LAW libertad *f* condicional

probe [proub] **1** *n* (*investigation*) investigación *f*; *scientific* sonda *f* **2** *v/t* examinar; (*investigate*) investigar

problem ['prɑːbləm] problema *m*; **no** ⌐! ¡claro!

procedure [prə'siːdʒər] procedimiento *m*; **proceed** (*go: of people*) dirigirse; *of work etc* proseguir, avanzar; **proceedings** (*events*) actos *mpl*; **proceeds** recaudación *f*

process ['prɑːses] **1** *n* proceso *m* **2** *v/t* food tratar; *raw materials, data* procesar; *application* tramitar; **procession** desfile *m*; *religious* procesión *f*; **processor** procesador *m*

prod [prɑːd] **1** *n* empujoncito *m* **2** *v/t* dar un empujoncito a; *with elbow* dar un codazo a

prodigy ['prɑːdɪdʒɪ] (*child*) niño(-a) *m(f)* prodigio

produce¹ ['prɑːduːs] *n* productos *mpl* del campo

produce² [prə'duːs] *v/t* producir; (*manufacture*) fabricar; (*bring out*) sacar

producer [prə'duːsər] productor(a) *m(f)*; (*manufacturer*) fabricante *m/f*; **product** producto *m*; **production** producción *f*; **productive** productivo; **productivity** productividad *f*

profess [prə'fes] manifestar; **profession** profesión *f*; **professional 1** *adj* profesional **2** *n* profesional *m/f*; **professionally** *play sport* profesionalmente; (*well, skillfully*) con profesionalidad

professor [prə'fesər] catedrático(-a) *m(f)*

proficient [prə'fɪʃnt] competente; (*skillful*) hábil

profile ['proufaɪl] *of face* perfil *m*; *biographical* reseña *f*

profit ['prɑːfɪt] *n* beneficio *m* **2** *v/i*: ⌐ **from** beneficiarse de; **profitability** rentabilidad *f*; **profitable** rentable

profound [prə'faund] profundo

prognosis [prɑːg'nousɪs] pronóstico *m*

program ['prougræm] **1** *n* programa *m* **2** *v/t* COMPUT programar; **programme** *Br* ☞ **program**; **programmer** programador(a) *m(f)*

progress 1 ['prɑːgres] *n* progreso *m* **2** [prə'gres] *v/i* (*advance in time*) avanzar; (*move on*) pasar; (*make* ⌐) progresar; **progressive** (*enlightened*) progresista; (*which progresses*) progresivo; **progressively** progresivamente

prohibit [prəˈhɪbɪt] prohibir;
prohibitive prices prohibiti-
vo

project¹ [ˈprɒdʒekt] *n* proyecto *m*; *edu* trabajo *m*;
(*housing area*) barriada *f* de
viviendas sociales

project² [prəˈdʒekt] **1** *v/t movie* proyectar; *figures, sales*
calcular **2** *v/i* (*stick out*) sobresalir

projection [prəˈdʒekʃn] (*forecast*) previsión *f*; **projector**
for slides proyector *m*

prolog [ˈprəʊlɒɡ] *Br* **prologue** [ˈprəʊ-
lɒːɡ] prólogo *m*

prolong [prəˈlɒŋ] prolongar

prominent [ˈprɒmɪnənt]
nose, chin prominente; (*significant*) destacado

promiscuity [prɒmɪˈskjuːətɪ]
promiscuidad *f*; **promiscu-
ous** promiscuo

promise [ˈprɒmɪs] **1** *n* promesa *f* **2** *v/t* prometer; **promising** prometedor

promote [prəˈməʊt] *employee*
ascender; (*encourage, foster*)
promover; COM promocio-
nar; **promoter** *of sports event*
promotor(a) *m(f)*; **promotion** *of employee* ascenso
m; *of scheme, idea,* COM promoción *f*

prompt [prɒmpt] **1** *adj* (*on
time*) puntual; (*speedy*) rápido **2** *v/t* (*cause*) provocar; *actor* apuntar; **promptly** *(on
time)* puntualmente; *(immediately)* inmediatamente

prone [prəʊn] **be ~ to** ser pro-

penso a

pronoun [ˈprəʊnaʊn] pronombre *m*

pronounce [prəˈnaʊns] *word*
pronunciar; *(declare)* declarar

pronto [ˈprɒntəʊ] F ya, en seguida

pronunciation [prənʌn-
sɪˈeɪʃn] pronunciación *f*

proof [pruːf] prueba(s) *f(pl)*

prop [prɒp] THEA accesorio
m

♦ **prop up** apoyar

propaganda [prɒpəˈɡændə]
propaganda *f*

propel [prəˈpel] propulsar;
propeller hélice *f*

proper [ˈprɒpə(r)] (*real*) de verdad; (*correct, fitting*) adecuado; **properly** (*correctly*) bien;
(*fittingly*) adecuadamente;
property propiedad *f*; *(land)*
propiedad(es) *f(pl)*

proportion [prəˈpɔːʃn] proporción *f*; **proportional** proporcional

proposal [prəˈpəʊzl] propuesta *f*; *of marriage* proposición *f*; **propose 1** *v/t* sugerir, proponer; *(plan)* proponerse **2** *v/i* (*make offer of
marriage*) pedir la mano (**to**
a); **proposition 1** *n* propuesta *f* **2** *v/t woman* hacer propo-
siciones a

proprietor [prəˈpraɪətə(r)] pro-
pietario(-a) *m(f)*

prosecute [ˈprɒsɪkjuːt] LAW
procesar; **prosecution** LAW
procesamiento *m*; lawyers

acusación f

prospect ['prɒspekt] (*chance, likelihood*) probabilidad f; (*thought of something in the future*) perspectiva f; **~s** perspectivas fpl (*de futuro*); **prospective** potencial

prosper ['prɒspər] prosperar; **prosperity** prosperidad f; **prosperous** próspero

prostitute ['prɒstɪtuːt] prostituta f; **male ~** prostituto m; **prostitution** prostitución f

protect [prə'tekt] proteger; **protection** protección f; **protective** protector; **protector** protector(a) m(f)

protein ['prəʊtiːn] proteína f

protest 1 ['prəʊtest] n protesta f **2** [prə'test] v/t protestar, quejarse de; (*object to*) protestar contra **3** [prə'test] v/i protestar

Protestant ['prɒtɪstənt] **1** n protestante m/f **2** adj protestante

protester [prə'testər] manifestante m/f

prototype ['prəʊtətaɪp] prototipo m

protrude [prə'truːd] sobresalir; **protruding** saliente; *ears, teeth* prominente

proud [praʊd] orgulloso; **proudly** con orgullo, orgullosamente

prove [pruːv] demostrar, probar

proverb ['prɒvɜːrb] proverbio m, refrán m

provide [prə'vaɪd] proporcionar; **~d (that)** (*on condition that*) con la condición de que, siempre que

province ['prɒvɪns] provincia f; **provincial** *city* provincial; *pej: attitude* de pueblo, provinciano

provision [prə'vɪʒn] (*supply*) suministro m; *of law, contract* disposición f; **provisional** provisional

provocation [prɒvə'keɪʃn] provocación f, **provocative** provocador; *sexually* provocativo; **provoke** provocar

prowl [praʊl] merodear; **prowler** merodeador(a) m(f)

proximity [prɒk'sɪmətɪ] proximidad f

proxy ['prɒksɪ] (*authority*) poder m; *person* apoderado(-a) m(f)

prudence ['pruːdns] prudencia f; **prudent** prudente

pry [praɪ] entrometerse

PS ['piːes] (= **postscript**) PD (= posdata f)

pseudonym ['suːdənɪm] pseudónimo m

psychiatric [saɪkɪ'ætrɪk] psiquiátrico; **psychiatrist** psiquiatra m/f; **psychiatry** psiquiatría f

psychoanalysis [saɪkəʊən'æləsɪs] psicoanálisis m; **psychoanalyst** psicoanalista m/f; **psychoanalyze** psicoanalizar

psychological [saɪkə'lɑːdʒɪkl] psicológico; **psychologist** psicólogo(-a) *m(f)*; **psychology** psicología *f*

psychopath ['saɪkoʊpæθ] psicópata *m/f*

psychosomatic [saɪkoʊsə-'mætɪk] psicosomático

pub [pʌb] *Br* bar *m*

public [ˈpʌblɪk] **1** *adj* público **2** *n*: **the ~** el público

publication [pʌblɪˈkeɪʃn] publicación *f*

public 'holiday día *m* festivo

publicity [pʌbˈlɪsətɪ] publicidad *f*; **publicize** (*make known*) publicar, hacer público; COM dar publicidad a

publicly [ˈpʌblɪklɪ] públicamente

'public school colegio *m* público; *Br* colegio *m* privado

publish [ˈpʌblɪʃ] publicar; **publisher** *person* editor(a) *m(f)*; *company* editorial *f*; **publishing** industria *f* editorial; **publishing company** editorial *f*

Puerto Rican [pwertoʊˈriːkən] **1** *adj* portorriqueño, puertorriqueño **2** *n* portorriqueño(-a) *m(f)*, puertorriqueño(-a) *m(f)*; **Puerto Rico** Puerto Rico

puff [pʌf] **1** *n* of wind racha *f*; from cigarette calada *f*; of smoke bocanada *f* **2** *v/i* (*pant*) resoplar; **puffy eyes**, **face** hinchado

pull [pʊl] **1** *n* on rope tirón *m*; F (*appeal*) gancho *m* F; F (*influence*) enchufe *m* F **2** *v/t*

(*drag*) arrastrar; (*tug*) tirar de; *tooth* sacar **3** *v/i* tirar

◆ **pull ahead** in race adelantarse

◆ **pull down** (*lower*) bajar; (*demolish*) derribar

◆ **pull in** of bus, train llegar

◆ **pull up 1** *v/t* (*raise*) subir; *item of clothing* subirse; *weeds* arrancar **2** *v/i* of car etc parar

pulley [ˈpʊlɪ] polea *f*

pulsate [pʌlˈseɪt] of heart palpitar; of music vibrar

pulse [pʌls] pulso *m*

pulverize [ˈpʌlvəraɪz] pulverizar

pump [pʌmp] **1** *n* bomba *f*; (*gas ~*) surtidor *m* **2** *v/t* bombear

pumpkin [ˈpʌmpkɪn] calabaza *f*

pun [pʌn] juego *m* de palabras

punch [pʌntʃ] **1** *n* blow puñetazo *m*; *implement* perforadora *f* **2** *v/t* with fist dar un puñetazo a; *hole*, *ticket* agujerear

punctual [ˈpʌŋktʃʊəl] puntual; **punctuality** puntualidad *f*

punctuation [pʌŋktʃʊˈeɪʃn] puntuación *f*

puncture [ˈpʌŋktʃər] **1** *n* perforación *f* **2** *v/t* perforar

punish [ˈpʌnɪʃ] castigar; **punishing** *schedule* exigente; *pace* fuerte; **punishment** castigo *m*

puny [ˈpjuːnɪ] person enclenque

oup [pʌp] cachorro *m*

pupil[1] ['pjuːpl] *of eye* pupila *f*

pupil[2] ['pjuːpl] *(student)* alumno(-a) *m(f)*

puppet ['pʌpɪt] *also fig* marioneta *f*

purchase[1] ['pɜːrtʃəs] **1** *n* adquisición *f*, compra *f* **2** *v/t* adquirir, comprar

purchase[2] ['pɜːrtʃəs] *n (grip)* agarre *m*

purchaser ['pɜːrtʃəsər] comprador(a) *m(f)*

pure [pjʊr] puro; *purely* puramente

purge [pɜːrdʒ] **1** *n of political party* purga *f* **2** *v/t* purgar *f*

purify ['pjʊrɪfaɪ] *water* depurar

puritan ['pjʊrɪtən] puritano(-a) *m(f)*

purity ['pjʊrɪtɪ] pureza *f*

purple [pɜːrps] *n (aim, object)* propósito *m*, objeto *m*; *on* ~ a propósito; *purposely* decididamente

purr [pɜːr] *of cat* ronronear

purse [pɜːrs] *(pocket book)* bolso *m*; *Br for money* monedero *m*

pursue [pərˈsuː] *person* perseguir; *career* ejercer; *course of action* proseguir; *pursuer* perseguidor(a) *m(f)*; *pursuit (chase)* persecución *f*; *of happiness etc* búsqueda *f*; *(activity)* actividad *f*

push [pʊʃ] **1** *n* empujón *m* **2** *v/t (shove)* empujar; *button* apretar, pulsar; *(pressurize)* presionar; F *drugs* pasar F

3 *v/i* empujar; *pusher F of drugs* camello *m* F; *push-up* flexión *f* (de brazos); *pushy* F avasallador, agresivo

puss, pussy (cat) [pʊs, ˈpʊsɪ (kæt)] F minino *m* F

put [pʊt] poner; *question* hacer; ~ *the cost at* estimar el costo en

◆ **put across** *idea etc* hacer llegar

◆ **put aside** *money* apartar; *work* dejar a un lado

◆ **put away** *in closet etc* guardar; *in institution* encerrar; F *(consume)* cepillarse F; *money* apartar; *animal* sacrificar

◆ **put back** *(replace)* volver a poner

◆ **put down** dejar; *deposit* entregar; *rebellion* reprimir; *(belittle)* dejar en mal lugar

◆ **put forward** *idea etc* proponer, presentar

◆ **put in** *meter; time* dedicar; *request, claim* presentar

◆ **put off** *light, TV* apagar; *(postpone)* posponer, aplazar; *(deter)* desalentar; *(repel)* desagradar

◆ **put on** *light, TV* encender; *L.Am.* prender; *tape, music* poner; *jacket, eye glasses* ponerse; *(pretend)* representar; *(assume)* fingir

◆ **put out** *hand* extender; *fire, light* apagar

◆ **put together** *(assemble, organize)* montar

◆ **put up** *hand, building* levantar; *person for the night* alojar; *prices* subir; *poster* colocar; *money* aportar

◆ **put up with** *v/t* aguantar

putty ['pʌtɪ] masilla *f*

puzzle ['pʌzl] **1** *n* (*mystery*) enigma *m*; *game* pasatiempos *mpl*; (*jigsaw*) puzzle *m*; (*crossword*) crucigrama *m* **2** *v/t* desconcertar; **puzzling** *adj* desconcertante

PVC [piːviːˈsiː] (= *polyvinyl chloride*) PVC *m* (= cloruro *m* de polivinilo)

pyjamas *Br* ☞ **pajamas**

pylon ['paɪlən] torre *f* de alta tensión

Pyrenees [pɪrəˈniːz]: **the** ~ los Pirineos

Q

quadrangle ['kwɑːdræŋgl] cuadrángulo *m*; *courtyard* patio *m*

quadruped ['kwɑːdruped] cuadrúpedo *m*

quail [kweɪl] temblar (**at** ante)

quaint [kweɪnt] *cottage* pintoresco; *ideas etc* extraño

quake [kweɪk] **1** *n* (*earthquake*) terremoto *m* **2** *v/i of earth, with fear* temblar

qualification [kwɑːlɪfɪˈkeɪʃn] *from university etc* título *m*; (*restricted*) limitado; **qualify 1** *v/t of degree, course etc* habilitar; *remark etc* matizar **2** *v/i* (*get degree etc*) titularse, *L.Am.* egresar; *in competition* calificarse

quality ['kwɑːlɪtɪ] calidad *f*; (*characteristic*) cualidad *f*; **quality control** control *m* de calidad

quandary ['kwɑːndərɪ] dilema *m*

quantify ['kwɑːntɪfaɪ] cuantificar

quantity ['kwɑːntɪtɪ] cantidad *f*

quarantine ['kwɑːrəntiːn] cuarentena *f*

quarrel ['kwɑːrəl] **1** *n* pelea *f* **2** *v/i* pelearse

quarry¹ ['kwɑːrɪ] *in hunt* presa *f*

quarry² ['kwɑːrɪ] *for mining* cantera *f*

quart [kwɔːrt] cuarto *m* de galón *(0,946 litre)*

quarter ['kwɔːrtər] cuarto *m* 25 *cents* cuarto *m* de dólar; *part of town* barrio *m*; **a ~ of an hour** un cuarto de hora; **a ~ of 5** las cinco menos cuarto, *L.Am.* cuarto para las cinco; **a ~ after 5** las cinco y cuarto; **quarter-final** cuarto *m* de final; **quarter-finalist** cuartofinalista *m/f*; **quarterly 1** *adj* trimestral **2** *adv* trimestralmente; **quarters** MIL alojamiento *m*; **quartet** MUS cuarteto *m*

quartz [kwɔːrts] cuarzo *m*

quash [kwɑːʃ] *rebellion* aplastar, sofocar; *court decision* revocar

quaver ['kweɪvər] **1** *n in voice* temblor *m* **2** *v/i of voice* temblar

queasy ['kwiːzɪ] mareado

queen [kwiːn] reina *f*

queer [kwɪr] *(peculiar)* raro, extraño

quell [kwel] *protest* acallar; *riot* aplastar, sofocar

quench [kwentʃ] *thirst* apagar, saciar; *flames* apagar

query ['kwɪrɪ] **1** *n* duda *f*, pregunta *f* **2** *v/t (express doubt about)* cuestionar; *(check)* comprobar

quest [kwest] busca *f*

question ['kwestʃən] **1** *n* pregunta *f*; *(matter)* cuestión *f*, asunto *m* **2** *v/t person* preguntar a; LAW interrogar; *(doubt)* cuestionar; **questionable** cuestionable; **questioning 1** *adj look* inquisitivo **2** *n* interrogatorio *m*; **question mark** signo *m* de interrogación; **questionnaire** cuestionario *m*

queue [kjuː] **1** *n Br* cola *f* **2** *v/i* hacer cola

quibble ['kwɪbl] discutir *(por algo insignificante)*

quick [kwɪk] rápido; **be ~!** ¡date prisa!; **quickly** rápida-

mente, rápido, deprisa; **quickwitted** agudo

quiet ['kwaɪət] tranquilo; *engine* silencioso; **~!** ¡silencio!; **quietly** *(not loudly)* silenciosamente; *(without fuss)* discretamente; *(peacefully)* tranquilamente; **speak ~** hablar en voz baja; **quietness** *of voice* suavidad *f*; *of night, street* silencio *m*, calma *f*

quilt [kwɪlt] *on bed* edredón *m*

quinine ['kwɪniːn] quinina *f*

quip [kwɪp] **1** *n joke* broma *f*, *remark* salida *f* **2** *v/i* bromear

quirk [kwɜːrk] peculiaridad *f*, rareza *f*; **quirky** peculiar, raro

quit [kwɪt] **1** *v/t job* dejar, abandonar **2** *v/i (leave job)* dimitir; COMPUT salir

quite [kwaɪt] *(fairly)* bastante; *(completely)* completamente; **~ a lot** bastante

quiver ['kwɪvər] estremecerse

quiz [kwɪz] **1** *n* concurso *m (de preguntas y respuestas)* **2** *v/t* interrogar *(about* sobre)

quota ['kwoʊtə] cuota *f*

quotation [kwoʊ'teɪʃn] *from author* cita *f*; *(price)* presupuesto *m*; **quotation marks** comillas *fpl*; **quote 1** *n from author* cita *f*; *(price)* presupuesto *m*; *(quotation mark)* comilla *f*; **in ~s** entre comillas **2** *v/t text* citar; *price* dar

R

rabbit ['ræbɪt] conejo *m*
rabble ['ræbl] chusma *f*, multitud *f*; **rabble-rouser** agitador(a) *m(f)*
rabies ['reɪbiːz] rabia *f*
raccoon [rə'kuːn] mapache *m*
race¹ [reɪs] *n* of people raza *f*
race² [reɪs] **1** *n* SP carrera *f* **2** *v/i* (*run fast*) correr **3** *v/t* correr contra; *I'll ~ you* te echo una carrera
'racecourse hipódromo *m*; **racehorse** caballo *m* de carreras; **race** riot disturbios *mpl* raciales; **racetrack** circuito *m*; for horses hipódromo *m*
racial ['reɪʃl] racial
racing ['reɪsɪŋ] carreras *fpl*
racism ['reɪsɪzm] racismo *m*; **racist** **1** *n* racista *m/f* **2** *adj* racista
rack [ræk] **1** *n* for bags on train portaequipajes *m inv*; for CDs mueble *m* **2** *v/t*: ~ *one's brains* devanarse los sesos
racket¹ ['rækɪt] SP raqueta *f*
racket² ['rækɪt] (*noise*) jaleo *m*; (*criminal activity*) negocio *m* sucio
radar ['reɪdɑːr] radar *m*
radiance ['reɪdɪəns] esplendor *m*; **radiant** *smile* resplandeciente; **radiate** of heat, light irradiar; **radiation** PHYS radiación *f*; **radiator** radiador *m*

radical ['rædɪkl] **1** *adj* radical **2** *n* POL radical *m/f*; **radicalism** POL radicalismo *m*; **radically** radicalmente
radio ['reɪdɪoʊ] radio *f*; **radioactive** radiactivo; **radioactivity** radiactividad *f*; **radio alarm** radio *m* despertador; **radiographer** técnico(-a) *m(f)* de rayos X; **radiography** radiografía *f*; **radio station** emisora *f* de radio
radius ['reɪdɪəs] radio *m*
raft [ræft] balsa *f*
rafter ['ræftər] viga *f*
rag [ræg] for cleaning etc trapo *m*
rage [reɪdʒ] **1** *n* ira *f*, cólera *f* **2** *v/i* of storm bramar
ragged ['rægɪd] andrajoso
raid [reɪd] **1** *n* by troops, FIN incursión *f*; by police redada *f*; by robbers atraco *m* **2** *v/t* of troops realizar una incursión en; of police realizar una redada en; of robbers atracar; fridge saquear; **raider** on bank etc atracador(a) *m(f)*
rail [reɪl] on track riel *m*, carril *m*; (hand~) pasamanos *m inv*, barandilla *f*; for towel barra *f*; **by** ~ en tren; **railings** around park etc verja *f*; **railroad** ferrocarril *m*; track vía *f* férrea; **railroad station** estación *f* de ferrocarril or de tren; **railway** Br ferrocarril

m; **track** vía *f* férrea

rain [reɪn] **1** *n* lluvia *f* **2** *v/i* llover; **it's** *~***ing** llueve; **rainbow** arco *m* iris; **raincheck: can I take a** *~* **on that?** F ¿lo podríamos aplazar para algún otro momento?; **raincoat** impermeable *m*; **raindrop** gota *f* de lluvia; **rainfall** pluviosidad *f*; **rain forest** selva *f*; **rainproof** *fabric* impermeable; **rainstorm** tormenta *f*, aguacero *m*; **rainy** lluvioso

raise [reɪz] **1** *n in salary* aumento *m* de sueldo **2** *v/t shelf etc* levantar; *offer* incrementar; *children* criar; *question* plantear; *money* reunir

rake [reɪk] *for garden* rastrillo *m*

rally ['rælɪ] *(meeting, reunion)* concentración *f*; *political* mitin *m*; *MOT* rally *m*; *in tennis* peloteo *m*

RAM [ræm] COMPUT *(= random access memory)* RAM *f* (= memoria *f* de acceso aleatorio)

ram [ræm] **1** *n* carnero *m* **2** *v/t ship, car* embestir

ramble ['ræmbl] **1** *n walk* caminata *f* **2** *v/i walk* caminar; *in speaking* divagar; *(talk incoherently)* hablar sin decir nada coherente; **rambling** *speech* inconexo

ramp [ræmp] rampa *f*; *for raising vehicle* elevador *m*

rampant ['ræmpənt] *inflation* galopante

rampart ['ræmpɑːrt] muralla *f*

R & D [ɑːrən'diː] *(= research and development)* I+D *f* (= investigación *f* y desarrollo)

random ['rændəm] **1** *adj* al azar; *~* **sample** muestra *f* aleatoria; **2** *n*: **at** *~* al azar

range [reɪndʒ] **1** *n of products* gama *f*; *of gun, airplane* alcance *m*; *of voice* registro *m*; *of mountains* cordillera *f*; **at close** *~* de cerca **2** *v/i*: *~* **from X to Y** ir desde X a Y; **ranger** guardabosques *m/f inv*

rank [ræŋk] **1** *n* MIL, *in society* rango *m* **2** *v/t* clasificar

♦ **rank among** figurar entre

ransack ['rænsæk] saquear

ransom ['rænsəm] rescate *m*

rap [ræp] **1** *n at door etc* golpe *m*; MUS rap *m* **2** *v/t table etc* golpear

rape[1] [reɪp] **1** *n* violación *f* **2** *v/t* violar

rape[2] [reɪp] *n* BOT colza *f*

rapid ['ræpɪd] rápido; **rapidity** rapidez *f*; **rapidly** rápidamente; **rapids** rápidos *mpl*

rapist ['reɪpɪst] violador(a) *m(f)*

rare [rer] raro; *steak* poco hecho; **rarely** raramente, raras veces; **rarity** rareza *f*

rash

rash¹ [ræʃ] n MED sarpullido m, erupción f cutánea

rash² [ræʃ] adj act precipitado; **rashly** precipitadamente

rat [ræt] rata f

rate [reɪt] of exchange tipo m; of pay tarifa f; (price) tarifa f, precio m; (speed) ritmo m; **at this ~** (at this speed) a este ritmo; (if we carry on like this) si seguimos así; **at any ~** (anyway) en todo caso; (at least) por lo menos

rather ['rɑːðər] (fairly, quite) bastante; **I would ~ stay here** preferiría quedarme aquí

ratification [rætɪfɪ'keɪʃn] ratificación f; **ratify** ratificar

rating agency ['reɪtɪŋ] FIN agencia f de calificación de riesgos, agencia f de calificación de deuda

ratings ['reɪtɪŋz] índice m de audiencia

ratio ['reɪʃɪəʊ] proporción f

ration ['ræʃn] 1 n ración f 2 v/t supplies racionar

rational ['ræʃənl] racional; **rationality** racionalidad f; **rationalization** racionalización f; **rationalize** 1 v/t racionalizar 2 v/i buscar una explicación racional; **rationally** racionalmente

rattle ['rætl] 1 n noise traqueteo m; toy sonajero m 2 v/t chains etc entrechocar 3 v/i of chains etc entrechocarse; of crates traquetear; **rattlesnake** serpiente f de casca-

bel

raucous ['rɔːkəs] estridente

rave [reɪv] 1 v/i (talk deliriously) delirar; (talk wildly) desvariar; **~ about sth** (be very enthusiastic) estar muy entusiasmado con algo 2 n party fiesta f tecno

ravenous ['rævənəs] famélico

ravine [rə'viːn] barranco m

raw [rɔː] meat, vegetable crudo; sugar sin refinar; iron sin tratar; **raw materials** materias fpl primas

ray [reɪ] rayo m

razor ['reɪzər] maquinilla f de afeitar; **razor blade** cuchilla f de afeitar

re [riː] COM con referencia a

reach [riːtʃ] 1 n: **within ~** al alcance; **out of ~** fuera del alcance 2 v/t llegar a; decision, agreement alcanzar

react [rɪ'ækt] reaccionar; **reaction** reacción f; **reactionary** 1 n POL reaccionario(-a) m(f) 2 adj POL reaccionario; **reactor** nuclear reactor m

read [riːd] leer
◆ **read out** aloud leer en voz alta

readable ['riːdəbl] writing legible; book ameno; **reader** person lector(a) m(f)

readily ['redɪlɪ] admit, agree de buena gana

reading ['riːdɪŋ] lectura f

readjust [riːə'dʒʌst] 1 v/t reajustar 2 v/i to conditions volver a adaptarse

ready ['redɪ] (*prepared*) listo, preparado; (*willing*) dispuesto; **get sth ~** preparar algo; **ready cash** dinero *m* contante y sonante; **ready-made** *stew etc* precocinado; *solution* ya hecho; **ready-to-wear** de confección

real [rɪːl] *real*; *surprise, genius* auténtico; **real estate** bienes *mpl* inmuebles; **real estate agent** agente *m/f* inmobiliario(-a); **realism** realismo *m*; **realist** realista *m/f*; **realistic** realista; **realistically** realísticamente; **reality** realidad *f*; **realize** darse cuenta de; FIN (*yield*) producir; (*sell*) realizar, liquidar; **really** *in truth* de verdad; *big, small* muy; **I am ~ sorry** lo siento en el alma; **real time** COMPUT tiempo *m* real; **real-time** COMPUT en tiempo real

realtor ['rɪːltər] agente *m/f* inmobiliario(-a); **realty** bienes *mpl* inmuebles

reappear [rɪːə'pɪr] reaparecer; **reappearance** reaparición *f*

rear [rɪr] **1** *n* parte *f* de atrás **2** *adj* *legs* de atrás; *seats, wheels, lights* trasero

rearm [rɪː'ɑːrm] **1** *v/t* rearmar **2** *v/i* rearmarse

rearrange [rɪːə'reɪnʒ] *flowers* volver a colocar; *furniture* reordenar; *schedule* cambiar

rear-view 'mirror espejo *m* retrovisor

reason ['rɪːzn] razón *f*; **rea-** sonable razonable; **reasonably** *act* razonablemente; (*quite*) bastante; **reasoning** razonamiento *m*

reassure [rɪːə'ʃur] tranquilizar; **reassuring** tranquilizador

rebate ['rɪːbeɪt] *money back* reembolso *m*

rebel 1 ['rebl] *n* rebelde *m/f* **2** [rɪ'bel] *v/i* rebelarse; **rebellion** rebelión *f*; **rebellious** rebelde; **rebelliousness** rebeldía *f*

rebound [rɪ'baund] *of ball etc* rebotar

rebuild [rɪː'bɪld] reconstruir

recall [rɪ'kɔːl] *goods* retirar del mercado; (*remember*) recordar

recap ['rɪːkæp] recapitular

recapture [rɪː'kæptʃər] MIL reconquistar; *criminal* volver a detener

recede [rɪ'sɪːd] *of flood waters* retroceder

receipt [rɪ'sɪːt] *for purchase* recibo *m*; **~s** FIN ingresos *mpl*; **receive** recibir; **receiver** *of letter* destinatario(-a) *m(f)*; TELEC auricular *m*; *for radio* receptor *m*; **receivership: be in ~** estar en suspensión de pagos

recent ['rɪːsnt] reciente; **recently** recientemente

reception [rɪ'sepʃn] recepción *f*; (*welcome*) recibimiento *m*; **reception desk** recepción *f*; **receptionist** recepcionista *m/f*; **receptive:**

be ~ to sth ser receptivo a algo

recess ['ri:ses] *in wall etc* hueco *m*; EDU recreo *m*; *of legislature* periodo *m* vacacional; **recession** *economic* recesión *f*

recharge [ri:'ʧɑ:rdʒ] *battery* recargar

recipe ['resəpi] receta *f*

recipient [rɪ'sɪpɪənt] *of parcel etc* destinatario(-a) *m(f)*; *of payment* receptor(a) *m(f)*

reciprocal [rɪ'sɪprəkl] recíproco

recite [rɪ'saɪt] *poem* recitar; *details, facts* enumerar

reckless ['reklɪs] imprudente; *driving* temerario; **recklessly** con imprudencia; *drive* con temeridad

reckon ['rekən] *(think, consider)* estimar, considerar
◆ **reckon on** contar con

reclaim [rɪ'kleɪm] *land from sea* ganar, recuperar; *lost property, rights* reclamar

recline [rɪ'klaɪn] reclinarse; **recliner** *chair* sillón *m* reclinable

recluse [rɪ'klu:s] solitario(-a) *m(f)*

recognition [rekəg'nɪʃn] *of state, achievements* reconocimiento *m*; **recognizable** reconocible; **recognize** reconocer

recoil [rɪ'kɔɪl] echarse atrás

recollect [rekə'lekt] recordar; **recollection** recuerdo *m*

recommend [rekə'mend] re-

comendar; **recommendation** recomendación *f*

recompense ['rekəmpens] recompensa *f*

reconcile ['rekənsaɪl] *people* reconciliar; *differences, facts* conciliar; **reconciliation** *of people* reconciliación *f*; *of differences, facts* conciliación *f*

recondition [ri:kən'dɪʃn] reacondicionar

reconnaissance [rɪ'kɑ:nɪsns] MIL reconocimiento *m*

reconsider [ri:kən'sɪdər] reconsiderar

reconstruct [ri:kən'strʌkt] reconstruir

record[1] ['rekɔ:rd] *n* MUS disco *m*; SP *etc* récord *m*; *written document, in database* registro *m*; **~s** archivos *mpl*; **have a criminal ~** tener antecedentes penales

record[2] [rɪ'kɔ:rd] *v/t electronically* grabar; *in writing* anotar

'record-breaking récord *inv*; **record holder** plusmarquista *m/f*

recording [rɪ'kɔ:rdɪŋ] grabación *f*

recount [rɪ'kaʊnt] *(tell)* relatar

re-count ['ri:kaʊnt] **1** *n of votes* segundo recuento *m* **2** *v/t (count again)* volver a contar

recoup [rɪ'ku:p] *financial losses* resarcirse de

recover [rɪˈkʌvər] **1** v/t sth lost recuperar; composure recobrar **2** v/i from illness recuperarse; **recovery** recuperación f

recreation [rekrɪˈeɪʃn] ocio m; **recreational** done for pleasure recreativo

recruit [rɪˈkruːt] **1** n MIL recluta m/f; to company nuevo(-a) trabajador(a) **2** v/t new staff contratar; **recruitment** MIL reclutamiento m; to company contratación f

rectangle [ˈrektæŋgl] rectángulo m; **rectangular** rectangular

rectify [ˈrektɪfaɪ] rectificar

recuperate [rɪˈkuːpəreɪt] recuperarse

recur [rɪˈkɜːr] of event repetirse; of symptoms reaparecer; **recurrent** recurrente

recycle [riːˈsaɪkl] reciclar; **recycling** reciclado m

red [red] rojo; in the ~ en números rojos; **Red Cross** Cruz f Roja

redecorate [riːˈdekəreɪt] paint volver a pintar; paper volver a empapelar

redeem [rɪˈdiːm] debt amortizar; REL redimir

redevelop [riːdɪˈveləp] part of town reedificar

redhead pelirrojo(-a) m(f); **red light** at traffic light semáforo m (en) rojo; **red light district** zona f de prostitución; **red meat** carne f roja; **redneck** F individuo racista y reaccionario, normalmente de clase trabajadora; **red tape** F burocracia f, papeleo m

reduce [rɪˈdjuːs] reducir; price rebajar; **reduction** reducción f; in price rebaja f

reek [riːk] apestar (of a)

reel [riːl] of film rollo m; of thread carrete m

re-e·lect reelegir; **re-election** reelección f

re-entry of spacecraft reentrada f

ref [ref] F árbitro(-a) m(f)

◆ **refer to** referirse a; dictionary etc consultar

referee [refəˈriː] SP árbitro(-a) m(f); for job: persona que pueda dar referencias; **reference** referencia f; **reference book** libro m de consulta; **reference number** número m de referencia

referendum [refəˈrendəm] referéndum m

refill [ˈriːfɪl] volver a llenar

refine [rɪˈfaɪn] refinar; technique perfeccionar; **refinement** to process, machine mejora f; **refinery** refinería f

reflect [rɪˈflekt] **1** v/t light reflejar **2** v/i (think) reflexionar; **reflection** in water, glass etc reflejo m; (consideration) reflexión f

reflex [ˈriːfleks] in body reflejo m

reform [rɪˈfɔːrm] **1** n reforma f **2** v/t reformar; **reformer** reformador(a) m(f)

refresh [rɪˈfreʃ] refrescar; refreshing *drink* refrescante; *experience* reconfortante; **refreshments** refrigerio *m*

refrigerate [rɪˈfrɪdʒəreɪt] *v/t* refrigerar; **refrigerator** frigorífico *m*, refrigerador *m*

refuel [riːˈfjuəl] **1** *v/t airplane* reabastecer de combustible a **2** *v/i of plane* repostar

refuge [ˈrefjuːdʒ] refugio *m*; **take ~** *from storm etc* refugiarse; **refugee** refugiado(-a) *m(f)*

refund [ˈriːfʌnd] *n* reembolso *m* **2** [rɪˈfʌnd] *v/t* reembolsar

refusal [rɪˈfjuːzl] negativa *f*; **refuse** **1** *v/i* negarse **2** *v/t help, food* rechazar; **~ to do sth** negarse a hacer algo

regain [rɪˈgeɪn] recuperar

regard [rɪˈgɑːrd] **1** *n*: **with ~ to** con respecto a; **(kind) ~s** saludos; **with no ~ for** sin tener en cuenta **2** *v/t*: **~ as** con respecto a; **regarding** con respecto a; **regardless** a pesar de todo; **~ of** sin tener en cuenta

regime [reɪˈʒiːm] *(government)* régimen *m*

regiment [ˈredʒɪmənt] regimiento *m*

region [ˈriːdʒən] región *f*; **regional** regional

register [ˈredʒɪstər] **1** *n* registro *m*; *at school* lista *f* **2** *v/t birth, death* registrar; *vehicle* matricular; *letter* certificar; *emotion* mostrar **3** *v/i at university* matricularse; *with po-*

lice registrarse; **registered letter** carta *f* certificada; **registration** registro *m*; *at university* matriculación *f*

regret [rɪˈgret] **1** *v/t* lamentar, sentir **2** *n* arrepentimiento *m*, pesar *m*; **regretful** arrepentido; **regrettable** lamentable

regular [ˈregjələr] **1** *adj* regular; *(normal)* normal **2** *n* *at bar etc* habitual *m/f*; **regularity** regularidad *f*; **regularly** regularmente

regulate [ˈregəleɪt] regular; **regulation** *(rule)* regla *f*, norma *f*

rehabilitate [riːhəˈbɪlɪteɪt] *ex-criminal* rehabilitar

rehearsal [rɪˈhɜːrsl] ensayo *m*; **rehearse** ensayar

reign [reɪn] **1** *n* reinado *m* **2** *v/i* reinar

reimburse [riːɪmˈbɜːrs] reembolsar

reinforce [riːɪnˈfɔːrs] *structure* reforzar; *beliefs* reafirmar; **reinforced concrete** hormigón *m* armado; **reinforcements** MIL refuerzos *mpl*

reinstate [riːɪnˈsteɪt] *in office* reincorporar; *in text* volver a colocar

reject [rɪˈdʒekt] rechazar; **rejection** rechazo *m*

relapse [ˈriːlæps] MED recaída *f*

related [rɪˈleɪtɪd] *by family* emparentado; *events, etc* relacionado; **relation in** *family* pariente *m/f*; *(connec-*

tion) relación f; **relationship** relación f; **relative 1** *n* pariente *m*/f **2** *adj* relativo; **relatively** relativamente

relax [rɪˈlæks] **1** *v/i* relajarse **2** *v/t muscle, pace* relajar; **~!** ¡tranquilízate!; **relaxation** relajación f; **relaxed** relajado; **relaxing** relajante

relay 1 [riːˈleɪ] *v/t message* pasar; *radio, TV signals* retransmitir **2** [ˈriːleɪ] *n:* **~ (race)** carrera f de relevos

release [rɪˈliːs] **1** *n from prison* liberación f; *of CD etc* lanzamiento *m; CD, record* trabajo *m* **2** *v/t prisoner* liberar; *parking brake* soltar; *information* hacer público

relegate [ˈreləgeɪt] relegar

relent [rɪˈlent] ablandarse; **relentless** *(determined)* implacable; *rain etc* que no cesa

relevance [ˈreləvəns] pertinencia f; **relevant** pertinente

reliability [rɪlaɪəˈbɪlətɪ] fiabilidad f; **reliable** fiable; **reliance** confianza f, dependencia f

relic [ˈrelɪk] reliquia f

relief [rɪˈliːf] alivio *m;* **relieve** *pain* aliviar; *(take over from)* relevar

religion [rɪˈlɪdʒən] religión f; **religious** religioso

relinquish [rɪˈlɪŋkwɪʃ] renunciar a

relish [ˈrelɪʃ] **1** *n sauce* salsa f; *(enjoyment)* goce *m* **2** *v/t idea, prospect* gozar de

relive [riːˈlɪv] *event* revivir

relocate [riːləˈkeɪt] *of business, employee* trasladarse

reluctance [rɪˈlʌktəns] reticencia f; **reluctant** reticente, reacio

◆ **rely on** [rɪˈlaɪ] depender de; **rely on s.o. to do sth** contar con alguien para hacer algo

remain [rɪˈmeɪn] *(be left)* quedar; *(stay)* permanecer; **remainder** *also* MATH resto *m;* **remaining** restante; **remains** *of body* restos *mpl* (mortales)

remake [ˈriːmeɪk] *of movie* nueva versión f

remark [rɪˈmɑːrk] **1** *n* comentario *m*, observación f **2** *v/t* comentar, observar; **remarkable** extraordinario; **remarkably** extraordinariamente

remarry [riːˈmærɪ] volver a casarse

remedy [ˈremədɪ] MED, *fig* remedio *m*

remember [rɪˈmembər] **1** *v/t* recordar, acordarse de **2** *v/i* recordar, acordarse

remind [rɪˈmaɪnd]: **~ s.o. of sth** recordar algo a alguien; **~ s.o. of s.o.** recordar alguien a alguien; **~ s.o. to do sth** recordar a alguien que haga algo; **reminder** recordatorio *m*

reminisce [remɪˈnɪs] contar recuerdos

remission [rɪˈmɪʃn] remisión f; **go into** MED remitir

remnant [ˈremnənt] resto *m*

remorse [rɪˈmɔːrs] remordimientos *mpl*; **remorseless** *person* despiadado; *pace, demands* implacable

remote [rɪˈmout] *village, possibility* remoto; *(aloof)* distante; *ancestor* lejano; **remote control** control *m* remoto; *for TV* mando a distancia; **remotely** remotamente

removable [rɪˈmuːvəbl] de quita y pon; **removal** eliminación *f*; **remove** eliminar; *lid* quitar; *coat etc* quitarse; *doubt, suspicion* despejar; *growth, organ* extirpar

rename [riːˈneɪm] cambiar el nombre a

rendez-vous [ˈrɑːndeɪvuː] *romantic* cita *f*; MIL encuentro *m*

renew [rɪˈnuː] *contract* renovar; *discussions* reanudar; **renewal** *of contract etc* renovación *f*; *of discussions* reanudación *f*

renounce [rɪˈnaʊns] renunciar a

renovate [ˈrenəveɪt] renovar; **renovation** renovación *f*

rent [rent] **1** *n* alquiler *m*; **for ~** se alquila **2** *v/t* alquilar, *Mex* rentar; **rental** *for apartment, TV* alquiler *m*, *Mex* renta *f*; **rental car** coche *m* de alquiler; **rent-free** sin pagar alquiler

reopen [riːˈoupn] **1** *v/t* reabrir; *negotiations* reanudar **2** *v/i* *of theater etc* volver a abrir

reorganization [riːɔːrgənaɪˈzeɪʃn] reorganización *f*; **reorganize** reorganizar

repaint [riːˈpeɪnt] repintar

repair [rɪˈper] **1** *v/t* reparar; *shoes* arreglar **2** *n* reparación *f*; *of shoes* arreglo *m*; **repairman** técnico *m*

repatriate [riːˈpætrieɪt] repatriar; **repatriation** repatriación *f*

repay [riːˈpeɪ] *money* devolver; *person* pagar; **repayment** devolución *f*; *installment* plazo *m*

repeal [rɪˈpiːl] *law* revocar

repeat [rɪˈpiːt] **1** *v/t* repetir **2** *n* TV *program* repetición *f*; **repeatedly** repetidamente, repetidas veces

repel [rɪˈpel] *attack* rechazar; *insects* repeler, ahuyentar; *(disgust)* repeler, repugnar; **repellent 1** *n* *(insect ~)* repelente *m* **2** *adj* repelente

repercussions [riːpərˈkʌʃnz] repercusiones *fpl*

repertoire [ˈrepərtwɑːr] repertorio *m*

repetition [repəˈtɪʃn] repetición *f*; **repetitive** repetitivo

replace [rɪˈpleɪs] *(put back)* volver a poner; *(take place of)* reemplazar, sustituir; **replacement** *person* sustituto(-a) *m(f)*; *thing* recambio *m*, reemplazo *m*; **replacement part** (pieza *f* de) recambio *m*

replay [ˈriːpleɪ] **1** *n* *recording* repetición *f* (de la jugada);

match repetición f (del partido) **2** v/t *match* repetir

replenish [rɪˈplenɪʃ] *container* rellenar; *supplies* reaprovisionar

replica [ˈreplɪkə] réplica f

reply [rɪˈplaɪ] **1** n respuesta f, contestación f **2** v/t & v/i responder, contestar

report [rɪˈpɔːrt] **1** n (*account*) informe m; *by journalist* reportaje m **2** v/t *facts* informar; *to authorities* informar de **3** v/i *of journalist* informar; (*present o.s.*) presentarse (*to* ante); **reporter** reportero(-a) m(f)

repossess [riːpəˈzes] COM embargar

represent [reprɪˈzent] representar; **representative 1** n representante m/f; POL representante m/f, diputado(-a) m(f) **2** adj (*typical*) representativo

repress [rɪˈpres] *revolt* reprimir; *feelings, laughter* reprimir, controlar; **repression** POL represión f; **repressive** POL represivo

reprieve [rɪˈpriːv] **1** n LAW indulto m; *fig* aplazamiento m **2** v/t *prisoner* indultar

reprimand [ˈreprɪmænd] reprender

reprint [ˈriːprɪnt] **1** n reimpresión f **2** v/t reimprimir

reprisal [rɪˈpraɪzl] represalia f

reproach [rɪˈprəʊtʃ] **1** n reproche m v/t: ~ *s.o.* **for sth** reprochar algo a alguien; re-

proachful de reproche

reproduce [riːprəˈduːs] **1** v/t *atmosphere, mood* reproducir **2** v/i BIO reproducirse; **reproduction** reproducción f; **reproductive** reproductivo

reptile [ˈreptaɪl] reptil m

republic [rɪˈpʌblɪk] república f; **republican** n republicano(-a) m(f)

repulsive [rɪˈpʌlsɪv] repulsivo

reputable [ˈrepjʊtəbl] reputado, acreditado; **reputation** reputación f

request [rɪˈkwest] **1** n petición f, solicitud f; **on** ~ por encargo **2** v/t pedir, solicitar

require [rɪˈkwaɪr] (*need*) requerir, necesitar; **required** (*necessary*) necesario; **requirement** (*need*) necesidad f; (*condition*) requisito m

requisition [rekwɪˈzɪʃn] requisar

re-route [riːˈruːt] desviar

rerun [ˈriːrʌn] **1** n of TV program reposición f **2** v/t *tape* volver a poner

reschedule [riːˈʃedjuːl] volver a programar

rescue [ˈreskjuː] **1** n rescate m **2** v/t rescatar

research [rɪˈsɜːrtʃ] investigación f; **research and development** investigación f y desarrollo; **researcher** investigador(a) m(f)

resemblance [rɪˈzembləns] parecido m, semejanza f; **resemble** parecerse a

resent [rɪˈzent] estar molesto

por; **resentful** resentido; **resentment** resentimiento *m*

reservation [rezər'veɪʃn] reserva *f*; **reserve 1** *n* reserva *f*; SP reserva *m/f* **2** *v/t* reservar; *judgment* reservarse; **reserved** *table, manner* reservado

reservoir ['rezərvwɑːr] *for water* embalse *m*

residence ['rezɪdəns] *fml: house etc* residencia *f*; *(stay)* estancia *f*; **resident** residente *m/f*; **residential** residencial

residue ['rezɪduː] residuo *m*

resign [rɪ'zaɪn] **1** *v/t position* dimitir de; **~ o.s. to** resignarse a **2** *v/i from job* dimitir; **resignation** *from job* dimisión *f*; *mental* resignación *f*

resilient [rɪ'zɪliənt] *personality* fuerte; *material* resistente

resist [rɪ'zɪst] **1** *v/t* resistir; *new measures* oponer resistencia a **2** *v/i* resistir; **resistance** resistencia *f*; **resistant** *material* resistente

resolution [rezə'luːʃn] resolución *f*; *at New Year etc* propósito *m*

resort [rɪ'zɔːrt] *place* centro *m* turístico; **as a last ~** como último recurso

◆ **resort to** recurrir a

◆ **resound with** [rɪ'zaʊnd] resonar con

resounding [rɪ'zaʊndɪŋ] *success, victory* clamoroso

resource [rɪ'sɔːrs] recurso *m*; **resourceful** *person* lleno de

recursos; *approach* ingenioso

respect [rɪ'spekt] **1** *n* respeto *m*; **in this / that ~** en cuanto a esto / eso; **in many ~s** en muchos aspectos **2** *v/t* respetar; **respectability** respetabilidad *f*; **respectable** respetable; **respectful** respetuoso; **respective** respectivo; **respectively** respectivamente

respiration [respɪ'reɪʃn] respiración *f*; **respirator** MED respirador *m*

respond [rɪ'spɑːnd] responder; **response** respuesta *f*

responsibility [rɪspɑːnsɪ'bɪlətɪ] responsabilidad *f*; **responsible** reponsable (**for** de); *job* de responsabilidad

rest¹ [rest] **1** *n* descanso *m* **2** *v/i* descansar **3** *v/t (lean, balance)* apoyar

rest² [rest]: **the ~** el resto

restaurant ['restrɑːnt] restaurante *m*

restful ['restfəl] tranquilo; **rest home** residencia *f* de ancianos; **restless** inquieto; **restlessly** sin descanso

restoration [restə'reɪʃn] restauración *f*; **restore** *building etc* restaurar; *(bring back)* devolver

restrain [rɪ'streɪn] contener; **restraint** *(moderation)* moderación *f*

restrict [rɪ'strɪkt] restringir; **restricted** *view* limitado; **restriction** restricción *f* '**rest room** aseo *m*, servicios *mpl*

result [rɪ'zʌlt] resultado *m*; **as a ~ of this** como resultado de esto

resume [rɪ'zuːm] **1** *v/t* reanudar **2** *v/i* continuar

résumé ['rezʊmeɪ] currículum *m* (vitae)

resumption [rɪ'zʌmpʃn] reanudación *f*

resurface [riː'sɜːfɪs] **1** *v/t* roads volver a asfaltar **2** *v/i* (reappear) reaparecer

resurrection [rezə'rekʃn] REL resurrección *f*

retail ['riːteɪl] **1** *adv*: **sell sth ~** vender algo al por menor **2** *v/i*: **it ~s at** su precio de venta al público es de; **retailer** minorista *m/f*

retain [rɪ'teɪn] conservar; *heat* retener; **retainer** FIN anticipo *m*

retaliate [rɪ'tælɪeɪt] tomar represalias; **retaliation** represalias *fpl*

rethink [riː'θɪŋk] replantear

reticence ['retɪsns] reserva *f*; **reticent** reservado

retire [rɪ'taɪr] *from work* jubilarse; **retired** jubilado; **retirement** jubilación *f*; **retiring** retraído

retort [rɪ'tɔːt] **1** *n* réplica *f* **2** *v/t* replicar

retract [rɪ'trækt] *claws* retraer; *undercarriage* replegar; *statement* retirar

'**re-train** reciclar

retreat [rɪ'triːt] **1** *v/i* retirarse

2 *n* MIL retirada *f*; *place* retiro *m*

retrieve [rɪ'triːv] recuperar

retroactive [retrəʊ'æktɪv] retroactivo; **retroactively** con retroactividad

retrograde ['retrəɡreɪd] retrógrado

retrospective [retrə'spektɪv] retrospectiva *f*

return [rɪ'tɜːn] **1** *n* to a place vuelta *f*, regreso *m*; (giving back) devolución *f*; COMPUT retorno *m*; *in tennis* resto *m*; (profit) rendimiento *m*; *Br ticket* billete *m* or *L.Am.* boleto *m* de ida y vuelta; **many happy ~s (of the day)** feliz cumpleaños; **in ~ for** a cambio de **2** *v/t* devolver; (put back) volver a colocar **3** *v/i* (go back, come back) volver, regresar; *of good times, doubts* volver

reunification [riːjuːnɪfɪ'keɪʃn] reunificación *f*

reunion [riː'juːnjən] reunión *f*; **reunite** reunir

reusable [riː'juːzəbl] reutilizable; **reuse** reutilizar

◆ **rev up** [rev] *engine* revolucionar

revaluation [riːvæljʊ'eɪʃn] revaluación *f*

reveal [rɪ'viːl] revelar; **revealing** *remark* revelador; *dress* insinuante, atrevido; **revelation** revelación *f*

revenge [rɪ'vendʒ] venganza *f*; **take one's ~** vengarse

revenue ['revənuː] ingresos

mpl

reverberate [rɪˈvɜːrbəreɪt] *of sound* reverberar

revere [rɪˈvɪr] reverenciar; **reverence** reverencia *f*; **reverent** reverente

reverse [rɪˈvɜːrs] **1** *adj sequence* inverso **2** *n (back)* dorso *m*; MOT marcha *f* atrás; **the ~** *(the opposite)* lo contrario **3** *v/i* MOT hacer marcha atrás

review [rɪˈvjuː] **1** *n of book, movie* reseña *f*; *of situation etc* revisión *f* **2** *v/t book, movie* reseñar; *troops* pasar revista a; *situation etc* revisar; EDU repasar; **reviewer** *of book, movie* crítico(-a) *m(f)*

revise [rɪˈvaɪz] *opinion, text* revisar; **revision** revisión *f*

revival [rɪˈvaɪvl] *of custom, old style* resurgimiento *m*; *of patient* reanimación *f*; **revive 1** *v/t custom, old style* hacer resurgir; *patient* reanimar **2** *v/i of business, exchange rate etc* reactivarse

revoke [rɪˈvouk] *law* derogar; *license* revocar

revolt [rɪˈvoult] **1** *n* rebelión *f* **2** *v/i* rebelarse; **revolting** repugnante; **revolution** POL, *(turn)* revolución *f*; **revolutionary 1** *n* POL revolucionario(-a) *m(f)* **2** *adj* revolucionario; **revolutionize** revolucionar

revolve [rɪˈvɑːlv] girar *(around* en torno a); **revolv-**

er revólver *m*

revulsion [rɪˈvʌlʃn] repugnancia *f*

reward [rɪˈwɔːrd] **1** *n* recompensa *f* **2** *v/t financially* recompensar; **rewarding** *experience* gratificante

rewind [riːˈwaɪnd] *film, tape* rebobinar

rewrite [riːˈraɪt] reescribir

rhetoric [ˈretərɪk] retórica *f*

rhyme [raɪm] **1** *n* rima *f* **2** *v/i* rimar

rhythm [ˈrɪðm] ritmo *m*

rib [rɪb] ANAT costilla *f*

ribbon [ˈrɪbən] cinta *f*

rice [raɪs] arroz *m*

rich [rɪtʃ] **1** *adj rich; food* sabroso **2** *npl:* **the ~** los ricos

ricochet [ˈrɪkəʃeɪ] rebotar

rid [rɪd]: **get ~ of** deshacerse de

ride [raɪd] **1** *n on horse, in vehicle* paseo *m*, vuelta *f*; *(journey)* viaje *m*; **do you want a ~ into town?** ¿quieres que te lleve al centro? **2** *v/t horse* montar a; *bike* montar en **3** *v/i on horse* montar; **rider** *on horse* jinete *m*, amazona *f*; *on bicycle* ciclista *m/f*; *on motorbike* motorista *m/f*

ridge [rɪdʒ] *borde m*; *of mountain* cresta *f*; *of roof* caballete *m*

ridicule [ˈrɪdɪkjuːl] **1** *n* burlas *fpl* **2** *v/t* ridiculizar; **ridiculous** ridículo; **ridiculously** *expensive, difficult* terriblemente

riding [ˈraɪdɪŋ] *on horseback*

equitación f

rifle ['raɪfl] rifle m

rift [rɪft] in earth grieta f; in party etc escisión f

rig [rɪg] **1** n (oil ~) plataforma f petrolífera; (truck) camión m **2** v/t elections amañar

right [raɪt] **1** adj (correct) correcto; (suitable) adecuado, apropiado; (not left) derecho; **be** ~ of answer estar correcto; of person tener razón; of clock ir bien; **put things** ~ arreglar las cosas; **that's all** ~ doesn't matter no te preocupes; when s.o. says thank you de nada; is quite good está bastante bien; **I'm all** ~ not hurt estoy bien; have got enough no, gracias **2** adv (directly) justo; (correctly) correctamente; (not left) a la derecha; ~ **now** ahora mismo **3** n civil, legal etc derecho m; not left, POL derecha f; **be in the** ~ tener razón

right-'angle ángulo m recto; **rightful** owner etc legítimo; **right-handed** person diestro; **right-hand man** mano f derecha; **right of way** in traffic preferencia f; across land derecho m de paso; **right wing** POL derecha f; SP banda f derecha; **right-wing** POL de derechas

rigid ['rɪdʒɪd] rígido

rigor ['rɪgər] rigor m; **rigorous** riguroso; **rigorously** check rigurosamente

rigour Br → **rigor**

rile [raɪl] F fastidiar, Span mosquear F

rim [rɪm] of wheel llanta f; of cup borde m; of eye glasses montura f

ring¹ [rɪŋ] n (circle) círculo m; on finger anillo m; in boxing cuadrilátero m, ring m; at circus pista f

ring² [rɪŋ] **1** n of bell timbrazo m; of voice tono m **2** v/t bell hacer sonar; Br TELEC llamar **3** v/i of bell sonar

'ringleader cabecilla m / f; **'ring-pull** anilla f

rink [rɪŋk] pista f de patinaje

rinse [rɪns] **1** n for hair color reflejo m **2** v/t aclarar

riot ['raɪət] **1** n disturbio m **2** v/i causar disturbios; **rioter** alborotador(a) m(f); **riot police** policía f antidisturbios

rip [rɪp] **1** n in cloth etc rasgadura f **2** v/t cloth rasgar

♦ **rip off** F customers robar F

ripe [raɪp] fruit maduro; **ripen** of fruit madurar; **ripeness** madurez f

'rip-off F robo m F

ripple ['rɪpl] on water onda f

rise [raɪz] **1** v/i from chair etc levantarse; of sun salir; of rocket ascender, subir; of price, temperature, water subir **2** n in price, temperature subida f, aumento m; in water level subida f; in salary aumento m

risk [rɪsk] **1** n riesgo m; **take a** ~ arriesgarse **2** v/t arriesgar; **risky** arriesgado

ritual ['rɪtʊəl] **1** n ritual m **2** adj ritual

rival ['raɪvl] **1** n rival m/f **2** v/t rivalizar con; **rivalry** rivalidad f

river ['rɪvər] río m; **riverbank** ribera f; **riverbed** lecho m; **riverside 1** adj **the ~** el Río de la Plata; **riverside 1** adj **the ~** a la orilla del río **2** n ribera f, orilla f del río

riveting ['rɪvɪtɪŋ] fascinante

road [roʊd] in country carretera f; in city calle f; **roadblock** control m de carretera; **road-holding** of vehicle adherencia f; **road map** mapa m de carreteras; **road safety** seguridad f vial; **roadsign** señal f de tráfico; **roadway** calzada f; **roadworthy** en condiciones de circular

roam [roʊm] vagar; **roaming** IT roaming m, itinerancia f

roar [rɔːr] **1** n of traffic estruendo m; of lion rugido m; of person grito m, bramido m **2** v/i of engine, lion rugir; of person gritar, bramar

roast [roʊst] **1** n of beef etc asado m **2** v/t asar **3** v/i of food asarse; **roast beef** rosbif m

rob [rɑːb] person robar a; bank atracar, robar; **robber** atracador(a) m(f); **robbery** atraco m, robo m

robe [roʊb] of judge toga f; of priest sotana f; (bath~) bata f

robot ['roʊbɑːt] robot m

robust [roʊˈbʌst] robusto;

material resistente

rock [rɑːk] **1** n roca f; MUS rock m **2** v/t baby acunar; cradle mecer; (surprise) impactar **3** v/i on chair mecerse; of boat balancearse; **rock-bottom** prices mínimo; **rock climber** escalador(a) m(f); **rock climbing** escalada f (en roca)

rocket ['rɑːkɪt] **1** n cohete m **2** v/i of prices etc dispararse

rocking chair ['rɑːkɪŋ] mecedora f; **rock 'n' roll** rock and roll m; **rocky** beach pedregoso

rod [rɑːd] vara f; for fishing caña f

rodent ['roʊdnt] roedor m

rogue [roʊg] granuja m/f

role [roʊl] papel m; **role model** ejemplo m

roll [roʊl] **1** n (bread) panecillo m; of film rollo m; (list, register) lista **2** v/i of ball etc rodar

◆ **roll over 1** v/i darse la vuelta **2** v/t person, object dar la vuelta a; (renew) renovar; (extend) refinanciar

'roll-call lista f; **roller** for hair rulo m; **roller blade**® patín m en línea; **roller coaster** montaña f rusa; **roller skate** patín m (de ruedas)

ROM [rɑːm] COMPUT (= read only memory) ROM f (= memoria f de sólo lectura)

Roman 'Catholic 1 n REL católico(-a) m(f) romano(-a) **2** adj católico romano

romance [rə'mæns] (*affair*) aventura *f* (amorosa); *novel* novela *f* rosa; *movie* película *f* romántica; **romantic** romántico

roof [ru:f] techo *m*, tejado *m*; **roof-rack** MOT baca *f*

rookie ['rʊkɪ] F novato(-a) *m(f)*

room [ru:m] habitación *f*; (*space*) espacio *m*, sitio *m*; **room clerk** recepcionista *m/f*; **roommate** compañero(-a) *m(f)* de habitación; *sharing apartment* compañero(-a) *m(f)* de piso; **room service** servicio *m* de habitaciones; **room temperature** temperatura *f* ambiente; **roomy** *car etc* espacioso; *clothes* holgado

root [ru:t] raíz *f*

rope [rəʊp] cuerda *f*; *thick* soga *f*

rosary ['rəʊzərɪ] REL rosario *m*

rose [rəʊz] BOT rosa *f*

roster ['rɒstər] turnos *mpl*; *actual document* calendario *m* con los turnos

rostrum ['rɒstrəm] estrado *m*

rosy ['rəʊzɪ] *cheeks* sonrosado; *future* de color de rosa

rot [rɒt] **1** *n in wood* putrefacción *f* **2** *v/i of food, wood* pudrirse; *of teeth* cariarse

rotate [rəʊ'teɪt] **1** *v/i* girar **2** *v/t* hacer girar; *crops* rotar; **rotation** rotación *f*

rotten ['rɒtn] *food, wood etc* podrido; F *weather, luck* horrible

rough [rʌf] **1** *adj surface, ground* accidentado; *hands, skin* áspero; *voice* ronco; (*violent*) bruto; *crossing* movido; *seas* bravo; (*approximate*) aproximado **2** *n in golf* rough *m*; **roughage** *in food* fibra *f*; **roughly** (*approximately*) aproximadamente; (*harshly*) brutalmente

roulette [ru:'let] ruleta *f*

round [raʊnd] **1** *adj* redondo **2** *n of mailman, drinks, competition* ronda *f*; *in boxing* round *m*, asalto *m* **3** *v/t corner* doblar **4** *adv & prep* ☞ **around**

◆ **round up** *figure* redondear (hacia la cifra más alta); *suspects, criminals* detener

roundabout ['raʊndəbaʊt] **1** *adj* indirecto **2** *n Br on road* rotonda *f*, *Span* glorieta *f*; **round-the-world** alrededor del mundo; **round trip** viaje *m* de ida y vuelta; **round-up** *of cattle* rodeo *m*; *of suspects* redada *f*; *of news* resumen *m*

rouse [raʊz] *from sleep* despertar; *emotions* excitar; **rousing** emocionante

route [raʊt] ruta *f*, recorrido *m*

routine [ru:'ti:n] **1** *adj* habitual **2** *n* rutina *f*

row¹ [rəʊ] *n* (*line*) hilera *f* **3 days in a ~** 3 días seguidos

row² [rəʊ] *v/i in boat* remar

rowboat bote *m* de remos

rowdy ['raʊdɪ] alborotador,

Span follonero

royal ['rɔɪəl] real; **royalty** realeza *f*; *on book etc* derechos *mpl* de autor

rub [rʌb] frotar

rubber ['rʌbər] **1** *n material* goma *f*, caucho *m* **2** *adj* de goma *or* caucho; **rubber band** goma *f* elástica

rubble ['rʌbl] escombros *mpl*

ruby ['ruːbɪ] *jewel* rubí *m*

rudder ['rʌdər] timón *m*

ruddy ['rʌdɪ] *face* rubicundo

rude [ruːd] *person, behavior* maleducado, grosero; *language* grosero; **rudely** (*impolitely*) groseramente; **rudeness** mala *f* educación, grosería *f*

rudimentary [ruːdɪ'mentərɪ] rudimentario; **rudiments** rudimentos *mpl*

rueful ['ruːfl] arrepentido; **ruefully** con arrepentimiento

ruffian ['rʌfɪən] rufián *m*

ruffle ['rʌfl] **1** *n on dress* volante *m* **2** *v/t hair* despeinar; *clothes* arrugar; *person* alterar

rug [rʌg] alfombra *f*; (*blanket*) manta *f* (de viaje)

rugby ['rʌgbɪ] rugby *m*

rugged ['rʌgɪd] *scenery* escabroso; *face* de rasgos duros; *resistance* decidido

ruin ['ruːɪn] **1** *n* ruina *f* **2** *v/t* arruinar

rule [ruːl] **1** *n* regla *f*; *of monarch* reinado *m*; **as a ~** por regla general **2** *v/t country*

gobernar **3** *v/i of monarch* reinar; **ruler** *for measuring* regla *f*; *of state* gobernante *m/f*; **ruling 1** *n* fallo *m*, decisión *f* **2** *adj party* gobernante, en el poder

rum [rʌm] *drink* ron *m*

rumble ['rʌmbl] *of stomach* gruñir; *of thunder* retumbar

rumor, *Br* **rumour** ['ruːmər] **1** *n* rumor *m* **2** *v/t*: **it is ~ed that ...** se rumorea que...

rump [rʌmp] *of animal* cuartos *mpl* traseros

rumple ['rʌmpl] arrugar

rump 'steak filete *m* de lomo

run [rʌn] **1** *n on foot, in pantyhose* carrera *f*; *Br: in car* viaje *m*; THEA: *of play* temporada *f*; **in the short / long ~** a corto / largo plazo **2** *v/i* correr; *of river* correr, discurrir; *of paint, make-up* correrse; *of play* estar en cartel; *of engine, software* funcionar; *in election* presentarse; **~ for President** presentarse a las elecciones presidenciales **3** *v/t race* correr; *business etc* dirigir; *software* usar; *car* tener; (*use*) usar

◆ **run away** salir corriendo, huir; *from home* escaparse

◆ **run down** *v/t* (*knock down*) atropellar; (*criticize*) criticar; *stocks* reducir *v/i of battery* agotarse

◆ **run off** *v/i* salir corriendo **2** *v/t* (*print off*) tirar

◆ **run out** *of contract* vencer; *of supplies* agotarse

◆ **run out of** quedarse sin
◆ **run over 1** *v/t (knock down)* atropellar **2** *v/i of water etc* desbordarse
◆ **run up** *debts* acumular

runaway ['rʌnəweɪ] *persona que se ha fugado de casa*; **run-down** *person* débil; *part of town* ruinoso

rung [rʌŋ] *of ladder* peldaño *m*

runner ['rʌnər] *athlete* corredor(a) *m(f)*; **runner beans** judías *fpl* verdes, *L.Am.* porotos *mpl* verdes, *Mex* ejotes *mpl*; **runner-up** subcampeón(-ona) *m(f)*; **running 1** *n* SP el correr; *(jogging)* footing *m*; *of business* gestión *f* **2** *adj*: **for two days** ~ durante dos días seguidos; **running water** agua *f* corriente; **running mixture** fluido; *nose que* moquea; **run-up** SP élan *m*; **in the ~ to** en el periodo previo a; **runway** pista *f* (de ate-

rrizaje / despegue)

rupture ['rʌptʃər] **1** *n* ruptura *f* **2** *v/i of pipe etc* romperse

rural ['ruərəl] rural

ruse [ru:z] artimaña *f*

rush [rʌʃ] **1** *n* prisa *f* **2** *v/t person* meter prisa a; *meal* comer a toda prisa **3** *v/i* darse prisa; **rush hour** hora *f* punta

Russia ['rʌʃə] Rusia; **Russian 1** *adj* ruso (-a) **2** *n* ruso(-a) *m(f)*; *language* ruso *m*

rust [rʌst] **1** *n* óxido *m* **2** *v/i* oxidarse; **rust-proof** inoxidable; **rusty** oxidado

rut [rʌt] *in road* rodada *f*; **be in a ~** *fig* estar estancado

ruthless ['ru:θlɪs] implacable, despiadado; **ruthlessly** sin compasión, despiadadamente; **ruthlessness** falta *f* de compasión

rye [raɪ] centeno *m*; **rye bread** pan *m* de centeno

S

sabotage ['sæbətɑːʒ] **1** *n* sabotaje *m* **2** *v/t* sabotear; **saboteur** saboteador(a) *m(f)*

sachet ['sæʃeɪ] sobrecito *m*

sack [sæk] **1** *n bag* saco *m*; *for groceries* bolsa *f* **2** *v/t* F echar

sacred ['seɪkrɪd] sagrado

sacrifice ['sækrɪfaɪs] **1** *n* sacrificio *m* **2** *v/t* sacrificar

sacrilege ['sækrɪlɪdʒ] sacrilegio *m*

sad [sæd] triste; *state of affairs* lamentable

saddle ['sædl] **1** *n* silla *f* de montar **2** *v/t horse* ensillar

sadism ['seɪdɪzm] sadismo *m*; **sadist** sádico(-a) *m(f)*; **sadistic** sádico

sadly ['sædlɪ] con tristeza; *(regrettably)* lamentablemente; **sadness** tristeza *f*

safe [seɪf] **1** *adj* seguro; *driver*

prudente; (*not in danger*) a
salvo **2** *n* caja *f* fuerte; **safe-
guard 1** *n* garantía *f* **2** *v/t* salvaguardar; **safely** *arrive* sin
percances; *drive* prudentemente; *assume* con certeza;
safety seguridad *f*; **safety
pin** imperdible *m*

sag [sæg] *of ceiling* combarse;
of rope destensarse; *of tempo*
disminuir

saga ['sɑːɡə] saga *f*

sage [seɪdʒ] *herb* salvia *f*

sail [seɪl] **1** *n of boat* vela *f*; *trip*
viaje *m* (en barco) **2** *v/i* navegar; (*depart*) zarpar; **sailboard** *n* tabla *f* de windsurf
2 *v/i* hacer windsurf; **sailboarding** windsurf *m*; **sailboat** barco *m* de vela, velero
m; **sailing** SP vela *f*; **sailor**
marinero(-a) *m(f)*; *in the navy* marino *m/f*

saint [seɪnt] santo *m*

sake [seɪk]: *for my ~* por mí

salad ['sæləd] ensalada *f*

salary ['sælərɪ] sueldo *m*, salario *m*

sale [seɪl] venta *f*; *reduced
prices* rebajas *fpl*; **be on ~** estar a la venta; *at reduced
prices* estar de rebajas; **sales
department** ventas *fpl*; **sales
clerk** dependiente(-a) *m(f)*;
sales figures cifras *fpl* de
ventas; **salesman** vendedor
m; **saleswoman** vendedora
f

salient ['seɪlɪənt] sobresaliente, destacado

saliva [sə'laɪvə] saliva *f*

salmon ['sæmən] salmón *m*

saloon [sə'luːn] (*bar*) bar *m*;
Br MOT turismo *m*

salt [sɔːlt] sal *f*; **salty** salado

salute [sə'luːt] **1** *n* MIL saludo
2 *v/t & v/i* MIL saludar

Salvadoran [sælvə'dɔːrən]
1 *adj* salvadoreño **2** *n* salvadoreño(-a) *m(f)*

salvage ['sælvɪdʒ] *from wreck*
rescatar

salvation [sæl'veɪʃn] *also fig*
salvación *f*

same [seɪm] **1** *adj* mismo **2**
pron: *the ~* lo mismo; *Happy
New Year* – *the ~ to you* Feliz Año Nuevo – igualmente;
all the ~ (*even so*) aun así **3**
adv: *the ~* igual

sample ['sæmpl] muestra *f*

sanction ['sæŋkʃn] **1** *n* (*approval*) consentimiento *m*;
(*penalty*) sanción *f* **2** *v/t* (*approve*) sancionar

sand [sænd] **1** *n* arena *f* **2** *v/t*
with sandpaper lijar

sandal ['sændl] sandalia *f*

'sandbag saco *m* de arena,
sand dune duna *f*; **sander**
tool lijadora *f*; **sandpaper**
1 *n* lija *f* **2** *v/t* lijar

sandwich ['sænwɪtʃ] *Span* bocadillo *m*, *L.Am.* sandwich
m

sandy ['sændɪ] *soil* arenoso;
feet, towel etc lleno de arena;
hair rubio oscuro; *~ beach*
playa *f* de arena

sane [seɪn] cuerdo

sanitarium [sænɪ'terɪəm] sanatorio *m*

sanitary ['sænɪterɪ] salubre, higiénico; **sanitary napkin** compresa *f*; **sanitation** instalaciones *fpl* sanitarias; *(removal of waste)* saneamiento *m*

sanity ['sænətɪ] razón *f*, juicio *m*

Santa Claus ['sæntəklɔːz] Papá Noel *m*, Santa Claus *m*

sap [sæp] **1** *n* in tree savia *f* **2** *v/t s.o.'s energy* consumir

sapphire ['sæfaɪr] zafiro *m*

sarcasm ['sɑːrkæzm] sarcasmo *m*; **sarcastic** sarcástico; **sarcastically** sarcásticamente

sardine [sɑːr'diːn] sardina *f*

sardonic [sɑːr'dɑːnɪk] sardónico

satellite ['sætəlaɪt] satélite *m*; **satellite dish** antena *f* parabólica; **satellite TV** televisión *f* por satélite

satin ['sætɪn] satén *m*

satire ['sætaɪr] sátira *f*; **satirical** [sə'tɪrɪkl] satírico; **satirize** satirizar

satisfaction [sætɪs'fækʃn] satisfacción *f*; **satisfactory** satisfactorio; *(just good enough)* suficiente; **satisfy** satisfacer; *conditions* cumplir

Saturday ['sætərdeɪ] sábado *m*

sauce [sɔːs] salsa *f*; **saucepan** cacerola *f*; **saucer** plato *m (de taza)*

Saudi Arabia [saudɪə'reɪbɪə] Arabia Saudí *or* Saudita; **Saudi Arabian 1** *adj* saudita,

saudí **2** *n* saudita *m/f*, saudí *m/f*

sausage ['sɔːsɪdʒ] salchicha *f*

savage ['sævɪdʒ] **1** *adj* salvaje; *criticism* feroz **2** *n* salvaje *m/f*; **savagery** crueldad *f*

save [seɪv] **1** *v/t (rescue)* rescatar, salvar; *money, time* ahorrar; *(collect)*, COMPUT guardar; *goal* parar; REL salvar **2** *v/i (put money aside)* ahorrar; SP hacer una parada **3** *n* SP parada *f*; **saver** *person* ahorrador(a) *m(f)*; **savings** ahorros *mpl*; **savings account** cuenta *f* de ahorros; **savings and loan** caja *f* de ahorros; **savings bank** caja *f* de ahorros

savior, *Br* **saviour** ['seɪvjər] REL salvador *m*

savor ['seɪvər] saborear; **savory** *not sweet* salado

savour *etc Br* → **savor** *etc*

saw [sɔː] **1** *n tool* serrucho *m*, sierra *f* **2** *v/t* aserrar; **sawdust** serrín *m*, aserrín *m*

saxophone ['sæksəfoun] saxofón *m*

say [seɪ] decir; *that is to ~* es decir; *saying* dicho *m*

scab [skæb] *on skin* costra *f*

scaffolding ['skæfəldɪŋ] *on building* andamiaje *m*

scald [skɔːld] escaldar

scale[1] [skeɪl] *n on fish* escama *f*

scale[2] [skeɪl] **1** *n (size)* escala *f*, tamaño *m*; *on thermometer, map*, MUS escala *f* **2** *v/t cliffs etc* escalar

scales [skeɪlz] *for weighing* báscula *f*, peso *m*

scallop ['skæləp] *shellfish* vieira *f*

scalp [skælp] cuero *m* cabelludo

scalpel ['skælpl] bisturí *m*

scam [skæm] F chanchullo *m* F

scampi ['skæmpɪ] gambas *fpl* rebozadas

scan [skæn] **1** *v/t horizon* otear; *page* ojear; COMPUT escanear **2** *n of brain* escáner *m*; *of fetus* ecografía *f*
◆ **scan in** COMPUT escanear

scandal ['skændl] escándalo *m*; **scandalize** escandalizar; **scandalous** escandaloso

scanner ['skænər] MED, COMPUT escáner *m*; *for fetus* ecógrafo *m*

scanty ['skæntɪ] *skirt* cortísimo; *bikini* mínimo

scapegoat ['skeɪpgoʊt] cabeza *f* de turco

scar [skɑːr] **1** *n* cicatriz *f* **2** *v/t* cicatrizar

scarce [skers] *in short supply* escaso; **scarcely:** ~ *anything* casi nada; *I* ~ *know her* apenas la conozco; **scarcity** escasez *f*

scare [sker] **1** *v/t* asustar, **be** ~**d of** tener miedo de **2** *n* (*panic, alarm*) miedo *m*, temor *m*; **scaremonger** alarmista *m/f*

scarf [skɑːrf] pañuelo *m*; *woollen* bufanda *f*

scarlet ['skɑːrlət] escarlata

scary ['skerɪ] espeluznante

scathing ['skeɪðɪŋ] feroz

scatter ['skætər] **1** *v/t leaflets* esparcir; *seeds* diseminar **2** *v/i of people* dispersarse; **scattered** disperso

scavenge ['skævɪndʒ] rebuscar; **scavenger** carroñero *m*; (*person*) persona *que busca comida entre la basura*

scenario [sɪ'nɑːrɪoʊ] situación *f*

scene [siːn] escena *f*; *of accident, crime* lugar *m*; (*argument*) escena *f*, número *m*; *behind the* ~**s** entre bastidores; **scenery** paisaje *m*; THEA escenario *m*

scent [sent] olor *m*; (*perfume*) perfume *m*, fragancia *f*

sceptic *etc Br* ► **skeptic** *etc*

schedule ['skedjuːl] **1** *n of events, work* programa *m*; *of exams* calendario *m*; *for train, work, of lessons* horario *m*; **be on** ~ *of work* ir según lo previsto; *of train* ir a la hora prevista; **be behind** ~ in con retraso **2** *v/t* (*put on* ~) programar; **scheduled flight** vuelo *m* regular

scheme [skiːm] **1** *n* (*plan*) plan *m*; (*plot*) confabulación *f* **2** *v/i* (*plot*) confabularse; **scheming** maquinador

schizophrenia [skɪtsə'friːnɪə] esquizofrenia *f*; **schizophrenic 1** *n* esquizofrénico(-a) *m(f)* **2** *adj* esquizofrénico

scholar ['skɒlər] erudito(-a) *m(f)*; **scholarly** erudito; **scholarship** *work* estudios *mpl*; *financial award* beca *f*

school[1] [skuːl] escuela *f*, colegio *m*; *(university)* universidad *f*; **school bag** cartera *f*; **schoolchildren** escolares *mpl*

science ['saɪəns] ciencia *f*; **scientific** científico; **scientist** científico(-a) *m(f)*

scissors ['sɪzərz] tijeras *fpl*

scoff[1] [skɒf] F *(eat fast)* zamparse F

scoff[2] [skɒf] *(mock)* burlarse, mofarse

scold [skould] regañar

scoop [skuːp] *n* cuchara *f*; *story* exclusiva *f*

scooter ['skuːtər] *with motor* escúter *m*; *child's* patinete *m*

scope [skoup] alcance *m*; *(freedom, opportunity)* oportunidad *f*

scorch [skɔːrtʃ] quemar; **scorching** abrasador

score [skɔːr] 1 *n* SP resultado *m*; *in competition* puntuación *f*; *(written music)* partitura *f*; *of movie etc* banda *f* sonora 2 *v/t goal, line* marcar; *point* anotar 3 *v/i* marcar; *(keep the ~)* llevar el tanteo; **scoreboard** marcador *m*; **scorer** *of goal* goleador(a) *m(f)*; *of point* anotador(a) *m(f)*

scorn [skɔːrn] 1 *n* desprecio *m* 2 *v/t idea* despreciar; **scornful** despreciativo

scornfully con desprecio

Scot [skɒt] escocés(-esa) *m(f)*; **Scotch** *(whiskey)* whisky *m* escocés; **Scotch tape**® celo *m*, *L.Am.* Durex® *m*; **Scotland** Escocia; **Scottish** escocés

scoundrel ['skaundrəl] canalla *m / f*

scour [skaur] *(search)* rastrear, peinar

scowl [skaul] 1 *n* ceño *m* 2 *v/i* fruncir el ceño

scramble ['skræmbl] 1 *n* *(rush)* prisa *f* 2 *v/t message* cifrar 3 *v/i* *(climb)* trepar; **scrambled eggs** huevos *mpl* revueltos

scrap [skræp] 1 *n* *metal* chatarra *f*; *(fight)* pelea *f*; *of food* trocito *m*; *of common sense* pizca *f* 2 *v/t plan* abandonar; *paragraph* borrar

scrape [skreip] 1 *n* *on paintwork etc* arañazo *m* 2 *v/t paintwork* rayar

'scrap metal chatarra *f*

scrappy ['skræpi] *work, play* desorganizado

scratch [skrætʃ] 1 *n* *mark* marca *f*; **start from ~** empezar desde cero; **not up to ~** insuficiente 2 *v/t* *(mark: skin)* arañar; *(mark: paint)* rayar; *because of itch* rascarse 3 *v/i* *of cat etc* arañar; *because of itch* rascarse

scrawl [skrɔːl] 1 *n* garabato *m* 2 *v/t* garabatear

scrawny ['skrɔːni] escuálido

scream [skriːm] *m* grito *m* 2

screech

494

v/i gritar

screech [skriːtʃ] **1** *n* of tires chirrido *m*; (scream) chillido *m* **2** *v/i* of tires chirriar; (scream) chillar

screen [skriːn] **1** *n* in room, hospital mampara *f*; protective cortina *f*; in movie theater, COMPUT pantalla *f* **2** *v/t* (protect, hide) ocultar; movie proyectar; for security reasons investigar; **screenplay** guión *m*; **screen saver** COMPUT salvapantallas *m inv*; **screen test** prueba *f*

screw [skruː] **1** *n* tornillo *m* **2** *v/t* atornillar (**to** a); V (have sex with) echar un polvo con V; F (cheat) timar F; **screwdriver** destornillador *m*; **screwed up** F acomplejado; **screwy** F chiflado F; idea, film descabellado F

scribble ['skrɪbl] **1** *n* garabato *m* **2** *v/t & v/i* garabatear

script [skrɪpt] *n* of movie guión *m*; form of writing caligrafía *f*; **scripture: the (Holy) Scriptures** las Sagradas Escrituras; **scriptwriter** guionista *m / f*

◆ **scroll down** [skroʊl] COMPUT avanzar

◆ **scroll up** COMPUT retroceder

scrounge [skraʊndʒ] gorronear; **scrounger** gorrón (-ona) *m(f)*

scrub [skrʌb] floors fregar; hands frotar

scruples ['skruːplz] escrúpu-

los *mpl*; **scrupulous** with moral principles escrupuloso; (thorough) meticuloso; attention to detail minucioso; **scrupulously** (meticulously) minuciosamente

scrutinize ['skruːtɪnaɪz] estudiar, examinar; **scrutiny** escrutinio *m*

scuba diving ['skuːbə] submarinismo *m*

scuffle ['skʌfl] riña *f*

sculptor ['skʌlptər] escultor(a) *m(f)*; **sculpture** escultura *f*

scum [skʌm] on liquid película *f* de suciedad; pej: people escoria *f*

sea [siː] mar *m*; **seabird** ave *f* marina; **seafood** marisco *m*; **seagull** gaviota *f*

seal¹ [siːl] *n* animal foca *f*

seal² [siːl] **1** *n* on document, tech sello *m* **2** *v/t* container sellar

seam [siːm] on garment costura *f*; of ore filón *m*

seaman marinero *m*; **seaport** puerto *m* marítimo

search [sɜːrtʃ] **1** *n* búsqueda *f* **2** *v/t* registrar

◆ **search for** buscar

searching ['sɜːrtʃɪŋ] look escrutador; question difícil; **searchlight** reflector *m*

seashore orilla *f*; **seasick** mareado; **get ~** marearse; **seaside** costa *f*, playa *f*

season ['siːzn] estación *f*; *for tourism etc* temporada *f*; **seasonal** *fruit, vegetables* del tiempo; *employment* temporal; **seasoned** *wood* seco; *traveler, campaigner* experimentado; **seasoning** condimento *m*; **season ticket** abono *m*

seat [siːt] asiento *m*; *in theater* butaca *f*; *of pants* culera *f*; *please take a ~* por favor, siéntese; **seat belt** cinturón *m* de seguridad

seaweed alga(s) *f(pl)*

secluded [sɪ'kluːdɪd] apartado

second ['sekənd] **1** *n of time* segundo *m* **2** *adj* segundo **3** *adv come in* en segundo lugar **4** *v/t motion* apoyar; **secondary** secundario; **second floor** primer piso *m*, *Br* segundo piso *m*; **second-hand** de segunda mano; **secondly** en segundo lugar; **second-rate** inferior

secrecy ['siːkrəsɪ] secretismo *m*; **secret** **1** *n* secreto *m* **2** *adj* secreto

secretarial [sekrə'terɪəl] de secretario; **secretary** secretario(-a) *m(f)*; POL ministro(-a) *m(f)*; **Secretary of State** *in USA* Secretario(-a) *m(f)* de Estado

secretive ['siːkrətɪv] reservado; **secretly** en secreto

sect [sekt] secta *f*

section ['sekʃn] sección *f*; *of building* zona *f*; *of apple* parte *f*

sector ['sektər] sector *m*

secular ['sekjələr] laico

secure [sɪ'kjʊr] **1** *adj shelf etc* seguro; *job, contract* fijo **2** *v/t shelf etc* asegurar; *help* conseguir; **se'curities market** FIN mercado *m* de valores; **security** seguridad *f*; *for investment* garantía *f*; **security alert** alerta *f*; **security forces** fuerzas *fpl* de seguridad; **security guard** guardia *m/f* de seguridad; **security risk** *person* peligro *m* (para la seguridad)

sedan [sɪ'dæn] MOT turismo *m*

sedate [sɪ'deɪt] sedar

sedative ['sedətɪv] sedante *m*

sedentary ['sedənterɪ] *job* sedentario

sediment ['sedɪmənt] sedimento *m*

seduce [sɪ'duːs] seducir; **seduction** seducción *f*; **seductive** *dress* seductor; *offer* tentador

see [siː] ver; *~ you!* F ¡hasta la vista!, ¡chao! F

◆ **see off** *at airport etc* despedir; *(chase away)* espantar

seed [siːd] semilla *f*; *in tennis* cabeza *f* de serie; **seedy** *bar, district* de mala calaña

seeing 'eye dog ['siːɪŋ] perro *m* lazarillo; **seeing (that)** dado que, ya que

seek [siːk] buscar

seem [siːm] parecer; **seemingly** aparentemente

seesaw ['si:sɔ:] subibaja *m*
'see-through transparente
segment ['segmənt] segmento *m*
segregate ['segrɪgeɪt] segregar; **segregation** segregación *f*
seismology [saɪz'mɑ:lədʒɪ] sismología *f*
seize [si:z] *s.o., s.o.'s arm* agarrar; *opportunity* aprovechar; *of Customs, police etc* incautarse de; **seizure** MED ataque *m*; *of drugs etc* incautación *f*; *amount seized* alijo *m*
seldom ['seldəm] raramente, casi nunca
select [sɪ'lekt] **1** *v/t* seleccionar **2** *adj (exclusive)* selecto; **selection** selección *f*; *(choosing)* elección *f*; **selective** selectivo
self [self] *ego m*; **self-assurance** confianza *f* en sí mismo; **self-assured** seguro de sí mismo; **self-centered**, *Br* **self-centred** egoísta; **self-confidence** confianza *f* en sí mismo; **self-confident** seguro de sí mismo; **self-conscious** tímido; **self-consciousness** timidez *f*; **self-control** autocontrol *m*; **self-defence** *Br*, **self-defense** autodefensa *f*; **in ~** en defensa propia; **self-employed** autónomo; **self-evident** evidente; **self-expression** autoexpresión *f*; **self-government** autogobierno *m*; **self-interest** interés *m* propio; **selfish** egoísta; **selfless** desinteresado; **self-made man** hombre *m* hecho a sí mismo; **self-pity** autocompasión *f*; **self-portrait** autorretrato *m*; **self-reliant** autosuficiente; **self-respect** amor *m* propio; **self-satisfied** *pej* pagado de sí mismo; **self-service** de autoservicio; **self-service restaurant** (restaurante *m*) autoservicio *m*; **self-taught** autodidacta
sell [sel] **1** *v/t* vender **2** *v/i of products* venderse; **sell-by date** fecha *f* límite de venta; **seller** vendedor(a) *m(f)*; **selling** COM ventas *fpl*; **selling point** COM ventaja *f*
Sellotape® ['seləteɪp] *Br* celo *m*, *L.Am.* Durex® *m*
semester [sɪ'mestər] semestre *m*
semi ['semɪ] *truck* camión *m* semirremolque; **semicircle** semicírculo *m*; **semiconductor** ELEC semiconductor *m*; **semifinal** semifinal *f*; **semifinalist** semifinalista *m/f*
seminar ['semɪnɑːr] seminario *m*
semi-skilled semicualificado
senate ['senət] senado *m*; **senator** senador(a) *m(f)*
send [send] enviar, mandar
♦ **send back** devolver
♦ **send for** mandar buscar
sender ['sendər] *of letter* remitente *m / f*
senile ['si:naɪl] senil; **senility**

senilidad f

senior ['si:njər] *(older)* mayor; *in rank* superior; **senior citizen** persona *f* de la tercera edad; **seniority** *in job* antigüedad *f*

sensation [sen'seɪʃn] sensación *f*; **sensational** sensacional

sense [sens] **1** *n (meaning, point, hearing etc)* sentido *m; (feeling)* sentimiento *m; (common sense)* sentido *m* común, sensatez *f*; **come to one's ~s** entrar en razón; **it doesn't make ~** no tiene sentido **2** *v/t s.o.'s presence* sentir, notar; **senseless** *(pointless)* absurdo

sensible ['sensəbl] sensato; *shoes etc* práctico, apropiado; **sensibly** con sensatez

sensitive ['sensɪtɪv] sensible; **sensitivity** sensibilidad *f*

sensor ['sensər] sensor *m*

sensual ['senʃuəl] sensual; **sensuality** sensualidad *f*

sensuous ['senʃuəs] sensual

sentence ['sentəns] **1** *n* GRAM oración *f*; LAW sentencia *f* **2** *v/t* LAW sentenciar, condenar

sentiment ['sentɪmənt] *(sentimentality)* sentimentalismo *m; (opinion)* opinión *f*; **sentimental** sentimental; **sentimentality** sentimentalismo *m*

sentry ['sentri] centinela *m*

separate 1 ['sepərət] *adj* separado **2** ['sepəreɪt] *v/t* separar **3** ['sepəreɪt] *v/i of couple* separarse; **separated** *couple* separado; **separately** *pay, treat* por separado; **separation** separación *f*

September [sep'tembər] septiembre *m*

septic ['septɪk] séptico

sequel ['si:kwəl] continuación *f*

sequence ['si:kwəns] secuencia *f*

serene [sɪ'ri:n] sereno

sergeant ['sɑːrdʒənt] sargento *m* / *f*

serial ['sɪrɪəl] serie *f*, serial *m; in magazine* novela *f* por entregas; **serialize** *novel on TV* emitir en forma de serie; *in newspaper* publicar por entregas; **serial number** *of product* número *m* de serie

series ['sɪriːz] serie *f*

serious ['sɪrɪəs] *situation, damage, illness* grave; *(person: earnest)* serio; *company* serio; **seriously** *injured* gravemente; **take s.o. ~** tomar a alguien en serio; **seriousness** *of person* seriedad *f; of situation* seriedad *f*, gravedad *f; of illness* gravedad *f*

sermon ['sɜːrmən] sermón *m*

servant ['sɜːrvənt] sirviente(-a) *m(f)*

serve [sɜːrv] **1** *n in tennis* servicio *m*, saque *m* **2** *v/t food, meal* servir; *customer in shop* atender; *one's country* servir a **3** *v/i* servir; *in tennis* servir, sacar; **server** *in tennis* jugador(a) *m(f)* al servicio; COM-

PUT servidor *m*; **service 1** *n to customers, community* servicio *m*; *for vehicle, machine* revisión *f*; *in tennis* servicio *m*, saque *m*; **~s** (*~ sector*) el sector servicios **2** *v/t vehicle, machine* revisar; **service charge** servicio *m* (tarifa); **serviceman** MIL militar *m*; **service station** estación *f* de servicio; **serving** *of food* ración *f*

session ['seʃn] sesión *f*; *with boss etc* reunión *f*

set [set] **1** *n of tools* juego *m*; *of books* colección *f*; *of people*) grupo *m*; MATH conjunto *m*; (THEA: *scenery*) decorado *m*; *where a movie is made* plató *m*; *in tennis* set *m* **2** *v/t* (*place*) colocar; *movie, novel etc* ambientar; *date, time, limit* fijar; *alarm* poner; *clock* poner en hora; *broken limb* recomponer; *jewel* engastar; **~ the table** poner la mesa **3** *v/i of sun* ponerse; *of glue* solidificarse **4** *adj ideas* fijo; (*ready*) preparado

◆ **set off 1** *v/i on journey* salir **2** *v/t bomb* hacer explotar; *chain reaction* desencadenar; *alarm* activar

◆ **set out 1** *v/i on journey* salir (**for** hacia) **2** *v/t ideas, goods* exponer

◆ **set up 1** *v/t company* establecer; *equipment, machine* instalar; *market stall* montar; *meeting* organizar; F (*frame*) tender una trampa a **2** *v/i in*

business emprender un negocio

'setback contratiempo *m*

settee [se'tiː] *Br* sofá *m*

setting ['setɪŋ] *of novel etc* escenario *m*; *of house* ubicación *f*

settle ['setl] **1** *v/i of bird, dust* posarse; *of house* hundirse; *to live* establecerse **2** *v/t dispute, uncertainty* resolver; *debts* saldar; *nerves, stomach* calmar

◆ **settle down** (*stop being noisy*) tranquilizarse; (*stop wild living*) sentar la cabeza; *in an area* establecerse

◆ **settle for** (*accept*) conformarse con

settled ['setld] *weather* estable; **settlement** *of claim* resolución *f*; *of debt* liquidación *f*; *of dispute* acuerdo *m*; (*payment*) suma *f*; *of building* hundimiento *m*; **settler** *in new country* colono *m*

'set-up (*structure*) estructura *f*; (*relationship*) relación *f*; F (*frame-up*) trampa *f*

seven ['sevn] siete; **seventeen** diecisiete; **seventeenth** décimoséptimo; **seventh** séptimo; **seventieth** septuagésimo; **seventy** setenta

sever ['sevər] cortar; *relations* romper

several ['sevrl] **1** *adj* varios **2** *pron* varios(-as) *mpl* (*fpl*)

severe [sɪ'vɪr] *illness* grave;

penalty, winter, weather severo; *teacher* estricto; **severely** *punish, speak* con severidad; *injured, disrupted* gravemente; **severity** severidad *f; of illness* gravedad *f*

Seville ['sə'ɪdʒ] Sevilla

sew [soʊ] coser

sewage ['suːɪdʒ] aguas *fpl* residuales; **sewer** alcantarilla *f,* cloaca *f*

sewing ['soʊɪŋ] *skill* costura *f; that being sewn* labor *f*

sex [seks] *sexo m;* **have ~ with** tener relaciones sexuales con; **sexist** 1 *adj* sexista 2 *n* sexista *m / f;* **sexual** sexual; **sexuality** sexualidad *f;* **sexually** sexualmente; **transmitted disease** enfermedad *f* de transmisión sexual; **sexy** sexy *inv*

shabbily ['ʃæbɪlɪ] *dressed* con desaliño; *treat* muy mal; **shabby** *coat etc* desgastado; *treatment* malo

shack [ʃæk] choza *f*

shade [ʃeɪd] 1 *n for lamp* pantalla *f; of color* persiana *f; on window* persiana *f;* **in the ~** a la sombra 2 *v/t from sun, light* proteger de la luz

shadow ['ʃædoʊ] sombra *f*

shady ['ʃeɪdɪ] *spot* umbrío; *character* sospechoso

shaft [ʃæft] TECH eje *m,* árbol *m; of mine* pozo *m*

shake [ʃeɪk] 1 *n* sacudida *f* 2 *v/t* agitar; *emotionally* conmocionar; **he shook his head** negó con la cabeza; **~**

hands with s.o. estrechar or dar la mano a alguien 3 *v/i of voice, building* temblar; **shaken** *emotionally* conmocionado; **shake-up** reestructuración *f;* **shaky** *table etc* inestable; *after illness* débil; *after shock* conmocionado; *grasp of sth* flojo; *voice, hand* tembloroso

shall [ʃæl] ◇ *future:* **I ~ do my best** haré todo lo que pueda ◇ *suggesting:* **~ we go?** ¿nos vamos?

shallow ['ʃæloʊ] *water* poco profundo; *person* superficial

shame [ʃeɪm] 1 *n* vergüenza *f, Col, Mex, Ven* pena *f;* **what a ~!** ¡qué pena or lástima! 2 *v/t* avergonzar, *Col, Mex, Ven* apenar; **shameful** vergonzoso; **shameless** desvergonzado

shampoo [ʃæm'puː] champú *m*

shanty town ['ʃæntɪ] *Span* barrio *m* de chabolas, *L.Am.* barriada *f, Arg* villa *f* miseria, *Chi* callampa *f, Mex* ciudad *f* perdida, *Urug* cantegril *m*

shape [ʃeɪp] 1 *n* forma *f* 2 *v/t clay* modelar; *character* determinar; *the future* dar forma a; **shapeless** *dress etc* amorfo; **shapely** *figure* esbelto

share [ʃer] 1 *n* parte *f,* FIN acción *f* 2 *v/t & v/i* compartir; **shareholder** accionista *m / f*

shark [ʃɑːrk] tiburón *m*

sharp [ʃɑːrp] **1** *adj knife* afilado; *mind* vivo; *pain* agudo; *taste* ácido **2** *adv* MUS demasiado alto; **at 3 o'clock ~** a las tres en punto; **sharpen** *knife* afilar; *skills* perfeccionar

shatter [ʃætər] **1** *v/t glass* hacer añicos; *illusions* destrozar **2** *v/i of glass* hacerse añicos; **shattered** F destrozado F; **shattering** *news* demoledor

shave [ʃeɪv] **1** *v/t* afeitar **2** *v/i* afeitarse **3** *n* afeitado *m*; **shaven** *head* afeitado; **shaver** *electric* máquinilla *f* de afeitar (eléctrica)

shawl [ʃɔːl] chal *m*

she [ʃiː] ella; **~ is a student** es estudiante

sheath [ʃiːθ] *for knife* funda *f*; *contraceptive* condón *m*

shed[1] [ʃed] *v/t blood, tears* derramar; *leaves* perder

shed[2] [ʃed] *n* cobertizo *m*

sheep [ʃiːp] oveja *f*; **sheepdog** perro *m* pastor; **sheep-herder** pastor *m*; **sheepish** avergonzado

sheer [ʃɪr] verdadero; *cliffs* escarpado

sheet [ʃiːt] sábana *f*; *of paper, glass* hoja *f*; *of metal* chapa *f*

shelf [ʃelf] estante *m*; **shelves** estanterías *fpl*

shell [ʃel] **1** *n of mussel etc* concha *f*; *of egg* cáscara *f*; *of tortoise* caparazón *m*; MIL proyectil *m* **2** *v/t peas* pelar; MIL bombardear (*con artillería*); **shellfire** fuego *m* de artillería; **shellfish** marisco *m*

shelter [ʃeltər] **1** *n* refugio *m* (*bus ~*) marquesina *f* **2** *v/i* refugiarse **3** *v/t* (*protect*) proteger; **sheltered** *place* resguardado; **lead a ~ life** llevar una vida protegida

shelve [ʃelv] *fig* posponer

shepherd [ʃepərd] pastor *m*

sheriff [ʃerɪf] sheriff *m/f*

shield [ʃiːld] **1** *n* escudo *m*; TECH placa *f* protectora; *of policeman* placa *f* **2** *v/t* (*protect*) proteger

shift [ʃɪft] **1** *n* cambio *m*; *at work* turno *m* **2** *v/t* (*move*) mover; *stains etc* eliminar **3** *v/i* (*move*) moverse; (*change*) trasladarse; *of wind* cambiar; **shifty** *pej* sospechoso

shin [ʃɪn] espinilla *f*

shine [ʃaɪn] **1** *v/i* brillar; *fig of student etc* destacar (**at** en) **2** *n on shoes etc* brillo *m*; **shiny** brillante

ship [ʃɪp] **1** *n* barco *m*, buque *m* **2** *v/t* (*send*) enviar; **3** *v/i of new product* distribuirse; **shipment** envío *m*; **shipowner** naviero(-a) *m(f)*, armador(a) *m(f)*; **shipping** (*sea traffic*) navíos *mpl*, buques *mpl*; (*sending*) envío *m*; **shipwreck** naufragio *m*; **shipyard** astillero *m*

shirt [ʃɜːrt] camisa *f*

shit [ʃɪt] **1** *n* P mierda *f* P **2** *v/i* P cagar P **3** *int* P mierda P

shitty F asqueroso F
shiver ['ʃɪvər] tiritar
shock [ʃɑːk] **1** n shock m, impresión f; ELEC descarga f; **be in ~** MED estar en estado de shock **2** v/t impresionar, dejar boquiabierto; **shock absorber** MOT amortiguador m; **shocking** escandaloso; F weather, spelling terrible
shoddy ['ʃɑːdɪ] goods de mala calidad; behavior vergonzoso
shoe [ʃuː] zapato m; **shoelace** cordón m; **shoemaker** zapatero(-a) m(f); **shoe mender** zapatero(-a) m(f) remendón(-ona); **shoestore** zapatería f
shoot [ʃuːt] **1** n BOT brote m **2** v/t disparar; and kill matar de un tiro; movie rodar
◆ **shoot down** airplane derribar; fig: suggestion echar por tierra
◆ **shoot up** of prices dispararse; of children crecer mucho; of new buildings etc aparecer de repente
shooting star ['ʃuːtɪŋ] estrella f fugaz
shop [ʃɑːp] **1** n tienda f **2** v/i comprar; **go ~ping** ir de compras; **shopkeeper** tendero(-a) m(f); **shoplifter** ladrón(-ona) m(f) (en tienda); **shoplifting** hurtos mpl (en tiendas); **shopper** comprador(a) m(f); **shopping** items compra f; **shopping bag**

bolsa f de la compra; **shopping list** lista f de la compra; **shopping mall** centro m comercial
shore [ʃɔːr] orilla f
short [ʃɔːrt] **1** adj corto; in height bajo; **we're ~ of fuel** nos queda poco combustible **2** adv: **cut ~** interrumpir; **go ~ of** pasar sin; **in ~** en resumen; **shortage** escasez f, falta f; **shortcoming** defecto m; **shortcut** atajo m; **shorten** dress, hair, vacation acortar; chapter, article abreviar; work day reducir; **shortfall** déficit m; **short-lived** efímero; **shortly** (soon) pronto; **~ before / after** justo antes / después; **shortness** of visit brevedad f; in height baja f estatura; **shorts** pantalones mpl cortos, shorts mpl; underwear calzoncillos mpl; **shortsighted** miope; fig corto de miras; **short-sleeved** de manga corta; **short-tempered** irascible; **short-term** a corto plazo
shot [ʃɑːt] from gun disparo m; (photo) fotografía f; (injection) inyección f; **shotgun** escopeta f
should [ʃʊd]: **what ~ I do?** ¿qué debería hacer?; **you ~n't do that** no deberías hacer eso; **you ~ have heard him!** ¡tendrías que haberle oído!
shoulder ['ʃoʊldər] ANAT hombro m

shout [ʃaʊt] **1** *n* grito *m* **2** *v/t & v/i* gritar; **shouting** griterío *m*

shove [ʃʌv] **1** *n* empujón *m* **2** *v/t & v/i* empujar

shovel ['ʃʌvl] pala *f*

show [ʃoʊ] **1** *n* THEA espectáculo *m*; TV programa *m*; *of emotion* muestra *f* **2** *v/t* mostrar; *at exhibition* exponer; *movie* proyectar **3** *v/i (be visible)* verse

◆ **show in** hacer pasar a

◆ **show off 1** *v/t skills* mostrar **2** *v/i pej* presumir, alardear

◆ **show up 1** *v/t shortcomings etc* poner de manifiesto **2** *v/i (be visible)* verse; F *(arrive)* aparecer

'**show business** el mundo del espectáculo; **showcase** vitrina *f*; *fig* escaparate *m*; **showdown** enfrentamiento *m*

shower ['ʃaʊər] **1** *n of rain* chaparrón *m*; *to wash* ducha *f*; *Mex* regadera *f*; *(party) fiesta con motivo de un bautizo, una boda etc., en la que los invitados hacen obsequios*; **take a ~** ducharse **2** *v/i* ducharse

'**show-off** *pej* fanfarrón(-ona) *m(f)*; **showroom** sala *f* de exposición *f*; **showy** llamativo

shred [ʃred] **1** *n of paper etc* trozo *m*; *of fabric* jirón *m* **2** *v/t paper* hacer trizas; *in cooking* cortar en tiras;

shredder *for documents* trituradora *f* (de documentos)

shrewd [ʃruːd] *person* astuto; *investment* inteligente; **shrewdness** *of person* astucia *f*; *of decision* inteligencia *f*

shriek [ʃriːk] **1** *n* alarido *m*, chillido *m* **2** *v/i* chillar

shrill [ʃrɪl] estridente, agudo

shrimp [ʃrɪmp] gamba *f*; *larger Span* langostino *m*, *L.Am.* camarón *m*

shrine [ʃraɪn] santuario *m*

shrink[1] [ʃrɪŋk] *v/i of material* encoger(se); *of support etc* reducirse

shrink[2] [ʃrɪŋk] *n* F *(psychiatrist)* psiquiatra *m/f*

shrivel ['ʃrɪvl] *of skin* arrugarse; *of leaves* marchitarse

shrub [ʃrʌb] arbusto *m*; **shrubbery** arbustos *mpl*

shrug [ʃrʌg]: ~ (**one's shoulders**) encoger los hombros

shudder ['ʃʌdər] **1** *n of fear, disgust* escalofrío *m*; *of earth* temblor *m* **2** *v/i with fear, disgust* estremecerse; *of earth* temblar

shuffle ['ʃʌfl] **1** *v/t cards* barajar **2** *v/i in walking* arrastrar los pies

shun [ʃʌn] rechazar

shut [ʃʌt] cerrar

◆ **shut down 1** *v/t business* cerrar; *computer* apagar **2** *v/i of business* cerrarse; *of computer* apagarse

◆ **shut up** F *(be quiet)* callarse; **shut up!**¡cállate!

shutter ['ʃʌtər] *on window* contraventana *f*; PHOT obturador *m*

'shuttlebus *at airport* autobús *m* de conexión

shy [ʃaɪ] tímido; **shyness** timidez *f*

sick [sɪk] enfermo; *sense of humor* morboso, macabro; **be ~** *Br (vomit)* vomitar; **sicken 1** *v/t (disgust)* poner enfermo; *(make ill)* hacer enfermar **2** *v/i*: **be ~ing for sth** estar incubando algo; **sickening** *stench* nauseabundo; *crime* repugnante; **sick leave** baja *f* (por enfermedad); **sickness** enfermedad *f*; *(vomiting)* vómitos *mpl*

side [saɪd] lado *m*; *of mountain* ladera *f*; *of person* costado *m*; SP equipo *m*; **take ~s** *(favor one ~)* tomar partido *(with* por*)*; **~ by ~** uno al lado del otro; **side effect** efecto *m* secundario; **sidestep** *fig* evadir; **side street** bocacalle *f*; **sidewalk** acera *f*, *Rpl* vereda *f*, *Mex* banqueta *f*; **sideways** de lado

siege [siːdʒ] sitio *m*

sieve [sɪv] tamiz *m*

sift [sɪft] tamizar; *data* examinar a fondo

sigh [saɪ] **1** *n* suspiro *m* **2** *v/i* suspirar

sight [saɪt] vista *f*; **~s** *of city* lugares *mpl* de interés; *know by* ~ conocer de vista; **sight-**

seeing: *go* ~ hacer turismo; **sightseer** turista *m/f*

sign [saɪn] **1** *n* señal *f*; *outside shop* cartel *m*, letrero *m* **2** *v/t & v/i* firmar

signal ['sɪɡnl] **1** *n* señal *f* **2** *v/i of driver* poner el intermitente

signatory ['sɪɡnətərɪ] signatario(-a) *m(f)*, firmante *m/f*

signature ['sɪɡnətʃər] firma *f*

significance [sɪɡ'nɪfɪkəns] importancia *f*, relevancia *f*; **significant** *event etc* importante, relevante; *(quite large)* considerable; **significantly** *larger, more expensive* considerablemente

signify ['sɪɡnɪfaɪ] significar, suponer

'sign language lenguaje *m* por señas; **signpost** señal *f*

silence ['saɪləns] **1** *n* silencio *m* **2** *v/t* hacer callar; **silent** silencioso

silhouette [sɪlu'et] silueta *f*

silicon ['sɪlɪkən] silicio *m*

silicone ['sɪlɪkoʊn] silicona *f*

silk [sɪlk] **1** *n* seda *f* **2** *adj shirt etc* de seda; **silky** sedoso

silliness ['sɪlɪnɪs] tontería *f*; **silly** tonto

silo ['saɪloʊ] silo *m*

silver ['sɪlvər] **1** *n* plata *f* **2** *adj ring* de plata; *hair* canoso; **silverware** plata *f*

similar ['sɪmɪlər] parecido, similar; **similarity** parecido *m*, similitud *f*; **similarly** de la misma manera

simple ['sɪmpl] sencillo; *per-*

son simple; **simple-minded** *pej* simplón; **simplicity** sencillez *f*, simplicidad *f*; **simplify** simplificar; **simplistic** simplista; **simply** sencillamente

simultaneous [saɪml'teɪnɪəs] simultáneo; **simultaneously** simultáneamente

sin [sɪn] **1** *n* pecado *m* **2** *v/i* pecar

since [sɪns] **1** *prep* desde **2** *adv* desde entonces **3** *conj* in *expressions of time* desde que; (*seeing that*) ya que, dado que

sincere [sɪn'sɪr] sincero; **sincerely** sinceramente; *Sincerely Yours* atentamente; **sincerity** sinceridad *f*

sinful ['sɪnfəl] *person* pecador; *things* pecaminoso

sing [sɪŋ] cantar

singe [sɪndʒ] chamuscar

singer ['sɪŋər] cantante *m/f*

single ['sɪŋgl] **1** *adj* único; (*not married*) soltero *m* **2** *n* MUS sencillo *m*; (*~ room*) habitación *f* individual; *person* soltero(-a) *m(f)*; *Br* ticket billete *m* or *L.Am.* boleto *m* de ida; *~s in tennis* individuales *mpl*; **single-handed** en solitario; **single-minded** determinado, resuelto; **single parent** padre *m* / madre *f* soltero(-a); **single parent family** familia *f* monoparental; **single room** habitación *f* individual

singular ['sɪŋgjʊlər] GRAM **1**

adj singular **2** *n* singular *m*

sinister ['sɪnɪstər] siniestro; *sky* amenazador

sink [sɪŋk] **1** *n* in *kitchen* fregadero *m*; in *bathroom* lavabo *m* **2** *v/i* of *ship*, *object* hundirse; of *sun* ponerse; of *interest rates etc* descender, bajar **3** *v/t ship* hundir; *funds* invertir

sinner ['sɪnər] pecador(a) *m(f)*

sip [sɪp] **1** *n* sorbo *m* **2** *v/t* sorber

sir [sɜr] señor *m*; *excuse me, ~* perdone, caballero

siren ['saɪrən] sirena *f*

sirloin ['sɜrlɔɪn] solomillo *m*

sister ['sɪstər] hermana *f*; **sister-in-law** cuñada *f*

sit [sɪt] estar sentado; (*~ down*) sentarse

♦ **sit down** sentarse

sitcom ['sɪtkɑːm] telecomedia *f*, comedia *f* de situación

site [saɪt] **1** *n* emplazamiento *m*; of *battle* lugar *m* **2** *v/t new offices etc* situar

sitting ['sɪtɪŋ] of *committee*, *for artist* sesión *f*; *for meals* turno *m*; **sitting room** sala *f* de estar, salón *m*

situated ['sɪtʊeɪtɪd] situado; **situation** situación *f*

six [sɪks] seis; **sixteen** dieciséis; **sixteenth** decimosexto; **sixth** sexto; **sixtieth** sexagésimo; **sixty** sesenta

size [saɪz] tamaño *m*; of *loan* importe *m*; of *jacket* talla *f*; of *shoes* número *m*; **sizeable** *house*, *order* considerable;

meal copioso

skate [skeɪt] **1** *n* patín *m* **2** *v/i* patinar; **skateboard** monopatín *m*; **skateboarding** patinaje *m* en monopatín; **skater** patinador(a) *m(f)*; **skating** patinaje *m*; **skating rink** pista *f* de patinaje

skeleton ['skelɪtn] esqueleto *m*

skeptic ['skeptɪk] escéptico(-a) *m(f)*; **skeptical** escéptico; **skepticism** escepticismo *m*

sketch [sketʃ] **1** *n* boceto *m*, esbozo *m*; THEA sketch *m* **2** *v/t* bosquejar; **sketchy** *knowledge etc* básico, superficial

ski [skiː] **1** *n* esquí *m* **2** *v/i* esquiar

skid [skɪd] **1** *n of car* patinazo *m*; *of person* resbalón *m* **2** *v/i of car* patinar; *of person* resbalar

skier ['skiːər] esquiador(a) *m(f)*; **skiing** esquí *m*

skilful *etc Br* ☞ **skillful** *etc*

skill [skɪl] destreza *f*, habilidad *f*; **skilled** capacitado; **skillful** hábil, habilidoso; **skillfully** con habilidad *or* destreza

skim [skɪm] *surface* rozar; *milk* desnatar, descremar

skimpy ['skɪmpɪ] *account etc* superficial; *dress* cortísimo; *bikini* mínimo

skin [skɪn] **1** *n* piel *f* **2** *v/t* despellejar, desollar; **skin diving** buceo *m*; **skinny** escuá-

lido; **skin-tight** ajustado

skip [skɪp] **1** *n* (*little jump*) brinco *m*, saltito *m* **2** *v/i* brincar **3** *v/t* (*omit*) pasar por alto; **skipper** capitán(-ana) *m(f)*

skirt [skɜːrt] falda *f*

skull [skʌl] cráneo *m*

skunk [skʌŋk] mofeta *f*

sky [skaɪ] cielo *m*; **skylight** claraboya *f*; **skyline** horizonte *m*; **skyscraper** rascacielos *m inv*

slab [slæb] *of stone* losa *f*; *of cake etc* trozo *m* grande

slack [slæk] *rope* flojo; *work* descuidado; *period* tranquilo; **slacken** *rope*, *pace* aflojar; **slacks** pantalones *mpl*

slam [slæm] **1** *v/t door* cerrar de un golpe **2** *v/i of door* cerrarse de golpe

slander ['slændər] **1** *n* difamación *f* **2** *v/t* difamar; **slanderous** difamatorio

slang [slæŋ] argot *m*, jerga *f*; *of a specific group* jerga *f*

slant [slænt] **1** *v/i* inclinarse **2** *n* inclinación *f*; *given to a story* enfoque *m*; **slanting** *roof* inclinado; *eyes* rasgado

slap [slæp] **1** *n* (*blow*) bofetada *f* **2** *v/t* dar una bofetada

slash [slæʃ] **1** *n cut* corte *m*, raja *f*; *in punctuation* barra *f* **2** *v/t skin etc* cortar; *prices* recortar drásticamente

slaughter ['slɔːtər] **1** *n of animals* sacrificio *m*; *of people*, *troops* matanza *f* **2** *v/t animals* sacrificar; *people*, *troops* masacrar; **slaughterhouse** matadero *m*

slave [sleɪv] esclavo(-a) *m(f)*

slay [sleɪ] asesinar; **slaying** (*murder*) asesinato *m*

sleaze [sliːz] POL corrupción *f*; **sleazy** *bar* sórdido; *person* de mala calaña

sleep [sliːp] **1** *n* sueño *m*; **go to ~** dormirse **2** *v/i* dormir
◆ **sleep with** (*have sex with*) acostarse con

sleeping bag ['sliːpɪŋ] saco *m* de dormir; **sleeping car** RAIL coche *m* cama; **sleeping pill** somnífero *m*, pastilla *f* para dormir; **sleepwalker** sonámbulo(-a) *m(f)*; **sleepwalking** sonambulismo *m*; **sleepy** adormilado, somnoliento; *town* tranquilo; **I'm ~** tengo sueño

sleet [sliːt] aguanieve *f*

sleeve [sliːv] manga *f*; **sleeveless** sin mangas

slender ['slendər] *figure, arms* esbelto; *margin* escaso; *chance* remoto

slice [slaɪs] **1** *n* of bread rebanada *f*; *of cake* trozo *m*; *of salami, cheese* loncha *f*; fig: *of profits etc* parte *f* **2** *v/t loaf etc* cortar (en rebanadas)

slick [slɪk] **1** *adj performance* muy logrado; (*pej: cunning*) con mucha labia **2** *n* *of oil* marea *f* negra

slide [slaɪd] **1** *n* for kids tobogán *m*; PHOT diapositiva *f* **2** *v/i* deslizarse; *of exchange rate etc* descender **3** *v/t* zar

slight [slaɪt] *person, figure* menudo; (*small*) pequeño; *accent* ligero; **no, not in the ~est** no, en absoluto; **slightly** un poco

slim [slɪm] delgado; *chance* remoto

slime [slaɪm] (*mud*) lodo *m*; *of slug etc* baba *f*; **slimy** *liquid* viscoso; *river bed* lleno de lodo

sling [slɪŋ] **1** *n* for arm cabestrillo *m* **2** *v/t* F (*throw*) tirar

slip [slɪp] **1** *n* (*mistake*) desliz *m* **2** *v/i* on ice etc resbalar; *of quality etc* empeorar
◆ **slip up** (*make mistake*) equivocarse

slipped 'disc [slɪpt] hernia *f* discal

slipper ['slɪpər] zapatilla *f* (*de estar por casa*)

slippery ['slɪpərɪ] *surface, road* resbaladizo; *fish* escurridizo

'slip-up (*mistake*) error *m*

slit [slɪt] **1** *n* (*tear*) raja *f*; (*hole*) rendija *f*; *in skirt* corte *m* **2** *v/t* abrir

sliver ['slɪvər] trocito *m*; *of wood, glass* astilla *f*

slob [slɑːb] F pej dejado(-a) *m/f*, guarro(-a) *m/f*

slog [slɑːg] F paliza *f*

slogan ['sloʊgən] eslogan *m*

slop [slɑːp] derramar

slope [sloʊp] **1** *n of roof* inclinación *f*; *of mountain* ladera *f* **2** *v/i* inclinarse

sloppy ['slɑːpɪ] descuidado;

too sentimental sensiblero

slot [slɑːt] ranura *f; in schedule* hueco *m;* **slot machine** *for cigarettes, food* máquina *f* expendedora; *for gambling* máquina *f* tragaperras

slovenly ['slʌvnlɪ] descuidado

slow [slou] lento; *be~ of clock* ir retrasado

◆ **slow down** 1 *v/t work, progress* restrasar; *traffic, production* ralentizar 2 *v/i in walking, driving* reducir la velocidad; *of production etc* relentizar

'slowdown *in production* ralentización *f;* **slowly** despacio, lentamente; **slowness** lentitud *f*

sluggish ['slʌgɪʃ] lento

slum [slʌm] suburbio *m,* arrabal

slump [slʌmp] 1 *n in trade* desplome *m* 2 *v/i economically, of person* desplomarse

slur [slɜːr] 1 *n on character* difamación *f* 2 *v/t words* arrastrar

slush [slʌʃ] nieve *f* derretida; *(pej: sentimental stuff)* sensiblería *f;* **slush fund** fondo *m* para corruptelas

slut [slʌt] *pej* fulana *f*

sly [slaɪ] ladino

small [smɔːl] pequeño, *L.Am.* chico

smart[1] [smɑːrt] *adj* elegante; *(intelligent)* inteligente; *pace* rápido

smart[2] [smɑːrt] *v/i (hurt)* escocer

'smart card tarjeta *f* inteligente; **smartly** *dressed* con elegancia

smash [smæʃ] 1 *n noise* estruendo *m; (car crash)* choque *m; in tennis* smash *m* 2 *v/t break* hacer pedazos *or* añicos 3 *v/i break* romperse

smattering ['smætərɪŋ] *of a language* nociones *fpl*

smear [smɪr] 1 *n of ink* borrón *m; of paint* mancha *f; Br* MED citología *f; on character* difamación *f* 2 *v/t character* difamar

smell [smel] 1 *n* olor *m;* **sense of~** sentido *m* del olfato 2 *v/t* oler 3 *v/i unpleasantly* oler (mal); *(sniff)* olfatear; **smelly** apestoso

smile [smaɪl] 1 *n* sonrisa *f* 2 *v/i* sonreír

smirk [smɜːrk] sonrisa *f* maligna

smoke [smouk] 1 *n* humo *m* 2 *v/t cigarettes* fumar; *bacon* ahumar 3 *v/i of person* fumar; **smoke-free** *zone* de no fumadores; **smoker** fumador(-a) *m(f);* **smoking: no ~** prohibido fumar; **smoky** lleno de humo

smolder, *Br* **smoulder** ['smouldər] *of fire* arder

smooth [smuːð] 1 *adj surface, skin* liso, suave; *sea* en calma; *(peaceful)* tranquilo; *ride, drive* sin vibraciones; *transition* sin problemas; *pej: person* meloso 2 *v/t hair* alisar; **smoothly** *without problems* sin incidentes

smother ['smʌðər] *flames* sofocar; *person* asfixiar

smudge [smʌdʒ] **1** *n of paint* mancha *f*; *of ink* borrón *m* **2** *v/t* emborronar; *paint* difuminar

smug [smʌg] engreído

smuggle ['smʌgl] pasar de contrabando; **smuggler** contrabandista *m/f*; **smuggling** contrabando *m*

smutty ['smʌtɪ] *joke* obsceno

snack [snæk] tentempié *m*, aperitivo *m*

snag [snæg] *(problem)* inconveniente *m*, pega *f*

snake [sneɪk] serpiente *f*

snap [snæp] **1** *n* chasquido *m*; PHOT foto *f* **2** *v/t break* romper **3** *v/i break* romperse **4** *adj decision, judgment* rápido, súbito; **snappy** *person, mood* irascible; *decision* rápido; *(elegant)* elegante; **snapshot** foto *f*

snarl [snɑːrl] **1** *n of dog* gruñido *m* **2** *v/i* gruñir

snatch [snætʃ] arrebatar; *(steal)* robar; *(kidnap)* secuestrar

snazzy ['snæzɪ] F vistoso, *Span* chulo F

sneakers ['sniːkərz] zapatillas *fpl* de deporte

sneaky ['sniːkɪ] F *(crafty)* ladino, cuco F

sneer [snɪr] **1** *n* mueca *f* desdeñosa **2** *v/i* burlarse (**at** de)

sneeze [sniːz] **1** *n* estornudo

m **2** *v/i* estornudar

snicker ['snɪkər] reírse (*en voz baja*)

sniff [snɪf] **1** *v/i to clear nose* sorberse los mocos; *of dog* olfatear **2** *v/t (smell)* oler; *of dog* olfatear

sniper ['snaɪpər] francotirador(a) *m(f)*

snitch [snɪtʃ] F **1** *n (telltale)* chivato(-a) *m(f)* **2** *v/i* chivarse

snivel ['snɪvl] gimotear

snob [snɑːb] presuntuoso(-a) *m(f)*; **snobbery** presuntuosidad *f*; **snobbish** presuntuoso

snoop [snuːp] fisgón(-ona) *m(f)*

snooty ['snuːtɪ] presuntuoso

snooze [snuːz] **1** *n* cabezada *f* **2** *v/i* echar una cabezada

snore [snɔːr] roncar; **snoring** ronquidos *mpl*

snorkel ['snɔːrkl] snorkel *m*, tubo *m* para buceo

snort [snɔːrt] *of bull, person* bufar, resoplar

snout [snaʊt] *of pig, dog* hocico *m*

snow [snoʊ] **1** *n* nieve *f* **2** *v/i* nevar; **snowball** bola *f* de nieve; **snowdrift** ventisca *f*; **snowman** muñeco *m* de nieve; **snowplow** quitanieves *f inv*; **snowstorm** tormenta *f* de nieve; **snowy** *weather* de nieve; *hills* nevado

snub [snʌb] **1** *n* desaire *m* **2** *v/t* desairar; **snub-nosed** con la nariz respingona

snug [snʌg] *(tight-fitting)*

ajustado

so [sou] **1** *adv* tan; *it was ~ easy* fue tan fácil; *I'm ~ cold* tengo tanto frío; *that was ~ kind of you* fue muy amable de tu parte; *not ~ much* no tanto; *~ much easier* mucho más fácil; *you shouldn't drink ~ much* no deberías beber tanto; *I miss you ~* te echo tanto de menos; *~ am I do I* yo también; *~ is she does she* ella también; *~ an* etcétera **2** *pron: I hope think ~* eso espero / creo; *you didn't tell me - I did* no me lo dijiste - sí que lo hice; *15 or ~* unos 15 **3** *conj for that reason as* que; *in order that* para que; *~ (that) I could come too* para que yo también pudiera venir; *~ what?* F ¿y qué?

soak [souk] (*steep*) poner en remojo; *of water* empapar; **soaked** empapado

soap [soup] *for washing* jabón *m*; *soap* (*opera*) telenovela *f*; **soapy** jabonoso

soar [sɔːr] *of rocket etc* elevarse; *of prices* disparar

sob [saːb] **1** *n* sollozo *m* **2** *v/i* sollozar

sober [ˈsoubər] sobrio; (*serious*) serio

so-called (*referred to as*) así llamado; (*incorrectly referred to as*) mal llamado

soccer [ˈsaːkər] fútbol *m*

sociable [ˈsouʃəbl] sociable

social [ˈsouʃl] social; **social**

democrat socialdemócrata *m/f*; **socialism** socialismo *m*; **socialist 1** *adj* socialista **2** *n* socialista *m/f*; **socialize** socializar; **social worker** asistente(-a) *m(f)* social

society [səˈsaɪətɪ] sociedad *f*

sociologist [sousɪˈɑːlədʒɪst] sociólogo(-a) *m(f)*; **sociology** sociología *f*

sock[1] [saːk] *n for wearing* calcetín *m*

sock[2] [saːk] *v/t* (*punch*) dar un puñetazo a

socket [ˈsaːkɪt] *for light bulb* casquillo *m*; *of arm* cavidad *f*; *of eye* cuenca *f*; *Br* ELEC enchufe *m*

soda [ˈsoudə] (*~ water*) soda *f*; (*soft drink*) refresco *m*; (*ice-cream ~*) refresco de soda con helado

sofa [ˈsoufə] sofá *m*

soft [saːft] *voice, light, skin* suave; *pillow, attitude* blando; **soften** *position* ablandar; *impact, blow* amortiguar; **softly** suavemente; **software** software *m*

soggy [ˈsaːgɪ] empapado

soil [sɔɪl] **1** *n* (*earth*) tierra *f* **2** *v/t* ensuciar

solar energy [ˈsoulər] energía *f* solar

soldier [ˈsouldʒər] soldado *m*

sole[1] [soul] *of foot* planta *f*; *of shoe* suela *f*

sole[2] [soul] *adj* único

solely [ˈsoulɪ] únicamente

solemn [ˈsaːləm] solemne; **solemnity** solemnidad *f*;

solemnly solemnemente

solicit [sə'lɪsɪt] of prostitute abordar clientes

solid ['sɑ:lɪd] 1 adj (without holes) compacto; gold, silver macizo; solidarity solidaridad f; solidify solidificarse; solidly built sólidamente, in favor of unánime

solitaire [sɑ:lɪ'ter] card game solitario m

solitary ['sɑ:lɪterɪ] life solitario; (single) único; solitude soledad f

solo ['souloʊ] 1 n MUS solo m 2 adj en solitario; soloist solista m/f

soluble ['sɑ:ljʊbl] substance, problem soluble; solution also mixture solución f

solve [sɑ:lv] problem solucionar, resolver; mystery resolver; solvent financially solvente

somber, Br sombre ['sɑ:mbər] (dark) oscuro; (serious) sombrío

some [sʌm] 1 adj: would you like ~ water / cookies? ¿quieres agua / galletas?; ~ countries algunos países; I gave him ~ money le di (algo de) dinero; ~ people say that ... hay quien dice... 2 pron: ~ of the group parte del grupo; would you like ~? ¿quieres? 3 adv (a bit): we'll have to wait ~ tendremos que esperar algo or un poco; somebody alguien; someday algún día; some-

how (by one means or another) de alguna manera; (for some unknown reason) por alguna razón; someone ☞ somebody; someplace ☞ somewhere

somersault ['sʌmərsɔ:lt] 1 n voltereta f 2 v/i of vehicle dar una vuelta de campana

'something algo; sometime: ~ last year en algún momento del año pasado; sometimes a veces; somewhat un tanto; somewhere 1 adv en alguna parte or algún lugar 2 pron: let's go ~ quiet vamos a algún sitio tranquilo; ~ to park un sitio donde aparcar

son [sʌn] hijo m

song [sɔ:ŋ] canción f

'son-in-law yerno m; son of a bitch V hijo m de puta P

soon [su:n] pronto; as ~ as tan pronto como; as ~ as possible lo antes posible; ~er or later tarde o temprano; the ~er the better cuanto antes mejor

soothe [su:ð] calmar

sophisticated [sə'fɪstɪkeɪtɪd] sofisticado; sophistication sofisticación f

sophomore ['sɑ:fəmɔːr] estudiante m/f de segundo año

soprano [sə'prænoʊ] singer soprano m/f; voice voz f de soprano

sordid ['sɔːrdɪd] sórdido

sore [sɔːr] 1 adj (painful) dolorido; F (angry) enojado,

Span mosqueado F; *is it ~?* ¿duele? **2** *n* llaga *f*

sorrow ['sɒrou] pena *f*

sorry ['sɒrɪ] *day, sight, (sad)* triste; *(I'm) ~!* *apologizing* ¡lo siento!

sort [sɔːt] **1** *n* clase *f*, tipo *m*; *~ of* F un poco, algo **2** *v/t* ordenar, clasificar; COMPUT ordenar

SOS [esou'es] SOS *m*; *fig* llamada *f* de auxilio

so-'so F así así F

soul [soul] REL, *fig* alma *f*; *character* personalidad *f*

sound[1] [saund] **1** *adj (sensible)*; *beaten* sano; *(healthy)* sano; *sleep* profundo **2** *adv*: *be ~ asleep* estar profundamente dormido

sound[2] [saund] **1** *n* sonido *m*; *(noise)* ruido *m* **2** *v/i* parecer; *that ~s interesting* parece interesante

soundly ['saundlɪ] *sleep* profundamente; *beaten* rotundamente; **soundproof** insonorizado; **soundtrack** banda *f* sonora

soup [suːp] sopa *f*

sour [saur] agrio

source [sɔːrs] fuente *f*; *of river* nacimiento *m*

south [sauθ] **1** *adj* sur, del sur **2** *n* sur *m* **3** *adv* al sur; **South Africa** Sudáfrica *f*; **South African 1** *adj* sudafricano **2** *n* sudafricano(-a) *m(f)*; **South America** Sudamérica, América del Sur; **South American 1** *adj* sudamericano **2**

n sudamericano(-a) *m(f)*; **south-east 1** *n* sudeste *m*, sureste *m* **2** *adj* sudeste, sureste **3** *adv* al sudeste *or* sureste; **southeastern** del sudeste; **southerly** *wind* sur; *direction* sur; **southern** sureño; **southerner** sureño(-a) *m(f)*; **southernmost** más al sur; **South Pole** Polo *m* Sur; **southward** hacia el sur; **southwest 1** *n* sudoeste *m*, suroeste *m* **2** *adj* sudoeste, suroeste **3** *adv* al sudoeste *or* suroeste; **southwestern** del sudoeste *or* suroeste

souvenir [suːvə'nɪr] recuerdo *m*

sovereign ['sɒvrɪn] *state* soberano; **sovereignty** *of state* soberanía *f*

sow[1] [sau] *n (female pig)* cerda *f*, puerca *f*

sow[2] [sou] *v/t seeds* sembrar

space [speɪs] espacio *m*; **space shuttle** transbordador *m* espacial; **space station** estación *f* espacial; **spacious** espacioso

spade [speɪd] pala *f*; *~s in card game* picas *fpl*

spaghetti [spə'getɪ] espaguetis *mpl*

spa hotel hotel *m* spa

Spain [speɪn] España

spam [spæm] COMPUT propaganda *f* electrónica

span [spæn] abarcar; *of bridge* cruzar

Spaniard ['spænjərd] español(a) *m(f)*; **Spanish 1** *adj* español 2 *n language* español *m*; **the ~** los españoles

spanner ['spænər] *Br* llave *f*

spare [sper] **1** *v/t*: **can you ~ me $50?** ¿me podrías dejar 50 dólares?; **can you ~ the time?** ¿tienes tiempo? **2** *adj pair of glasses, set of keys* de repuesto **3** *n* recambio *m*, repuesto *m*; **spare part** pieza *f* de recambio *or* repuesto; **spare ribs** costillas *fpl* de cerdo; **spare room** habitación *f* de invitados; **spare time** tiempo *m* libre; **spare wheel** MOT rueda *f* de recambio; **sparing** moderado; **sparingly** con moderación

spark [spɑːrk] chispa *f*

sparkle ['spɑːrkl] destellar; **sparkling wine** vino *m* espumoso; **spark plug** bujía *f*

sparse [spɑːrs] *vegetation* escaso

spartan ['spɑːrtn] *room* espartano

spasmodic [spæz'mɑːdɪk] intermitente

spate [speɪt] *fig* oleada *f*

spatial ['speɪʃl] espacial

speak [spiːk] **1** *v/i* hablar (**to, with** con); (*make a speech*) dar una charla; **~ing** TELEC al habla **2** *v/t foreign language* hablar; **speaker** *at conference* conferenciante *m/f*; (*orator*) orador(a) *m(f)*; *of sound system* altavoz *m*, *L.Am.* altoparlante *m*; *of language* hablante *m/f*

special ['speʃl] especial; **specialist** especialista *m/f*; **specialize** especializarse (**in** en); **specially** *☞* **especially**; **specialty** especialidad *f*

species ['spiːʃiːz] especie *f*

specific [spə'sɪfɪk] específico; **specifically** específicamente; **specifications** *of machine etc* especificaciones *fpl*; **specify** especificar

specimen ['spesɪmən] muestra *f*

spectacular [spek'tækjʊlər] espectacular

spectator [spek'teɪtər] espectador(a) *m(f)*

spectrum ['spektrəm] *fig* espectro *m*

speculate ['spekjʊleɪt] *also* FIN especular; **speculation** *also* FIN especulación *f*; **speculator** FIN especulador(a) *m(f)*

speech [spiːtʃ] (*address*) discurso *m*; *in play* parlamento *m*; (*ability to speak*) habla *f*, dicción *f*; (*way of speaking*) forma *f* de hablar; **speechless** sin habla

speed [spiːd] **1** *n* velocidad *f*; (*promptness*) rapidez *f* **2** *v/i* *run* correr; *drive too quickly* sobrepasar el límite de velocidad; **speedboat** motora *f*, planeadora *f*; **speed bump** resalto *m* (*para reducir la velocidad del tráfico*), *Arg* despertador *m*, *Mex* tope *m*; **speed-dial button** botón *m* de marcado rápido; **speedi-**

ly con rapidez; **speeding:
fined for ~** multado por exceso de velocidad; **speed
limit** límite *m* de velocidad;
speedometer velocímetro
m; **speedy** rápido

spell[1] [spel] *v/t word* deletrear; **how do you~ ...?** ¿cómo se escribe... ? **2** *v/i* deletrear

spell[2] [spel] *n* of time periodo
m, temporada *f*

spelling ['spelɪŋ] ortografía *f*

spend [spend] *money* gastar;
time pasar; **spendthrift** *pej*
derrochador(a) *m(f)*

sperm [spɜːm] espermatozoide *m*; *(semen)* esperma *f*

sphere [sfɪr] *also fig* esfera *f*

spice [spaɪs] *(seasoning)* especia *f*; **spicy** food con especias; *(hot)* picante

spider ['spaɪdər] araña *f*; **spiderweb** telaraña *f*

spike [spaɪk] pincho *m*; *on
running shoe* clavo *m*

spill [spɪl] **1** *v/t* derramar **2**
v/i derramarse **3** *n* derrame
m

spin[1] [spɪn] **1** *n (turn)* giro *m* **2**
v/t hacer girar **3** *v/i* of wheel
girar

spin[2] [spɪn] *v/t cotton* hilar;
web tejer

spinach ['spɪnɪdʒ] espinacas
fpl

spinal ['spaɪnl] de la columna
vertebral; **spinal column**
columna *f* vertebral; **spinal
cord** médula *f* espinal; **spine**
of person, animal co-

lumna *f* vertebral; *of book*
lomo *m*; *on plant, hedgehog*
espina *f*; **spineless** *(cowardly)* débil

'spin-off producto *m* derivado

spiny ['spaɪnɪ] espinoso

spiral ['spaɪrəl] **1** *n* espiral **2**
v/i (rise quickly) subir vertiginosamente

spire [spaɪr] aguja *f*

spirit ['spɪrɪt] espíritu *m*;
(courage) valor *m*; **spirited**
(energetic) enérgico; **spirits**
(morale) la moral; **be in
good / poor ~** tener la moral alta / baja; **spiritual** espiritual

spit [spɪt] *of person* escupir

spite [spaɪt] rencor *m*; **in ~ of**
a pesar de; **spiteful** malo,
malicioso; **spitefully** con
maldad *or* malicia

splash [splæʃ] **1** *n small
amount of liquid* chorrito
m; *of color* mancha *f* **2** *v/t
person* salpicar **3** *v/i* chapotear; *of water* salpicar

◆ **splash down** *of spacecraft*
amerizar

splendid ['splendɪd] espléndido; **splendor**, Br **splendour** esplendor *m*

splint [splɪnt] MED tablilla *f*

splinter ['splɪntər] **1** *n* astilla *f*
2 *v/i* astillarse

split [splɪt] **1** *n damage* raja *f*;
(disagreement) escisión *f*; *(division, share)* reparto *m* **2** *v/t
damage* rajar; *logs* partir en
dos; *(cause disagreement) in*

escindir; (*share*) repartir **3** *v/i*
(*tear*) rajarse; (*disagree*) es-
cindirse

◆ **split up** *of couple* separarse

spoil [spɔɪl] estropear, arruinar; **spoilsport** F aguafiestas *m/f inv* F; **spoilt** *child*
consentido, mimado

spoke [spəʊk] *of wheel* radio
m

spokesperson ['spəʊks-
pɜːrsən] portavoz *m/f*

sponge [spʌndʒ] esponja *f*;
sponger F gorrón(-ona)
m(f) F

sponsor ['spɒnsər] **1** *n* patrocinador *m* **2** *v/t* patrocinar;
sponsorship patrocinio *m*

spontaneous [spɒn'teɪnɪəs]
espontáneo; **sponta-
neously** espontáneamente

spool [spuːl] carrete *m*

spoon [spuːn] cuchara *f*;
spoonful cucharada *f*

sporadic [spə'rædɪk] esporádico

sport [spɔːrt] deporte *m*;
sporting deportivo; **sports
car** (coche *m*) deportivo *m*;
sportsman deportista *m*;
sportswoman deportista *f*;
sporty *person* deportista;
clothes deportivo

spot[1] [spɒt] *n* (*pimple etc*)
grano *m*; (*in pattern*) lunar *m*

spot[2] [spɒt] *n* (*place*) lugar *m*,
sitio *m*

spot[3] [spɒt] *v/t* (*notice*) ver

'**spot check** control *m* al
azar; **spotless** inmaculado;
spotlight foco *m*; **spotty**

with pimples con granos

spouse [spaʊs] *fml* cónyuge
m/f

spout [spaʊt] **1** *n* pitorro *m* **2**
v/i of liquid chorrear **3** *v/t* F
soltar F

sprain [spreɪn] **1** *n* esguince *m*
2 *v/t* hacerse un esguince en

sprawl [sprɔːl] despatarrarse;
of city expandirse; **sprawl-
ing** *city* extendido

spray [spreɪ] **1** *n of sea water*
rociada *f*; *for hair* spray *m*;
container aerosol *m*, spray
m **2** *v/t* rociar; **spraygun** pistola *f* pulverizadora

spread [spred] **1** *n of disease,
religion etc* propagación *f*;
(*big meal*) comilona *f* F **2**
v/t (*lay*) extender; *butter* untar; *rumor* difundir; *disease*
propagar; *arms, legs* extender **3** *v/i of disease, fire* pro-
pagarse; *of rumor, news* difundirse; **spreadsheet** COM-
PUT hoja *f* de cálculo

sprightly ['spraɪtlɪ] lleno de
energía

spring[1] [sprɪŋ] *n season* primavera *f*

spring[2] [sprɪŋ] *n device* muelle *m*

spring[3] [sprɪŋ] **1** *n* (*jump*) salto *m*; (*stream*) manantial *m* **2**
v/i saltar

'**springboard** trampolín *m*;
springtime primavera *f*

sprinkle ['sprɪŋkl] espolvore-
ar; **sprinkler** *for garden* as-
persor *m*; *in ceiling* rociador
m contra incendios

sprint [sprɪnt] **1** n esprint m; SP carrera f de velocidad **2** v/i (run fast) correr a toda velocidad; of runner esprintar; **sprinter** SP esprínter m/f, velocista m/f

spy [spaɪ] **1** n espía m/f **2** v/i espiar **3** v/t (see) ver

◆ **spy on** espiar

squabble ['skwɑːbl] **1** n riña f **2** v/i reñir

squalid ['skwɒlɪd] inmundo, miserable; **squalor** inmundicia f

squander ['skwɒndər] money despilfarrar

square [skwer] **1** adj in shape cuadrado; ∼ **miles** millas cuadradas **2** n also MATH cuadrado m; in town plaza f; in board game casilla f

squash[1] ['skwɑːʃ] n vegetable calabacera f

squash[2] [skwɑːʃ] n game squash m

squash[3] [skwɑːʃ] v/t (crush) aplastar

squat [skwɑːt] **1** adj person chaparro; figure, buildings bajo **2** v/i sit agacharse

squeak [skwiːk] **1** n of mouse chillido m; of hinge chirrido m **2** v/i of mouse chillar; of hinge chirriar

squeal [skwiːl] **1** n chillido m **2** v/i chillar; of brakes armar un estruendo

squeamish ['skwiːmɪʃ] aprensivo

squeeze [skwiːz] (press) apretar; (remove juice from) ex-

primir

squid [skwɪd] calamar m

squirm [skwɜːrm] retorcerse

St (= **saint**) Sto; Sta (= santo m; santa f); (= **street**) c/ (= calle f)

stab [stæb] apuñalar

stability [stə'bɪlətɪ] estabilidad f; **stabilize 1** v/t prices, boat estabilizar **2** v/i of prices etc estabilizarse; **stable 1** adj estable; patient's condition estacionario **2** n for horses establo m

stack [stæk] **1** n (pile) pila f **2** v/t apilar

stadium ['steɪdɪəm] estadio m

staff [stæf] (employees) personal m; (teachers) profesorado m

stage[1] [steɪdʒ] n in project etc etapa f

stage[2] [steɪdʒ] **1** n THEA escenario m **2** v/t play escenificar; demonstration llevar a cabo

stagger ['stægər] **1** v/i tambalearse **2** v/t (amaze) dejar anonadado; coffee breaks etc escalonar; **staggering** asombroso

stagnant ['stægnənt] also fig estancado; **stagnate** fig estancarse

'**stag party** despedida f de soltero

stain [steɪn] **1** n (dirty mark) mancha f; for wood tinte m **2** v/t (dirty) manchar; wood teñir; **stained-glass window** vidriera f; **stainless**

steel acero *m* inoxidable

stair [ster] escalón *m*; **the ~s** la(s) escalera(s); **staircase** escalera(s) *f(pl)*

stake [steɪk] **1** *n of wood* estaca *f*; *when gambling* apuesta *f*; *(investment)* participación *f*; **be at ~** estar en juego **2** *v/t money* apostar; *participate* jugarse; *person* ayudar *(económicamente)*

stale [steɪl] *bread* rancio; *air* viciado; *fig: news* viejo

stalk[1] [stɔːk] *n of fruit, plant* tallo *m*

stalk[2] [stɔːk] *v/t (follow)* acechar; *person* seguir

stall[1] [stɔːl] *n at market* puesto *m*; *for cow, horse* casilla *f*

stall[2] [stɔːl] **1** *v/i of engine* calarse; *(play for time)* intentar ganar tiempo **2** *v/t engine* calar; *person* retener

stalls [stɔːlz] patio *m* de butacas

stalwart ['stɔːlwərt] *support* incondicional

stamina ['stæmɪnə] resistencia *f*

stammer ['stæmər] **1** *n* tartamudeo *m* **2** *v/i* tartamudear

stamp[1] [stæmp] **1** *n for letter* sello *m*, *L.Am.* estampilla *f*, *Mex* timbre *m*; *device* tampón *m*; *mark made with device* sello *m* **2** *v/t* sellar

stamp[2] [stæmp] *v/t:* **~ one's feet** patear

stance [stæns] *(position)* postura *f*

stand [stænd] **1** *n at exhibition*

puesto *m*, stand *m*; *(witness ~)* estrado *m*; *(support, base)* soporte *m*; **take the ~** LAW subir al estrado **2** *v/i of building* encontrarse, hallarse; *as opposed to sit* estar de pie; *(rise)* ponerse de pie **3** *v/t (tolerate)* soportar; *(put)* colocar

◆ **stand by 1** *v/i (not take action)* quedarse sin hacer nada; *(be ready)* estar preparado **2** *v/t person* apoyar; *decision* atenerse a

◆ **stand down** *(withdraw)* retirarse

◆ **stand for** *(tolerate)* aguantar; *(represent)* significar

◆ **stand out** destacar

◆ **stand up 1** *v/i* levantarse **2** *v/t* F plantar F

◆ **stand up for** defender

◆ **stand up to** hacer frente a

standard ['stændərd] **1** *adj (usual)* habitual **2** *n (level)* nivel *m*; TECH estándar *m*; **standardize** normalizar; **standard of living** nivel *m* de vida

'**standby** *fly* con un billete stand-by; **standing** *in society etc* posición *f*; *(repute)* reputación *f*; **standoffish** distante; **standpoint** punto *m* de vista; **standstill**: **be at a ~** estar paralizado; **bring to a ~** paralizar

staple[1] ['steɪpl] *n foodstuff* alimento *m* básico

staple[2] ['steɪpl] **1** *n (fastener)* grapa *f* **2** *v/t* grapar

stapler ['steɪplər] grapadora f
star [stɑːr] **1** n also person estrella f **2** v/t of movie estar protagonizado por; **starboard** de estribor

stare [ster] mirar fijamente; **~ at** mirar fijamente

stark [stɑːrk] **1** adj landscape desolado; reminder, picture etc desolador **2** adv: **~ naked** completamente desnudo

starry ['stɑːrɪ] night estrellado; **Stars and Stripes** la bandera estadounidense

start [stɑːrt] **1** n comienzo m, principio m; of race salida f **2** v/t & v/i empezar, comenzar; of engine arrancar; **~ing from tomorrow** a partir de mañana **3** v/t business montar; starter (of meal) entrada f; of car motor m de arranque

startle ['stɑːrtl] sobresaltar; **startling** sorprendente

starvation [stɑːr'veɪʃn] inanición f, hambre f; **starve** v/i pasar hambre; **I'm starving** F me muero de hambre F

state¹ [steɪt] **1** n (condition, country) estado m; **the States** (los) Estados Unidos **2** adj capital etc estatal; banquet etc de estado

state² [steɪt] v/t declarar

'State Department Departamento m de Estado, Ministerio m de Asuntos Exteriores; **statement** declaración f; (bank **~**) extracto m; **state of emergency** estado m de emergencia; **state-of-the-art** modernísimo; **statesman** hombre m de estado

static (**electricity**) ['stætɪk] electricidad f estática

station ['steɪʃn] **1** n RAIL estación f; RAD emisora f; TV canal m **2** v/t guard etc apostar; **stationary** parado

stationery ['steɪʃənerɪ] artículos mpl de papelería

'station wagon ranchera f

statistical [stə'tɪstɪkl] estadístico; **statistically** estadísticamente; **statistician** estadístico(-a) m(f); **statistics** science estadística f; figures estadísticas fpl

statue ['stætʃuː] estatua f; **Statue of Liberty** Estatua f de la Libertad

status ['stætəs] categoría f, posición f; **status symbol** símbolo m de prestigio

statute ['stætuːt] estatuto m

staunch [stɔːntʃ] supporter incondicional; friend fiel

stay [steɪ] **1** n estancia f, L.Am. estadía f **2** v/i in a place quedarse; in a condition permanecer; **~ in a hotel** alojarse en un hotel

◆ **stay behind** quedarse

◆ **stay up** (not go to bed) quedarse levantado

steadily ['stedɪlɪ] improve etc constantemente; **steady 1** adj (not shaking) firme; (continuous) continuo; beat regular; boyfriend estable **2** adv: **they've been going ~ for**

two years llevan saliendo dos años 3 *v/t* afianzar; **voice** calmar

steak [steɪk] filete *m*

steal [stiːl] **1** *v/t* robar **2** *v/i* (*be a thief*) robar; ~ *in* / *out* entrar / salir furtivamente

stealthy ['stelθɪ] sigiloso

steam [stiːm] **1** *n* vapor *m* **2** *v/t food* cocinar al vapor; **steamed up** F (*angry*) enojado, *Span* mosqueado F; **steamer** *for cooking* olla *f* para cocinar al vapor

steel [stiːl] **1** *n* acero *m* **2** *adj* (*made of* ~) de acero; **steelworker** trabajador(a) *m(f)* del acero

steep[1] [stiːp] *adj* hill etc empinado; F *prices* caro

steep[2] [stiːp] *v/t* (*soak*) poner en remojo

steer[1] [stɪr] *n animal* buey *m*

steer[2] [stɪr] *v/t car* conducir, *L.Am.* manejar; *boat* gobernar; *person* guiar; *conversation* llevar; **steering** MOT dirección *f*; **steering wheel** volante *m*, *S.Am.* timón *m*

stem[1] [stem] *n. of plant* tallo *m*; *of glass* pie *m*; *of word* raíz *f*

stem[2] [stem] *v/t* (*block*) contener

stench [stentʃ] peste *f*

stencil ['stensɪl] **1** *n* plantilla *f* **2** *v/t pattern* estarcir

step [step] **1** *n* (*pace*) paso *m*; (*stair*) escalón *m*; (*measure*) medida *f* **2** *v/i*: ~ *on sth* pisar algo

◆ **step down** *from post etc* dimitir

◆ **step up** (*increase*) incrementar

'stepbrother hermanastro *m*; **stepdaughter** hijastra *f*; **stepfather** padrastro *m*; **stepladder** escalera *f* de tijera; **stepmother** madrastra *f*; **stepsister** hermanastra *f*; **stepson** hijastro *m*

stereo ['sterɪoʊ] (*sound system*) equipo *m* de música; **stereotype** estereotipo *m*

sterile ['steraɪl] estéril; **sterilize** esterilizar

sterling ['stɜːrlɪŋ] FIN libra *f* esterlina

stern[1] [stɜːrn] *adj* severo

stern[2] [stɜːrn] *n* NAUT popa *f*

sternly con severidad

steroids ['sterɔɪdz] esteroides *mpl*

stew [stuː] *n* guiso *m*

steward ['stuːərd] *on plane* auxiliar *m* de vuelo; *on ship* camarero *m*; *at demonstration* miembro *m* de la organización; **stewardess** *on plane* auxiliar *f* de vuelo; *on ship* camarera *f*

stick[1] [stɪk] *n* palo *m*; *of policeman* porra *f*; (*walking* ~) bastón *m*

stick[2] [stɪk] **1** *v/t with adhesive* pegar; F (*put*) meter **2** *v/i* (*jam*) atascarse; (*adhere*) pegarse

◆ **stick by** F apoyar, no abandonar

◆ **stick to** *of sth sticky* pegar

se a; F *plan etc* seguir; F (*trail, follow*) pegarse a F

◆ **stick up for** F defender

sticker ['stɪkər] pegatina f; **stick-in-the-mud** F aburrido(-a) m(f) F; **sticky** pegajoso; *label* adhesivo

stiff [stɪf] *board, manner* rígido; *brush, penalty, competition* duro; *muscle* agarrotado; *drink* cargado; **stiffness** *of muscles* agarrotamiento m; *of manner* rigidez f

stifle ['staɪfl] reprimir; **stifling** sofocante

stigma ['stɪgmə] estigma m

still[1] [stɪl] **1** *adj* (*not moving*) quieto; *with no wind* sin viento **2** *adv*: **keep ~!** ¡estate quieto!

still[2] [stɪl] *adv* (*yet*) todavía, aún; (*nevertheless*) de todas formas

'**stillborn**: **be ~** nacer muerto; **still life** naturaleza f muerta

stilted ['stɪltɪd] forzado

stimulant ['stɪmjʊlənt] estimulante m; **stimulate** estimular; **stimulating** estimulante; **stimulation** estimulación f; **stimulus** (*incentive*) estímulo m

sting [stɪŋ] **1** *from bee, jellyfish* picadura f **2** *v/t of bee, jellyfish* picar **3** *v/i of eyes, scratch* escocer; **stinging** *criticism* punzante

stink [stɪŋk] **1** *n* (*bad smell*) peste f; F (*fuss*) escándalo F **2** *v/i* (*smell bad*) apestar; F (*be very bad*) dar asco

stipulate ['stɪpjʊleɪt] estipular; **stipulation** estipulación f

stir [stɜːr] **1** *v/t* remover, dar vueltas a **2** *v/i of sleeping person* moverse; **stirring** *music, speech* conmovedor

stitch [stɪtʃ] **1** *n in sewing* puntada f; *in knitting* punto m; **~es** MED puntos mpl **2** *v/t sew* coser; **stitching** (*stitches*) cosido m

stock [staːk] **1** *n* (*reserves*) reservas fpl; COM *of store* existencias fpl; (*animals*) ganado m; FIN acciones fpl; *for soup etc* caldo m; **in ~** en existencias; **out of ~** agotado **2** *v/t* COM (*have*) tener en existencias; COM (*sell*) vender; **stockbreeder** ganadero(-a) m(f); **stockbroker** corredor(a) m(f) de bolsa; **stock exchange** bolsa f (de valores); **stockholder** accionista m/f; **stockist** distribuidor(a) m(f); **stock market** mercado m de valores; **stockpile 1** *n of food, weapons* reservas fpl **2** *v/t* acumular

stocky ['staːkɪ] bajo y robusto

stodgy ['staːdʒɪ] *food* pesado

stoical ['stoʊɪkl] estoico; **stoicism** estoicismo m

stomach ['stʌmək] **1** *n* estómago m, tripa f **2** *v/t* (*tolerate*) soportar

stone [stoʊn] piedra f; **stoned** (*on drugs*) colocado F

stool [stuːl] (*seat*) taburete m

stoop[1] [stuːp] v/i (bend down) agacharse

stoop[2] [stuːp] n (porch) porche m

stop [stɒp] **1** n for train, bus parada f **2** v/t (put an end to) poner fin a; (prevent) impedir; (cease), person in street parar; car, bus, train: of driver detener; check bloquear; ~ doing sth dejar de hacer algo **3** v/i (come to a halt) pararse, detenerse; in a particular place: of bus, train parar
◆ **stop over** hacer escala

'stopgap solución f intermedia; **stoplight** (traffic light) semáforo m; (brake light) luz m de freno; **stopper** for bottle tapón m; **stop sign** (señal f de) stop m; **stopwatch** cronómetro m

storage ['stɔːrɪdʒ] almacenamiento m; **store 1** n tienda f; (stock) reserva f; (storehouse) almacén m **2** v/t almacenar; COMPUT guardar; **storefront** fachada f de tienda; **storekeeper** tendero(-a) m(f); **store window** escaparate m, L.Am. vidriera f, Mex aparador m

storey Br ▶ **story**[2]

storm [stɔːrm] tormenta f; **stormy** tormentoso

story[1] ['stɔːrɪ] (tale) cuento m; (account) historia f; (newspaper article) artículo m; F (lie) cuento m

story[2] ['stɔːrɪ] of building piso m, planta f

stout [staʊt] person relleno, corpulento

stove [stoʊv] for cooking cocina f, Col, Mex, Ven estufa f; for heating estufa f

stow [stoʊ] guardar
◆ **stow away** viajar de polizón

'stowaway polizón m

straight [streɪt] **1** adj line, back recto; hair liso; (honest, direct) franco; whiskey solo; (tidy) en orden; (conservative) serio; (not homosexual) heterosexual **2** adv (in a straight line) recto; (directly, immediately) directamente; (clearly) con claridad; go ~ F of criminal reformarse; ~away, ~ off en seguida; ~ out directamente; ~ up without ice solo; ~ ahead be situated todo derecho; walk, drive todo recto; look hacia delante; **straighten** enderezar; **straightforward** (honest, direct) franco; (simple) simple

strain[1] [streɪn] **1** n on rope tensión f; on engine, heart esfuerzo m; on person agobio m **2** v/t finances crear presión en; ~ one's back hacerse daño en la espalda

strain[2] [streɪn] v/t vegetables escurrir; oil, fat etc colar

strained [streɪnd] relations tirante; **strainer** for vegetables etc colador m

strike

strait [streɪt] estrecho *m*;
straitlaced mojigato

strange [streɪndʒ] (*odd, curious*) extraño, raro; (*unknown, foreign*) extraño; **strangely** (*oddly*) de manera extraña; **~ enough** aunque parezca extraño; **stranger** (*person you don't know*) extraño(-a) *m(f)*, desconocido(-a) *m(f)*; **I'm a ~ here myself** yo tampoco soy de aquí

strangle ['stræŋgl] strangular

strap [stræp] *of purse, watch* correa *f*; *of bra, dress* tirante *m*; *of shoe* tira *f*; **strapless** sin tirantes

strategic [strə'tiːdʒɪk] estratégico; **strategy** estrategia *f*

straw [strɔː] *1* paja *f*; *for drink* pajita *f*; **strawberry** fresa *f*, *S.Am.* frutilla *f*

stray [streɪ] *1 adj animal* callejero; *bullet* perdido *2 n dog* perro *m* callejero; *cat* gato *m* callejero *3 v/i* extraviarse, perderse; *fig: of eyes, thoughts* desviarse

streak [striːk] *1 n of dirt, paint* raya *f*; *in hair* mechón *m*; *fig: of nastiness etc* vena *f* *2 v/i move quickly* pasar disparado

stream [striːm] riachuelo *m*; *fig: of people* oleada *f*; **streamline** *fig* racionalizar; **streamlined** *car, plane* aerodinámico; *organization* racionalizado

street [striːt] calle *f*; **streetcar** tranvía *m*; **streetlight** farola *f*; **street people** los sin techo; **street value of drugs** valor *m* en la calle

strength [streŋθ] fuerza *f*; *fig* (*strong point*) punto *m* fuerte; *of friendship etc* solidez *f*; *of emotion* intensidad *f*; *of currency* fortaleza *f*; **strengthen** *1 v/t muscles, currency* fortalecer; *bridge* reforzar; *country, relationship* consolidar *2 v/i of bonds, ties* consolidarse; *of currency* fortalecerse

strenuous ['strenjuəs] agotador; **strenuously** *deny* tajantemente

stress [stres] *1 n* (*emphasis*) énfasis *m*; (*tension*) estrés *m*; *on syllable* acento *m* *2 v/t syllable* acentuar; *importance etc* hacer hincapié en; **stressed out** F estresado; **stressful** estresante

stretch [stretʃ] *1 n of land, water* extensión *f*; *of road* tramo *m* *2 adj fabric* elástico *3 v/t material, income* estirar; F *rules* ser flexible con *4 v/i to relax, reach* estirarse; (*spread*) extenderse; **stretcher** camilla *f*

strict [strɪkt] estricto; **strictly** con rigor; **it is ~ forbidden** está terminantemente prohibido

stride [straɪd] *1 n* zancada *f* *v/i* caminar dando zancadas

strident ['straɪdnt] estridente

strike [straɪk] *1 n of workers*

huelga *f*; *in baseball* strike *m*; *of oil* descubrimiento *m*; **be on ~** estar en huelga **2** *v/i of workers* hacer huelga; *(attack)* atacar; *of disaster* sobrevenir; *of clock* dar las horas **3** *v/t (hit)* golpear; *of disaster* sacudir; *match* encender; *oil* descubrir

◆ **strike out** *(delete)* tachar; *in baseball* eliminar a, *L.Am.* ponchar

'**strikebreaker** esquirol(a) *m(f)*; **striker** *(person on strike)* huelguista *m* / *f*; *in soccer* delantero(-a) *m(f)*; **striking** *(marked)* sorprendente, llamativo; *(eye-catching)* deslumbrante

string [strɪŋ] cuerda *f*; **stringed instrument** instrumento *m* de cuerda

stringent ['strɪndʒənt] riguroso

strip [strɪp] **1** *n of land* franja *f*; *(comic ~)* tira *f* cómica **2** *v/t (remove)* quitar; *(undress)* desnudar **3** *v/i (undress)* desnudarse; *of stripper* hacer striptease; **strip club** club *m* de striptease

stripe [straɪp] raya *f*; *indicating rank* galón *m*; **striped** a rayas

stripper ['strɪpər] artista *m/f* de striptease; **striptease** striptease *m*

stroke [stroʊk] **1** *n* MED derrame *m* cerebral; *in painting* pincelada *f*; *(style of swimming)* estilo *m* **2** *v/t* acariciar

stroll [stroʊl] **1** *n* paseo *m* **2** *v/i* caminar; **stroller** *for baby* silla *f* de paseo

strong [strɒŋ] fuerte; *structure* resistente; *candidate* claro, con muchas posibilidades; *support, supporter, views, objection* firme; **strongly** fuertemente; **strong-minded** decidido; **strong point** (punto *m*) fuerte *m*; **strongroom** cámar *f* acorazada; **strong-willed** tenaz

structural ['strʌktʃərəl] estructural; **structure 1** *n (something built)* construcción *f*; *of novel, society etc* estructura *f* **2** *v/t* estructurar

struggle ['strʌɡl] **1** *n* lucha *f* **2** *v/i with a person* forcejear; *(have a hard time)* luchar

strut [strʌt] pavonearse

stub [stʌb] *of cigarette* colilla *f*; *of check* matriz *f*; *of ticket* resguardo *m*

stubborn ['stʌbərn] *person* testarudo, terco; *defense, refusal* tenaz, pertinaz

stubby ['stʌbi] regordete

stuck [stʌk] F: **be~ on s.o.** estar colado por alguien F

student ['stuːdnt] estudiante *m/f*; *at high school* alumno(-a) *m(f)*

studio ['stuːdɪoʊ] estudio *m*

studious ['stuːdɪəs] estudioso; **study 1** *n* estudio *m* **2** *v/t & v/i* estudiar

stuff [stʌf] **1** *n (things)* cosas *fpl*; **what's that ~?** ¿qué es eso? **2** *v/t turkey* rellenar;

sth into sth meter algo dentro de algo; **stuffing** relleno *m*; **stuffy** *room* cargado; *person* estirado

stumble ['stʌmbl] tropezar; **stumbling-block** escollo *m*

stump [stʌmp] **1** *n of tree* tocón *m* **2** *v/t of question* dejar perplejo

stun [stʌn] *of blow* dejar sin sentido; *of news* dejar atonito; **stunning** (*amazing*) increíble; (*very beautiful*) imponente

stunt [stʌnt] *for publicity* truco *m*; *in movie* escena *f* peligrosa; **stuntman** *in movie* doble *m*, especialista *m*

stupefy ['stu:pɪfaɪ] dejar perplejo

stupendous [stu:'pendəs] extraordinario

stupid ['stu:pɪd] estúpido; **stupidity** estupidez *f*

sturdy ['stɜ:rdɪ] *person* robusto; *table, plant* resistente

stutter ['stʌtər] tartamudear

style [staɪl] estilo *m*; (*fashion*) moda *f*; **stylish** elegante; **stylist** (*hair ~*) estilista *m/f*

subcommittee ['sʌbkəmɪtɪ] subcomité *m*

subconscious [sʌb'kɑ:nʃəs] subconsciente; **subconsciously** inconscientemente

subcontract [sʌbkə:n'trækt] subcontratar; **subcontractor** subcontratista *m/f*

subdivide [sʌbdɪ'vaɪd] subdividir

subdue [səb'du:] someter

subheading ['sʌbhedɪŋ] subtítulo *m*

subhuman [sʌb'hju:mən] inhumano

subject 1 ['sʌbdʒɪkt] *n* (*topic*) tema *m*; (*branch of learning*) asignatura *f*, materia *f*; GRAM sujeto *m*; *of monarch* súbdito(-a) *m(f)* **2** ['sʌbdʒɪkt] *adj*: **be ~ to** have tendency *to* ser propenso a; **be regulated by** estar sujeto a **3** [səb'dʒekt] *v/t* someter; **subjective** subjetivo

sublet ['sʌblet] realquilar

submachine gun [sʌbmə'ʃi:ngʌn] metralleta *f*

submarine ['sʌbməri:n] submarino *m*

submission [səb'mɪʃn] (*surrender*) sumisión *f*; *to committee etc* propuesta *f*; **submissive** sumiso; **submit 1** *v/t plan* presentar **2** *v/i* someterse

subordinate [sə'bɔ:rdɪneɪt] **1** *adj position* subordinado **2** *n* subordinado(-a) *m(f)*

subpoena [sə'pi:nə] **1** *n* citación *f* **2** *v/t person* citar

◆ **subscribe to** [səb'skraɪb] *magazine etc* suscribirse a; *theory* suscribir

subscriber [səb'skraɪbər] *to magazine* suscriptor(a) *m(f)*; **subscription** suscripción *f*

subsequent ['sʌbsɪkwənt] posterior

subside [səb'saɪd] *of waters*

bajar; *of winds* amainar; *of building* hundirse; *of fears* calmarse

subsidiary [səbˈsɪdɪərɪ] filial *f*

subsidize [ˈsʌbsɪdaɪz] subvencionar; **subsidy** subvención *f*

substance [ˈsʌbstəns] sustancia *f*

substandard [sʌbˈstændərd] deficiente

substantial [səbˈstænʃl] sustancial, considerable; **substantially** (*considerably*) considerablemente; (*in essence*) sustancialmente

substantive [səbˈstæntɪv] significativo

substitute [ˈsʌbstɪtuːt] **1** *n* sustituto *m*; SP suplente *m/f* **2** *v/t* sustituir; **~ X for Y** sustituir Y por X; **substitution** sustitución *f*

subtitle [ˈsʌbtaɪtl] subtítulo *m*

subtle [ˈsʌtl] sutil

subtract [səbˈtrækt] restar

suburb [ˈsʌbɜːrb] zona *f* residencial de la periferia; **suburban** de la periferia; (*attitudes, lifestyle* aburguesado

subversive [səbˈvɜːrsɪv] **1** *adj* subversivo **2** *n* subversivo(-a) *m(f)*

subway [ˈsʌbweɪ] metro *m*

succeed [səkˈsiːd] **1** *v/i* tener éxito; **~ to the throne** suceder en el trono; **~ in doing sth** conseguir hacer algo **2** *v/t* (*come after*) suceder; **suc-**

cess éxito *m*; **successful** *person* con éxito; **be ~ in doing sth** lograr hacer algo; **successfully** con éxito; **successive** sucesivo; **successor** sucesor(a) *m(f)*

succinct [səkˈsɪŋkt] sucinto

succumb [səˈkʌm] (*give in*) sucumbir

such [sʌtʃ] **1** *adj* (*of that kind*) tal; **~ men are dangerous** los hombres así son peligrosos; *don't make* **~** *a fuss* no armes tanto alboroto; **~ as** como; *there is no* **~** *word as* ... no existe la palabra ... **2** *adv* tan; *as* **~** como tal; **~ a nice day** un día tan bueno;

suck [sʌk] *v/t candy etc* chupar **2** *v/i* P: *it ~s* es una mierda P; **sucker** F (*person*) primo(-a) *m/f*; F (*lollipop*) piruleta *f*; **suction** succión *f*

sudden [ˈsʌdn] repentino; **suddenly** de repente

sue [suː] demandar

suede [sweɪd] ante *m*

suffer [ˈsʌfər] **1** *v/i* sufrir; (*deteriorate*) deteriorarse **2** *v/t loss, setback* sufrir; **suffering** sufrimiento *m*

sufficient [səˈfɪʃnt] suficiente; **sufficiently** suficientemente

suffocate [ˈsʌfəkeɪt] **1** *v/i* asfixiarse **2** *v/t* asfixiar; **suffocation** asfixia *f*

sugar [ˈʃʊɡər] **1** *n* azúcar *m or f* **2** *v/t* echar azúcar a

suggest [səˈdʒest] sugerir; **suggestion** sugerencia *f*

suicide ['suːɪsaɪd] suicidio *m*

suit [suːt] **1** *n* traje *m*; *in cards* palo *m* **2** *v/t of clothes, color* sentar bien a; **suitable** apropiado; **suitably** apropiadamente; **suitcase** maleta *f*, *L.Am.* valija *f*

suite [swiːt] *of rooms*, MUS suite *f*; *furniture* tresillo *m*

sulk [sʌlk] enfurruñarse; **sulky** enfurruñado

sullen ['sʌlən] malhumorado, huraño

sultry ['sʌltrɪ] sofocante, bochornoso; *sexually* sensual

sum [sʌm] *(total)*, *in arithmetic* suma *f*; *(amount)* cantidad *f*
◆ **sum up 1** *v/t (summarize)* resumir; *(assess)* catalogar **2** *v/i* LAW recapitular

summarize ['sʌməraɪz] resumir; **summary** resumen *m*

summer ['sʌmər] verano *m*

summit ['sʌmɪt] *also* POL cumbre *f*

summon ['sʌmən] llamar; *meeting* convocar; **summons** LAW citación *f*

sun [sʌn] sol *m*; **sunbathe** tomar el sol; **sunbed** cama *f* de rayos UVA; **sunblock** crema *f* solar de alta protección; **sunburn** quemadura *f* (del sol); **sunburnt** quemado (por el sol); **Sunday** domingo *m*; **sunglasses** gafas *fpl* or *L.Am.* anteojos *mpl* de sol; **sunny** soleado; *disposition* radiante; *it's* ~ hace sol; **sunrise** amanecer *m*; **sunset** atardecer *m*, puesta

f de sol; **sunshade** sombrilla *f*; **sunshine** sol *m*; **sunstroke** insolación *f*; **suntan** bronceado *m*

super ['suːpər] **1** *adj* F genial F, estupendo F **2** *n (janitor)* portero(-a) *m(f)*

superb [suˈpɜːrb] excelente

superficial [suːpərˈfɪʃl] superficial

superfluous [suˈpɜːrfluəs] superfluo

superintendent [suːpərɪnˈtendənt] *of apartment block* portero(-a) *m(f)*

superior [suˈpɪrɪər] **1** *adj (better)* superior; *pej: attitude* arrogante **2** *n in organization* superior *m*

superlative [suːˈpɜːrlətɪv] **1** *adj* excelente **2** *n* GRAM superlativo *m*

'supermarket supermercado *m*

'superpower POL superpotencia *f*

supersonic [suːpərˈsɑːnɪk] supersónico

superstition [suːpərˈstɪʃn] superstición *f*; **superstitious** supersticioso

supervise ['suːpərvaɪz] *class* vigilar; *workers* supervisar; *activities* dirigir; **supervisor** *at work* supervisor(a) *m(f)*

supper ['sʌpər] cena *f*, *L.Am.* comida *f*

supplement ['sʌplɪmənt] *(extra payment)* suplemento *m*

supplier [səˈplaɪər] COM proveedor *m*; **supply** *n* suminis-

tro *m*, abastecimiento *m*;
supplies *of food* provisiones
fpl; **~ and demand** la oferta
y la demanda **2** *v/t goods* suministrar

support [sə'pɔːrt] **1** *n for structure* soporte *m*; (*backing*) apoyo *m* **2** *v/t structure* soportar; (*financially*) mantener; (*back*) apoyar; **supporter** partidario(-a) *m(f)*; *of football team etc* seguidor(a) *m(f)*; **supportive** comprensivo; **be ~** apoyar (**toward, of** a)

suppose [sə'pəʊz] (*imagine*) suponer; **you are not ~d to ...** (*not allowed to*) no deberías...; **supposing ... y si...**; **supposedly** supuestamente

suppress [sə'pres] reprimir, sofocar; **suppression** represión *f*

supremacy [suː'preməsɪ] supremacía *f*; **supreme** supremo; **Supreme Court** Tribunal *m* Supremo, *L.Am.* Corte *f* Suprema

surcharge ['sɜːrtʃɑːrdʒ] recargo *m*

sure [ʃʊr] **1** *adj* seguro; **make ~ that ...** asegurarse de que... **2** *adv*: **~ enough** efectivamente; **it ~ is hot today** *F* vaya calor que hace *F*; **~!** *F* ¡claro!; **surety** *for loan* fianza *f*

surf [sɜːrf] **1** *n* surf *m* **2** *v/t*: **~ the Net** navegar por Internet
surface ['sɜːrfɪs] **1** *n* superficie *f* **2** *v/i from water* salir a la

superficie; (*appear*) aparecer; **surface mail** correo *m* terrestre

'surfboard tabla *f* de surf; **surfer** surfista *m/f*; **surfing** surf *m*; **go ~** ir a hacer surf

surge [sɜːrdʒ] *in electric current* sobrecarga *f*; *in demand etc* incremento *m* repentino

surgeon ['sɜːrdʒən] cirujano(-a) *m(f)*; **surgery** cirugía *f*; **surgical** quirúrgico; **surgically** quirúrgicamente

surly ['sɜːrlɪ] arisco, hosco

surmount [sər'maʊnt] *difficulties* superar

surname ['sɜːrneɪm] apellido *m*

surpass [sər'pæs] superar

surplus ['sɜːrpləs] **1** *n* excedente *m* **2** *adj* excedente

surprise [sər'praɪz] **1** *n* sorpresa *f* **2** *v/t* sorprender; **be / look ~d** quedarse / parecer sorprendido; **surprising** sorprendente; **surprisingly** sorprendentemente

surrender [sə'rendər] **1** *v/i army* rendirse **2** *v/t weapons etc* entregar **3** *n* rendición *f*; (*handing in*) entrega *f*

surrogate 'mother ['sʌrəgət] madre *f* de alquiler

surround [sə'raʊnd] **1** *v/t* rodear **2** *n of picture etc* marco *m*; **surrounding** circundante; **surroundings** *of village etc* alrededores *mpl*; (*environment*) entorno *m*

survey 1 ['sɜːrveɪ] *n of modern literature etc* estudio *m*;

Br: of building tasación *f*, peritaje; *poll* encuesta *f* **2** [sər'veɪ] *v/t (look at)* contemplar; *Br: building* tasar, peritar; **surveyor** *m(f)* tasador(a) *m(f)* o perito (-a) *m(f)* de la propiedad

survival [sər'vaɪvl] supervivencia *f*; **survive 1** *v/i* sobrevivir **2** *v/t accident etc* sobrevivir a; *(outlive)* sobrevivir; **survivor** superviviente *m/f*

suspect 1 ['sʌspekt] *n* sospechoso(-a) *m(f)* **2** [sə'spekt] *v/t person* sospechar de; *(suppose)* sospechar; **suspected** *murderer* presunto; *cause, heart attack etc* supuesto

suspend [sə'spend] *v/t; from office* suspender; **suspenders** *for pants* tirantes *mpl, S.Am.* suspensores *mpl; Br: for stockings* liga *f*

suspense [sə'spens] *Span* suspense *m, L.Am.* suspenso *m*; **suspension** MOT, *from duty* suspensión *f*

suspicion [sə'spɪʃn] sospecha *f*; **suspicious** *(causing suspicion)* sospechoso; *(feeling suspicion)* receloso; **suspiciously** *behave* de manera sospechosa; *ask* con recelo

sustain [sə'steɪn] sostener; **sustainable** sostenible

SUV [esjuː'viː] (*= sport utility vehicle*) SUV *m*, todoterreno *m* ligero

swab [swɑːb] *material* torunda *f; test* muestra *f*

swallow[1] ['swɑːloʊ] *v/t & v/i*

tragar

swallow[2] ['swɑːloʊ] *n bird* golondrina *f*

swamp [swɑːmp] **1** *n* pantano *m* **2** *v/t: be ~ed with* estar inundado de; **swampy** pantanoso

swap [swɑːp] **1** *v/t* cambiar **2** *v/i* hacer un cambio

swarm [swɔːrm] **1** *n* of bees enjambre *m* **2** *v/i: the town was ~ing with ...* la ciudad estaba abarrotada de...

swarthy ['swɔːrðɪ] moreno

swat [swɑːt] *insect* aplastar

sway [sweɪ] **1** *n (influence)* dominio *m* **2** *v/i* tambalearse

swear [swer] **1** *v/i (use swearword)* decir palabrotas *o* tacos **2** *v/t (promise)*, LAW jurar
♦ **swear in** *witnesses etc* tomar juramento a

'swearword palabrota *f*, taco *m*

sweat [swet] **1** *n* sudor *m* **2** *v/i* sudar; **sweatband** banda *f* (en la frente); *on wrist* muñequera *f*; **sweater** suéter *m*, *Span* jersey *m*; **sweatshirt** sudadera *f*; **sweaty** sudoroso

Swede [swiːd] sueco(-a) *m(f)*; **Sweden** Suecia; **Swedish** *adj* sueco **2** *n* sueco *m*

sweep [swiːp] **1** *v/t floor, leaves* barrer **2** *n (long curve)* curva *f*; **sweeping** *statement* demasiado generalizado; *changes* radical

sweet [swiːt] dulce; F *(kind)*

amable; F (cute) mono;
sweetcorn maíz m, S.Am.
choclo m; **sweeten** endulzar; **sweetheart** novio(-a)
m(f)
swell [swel] **1** v/i of wound,
limb hincharse **2** adj F (good)
genial F **3** n of the sea oleaje
m; **swelling** MED hinchazón
f
swerve [swɜːrv] of driver, car
girar bruscamente
swift [swɪft] rápido
swim [swɪm] **1** v/i nadar **2** n
baño m; **go for a ~** ir a darse
un baño; **swimmer** nadador(a) m(f); **swimming** natación f; **swimming pool**
piscina f, Mex alberca f,
Rpl pileta f; **swimsuit** traje
m de baño, bañador m
swindle [ˈswɪndl] **1** n estafa f
2 v/t estafar; **~ s.o. out of sth**
estafar algo a alguien
swing [swɪŋ] **1** n oscilación f;
for child columpio m **2** v/t balancear; hips menear **3** v/i
balancearse; (turn) girar; of
opinion etc cambiar
Swiss [swɪs] **1** adj suizo **2** n
person suizo(-a) m(f); **the ~**
los suizos
switch [swɪtʃ] **1** n for light interruptor m; (change) cambio m **2** v/t (change) cambiar
de **3** v/i (change) cambiar
◆ **switch off** apagar
◆ **switch** on encender,
L.Am. prender
Switzerland [ˈswɪtsərlənd]
Suiza

swivel [ˈswɪvl] girar
swollen [ˈswəʊlən] hinchado
'swordfish pez f espada
syllabus [ˈsɪləbəs] plan m de
estudios
symbol [ˈsɪmbəl] símbolo m;
symbolic simbólico; **symbolism** simbolismo m; **symbolist** simbolista m/f; **symbolize** simbolizar
symmetrical [sɪˈmetrɪkl] simétrico; **symmetry** simetría
f
sympathetic [sɪmpəˈθetɪk]
(showing pity) compasivo;
(understanding) comprensivo
◆ **sympathize with** [ˈsɪmpəθaɪz] comprender
sympathizer [ˈsɪmpəθaɪzər]
POL simpatizante m/f; **sympathy** (pity) compasión f;
(understanding) comprensión f
symphony [ˈsɪmfənɪ] sinfonía f
symptom [ˈsɪmptəm] also fig
síntoma m
synchronize [ˈsɪŋkrənaɪz]
sincronizar
synonym [ˈsɪnənɪm] sinónimo m; **synonymous** sinónimo
synthesizer [ˈsɪnθəsaɪzər]
MUS sintetizador m; **synthetic** sintético
syphilis [ˈsɪfɪlɪs] sífilis f
Syria [ˈsɪrɪə] Siria; **Syrian 1**
adj sirio **2** n sirio(-a) m(f)
syringe [sɪˈrɪndʒ] jeringuilla f
syrup [ˈsɪrəp] almíbar m

system ['sɪstəm] sistema *m*; **systematic** sistemático; **systematically** sistemática-

mente; **systems analyst** COMPUT analista *m/f* de sistemas

T

table ['teɪbl] mesa *f*; *of figures* cuadro *m*; **tablecloth** mantel *m*; **table lamp** lámpara *f* de mesa; **table of contents** índice *m* (de contenidos); **tablespoon** *object* cuchara *f* grande; *quantity* cucharada *f* grande

tablet ['tæblɪt] MED pastilla *f*; IT tableta *f*; **tablet computer** IT ordenador *m* tableta, *L.Am.* computadora *f* tableta; **tablet PC** IT PC *m* tableta

tabloid ['tæblɔɪd] *newspaper* periódico *m* sensacionalista (*de tamaño tabloide*)

taboo [tə'buː] tabú *inv*

tacit ['tæsɪt] tácito

tack [tæk] **1** *n* (*nail*) tachuela *f* **2** *v/t* (*sew*) hilvanar **3** *v/i* of *yacht* dar bordadas

tackle ['tækl] **1** *n* (*equipment*) equipo *m*; SP entrada *f* **2** *v/t* SP entrar a; *problem* abordar; *intruder* hacer frente a

tacky ['tækɪ] *glue* pegajoso; F (*poor quality*) chabacano, *Span* hortera F; *behavior* impresentable

tact [tækt] tacto *m*; **tactful** diplomático; **tactfully** diplomáticamente

tactical ['tæktɪkl] táctico; **tactics** ['tæktɪks] táctica *f*

tactless ['tæktlɪs] indiscreto

tag [tæg] (*label*) etiqueta *f*

tail [teɪl] cola *f*; **tail light** luz *f* trasera

tailor ['teɪlər] sastre *m*; **tailor-made** *also fig* hecho a medida

'tailpipe *of car* tubo *m* de escape

take [teɪk] (*remove*) llevarse, *Span* quitar; (*steal*) llevarse; (*transport, accompany*) llevar; (*accept: money, credit cards*) aceptar; (*study: math, French*) hacer, estudiar; *photograph, photocopy* hacer, sacar; *exam, degree* hacer; *shower* darse; *medicine, s.o.'s temperature, taxi* tomar; (*endure*) aguantar

◆ **take after** parecerse a

◆ **take away** *pain* hacer desaparecer; *object* quitar; MATH restar

◆ **take back** (*return: object*) devolver; *person* llevar de vuelta; (*accept back: husband etc*) dejar volver

◆ **take down** *from shelf* bajar; *scaffolding* desmontar; *trousers* bajarse; (*write down*) anotar, apuntar

◆ **take in** (*take indoors*) recoger; (*give accommodation to*)

acoger; (make narrower) meter; (deceive) engañar; (include) incluir

◆ **take off 1** v/t clothes, hat quitarse; 10% etc descontar; (mimic) imitar; (cut off) cortar **2** v/i of airplane despegar, L.Am. decolar; (become popular) empezar a cuajar

◆ **take on** job aceptar; staff contratar

◆ **take out** from bag, from bank, tooth sacar; word from text quitar; insurance policy suscribir; **he took her out to dinner** la llevó a cenar

◆ **take over 1** v/t company etc adquirir **2** v/i of new management etc asumir el cargo; of new government asumir el poder; (do sth in s.o.'s place) tomar el relevo

◆ **take up** carpet etc levantar; (carry up) subir; (shorten: dress etc) acortar; hobby empezar a hacer; subject empezar a estudiar; offer aceptar; new job comenzar; space, time ocupar

'takeoff of airplane despegue m, L.Am. decolaje m; (impersonation) imitación f; **takeover** COM adquisición f; **takeover bid** oferta f pública de adquisición, OPA f; **takings** recaudación f

tale [teɪl] cuento m, historia f

talent ['tælənt] talento m; **talented** con talento; **talent scout** cazatalentos m inv

talk [tɔːk] **1** v/t & v/i hablar; ~

business hablar de negocios **2** n (conversation) charla f, C.Am., Mex plática f; (lecture) conferencia f, ~**s** negociaciones fpl

◆ **talk back** responder, contestar

talkative ['tɔːkətɪv] hablador; **talk show** programa m de entrevistas

tall [tɔːl] alto

tally ['tælɪ] **1** n cuenta f **2** v/i cuadrar, encajar

tame [teɪm] animal manso, domesticado; joke etc soso

◆ **tamper with** ['tæmpər] lock intentar forzar; brakes tocar

tampon ['tæmpɔːn] tampón m

tan [tæn] **1** n from sun bronceado m; (color) marrón m claro **2** v/i in sun broncearse **3** v/t leather curtir

tangent ['tændʒənt] MATH tangente f

tangible ['tændʒɪbl] tangible

tangle ['tæŋgl] lío m

tango ['tæŋgoʊ] tango m

tank [tæŋk] for water depósito m, tanque m; for fish pecera f; MOT depósito m; MIL, for skin diver tanque m; **tanker** truck camión m cisterna; ship buque m cisterna; for oil petrolero m

tanned [tænd] moreno, bronceado

tantalizing ['tæntəlaɪzɪŋ] sugerente

tantrum ['tæntrəm] rabieta f

tap [tæp] **1** *n Br* (*faucet*) grifo *m*, *L.Am.* llave *f* **2** *v/t* (*knock*) dar un golpecito en; *phone* intervenir

tape [teɪp] **1** *n* cinta *f* **2** *v/t conversation etc* grabar; *with sticky tape* pegar con cinta adhesiva; **tape deck** pletina *f*; **tape drive** COMPUT unidad *f* de cinta; **tape measure** cinta *f* métrica

taper ['teɪpər] estrecharse

'tape recorder magnetófono *m*, *L.Am.* grabador *m*; **tape recording** grabación *f* (magnetofónica)

tar [tɑːr] alquitrán *m*

tardy ['tɑːrdɪ] tardío

target ['tɑːrgɪt] *n in shooting* blanco *m*; *for sales, production* objetivo *m* **2** *v/t market* apuntar a; **target audience** audiencia *f* objetivo; **target date** fecha *f* fijada; **target market** mercado *m* objetivo

tariff ['tærɪf] (*price*) tarifa *f*; (*tax*) arancel *m*

tarmac ['tɑːrmæk] *for road surface* asfalto *m*; *at airport* pista *f*

tarnish ['tɑːrnɪʃ] *metal* deslucir; *reputation* empañar

tarpaulin [tɑːr'pɔːlɪn] lona *f* (*impermeable*)

tart [tɑːrt] tarta *f*, pastel *m*

task [tæsk] tarea *f*; **task force** *for a special job* equipo *m* de trabajo; MIL destacamento *m*

taste [teɪst] **1** *n* gusto *m*; *of food etc* sabor *m* **2** *v/t also*

fig probar **3** *v/i*: **it ~s like ...** sabe a ...; **tasteful** de buen gusto; **tastefully** con buen gusto; **tasteless** *food* insípido; *remark* de mal gusto; **tasting** *of wine* cata *f*, degustación *f*; **tasty** sabroso, rico

tattered ['tætərd] *clothes* andrajoso; *book* destrozado

tattoo [tə'tuː] tatuaje *m*

taunt [tɔːnt] **1** *n* pulla *f* **2** *v/t* mofarse de

taut [tɔːt] tenso

tax [tæks] **1** *n* impuesto *m* **2** *v/t people* cobrar impuestos a; *product* gravar; **taxable income** ingresos *mpl* gravables; **taxation** (*act of taxing*) imposición *f* de impuestos; (*taxes*) fiscalidad *f*, impuestos *mpl*; **tax bracket** banda *f* impositiva; **tax-deductible** desgravable; **tax evasion** evasión *f* fiscal; **tax-free** libre de impuestos; **tax haven** paraíso *m* fiscal

taxi ['tæksɪ] taxi *m*; **taxi driver** taxista *m/f*

taxing ['tæksɪŋ] difícil

'taxi stand, *Br* **'taxi rank** parada *f* de taxis

'taxpayer contribuyente *m/f*; **tax return** declaración *f* de la renta; **tax year** año *m* fiscal

TB [tiː'biː] (= *tuberculosis*) tuberculosis *f*

tea [tiː] *drink* té *m*; *meal* merienda *f*; **teabag** bolsita *f* de té

teach [ti:tʃ] **1** *v/t* enseñar **2** *v/i*: **he always wanted to ~** siempre quiso ser profesor; **teacher** *at primary school* maestro(-a) *m(f)*; *at secondary school, university* profesor(a) *m(f)*; **teaching** *profession* enseñanza *f*, docencia *f*

'tea-cup taza *f* de té

teak [ti:k] teca *f*

team [ti:m] equipo *m*; **team spirit** espíritu *m* de equipo; **teamster** camionero(-a) *m(f)*; **teamwork** trabajo *m* en equipo

'teapot tetera *f*

tear[1] [ter] **1** *n in cloth etc* desgarrón *m*, rotura *f* **2** *v/t paper, cloth* rasgar **3** *v/i* (*run fast, drive fast*) ir a toda velocidad

◆ **tear down** *poster* arrancar; *building* derribar

◆ **tear out** *page* arrancar

◆ **tear up** romper

tear[2] [tɪr] *n in eye* lágrima *f*; **be in ~s** estar llorando; **tearful** lloroso; **tear gas** gas *m* lacrimógeno

tease [ti:z] tomar el pelo a; *animal* hacer rabiar

'teaspoon *object* cucharilla *f*; *quantity* cucharadita *f*

technical ['teknɪkl] técnico; **technically** técnicamente; **technician** técnico(-a) *m(f)*; **technique** técnica *f*

technological [teknə'lɑ:dʒɪkl] tecnológico; **technology** tecnología *f*; **technophobia** rechazo *m* de las nuevas tecnologías

teddy bear ['tedɪber] osito *m* de peluche

tedious ['ti:dɪəs] tedioso

tee [ti:] *in golf* tee *m*

teenage ['ti:neɪdʒ] *fashions* adolescente, juvenil; **teenager** adolescente *m/f*

teens [ti:nz] adolescencia *f*

teeny ['ti:nɪ] F chiquitín F

teeth [ti:θ] *pl* ☞ **tooth**

teethe [ti:ð] echar los dientes

telecommunications [telɪkəmju:nɪ'keɪʃnz] telecomunicaciones *fpl*

telegraph pole ['telɪgræf] *Br* poste *m* telegráfico

telepathic [telɪ'pæθɪk] telepático; **telepathy** telepatía *f*

telephone ['telɪfoʊn] **1** *n* teléfono *m* **2** *v/t & v/i* telefonear; **telephone book** guía *f* telefónica, listín *m* telefónico; **telephone booth** cabina *f* telefónica; **telephone call** llamada *f* telefónica; **telephone conversation** conversación *f* por teléfono *or* telefónica; **telephone directory** guía *f* telefónica, listín *m* telefónico; **telephone number** número *m* de teléfono

telephoto lens [telɪ'foʊtoʊlenz] teleobjetivo *m*

telesales ['telɪseɪlz] televentas *fpl*

telescope ['telɪskoʊp] telescopio *m*

televise ['telɪvaɪz] televisar

television ['telɪvɪʒn] televisión *f*; **on ~** en la televisión;

television program, Br television programme programa m televisivo; television studio estudio m de televisión

tell [tel] 1 v/t contar; I can't ~ the difference no veo la diferencia; ~ s.o. sth decir algo a alguien; ~ s.o. to do sth decir a alguien que haga algo 2 v/i (have effect) hacerse notar; teller in bank cajero(-a) m(f); telling off regañina f; telltale 1 adj signs revelador 2 n chivato(-a) m(f)

temp [temp] 1 n employee trabajador(a) m(f) temporal 2 v/i hacer trabajo temporal

temper ['tempər] (bad ~) mal humor m; lose one's ~ perder los estribos

temperament ['tempərmənt] temperamento m; temperamental (moody) temperamental

temperate ['tempərət] templado

temperature ['temprətfər] temperatura f; (fever) fiebre f

temple¹ ['templ] REL templo m

temple² ['templ] ANAT sien f

tempo ['tempou] tempo m

temporarily [tempə'rerili] temporalmente; temporary temporal

tempt [tempt] tentar; temptation tentación f; tempting tentador

ten [ten] diez

tenacious [tɪ'neɪʃəs] tenaz; tenacity tenacidad f

tenant ['tenənt] of building inquilino(-a) m(f); of land arrendatario(-a) m(f)

tend¹ [tend] v/t (look after) cuidar (de)

tend² [tend] v/i: ~ to do sth soler hacer algo

tendency ['tendənsɪ] tendencia f

tender¹ ['tendər] adj (sore) sensible(e); (affectionate) cariñoso; tierno; steak tierno

tender² ['tendər] n COM oferta f

tenderness ['tendərnɪs] (soreness) dolor m; of kiss etc cariño m, ternura f

tendon ['tendən] tendón m

tennis ['tenɪs] tenis m; tennis ball pelota f de tenis; tennis court pista f de tenis, cancha f de tenis; tennis player tenista m/f

tenor ['tenər] MUS tenor m

tense¹ [tens] n gram tiempo m

tense² [tens] adj muscle, voice tenso

tension ['tenʃn] tensión f

tent [tent] tienda f

tentative ['tentətɪv] move, offer provisional

tenth [tenθ] 1 adj décimo m; of second, degree décima f

tepid ['tepɪd] tibio

term [tɜːrm] in office etc mandato m; Br EDU trimestre m; (condition, word) término m;

be on good / bad ~s with s.o. llevarse bien / mal con alguien; *in the long / short ~* a largo / corto plazo

terminal ['tɜːmɪnl] **1** *n* at airport, for buses terminal *f*; ELEC, COMPUT terminal *m*; of battery polo *m* **2** *adj* illness terminal; *terminally: ~ ill* en la fase terminal de una enfermedad; **terminate 1** *v/t* contract rescindir; *pregnancy* interrumpir **2** *v/i* finalizar; **termination** *of contract* rescisión *f*; *of pregnancy* interrupción *f*

terminus ['tɜːmɪnəs] *for buses* final *m* de trayecto; *for trains* estación *f* terminal

terrace ['terəs] terraza *f*

terrain [te'reɪn] terreno *m*

terrible ['terəbl] terrible; **terribly** (*very*) tremendamente

terrific [tə'rɪfɪk] estupendo; **terrifically** (*very*) tremendamente

terrify ['terɪfaɪ] aterrorizar; **terrifying** aterrador

territorial [terɪ'tɔːriəl] territorial; **territory** territorio *m*

terror ['terər] terror *m*; **terrorism** terrorismo *m*; **terrorist** terrorista *m/f*; **terrorist attack** atentado *m* terrorista; **terrorize** aterrorizar

terse [tɜːs] tajante, seco

test [test] **1** *n* prueba *f*; *academic*, *for driving* examen *m* **2** *v/t* probar; **test-drive** *car* probar en carretera

testicle ['testɪkl] testículo *m*

testify ['testɪfaɪ] LAW testificar, prestar declaración

testimony ['testɪmənɪ] LAW testimonio *m*

testy ['testɪ] irritable

tetanus ['tetənəs] tétanos *m*

text [tekst] **1** *n* texto *m*; (*~ message*) mensaje *m* **2** *v/t* mandar un mensaje a; **textbook** libro *m* de texto

textile ['tekstaɪl] textil *m*

text message mensaje *m* de texto

texture ['tekstʃər] textura *f*

than [ðæn] que; *with numbers* de; *bigger ~ me* más grande que yo

thank [θæŋk] dar las gracias a; *~ you* gracias; **thankful** agradecido; **thankfully** (*luckily*) afortunadamente; **thankless** *task* ingrato; **thanks** gracias *fpl*; **Thanksgiving (Day)** Día *m* de Acción de Gracias

that [ðæt] **1** *adj* ese *m*, esa *f*; *more remote* aquel *m*, aquella; *~ one* ése *m*, ésa; *more remote* aquél *m*, aquella *f*; *what is ~?* ¿qué es eso?; *who is ~?* ¿quién es ése?; *~'s tea* es té; *~'s very kind* qué amable; **3** *rel pron* que; *the car ~ you see* el coche que ves **4** *conj* que; *I think ~ ...* creo que... **5** *adv* (*so*) tan; *~ expensive* tan caro

thaw [θɔː] *of snow* derretirse, fundirse; *of frozen food* descongelarse

the [ðə] el, la; *plural* los, las; **~ sooner ~ better** cuanto antes, mejor

theater, *Br* **theatre** ['θɪətər] teatro *m*; **theatrical** *also fig* teatral

theft [θeft] robo *m*

their [ðer] su; **theirs** el suyo, la suya; **that book is ~** ese libro es suyo; **a friend of ~** un amigo suyo

them [ðem] *direct object* los *mpl*, las *fpl*; *indirect object* les; *after prep* ellos *mpl*, ellas *fpl*; **I know ~** los / las conozco; **I gave ~ the keys** les di las llaves; **I sold it to ~** se lo vendí; **with ~** con ellos / ellas; **it's ~** son ellos / ellas; **if a person asks for help, you should help ~** si una persona pide ayuda, hay que ayudarla

theme [θiːm] tema *m*; **theme park** parque *m* temático

themselves [ðem'selvz] *reflexive* se; *emphatic* ellos mismos *mpl*, ellas mismas *fpl*; **they hurt ~** se hicieron daño

then [ðen] *(at that time, deducing)* entonces; *(after that)* luego, después; **by ~** para entonces

theoretical [θɪə'retɪk] teórico; **theoretically** en teoría; **theory** teoría *f*

therapeutic [θerə'pjuːtɪk] terapéutico; **therapist** terapeuta *m/f*; **therapy** terapia *f*

there [ðer] allí, ahí, allá; **down ~** allí *or* ahí *or* allá abajo; **~ is / are ...** hay...; **~ is / are not ...** no hay...; **~ you are** *giving sth* aquí tienes; *finding sth* aquí está; *completing sth* ya está; **~ and back** ida y vuelta; **it's 5 miles ~ and back** entre ida y vuelta hay cinco millas; **~ he is!** ¡ahí está!, **~!** ¡venga!; **thereabouts** aproximadamente; **therefore** por (lo) tanto

thermometer [θər'mɑːmɪtər] termómetro *m*

thermos flask ['θɜːrməs] termo *m*

these [ðiːz] **1** *adj* estos(-as) **2** *pron* éstos *mpl*, éstas *fpl*

thesis ['θiːsɪs] tesis *f inv*

they [ðeɪ] ellos *mpl*, ellas *fpl*; **~ are Mexican** son mexicanos; **if anyone looks at this, ~ will see that ...** si alguien mira esto, verá que...; **~ say that ...** dicen que...

thick [θɪk] *soup* espeso; *fog* denso; *wall, book* grueso; *hair* poblado; F *(stupid)* corto; **thicken** *sauce* espesar; **thickskinned** *fig* insensible

thief [θiːf] ladrón(-ona) *m(f)*

thigh [θaɪ] muslo *m*

thin [θɪn] *person* delgado; *hair* ralo, escaso; *soup* claro; *coat, line* fino

thing [θɪŋ] cosa *f*

think [θɪŋk] pensar; *hold an opinion* pensar, creer; **I ~ so** creo que sí; **I don't ~ so** creo que no; **what do you ~ of it?** ¿qué te parece

◆ **think over** reflexionar so-

bre
♦ **think through** pensar bien
♦ **think up** *plan* idear
'**think tank** grupo *m* de expertos
thin-skinned [θɪn'skɪnd] sensible
third [θɜːrd] **1** *adj* tercero **2** *n* tercero(a) *m(f)*; *fraction* tercio *m*, tercera parte *f*; **thirdly** en tercer lugar; **third party** tercero *m*; **third-party insurance** seguro *m* a terceros; **Third World** Tercer Mundo *m*
thirst [θɜːrst] sed *f*; **thirsty** sediento; **be ~** tener sed
thirteen [θɜːr'tiːn] trece; **thirteenth** decimotercero; **thirtieth** trigésimo; **thirty** treinta
this [ðɪs] **1** *adj* este *m*, esta *f*; **~ one** éste *m*, ésta *f*; **~ is good** esto es bueno; **is ... introducing s.o.** éste / ésta es...; TELEC soy... **3** *adv*: **~ high** así de alto
thorn [θɔːrn] espina *f*; **thorny** *also fig* espinoso
thorough ['θɜːroʊ] *search* minucioso; *knowledge* profundo; *person* concienzudo; **thoroughbred** *horse* pura-sangre *m*; **thoroughly** completamente; **clean up** a fondo; *search* minuciosamente
those [ðoʊz] **1** *adj* esos *mpl*, esas *fpl*; *more remote* aquellos *mpl*, aquellas *fpl* **2** *pron* ésos *mpl*, ésas *fpl*; *more remote* aquéllos *mpl*, aquéllas

mpl
though [ðoʊ] **1** *conj* (*although*) aunque; **as ~** como si **2** *adv* sin embargo
thought [θɔːt] *single idea f*; *collective* pensamiento *m*; **thoughtful** pensativo; *book* serio; (*considerate*) atento; **thoughtless** desconsiderado
thousand ['θaʊznd] mil *m*; **thousandth** milésimo
thrash [θræʃ] *also* SP dar una paliza a
♦ **thrash out** *solution* alcanzar
thrashing ['θræʃɪŋ] *also* SP paliza *f*
thread [θred] **1** *n* hilo *m*; *of screw* rosca *f* **2** *v/t needle* enhebrar; *beads* ensartar; **threadbare** raído
threat [θret] amenaza *f*; **threaten** amenazar; **threatening** amenazador
three [θriː] tres; **three-quarters** tres cuartos *mpl*
threshold ['θreʃhoʊld] *of house, new age* umbral *m*
thrifty ['θrɪftɪ] ahorrativo
thrill [θrɪl] **1** *n* emoción *f*, estremecimiento *m* **2** *v/t*: **be ~ed** estar entusiasmado; **thriller** *movie* película *f* de Span suspense *or L.Am.* suspenso; *novel* novela *f* de Span suspense *or L.Am.* suspenso; **thrilling** emocionante
thrive [θraɪv] *of plant* medrar; *of business* prosperar

throat [θrəʊt] garganta f;
throat lozenge pastilla f para la garganta

throb [θrɒb] **1** n of heart latido m; of music zumbido m **2** v/i of heart latir; of music zumbar

throne [θrəʊn] trono m

throttle ['θrɒtl] **1** n on motorbike acelerador m; on boat palanca f del gas **2** v/t (strangle) estrangular

through [θruː] **1** prep ◇ (across) a través de; **go ~ the city** atravesar la ciudad ◇ (during) durante; **Monday ~ Friday** de lunes a viernes ◇ (by means of) por medio de; **arranged ~ him** acordado por él **2** adv: **wet ~** completamente mojado **3** adj: **be ~ of couple** haber terminado; **I'm ~ with ...** (finished with) he terminado con...; **throughout 1** prep durante, a lo largo de **2** adv (in all parts) en su totalidad

throw [θrəʊ] **1** v/t tirar; (disconcert) desconcertar; party dar **2** n lanzamiento m
◆ **throw away** tirar, L.Am. botar
◆ **throw out** old things tirar, L.Am. botar; from bar, job, home echar; from country expulsar; plan rechazar
◆ **throw up 1** v/t ball lanzar hacia arriba **2** v/i (vomit) vomitar
'throw-away remark insus-

tancial, pasajero; (disposable) desechable; **throw-in** SP saque m de banda

thru [θruː] → **through**

thrust [θrʌst] (push hard) empujar; knife hundir

thud [θʌd] golpe m sordo

thug [θʌg] matón m

thumb [θʌm] **1** n pulgar m **2** v/t: **~ a ride** hacer autoestop; **thumbtack** chincheta f

thunder ['θʌndər] truenos mpl; **thunderous** applause tormenta f; **thunderstorm** tormenta f (con truenos); **thunderstruck** atónito; **thundery** weather tormentoso

Thursday ['θɜːrzdeɪ] jueves m inv

thus [ðʌs] (in this way) así

thwart [θwɔːrt] frustrar

tick [tɪk] **1** n of clock tictac m; Br (checkmark) señal f de visto bueno **2** v/i of clock hacer tictac

ticket ['tɪkɪt] for bus, train, lottery billete m, L.Am. boleto m; for airplane billete m, L.Am. pasaje m; for theater, museum entrada f, L.Am. boleto m; for speeding etc multa f; **ticket machine** máquina f expendedora de billetes; **ticket office** at station ostrador m de venta de billetes; THEA taquilla f, L.Am. boletería f

ticking ['tɪkɪŋ] noise tictac m

tickle ['tɪkl] **1** v/t person hacer cosquillas a **2** v/i of material

tidal wave

hacer cosquillas

tidal wave ['taɪdlweɪv] mare-moto *m* (*ola*)

tide [taɪd] marea *f*

tidiness ['taɪdɪnɪs] orden *m*; tidy ordenado

◆ **tidy up 1** *v/t* ordenar; **tidy o.s. up** arreglarse **2** *v/i* recoger

tie [taɪ] **1** *n* (*necktie*) corbata *f*; SP (*even result*) empate *m*; **he doesn't have any ~s** no está atado a nada **2** *v/t knot, hands* atar **3** *v/i* SP empatar

◆ **tie down** *also fig* atar

◆ **tie up** *person, laces* atar; *boat* amarrar; *hair* recoger

tier [tɪr] *of hierarchy* nivel *m*; *in stadium* grada *f*

tight [taɪt] **1** *adj clothes* ajusta-do, estrecho; *security* estric-to; (*hard to move*) apretado; (*properly shut*) cerrado; (*not leaving much time*) justo de tiempo; F (*drunk*) como una cuba F **2** *adv hold* fuerte; *shut* bien; **tighten** *screw* apretar; *control* endurecer; *security* intensificar; **tight-fisted** agarrado; **tightly** *tight*; **tightrope** cuerda *f* flo-ja; **tights** Br medias *fpl*, panti *mpl*

tile [taɪl] *on floor* baldosa *f*; *on wall* azulejo *m*; *on roof* teja *f*

till¹ [tɪl] → **until**

till² [tɪl] (*cash register*) caja *f* (registradora)

tilt [tɪlt] **1** *v/t* inclinar **2** *v/i* in-clinarse

timber ['tɪmbər] madera *f* (de construcción)

time [taɪm] **1** *n* tiempo *m*; (*occasion*) vez *f*; **have a good ~** pasarlo bien; **what's the ~?** ¿qué hora es?; **the first ~** la primera vez; **all the ~** todo el rato; **at the same ~** *speak, reply etc* a la vez; (*however*) al mismo tiempo; *on ~* pun-tual; **in ~** con tiempo **2** *v/t* cronometrar; **time bomb** bomba *f* de relojería; **time difference** diferencia *f* hora-ria; **time-lag** intervalo *m*; **time limit** plazo *m*; **timely** oportuno; **time out** SP tiem-po *m* muerto; **timer** *device* temporizador *m*; **timesaving** ahorro *m* de tiempo; **timescale** *of project* plazo *m* (de tiempo); **time switch** temporizador *m*; **time zone** huso *m* horario

timid ['tɪmɪd] tímido

tin [tɪn] *metal* estaño *m*; Br (*can*) lata *f*; **tinfoil** papel *m* de aluminio

tinge [tɪndʒ] matiz *m*

tingle ['tɪŋgl] hormigueo *m*

tinkle ['tɪŋkl] *of bell* tintineo *m*

tinsel ['tɪnsl] espumillón *m*

tint [tɪnt] **1** *n of color* matiz *m*; *in hair* tinte *m* **2** *v/t hair* teñir; **tinted** *glasses* con un tinte; *paper* coloreado

tiny ['taɪnɪ] diminuto, minús-culo

tip¹ [tɪp] *n of stick, finger* pun-ta *f*; *of mountain* cumbre *f*; *of cigarette* filtro *m*

tip² [tɪp] **1** n advice consejo m; money propina f **2** v/t waiter etc dar propina a

◆ **tip off** avisar

tip-off soplo m

tipped [tɪpt] cigarettes con filtro

tippy-toe ['tɪpɪtoʊ]: **on ~** de puntillas

tipsy ['tɪpsɪ] achispado

tire¹ [taɪr] n neumático m, L.Am. llanta f

tire² [taɪr] **1** v/t cansar, fatigar **2** v/i cansarse, fatigarse

tired [taɪrd] cansado, fatigado; **tiredness** cansancio m, fatiga f; **tireless** efforts incansable, infatigable; **tiresome** (annoying) pesado; **tiring** agotador

tissue ['tɪʃuː] ANAT tejido m; (handkerchief) pañuelo m de papel, Kleenex® m; **tissue paper** papel m de seda

title ['taɪtl] título m; LAW título m de propiedad; **titleholder** SP campeón(-ona) m(f)

to [tuː] **1** prep a; **~ Japan / Chicago** a Japón / Chicago; **~ the north of ...** al norte de...; **give sth ~ s.o.** dar algo a alguien; **from Monday ~ Wednesday** de lunes a miércoles; **from 10 ~ 15 people** de 10 a 15 personas; **with verbs: ~ speak** hablar; **learn ~ swim** aprender a nadar; **too heavy ~ carry** demasiado pesado para llevarlo **2** adv: **~ and fro** de un lado pa-

ra otro

toast [toʊst] **1** n pan m tostado; when drinking brindis m inv **2** v/t when drinking brindar por; **toaster** tostador(a) m(f)

tobacco [təˈbækoʊ] tabaco m

today [təˈdeɪ] hoy

toddler ['tɑːdlər] niño m pequeño

to-do [təˈduː] F revuelo m

toe [toʊ] dedo m del pie; of shoe puntera f; **toenail** uña f del pie

together [təˈɡeðər] juntos (-as); (at the same time) a la vez

toilet ['tɔɪlɪt] place cuarto m de baño, servicio m; equipment retrete m; **toilet paper** papel m higiénico; **toiletries** artículos mpl de tocador

token ['toʊkən] (sign) muestra f; Br (gift~) vale m; (disk) ficha f

tolerable ['tɑːlərəbl] pain etc soportable; (quite good) aceptable; **tolerance** tolerancia f; **tolerant** tolerante; **tolerate** tolerar

toll¹ [toʊl] v/i of bell tañer

toll² [toʊl] n (deaths) mortandad f

toll³ [toʊl] n for bridge, road peaje m; telec tarifa f

'toll booth cabina f de peaje; **toll-free** TELEC gratuito

tomato [təˈmeɪtoʊ] tomate m, Mex jitomate m; **tomato ketchup** ketchup m

tomb [tuːm] tumba f; **tomb-**

stone lápida f

tomcat ['tɒmkæt] gato m

tomorrow [tə'mɔːrou] mañana; *the day after* ~ pasado mañana; *~ morning* mañana por la mañana

ton [tʌn] tonelada f (907 kg)

tone [toun] *of color, conversation* tono m; *of musical instrument* timbre m; *of neighborhood* nivel m; **toner** tóner m

tongue [tʌŋ] lengua f

tonic ['tɒnɪk] MED tónico m; **tonic (water)** (agua f) tónica f

tonight [tə'naɪt] esta noche

too [tuː] (*also*) también; (*excessively*) demasiado; *me* ~ yo también; *~ much rice* demasiado arroz

tool [tuːl] herramienta f

tooth [tuːθ] diente m; **toothache** dolor m de muelas; **toothbrush** cepillo m de dientes; **toothpaste** pasta f de dientes, dentífrico m; **toothpick** palillo m

top [tɒp] **1** n *of mountain* cima f; *of tree* copa f; *of wall, screen, page* parte f superior; (*lid: of bottle etc*) tapón m; *of pen* capucha f; *clothing* camiseta f, top m; (MOT: *gear*) directa f; *on* ~ *of* encima de, sobre; *be ~ of the league* ser el primero de la liga; *get to the* ~ *of country, mountain* llegar a la cumbre **2** *adj branches* superior; *floor* de arriba, último; *management*, *official* alto; *player* mejor; *speed, note* máximo

topic ['tɒpɪk] tema m; **topical** de actualidad

topless ['tɒplɪs] en topless; **topmost** superior; **topping** *on pizza* ingrediente m

topple ['tɒpl] **1** v/i derrumbarse **2** v/t *government* derrocar

top 'secret altamente confidencial

topsy-turvy [tɒpsɪ'tɜːrvɪ] (*in disorder*) desordenado; *world* al revés

torment ['tɔːrment] n tormento m **2** [tɔːr'ment] v/t atormentar

tornado [tɔːr'neɪdou] tornado m

torpedo [tɔːr'piːdou] **1** n torpedo m **2** v/t *also fig* torpedear

torrent ['tɒrənt] *also fig* torrente m; *of lava* colada f

torture ['tɔːrtʃər] **1** n tortura f **2** v/t torturar

toss [tɒs] *ball* lanzar; *rider* desmontar; *salad* remover

total ['toutl] **1** n total m **2** adj *amount* total; *disaster, stranger* completo; *idiot* de tomo y lomo; *totalitarian* totalitario; **totally** totalmente

totter ['tɒtər] tambalearse

touch [tʌtʃ] **1** n toque m; *sense* tacto m; *lose* ~ *with s.o.* perder el contacto con alguien; *in* ~ SP fuera **2** v/t tocar; *emotionally* conmover **3** v/i tocar; *of two lines etc* tocarse

◆ **touch down** *of airplane* aterrizar; SP marcar un ensayo

'**touchdown** *of airplane* aterrizaje *m*; SP touchdown *m*, ensayo *m*; **touching** conmovedor; **touchline** SP línea *f* de banda; **touch screen** pantalla *f* táctil; **touchy** *person* susceptible

tough [tʌf] *person, meat, punishment* duro; *question, exam* difícil; *material* resistente, fuerte

tour [tur] **1** *n of museum etc* recorrido *m*, *of area* viaje *m* (**of** por); *of band etc* gira *f* **2** *v/t area* recorrer **3** *v/i of band etc* estar de gira; **tour guide** guía *m/f* turístico(-a); **tourism** turismo *m*; **tourist** turista *m/f*; **tourist industry** industria *f* turística; **tourist (information) office** oficina *f* de turismo

tournament ['tʊrnəmənt] torneo *m*

'**tour operator** operador *m* turístico

tow [tou] remolcar

◆ **tow away** *car* llevarse

toward [tɔːrd] hacia

towel ['tauəl] toalla *f*

tower ['tauər] torre *f*

town [taun] ciudad *f*; *small* pueblo *m*; **town center**, *Br* **town centre** centro *m* de la ciudad / del pueblo; **town council** ayuntamiento *m*; **town hall** ayuntamiento *m*

toxic ['tɑːksɪk] tóxico; **toxin**

toxina *f*

toy [tɔɪ] juguete *m*

trace [treɪs] **1** *n of substance* resto *m* **2** *v/t* (*find*) localizar; (*follow: footsteps of*) seguir el rastro a; (*draw*) trazar

track [træk] (*path*) senda *f*, camino; *for horses* hipódromo *m*; *for cars* circuito *m*; *for athletics* pista *f*; *on CD* canción *f*, corte *m*; RAIL vía *f*; **keep ~ of sth** llevar la cuenta de algo

◆ **track down** localizar

'**tracksuit** *Br* chándal *m*

tractor ['træktər] tractor *m*

trade [treɪd] **1** *n* (*commerce*) comercio *m*; (*profession, craft*) oficio *m* **2** *v/i* (*do business*) comerciar **3** *v/t* (*exchange*) intercambiar; **trade fair** feria *f* de muestras; **trademark** marca *f* registrada; **trade mission** misión *f* comercial; **trader** comerciante *m*

tradition [trə'dɪʃn] tradición *f*; **traditional** tradicional; **traditionally** tradicionalmente

traffic ['træfɪk] tráfico *m*

◆ **traffic in** *drugs* traficar con

'**traffic circle** rotonda *f*, *Span* glorieta; **traffic cop** F poli *m* de tráfico F; **traffic jam** atasco *m*; **traffic light** semáforo *m*; **traffic sign** señal *f* de tráfico

tragedy ['trædʒədɪ] tragedia *f*; **tragic** trágico

trail [treɪl] **1** *n* (*path*) camino

m, senda *f*; *of blood* rastro *m*
2 *v/t* (*follow*) seguir la pista
de; (*tow*) arrastrar **3** *v/i* (*lag
behind*) ir a la zaga; *trailer
pulled by vehicle* remolque
m; (*mobile home*) caravana
f; *of movie* avance *m*, tráiler
m

train¹ [treɪn] *n* tren *m*

train² [treɪn] **1** *v/t team, athlete*
entrenar; *employee* formar;
dog adiestrar **2** *v/i of team,
athlete* entrenarse; *of teacher
etc* formarse

trainee aprendiz(a) *m(f)*

trainer SP entrenador(a)
m(f); *of dog* adiestrador(a)
m(f); **~s** Br: *shoes* zapatillas
fpl de deporte; **training** *of
staff* formación *f*; SP entrenamiento *m*

'train station estación *f* de
tren

traitor ['treɪtər] traidor(a)
m(f)

◆ **trample on** pisotear

trampoline ['træmpəliːn] cama *f* elástica

tranquil ['træŋkwɪl] tranquilo; **tranquility**, Br **tranquility** tranquilidad *f*; **tranquiliz-
er**, Br **tranquillizer** tranquili-
zante *m*

transaction [træn'zækʃn] *action* transacción *f*; *deal* negociación *f*

transatlantic
[trænzət'læntɪk] transatlántico

transcript ['trænskrɪpt] transcripción *f*

transfer 1 [træns'fɜːr] *v/t*
transferir **2** [træns'fɜːr] *v/i
in traveling* hacer transbordo
3 ['trænsfɜːr] *n also of money*
transferencia *f*; *in travel*
transbordo *m*; **transferable**
ticket transferible; **transfer
fee** *for football player* traspaso *m*

transform [træns'fɔːrm]
transformar; **transformation** transformación *f*;
transformer ELEC transformador *m*

transfusion [træns'fjuːʒn]
transfusión *f*

transit ['trænzɪt]: **in ~** en
tránsito; **transition** transición *f*; **transitional** de transición; **transit lounge** *at airport* sala *f* de tránsito; **transit
passenger** pasajero *m* en
tránsito

translate [træns'leɪt] traducir;
translation traducción *f*;
translator traductor(a) *m(f)*

transmission [trænz'mɪʃn] *of
news, program* emisión *f*; *of
disease*, MOT transmisión *f*;
transmit *program* emitir;
disease transmitir; **trans-
mitte** *for radio, TV* emisora *f*

transparency
[træns'pærənsɪ] PHOT diapositiva *f*; **transparent** *f*; transparente; (*obvious*) obvio

transplant MED **1**
[træns'plænt] *v/t* trans-
plantar **2** ['trænsplænt] *n*
transplante *m*

transport 1 [træn'spɔːrt] *v/t*

transportar 2 ['trænspɔːt] n transporte m; **transportation** transporte m

transvestite [træns'vestaɪt] travestí m, travestido m

trap [træp] 1 n trampa f 2 v/t atrapar; **trappings** *of power* parafernalia f

trash [træʃ] (*garbage*) basura f; (*poor product*) bazofia f; (*despicable person*) escoria f; **trashcan** cubo m de la basura; **trashy** *goods* barato

traumatic [trɔ'mætɪk] traumático; **traumatize** traumatizar

travel ['trævl] 1 n viajes mpl 2 v/t & v/i viajar; **travel agency** agencia f de viajes; **travel agent** agente m de viajes; **traveler,** *Br* **traveller** viajero(-a) m(f); **traveler's check,** *Br* **traveller's cheque** cheque m de viaje; **travel expenses** gastos mpl de viaje; **travel insurance** seguro m de asistencia en viaje

trawler ['trɔːlər] (*barco m*) arrastrero m

tray [treɪ] bandeja f

treacherous ['tretʃərəs] traicionero; **treachery** traición f

tread [tred] 1 n pasos mpl; *of staircase* huella f (del peldaño); *of tire* dibujo m 2 v/i andar

treason ['triːzn] traición f

treasure ['treʒər] 1 n *also person* tesoro m 2 v/t *gift etc* apreciar mucho; **treasurer**

tesorero(-a) m(f); **Treasury Department** Ministerio m de Hacienda

treat [triːt] 1 n placer; *it's my ~* (*I'm paying*) yo invito 2 v/t tratar; **~ s.o. to sth** invitar a alguien a algo; **treatment** tratamiento m

treaty ['triːtɪ] tratado m

treble ['trebl] 1 adv: **~ the price** el triple del precio 2 v/i triplicarse

tree [triː] árbol m

trekking ['trekɪŋ] SP trekking m; **trekking bike** SP bicicleta f de trekking; **trekking boot** SP bota f de trekking; **trekking shoe** SP zapato m de trekking

tremble ['trembl] temblar

tremendous [trɪ'mendəs] (*very good*) estupendo; (*enormous*) enorme; **tremendously** (*very*) tremendamente; (*a lot*) enormemente

tremor ['tremər] *of earth* temblor m

trench [trentʃ] trinchera f

trend [trend] tendencia f; (*fashion*) moda f; **trendy** de moda; *views* moderno

trespass ['trespæs] entrar sin autorización; **no ~ing** prohibido el paso; **trespasser** intruso(-a) m(f)

trial ['traɪəl] LAW juicio m; *of equipment* prueba f; **be on ~** LAW estar siendo juzgado

triangle ['traɪæŋgl] triángulo m; **triangular** triangular

tribe [traɪb] tribu *f*

tribunal [traɪˈbjuːnl] tribunal *m*

tributary [ˈtrɪbjətərɪ] *of river* afluente *m*

trick [trɪk] **1** *n* (*to deceive, knack*) truco *m* **2** *v/t* engañar; **trickery** engaños *mpl*

trickle [ˈtrɪkl] **1** *n* hilo *m*, reguero *m*; *fig: of money* goteo *m* **2** *v/i* gotear

tricky [ˈtrɪkɪ] (*difficult*) difícil

trifling [ˈtraɪflɪŋ] insignificante

trigger [ˈtrɪɡər] *on gun* gatillo *m*

◆ **trigger off** desencadenar

trim [trɪm] **1** *adj* (*neat*) muy cuidado; *figure* delgado **2** *v/t hair, costs* recortar; (*decorate: dress*) adornar **3** *n* (*light cut*) recorte *m*

trinket [ˈtrɪŋkɪt] baratija *f*

trip [trɪp] **1** *n* (*journey*) viaje *m* **2** *v/i* (*stumble*) tropezar **3** *v/t* (*make fall*) poner la zancadilla a

◆ **trip up 1** *v/t* (*make fall*) poner la zancadilla a; (*cause to go wrong*) confundir **2** *v/i* (*stumble*) tropezar; (*make a mistake*) equivocarse

triple [ˈtrɪpl] ☞ **treble**

trite [traɪt] manido

triumph [ˈtraɪʌmf] triunfo *m*

trivial [ˈtrɪvɪəl] trivial; **triviality** trivialidad *f*

trolley [ˈtrɑːlɪ] (*streetcar*) tranvía *m*

troops [truːps] tropas *fpl*

trophy [ˈtroʊfɪ] trofeo *m*

tropic [ˈtrɑːpɪk] trópico *m*; **tropical** tropical; **tropics** trópicos *mpl*

trot [trɑːt] trotar

trouble [ˈtrʌbl] **1** *n* (*difficulties*) problema *m*, problemas *mpl*; (*inconvenience*) molestia *f*; (*disturbance*) conflicto *m*; **get into ~** meterse en líos **2** *v/t* (*worry*) preocupar; (*bother, disturb*) molestar; **troublemaker** alborotador(a) *m(f)*; **troubleshooting** resolución *f* de problemas; **troublesome** problemático

trousers [ˈtraʊzərz] *Br* pantalones *mpl*

trout [traʊt] trucha *f*

truant [ˈtruːənt]: **play ~** hacer novillos, *Mex* irse de pinta, *S.Am.* hacerse la rabona

truce [truːs] tregua *f*

truck [trʌk] camión *m*; **truck driver** camionero(-a) *m(f)*; **truck stop** restaurante *m* de carretera

trudge [trʌdʒ] **1** *v/i* caminar fatigosamente **2** *n* caminata *f*

true [truː] verdadero, cierto; *friend, American* auténtico; **come ~** *of hopes, dream* hacerse realidad; **truly** verdaderamente; **Yours ~** le saluda muy atentamente

trumpet [ˈtrʌmpɪt] trompeta *f*

trunk [trʌŋk] *of tree, body* tronco *m*; *of elephant* trompa *f*; (*large case*) baúl *m*; *of car* maletero *m*, *C.Am.*, *Mex* cajuela f, Rpl baúl m

trust [trʌst] **1** n confianza f; FIN fondo m de inversión **2** v/t confiar en; **trusted** de confianza; **trustee** fideicomisario(-a) m(f); **trustful, trusting** confiado; **trustworthy** de confianza

truth [truːθ] verdad f; truthful sincero; **account** verdadero

try [traɪ] probar; LAW juzgar; ~ **to do sth** intentar hacer algo, tratar de hacer algo; **trying** (annoying) molesto

T-shirt [ˈtiːʃɜːrt] camiseta f

tub [tʌb] (bath) bañera f, L.Am. tina f; for liquid cuba f; of yoghurt envase m; **tubby** rechoncho

tube [tuːb] tubo m; **tubeless** tire sin cámara de aire

Tuesday [ˈtuːzdeɪ] martes m inv

tuft [tʌft] of hair mechón m; of grass mata f

tug [tʌg] **1** n (pull) tirón m; NAUT remolcador m **2** v/t (pull) tirar de

tuition [tuˈɪʃn] clases fpl

tumble [ˈtʌmbl] caer, caerse; **tumbledown** destartalado; **tumbler** for drink vaso m; in circus acróbata m f

tummy [ˈtʌmɪ] F tripa f F, barriga f F; **tummy ache** dolor m de tripa or barriga

tumor, Br **tumour** [ˈtuːmər] tumor m

tumult [ˈtuːmʌlt] tumulto m; **tumultuous** tumultuoso

tuna [ˈtuːnə] atún m

tune [tuːn] **1** n melodía f **2** v/t instrument afinar

◆ **tune up 1** v/i of orchestra afinar **2** v/t engine poner a punto

tuneful [ˈtuːnfəl] melodioso; **tune-up** of engine puesta f a punto

tunnel [ˈtʌnl] túnel m

turbine [ˈtɜːrbaɪn] turbina f

turbulence [ˈtɜːrbjələns] in air travel turbulencia f; **turbulent** turbulento

turf [tɜːrf] césped m; piece tepe m

turkey [ˈtɜːrkɪ] pavo m

turmoil [ˈtɜːrmɔɪl] desorden m, agitación f

turn [tɜːrn] **1** n (rotation) vuelta f; in road curva f; junction giro m; in vaudeville número m; **take ~s in doing sth** turnarse para hacer algo; **it's my ~** me toca a mí **2** v/t wheel girar; corner dar la vuelta a **3** v/i of driver, car, wheel girar; of person: turn around volverse; **it has ~ed cold** se ha enfriado

◆ **turn around 1** v/t object dar la vuelta a; company dar un vuelco a; COM (deal with) procesar **2** v/i of person volverse; of driver dar la vuelta

◆ **turn away 1** v/t (send away) rechazar **2** v/i (walk away) marcharse; (look away) desviar la mirada

◆ **turn back 1** v/t edges doblar **2** v/i of walkers etc volver; *in course of action* echarse atrás

◆ **turn down** *offer* rechazar; *volume, heating* bajar; *edge* doblar

◆ **turn off 1** *v/t TV, engine* apagar; *faucet* cerrar; *heater* apagar **2** *v/i of car, driver* doblar

◆ **turn on 1** *v/t TV, engine, heating* encender, *L.Am.* prender; *faucet* abrir; *F sexually* excitar **F 2** *v/i of machine* encenderse, *L.Am.* prenderse

◆ **turn over 1** *v/i in bed* darse la vuelta; *of vehicle* volcar **2** *v/t* (*put upside down*) dar la vuelta a; *page* pasar; *FIN* facturar

◆ **turn up 1** *v/t collar* subirse; *volume, heating* subir **2** *v/i* (*arrive*) aparecer

turning ['tɜːrnɪŋ] giro *m*; **turning point** punto *m* de inflexión; **turnout** *of people* asistencia *f*; **turnover** FIN facturación *f*; **turnpike** autopista *f* de peaje; **turn signal** *on car* intermitente *m*

turquoise ['tɜːrkwɔɪz] turquesa

turtle ['tɜːrtl] tortuga *f* (marina); **turtleneck sweater** suéter *m* de cuello alto

tusk [tʌsk] colmillo *m*

tutor ['tuːtər] *Br: at university* tutor *m*; (*private*) ~ profesor(a) *m(f)* particular

tuxedo [tʌk'siːdou] esmoquin *m*

TV [tiː'viː] televisión *f*; **on** ~ en la televisión; **TV dinner** menú *m* precocinado; **TV guide** guía *f* televisiva; **TV program**, *Br* **TV programme** programa *m* de televisión

twang [twæŋ] **1** *n in voice* entonación *f* nasal **2** *v/t guitar string* puntear

tweezers ['twiːzərz] pinzas *fpl*

twelfth [twelfθ] duodécimo; **twelve** doce

twentieth ['twentɪθ] vigésimo; **twenty** veinte

twice [twaɪs] dos veces; ~ **as much** el doble

twig [twɪg] ramita *f*

twilight ['twaɪlaɪt] crepúsculo *m*

twin [twɪn] gemelo *m*; **twin beds** camas *fpl* gemelas

twinge [twɪndʒ] *of pain* punzada *f*

twinkle ['twɪŋkl] *of stars* parpadeo *m*; *of eyes* brillo *m*

twin 'room habitación *f* con camas gemelas

twirl [twɜːrl] **1** *v/t* hacer girar **2** *n of cream etc* voluta *f*

twist [twɪst] **1** *v/t* retorcer; **one's ankle** torcerse el tobillo **2** *v/i of road, river* serpentear **3** *n in rope, road* vuelta *f*; *in plot* giro *m* inesperado; **twisty** *road* serpenteante

twitch [twɪtʃ] *nervous* tic *m*

twitter ['twɪtər] gorjear; IT twittear

two [tuː] dos; **the** ~ **of them** los dos, ambos

tycoon [taɪˈkuːn] magnate *m*

type [taɪp] **1** *n* (*sort*) tipo *m*, clase *f* **2** *v/i* (*use a keyboard*) escribir a máquina **3** *v/t* with a typewriter escribir a máquina

typhoon [taɪˈfuːn] tifón *m*

typhus [ˈtaɪfəs] tifus *m*

typical [ˈtɪpɪkl] típico; **typi-**cally típicamente

typist [ˈtaɪpɪst] mecanógrafo(-a) *m(f)*

tyrannical [tɪˈrænɪkl] tiránico; **tyrannize** tiranizar; **tyranny** tiranía *f*; **tyrant** tirano(-a) *m(f)*

tyre *Br* ☞ **tire**[1]

U

ugly [ˈʌɡlɪ] feo

UK [juːˈkeɪ] (= *United Kingdom*) RU *m* (= Reino Unido)

ulcer [ˈʌlsər] úlcera *f*; *in mouth* llaga *f*

ultimate [ˈʌltɪmət] (*final*) final; (*fundamental*) esencial; **ultimately** (*in the end*) en última instancia

ultimatum [ʌltɪˈmeɪtəm] ultimátum *m*

ultrasound [ˈʌltrəsaund] MED ultrasonido *m*; (*scan*) ecografía *f*

ultraviolet [ʌltrəˈvaɪələt] ultravioleta

umbrella [ʌmˈbrelə] paraguas *m inv*

umpire [ˈʌmpaɪr] árbitro *m*; *in tennis* juez *m/f* de silla

UN [juːˈen] (= *United Nations*) ONU *f* (= Organización *f* de las Naciones Unidas)

unable [ʌnˈeɪbl]: *be* ~ *to do sth not know how* no saber hacer algo; *not be in a posi-*tion no poder hacer algo

unacceptable [ʌnəkˈseptəbl] inaceptable

unaccountable [ʌnəˈkauntəbl] inexplicable

un-American [ʌnəˈmerɪkən] poco americano; *activities* antiamericano

unanimous [juːˈnænɪməs] *verdict* unánime; **unanimously** unánimemente

unapproachable [ʌnəˈproutʃəbl] *person* inaccesible

unarmed [ʌnˈɑːrmd] *person* desarmado

unassuming [ʌnəˈsuːmɪŋ] sin pretensiones

unattached [ʌnəˈtætʃt] *without a partner* sin compromiso, sin pareja

unattended [ʌnəˈtendɪd] desatendido

unauthorized [ʌnˈɔːθəraɪzd] no autorizado

unavoidable [ʌnəˈvɔɪdəbl] inevitable

unbalanced [ʌnˈbælənst] *also* PSYCH desequilibrado

unbearable [ʌnˈberəbl] insoportable

unbeatable [ʌnˈbiːtəbl] *team* invencible; *quality* insuperable

unbeaten [ʌnˈbiːtn] *team* invicto

unbelievable [ʌnbɪˈliːvəbl] *also* F increíble

unbias(s)ed [ʌnˈbaɪəst] imparcial

unblock [ʌnˈblɑːk] *pipe* desatascar

unbreakable [ʌnˈbreɪkəbl] *plates* irrompible; *world record* inalcanzable

unbutton [ʌnˈbʌtn] desabotonar

uncanny [ʌnˈkænɪ] *resemblance* increíble; *skill* inexplicable; *(worrying: feeling)* extraño, raro

unceasing [ʌnˈsiːsɪŋ] incesante

uncertain [ʌnˈsɜːrtn] *future, origins* incierto; **uncertainty** incertidumbre *f*

uncle [ˈʌŋkl] tío *m*

uncomfortable [ʌnˈkʌmftəbl] *chair* incómodo

uncommon [ʌnˈkɑːmən] poco corriente, raro

uncompromising [ʌnˈkɑːmprəmaɪzɪŋ] inflexible

unconditional [ʌnkənˈdɪʃnl] incondicional

unconscious [ʌnˈkɑːnʃəs] MED, PSYCH inconsciente

uncontrollable [ʌnkənˈtroʊləbl] incontrolable

unconventional [ʌnkən-

venˈʃnl] poco convencional

uncooperative [ʌnkoʊˈɑːpərətɪv]: *be* ~ no estar dispuesto a colaborar

uncover [ʌnˈkʌvər] *remove cover from* destapar; *plot, remains* descubrir

undamaged [ʌnˈdæmɪdʒd] intacto

undecided [ʌndɪˈsaɪdɪd] *question* sin resolver; *be* ~ *about* estar indeciso sobre

undeniable [ʌndɪˈnaɪəbl] innegable

under [ˈʌndər] debajo de, bajo; *(less than)* menos de; *it is* ~ *investigation* está siendo investigado

'undercarriage tren *m* de aterrizaje

'undercover *agent* secreto

under'cut COM vender más barato que

under'done *meat* poco hecho

under'estimate subestimar

under'fed malnutrido

under'go *surgery* ser sometido a; *experiences* sufrir

under'graduate estudiante *m/f* universitario(-a) *(todavía no licenciado(-a))*

'underground 1 *adj* subterráneo; POL clandestino **2** *adv work* bajo tierra

under'hand *(devious)* poco honrado

under'line *text* subrayar

under'lying subyacente

under'mine *position* minar

underneath [ʌndərˈniːθ] **1** *prep* debajo de, bajo **2** *adv* debajo

'**underpants** calzoncillos *mpl*

'**underpass** *for pedestrians* paso *m* subterráneo

underprivileged [ʌndər'prɪvɪlɪdʒd] desfavorecido

under'rate subestimar

understaffed [ʌndər'stæft] sin suficiente personal

under'stand entender, comprender; *language* entender; **understandable** comprensible; **understandably** comprensiblemente; **understanding 1** *adj person* comprensivo **2** *n* interpretación *f*; *(agreement)* acuerdo *m*

under'take *task* emprender; **~ to do sth** *(agree to)* encargarse de hacer algo; **undertaking** *(enterprise)* proyecto *m*, empresa *f*

under'value infravalorar

'**underwear** ropa *f* interior

'**underworld** *criminal* hampa *f*; *in mythology* Hades *m*

under'write FIN asegurar

undeserved [ʌndɪ'zɜːrvd] inmerecido

undesirable [ʌndɪ'zaɪrəbl] *features* no deseado; *person* indeseable

undisputed [ʌndɪ'spjuːtɪd] *champion* indiscutible

undo [ʌn'duː] *parcel* abrir; *buttons, shirt* desabrochar; *shoelaces* desatar; *s.o.'s work* deshacer

undoubtedly [ʌn'daʊtɪdlɪ] indudablemente

undress [ʌn'dres] **1** *v/t* desvestir; **get ~ed** desvestirse **2** *v/i* desvestirse

undue [ʌn'duː] *(excessive)* excesivo; **unduly** injustamente; *(excessively)* excesivamente

unearth [ʌn'ɜːrθ] descubrir; *remains* desenterrar

uneasy [ʌn'iːzɪ] *relationship, peace* tenso

uneatable [ʌn'iːtəbl] incomible

uneconomic [ʌniːkə'nɑːmɪk] antieconómico

uneducated [ʌn'edʒəkeɪtɪd] inculto, sin educación

unemployed [ʌnɪm'plɔɪd] desempleado, *Span* parado; **unemployment** desempleo *m*, *Span* paro *m*

unequal [ʌn'iːkwəl] desigual

unerring [ʌn'erɪŋ] *judgement, instinct* infalible

uneven [ʌn'iːvn] *quality* desigual; *surface* irregular

uneventful [ʌnɪ'ventfəl] *day, journey* sin incidentes

unexpected [ʌnɪk'spektɪd] inesperado; **unexpectedly** inesperadamente

unfair [ʌn'fer] injusto

unfaithful [ʌn'feɪθfəl] *husband, wife* infiel; **be ~ to s.o.** ser infiel a alguien

unfamiliar [ʌnfə'mɪljər] desconocido, extraño

unfasten [ʌn'fæsn] *belt* desabrochar

unfavorable, *Br* **unfavourable** [ʌn'feɪvərəbl] desfavorable

unfinished [ʌnˈfɪnɪʃt] inacabado

unfold [ʌnˈfould] **1** v/t *letter* desdoblar; *arms* descruzar **2** v/i *of story etc* desarrollarse; *of view* abrirse

unforeseen [ʌnfɔːrˈsiːn] imprevisto

unforgettable [ʌnfərˈgetəbl] inolvidable

unforgivable [ʌnfərˈgɪvəbl] imperdonable

unfortunate [ʌnˈfɔːrtʃənət] desafortunado; *event* desgraciado; **unfortunately** desgraciadamente

unfounded [ʌnˈfaundɪd] infundado

unfriendly [ʌnˈfrendlɪ] *person* antipático; *place* desagradable; *welcome* hostil

ungrateful [ʌnˈɡreɪtfəl] desagradecido

unhappiness [ʌnˈhæpɪnɪs] infelicidad *f*; **unhappy** infeliz; *day* triste; *customer etc* descontento

unharmed [ʌnˈhɑːrmd] ileso

unhealthy [ʌnˈhelθɪ] enfermizo; *food, economy* poco saludable

unheard-of [ʌnˈhɜːrdəv] inaudito

unhygienic [ʌnhaɪˈdʒiːnɪk] antihigiénico

unification [juːnɪfɪˈkeɪʃn] unificación *f*

uniform [ˈjuːnɪfɔːrm] **1** *n* uniforme *m* **2** *adj* uniforme

unify [ˈjuːnɪfaɪ] unificar

unilateral [juːnɪˈlætərəl] unilateral

unimaginable [ʌnɪˈmædʒɪnəbl] inimaginable

unimaginative [ʌnɪˈmædʒɪnətɪv] sin imaginación

unimportant [ʌnɪmˈpɔːrtənt] poco importante

uninhabitable [ʌnɪnˈhæbɪtəbl] inhabitable; **uninhabited** *building* deshabitado; *region* desierto

unintentional [ʌnɪnˈtenʃnl] no intencionado; **unintentionally** sin querer

uninteresting [ʌnˈɪntrəstɪŋ] sin interés

uninterrupted [ʌnɪntəˈrʌptɪd] ininterrumpido

union [ˈjuːnjən] POL unión *f*; *(labor ~)* sindicato *m*

unique [juːˈniːk] único

unit [ˈjuːnɪt] unidad *f*

unite [juːˈnaɪt] **1** v/t unir **2** v/i unirse; **united** unido; **United Kingdom** Reino *m* Unido; **United Nations** Naciones *fpl* Unidas; **United States (of America)** Estados *mpl* Unidos (de América)

unity [ˈjuːnətɪ] unidad *f*

universal [juːnɪˈvɜːrsl] universal; **universe** universo *m*

university [juːnɪˈvɜːrsətɪ] universidad *f*

unjust [ʌnˈdʒʌst] injusto

unkind [ʌnˈkaɪnd] desagradable, cruel

unknown [ʌnˈnoun] desconocido

unleaded [ʌnˈledɪd] sin plomo

unless [ən'les] a menos que, a no ser que

unlikely [ʌn'laɪklɪ] improbable; *explanation* inverosímil

unlimited [ʌn'lɪmɪtɪd] ilimitado

unload [ʌn'ləʊd] descargar

unlock [ʌn'lɑːk] abrir

unluckily [ʌn'lʌkɪlɪ] desgraciadamente, por desgracia; **unlucky** *day* aciago, funesto; *person* sin suerte; **that was so ~ for you!** ¡qué mala suerte tuviste!

unmanned [ʌn'mænd] *spacecraft* no tripulado

unmarried [ʌn'mærɪd] soltero

unmistakable [ʌnmɪ'steɪkəbl] inconfundible

unnatural [ʌn'nætʃrəl] anormal

unnecessary [ʌn'nesəserɪ] innecesario

unnerving [ʌn'nɜːrvɪŋ] desconcertante

unobtainable [ʌnəb'teɪnəbl] *goods* no disponible; TELEC desconectado

unobtrusive [ʌnəb'truːsɪv] discreto

unoccupied [ʌn'ɑːkjʊpaɪd] *building* desocupado; *post* vacante

unofficial [ʌnə'fɪʃl] no oficial; **unofficially** extraoficialmente

unorthodox [ʌn'ɔːrθədɑːks] poco ortodoxo

unpack [ʌn'pæk] **1** *v/t* deshacer **2** *v/i* deshacer el equipaje

unpaid [ʌn'peɪd] *work* no re-

munerado

unpleasant [ʌn'pleznt] desagradable

unplug [ʌn'plʌg] *TV, computer* desenchufar

unpopular [ʌn'pɑːpjələr] impopular

unprecedented [ʌn'presɪdentɪd] sin precedentes

unpredictable [ʌnprɪ'dɪktəbl] imprevisible, impredecible

unpretentious [ʌnprɪ'tenʃəs] modesto, sin pretensiones

unproductive [ʌnprə'dʌktɪv] *meeting* infructuoso; *soil* improductivo

unprofessional [ʌnprə'feʃnl] poco profesional

unprofitable [ʌn'prɑːfɪtəbl] no rentable

unprovoked [ʌnprə'vəʊkt] *attack* no provocado

unqualified [ʌn'kwɑːlɪfaɪd] sin titulación

unquestionably [ʌn'kwestʃnəblɪ] indiscutiblemente; **unquestioning** *attitude* incondicional

unreadable [ʌn'riːdəbl] *book* ilegible

unrealistic [ʌnrɪə'lɪstɪk] poco realista

unreasonable [ʌn'riːznəbl] irrazonable

unrelated [ʌnrɪ'leɪtɪd] *issues* no relacionado; *people* no emparentado

unrelenting [ʌnrɪ'lentɪŋ] implacable

unreliable [ʌnrɪ'laɪəbl] *ma-*

chine poco fiable; *person* informal

unrest [ʌn'rest] malestar *m*; *(rioting)* disturbios *mpl*

unrestrained [ʌnrɪ'streɪnd] *emotions* incontrolado

unroll [ʌn'rəʊl] desenrollar

unruly [ʌn'ruːlɪ] revoltoso

unsanitary [ʌn'sænɪterɪ] insalubre

unsatisfactory [ʌnsætɪs'fæktərɪ] insatisfactorio

unscathed [ʌn'skeɪðd] *(not injured)* ileso; *(not damaged)* intacto

unscrew [ʌn'skruː] *top* desenroscar; *hooks* desatornillar

unscrupulous [ʌn'skruːpjələs] sin escrúpulos

unselfish [ʌn'selfɪʃ] generoso

unsettled [ʌn'setld] *issue* sin decidir; *weather, lifestyle* inestable; *bills* sin pagar

unshaven [ʌn'ʃeɪvn] sin afeitar

unskilled [ʌn'skɪld] no cualificado

unsophisticated [ʌnsə'fɪstɪkeɪtɪd] sencillo; *equipment* simple

unstable [ʌn'steɪbl] inestable

unsteady [ʌn'stedɪ] *hand* tembloroso; *ladder* inestable

unsuccessful [ʌnsək'sesfəl] *writer etc* fracasado; *candidate* perdedor; *party, attempt* fallido; **unsuccessfully** sin éxito

unsuitable [ʌn'suːtəbl] inadecuado; *thing to say* inoportuno

unswerving [ʌn'swɜːrvɪŋ] *loyalty* inquebrantable

unthinkable [ʌn'θɪŋkəbl] impensable

untidy [ʌn'taɪdɪ] *room, desk* desordenado; *hair* revuelto

untie [ʌn'taɪ] desatar

until [ən'tɪl] **1** *prep* hasta que; **not ~ Friday** no antes del viernes **2** *conj* hasta que; **can you wait ~ I'm ready?** ¿puedes esperar hasta que esté listo?

untiring [ʌn'taɪrɪŋ] *efforts* incansable

untold [ʌn'təʊld] *suffering* indecible; *riches* inconmensurable; *story* nunca contado

untrue [ʌn'truː] falso

unused [ʌn'juːzd] *goods* sin usar

unusual [ʌn'juːʒl] poco corriente; **it is ~ ...** es raro or extraño...; **unusually** inusitadamente

unveil [ʌn'veɪl] *statue etc* desvelar

unwell [ʌn'wel] indispuesto, mal

unwilling [ʌn'wɪlɪŋ] poco dispuesto, reacio; **unwillingly** de mala gana

unwind [ʌn'waɪnd] *of story* irse desarrollando; *(relax)* relajarse

unwise [ʌn'waɪz] imprudente

unwrap [ʌn'ræp] desenvolver

unzip [ʌn'zɪp] abrir la cremallera de; COMPUT descomprimir

up [ʌp] **1** *adv position* arriba;

movement hacia arriba; **~ here / there** aquí / allí arriba; **be ~** (*out of bed*) estar levantado; *of sun* haber salido; *of temperature* haber subido; (*have expired*) haberse acabado; **he came ~?** F ¿qué pasa?; **~ to 1989** hasta el año 1989; **he came ~ to me** se me acercó; **what are you ~ to these days?** ¿qué es de tu vida?; **be ~ to something** (*bad*) estar tramando algo; **I don't feel ~ to it** no me siento en condiciones de hacerlo; **it's ~ to you** tú decides; **it is ~ to them to solve it** (*their duty*) les corresponde a ellos resolverlo **2** *prep*: **further ~ the mountain** más arriba de la montaña; **they ran ~ the street** corrieron por la calle; **we traveled ~ to Chicago** subimos hasta Chicago **3** *n*: **~s and downs** altibajos *mpl*

'**upbringing** educación *f*

up'date *file* actualizar

up'grade modernizar; **~ s.o. to business class** cambiar a alguien a clase ejecutiva

upheaval [ʌpˈhiːvl] *emotional* conmoción *f*; *physical* trastorno *m*; *political, social* sacudida *f*

up'hold *rights* defender, conservar; (*vindicate*) confirmar

'**upkeep** mantenimiento *m*

up'load COMPUT cargar

up'market *Br restaurant, hotel* de categoría

upon [əˈpɒn] ☞ **on**

upper [ˈʌpər] superior

'**upright 1** *adj citizen* honrado **2** *adv sit* derecho; **upright** (*piano*) piano *m* vertical

'**uprising** levantamiento *m*

up'roar alboroto *m*; (*protest*) tumulto *m*

up'set 1 *v/t* tirar; *emotionally* disgustar **2** *adj emotionally* disgustado; **upsetting** triste

upside 'down boca abajo

up'stairs 1 *adv* arriba **2** *adj room* de arriba

up'stream río arriba

up'tight F (*nervous*) tenso; (*inhibited*) estrecho

up-to-'date *information* actualizado

'**upturn** *in economy* mejora *f*

upward [ˈʌpwərd] hacia arriba; **~ of 100** más de 100

uranium [juˈreɪnɪəm] uranio *m*

urban [ˈɜːrbən] urbano

urge [ɜːrdʒ] **1** *n* impulso *m* **2** *v/t*: **~ s.o. to do sth** rogar a alguien que haga algo; **urgency** urgencia *f*; **urgent** urgente

urinate [ˈjʊərəneɪt] orinar; **urine** orina *f*

Uruguay [ˈjʊərəgwaɪ] Uruguay; **Uruguayan 1** *adj* uruguayo **2** *n* uruguayo(-a) *m(f)*

US [juːˈes] (= *United States*) EE.UU. *mpl* (= *Estados mpl* Unidos)

us [ʌs] nos; *after prep* nosotros (-as); **that's for ~** eso es para nosotros; **who's that? – it's ~**

¿quién es? - ¡somos nosotros!

USA [juːesˈeɪ] (= **United States of America**) EE.UU. *mpl* (= Estados *mpl* Unidos)

usage [ˈjuːzɪdʒ] uso *m*

USB cable IT cable *m* USB; **USB drive** IT memoria *f* USB; **USB stick** IT memoria *f* USB, llave *f* de memoria USB

use 1 [juːz] *v/t tool, word* utilizar, usar; *skills, car* usar; *a lot of gas* consumir; *pej: person* utilizar **2** [juːs] *n* uso *m*, utilización *f*; **it's no ~ waiting** no sirve de nada esperar
♦ **use up** agotar

used¹ [juːzd] *adj car etc* de segunda mano

used² [juːst]: **be ~ to** estar acostumbrado a; **get ~ to** acostumbrarse a

used³ [juːst]: **I ~ to like him** antes me gustaba; **they ~ to meet every Saturday** solían verse todos los sábados

useful [ˈjuːsfəl] útil; **usefulness** utilidad *f*; **useless** inútil; *machine* inservible; **user** usuario(-a) *m(f)*; **user account** IT cuenta *f* de usuario; **user-friendly** de fácil manejo; **user ID**, **user identification** IT identidad *f* de usuario; **user name** IT nombre *m* de usuario

usual [ˈjuːʒl] habitual; **as ~** como de costumbre; **usually** normalmente

utensil [juːˈtensl] utensilio *m*

utilize [ˈjuːtɪlaɪz] utilizar

utter [ˈʌtə] **1** *adj* completo **2** *v/t sound* decir; **utterly** completamente

V

vacant [ˈveɪkənt] *building* vacío; *position* vacante; *look* vago, distraído; **vacantly** distraídamente; **vacate room** desalojar

vacation [veɪˈkeɪʃn] vacaciones *fpl*; **be on ~** estar de vacaciones

vaccinate [ˈvæksɪneɪt] vacunar; **vaccination** *action* vacunar; **vaccination** *action* vacunación *f*; (*vaccine*) vacuna *f*; **vaccine** vacuna *f*

vacuum [ˈvækjʊəm] **1** *n* vacío

m **2** *v/t floors* aspirar

vagrant [ˈveɪɡrənt] vagabundo(-a) *m(f)*

vague [veɪɡ] vago; **vaguely** vagamente

vain [veɪn] **1** *adj* vanidoso; *hope* vano **2** *n*: **in ~** en vano

valiant [ˈvæljənt] valiente

valid [ˈvælɪd] válido; **validate** *with official stamp* sellar; *alibi* dar validez a; **validity** validez *f*

valley [ˈvælɪ] valle *m*

valuable ['væljʊbl] **1** *adj* valioso **2** *n*: **~s** objetos *mpl* de valor; **valuation** tasación *f*, valoración *f*; **value 1** *n* valor *m* **2** *v/t* valorar

valve [vælv] válvula *f*

van [væn] camioneta *f*, furgoneta *f*

vandal ['vændl] vándalo *m*; **vandalism** vandalismo *m*; **vandalize** destrozar (*intencionadamente*)

vanilla [vəˈnɪlə] **1** *n* vainilla *f* **2** *adj* de vainilla

vanish ['vænɪʃ] desaparecer

vanity ['vænɪtɪ] vanidad *f*

vapor ['veɪpər] vapor *m*; **vaporize** vaporizar; **vapour** *Br* ☞ **vapor**

variable ['verɪəbl] **1** *adj* variable **2** *n* variable *f*; **variant** variante *f*; **variation** variación *f*; **varied** variado; **variety** variedad *f*; **various** (*several*) varios; (*different*) diversos

varnish ['vɑːrnɪʃ] **1** *n* for wood barniz *m*; for fingernails esmalte *m* **2** *v/t* wood barnizar

vary ['verɪ] variar; **it varies** depende

vase [veɪz] jarrón *m*

vast [væst] vasto; *number, improvement* enorme; **vastly** enormemente

Vatican ['vætɪkən]: **the ~** el Vaticano

vault[1] [vɔːlt] *n* in roof bóveda *f*; **~s** (*cellar*) sótano *m*; of bank cámara *f* acorazada

vault[2] [vɔːlt] **1** *n* SP salto *m* **2**

v/t beam etc saltar

VCR [viːsiːˈɑːr] (= **video cassette recorder**) aparato *m* de *Span* vídeo *or L.Am.* video

veal [viːl] ternera *f*

veer [vɪr] girar, torcer

vegetable ['vedʒtəbl] hortaliza *f*; **~s** verduras *fpl*; **vegetarian 1** *n* vegetariano(-a) *m(f)* **2** *adj* vegetariano; **vegetation** vegetación *f*

vehement ['viːəmənt] vehemente

vehicle ['viːɪkl] vehículo *m*

veil [veɪl] velo *m*

vein [veɪn] ANAT vena *f*

velocity [vɪˈlɑːsɪtɪ] velocidad *f*

velvet ['velvɪt] terciopelo *m*

vendetta [venˈdetə] vendetta *f*

vending machine ['vendɪŋ] máquina *f* expendedora; **vendor** LAW parte *f* vendedora

veneer [vəˈnɪr] on wood chapa *f*; of politeness etc apariencia *f*

venerable ['venərəbl] venerable; **veneration** veneración *f*

venereal disease [vɪˈnɪrɪəl] enfermedad *f* venérea

venetian 'blind [vəˈniːʃn] persiana *f* veneciana

Venezuela [venɪˈweɪlə] Venezuela; **Venezuelan 1** *adj* venezolano **2** *n* venezolano(-a) *m(f)*

venom ['venəm] veneno *m*

ventilate ['ventɪleɪt] ventilar;

ventilation ventilación f;
ventilator ventilador m;
MED respirador m

venture ['ventʃər] **1** n (undertaking) iniciativa f; COM empresa f **2** v/i aventurarse

venue ['venjuː] for meeting lugar m; for concert local m, sala f

veranda [vəˈrændə] porche m

verb [vɜːrb] verbo m; **verbal**
(spoken) verbal; **verbally** de
palabra

verdict ['vɜːrdɪkt] veredicto
m

verge [vɜːrdʒ] of road arcén
m; **be on the ~ of** ruin estar
al borde de; tears estar a
punto de

verification [verɪfɪˈkeɪʃn]
(checking) verificación f;
(confirmation) confirmación
f; **verify** (check) verificar;
(confirm) confirmar

vermin ['vɜːrmɪn] bichos mpl,
alimañas fpl

vermouth [vɜːrˈmuːθ] vermut
m

versatile ['vɜːrsətl] polifacético, versátil; **versatility** po-
livalencia f, versatilidad f

verse [vɜːrs] verso m

version ['vɜːrʃn] versión f

versus ['vɜːrsəs] contra

vertical ['vɜːrtɪkl] vertical

vertigo ['vɜːrtɪgoʊ] vértigo m

very ['verɪ] **1** adv muy; **the ~
best** el mejor de todos **2**
adj: **at that ~ moment** en
ese mismo momento; **that's
the ~ thing I need** eso es

precisamente lo que necesito

vessel ['vesl] NAUT buque m

vest [vest] chaleco m; Br camiseta f interior

vestige ['vestɪdʒ] vestigio m

vet[1] [vet] n (veterinary surgeon) veterinario(-a) m(f)

vet[2] [vet] v/t applicants etc
examinar, investigar

vet[3] [vet] n mil veterano(-a)
m(f)

veteran ['vetərən] **1** n vetera-
no(-a) m(f) **2** adj veterano

veterinarian [vetərəˈneriən]
veterinario(-a) m(f)

veto ['viːtoʊ] **1** n veto m **2** v/t
vetar

via ['vaɪə] vía

viable ['vaɪəbl] viable

vibrate [vaɪˈbreɪt] vibrar; **vibration** vibración f

vice[1] [vaɪs] n vicio m

vice[2] [vaɪs] Br → **vise**

vice 'president vicepresiden-
te(-a) m(f)

vice versa [vaɪsˈvɜːrsə] viceversa

vicious ['vɪʃəs] dog fiero; attack, temper feroz; **viciously**
con brutalidad

victim ['vɪktɪm] víctima f; **vic-
timize** tratar injustamente

victorious [vɪkˈtɔːrɪəs] victorioso; **victory** victoria f

video ['vɪdɪoʊ] **1** n Span vídeo
m, L.Am. video m **2** v/t grabar en Span vídeo or L.Am.
video; **video call** IT, TELEC
videollamada f; **video camera** videocámara f; **video**

cassette videocasete *m*; **video recorder** aparato *m* de *Span* vídeo *or* *L.Am.* video; **videotape** cinta *f* de *Span* vídeo *or* *L.Am.* video

vie [vaɪ] competir

Vietnam [vɪet'næm] Vietnam; **Vietnamese 1** *adj* vietnamita **2** *n* vietnamita *m/f*; *language* vietnamita *m*

view [vjuː] **1** *n* *of situation* opinión *f*; **in ~ of** teniendo en cuenta **2** *v/t* ver **3** *v/i* (*watch TV*) ver la televisión; **viewer** TV telespectador(a) *m(f)*; **viewpoint** punto *m* de vista

vigor ['vɪɡər] vigor *m*; **vigorous** vigoroso; *person* enérgico; *denial* rotundo; **vigorously** con vigor; *deny, defend* rotundamente; **vigour** *Br* → **vigor**

village ['vɪlɪdʒ] pueblo *m*; **villager** aldeano(-a) *m(f)*

villain ['vɪlən] malo(a) *m(f)*

vindicate ['vɪndɪkeɪt] (*show to be correct*) dar la razón a; (*show to be innocent*) vindicar

vindictive [vɪn'dɪktɪv] vengativo

vine [vaɪn] vid *f*

vinegar ['vɪnɪɡər] vinagre *m*

vineyard ['vɪnjɑːrd] viñedo *m*

vintage ['vɪntɪdʒ] **1** *n of wine* cosecha *f* **2** *adj* clásico *m*

violate ['vaɪəleɪt] violar; **violation** violación *f*; (*traffic ~*) infracción *f*

violence ['vaɪələns] violencia *f*; **violent** violento

violin [vaɪə'lɪn] violín *m*; **violinist** violinista *m/f*

VIP [viːaɪ'piː] (= *very important person*) VIP *m*

viral ['vaɪrəl] vírico, viral

virgin ['vɜːrdʒɪn] virgen *m/f*; **virginity** virginidad *f*

virile ['vɪrəl] viril; **virility** virilidad *f*

virtual ['vɜːrtʃʊəl] virtual; **virtually** (*almost*) virtualmente

virtue ['vɜːrtʃuː] virtud *f*; **virtuous** virtuoso

virus ['vaɪrəs] virus *m inv*

visa ['viːzə] visa *f*, visado *m*

vise [vaɪs] torno *m* de banco

visibility [vɪzə'bɪlətɪ] visibilidad *f*; **visible** visible; *anger* evidente

vision ['vɪʒn] visión *f*

visit ['vɪzɪt] **1** *n* visita *f* **2** *v/t* visitar; **visitor** visita *f*; (*tourist*), *to museum etc* visitante *m/f*

visor ['vaɪzər] visera *f*

visual ['vɪʒʊəl] visual; **visualize** visualizar; (*foresee*) prever; **visually** visualmente

vital ['vaɪtl] (*essential*) vital; **vitality** vitalidad *f*; **vitally**: **~ important** de importancia vital

vitamin ['vaɪtəmɪn] vitamina *f*; **vitamin pill** pastilla *f* vitamínica

vivacious [vɪ'veɪʃəs] vivaz; **vivacity** vivacidad *f*

vivid ['vɪvɪd] *color* vivo; *imagination* vívido; **vividly** (*brightly*) vivamente; (*clear-*

ly) vívidamente

V-neck ['vi:nek] cuello *m* de pico

vocabulary [vou'kæbjuləri] vocabulario *m*

vocal ['voukl] vocal; *expressing opinions* ruidoso; **vocalist** MUS vocalista *m/f*

vocation [vo'keɪʃn] vocación *f*; *(profession)* profesión *f*; **vocational** *guidance* profesional

vodka ['vɑ:dkə] vodka *m*

vogue [voug] moda *f*; **be in ~** estar en boga

voice [vɔɪs] **1** *n* voz *f*; *of opinions* expresar; **voicemail** correo *m* de voz

volcano [vɑl'keɪnou] volcán *m*

volley ['vɑ:lɪ] *of shots* ráfaga *f*; *in tennis* volea *f*

volt [voult] voltio *m*; **voltage** voltaje *m*

volume ['vɑ:ljəm] volumen

m; *of container* capacidad *f*

voluntarily [vɑ:lən'terɪlɪ] voluntariamente; **voluntary** voluntario; **volunteer 1** *n* voluntario(-a) *m(f)* **2** *v/i* ofrecerse voluntariamente

vomit ['vɑ:mɪt] **1** *n* vómito *m* **2** *v/i* vomitar

voracious [və'reɪʃəs] voraz

vote [vout] **1** *n* voto *m* **2** *v/i* POL votar; **~ for / against** votar a favor / en contra; **voter** POL votante *m/f*; **voting** POL votación *f*

◆ **vouch for** [vautʃ] *truth* dar fe de; *person* responder por

vow [vau] **1** *n* voto *m* **2** *v/t:* **~ to do** prometer hacer

vowel [vaul] vocal *f*

voyage ['vɔɪdʒ] viaje *m*

vulgar ['vʌlgər] vulgar, grosero

vulnerable ['vʌlnərəbl] vulnerable

vulture ['vʌltʃər] buitre *m*

W

waddle ['wɑ:dl] *of duck* caminar; *of person* anadear

wade [weɪd] caminar en el agua

wafer ['weɪfər] *cookie* barquillo *m*; REL hostia *f*

waffle ['wɑ:fl] *to eat* gofre *m*

wag [wæg] **1** *v/t* menear **2** *v/i of tail* menearse

wages ['weɪdʒɪz] salario *m*, sueldo *m*

waggle ['wægl] *hips* menear;

loose screw etc mover

wail [weɪl] *of person* gemir; *of siren* sonar, aullar

waist [weɪst] cintura *f*

wait [weɪt] **1** *n* espera *f* **2** *v/i* esperar

◆ **wait for** esperar

◆ **wait on** *(serve)* servir; *(wait for)* esperar

◆ **wait up** esperar levantado

waiter ['weɪtər] camarero *m*; **waiting list** lista *f* de espera;

waiting room sala *f* de espera; **waitress** camarera *f*

waive [weɪv] *right* renunciar; *requirement* no aplicar

wake [weɪk] **1** *v/i*: ~ **(up)** despertarse **2** *v/t*: ~ **(up)** despertar

walk [wɔ:k] **1** *n* paseo *m*; *longer* caminata *f*; *(path)* camino *m*; **go for a** ~ salir a dar un paseo **2** *v/i* caminar, andar; *as opposed to driving* ir a pie **3** *v/t dog* sacar a pasear

◆ **walk out** *of spouse* marcharse; *from theater etc* salir; *(go on strike)* declararse en huelga

walker ['wɔ:kər] *(hiker)* excursionista *m/f*; *for baby, old person* andador *m*; **walking** *(hiking)* excursionismo *m*; **walkout** *(strike)* huelga *f*; **walkover** *(easy win)* paseo *m*

wall [wɔ:l] muro *m*; *inside* pared *f*

wallet ['wɔ:lɪt] *(billfold)* cartera *f*

'**wallpaper 1** *n* papel *m* pintado **2** *v/t* empapelar; **wall-to-wall** *Span* moqueta *f*, *L.Am.* alfombra *f*

waltz [wɔ:lts] vals *m*

wan [wɔːn] *face* pálido *m*

wander ['wɒndər] *(roam)* vagar, deambular; *(stray)* extraviarse

wangle ['wæŋgl] F agenciarse F

want [wɒnt] **1** *n*: **for ~ of** por falta de **2** *v/t* querer; *(need)*

necesitar; ~ **to do sth** querer hacer algo; **I** ~ **to stay here** quiero quedarme aquí; **she** ~**s you to go back** quiere que vuelvas **3** *v/t*: **he** ~**s for nothing** no le falta nada; **wanted** *by police* buscado por la policía

war [wɔ:r] *also fig* guerra *f*

ward [wɔ:rd] *in hospital* sala *f*; *child* pupilo(-a) *m(f)*

◆ **ward off** *blow* parar; *attacker* rechazar; *cold* evitar

warden ['wɔ:rdn] *of prison* director(-a) *m(f)*; *Br of hostel* vigilante *m/f*

'**wardrobe** *for clothes* armario *m*; *(clothes)* guardarropa *m*

'**warehouse** ['werhaus] almacén *m*

'**warfare** guerra *f*; **warhead** ojiva *f*

warily ['werɪlɪ] cautelosamente

warm [wɔ:rm] *hands, room, water* caliente; *weather, welcome* cálido; *coat* de abrigo

◆ **warm up 1** *v/t* calentar **2** *v/i* calentarse; *of athlete etc* calentar

warmly ['wɔ:rmlɪ] calurosamente; **warmth** calor *m*; **warm-up** SP calentamiento *m*

warn [wɔ:rn] advertir, avisar; **warning** advertencia *f*, aviso *m*

warp [wɔ:rp] *of wood* combarse; **warped** *fig* retorcido

warrant ['wɔ:rənt] **1** *n* orden *f* judicial **2** *v/t* justificar; **war-**

ranty garantía f

warrior ['wɔːriər] guerrero(-a) m(f)

wart [wɔːrt] verruga f

wary ['weri] cauto

wash [wɑːʃ] 1 n lavado m; **have a ~** lavarse 2 v/t lavar 3 v/i lavarse

◆ **wash up** (wash one's hands and face) lavarse

washable ['wɑːʃəbl] lavable; **washbasin, washbowl** lavabo m; **washcloth** toallita f; **washed** out agotado; **washer** for faucet etc arandela f; **washing** (clothes washed) ropa f limpia; (dirty clothes) ropa f sucia; **do the ~** lavar la ropa sucia; **washing machine** lavadora f; **washroom** lavabo m, aseo m

wasp [wɑːsp] avispa f

waste [weist] 1 n desperdicio m; from industrial process desechos mpl; **it's a ~ of time / money** es una pérdida de tiempo / dinero 2 adj residual 3 v/t derrochar; money gastar; time perder; **waste basket** papelera f; **waste disposal (unit)** trituradora f de basuras; **wasteful** derrochador; **wasteland** erial m; **wastepaper** papel m usado

watch [wɑːtʃ] 1 n timepiece reloj m; **keep ~** hacer la guardia, vigilar 2 v/t film, TV ver; (look after) vigilar 3 v/i mirar, observar; **watchful** vigilante

water ['wɔːtər] 1 n agua f 2 v/t plant regar 3 v/i: **my mouth is ~ing** se me hace la boca agua; **watercolour,** Br **watercolour** acuarela f; **watered down** fig dulcificado; **waterfall** cascada f; **waterline** línea f de flotación; **waterlogged** anegado; boat lleno de agua; **watermelon** sandía f; **waterproof** impermeable; **waterside** orilla f; **waterskiing** esquí m acuático; **watertight** compartment estanco; fig irrefutable; **waterway** curso m de agua navegable; **watery** aguado

watt [wɑːt] vatio m

wave[1] n in sea ola f

wave[2] [weiv] 1 n of hand saludo m 2 v/i with hand saludar con la mano 3 v/t flag etc agitar

'wavelength RAD longitud f de onda; **be on the same ~** fig estar en la misma onda

waver ['weivər] vacilar

wavy ['weivi] ondulado

wax [wæks] cera f

way [wei] (method) manera f; (manner also) modo m; (route) camino m; **this ~** (like this) así; (in this direction) por aquí; **by the ~** (incidentally) a propósito; **in a ~** (in certain respects) en cierto sentido; **lose one's ~** perderse; **be in the ~** (be an obstruction) estar en medio; **no ~!** ¡ni hablar!; **way in** entrada f; **way of life** modo m de vida; **way**

welfare

out salida f

we [wiː] nosotros *mpl*, nosotras *fpl*; **~ are the best** somos los mejores

weak [wiːk] débil; *tea, coffee* poco cargado; **weaken 1** *v/t* debilitar **2** *v/i* debilitarse; **weakness** debilidad f

wealth [welθ] riqueza f; **wealthy** rico

weapon ['wepən] arma f

wear [wer] **1** *n*: **~ (and tear)** desgaste m **2** *v/t* (*have on*) llevar; (*damage*) desgastar **3** *v/i* (*wear out*) desgastarse; (*last*) durar

◆ **wear down** agotar

◆ **wear off** *of effect* pasar

◆ **wear out 1** *v/t* (*tire*) agotar; *shoes* desgastar **2** *v/i of shoes, carpet* desgastarse

wearily ['wɪrɪlɪ] cansinamente; **weary** cansado

weather ['weðər] **1** *n* tiempo m **2** *v/t crisis* capear; superar; **weather-beaten** curtido; **weather forecast** pronóstico m del tiempo; **weatherman** hombre m del tiempo

weave [wiːv] **1** *v/t* tejer **2** *v/i move* zigzaguear

web [web] *of spider* tela f; **the Web** COMPUT la Web; **web page** página f web; **web site** sitio m web

wedding ['wedɪŋ] boda f; **wedding anniversary** aniversario m de boda; **wedding day** día m de la boda; **wedding dress** vestido m de boda or novia; **wedding**

ring anillo m de boda

wedge [wedʒ] cuña f; *of cheese etc* trozo m

Wednesday ['wenzdeɪ] miércoles m inv

weed [wiːd] **1** *n* mala hierba **2** *v/t* escardar; **weed-killer** herbicida m; **weedy** F esmirriado, enclenque

week [wiːk] semana f; **a ~ tomorrow** de mañana en una semana; **weekday** día m de la semana; **weekend** fin m de semana; **on the ~** el fin de semana; **weekly 1** *adj* semanal **2** *n magazine* semanario m **3** *adv* semanalmente

weep [wiːp] llorar

wee-wee ['wiːwiː] F pipí m; **do a ~** hacer pipí

weigh [weɪ] pesar

◆ **weigh up** (*assess*) sopesar

weight [weɪt] peso m; **weightlessness** ingravidez f; **weightlifter** levantador(a) m(f) de pesas; **weightlifting** halterofilia f, levantamiento m de pesas; **weighty** *fig* (*important*) serio

weir [wɪr] presa f (*rebasadero*)

weird [wɪrd] extraño, raro; **weirdo** F bicho m raro F

welcome ['welkəm] **1** *adj* bienvenido; **you're ~!** ¡de nada! **2** *n* bienvenida f **3** *v/t guests etc* dar la bienvenida a; *decision etc* acoger positivamente

weld [weld] soldar

welfare ['welfer] bienestar m; *financial assistance* subsidio *m* estatal; **welfare check** cheque con el importe del subsidio estatal; **welfare state** estado *m* del bienestar; **welfare worker** asistente *m/f* social

well¹ [wel] *n for water, oil* pozo *m*

well² [wel] **1** *adv* bien; **as ~** (*too*) también; **as ~ as** (*in addition to*) así como; **very ~** muy bien; **~ !** *surprise* ¡caramba!; **~ ...** *uncertainty* bueno... **2** *adj*: **be ~** estar bien; **well-balanced** equilibrado; **well-behaved** educado; **well-being** bienestar *m*; **well-done** *meat* muy hecho; **well-dressed** bien vestido; **well-earned** merecido; **well-heeled** F adinerado, *Span* con pasta F; **well-informed** bien informado; **well-known** conocido; **well-meaning** bienintencionado; **wellness** bienestar *m*; **wellness center**, *Br* **wellness centre** centro *m* de bienestar; **wellness hotel** hotel *m* de bienestar; **well-off** acomodado; **well-timed** oportuno; **well-wisher** admirador(a) *m(f)*

west [west] **1** *n* oeste *m*; **the West** (*Western nations*) el Occidente; (*western part of a country*) el oeste **2** *adj* del oeste **3** *adv travel* hacia el oeste; **westerly** *wind* del oeste; *direction* hacia el oeste; **western 1** *adj* occidental

2 *n movie* western *m*, película *f* del oeste; **Westerner** occidental *m/f*; **westernized** occidentalizado; **West Indian 1** *adj* antillano **2** *n* antillano(-a) *m(f)*; **West Indies: the ~** las Antillas; **westward** hacia el oeste

wet [wet] mojado; (*damp*) húmedo; (*rainy*) lluvioso; **wet suit** traje *m* de neopreno

whack [wæk] F (*blow*) porrazo *m* F

whale [weɪl] ballena *f*

what [wɑːt] **1** *pron* qué; **~ is it?** (*what do you want*) ¿qué quieres?; **~ about heading home?** ¿y si nos fuéramos a casa?; **~ for?** (*why*) ¿para qué?; **so ~?** ¿y qué?; **take ~ you need** toma lo que te haga falta **2** *adj* qué; **~ color is the car?** ¿de qué color es el coche?; **whatever: ~ the season** en cualquier estación; **ok ~** vale, lo que tú digas

wheat [wiːt] trigo *m*

wheel [wiːl] rueda *f*; (*steering ~*) volante *m*; **wheelchair** silla *f* de ruedas; **wheel clamp** *Br* cepo *m*

wheeze [wiːz] resoplido *m*

when [wen] **1** *adv* cuándo; **~ do you open?** ¿a qué hora abren? **2** *conj* cuando; **~ I was a child** cuando era niño; **whenever** (*each time*) cada vez que; **~ you like** cuando quieras

where [wer] **1** *adv* dónde;

wide

from? ¿de dónde?; **~ to?** ¿a dónde? **2** *conj whereas* mientras que; **this is ~ I used to live** aquí es donde vivía antes; **whereas** mientras que; **wherever 1** *conj* dondequiera que; **sit ~ you like** siéntate donde prefieras **2** *adv* dónde?; **~ can it be?** ¿dónde puede estar?

whet [wet] *appetite* abrir

whether ['weðər] si; **~ you approve or not** te parezca bien o no

which [wɪtʃ] **1** *adj* qué; **~ one is yours?** ¿cuál es tuyo? **2** *pron interrogative* cuál; *relative* que; **take one, it doesn't matter ~** toma uno, no importa cuál

whiff [wɪf] *(smell)* olorcillo *m*

while [waɪl] **1** *conj* mientras; *(although)* si bien **2** *n* rato *m*

whim [wɪm] capricho *m*

whimper ['wɪmpər] gimotear

whine [waɪn] *of dog* gimotear; F *(complain)* quejarse

whip [wɪp] **1** *n* látigo *m* **2** *v/t (beat)* azotar; *cream* batir; F *(defeat)* dar una paliza a F

whirlpool ['wɜːrlpuːl] *in river* remolino *m; for relaxation* bañera *f* de hidromasaje

whisk [wɪsk] **1** *n kitchen implement* batidora *f* **2** *v/t eggs* batir

whiskey ['wɪskɪ] whisky *m*

whisper ['wɪspər] susurrar

whistle ['wɪsl] **1** *n sound* silbido *m; device* silbato *m* **2** *v/t & v/i* silbar

white [waɪt] **1** *n* blanco *m; of egg* clara *f; person* blanco(-a) *m(f)* **2** *adj* blanco; **white-collar worker** persona *f* que trabaja en una oficina; **White House** Casa *f* Blanca; **white lie** mentira *f* piadosa; **white-wash 1** *n* cal *f; fig* encubrimiento *m* **2** *v/t* encalar; **white wine** vino *m* blanco

whittle ['wɪtl] *wood* tallar

♦ **whittle down** reducir

who [huː] *interrogative* ¿quién?; *relative* que; **do you want to speak to?** ¿con quién quieres hablar? **whoever** quienquiera

whole [hoʊl] **1** *adj* entero; **the ~ country** todo el país **2** *n* totalidad *f; on the ~* en general; **whole-hearted** incondicional; **wholesale** al por mayor; *fig* indiscriminado; **wholesaler** mayorista *m/f;* **wholesome** saludable, sano; **wholly** completamente

whom [huːm] *fml* quién

whore [hɔːr] prostituta *f*

whose [huːz] *interrogative* de quién; *relative* cuyo(-a); **~ is this?** ¿de quién es esto?; **a country ~ economy …** un país cuya economía…

why [waɪ] por qué

wicked ['wɪkɪd] malvado

wicker ['wɪkər] de mimbre

wicket ['wɪkɪt] *in station, bank etc* ventanilla *f*

wide [waɪd] ancho; *experience, range* amplio; *be 12 feet ~* tener 12 pies de ancho; **widely** ampliamente;

widen 1 *v/t* ensanchar **2** *v/i* ensancharse; **wide-open** abierto de par en par; **wide-ranging** amplio; **widespread** extendido

widow ['wɪdəʊ] viuda *f*; **widower** viudo *m*

width [wɪdθ] anchura *f*, ancho *m*

wield [wiːld] *weapon* empuñar; *power* detentar

wife [waɪf] mujer *f*, esposa *f*

wi-fi ['waɪfaɪ] *IT* Wi-Fi *m or f*

wig [wɪɡ] peluca *f*

wiggle ['wɪɡl] menear

wild [waɪld] *animal* salvaje; *flower* silvestre; *teenager, party* descontrolado; (*crazy: scheme*) descabellado; *applause* arrebatado

wilderness ['wɪldərnɪs] desierto *m*, yermo *m*

'wildlife flora *f* y fauna *f*

wilful *Br* ☞ **willful**

will¹ [wɪl] *n* law testamento *m*

will² [wɪl] *n* (*willpower*) voluntad *f*

will³ [wɪl] *v/aux:* **I ~ let you know tomorrow** te lo diré mañana; **the car won't start** el coche no arranca; **~ you tell her that …?** ¿le quieres decir que…?; **~ you stop that!** ¡basta ya!

willful ['wɪlfʊl] *person* tozudo, obstinado; *action* deliberado, intencionado; **willing** dispuesto; **willingly** gustosamente; **willingness** buena disposición *f*; **willpower**

fuerza *f* de voluntad

willy-nilly [wɪlɪ'nɪlɪ] (*at random*) a la buena de Dios

wilt [wɪlt] *of plant* marchitarse

wily ['waɪlɪ] astuto

wimp [wɪmp] F enclenque *m/f* F, blandengue *m/f* F

win [wɪn] **1** *n* victoria *f*, triunfo *m* **2** *v/t & v/i* ganar

wince [wɪns] hacer una mueca de dolor

wind¹ [wɪnd] *n* viento *m*; (*flatulence*) gases *mpl*

wind² [waɪnd] **1** *v/i* serpentear **2** *v/t* enrollar

◆ **wind up 1** *v/t* clock dar cuerda a; *car window* subir, cerrar; *speech* finalizar; *business* concluir; *company* cerrar **2** *v/i* (*finish*) concluir

windfall *fig* dinero *m* inesperado

winding ['waɪndɪŋ] serpenteante

window ['wɪndəʊ] *also* COMPUT ventana *f*; **in the ~ of** *store* en el escaparate *or* L.Am. la vidriera; **window seat** asiento *m* de ventana; **window-shop:** *go ~ping* ir de escaparates *or* L.Am. vidrieras; **windowsill** alféizar *m*; **windshield**, *Br* **windscreen** parabrisas *m inv*; **windshield wiper** limpiaparabrisas *m inv*; **windsurfer** windsurfista *m/f*; *board* tabla *f* de windsurf; **windsurfing** el windsurf; **windy** ventoso

wine [waɪn] vino *m*; **wine cellar** bodega *f*; **wine list** lista *f* de vinos; **winery** bodega f

wing [wɪŋ] ala f; SP lateral m/f, extremo m/f; **wingspan** envergadura f

wink [wɪŋk] of person guiñar, hacer un guiño

winner ['wɪnər] ganador(a) m(f), vencedor(a) m(f); of lottery acertante m/f; **winning** ganador; **winning post** meta f; **winnings** ganancias fpl

winter ['wɪntər] invierno m; **winter sports** deportes mpl de invierno; **wintry** invernal

wipe [waɪp] limpiar; tape borrar

wiper ['waɪpər] ☞ **windshield wiper**

wire [waɪr] alambre m; ELEC cable m; **wireless hotspot** IT hotspot m Wi-Fi; **wireless phone** teléfono m inalámbrico; **wiring** ELEC cableado m; **wiry** person fibroso

wisdom ['wɪzdəm] of person sabiduría f; of action prudencia f, sensatez f

wise [waɪz] sabio; action, decision prudente, sensato; **wisecrack** F chiste m; **wisely** act prudentemente, sensatamente

wish [wɪʃ] **1** n deseo m; **best ~es** un saludo cordial **2** v/t desear

◆ **wish for** desear

wisp [wɪsp] of hair mechón m; of smoke voluta f

wistful ['wɪstfəl] nostálgico; **wistfully** con nostalgia

wit [wɪt] ingenio m; person ingenioso(-a) m/f

witch [wɪtʃ] bruja f; **witch-hunt** fig caza f de brujas

with [wɪð] con; **shivering ~ fear** temblando de miedo; **a girl ~ brown eyes** una chica de ojos castaños; **are you ~ me?** (do you understand) ¿me sigues?; **~ no money** sin dinero

withdraw [wɪð'drɔː] **1** v/t retirar **2** v/i retirarse; **withdrawal** retirada f; of money reintegro m; **withdrawal symptoms** síndrome m de abstinencia; **withdrawn** person retraído

wither ['wɪðər] marchitarse

with'hold information ocultar; payment retener; consent negar

with'in dentro de; in expressions of time en menos de

with'out sin

with'stand resistir, soportar

witness ['wɪtnɪs] **1** n testigo m/f **2** v/t ser testigo de

witticism ['wɪtɪsɪzm] comentario m gracioso; **witty** ingenioso, agudo

wobble ['wɑːbl] tambalearse; **wobbly** tambaleante

wolf [wʊlf] **1** n lobo m **2** v/t: ~ (**down**) engullir

woman ['wʊmən] mujer f; **womanizer** mujeriego(-a) m(f); **womanly** femenino

womb [wuːm] matriz f, útero m

m

women ['wɪmɪn] *pl* ☞ **woman**; **women's lib** la liberación de la mujer

wonder ['wʌndər] **1** *n* (*amazement*) asombro *m*; **no ~!** ¡no me sorprende! **2** *v/i* preguntarse; **I ~ if you could help** ¿le importaría ayudarme?; **wonderful** maravilloso; **wonderfully** maravillosamente

won't [wount] ☞ **will not**

wood [wud] madera *f*; *for fire* leña *f*; (*forest*) bosque *m*; **wooded** arbolado; **wooden** (*made of wood*) de madera; **woodpecker** pájaro *m* carpintero; **woodwork** carpintería *f*

wool [wul] lana *f*; **woolen**, *Br* **woollen 1** *adj* de lana **2** *n* prenda *f* de lana

word [wɜːrd] **1** *n* palabra *f* **2** *v/t letter* redactar; **word processor** procesador *m* de textos

work [wɜːrk] **1** *n* trabajo *m*; **out of ~** desempleado, *Span* en el paro **2** *v/i of person* trabajar; *of machine,* (*succeed*) funcionar

♦ **work out 1** *v/t problem* resolver; *solution* encontrar **2** *v/i of gym* hacer ejercicios; *of relationship etc* funcionar, ir bien

workable ['wɜːrkəbl] *solution* viable; **workaholic** F *persona adicta al trabajo*; **workday** (*hours of work*) jornada *f* laboral; (*not a holiday*) día *m* de trabajo; **worker** trabajador(a) *m(f)*; **workforce** trabajadores *mpl*; **work hours** horas *fpl* de trabajo; **working class** clase *f* trabajadora; **working-class** de clase trabajadora; **working hours** ☞ **workhours**; **workload** cantidad *f* de trabajo; **workman** obrero *m*; **workmanlike** competente; **workmanship** factura *f*, confección *f*; **work of art** obra *f* de arte; **workout** sesión *f* de ejercicios; **work permit** permiso *m* de trabajo; **workshop** *also seminar* taller *m*

world [wɜːrld] mundo *m*; **world-class** de categoría mundial; **World Cup** Mundial *m*, Copa *f* del Mundo; **world-famous** mundialmente famoso; **worldly** mundano; **world record** récord *m* mundial *or* del mundo; **world war** guerra *f* mundial; **worldwide 1** *adj* mundial **2** *adv* en todo el mundo

worn-out gastado; *person* agotado

worried ['wʌrɪd] preocupado; **worry 1** *n* preocupación *f* **2** *v/t* preocupar **3** *v/i* preocuparse; **worrying** preocupante

worse [wɜːrs] peor; **get ~** empeorar; **worsen** empeorar

worship ['wɜːrʃɪp] **1** *n* culto *m* **2** *v/t* adorar

worst [wɜːrst] peor

worth [wɜːrθ]: *be* ~ ... valer...; *be* ~ *it* valer la pena; **worthwhile** que vale la pena

worthy ['wɜːrði] digno; *cause* justo

would [wʊd]: *I* ~ *help if I could* te ayudaría si pudiera; ~ *you like to go to the movies?* ¿te gustaría ir al cine?; ~ *you close the door?* ¿podrías cerrar la puerta?

wound [wuːnd] **1** *n* herida *f* **2** *v/t* herir

wrap [ræp] envolver; **wrapping** envoltorio *m*; **wrapping paper** papel *m* de envolver

wrath [ræθ] ira *f*

wreath [riːθ] corona *f* de flores

wreck [rek] **1** *n* restos *mpl* **2** *v/t ship* hundir; *car* destrozar; *plans, marriage* arruinar; **wreckage** *of car, plane* restos *mpl*; *of marriage, career* ruina *f*; **wrecker** grúa *f*

wrench [rentʃ] **1** *n tool* llave *f* **2** *v/t* (*pull*) arrebatar

wrestle ['resl] luchar; **wrestler** luchador(a) *m(f)* (de lucha libre); **wrestling** lucha *f* libre

wriggle ['rɪgl] (*squirm*) menearse; *along the ground* arrastrarse; *into small space* escurrirse

wrinkle ['rɪŋkl] arruga *f*

wrist [rɪst] muñeca *f*; **wristwatch** reloj *m* de pulsera

write [raɪt] escribir; *check* extender

♦ **write off** *debt* cancelar; *car* destrozar

writer ['raɪtər] escritor(a) *m(f)*; *of book, song* autor(a) *m(f)*; **write-up** reseña *f*

writhe [raɪð] retorcerse

writing ['raɪtɪŋ] *words, text* escritura *f*; (*hand-*~) letra *f*; *in* ~ por escrito; **writing paper** papel *m* de escribir

wrong [rɔːŋ] **1** *adj answer* equivocado; *decision* erróneo; *be* ~ *of person* estar equivocado; *of answer* ser incorrecto; *morally* ser injusto; *what's* ~? ¿qué pasa?; *you have the* ~ *number* TELEC se ha equivocado **2** *adv* mal **3** *n* mal *m*; **wrongful** ilegal; **wrongly** erróneamente

wry [raɪ] socarrón

X

xenophobia [zenoʊˈfoʊbɪə] xenofobia *f*

X-ray ['eksreɪ] **1** *n picture* radiografía *f* **2** *v/t* radiografiar

Y

yacht [jɑːt] yate *m*; **yachting**
vela *f*

Yank [jæŋk] F yanqui *m/f*

yank [jæŋk] tirar de

yard[1] *of prison etc* patio *m*; *behind house* jardín *m*;
for storage almacén *m* (*al aire libre*)

yard[2] [jɑːrd] *measurement*
yarda *f*

'yardstick patrón *m* F

yarn [jɑːrn] (*thread*) hilo *m*; F
(*story*) batallita *f* F

yawn [jɔːn] **1** *n* bostezo *m* **2** *v/i*
bostezar

year [jɪr] año *m*; **be six ~s old**
tener seis años (de edad);
yearly 1 *adj* anual **2** *adv*
anualmente

yeast [jiːst] levadura *f*

yell [jel] **1** *n* grito *m* **2** *v/t & v/i*
gritar

yellow ['jeloʊ] amarillo

yelp [jelp] **1** *n* aullido *m* **2** *v/i*
aullar

yes [jes] sí; **yes man** *pej* pelotillero *m*

yesterday ['jestərdeɪ] ayer;
the day before ~ anteayer

yet [jet] **1** *adv* todavía, aún;
have you finished ~? ¿has
acabado ya?; **he hasn't arrived ~** todavía *or* aún no
ha llegado **2** *conj* (*however*)
sin embargo

yield [jiːld] **1** *n from fields etc*
cosecha *f*; *from investment*

rendimiento *m* **2** *v/t fruit,
good harvest* proporcionar;
interest rendir **3** *v/i* (*give
way*) ceder; *of driver* ceder
el paso

yoga ['joʊgə] yoga *m*

yoghurt ['joʊgərt] yogur *m*

yolk [joʊk] yema *f*

you [juː] ◇ *as subject, singular*
tú, *L.Am.* usted, *Rpl, C.Am.*
vos; *formal* usted; *plural:
Span* vosotros, vosotras,
L.Am. ustedes; *formal* ustedes; **do ~ know him?** ¿lo conoces / conoce?
◇ *as object, singular* te,
L.Am. le; *formal* le; *plural:
Span* os, *L.Am.* les; *formal*
les
◇*with preps, singular* ti (*other forms as subject*)
◇ *people, one:* **~ never know**
nunca se sabe; **~ have to pay**
hay que pagar; **exercise is
good for ~** es bueno hacer
ejercicio

young [jʌŋ] joven; **youngster**
joven *m/f*

your [jʊr] *singular* tu, *L.Am.*
su; *formal* su; *plural: Span*
vuestro, *L.Am.* su; *formal* su

yours [jʊrz] *singular* el tuyo,
la tuya, *L.Am.* el suyo, la suya; *formal* el suyo, la suya;
plural el vuestro, la vuestra,
L.Am. el suyo, la suya; *formal* el suyo, la suya; **it's ~**

zucchini

es tuyo etc; **a friend of** ~ un amigo tuyo / suyo / vuestro; ~ **at end of letter** un saludo

yourself [jur'self] *reflexive* te, *L.Am.* se; *formal* se; *emphatic* tú mismo *m*, tú misma *f*, *L.Am.* usted mismo, usted misma; *Rpl, C.Am.* vos mismo, vos misma; *formal* usted mismo, usted misma; **did you hurt ~?** ¿te hiciste / se hizo daño?; **yourselves** *reflexive* os, *L.Am.* se; *formal*

se; *emphatic* vosotros mismos *mpl*, vosotras mismas *fpl*, *L.Am.* ustedes mismos, ustedes mismas; *formal* ustedes mismos, ustedes mismas; **did you hurt ~?** ¿os hicisteis / se hicieron daño?

youth [ju:θ] juventud *f*; (*young man*) joven *m/f*; **youth club** club *m* juvenil; **youthful** joven; *fashion, idealism* juvenil

yuppie ['jʌpɪ] F yupi *m/f*

Z

zap [zæp] F (COMPUT: *delete*) borrar; (*kill*) liquidar F; (*hit*) golpear; (*send*) enviar

zeal [zi:l] celo *m*

zero ['zɪrou] cero *m*

zest [zest] entusiasmo *m*

zigzag ['zɪgzæg] **1** *n* zigzag *m* **2** *v/i* zigzaguear

zilch [zɪltʃ] F nada de nada

zip [zɪp] *Br* cremallera *f*

◆ **zip up** *dress, jacket* cerrar la

cremallera de; COMPUT compactar

'zip code código *m* postal; **zipper** cremallera *f*

zone [zoun] zona *f*

zoo [zu:] zoo *m*

zoology [zu:'ɑ:lədʒɪ] zoología *f*

'zoom lens zoom *m*

zucchini [zu:'ki:nɪ] calabacín *m*

Los verbos irregulares ingleses

Se citan las tres partes principales de cada verbo: infinitivo, pretérito, participio del pasado.

arise – arose – arisen

awake – awoke – awoken, awaked

be (am, is, are) – was (were) – been

bear – bore – borne

beat – beat – beaten

become – became – become

begin – began – begun

bend – bent – bent

bet – bet, betted – bet, betted

bid – bid – bid

bind – bound – bound

bite – bit – bitten

bleed – bled – bled

blow – blew – blown

break – broke – broken

breed – bred – bred

bring – brought – brought

broadcast – broadcast – broadcast

build – built – built

burn – burnt, burned – burnt, burned

burst – burst – burst

buy – bought – bought

cast – cast – cast

catch – caught – caught

choose – chose – chosen

cling – clung – clung

come – came – come

cost (v/i) – cost – cost

creep – crept – crept

cut – cut – cut

deal – dealt – dealt

dig – dug – dug

dive – dived, dove [douv] (1) – dived

do – did – done

draw – drew – drawn

dream – dreamt, dreamed – dreamt, dreamed

drink – drank – drunk

drive – drove – driven

eat – ate – eaten

fall – fell – fallen

feed – fed – fed

feel – felt – felt

fight – fought – fought

find – found – found

flee – fled – fled

fling – flung – flung

fly – flew – flown

forbid – forbad(e) – forbidden

forecast – forecast(ed) – forecast(ed)

forget – forgot – forgotten

forgive – forgave – forgiven

freeze – froze – frozen

get – got – got, gotten (2)

give – gave – given

go – went – gone

grind – ground – ground

grow – grew – grown

hang – hung, hanged – hung, hanged (3)

have – had – had

hear – heard – heard

hide – hid – hidden

hit – hit – hit

hold – held – held

hurt – hurt – hurt

keep – kept – kept

kneel – knelt, kneeled – knelt, kneeled

know – knew – known

lay – laid – laid

lead – led – led

lean – leaned, leant – leaned, leant (4)

leap – leaped, leapt – leaped, leapt (4)

learn – learned, learnt – learned, learnt (4)

leave – left – left

lend – lent – lent

let – let – let

lie – lay – lain

light – lighted, lit – lighted, lit

lose – lost – lost

make – made – made

mean – meant – meant

meet – met – met

mow – mowed – mowed, mown

pay – paid – paid

plead – pleaded, pled – pleaded, pled (5)

prove – proved – proved, proven

put – put – put

quit – quit(ted) – quit(ted)

read – read [red] – read [red]

ride – rode – ridden

ring – rang – rung

rise – rose – risen

run – ran – run

saw – sawed – sawn, sawed

say – said – said

see – saw – seen

seek – sought – sought

sell – sold – sold

send – sent – sent

set – set – set

sew – sewed – sewed, sewn

shake – shook – shaken

shed – shed – shed

shine – shone – shone

shit – shit(ted), shat – shit(ted), shat

shoot – shot – shot

show – showed – shown

shrink – shrank – shrunk

shut – shut – shut

sing – sang – sung

sink – sank – sunk

sit – sat – sat

slay – slew – slain

sleep – slept – slept

slide – slid – slid

sling – slung – slung	**stride** – strode – stridden
slit – slit – slit	**strike** – struck – struck
smell – smelt, smelled – smelt, smelled	**swear** – swore – sworn
	sweep – swept – swept
sow – sowed – sown, sowed	**swell** – swelled – swollen
speak – spoke – spoken	**swim** – swam – swum
speed – sped, speeded – sped, speeded	**swing** – swung – swung
	take – took – taken
spell – spelt, spelled – spelt, spelled (4)	**teach** – taught – taught
	tear – tore – torn
spend – spent – spent	**tell** – told – told
spill – spilt, spilled – spilt, spilled	**think** – thought – thought
spin – spun – spun	**thrive** – throve – thriven, thrived (6)
spit – spat – spat	
split – split – split	**throw** – threw – thrown
spoil – spoiled, spoilt – spoiled, spoilt	**thrust** – thrust – thrust
	tread – trod – trodden
spread – spread – spread	**wake** – woke, waked – woken, waked
spring – sprang, sprung – sprung	
	wear – wore – worn
stand – stood – stood	**weave** – wove – woven (7)
steal – stole – stolen	**weep** – wept – wept
stick – stuck – stuck	**win** – won – won
sting – stung – stung	**wind** – wound – wound
stink – stunk, stank – stunk	**write** – wrote – written

(1) **dove** no se usa en inglés británico
(2) **gotten** no se usa en inglés británico
(3) **hung** para un cuadro; **hanged** para un ajusticiado
(4) en inglés americano se suele emplear la forma terminada en **-ed**
(5) **pled** se usa en inglés americano y escocés
(6) **thrived** es la forma más común
(7) aunque **weaved** en la acepción *zigzaguear*

Numbers – Numerales

Cardinal Numbers – Números cardinales

0	cero *zero*, Br tb *nought*
1	uno, una *one*
2	dos *two*
3	tres *three*
4	cuatro *four*
5	cinco *five*
6	seis *six*
7	siete *seven*
8	ocho *eight*
9	nueve *nine*
10	diez *ten*
11	once *eleven*
12	doce *twelve*
13	trece *thirteen*
14	catorce *fourteen*
15	quince *fifteen*
16	dieciséis *sixteen*
17	diecisiete *seventeen*
18	dieciocho *eighteen*
19	diecinueve *nineteen*
20	veinte *twenty*
21	veintiuno *twenty-one*
22	veintidós *twenty-two*
30	treinta *thirty*
31	treinta y uno *thirty-one*
40	cuarenta *forty*
50	cincuenta *fifty*
60	sesenta *sixty*
70	setenta *seventy*

80	ochenta *eighty*
90	noventa *ninety*
100	cien(to) *a hundred, one hundred*
101	ciento uno *a hundred and one*
110	ciento diez *a hundred and ten*
200	doscientos, -as *two hundred*
300	trescientos, -as *three hundred*
324	trescientos, -as venticuatro *three hundred and twenty-four*
400	cuatrocientos, -as *four hundred*
500	quinientos, -as *five hundred*
600	seiscientos, -as *six hundred*
700	setecientos, -as *seven hundred*
800	ochocientos, -as *eight hundred*
900	novecientos, -as *nine hundred*
1000	mil *a thousand, one thousand*
1959	mil novecientos cincuenta y nueve *one thousand nine hundred and fifty-nine*
2000	dos mil *two thousand*
1 000 000	un millón *a million, one million*
2 000 000	dos millones *two million*

Notes:

i) In Spanish numbers a comma is used for decimals:
1,25 **one point two five** uno coma veinticinco

ii) A period is used where, in English, we would use a comma:
1.000.000 = 1,000,000

Numbers like this can also be written using a space instead of a comma:
1 000 000 = 1,000,000

Ordinal Numbers – Números ordinales

1°	primero	**1st**	*first*
2°	segundo	**2nd**	*second*
3°	tercero	**3rd**	*third*
4°	cuarto	**4th**	*fourth*
5°	quinto	**5th**	*fifth*
6°	sexto	**6th**	*sixth*
7°	séptimo	**7th**	*seventh*
8°	octavo	**8th**	*eighth*
9°	noveno, nono	**9th**	*ninth*
10°	décimo	**10th**	*tenth*
11°	undécimo	**11th**	*eleventh*
12°	duodécimo	**12th**	*twelfth*
13°	decimotercero	**13th**	*thirteenth*
14°	decimocuarto	**14th**	*fourteenth*
15°	decimoquinto	**15th**	*fifteenth*
16°	decimosexto	**16th**	*sixteenth*
17°	decimoséptimo	**17th**	*seventeenth*
18°	decimoctavo	**18th**	*eighteenth*
19°	decimonoveno, decimonono	**19th**	*nineteenth*
20°	vigésimo	**20th**	*twentieth*
21°	vigésimo prim(er)o	**21st**	*twenty-first*
22°	vigésimo segundo	**22nd**	*twenty-second*
30°	trigésimo	**30th**	*thirtieth*
31°	trigésimo prim(er)o	**31st**	*thirty-first*
40°	cuadragésimo	**40th**	*fortieth*
50°	quincuagésimo	**50th**	*fiftieth*
60°	sexagésimo	**60th**	*sixtieth*
70°	septuagésimo	**70th**	*seventieth*
80°	octogésimo	**80th**	*eightieth*
90°	nonagésimo	**90th**	*ninetieth*

100°	centésimo	**100th** *hundredth*
101°	centésimo primero	**101st** *hundred and first*
110°	centésimo décimo	**110th** *hundred and tenth*
200°	ducentésimo	**200th** *two hundredth*
300°	tricentésimo	**300th** *three hundredth*
400°	cuadringentésimo	**400th** *four hundredth*
500°	quingentésimo	**500th** *five hundredth*
600°	sexcentésimo	**600th** *six hundredth*
700°	septingentésimo	**700th** *seven hundredth*
800°	octingentésimo	**800th** *eight hundredth*
900°	noningentésimo	**900th** *nine hundredth*
1000°	milésimo	**1000th** *thousandth*
2000°	dos milésimo	**2000th** *two thousandth*
1 000 000°	millonésimo	**1,000,000th** *millionth*
2 000 000°	dos millonésimo	**2,000,000th** *two millionth*

Note:

Spanish ordinal numbers are ordinary adjectives and consequently must agree:

her 13th granddaughter
su decimotercera nieta

Dates – Fechas

1996	mil novecientos noventa y seis	*nineteen ninety-six*
2005	dos mil cinco	*two thousand (and) five*

el diez de noviembre, el 10 de noviembre
(on) November 10, *Br* (on) the 10th of November

el uno de marzo, *L.Am.* **el primero de marzo, el 1° de marzo**
(on) March 1, *Br* (on) the 1st of March